# Lecture Notes in Computer Science 14143

Founding Editors

Gerhard Goos

Juris Hartmanis

The series Lecture Notes in Computer Science (LNCS), including its subseries Lecture Notes in Artificial Intelligence (LNAI) and Lecture Notes in Bioinformatics (LNBI), has established itself as a medium for the publication of new developments in computer science and information technology research, teaching, and education.

LNCS enjoys close cooperation with the computer science R & D community, the series counts many renowned academics among its volume editors and paper authors, and collaborates with prestigious societies. Its mission is to serve this international community by providing an invaluable service, mainly focused on the publication of conference and workshop proceedings and postproceedings. LNCS commenced publication in 1973.

José Abdelnour Nocera ·
Marta Kristín Lárusdóttir · Helen Petrie ·
Antonio Piccinno · Marco Winckler
Editors

# Human-Computer Interaction – INTERACT 2023

19th IFIP TC13 International Conference
York, UK, August 28 – September 1, 2023
Proceedings, Part II

- WG 13.2 (Methodology for User-Centred System Design) aims to foster research, dissemination of information and good practice in the methodical application of HCI to software engineering.
- WG 13.3 (Human Computer Interaction, Disability and Aging) aims to make HCI designers aware of the needs of people with disabilities and older people and encourage development of information systems and tools permitting adaptation of interfaces to specific users.
- WG 13.4/WG2.7 (User Interface Engineering) investigates the nature, concepts and construction of user interfaces for software systems, using a framework for reasoning about interactive systems and an engineering model for developing user interfaces.
- WG 13.5 (Resilience, Reliability, Safety and Human Error in System Development) seeks a framework for studying human factors relating to systems failure, develops leading-edge techniques in hazard analysis and safety engineering of computer-based systems, and guides international accreditation activities for safety-critical systems.
- WG 13.6 (Human-Work Interaction Design) aims at establishing relationships between extensive empirical work-domain studies and HCI design. It will promote the use of knowledge, concepts, methods and techniques that enable user studies to procure a better apprehension of the complex interplay between individual, social and organisational contexts and thereby a better understanding of how and why people work in the ways that they do.
- WG 13.7 (Human–Computer Interaction and Visualization) aims to establish a study and research program that will combine both scientific work and practical applications in the fields of Human–Computer Interaction and Visualization. It will integrate several additional aspects of further research areas, such as scientific visualization, data mining, information design, computer graphics, cognition sciences, perception theory, or psychology into this approach.
- WG 13.8 (Interaction Design and International Development) aims to support and develop the research, practice and education capabilities of HCI in institutions and organisations based around the world taking into account their diverse local needs and cultural perspectives.
- WG 13.9 (Interaction Design and Children) aims to support practitioners, regulators and researchers to develop the study of interaction design and children across international contexts.
- WG 13.10 (Human-Centred Technology for Sustainability) aims to promote research, design, development, evaluation, and deployment of human-centred technology to encourage sustainable use of resources in various domains.

IFIP TC13 recognises contributions to HCI through both its Pioneer in HCI Award and various paper awards associated with each INTERACT conference. Since the processes to decide the various awards take place after papers are sent to the publisher for publication, the recipients of the awards are not identified in the proceedings.

The IFIP TC13 Pioneer in Human-Computer Interaction Award recognises the contributions and achievements of pioneers in HCI. An IFIP TC13 Pioneer is one who, through active participation in IFIP Technical Committees or related IFIP groups, has made outstanding contributions to the educational, theoretical, technical, commercial, or professional aspects of analysis, design, construction, evaluation, and use of interactive systems. The IFIP TC13 Pioneer Awards are presented during an awards ceremony at each INTERACT conference.

In 1999, TC13 initiated a special IFIP Award, the Brian Shackel Award, for the most outstanding contribution in the form of a refereed paper submitted to and delivered at each INTERACT Conference, which draws attention to the need for a comprehensive human-centred approach in the design and use of information technology in which the human and social implications have been considered. The IFIP TC13 Accessibility Award, launched in 2007 by IFIP WG 13.3, recognises the most outstanding contribution with international impact in the field of ageing, disability, and inclusive design in the form of a refereed paper submitted to and delivered at the INTERACT Conference. The IFIP TC13 Interaction Design for International Development Award, launched in 2013 by IFIP WG 13.8, recognises the most outstanding contribution to the application of interactive systems for social and economic development of people around the world taking into account their diverse local needs and cultural perspectives. The IFIP TC13 Pioneers' Award for Best Doctoral Student Paper at INTERACT, first awarded in 2019, is selected by the past recipients of the IFIP TC13 Pioneer title. The award is made to the best research paper accepted to the INTERACT Conference which is based on the doctoral research of the student and authored and presented by the student.

In 2015, TC13 approved the creation of a steering committee for the INTERACT conference. The Steering Committee (SC) is currently chaired by Marco Winckler and is responsible for:

- Promoting and maintaining the INTERACT conference as the premiere venue for researchers and practitioners interested in the topics of the conference (this requires a refinement of the topics above).
- Ensuring the highest quality for the contents of the event.
- Setting up the bidding process to handle future INTERACT conferences. Decision is made up at TC13 level.
- Providing advice to the current and future chairs and organizers of the INTERACT conference.
- Providing data, tools, and documents about previous conferences to future conference organizers.
- Selecting the reviewing system to be used throughout the conference (as this impacts the entire set of reviewers).
- Resolving general issues involved with the INTERACT conference.
- Capitalizing on history (good and bad practices).

Further information is available at the IFIP TC13 website: http://ifip-tc13.org/.

# IFIP TC13 Members

## Officers

**Chair**

Paula Kotzé, South Africa

**Vice-chair for Conferences**

Marco Winckler, France

**Vice-chair for Equity
and Development**

José Abdelnour-Nocera, UK

**Vice-chair for Media
and Communications**

Helen Petrie, UK

**Vice-chair for Membership
and Collaboration**

Philippe Palanque, France

**Vice-chair for Working Groups**

Simone D. J. Barbosa, Brazil

**Vice-chair for Finance (Treasurer)**

Regina Bernhaupt, The Netherlands

**Secretary**

Janet Wesson, South Africa

**INTERACT Steering Committee Chair**

Marco Winckler, France

## Country Representatives

**Australia**

Henry B. L. Duh
Australian Computer Society

**Austria**

Christopher Frauenberger
Austrian Computer Society

**Belgium**

Bruno Dumas
IMEC – Interuniversity
Micro-Electronics Center

**Brazil**

André Freire
Simone D. J. Barbosa (section b)
Sociedade Brasileira de Computação
(SBC)

**Bulgaria**

Petia Koprinkova-Hristova
Bulgarian Academy of Sciences

## Croatia

Andrina Granić
Croatian Information Technology
Association (CITA)

## Cyprus

Panayiotis Zaphiris
Cyprus Computer Society

## Czech Republic

Zdeněk Míkovec
Czech Society for Cybernetics and
Informatics

## Denmark

Jan Stage
Danish Federation for Information
Processing (DANFIP)

## Finland

Virpi Roto
Finnish Information Processing
Association

## France

Philippe Palanque
Marco Winckler (section b)
Société informatique de France (SIF)

## Germany

Tom Gross
Gesellschaft fur Informatik e.V.

## Ireland

Liam J. Bannon
Irish Computer Society

## Italy

Fabio Paternò
Associazione Italiana per l' Informatica ed
il Calcolo Automatico (AICA)

## Japan

Yoshifumi Kitamura
Information Processing Society of Japan

## Netherlands

Regina Bernhaupt
Koninklijke Nederlandse Vereniging
van Informatieprofessionals (KNVI)

## New Zealand

Mark Apperley
Institute of IT Professionals New Zealand

## Norway

Frode Eika Sandnes
Norwegian Computer Society

## Poland

Marcin Sikorski
Polish Academy of Sciences (PAS)

## Portugal

Pedro Filipe Pereira Campos
Associacão Portuguesa para o
Desenvolvimento da Sociedade da
Informação (APDSI)

## Serbia

Aleksandar Jevremovic
Informatics Association of Serbia (IAS)

**Singapore**

Shengdong Zhao
Singapore Computer Society

**Slovakia**

Wanda Benešová
Slovak Society for Computer Science

**Slovenia**

Matjaž Kljun
Slovenian Computer Society
INFORMATIKA

**South Africa**

Janet L. Wesson
Paula Kotzé (section b)
Institute of Information Technology
Professionals South Africa (IITPSA)

**Sri Lanka**

Thilina Halloluwa
Computer Society of Sri Lanka (CSSL)

**Sweden**

Jan Gulliksen
Swedish Interdisciplinary Society for
Human-Computer Interaction
Dataföreningen i Sverige

**Switzerland**

Denis Lalanne
Schweizer Informatik Gesellschaft (SI)

**United Kingdom**

José Luis Abdelnour Nocera
Helen Petrie (section b)
British Computer Society (BCS),
Chartered Institute for IT

## International Members at Large Representatives

**ACM**

Gerrit van der Veer
Association for Computing
Machinery

**CLEI**

César Collazos
Centro Latinoamericano de Estudios en
Informatica

## Expert Members

Anirudha Joshi, India
Constantinos Coursaris, Canada
Carmelo Ardito, Italy
Daniel Orwa Ochieng, Kenya
David Lamas, Estonia
Dorian Gorgan, Romania
Eunice Sari, Australia/Indonesia
Fernando Loizides, UK/Cyprus
Geraldine Fitzpatrick, Austria

Ivan Burmistrov, Russia
Julio Abascal, Spain
Kaveh Bazargan, Iran
Marta Kristin Lárusdóttir, Iceland
Nikolaos Avouris, Greece
Peter Forbrig, Germany
Torkil Clemmensen, Denmark
Zhengjie Liu, China

## Working Group Chairpersons

**WG 13.1 (Education in HCI and HCI Curricula)**

Konrad Baumann, Austria

**WG 13.2 (Methodologies for User-Centered System Design)**

Regina Bernhaupt, Netherlands

**WG 13.3 (HCI, Disability and Aging)**

Helen Petrie, UK

**WG 13.4/2.7 (User Interface Engineering)**

Davide Spano, Italy

**WG 13.5 (Human Error, Resilience, Reliability, Safety and System Development)**

Tilo Mentler, Germany

**WG13.6 (Human-Work Interaction Design)**

Barbara Rita Barricelli, Italy

**WG13.7 (HCI and Visualization)**

Gerrit van der Veer, Netherlands

**WG 13.8 (Interaction Design and International Development)**

José Adbelnour Nocera, UK

**WG 13.9 (Interaction Design and Children)**

Gavin Sim, UK

**WG 13.10 (Human-Centred Technology for Sustainability)**

Masood Masoodian, Finland

# Organization

## General Chairs

Helen Petrie                           University of York, UK
Jose Abdelnour-Nocera                  University of West London, UK and ITI/Larsys,
                                          Portugal

## Technical Program Chair

Marco Winckler                         Université Côte d'Azur, France

## Full Papers Chairs

Antonio Piccinno                       University of Bari Aldo Moro, Italy
Marta Kristin Lárusdóttir              Reykjavik University, Iceland

## Short Papers Chairs

Marta Rey-Babarro                      Zillow, USA
Frode Eika Sandnes                     Oslo Metropolitan University, Norway
Grace Eden                             University of York, UK

## Poster Chairs

Alena Denisova                         University of York, UK
Burak Merdenyan                        University of York, UK

## Workshops Chairs

Jan Stage                              Aalborg University, Denmark
Anna Bramwell-Dicks                    University of York, UK

## Panels Chairs

Effie Lai-Chong Law            Durham University, UK
Massimo Zancanaro             University of Trento, Italy

## Student Volunteers Chairs

Sanjit Samaddar              University of York, UK
Daniel Lock                 University of York, UK

## Interactive Demonstrations Chairs

Barbara Rita Barricelli         University of Brescia, Italy
Jainendra Shukla              Indraprastha Institute of Information Technology,
                          India

## Courses Chairs

Nikos Avouris               University of Patras, Greece
André Freire                Federal University of Lavras, Brazil

## Doctoral Consortium Chairs

David Lamas                Tallinn University, Estonia
Geraldine Fitzpatrick           TU Wien, Austria
Tariq Zaman                University of Technology Sarawak, Malaysia

## Industrial Experiences Chairs

Helen Petrie                University of York, UK
Jose Abdelnour-Nocera          University of West London, UK and ITI/Larsys,
                          Portugal

## Publicity Chairs

Delvin Varghese              Monash University, Australia
Lourdes Moreno              Universidad Carlos III de Madrid, Spain

# Advisors

| | |
|---|---|
| Marco Winckler | University of the Côte d'Azur, France |
| Fernando Loizides | Cardiff University, UK |
| Carmelo Ardito | LUM Giuseppe Degennaro University, Italy |

# Web Master

| | |
|---|---|
| Edmund Wei | University of York, UK |

# INTERACT Subcommittee Chairs

| | |
|---|---|
| Anirudha Joshi | Industrial Design Centre, IIT Bombay, India |
| Célia Martinie | IRIT, Université Toulouse III - Paul Sabatier, France |
| Fabio Paternò | CNR-ISTI, Pisa, Italy |
| Frank Steinicke | Universität Hamburg, Germany |
| Gerhard Weber | TU Dresden, Germany |
| Helen Petrie | University of York, UK |
| José Campos | University of Minho, Portugal |
| Nikolaos Avouris | University of Patras, Greece |
| Philippe Palanque | IRIT, Université Toulouse III - Paul Sabatier, France |
| Rosa Lanzilotti | University of Bari, Italy |
| Rosella Gennari | Free University of Bozen-Bolzano, Switzerland |
| Simone Barbosa | PUC-Rio, Brazil |
| Torkil Clemmensen | Copenhagen Business School, Denmark |
| Yngve Dahl | Norwegian University of Science and Technology, Norway |

# INTERACT Steering Committee

| | |
|---|---|
| Anirudha Joshi | Industrial Design Centre, IIT Bombay, India |
| Antonio Piccinno | University of Bari, Italy |
| Carmelo Arditto | University of Bari, Italy |
| Fernando Loizides | University of Cardiff, UK |
| Frode Sandnes | Oslo Metropolitan University, Norway |
| Helen Petrie | University of York, UK |
| Janet Wesson | Nelson Mandela University, South Africa |
| Marco Winckler (Chair) | Université Côte d'Azur, France |
| Marta Lárusdóttir | Reykjavik University, Iceland |

| Paolo Buono | University of Bari, Italy |
| Paula Kotzé | University of Pretoria, South Africa |
| Philippe Palanque | IRIT, Université Toulouse III - Paul Sabatier, France |
| Raquel Oliveira Prates | Universidade Federal de Minas Gerais, Brazil |
| Tom Gross | University of Bamberg, Germany |

## Program Committee

| Alan Chamberlain | University of Nottingham, UK |
| Alessandra Melonio | Ca' Foscari University of Venice, Italy |
| Alessandro Pagano | University of Bari, Italy |
| Andrea Marrella | Sapienza Università di Roma, Italy |
| Andrés Lucero | Aalto University, Finland |
| Anna Sigríður Islind | Reykjavik University, Iceland |
| Antonio Piccinno | University of Bari, Italy |
| Ashley Colley | University of Lapland, Finland |
| Aurora Constantin | University of Edinburgh, UK |
| Barbara Rita Barricelli | Università degli Studi di Brescia, Italy |
| Bridget Kane | Karlstad University Business School, Sweden |
| Bruno Dumas | University of Namur, Belgium |
| Carla Dal Sasso Freitas | Federal University of Rio Grande do Sul, Brazil |
| Célia Martinie | Université Toulouse III - Paul Sabatier, France |
| Chi Vi | University of Sussex, UK |
| Christopher Power | University of Prince Edward Island, Canada |
| Christopher Clarke | University of Bath, UK |
| Cristian Bogdan | KTH, EECS, HCT, Sweden |
| Cristina Gena | Università di Torino, Italy |
| Dan Fitton | University of Central Lancashire, UK |
| Daniela Fogli | University of Brescia, Italy |
| Daniela Trevisan | Universidade Federal Fluminense, Brazil |
| Denis Lalanne | University of Fribourg, Switzerland |
| Dipanjan Chakraborty | BITS Pilani, Hyderabad Campus, India |
| Fabio Buttussi | University of Udine, Italy |
| Federico Cabitza | University of Milano-Bicocca, Italy |
| Fernando Loizides | Cardiff University, UK |
| Frode Eika Sandnes | Oslo Metropolitan University, Norway |
| Gerd Bruder | University of Central Florida, USA |
| Gerhard Weber | TU Dresden, Germany |
| Giuliana Vitiello | Università di Salerno, Italy |
| Giuseppe Desolda | University of Bari Aldo Moro, Italy |

| | |
|---|---|
| Sumita Sharma | University of Oulu, Finland |
| Sven Mayer | LMU Munich, Germany |
| Tania Di Mascio | Università dell'Aquila, Italy |
| Theodoros Georgiou | Heriot-Watt University, UK |
| Thilina Halloluwa | University of Colombo, Sri Lanka |
| Tilo Mentler | Trier University of Applied Sciences, Germany |
| Timothy Merritt | Aalborg University, Denmark |
| Tom Gross | University of Bamberg, Germany |
| Valentin Schwind | Frankfurt University of Applied Sciences, Germany |
| Virpi Roto | Aalto University, Finland |
| Vita Santa Barletta | University of Bari Aldo Moro, Italy |
| Vivian Genaro Motti | George Mason University, USA |
| Wricha Mishra | MIT Institute of Design, India |
| Zdeněk Míkovec | Czech Technical University Prague, Czech Republic |
| Zeynep Yildiz | Koç University, Turkey |

## Additional Reviewers

Abhishek Shrivastava
Adalberto Simeone
Aditya Prakash Kulkarni
Adrien Chaffangeon Caillet
Adrien Coppens
Aekaterini Mavri
Ahmad Samer Wazan
Aidan Slingsby
Aimee Code
Aizal Yusrina Idris
Akihisa Shitara
Aku Visuri
Alberto Monge Roffarello
Alessandro Forgiarini
Alessio Malizia
Alex Binh Vinh Duc Nguyen
Alex Chen
Alexander Maedche
Alexander Meschtscherjakov
Alexander Wachtel
Alexandra Voit
Alexandre Canny
Ali Gheitasy

Aline Menin
Alisson Puska
Alma Cantu
Amy Melniczuk
An Jacobs
Ana Serrano
Anderson Maciel
André Freire
Andre Salgado
Andre Suslik Spritzer
Andrea Antonio Cantone
Andrea Bellucci
Andrea Esposito
Andreas Fender
Andreas Mallas
Andreas Sonderegger
Andres Santos-Torres
Ángel Cuevas
Angela Locoro
Angus Addlesee
Angus Marshall
Anicia Peters
Anirudh Nagraj

Ankica Barisic
Anna Spagnolli
Annika Schulz
Anthony Perritano
Antigoni Parmaxi
Antje Jacobs
Antonella Varesano
Antonio Bucchiarone
Antonio Piccinno
Anupriya Tuli
Argenis Ramirez Gomez
Arminda Lopes
Arnaud Blouin
Ashwin Singh
Ashwin T. S.
Asim Evren Yantac
Axel Carayon
Aykut Coşkun
Azra Ismail
Barsha Mitra
Basmah Almekhled
Beat Signer
Beenish Chaudhry
Behnaz Norouzi
Benjamin Schnitzer
Benjamin Tag
Benjamin Weyers
Berardina De Carolis
Bharatwaja Namatherdhala
Bhumika Walia
Biju Thankachan
Bram van Deurzen
Çağlar Genç
Canlin Zhang
Carolyn Holter
Céline Coutrix
Chameera De Silva
Charlotte Magnusson
Chiara Ceccarini
Chiara Natali
Chikodi Chima
Christian Frisson
Christophe Kolski
Christopher Frauenberger
Christos Katsanos

Christos Sintoris
Cléber Corrêa
Cleidson de Souza
Daisuke Sato
Damianos Dumi Sigalas
Damon Horowitz
Dan Fitton
Daniel Görlich
Daniel Zielasko
Danielle Langlois
Daphne Chang
Dario Bertero
David Gollasch
David Navarre
Davide D'Adamo
Davide Mulfari
Davide Spallazzo
Debjani Roy
Diana Korka
Diego Morra
Dilrukshi Gamage
Diogo Cabral
Dixie Ching
Domenico Gigante
Dominic Potts
Donald McMillan
Edwige Pissaloux
Edy Portmann
Effie Law
Eike Schneiders
Elisa Mekler
Elise Grevet
Elizabeth Buie
Elodie Bouzbib
Emanuele Pucci
Enes Yigitbas
Eric Barboni
Estela Peralta
Euan Freeman
Evangelia Chrysikou
Evelyn Eika
Fabiana Vernero
Fabio Cassano
Fabrizio Balducci
Fanny Vainionpää

Fausto Medola
Favour Aladesuru
Federica Cena
Federico Botella
Florian Gnadlinger
Francesco Cauteruccio
Francesco Chiossi
Francesco Ferrise
Francesco Greco
Francisco Iniesto
Francisco Maria Calisto
Frank Beruscha
Frank Fischer
Frank Nack
Frida Milella
Funmi Adebesin
Gavin Sim
George Adrian Stoica
George Raptis
Georgios Papadoulis
Gianluca Schiavo
Girish Dalvi
Grischa Liebel
Guanhua Zhang
Guilherme Schardong
Gustavo Rovelo Ruiz
Hanne Sørum
Heidi Hartikainen
Himanshu Verma
Holger Regenbrecht
Hsin-Jou Lin
Hui-Yin Wu
Ikram Ur Rehman
Isabela Gasparini
Ivo Malý
Jack Jamieson
James Simpson
Jan Leusmann
Jana Jost
Jannes Peeters
Jari Kangas
Jayden Khakurel
Jean Hallewell Haslwanter
Jemma König
Jermaine Marshall

Jeroen Ceyssens
Jesper Gaarsdal
Jessica Sehrt
Jiaying Liu
Job Timmermans
Joe Cutting
Jonas Moll
Jonathan Hook
Joni Salminen
Joongi Shin
Jorge Wagner
José Campos
Joseph O'Hagan
Judith Borghouts
Julia Hertel
Julio Reis
Kajetan Enge
Kasper Rodil
Kate Rogers
Katerina Cerna
Katherine Seyama
Kathia Oliveira
Kathrin Gerling
Khyati Priya
Konstantin Biriukov
Kostantinos Moustakas
Krishna Venkatasubramanian
Laden Husamaldin
Lars Lischke
Lars Oestreicher
Laura Helsby
Leena Ventä-Olkkonen
Lele Sha
Leonardo Sandoval
Lorena Riol-Blanco
Lorenzo Torrez
Louise Barkhuus
Luis Leiva
Luis Teran
M. Cristina Vannini
Maälis Lefebvre
Magdaléna Kejstová
Malay Dhamelia
Manik Gupta
Manuel J. Fonseca

Marco de Gemmis
Marco Manca
Marco Romano
Margarita Anastassova
Margault Sacré
Margherita Andrao
Mari Karhu
Maria Fernanda Antunes
María Óskarsdóttir
Marianna Di Gregorio
Marika Jonsson
Marios Constantinides
Mark Apperley
Mark Lochrie
Marko Tkalcic
Markus Löchtefeld
Markus Tatzgern
Marta Serafini
Martin Hedlund
Martin Kocur
Massimo Zancanaro
Mateusz Dubiel
Matthias Baldauf
Matthias Heintz
Max Birk
Maxime Savary-Leblanc
Maximiliano Jeanneret Medina
Mehdi Rizvi
Mengyu Chen
Michael Burch
Michael Rohs
Michalis Xenos
Mihail Terenti
Min Zhang
Mireia Ribera
Mirko De Vincentiis
Miroslav Macík
Mohd Kamal Othman
Monica Divitini
Monisha Pattanaik
Mrim Alnfiai
Murali Balusu
Nada Attar
Nadine Flegel
Nadine Vigouroux

Nadir Weibel
Nahal Norouzi
Najla Aldaraani
Nancy Alajarmeh
Nicholas Vanderschantz
Nicoletta Adamo
Niels van Berkel
Nikolaos Avouris
Nils Beese
Nivan Ferreira
Nurha Yingta
Ohoud Alharbi
Omar Al Hashimi
Pallabi Bhowmick
Pallavi Rao Gadahad
Panayiotis Koutsabasis
Paolo Massa
Parisa Saadati
Pascal Lessel
Patricia Arias-Cabarcos
Paula Alexandra Silva
Pavel Slavik
Peter Bago
Philippe Truillet
Pinar Simsek Caglar
Po-Ming Law
Prabodh Sakhardande
Pranjal Protim Borah
Quynh Nguyen
Radovan Madleňák
Ragad Allwihan
Rahat Jahangir Rony
Rajni Sachdeo
Razan Bamoallem
Rekha Sugandhi
Rishi Vanukuru
Rogério Bordini
Rohan Gaikwad
Romane Dubus
Rosella Gennari
Rui José
Sabrina Burtscher
Sabrina Lakhdhir
Sahar Mirhadi
Saif Hadj Sassi

Salvatore Andolina
Salvatore Sorce
Samangi Wadinambi Arachchi
Sanika Doolani
Sanjit Samaddar
Sara Capecchi
Sarah Hodge
Saumya Pareek
Scott MacKenzie
Scott Trent
Sebastian Feger
Sebastian Günther
Sebastian Weiß
Sébastien Scannella
Shah Rukh Humayoun
Shunyao Wu
Siddharth Gulati
Siiri Paananen
Silvia Espada
Silvia Gabrielli
Simon Ruffieux
Simon Voelker
Simone Barbosa
Siti Haris
Sónia Brito-Costa
Sophie Dupuy-Chessa
Sophie Lepreux
Soraia M. Alarcão
Srishti Gupta
Stefan Johansson
Stéphanie Fleck
Stine Johansen
Subrata Tikadar
Suzanna Schmeelk
Sybille Caffiau
Sylvain Malacria
Taejun Kim
Tahani Alahmadi
Tahani Albalawi
Takumi Yamamoto
Tariq Zaman
Tathagata Ray
Telmo Zarraonandia
Teresa Onorati
Tero Jokela
Theodoros Georgiou

Thomas Kosch
Tilman Dingler
Tom Veuskens
Tomas Alves
Tomáš Pagáč
Tomi Heimonen
Tommaso Turchi
Tong Wu
Tzu-Yang Wang
Valentino Artizzu
Vanessa Cesário
Vanessa Maike
Vania Neris
Vasiliki Mylonopoulou
Vera Memmesheimer
Vickie Nguyen
Victor Adriel de Jesus Oliveira
Vidushani Dhanawansa
Vikas Upadhyay
Vincent Zakka
Vincenzo Dentamaro
Vincenzo Gattulli
Vinitha Gadiraju
Vit Rusnak
Vittoria Frau
Vivek Kant
Way Kiat Bong
Weiqin Chen
Wenchen Guo
William Delamare
Xiying Wang
Yann Savoye
Yao Chen
Yaoli Mao
Yaxiong Lei
Yilin Liu
Ying Ma
Yingying Zhao
Yong-Joon Thoo
Yoselyn Walsh
Yosra Rekik
Yuan Chen
Yubo Kou
Zhiyuan Wang
Zi Wang

## Sponsors and Partners

**Sponsors**

**Partners**

International Federation for Information Processing

In-cooperation with ACM

In-cooperation with SIGCHI

# Contents – Part II

**Interacting with Children**

**Interaction with Conversational Agents I and II**

## Methodologies for HCI

## Model-Based UI Design and Testing

## Motion Sickness, Stress and Risk perception in 3D Environments

## Multisensory Interaction and VR Experiences

# Human-Robot Interaction

# Pedestrian Interaction with a Snow Clearing Robot

Ashley Colley[1]($^{(\boxtimes)}$) , Marko Tiitto[2], Bastian Pfleging[3] , and Jonna Häkkilä[1]

[1] University of Lapland, Rovaniemi, Finland
{ashley.colley,jonna.hakkila}@ulapland.fi
[2] Lapland University of Applied Sciences, Rovaniemi, Finland
marko.tiitto@edu.lapinamk.fi
[3] TU Bergakademie Freiberg, Freiberg, Germany
bastian.pfleging@informatik.tu-freiberg.de

**Abstract.** In this paper, we investigate pedestrian interaction with a large autonomous robot that clears snow from the sidewalk. Through a virtual reality (VR) based user study, simulating different robot behaviors, we report on perceptions of encountering a potentially dangerous robot on the sidewalk. Overall, participants considered their actions in VR to be representative of their real-world actions. However, we note that VR headsets are not able to reproduce the high dynamic range required to realistically reproduce the high-intensity warning lights and sounds associated with close proximity to a large industrial machine. Participants expressed concern about interrupting the robot's work, and that the robot's safety-driven behavior should not delay passing by it on the sidewalk.

**Keywords:** robots · virtual reality · user experience · user studies · digital twin

## 1 Introduction

Autonomous vehicles and robots are becoming an increasingly frequent sight in everyday life contexts, as they can operate in various conditions, and complete tasks that are repetitive or dull for humans to conduct. Domestic robots performing household maintenance tasks such as vacuum cleaning and lawn mowing [3] are already commonplace, and a variety of robots and unmanned vehicles are increasingly being used in public service functions in outdoor settings [9].

Recently Starship[1] food delivery robots have become visible in many cities and university campuses around the globe. These robots are generally perceived

---

[1] https://www.starship.xyz/.

---

**Supplementary Information** The online version contains supplementary material available at https://doi.org/10.1007/978-3-031-42283-6_1.

as cute by passers-by, who express affection towards them and care for them, e.g. helping them when they get stuck [16]. Conversely, there have been reports of violence towards robots in public spaces, e.g. kicking a robot dog in the head [28].

In our work, we are interested to explore public perceptions, not towards small cute robots, but toward relatively large, noisy robots with rotating blades that autonomously clean snow from the sidewalks of cities (Fig. 1. Such robots) clearly have the potential to injure those accidentally wandering into their path when passing them on the sidewalk. The use case of encountering a snow cleaning robot is a common occasion in northern winter use context, and the related safety issues a relevant concern.

As a contribution, we extend prior works on human-robot interaction, which has so far primarily focused on factory floor and autonomous vehicle (AV) contexts, to a more uncontrolled environment where dangerous machines operate in close proximity to the general public. Through a virtual reality (VR) simulation-based user study, we report on perceptions of different robot behavior patterns. Our research is focused on the user experience and overall perception of a large maintenance robot in a realistic setting. not measured reaction times, quantified user tasks, or similar.

Fig. 1. The snow cleaning robot model used in the study.

## 2   Related Work

To position our work, we review prior works focusing on autonomous robots' interaction with humans, particularly searching for work in public, outdoor settings or with potentially dangerous robots. Our primary focus is on robots that move location, rather than static arm-type robots. Additionally, to validate our VR-based user study method, we present works that have applied a similar approach.

### 2.1   Robots Signaling to Humans

Research into the rapidly growing area of autonomous vehicles (AV) has explored different signaling mechanisms between the AV and the surrounding people (mostly pedestrians and other vulnerable road users) to increase safety and trust [7,13,17]. The works have generally highlighted the importance of vehicle kinematics as a communication signal, e.g. a vehicle beginning to slow down is the most natural and well-understood signal to pedestrians in a street crossing situation [17,21]. However, whilst the kinematics of cars are well understood by pedestrians, the same may not be true for the movements of robots that clean snow from the sidewalk. Thus, in our use case, we expect the need for explicit signaling to be higher than that for AVs driving on the roads.

Prior works exploring industrial factory floor robots have highlighted that anticipatory movement, e.g. as emphasized in animated cartoons, can be a useful indicator of a robot's movement intent [10]. A large number of works in this context have proposed the projection of the robot's movement direction [5] or intended path [4,11] on the floor as promising solutions. These kinds of solutions are plausible proposals in an indoors setting, where the space is defined and lighting conditions are controlled, but harder to extend to outdoors maintenance contexts.

The use of colored light has also been a commonly explored form of communication between robots and humans [8,13,23]. Here, different approaches have been applied. For example, in Holländer et al. [13] green is used to indicate that it is safe to cross in front of the AV, whilst Pörtner et al. [23] use a green lamp to indicate that the robot is active.

In the area of social robots [2], robot behavior and signaling to humans has gained attention as an important part of social context and communications. In the social robotics domain, robots typically employ a humanoid form factor, which highlights the function of body movements in communication, such as the ability to move the head, eyes, and arms. For example, the use of nodding, head movement, and gaze [18] as well as body posture [27] have an effect on people's perception of, and communication with, a robot. In the case of mobile robots, Hart et al. [12] reported that a gaze direction cue given by a robot head was more easily interpreted than an equivalent lighting-based signal.

## 2.2   VR as a User Study Methodology

Using a VR-simulated environment to conduct user studies has become increasingly common, as immersive VR technologies are today readily available. In VR different usage scenarios can often be more easily constructed and are more controlled than equivalent real-world settings. Covid-19 accelerated the use of VR, due to limitations on running physical user studies [20,24]. When comparing conducting a user study on public displays in VR and in the physical world, Mäkelä et al. report that participants' behavior was very similar in both studies [19]. Voit et al. [29] compared different study settings, including VR and in-situ, for investigating interaction with smart artifacts. They report similar results in both conditions and highlight the ability to control the study setting and not needing to construct physical prototypes as the benefits of a VR study. In prior art, VR settings have been used to study a broad range of user experiences, ranging from autonomous cars [13] to shoulder surfing [1]. Recently, Kassem and Michahelles [14] have investigated people's perceptions of robot behavior in a VR simulation-based study, focusing on the effect of multimodal cues.

In our research, we utilize an immersive VR set-up to study the perceptions of different behaviors of a snow-cleaning robot. This arrangement allowed us to simulate the use context, i.e. winter outdoors, and come up with a well-controlled study design.

**Fig. 2.** Interaction in the VR environment. Left: User navigation is by physical movement within the 3 m × 4 m zone or by teleporting. Right: The user interaction in the trash collection task.

## 3   Study

Our study aimed to extract data on the perceptions, actions, and feelings of people confronted with a snow-clearing robot when walking on the sidewalk. To address this, we developed a VR simulation environment where a test participant was required to walk past a moving snow-clearing robot on a narrow sidewalk. In an additional task, participants were approached by the robot from behind, whilst engaged in a trash collection task.

### 3.1   Study Design

The simulation environment was constructed from freely available 3D assets sourced from Quixel Bridge and Unreal Marketplace. These were used to create an environment with enough detail to immerse the participant in the scenarios. In addition, ambient and motor sounds were added to the environment and robot to increase the level of immersion. The robot model used in the test was loosely based on the Spyker Kat snow blower[2]. The developed model was scaled to fit realistically in the VR environment, with approximate dimensions 2.3 m long, 1.2 m wide, and 1.4 m high (see Fig. 3).

---

[2] https://spykerworkshop.com.

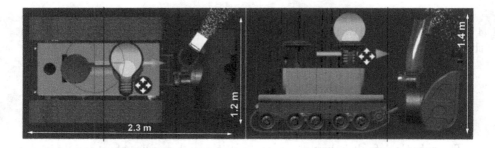

**Fig. 3.** Robot size in simulation. One grid square is 10 cm.

Two different maps were used in the study. The first map was designed to steer the participant to interact with the robot. In this scenario, the robot moved along the sidewalk toward the participant. The participant was required to navigate to a position behind the robot, marked with traffic cones. To create a challenging and informative point of interaction, the sidewalk narrowed in the area where the participant and robot would meet if the participant progressed at normal walking speed (see Fig. 4). The second map was designed to explore participant behavior when they were surprised by an approaching robot while engaged in a distraction task. As the distraction task, participants were tasked to collect six pieces of trash from the ground and deposit them into a trashcan. The trigger which spawned the robot was placed such that the robot would appear behind the participant and surprise them (Fig. 2: Right)

To move within the VR environment, participants were able to walk around freely in a 3 × 4 m area and to teleport, i.e. to use the hand controllers to target a position on the floor and immediately move to that position when releasing the hand controller trigger (Fig. 2: Left). To make the movement realistic, the teleporting distance was restricted to approximately two meters per step and at one second intervals. This restriction prevented the test participants from simply teleporting past the robot.

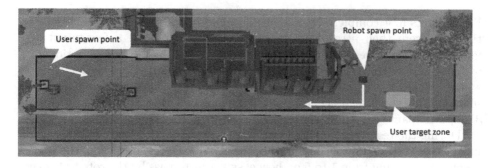

**Fig. 4.** User study environment. To complete the task the test participant must pass by the snow robot to reach the target zone.

To explore different possibilities for robot-human interaction, the robot had 4 different movement variations, which were each used as a test condition. When the robot sensed it was near the participant it would:

Condition 1: Continue unchanged
Condition 2: Stop
Condition 3: Reverse
Condition 3: Steer to go around the participant

The robot's default behavior was to move through a series of set points in the map, in the direction of the participant with its orange warning light flashing. An orange flashing warning light is typical for human-controlled machinery in public domains, e.g. street sweepers. In the first condition, the robot did not react to the participant at all. It maintained its set path and would drive over the participant if they were in its way. In the second condition, when the participant got too close to the robot, it completely stopped and changed the state of its warning light to show solid green. This lighting protocol is a logical extension of the default flashing orange warning when the robot is operating (c.f. [13]). When the participant moved away from the robot, the robot would resume its movement after 2 s. In the third condition, the robot would reverse by about 2 m when the participant got too close to the front of the robot and then stop. As in the previous condition, the warning light changed to show solid green. If the participant approached the robot from the rear, the robot would stop, as in the second condition. The fourth robot movement variation was only used in the trash-collecting task. In this variation, the robot would adjust its path to avoid the participant, but it would never stop.

The simulation was developed in Unreal Engine 5.0.3 and run on a high-performance Windows 10 computer (Nvidia GTX 1060 6 GB, Intel i7-7700K, 16 GB of ram). The VR setup consisted of a Meta Quest 2 VR headset and a 5G router. The simulation was run wirelessly through the Oculus Air Link from the computer to the headset.

### 3.2   Test Process

Participants first completed a consent form and background questionnaire. Participants were then fitted with the VR headset and given a few minutes to familiarize themselves with the VR environment and the movement options, i.e. walking and teleporting. After participants felt comfortable, the 3 test cases which required the participant to walk to the traffic cones target zone were presented. The case presentation order was counterbalanced using a Latin square. The participants were not informed which behavior the robot would take.

During the test, participants were encouraged to think-aloud, and their comments were recorded by the test moderator. After each test condition, the participant gave a rating from 1 to 5 on how easy it was to pass by the robot (1 = very difficult, 5 = very easy) and described what happened, why they acted as they did, and what were their feelings. These questions were asked verbally by the

**Fig. 5.** User study with Meta Quest 2 VR headset.

test moderator who recorded the answers. After completing the first 3 test cases, the participants completed the trash collection as a final task.

After all of the cases were completed, the participant removed the VR headset and completed an end questionnaire. The end questionnaire asked participants' opinions of the immersiveness of the simulation if they would behave the same way in real life, and how much they would trust such a street cleaning robot operating near them. The total test time was approximately 30 min. During this time participants spent between 10 and 20 min wearing the VR headset, Fig. 5.

### 3.3   Participants

A total of 12 people (5 female, 7 male) within the age range 21 to 47 ($\overline{x} = 30, s.d. = 7$) were recruited from the university's volunteer pool. There were no particular recruitment conditions. One (8%) of the participants had previously encountered an autonomous robot on the street. Half (50%) had some experience with robot vacuum cleaners or lawnmowers.

The participants reported a wide range of prior experience with VR; one participant (8%) reported no experience, 5 (25%) reported being very familiar, and the remainder of participants were placed between these extremes. Experience with robots was less common, with 8 (67%) reporting little or no experience, and the remainder reporting some experience.

## 4   Findings

We first present the quantitative results from the user study. Following this, we present the themes emerging from participants' subjective comments during the test and from the end questionnaire.

### 4.1   Passing the Robot on the Sidewalk and Collecting Trash

All participants were able to successfully complete all of the test tasks. Participants' ratings for the 3 test conditions where they were required to walk past the robot are shown in Fig. 6. Generally, the ratings were on the positive side, indicating participants considered it relatively easy to pass by the robot in all conditions. A Friedman repeated measures test indicated there was no significant difference between the test conditions, $\tilde{\chi}^2(2) = 2.36$, p $= .307$.

Figure 7 illustrates exemplary routes taken by participants (plotted data is from participant 7). Strategies included stepping into a safe area and waiting for the robot to pass by (Fig. 7, blue route), stepping into the road (Fig. 7, green route), and walking directly past the robot (Fig. 7, yellow route). The waiting strategy was described, "The robot came towards me on the sidewalk and I dodged out of its way to the side of the house. I waited for the robot to pass and then continued after that" (Participant 8 condition 1).

**Fig. 6.** Participants' rating on ease of walking past the robot in each condition

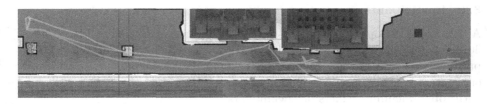

**Fig. 7.** The movement tracks of participant 7 in the 3 conditions. Blue = Condition 2, Green = Condition 3, Yellow = Condition 1 (Color figure online)

### 4.2   Emerging Themes

Several themes were identified based on the participants' subjective comments, being frightened, familiarity with the situation, interaction, social robotics and trust, and immersion in the simulation. In the following analysis, participants' subjective feedback from the test cases plus responses to the end questionnaire are combined.

**Being Frightened and Avoiding the Robot.** Many of the participants expressed a feeling of being frightened by the robot heading towards them, for example commenting, "I was just standing on the street and the robot wanted to drive over me. At the last second I jumped out of the way. It was terrifying to watch the dangerous-looking robot with spinning blades coming towards me" (P4, condition 1). Another participant commented similarly, "The device was scary, which made me jump to the side, the point where I met the robot was narrow, which even created a feeling of tightness and anxiety. I wondered if it would have run over me if I didn't jump away!" (P1 condition 1). Maintaining a comfortable distance from the robot was noted by several participants, e.g. "I felt like walking on the other side of the road" (P11 condition 3). In the trash collection task, it was noted by one participant that although the robot itself was at a comfortable distance, it was throwing snow onto the participant, "The robot threw snow on me when it was passing by me" (P6, trash collection).

**Familiarity and Expectation.** The most common expectation for robot behavior was that it would stop when it became close to the participant. Participants commented, e.g. "The robot didn't recognize me and drove through me and I died. I thought that the robot will stop moving" (P6, condition 1), and "I just stayed still and let the robot drive through me because I thought that the robot would stop" (P7, condition 1). One participant used their familiarity with the context to guide their strategy, "Every time I took the road instead of the sidewalk, probably because it had already been plowed and it would be easier to walk there" (P12, condition 1). Learning effects in the test process were apparent, e.g. "As it was my second time with the robot I was not afraid of it" (P1, condition 2), and "The robot was already familiar this time, so I knew where it was going..." (P11 condition 2).

**Interaction.** Several participants highlighted that they had little idea of the robot's intention, e.g. "...it was slow and I didn't understand its intentions to stop or continue" (P9, condition). The slow movement speed of the robot appeared to add to the frustration, e.g. "...it was annoying to wait for it to pass as it was slow" (P9 condition 2), and "I wasn't sure if it is going to back up, stop or keep on going. It stopped at the point I couldn't pass it, so I gave way to it. It still didn't move, so I took a step forward and it started moving. Waiting and not knowing to which direction it is heading was the most challenging part" (P10 condition 2). Potentially, this lack of understanding could lead to hesitation, "...I was happy that I didn't interrupt the robot and I didn't have to do the who-goes-first dance with it" (P10 condition 1).

Overall the interaction condition 2, where the robot stopped when it sensed a human in its proximity was preferred: "It was very nice that the robot noticed me and waited" (P4 condition2), "...as I passed by the robot it stopped in time, no issues passing the robot" (P5 condition 2), and "The robot stopped and it was easy to pass" (P12 condition 2). The reversing interaction (condition 3) was liked by some participants, e.g. "I liked this robot as it gave me space to walk on the narrow sidewalk" (P1 condition 3), and "The robot stopped and started backing out of my way. The event went smoothly" (P8, condition 3). The negative side of the reversing interaction was noted in that it potentially slows passing by the robot, e.g. "It was a bit annoying still to wait for it to go back. But not needing to step out of its path felt good" (P9 condition 3). The avoidance algorithm used in the trash collection case was observed as working well by some participants, e.g. "As I was picking up the trash the robot passed by uneventfully and moved to the side preemptively, I didn't need to move myself" (P5, trash collection task).

Only one participant commented specifically on the robot's indication lights, but was confused as to their meaning, "I noticed the light on top of the robot is indicating if it detects me or not. This was a good feature. But, if I am not wrong, it was showing green when I am in its way and yellow when it is moving forward. I somehow was a bit confused about this color mapping..." (P9 condition 3). Generally, it appeared participants wished for some indication of the robots' planned route. e.g. "I also wasn't sure about its path and where it would go next" (P2, trash collection task).

**Social Robotics and Trust.** Some participants acted to test the limits of the robot's reactions. In some cases this was playful but sometimes became malevolent, e.g. "I tested again if the robot would stop, and it did!" (P6 condition 2). Other participants were more proactive, e.g. "I wanted to test the limits of the robot, so I even walked back and towards the sides of the robot" (P8 condition 2), and "I noticed that the robot tried to avoid me at all costs, even when I was trying actively to get in the way" (P7, trash collection task).

Some participants were concerned that they were disturbing the robot's work. This was particularly commented in the reversing interaction (condition 3), e.g. "I didn't like it, because I felt I was disturbing its work. But I feel like people could abuse this system, e.g. children pushing it onto a road" P4 condition 3, and "I felt a bit rude to interrupt it from its work" P10 condition 3.

**Immersion in the Simulation.** Participants considered the simulation to be representative of real life, rating how well the simulation felt like real life as 3.6/5, on a scale of 1 = not at all, 5 = very like real life. 8/12 (67%) of participants commented that they would be more cautious in real life than in the simulation, e.g. keeping a bigger distance between themselves and the robot. One participant commented that the real-world soundscape would be one factor that could make them behave differently, e.g. to keep further from a noisy robot.

For some participants the simulation was immersive enough that they applied real-world knowledge, e.g. "I started from the snow and moved towards the cones using the road. I decided to use the road because of my real-life experiences with snow. I don't like getting my shoes wet and thus the road that is cleaned from snow is a more appealing alternative than deep snow" P2, condition 1.

# 5   Discussion

The areas of interest arising from our study findings relate to 1) the approach to communicating the robot's intention to pedestrians, and 2) the realism of the simulation environments. Additionally, we discuss some methodological issues related to our study design and approach.

## 5.1   Communicating the Robot's Intent

The traffic lights metaphor (flashing orange = warning, green = safe to walk) we used on the robot's warning light was either misunderstood or not noticed at all by participants. One contributing factor to the lack of visibility is the difficulty in rendering realistic bright lights in VR (see section Simulation Realism). Considering the functionality of the warning light, the choice between signaling instruction to others vs. presenting one's own intention has been previously raised in the domain of autonomous vehicles, e.g. by Zhang et al. [30]. We note also Hollander et al.'s conclusion that, in scenarios where there are multiple pedestrians, instructional displays on autonomous vehicles should be avoided, as they risk presenting conflicting or mistargeted instructions [13]. In the sidewalk snow-clearing context, it is highly likely that there will be multiple passers-by in the robot's vicinity. Here, inspiration for future work may be taken from Han et al.'s projected indoor robot paths [11], and for projection in a street context from Dancu et al.'s on-road intent projection for cyclists [6].

Prior art has reported, how in collaborative human-robot tasks, combining audio, visual, and haptic cues about the robot's intention led to higher collaborative task performance than using a single modality [14]. The case however used a small robot hidden behind a wall in a collaborative indoor task, which is quite different from a large, noisy, moving outdoor robot. Still, when designing the snow robot's signaling mechanics, a combination of different cues would be worth studying in future research.

## 5.2   Simulation Realism

Prior work exploring VR simulations of comparable contexts has largely reported strong correlations between virtual and real-life behaviors, e.g. in the cases of police training [15], shopping [22] and pedestrian behavior [26]. This suggests that, in general, there is good transferability between simulation and real-life. However, users' prior experience with VR has been reported as increasing perceived pragmatic quality and reducing the hedonic quality [25].

In our study, the participants generally reported that they found the study's virtual environment to be immersive. This was supported by the numerous participants that reported feeling frightened by the test scenario. However, there were clearly several points where the simulation did not expose participants' real-life behavior. Due to the limited tracking space, participants needed to make teleport jumps to navigate to the goal area. It appears our approach of limiting teleport to 2 m jumps and once per second was quite effective in maintaining the feeling of walking, as there were few participant comments about the tele-port function. However, for improved realism, future studies should utilize larger tracking areas or design different study tasks that require less movement.

Only one participant noted the warning light on the top of the robot. We note that is difficult to recreate such high-intensity lighting in a VR simulation, due to the limited dynamic range of the headset screen. Similarly, negative comments related to the soundscape in the game not representing real life. This is likely of particular importance with such loud sounds (and low frequency vibrations) that would be made by a snow-clearing robot, which naturally acts as a warning to keep one's distance. Such dynamics are challenging to recreate using headphones.

### 5.3  Methodology Reflections

As our interest was in studying the user experience that would occur in-the-wild, we did not focus on measuring user reactions or performance. One main interest was to understand how people react the very first time they encounter a snow-clearing robot in real life. With our within-subjects study method, it was clear that there was a very strong novelty effect and after completing the first test condition participants were already much more comfortable with interacting with the robot. Hence future studies targeting understanding of first encounters should adopt a between-subjects method and an accordingly larger sample size.

### 5.4  Future Work

As future work, we will explore the potential of movement intent path projection and seek to validate our findings in the virtual environment through real-world experiments.

## 6  Conclusion

Through a VR-based user study, perceptions of different behavior patterns for an autonomous snow-clearing robot were explored. Participants considered their actions in VR to be representative of their real-world actions and expressed concern about interrupting the robot's work and being delayed by the robot's safety-driven behavior. We note that the visual and audible dynamic range of VR headsets is insufficient to realistically reproduce high-intensity warning lights and close-proximity large machine sounds.

**Acknowledgments.** This research has been supported by the Lapland Robotics and Innovation in Lapland through Design and Art (ILO) projects, funded by the European Regional Development Fund (ERDF).

# References

1. Abdrabou, Y., et al.: Understanding shoulder surfer behavior and attack patterns using virtual reality. In: Proceedings of the 2022 International Conference on Advanced Visual Interfaces, pp. 1–9 (2022)
2. Bartneck, C., Forlizzi, J.: A design-centred framework for social human-robot interaction. In: RO-MAN 2004, 13th IEEE International Workshop on Robot and Human Interactive Communication (IEEE Catalog No. 04TH8759), pp. 591–594. IEEE (2004)
3. Bogue, R.: Domestic robots: has their time finally come? Ind. Robot Int. J. (2017)
4. Chadalavada, R.T., Andreasson, H., Krug, R., Lilienthal, A.J.: That's on my mind! Robot to human intention communication through on-board projection on shared floor space. In: 2015 European Conference on Mobile Robots (ECMR), pp. 1–6. IEEE (2015)
5. Coovert, M.D., Lee, T., Shindev, I., Sun, Y.: Spatial augmented reality as a method for a mobile robot to communicate intended movement. Comput. Hum. Behav. **34**, 241–248 (2014)
6. Dancu, A., et al.: Gesture bike: examining projection surfaces and turn signal systems for urban cycling. In: Proceedings of the 2015 International Conference on Interactive Tabletops and Surfaces, pp. 151–159 (2015)
7. Dey, D., et al.: Taming the EHMI jungle: a classification taxonomy to guide, compare, and assess the design principles of automated vehicles' external human-machine interfaces. Transport. Res. Interdisc. Perspect. **7**, 100174 (2020)
8. Dey, D., Habibovic, A., Pfleging, B., Martens, M., Terken, J.: Color and animation preferences for a light band EHMI in interactions between automated vehicles and pedestrians. In: Proceedings of the 2020 CHI Conference on Human Factors in Computing Systems. CHI '20, pp. 1–13. Association for Computing Machinery, New York, NY, USA (2020). https://doi.org/10.1145/3313831.3376325
9. Galar, D., Kumar, U., Seneviratne, D.: Robots, Drones, UAVs and UGVs for Operation and Maintenance. CRC Press, Boca Raton (2020)
10. Gielniak, M.J., Thomaz, A.L.: Generating anticipation in robot motion. In: 2011 RO-MAN, pp. 449–454. IEEE (2011)
11. Han, Z., Parrillo, J., Wilkinson, A., Yanco, H.A., Williams, T.: Projecting robot navigation paths: hardware and software for projected ar. arXiv preprint arXiv:2112.05172 (2021)
12. Hart, J., et al.: Using human-inspired signals to disambiguate navigational intentions. In: Wagner, A.R., et al. (eds.) ICSR 2020. LNCS (LNAI), vol. 12483, pp. 320–331. Springer, Cham (2020). https://doi.org/10.1007/978-3-030-62056-1_27
13. Holländer, K., Colley, A., Mai, C., Häkkilä, J., Alt, F., Pfleging, B.: Investigating the influence of external car displays on pedestrians' crossing behavior in virtual reality. In: Proceedings of the 21st International Conference on Human-Computer Interaction with Mobile Devices and Services. MobileHCI '19. Association for Computing Machinery, New York, NY, USA (2019). https://doi.org/10.1145/3338286.3340138
14. Kassem, K., Ungerböck, T., Wintersberger, P., Michahelles, F.: What is happening behind the wall? Towards a better understanding of a hidden robot's intent by multimodal cues. Proc. ACM Hum.-Comput. Interact. **6**(MHCI), 1–19 (2022)
15. Kleygrewe, L., Hutter, R.V., Koedijk, M., Oudejans, R.R.: Virtual reality training for police officers: a comparison of training responses in VR and real-life training. Police Pract. Res. 1–20 (2023)

16. Lee, A., Toombs, A.L.: Robots on campus: understanding public perception of robots using social media. In: Conference Companion Publication of the 2020 on Computer Supported Cooperative Work and Social Computing, pp. 305–309 (2020)
17. Lee, Y.M., et al.: Learning to interpret novel EHMI: the effect of vehicle kinematics and EHMI familiarity on pedestrian' crossing behavior. J. Safety Res. **80**, 270–280 (2022)
18. Liu, C., Ishi, C.T., Ishiguro, H., Hagita, N.: Generation of nodding, head tilting and eye gazing for human-robot dialogue interaction. In: 2012 7th ACM/IEEE International Conference on Human-Robot Interaction (HRI), pp. 285–292. IEEE (2012)
19. Mäkelä, V., et al.: Virtual field studies: conducting studies on public displays in virtual reality. In: Proceedings of the 2020 CHI Conference on Human Factors in Computing Systems, pp. 1–15 (2020)
20. Mathis, F., et al.: Remote XR studies: the golden future of HCI research. In: Proceedings of the CHI 2021 Workshop on XR Remote Research (2021). https://mat.qmul.ac.uk/events/xr-chi-2021
21. Moore, D., Currano, R., Strack, G.E., Sirkin, D.: The case for implicit external human-machine interfaces for autonomous vehicles. In: Proceedings of the 11th International Conference on Automotive User Interfaces and Interactive Vehicular Applications. AutomotiveUI '19, pp. 295–307. Association for Computing Machinery, New York, NY, USA (2019). https://doi.org/10.1145/3342197.3345320
22. Pizzi, G., Scarpi, D., Pichierri, M., Vannucci, V.: Virtual reality, real reactions?: Comparing consumers' perceptions and shopping orientation across physical and virtual-reality retail stores. Comput. Hum. Behav. **96**, 1–12 (2019)
23. Pörtner, A., Schröder, L., Rasch, R., Sprute, D., Hoffmann, M., König, M.: The power of color: a study on the effective use of colored light in human-robot interaction. In: 2018 IEEE/RSJ International Conference on Intelligent Robots and Systems (IROS), pp. 3395–3402. IEEE (2018)
24. Rivu, R., et al.: Remote VR studies-a framework for running virtual reality studies remotely via participant-owned HMDs. arXiv preprint arXiv:2102.11207 (2021)
25. Sagnier, C., Loup-Escande, E., Valléry, G.: Effects of gender and prior experience in immersive user experience with virtual reality. In: Ahram, T., Falcão, C. (eds.) AHFE 2019. AISC, vol. 972, pp. 305–314. Springer, Cham (2020). https://doi.org/10.1007/978-3-030-19135-1_30
26. Schneider, S., Bengler, K.: Virtually the same? Analysing pedestrian behaviour by means of virtual reality. Transport. Res. F: Traffic Psychol. Behav. **68**, 231–256 (2020)
27. Vázquez, M., Carter, E.J., McDorman, B., Forlizzi, J., Steinfeld, A., Hudson, S.E.: Towards robot autonomy in group conversations: Understanding the effects of body orientation and gaze. In: 2017 12th ACM/IEEE International Conference on Human-Robot Interaction (HRI), pp. 42–52. IEEE (2017)
28. Vice: Robot dog attack (2023). https://www.vice.com/en/article/3ad9zj/dollar15000-robot-dog-walks-30-seconds-on-brisbane-street-before-someone-punts-it-in-the-head. Accessed 26 Jan 2023
29. Voit, A., Mayer, S., Schwind, V., Henze, N.: Online, VR, AR, lab, and in-situ: comparison of research methods to evaluate smart artifacts. In: Proceedings of the 2019 CHI Conference on Human Factors in Computing Systems, pp. 1–12 (2019)
30. Zhang, J., Vinkhuyzen, E., Cefkin, M.: Evaluation of an autonomous vehicle external communication system concept: a survey study. In: Stanton, N.A. (ed.) AHFE 2017. AISC, vol. 597, pp. 650–661. Springer, Cham (2018). https://doi.org/10.1007/978-3-319-60441-1_63

# Robot Collaboration and Model Reliance Based on Its Trust in Human-Robot Interaction

Basel Alhaji[1]([✉])(iD), Michael Prilla[1](iD), and Andreas Rausch[2](iD)

[1] Computer Science and Applied Cognitive Science, University of Duisburg-Essen,
Duisburg, Germany
{basel.alhaji,michael.prilla}@uni-due.de
[2] Institute for Software and Systems Engineering, Clausthal University
of Technology, Clausthal-Zellerfeld, Germany
andreas.rausch@tu-clausthal.de

**Abstract.** Safety and performance are essential for fruitful teams consisting of a human and an autonomous robot. The collaboration in such a team requires that both parties are able to anticipate and understand each others' behavior. However, as both involved agents act autonomously, this form of collaboration has many sources of uncertainty, under which many decisions have to be made by both agents. In the case of interdependent set of actions, this also makes both agents vulnerable to each other's behavior. Depending on how critical the collaboration is, failing might significantly jeopardize safety and performance of the team. In interaction forms that contain uncertainty and vulnerability, trust plays an important role in making decisions, and consequently, in the outcome of the interaction. This applies for both agents, meaning that not only human trust is important but also robot trust. Having an adequate trust level can lead to safer and more natural collaboration. In this paper, we develop a robot trust model that allows the robot to reason about past interactions and use them to update its current belief about the human intentions. Using this model, the robot decides on how much to rely on the models it has and subsequently, trades-off between safety and performance. For evaluation, we conduct a human-subject experiment with 22 participants. The results show that including a sense of robotic trust in the decision-making of the robot enhances the interaction objectively and subjectively.

## 1 Introduction

Traditional robotic systems are being enhanced by adding AI-based and machine-learned components to their decision-making processes allowing them to

This publication is based upon work supported and financed by the Simulation Science Center Clausthal-Göttingen (SWZ) through the project HerMes.

handle more complex and unplanned situations more efficiently. As their intelligence is continually increasing, the new generation of robotic systems is not physically separated from humans anymore, but rather works autonomously and safely alongside them in many different domains. Examples include social robots supporting humans doing their daily activities [10,49], search and rescue robots [5,11], and in industrial domains where humans and robots work together to assemble physical objects [8,30]. Consequently, due to the different and complementary capabilities of humans and robots, the new topic of discussion is about designing and building hybrid teams [1,18,38] consisting of robots and humans, which undertake more intricate tasks than either party can do alone.

Interaction in hybrid teams may have different forms depending on the overlap of working time and workspace (and other factors) of the involved parties. For example, there is a clear differentiation between cooperation and collaboration forms of interaction [39,45] in both of which the human and the robot have a shared goal. In the cooperation form, the tasks are executed in a sequential way or in parallel where the human and the robot have different tasks to do. In the collaboration form, on the other hand, the dependency on each others behavior is the highest, where the human and the robot execute the tasks at the same time and they work together in the same workspace [39,45].

Cooperation and collaboration in a hybrid team where both agents are acting autonomously toward a shared goal, however, entails many challenges such as being mutually predictable and the agents should be able to understand and model each other's intentions [27]. For the robot to be able to do so, it needs to address the inherent uncertainty about the behavior and decisions of the human. This is especially challenging when the robot does not know in advance on what part of the task it should work. As humans have higher priority than robots, in such a case, the robot should observe the human behavior and use these observations up to a certain time point to infer the human intention and act accordingly. However, inference is always associated with uncertainty. Therefore, planning problems should take that explicitly into account [6]. In addition to uncertainty, the inter-dependency of agents' actions makes both of them vulnerable to each other's behavior. The vulnerability of the robot is due to the possibility of failing and the potential harm that it might cause especially to the human partner [2].

Humans deploy an effective mechanism when they face situations in which they are uncertain about and vulnerable to the behavior of another agent (another human or a robot), which is trust [33,35]. It contributes strongly to the level of reliance on others depending on previous experience [32]. It is also argued that trust is essential for working in teams [16,44,48].

There are many definitions of trust in the literature from different research fields. In the human-robot interaction literature, the most widely used one is put forward by Lee and See, who define trust as *"the attitude that an agent will help achieve an individual's goals in a situation characterized by uncertainty and vulnerability"* [32]. These characteristics, which make trust a relevant factor to consider in the interaction, are also mentioned by almost all other trust definitions [28,35,43]. Since the robot is uncertain about and vulnerable to the human behavior, it may benefit from using the concept of trust as an additional *soft* information that helps in making better decisions. It can be used to adjust the level of reliance on the human or on the models the robot has that describe the human behavior depending on how well the robot can understand its human partner behavior. Although trust of humans toward robots and autonomous machines has been deeply investigated for a couple of decades (see [26] for a review), researchers did not take the perspective of the robot into consideration as this concept does not exist naturally. Though, it is highly relevant. We strongly believe that robot trust can enhance the interaction with humans and other autonomous robots.

As mentioned earlier, predictability is one of the most important factors for team formation [27]. It is as well a paramount factor for trust formation [3,36,42]. Because the robot has to make predictions about the human behavior in order to be able to act collaboratively, robot trust should include the reliability of the prediction models and the accuracy of the inferences as input. To this end, in this work, we include a predictability-based trust function in the decision-making process of the robot and show the benefits of that in an objective way, where the idle and completion times of the designed task are recorded, and in a subjective way, where we evaluate the human perception of anthropomorphism, likeability, perceived intelligence, perceived safety, and human trust. Thus, our contribution is twofold: first, the development of the trust model and its integration with the decision making process of the robot. Second, a human-subject study that shows the influence of the proposed approach and the resulted robot behavior on the human perception of interacting with the robot.

## 2   Related Work

The human in a hybrid team can take different roles. Such as *supervisor, operator, cooperator, collaborator,* and *bystander* [39]. In the special case when the human and the robot act autonomously in a *team*, this reduces to two interaction forms. They are *cooperation* and *collaboration*. As collaborators, the human and the robot have similar hierarchical levels. They work simultaneously and continuously toward a joint task completion [39] in the same workspace. As cooperators, the agents work independently and they have strict task allocation [39]. Considering working time and space, cooperation is the case when the human and the robot work either sequentially, or separated in space. Collaboration, on the other hand, is the case when they work simultaneously sharing the same workspace [1].

In both forms of interaction, teamwork requires mutual understanding between involved members which is also important for hybrid teams [46]. For the robot to understand the human, it needs a model that describes the human behavior. There is much research work that concentrates on developing accurate human models that allow the robot to predict humans behavior and efficiently interact with them. For example, the authors in [25] used Hidden Markov models

(HMMs) in which they encoded the human goals as hidden states. They trained the HMMs for each human activity in an activity modeling phase in which the transition probabilities are obtained. In an intention recognition phase, the robot uses its observation and the trained HMMs to infer the human intended activity which they considered to be the one with the highest probability.

Using anticipatory temporal conditional random field with object affordance, the authors in [29] predicted the human intended activities a couple of seconds in advance given the observations.

The use of maximum entropy inverse reinforcement learning [50] (a.k.a. noisy rationality) is also popular to make predictions about the human intentions and activities. For example, in a navigation task, the authors in [31] used this approach to reason about the entire trajectories to generate a probability distribution over possible human navigational behaviors. In a shared control setting, the authors in [12,13] used the same concept to predict the human intended goal for the purpose of assisting the human doing a given task. Using a similar modeling technique, the authors in [40] inferred a probability distribution over possible human intended objects, which allows the robot to avoid working on them at the same time and complete its independent set of tasks.

None of these approaches considers the case when the model fails in describing the human behavior and what the robot should do in such a case. To handle this problem, the authors in [15] used the noisy rational model of human behavior in a navigation setting and inferred the rationality parameter online as an indicator for the robot confidence in order to produce safer plans. They used the model to predict the human policy as a probability distribution over set of actions in a state given a goal and not to predict the human goal itself.

It can be observed that most of the methods used in the literature for predicting the human intention and behavior return a probability distribution over a set of possibilities which naturally entails *uncertainties*. Based on this probabilities the robot makes its own decision. Teaming up with humans adds another important characteristic to the interaction, which is vulnerability of each agent to the behavior of the other. These two characteristics (uncertainty and vulnerability) make trust an essential factor to consider by definition [28,32] from the perspective of both agents.

Although there is a huge body of literature about humans trust in teamwork with each other [22] and with technological artefacts such as robots [17] and other forms of AI-based systems and autonomous machines [20], trust from the robot perspective when interacting with humans is not well covered. Recently, a couple of robot trust models have been proposed. For example, the authors in [47] put forward a probabilistic model to estimate the human trustworthiness as a source of information to the robot. They use a training session with participants to collect the data needed for building a Bayesian network, and an episodic memory to recall surprising interactions. In this work, no physical collaboration was involved.

The authors in [4] proposed a capability-based trust model. They used the tasks requirements and the known agent capabilities as inputs to the trust model which then generates the probability of succeeding in the task. However, this is not enough because although humans might possess the capabilities needed for a certain task, many factors might influence the way in which the human behaves for the same task.

The authors in [41] adopted a performance-centric human trust model based on performance and faults and used it for the purpose of optimal task allocation.

The authors in [2] proposed a trust function based on the transition probabilities of the used interaction model. The model first quantifies the difference in probabilities between the robot's expected state and the real one in the last step of the interaction and used this as an input to a simple trust function. Based on the current trust level, the robot decides to either follow the optimal policy or to behave conservatively until it gains more trust in the model.

Unlike the previous work, in this work, we address the uncertainty in the interaction with the human by integrating a predictability-based robot trust function in the robot decision-making process and use it to adjust the *reliance* on the model the robot has for the human behavior. Thus, it has a similar effect to human trust (i.e., moderating reliance). The reason for using predictability as the main factor of trust is that it forms the main issue in such interaction form. Additionally, it is one of the most important factors that affect trust in general [3,17,42]. We show that this integration allows the robot to change the interaction form between cooperation and collaboration, which consequently trades-off between safety and performance.

## 3  Formalism

### 3.1  Collaboration Model

As already stated, dealing with environments that include uncertainty requires the robot to probabilistically model the environment including the human behavior or intention. For this, the robot maintains a belief about the current system state and makes decisions based on it. Partially observable Markov decision process (POMDP) is a powerful formal framework that allows the robot to make sequential decisions under uncertainty and partial state observability [24]. It considers both the uncertainty about the current state and the effect of the agent actions.

In our work, we deploy the POMDP framework to model the interaction between the human and the robot. It consists of a tuple $\{S, A, T, R, O, \Omega\}$, where:

- $S$ is the set of all system states.
- $A$ is the set of all possible control actions that the robot can execute.
- $T : S \times A \to \Pi(S)$ is the transition function that returns the probability of reaching a given state $s'$ from the current state $s$ if action $a$ is executed ($T(s, a, s') = p(s'|s, a)$).
- $R$ is the reward function that gives the robot the immediate reward for taking action $a$ in state $s$.
- $O$ is the set of all possible observations the robot can make.

– $\Omega : S \times A \rightarrow \Pi(O)$ is the observation function that returns the probability of making observation $o$ if action $a$ is taken in state $s$ ($\Omega(o, a, s) = p(o|s, a)$).

For simplification, we assume that the robot can observe its own states perfectly which we denote as $x \in X$. In order for the robot to act collaboratively, it needs to predict the human intended goal $g \in G$, which is latent and can not be directly observable. Therefore, similar to [9,21,40], we augment the robot state with the human intended goal and use it as the system state $s = (x, g)$ and we maintain a belief about the human intention. Taking a human-centric perspective, the human is considered the leader of the interaction. Accordingly, we assume that the human does not adapt to the robot behavior, and the robot actions cannot influence the human intentions[1]. As a result, the robot's actions only affect the robot state and the observation function becomes independent of the actions and can be rewritten as $\Omega(o, s) = p(o|s) = p(o|g)$.

Using the observations received by the robot sensors up to the current time step (e.g., the pose of the human hand over time), the robot creates and updates its belief $b$ about the system state (i.e., $b(s) = p(s|o_{1:k})$). Given that the uncertain part of the system state is the human intention (i.e., the human intended goal), the belief represents a probability distribution over the possible goals. Accordingly, the belief can be written as $b(s) = b(g) = p(g|o_{1:k})$ [21,40] which gets updated with new observations using Bayes' rule that is shown in (1).

$$b(s) = b(g) = p(g|o_{1:k}) = \frac{p(o_{1:k}|g)p(g)}{\sum_{g'} p(o_{1:k}|g')p(g')} \tag{1}$$

Inferring the human latent intention (or other latent information in the environment) requires a model that links the observations to the possible intended goals. Due to the general imperfection of models, the robot should be able to detect and quantify the deviation between its expectations, that are derived from the models, and the real executions (e.g., the outcome at the end of the task). Using this information, the robot can adjust its behavior in order to enhance the team performance or to avoid failures in the future interactions. Considering these deviations is of special importance when interacting with humans due to the inconsistent human behavior that differs between individuals and over time. Even the same human may change the behavior and preferences multiple times for a certain task. Humans may also be affected by many human factors such as anxiety, workload, loss of situation awareness, risk cognition, lack of trust, and many more [19]. At these times, the models might fail in describing and predicting the human actions, which negatively affects both safety and performance of the team. Robot trust can play an important rule in avoiding the ramifications associated with the discrepancy between the model and reality due to the lack of predictability.

Assuming that the robot is already empowered with the sense of trust using a trust function that evaluates the trustworthiness of the inference model based on

---

[1] This assumption also simplifies the formalization of the problem. Relaxing it does not affect how trust is modeled. It mainly complicates the prediction model.

the history of experience ($Tr \in [-1, 1]$ where $-1$ is fully untrustworthy inference and $1$ is the other end where the inference is fully trustworthy), we intend to merge this *soft* and *partially subjective* source of information with the belief update process which results in a trust-based belief given in (2)

$$b_{Tr}(g) = p(g|o_{1:k}, Tr) = f(b, Tr) \tag{2}$$

where $b_{Tr}$ in this case is the new belief that takes the current value of trust into account, and $f$ is the mapping between the original *objective* belief to a new one which is trust dependent.

Before modeling the $f$ function of (2), we need to emphasize the difference between the *hard* observations $O$, and the *soft* observations $Tr$ that are derived from the robot trust function. While $O$'s help in recognizing the current system states, $Tr$'s do not provide direct information in this regard, but rather they primarily assist in determining the appropriate level of model reliance. Accordingly, when robot trust is high, there should be less uncertainty in the belief distribution and higher uncertainty otherwise (compared to the default where robot trust is not considered). Since we previously assumed trust to have values in the interval $[-1, 1]$, we model the mapping function $f$ to be as follows

$$f(b, Tr) = \alpha.b.b^{Tr} = \alpha.b^{1+Tr} \tag{3}$$

with $\alpha$ representing a (re)normalizing factor, and $b$ is the original objective belief derived from (1).

To show the effect of integrating trust in calculating the belief using the proposed function, we consider the extreme ends of the trust interval. Once the robot trust reaches its lowest value ($Tr = -1$), the uncertainty in the belief distribution will be at its highest value as the belief $b_{Tr}$ will be a uniform distribution and the entropy of the distribution (given in (4)) will be maximized.

$$H = -\sum_{i=1}^{n} p_i \log(p_i) \tag{4}$$

On the other end, when trust reaches its highest value ($Tr = 1$), the entropy of the distribution will be lower than the case when trust is not considered or it is at its neutral level ($Tr = 0$), and consequently the uncertainty in the belief distribution will be lower. Figure 1 depicts the effect of trust on the belief.

At this point, in order for the robot to predict the human intended goals, it needs a model that relates the human behavior (e.g., human hand motion) to the possible goals. For this, we follow the approach used in [12, 40] and use the maximum entropy inverse optimal control (MaxEnt IOC) [50]. In this formulation, the goals with higher costs given the history of observations will be exponentially less likely to be the intended ones. Dragan and Srinivasa [12], show that using Laplace's method, the likelihood function of (1) can be approximated by the following (interested readers are referred to [12] for details about the derivation)

$$p(o_{1:k}|g) \propto \frac{\exp(-C_g(o_{1:k}) - C_g(o_{k:n}^*))}{\exp(-C_g(o_{1:n}^*))} \tag{5}$$

**Fig. 1.** Robot trust effect on the belief distribution. When trust is high (low), the robot is more (less) certain about its predictions.

where $o^*_{k:n}$ is the optimal observations (i.e., optimal trajectory) from the current time step $k$ until the end of the task (i.e., reaching the goal), and $o^*_{1:n}$ is the hypothetical optimal observations from the beginning until the end.

### 3.2 Modeling Robot Trust

As mentioned earlier, predictability is a paramount factor for human trust [3,14, 36,42]. It is also essential for hybrid team formation [27]. Therefore, we extend the work by Alhaji et al. [2] and use a trust model based on predictability of the interactions. In order to quantify predictability, the authors define a new term called *events magnitude* denoted as $E_m \in [0,1]$ based on the transition probability of a fully observable Markov decision process (MDP). It measures the difference in probability between an expected and a real world transitions. Since we formally model the interaction as POMDP, in which the decisions are made based on a belief about the state (particularity the human goal which is not fully observable), we redefine this term to suit our formulation.

At each time step, the robot belief about the human goal can be visualized as Fig. 2 shows. During the execution of a given task, the robot derives its expectations about the task outcome and starts working toward its part of the task. At this time point, the robot clones the belief distribution. At the end of the execution, the robot measures the difference between the expected and the real outcome based on the cloned belief. Accordingly, the events magnitude can be calculated as in (6)

$$E_m = p_{expect} - p_{actual} \tag{6}$$

where $p_{expect}$ is the probability of the expected goal at the time when the robot starts working on its part of the task (i.e., initiates motion), which is simply

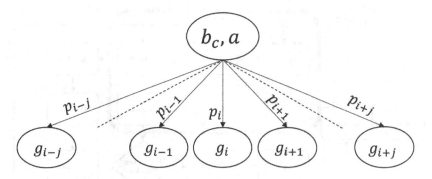

**Fig. 2.** Belief probability distribution.

the maximum of the belief distribution, and $p_{actual}$ is the probability of the real human goal based on the cloned belief, which cannot be deterministically known until the end of the task.

Predictability is then defined as the complement of the events magnitude and can be derived as in (7).

$$Pr = 1 - E_m \tag{7}$$

The robot trust function then takes the predictability as an input and evolves over tasks. It starts from an initial value ($Tr_{init}$) and gets updated after each interaction (i.e., after each sub-task). The proposed trust function is shown in (8), which is similar to the one presented in [2].

$$\begin{aligned} Tr_0 &= Tr_{init} \\ Tr_i &= Tr_{i-1} + (Pr - Pr_{th}) \quad i > 0 \\ Tr_{min} &\leq Tr_i \leq Tr_{max} \end{aligned} \tag{8}$$

where $Pr_{th}$ is a predefined threshold over which the interaction is considered predictable and trust increases (as $Pr - Pr_{th} > 0$). Otherwise trust decreases (as $Pr - Pr_{th} < 0$). $Tr_{min} = -1$ and $Tr_{max} = 1$ are the minimum and maximum allowed trust values, respectively.

$Pr_{thr}$ controls how fast trust accumulates and dissipates. Setting it to a high value (e.g., 90%) makes the dissipation of trust faster than its accumulation, which emulates human trust dynamics [3,23].

### 3.3 Decision Process

After formalizing the trust function, the robot can now use the trust-based belief $b_{Tr}$ to make decisions. Figure 3 shows the full process of decision making with robot trust integrated.

The robot starts with an initial trust value and using its observations it infers the human intended goal and creates its objective belief (using (1)). The robot then selects an action based on this belief but does not execute it. It uses it to check whether the information received so far is enough to start working on the task (e.g., initiate motion action) based on the original default model to trigger

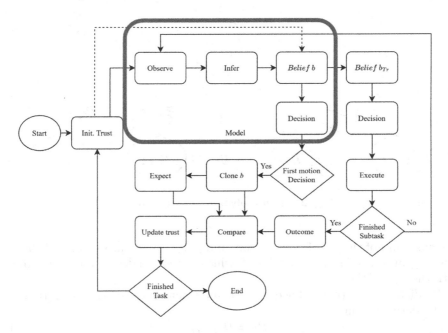

**Fig. 3.** Decision making process with robot trust integrated. The block in red contains the default decision making process. (Color figure online)

the cloning of the belief and derive the expectation. From the objective belief $b$, it derives the trust-based one $b_{T_r}$ (using (2)) and makes a decision and executes the action based on this one. Once the current sub-task is finished (e.g., the goal is reached), the robot does not have uncertainty about the human intended goal any more but rather knows it deterministically. At this point the robot compares the probability of this goal based on the cloned belief with the probability of the expected one to quantify the predictability (using (6) and (7)). Depending on the predictability value, the robot updates its trust (using (8)), which then changes the initial trust value for the next sub-task. If the task is finished, the robot saves the current value of trust to be used as initial value when interacting later with the same user.

## 4   Human-Subject Experiment

In this section, we describe the human subject experiment we ran to evaluate the outcome of our approach objectively and subjectively.

### 4.1   Apparatus

We implemented our approach on the collaborative robotic arm (aka. cobot) Panda from Franka Emika[2], which we programmed using Python within the

---

[2] http://www.franka.de/.

Robot Operating System (ROS) framework. For environment perception, we used the Microsoft HoloLens[3] 2 which we programmed using Unity[4] game engine and C#. The use of the HoloLens allows us to create virtual sensors that facilitate the implementation to a great extent. By overlaying virtual objects on the real ones, we kept track of the relative position of the human hand with respect to the setup. Additionally, they helped in detecting which object has been grasp after each step.

The communication between the HoloLens and the robot was established using ROS-Sharp[5] from the HoloLens side and ROSbridge[6] from the robot side.

## 4.2  Design and Implementation

We considered a packaging scenario for our experiment where a human and a robot work together on collecting objects located on a table in the accessible workspace of the robot and pack them into a cardboard box. Figure 4 shows the collaboration setting in our experiment.

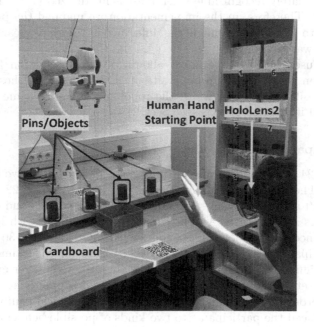

**Fig. 4.** Experiment setup.

There are multiple types of objects (four in this experiment) of different colors that need to be packed in the box in a given sequence. The objects are

---

[3] https://www.microsoft.com/en-us/hololens/.

[4] http://unity.com/.

[5] http://github.com/siemens/ros-sharp.

[6] http://wiki.ros.org/rosbridge_suite.

arranged in four stacks. Two of them are marked with green, and the other two are black. As described before, the robot does not know in advance which object it should grasp and pack. It only knows the roles, which say: pick an object of similar color as the human from the corresponding related stack. Thus, if the human grasps an object from the right green stack, the correct robot action is to grasp another green object from the stack in the middle, and similarly for the black objects (see Fig. 4). Grasping any other object is considered a failure. Each agent should manipulate a single object at a time.

According to this setup, the human possible intended goals are $G = \{obj_{i,\ i\in\{1,2,3,4\}}\}$, and the robot can be in five different states $X = \{Grasping(obj_{i,\ i\in\{1,2,3,4\}}), Waiting\}$. Therefore, the total number of different system states is $|S| = 20$, which is a mix of possible human goals and robot states. The robot available set of actions is $A = \{Keep, Abort, InitiateGrasping(obj_{i,\ i\in\{1,2,3,4\}})\}$. To solve the POMDP and choose the appropriate robot actions, we use QMDP approach [34].

For the trust function, we noticed, based on a pre-test, that the early reaction of the robot is barely recognizable when trust is maximized ($Tr = 1$) compared to the default. Therefore, in the implementation we mapped the positive trust interval $[0, 1]$ to $[0, 10]$, which made the difference in reactions clearer. The negative interval was kept as is.

The task used in this experiment allows for two interaction forms. They are cooperation (in which the robot waits until the human finishes packing an object), and collaboration (in which the robot moves at the same time as the human toward its related object) (see Sect. 2).

### 4.3 Participants and Procedure

We recruited 24 participants from our university and excluded two due to technical issues. Therefore, the sample size for this study is $n = 22$ (12 identify as men and 10 as women aged between 18 and 33), and we conducted it in a within-subjects study design. All participants were students with little ($< 2\,h$) to no experience with cobots. The experiment lasted between 30 and 45 min and all participants were compensated with 10 Euro for their time. First, the participants signed an informed consent, and then the researcher explained the task and the setup. Afterwards, the participants did a practicing session with the robot in order to get familiar with task and the technical equipment.

We introduced the participants to two kinds of possible behaviors. They are *Normal* and *Abnormal*. For the Normal behavior, the participants were asked to grasp their intended objects in a direct way from a starting point (a virtual object shown through the HoloLens). In the Abnormal behavior, the participants were asked to try to trick the robot by pretending that they are going to grasp a given object but in the middle of the way they change their intention and grasp another object. The reason for using this Normal and Abnormal conditions instead of free interaction style is that we want to test the effectiveness of the proposed approach in both correct and faulty cases. It might take a very long time until the model deviates from reality. There were no restrictions on the order of object selection. This behavior emulates the case when the human changes the behavior/preferences or makes mistakes during the interaction.

To evaluate the effect of our approach, we designed four conditions. They are *Default-Normal, Default-Abnormal*, in which robot trust was not considered, and *Trust-Normal, Trust-Abnormal* in which the robot uses the trust function to adjust its belief. All participants went through the conditions in the presented order and each condition was repeated twice and the participants filled a questionnaire (see Tables 4 and 5 in the Appendix) directly after each condition.

### 4.4   Dependent Variables

We evaluate our approach in a subjective and an objective senses. The objective dependent variables are *Human idle time, Task completion time*, which represent the metrics of team performance in this study, and *Failure rate* represents the metric for safety. Human idle time is measured as the sum of times the human has to wait until the robot finishes its part of the sub-task. Task completion time was measured as the sum of times between the human initial motion and the robot final motion (returning back to the initial configuration).

The subjective dependent variables used in this study are the key HRI concepts proposed by Bartneck et al., [7], which are: Anthropomorphism, Likeability, Perceived intelligence, Perceived safety, and Human trust. Human trust was measured by Muir questionnaire [37], whereas the other variables were measured by the Godspeed questionnaire [7] on 7-points Likert scales.

### 4.5   Results

**Objective Results.** We first calculate the number of failures occurred during each condition. The total number of steps for all participants is 264 as each participant (n = 22) repeated the grasping action 12 times. In the Default-Normal condition, the total number of failures for all participants was only 2 out of 264 steps. This is because the participants in this condition did the grasping actions in a way that is understandable and predictable by the robot's model. However, in the Default-Abnormal condition, the number of failures was very high (104) as the model fails to describe the human intention correctly. There were no failures when the trust function was used in both Normal and Abnormal behaviors. The reason for the absence of failure is the use of the virtual sensors (see Sect. 4.1). They checked which object has been touched by the human hand based on the collision with the virtual objects. This is necessary to deterministically determine the outcome of the interaction. The data are given in Table 1.

The idle and completion times for the Default-Abnormal condition are not given due to the high number of failures. Although there were 160 successful steps in this condition, their mean and standard deviation of the idle and completion times are the same as the Default-Normal since the same default model was used (without trust integration).

The data of the variables idle and completion times are normally distributed in all conditions according to Shapiro-Wilk test. Therefore, for a comparison of

**Table 1.** Objective variables descriptive data. M is the mean, and SD is the standard deviation. N stands for Normal, and A stands for Abnormal behaviors.

|          | No. of failures | | Idle time M (SD) | | Completion time M (SD) | |
|----------|------|---------|----------|---------|----------|---------|
|          | N    | A       | N        | A       | N        | A       |
| **Default** | 2/264 | 104/264 | 181 (10) | –     | 230 (7) | –       |
| **Trust**   | 0/264 | 0/264   | 173 (9)  | 189 (8) | 220 (8) | 248 (10) |

the variables between the Default-Normal and Trust-Normal/Abnormal conditions, we use the dependent T-test.

The comparison between the conditions Default-Normal and Trust-Normal shows that the idle time is statistically significantly lower ($t(42) = 4.45, p = 0.000***$) in the Trust-Normal condition ($M = 173, SD = 9$) compared to the Default-Normal one ($M = 181, SD = 10$). On the other hand, it is significantly higher ($t(42) = -3.29, p = 0.003**$) in the Trust-Abnormal condition ($M = 189, SD = 8$) compared to the Default-Normal. Figure 5 depicts these results.

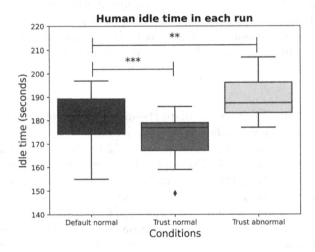

**Fig. 5.** Human idle time in the conditions: Default-Normal, Trust-Normal, and Trust-Abnormal. When robot trust is considered, the idle time is lower in case of normal behavior and higher otherwise with statistical significance ($p < 0.05$).

By extension, the task completion time is statistically significantly lower ($t(42) = 5.02, p = 0.000***$) in the Trust-Normal condition ($M = 220, SD = 8$) compared to the Default-Normal ($M = 230, SD = 7$), whereas it is statistically significantly higher ($t(42) = -6.74, p = 0.000***$) in the Trust-Abnormal condition ($M = 248, SD = 10$) compared to the Default-Normal one. The results can be seen in Fig. 6. Accordingly, considering the robot trust decreases the Human

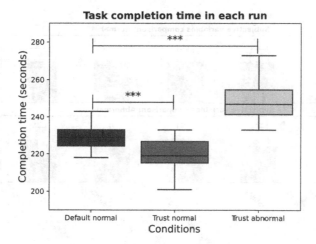

**Fig. 6.** Task completion time in the conditions: Default-Normal, Trust-Normal, and Trust-Abnormal. When robot trust is considered, the completion time is lower in case of normal behavior and higher otherwise with statistical significance ($p < 0.05$).

idle time and the Task completion time in the case of normal behavior (adhering to the model), and increases them when the behavior is abnormal (deviation from the assumed behavior).

**Subjective Results.** We compare our participants subjective reporting in the default behavior with the trust-based one with regard to all our dependent variables (see Sect. 4.4). Since our subjective data are ordinal in nature, we use the non-parametric Wilcoxon signed rank test for evaluation due to the within-subjects design.

*Normal Behavior.* No statistically significant difference between the Default-Normal and Trust-Normal conditions has been found for all subjectively measured variables except for anthropomorphism which shows a statistically significant difference ($W = 28, p = 0.004**$) between the two conditions as shown in Fig. 7 (top). Table 2 summarizes the statistical results of these tests.

*Abnormal Behavior.* Unlike the normal behavior, in the case of abnormal behavior, all subjective dependent variables show a statistically significant difference between the Default-Abnormal and Trust-Abnormal conditions as shown in Fig. 7 (bottom). The results of the statistical tests are presented in Table 3.

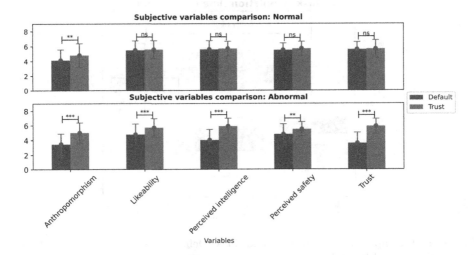

**Fig. 7.** Comparisons between the subjectively measured variables with and without trust in the normal and abnormal behavior.

**Table 2.** Results of Wilcoxon signed rank test for all subjective variables in the *normal* execution phase. M is the mean, and SD is the standard deviation.

|  | Default M (SD) | Trust M (SD) | Statistics W | p |
|---|---|---|---|---|
| **Anthropomorphism** | 4.14 (1.43) | 4.81 (1.60) | 28.0 | 0.004** |
| **Likeability** | 5.47 (1.26) | 5.56 (1.19) | 78.0 | 0.743 |
| **Perceived intelligence** | 5.57 (1.17) | 5.67 (0.97) | 80.0 | 0.544 |
| **Perceived safety** | 5.48 (0.91) | 5.67 (0.95) | 69.0 | 0.467 |
| **Human trust** | 5.56 (1.0) | 5.64 (1.16) | 81.5 | 0.580 |

**Table 3.** Results of Wilcoxon signed rank test for all subjective variables in the *abnormal* execution phase. M is the mean, and SD is the standard deviation.

|  | Default M (SD) | Trust M (SD) | Statistics W | p |
|---|---|---|---|---|
| **Anthropomorphism** | 3.45 (1.40) | 4.99 (1.39) | 11.5 | 0.000*** |
| **Likeability** | 4.74 (1.46) | 5.70 (1.25) | 9.0 | 0.000*** |
| **Perceived intelligence** | 3.99 (1.45) | 5.89 (1.09) | 8.0 | 0.000*** |
| **Perceived safety** | 4.77 (1.40) | 5.47 (1.01) | 34.0 | 0.004** |
| **Human trust** | 3.56 (1.45) | 5.89 (1.02) | 1.0 | 0.000*** |

# 5   Discussion

The results of our study show improvement in the interaction with collaborative robots subjectively and objectively. Regarding the latter, in the periods of time when the model succeeds in predicting and understanding the human actions, our approach allows the robot to gradually enhance the team performance by initiating early motions toward its goals, which consequently reduces the human idle time and the task completion time (see Figs. 5 and 6). The robot does this by increasing its reliance on the model and weighing its belief about the human intention with the value of trust it has based on the history of interactions it had with this particular user. Because the robot succeeds multiple times, it starts to believe that the interaction is safe and it can work toward enhancing the performance of the team by increasing the simultaneous motion with the human. On the other hand, when the model frequently fails in describing the observations (in the case of abnormal behavior), our approach allows the robot to reduce its reliance on the model and gradually sacrifice the team performance for safety by forcing the robot to wait longer until it gains more confidence in its predictions, and in the extreme case ($Tr = -1$) until the human finishes his/her part of the task. Although this behavior negatively affects the performance of the team by increasing the human idle time and task completion time (see Fig. 5 and Fig. 6), it significantly reduces the number of failures the robot commits over the whole interaction period (see Table 1). Thus, the main effect of our approach is the trade-off between performance and safety. In addition to that, our approach enables the robot to change the interaction form back and forth between cooperation (sequential execution) and collaboration (simultaneous execution) (see Sect. 2), and the continuum in between, depending on its trust in the models it has. This can be very effective in situations where any model is very likely to fail, which is the case for humans inconsistent behavior.

Regarding the subjective variables measured in this study, the results show a higher anthropomorphic attribution when trust is used with normal behavior compared to default. Hence, the participants perceived the robot behavior as more human-like when it uses trust and act earlier. However, this behavior does not seem to have a clear influence on the other measured variables (see Fig. 7 (top)). Conversely, including trust seems to have a positive effect on all measured variables in the case of abnormal behavior (see Fig. 7 (bottom)). This is probably due to the fact that the robot did not make any failure when trust is implemented, while most participants expected it to fail when they trick it.

The trust model used in this work can be designed in different ways depending on the goal of adding it. In this work, it was used to address the uncertainty associated with interacting with humans. Therefore, it has a similar effect on robot's behavior as humans' trust on theirs. This differentiates this work from previous works (see Sect. 2). The model can also be integrated in different ways. This is the reason why we referred to it before as *partially subjective* information. It should also be mentioned, that integrating trust in the way we proposed makes it independent of the model used for human intention prediction. It can be used with any model that returns a probability distribution over the possible intended goals.

## 6   Limitations and Future Work

Our work has some limitations. First, in our implementation, the robot trust keeps constant within the execution of a sub-task and only changes at the end of it when the human goal is already known. It would be very interesting to influence the robot behavior within a sub-task execution. Nevertheless, this is very challenging as the robot will not know the human goal until the end of an execution. Therefore, the robot cannot accurately judge the correctness of the model. Second, integrating trust in the proposed way should be done carefully as this will make the robot overly confident about its inference although the evidence for that is missing. In spite of the fact that our usage of robot trust imitates the way humans use their trust, it could raise some concerns to use it this way due to safety issues and other constraints. Finally, we evaluated the approach with a relatively small sample of university students as participants in a lab environment and fully structured experiment, which might not reflect a real industrial collaboration setting.

Our future work involves bidirectional flow of information as the robot can also share its intentions and understandings with the human virtually through the HoloLens. Additionally, we would like to include both a human and a robot trust models so that we can study the influence of each one on the other.

## 7   Conclusion

This research aims at developing and integrating a robot sense of trust with the decision-making process of robots due to its relevance. We modeled the interaction between the human and the robot as a POMDP which allows the robot to maintain a belief about the human intentions, from which the robot derives its expectations in this regard. The robot then derives a new trust-based belief and makes decision based on it. At the end of each sub-task, the robot quantifies the predictability of the last step and feeds this information forward into a time-series trust function, which generates a new trust value that can be used for the next sub-task execution. Using our approach, the robot sacrifices performance for safety when the model's ability to correctly describe the human behavior degrades, and gradually boosts performance with successful task executions. On the interaction level, the robot dynamically moves the interaction between cooperation and collaboration using its trust function. We evaluated our approach in a human-subject experiment and showed that considering trust actually enhances the interaction in a subjective and objective ways.

# Appendix

**Table 4.** Godspeed Questionnaire

| Question | | 1 | 2 | 3 | 4 | 5 | 6 | 7 | |
|---|---|---|---|---|---|---|---|---|---|
| please rate your impression of the robot on these scales (Anthropomorphism) | Fake | O | O | O | O | O | O | O | Natural |
| | Machinelike | O | O | O | O | O | O | O | Humanlike |
| | Unconscious | O | O | O | O | O | O | O | Conscious |
| | Artificial | O | O | O | O | O | O | O | Lifelike |
| | Moving rigidly | O | O | O | O | O | O | O | Moving elegantly |
| please rate your impression of the robot on these scales (Likeability) | Dislike | O | O | O | O | O | O | O | Like |
| | Unfriendly | O | O | O | O | O | O | O | Friendly |
| | Unkind | O | O | O | O | O | O | O | Kind |
| | Unpleasant | O | O | O | O | O | O | O | Pleasant |
| | Awful | O | O | O | O | O | O | O | Nice |
| please rate your impression of the robot on these scales (Perceived intelligence) | Incompetent | O | O | O | O | O | O | O | Competent |
| | Ignorant | O | O | O | O | O | O | O | Knowledgeable |
| | Irresponsible | O | O | O | O | O | O | O | Responsible |
| | Unintelligent | O | O | O | O | O | O | O | Intelligent |
| | Foolish | O | O | O | O | O | O | O | Sensible |
| please rate your emotional state on these scales (Perceived safety) | Anxious | O | O | O | O | O | O | O | Relaxed |
| | Agitated | O | O | O | O | O | O | O | Calm |
| | Quiescent | O | O | O | O | O | O | O | Surprised |

**Table 5.** Trust Questionnaire

| To what extent can the robot's behavior be predicted? | | | | | | | | |
|---|---|---|---|---|---|---|---|---|
| | 1 | 2 | 3 | 4 | 5 | 6 | 7 | |
| Not at all | O | O | O | O | O | O | O | To a great extent |

| To what extent can you count on panda to do its job? | | | | | | | | |
|---|---|---|---|---|---|---|---|---|
| | 1 | 2 | 3 | 4 | 5 | 6 | 7 | |
| Not at all | O | O | O | O | O | O | O | To a great extent |

| To what extent do you believe that the robot will be able to cope with all situations in the future? | | | | | | | | |
|---|---|---|---|---|---|---|---|---|
| | 1 | 2 | 3 | 4 | 5 | 6 | 7 | |
| Not at all | O | O | O | O | O | O | O | To a great extent |

| Overall, how much do you trust the robot? | | | | | | | | |
|---|---|---|---|---|---|---|---|---|
| | 1 | 2 | 3 | 4 | 5 | 6 | 7 | |
| Not at all | O | O | O | O | O | O | O | To a great extent |

# References

1. Alhaji, B., et al.: Engineering human-machine teams for trusted collaboration. Big Data Cogn. Comput. **4**(4), 35 (2020). https://doi.org/10.3390/bdcc4040035
2. Alhaji, B., Prilla, M., Rausch, A.: Trust, but verify: autonomous robot trust modeling in human-robot collaboration. In: Proceedings of the 9th International Conference on Human-Agent Interaction, pp. 402–406. HAI 2021, Association for Computing Machinery, New York, NY, USA (2021). https://doi.org/10.1145/3472307.3484672
3. Alhaji, B., Prilla, M., Rausch, A.: Trust dynamics and verbal assurances in human robot physical collaboration. Front. Artif. Intell. **4**, 703504 (2021). https://doi.org/10.3389/frai.2021.703504
4. Azevedo-Sa, H., Yang, X.J., Robert, L.P., Tilbury, D.M.: A unified bi-directional model for natural and artificial trust in human-robot collaboration. IEEE Robot. Autom. Lett. **6**(3), 5913–5920 (2021). https://doi.org/10.1109/LRA.2021.3088082
5. Bagosi, T., Hindriks, K.V., Neerincx, M.A.: Ontological reasoning for human-robot teaming in search and rescue missions. In: 2016 11th ACM/IEEE International Conference on Human-Robot Interaction (HRI), pp. 595–596. IEEE, Christchurch, New Zealand (2016). https://doi.org/10.1109/HRI.2016.7451873
6. Bandyopadhyay, T., Won, K.S., Frazzoli, E., Hsu, D., Lee, W.S., Rus, D.: Intention-aware motion planning. In: Frazzoli, E., Lozano-Perez, T., Roy, N., Rus, D. (eds.) Algorithmic Foundations of Robotics X. STAR, vol. 86, pp. 475–491. Springer, Heidelberg (2013). https://doi.org/10.1007/978-3-642-36279-8_29
7. Bartneck, C., Kulić, D., Croft, E., Zoghbi, S.: Measurement instruments for the anthropomorphism, animacy, likeability, perceived intelligence, and perceived safety of robots. Int. J. Soc. Robot. **1**(1), 71–81 (2009). https://doi.org/10.1007/s12369-008-0001-3
8. Bruno, G., Antonelli, D.: Dynamic task classification and assignment for the management of human-robot collaborative teams in workcells. Int. J. Adv. Manufact. Technol. **98**(9), 2415–2427 (2018). https://doi.org/10.1007/s00170-018-2400-4
9. Chen, M., Nikolaidis, S., Soh, H., Hsu, D., Srinivasa, S.: Planning with trust for human-robot collaboration. In: Proceedings of the 2018 ACM/IEEE International Conference on Human-Robot Interaction - HRI 2018, pp. 307–315. ACM Press, Chicago, IL, USA (2018). https://doi.org/10.1145/3171221.3171264
10. Cross, E.S., Hortensius, R., Wykowska, A.: From social brains to social robots: applying neurocognitive insights to human-robot interaction. Philosop. Trans. Roy. Soc. B: Biolog. Sci. **374**(1771), 20180024 (2019). https://doi.org/10.1098/rstb.2018.0024
11. Delmerico, J., et al.: The current state and future outlook of rescue robotics. J. Field Robot. **36**(7), 1171–1191 (2019). https://doi.org/10.1002/rob.21887
12. Dragan, A.D., Lee, K.C., Srinivasa, S.S.: Legibility and predictability of robot motion. In: 2013 8th ACM/IEEE International Conference on Human-Robot Interaction (HRI), pp. 301–308. IEEE, Tokyo, Japan (2013). https://doi.org/10.1109/HRI.2013.6483603
13. Dragan, A.D., Srinivasa, S.S.: A policy-blending formalism for shared control. Int. J. Robot. Res. **32**(7), 790–805 (2013). https://doi.org/10.1177/0278364913490324
14. Feltovich, P.J., Bradshaw, J.M., Clancey, W.J., Johnson, M.: Toward an ontology of regulation: socially-based support for coordination in human and machine joint activity. In: O'Hare, G.M.P., Ricci, A., O'Grady, M.J., Dikenelli, O. (eds.) ESAW 2006. LNCS (LNAI), vol. 4457, pp. 175–192. Springer, Heidelberg (2007). https://doi.org/10.1007/978-3-540-75524-1_10

15. Fisac, J., et al.: Probabilistically safe robot planning with confidence-based human predictions, vol. 14 (2018)
16. Groom, V., Nass, C.: Can robots be teammates? Benchmarks in human-robot teams. Interact. Stud. **8**(3), 483–500 (2007). https://doi.org/10.1075/is.8.3.10gro
17. Hancock, P.A., Kessler, T.T., Kaplan, A.D., Brill, J.C., Szalma, J.L.: Evolving trust in robots: specification through sequential and comparative meta-analyses. J. Hum. Fact. Ergon. Soc. **63**, 1196–1229 (2020). https://doi.org/10.1177/0018720820922080
18. Hoffman, G., Breazeal, C.: Collaboration in human-robot teams. In: AIAA 1st Intelligent Systems Technical Conference. American Institute of Aeronautics and Astronautics, Chicago, Illinois (2004). https://doi.org/10.2514/6.2004-6434
19. Hopko, S., Wang, J., Mehta, R.: Human factors considerations and metrics in shared space human-robot collaboration: a systematic review. Front. Robot. AI **9**, 799522 (2022). https://doi.org/10.3389/frobt.2022.799522
20. Jacovi, A., Marasović, A., Miller, T., Goldberg, Y.: Formalizing trust in artificial intelligence: prerequisites, causes and goals of human trust in AI. In: Proceedings of the 2021 ACM Conference on Fairness, Accountability, and Transparency, pp. 624–635. ACM, Virtual Event Canada (2021). https://doi.org/10.1145/3442188.3445923
21. Javdani, S., Admoni, H., Pellegrinelli, S., Srinivasa, S.S., Bagnell, J.A.: Shared autonomy via hindsight optimization for teleoperation and teaming. Int. J. Robot. Res. **37**(7), 717–742 (2018). https://doi.org/10.1177/0278364918776060
22. Jones, G.R., George, J.M.: The experience and evolution of trust: implications for cooperation and teamwork. Acad. Manag. Rev. **23**(3), 531–546 (1998). https://doi.org/10.5465/amr.1998.926625
23. Juvina, I., Collins, M.G., Larue, O., Kennedy, W.G., Visser, E.D., Melo, C.D.: Toward a unified theory of learned trust in interpersonal and human-machine interactions. ACM Trans. Inter. Intell. Syst. **9**(4), 1–33 (2019). https://doi.org/10.1145/3230735
24. Kaelbling, L.P., Littman, M.L., Cassandra, A.R.: Planning and acting in partially observable stochastic domains. Artif. Intell. **101**(1–2), 99–134 (1998). https://doi.org/10.1016/S0004-3702(98)00023-X
25. Kelley, R., Tavakkoli, A., King, C., Nicolescu, M., Nicolescu, M., Bebis, G.: Understanding human intentions via hidden Markov models in autonomous mobile robots. In: Proceedings of the 3rd international conference on Human robot interaction - HRI 2008, p. 367. ACM Press, Amsterdam, The Netherlands (2008). https://doi.org/10.1145/1349822.1349870
26. Khavas, Z.R., Ahmadzadeh, S.R., Robinette, P.: Modeling trust in human-robot interaction: a survey. In: Wagner, A.R., et al. (eds.) ICSR 2020. LNCS (LNAI), vol. 12483, pp. 529–541. Springer, Cham (2020). https://doi.org/10.1007/978-3-030-62056-1_44
27. Klein, G., Woods, D., Bradshaw, J., Hoffman, R., Feltovich, P.J.: Ten challenges for making automation a "team player" in joint human-agent activity. Intell. Syst. IEEE **19**, 91–95 (2004). https://doi.org/10.1109/MIS.2004.74
28. Kok, B.C., Soh, H.: Trust in robots: challenges and opportunities. Curr. Robot. Rep. **1**(4), 297–309 (2020). https://doi.org/10.1007/s43154-020-00029-y
29. Koppula, H.S., Saxena, A.: Anticipating human activities using object affordances for reactive robotic response. IEEE Trans. Pattern Anal. Mach. Intell. **38**(1), 14–29 (2016). https://doi.org/10.1109/TPAMI.2015.2430335

30. Krüger, J., Lien, T.K., Verl, A.: Cooperation of human and machines in assembly lines. CIRP Ann. **58**(2), 628–646 (2009). https://doi.org/10.1016/j.cirp.2009.09.009
31. Kuderer, M., Kretzschmar, H., Sprunk, C., Burgard, W.: Feature-based prediction of trajectories for socially compliant navigation. In: Robotics: Science and Systems (2012). https://doi.org/10.15607/RSS.2012.VIII.025
32. Lee, J.D., See, K.A.: Trust in automation: designing for appropriate reliance. Hum. Factors **46**(1), 50–80 (2004). https://doi.org/10.1518/hfes.46.1.50_30392
33. Lewis, M., Sycara, K., Walker, P.: The role of trust in human-robot interaction. In: Abbass, H.A., Scholz, J., Reid, D.J. (eds.) Foundations of Trusted Autonomy. SSDC, vol. 117, pp. 135–159. Springer, Cham (2018). https://doi.org/10.1007/978-3-319-64816-3_8
34. Littman, M.L., Cassandra, A.R., Kaelbling, L.P.: Learning policies for partially observable environments: scaling up. In: Machine Learning Proceedings 1995, pp. 362–370. Elsevier (1995). https://doi.org/10.1016/B978-1-55860-377-6.50052-9
35. Mayer, R.C., Davis, J.H., Schoorman, F.D.: An integrative model of organizational trust. Acad. Manag. Rev. **20**(3), 709–734 (1995). https://doi.org/10.2307/258792
36. Muir, B.M., Moray, N.: Trust in automation. Part II. Experimental studies of trust and human intervention in a process control simulation. Ergonomics **39**(3), 429–460 (1996). https://doi.org/10.1080/00140139608964474
37. Muir, B.M.: Operators' trust in and use of automatic controllers in a supervisory process control task, Ph. D. thesis, National Library of Canada, Ottawa (1990), ISBN: 9780315510142 OCLC: 31514812
38. Müller, S.L., Schröder, S., Jeschke, S., Richert, A.: Design of a robotic workmate. In: Duffy, V.G. (ed.) DHM 2017. LNCS, vol. 10286, pp. 447–456. Springer, Cham (2017). https://doi.org/10.1007/978-3-319-58463-8_37
39. Onnasch, L., Roesler, E.: A taxonomy to structure and analyze human–robot interaction. Int. J. Soc. Robot. **13**(4), 833–849 (2020). https://doi.org/10.1007/s12369-020-00666-5
40. Pellegrinelli, S., Admoni, H., Javdani, S., Srinivasa, S.: Human-robot shared workspace collaboration via hindsight optimization. In: 2016 IEEE/RSJ International Conference on Intelligent Robots and Systems (IROS), pp. 831–838. IEEE, Daejeon, South Korea (2016). https://doi.org/10.1109/IROS.2016.7759147
41. Rahman, S.M., Wang, Y.: Mutual trust-based subtask allocation for human-robot collaboration in flexible lightweight assembly in manufacturing. Mechatronics **54**, 94–109 (2018). https://doi.org/10.1016/j.mechatronics.2018.07.007
42. Rempel, J.K., Holmes, J.G., Zanna, M.P.: Trust in close relationships. J. Pers. Soc. Psychol. **49**(1), 95–112 (1985). https://doi.org/10.1037/0022-3514.49.1.95
43. Rousseau, D.M., Sitkin, S.B., Burt, R.S., Camerer, C.: Not so different after all: a cross-discipline view of trust. Acad. Manag. Rev. **23**(3), 393–404 (1998). https://doi.org/10.5465/amr.1998.926617
44. Schaefer, K.E., Hill, S.G., Jentsch, F.G.: Trust in human-autonomy teaming: a review of trust research from the us army research laboratory robotics collaborative technology alliance. In: Chen, J. (ed.) AHFE 2018. AISC, vol. 784, pp. 102–114. Springer, Cham (2019). https://doi.org/10.1007/978-3-319-94346-6_10
45. Schmidtler, J., Knott, V., Hölzel, C., Bengler, K.: Human centered assistance applications for the working environment of the future. Occup. Ergon. **12**(3), 83–95 (2015). https://doi.org/10.3233/OER-150226
46. Sciutti, A., Mara, M., Tagliasco, V., Sandini, G.: Humanizing human-robot interaction: on the importance of mutual understanding. IEEE Technol. Soc. Mag. **37**(1), 22–29 (2018). https://doi.org/10.1109/MTS.2018.2795095

47. Vinanzi, S., Patacchiola, M., Chella, A., Cangelosi, A.: Would a robot trust you? Developmental robotics model of trust and theory of mind. Philosop. Trans. Roy. Soc. B Biol. Sci. **374**(1771), 20180032 (2019). https://doi.org/10.1098/rstb.2018.0032
48. de Visser, E.J., et al.: Towards a theory of longitudinal trust calibration in human–robot teams. Int. J. Soc. Robot. **12**(2), 459–478 (2019). https://doi.org/10.1007/s12369-019-00596-x
49. Young, J.E., Hawkins, R., Sharlin, E., Igarashi, T.: Toward acceptable domestic robots: applying insights from social psychology. Int. J. Soc. Robot. **1**(1), 95–108 (2009). https://doi.org/10.1007/s12369-008-0006-y
50. Ziebart, B.D., Maas, A., Bagnell, J.A., Dey, A.K.: Maximum entropy inverse reinforcement learning. In: Proceedings of the 23rd national conference on Artificial intelligence - vol. 3, pp. 1433–1438. AAAI2008, AAAI Press, Chicago, Illinois (2008)

# User Experience in Large-Scale Robot Development: A Case Study of Mechanical and Software Teams

Sara Nielsen[1]([✉]) [iD], Mikael B. Skov[2] [iD], and Anders Bruun[2] [iD]

[1] Department of Electronic Systems, Aalborg University, Fredrik Bajers Vej 7B,
Aalborg 9220, Denmark
snie@es.aau.dk
[2] Department of Computer Science, Aalborg University, Selma Lagerlöfs Vej 300,
Aalborg 9220, Denmark
{dubois,bruun}@cs.aau.dk

**Abstract.** User experience integration within software companies has been studied extensively, but studies on organizations that develop robots are scant. The physical and socially situated presence of robots poses unique design and development challenges, which companies should be able to address. This case study examines *how* mechanical and software teams involved in a large-scale robot development project embed UX in robot design. The case offers new perspectives on HCI research, which traditionally explores UX integration in companies from the point of views of UX specialists and software developers, with little consideration of how mechanical and software design interact. During our 12+ months collaboration with the company, we conducted non-participant observations of 30 project SCRUM meetings. Based on this data, we identify four themes concerning the role of UX in robot development, workarounds in design evaluation, requirements handling, and coordination mechanisms.

**Keywords:** UX of robots · UX in development · Robot development · Case study · Mechanical development · Software development

## 1 Introduction

Integrating user experience (UX) in software development has proven difficult and based on an industry report by McKinsey & Company [35], above 40% of 300 companies followed over 5 years did not speak to end-users during development. Lack of user involvement in product development has damaging implications on return on investment. To illustrate this, McKinsey & Company [35] found companies with strong design (i.e., UX, user-centered design, and design management) capabilities outperformed industry-benchmark growth by two to one. Despite of this, UX seems more elusive in SCRUM and agile [10,40], which makes UX integration challenging. For example, handover of UX outcomes to developers proves problematic [10] partly because UX outcomes are accumulated in reports

J. Abdelnour Nocera et al. (Eds.): INTERACT 2023, LNCS 14143, pp. 40–61, 2023.
https://doi.org/10.1007/978-3-031-42283-6_3

[11], which does not go well with agile principles of reducing documentation. Contrarily, communicating UX outcomes verbally makes it difficult for developers to revisit and remember [46]. Furthermore, UX specialists struggle to impact product development, because they often work in silos away from development teams [10]. These challenges can result in developers deciding on implementations they find interesting without involving the team and stakeholders as well as lead to favoritism of own expert knowledge over users' lived experiences [12,42]. Despite tremendous research interest in UX integration in software development, there are companies in industries with traditions and legacies distinct from software companies, but who also design products for people. Examples of such industries are car manufacturing and facility management who in early days did not have a single line of code running in their products. Over time, such industries went through digital transformation; maturing products from purely mechanical to now being inherently controlled by software. Some companies now, additionally, combine their mechanical expertise with software to develop robots. However, developing robots is complicated as it relies on successful collaboration and design management within highly multidisciplinary teams [3]. Mechanical, hardware, electrical, and industrial design as well as supply chain management are examples of competencies additionally needed in robot development. Furthermore, the physical dimension and embodiment of robots adds an extra layer of complexity compared to software development [43]. Consequently, we have companies with substantially different legacies, organizational structures, and in-house competencies compared to purely software-driven companies, and we have only to a lesser extent systematically explored UX in such contexts.

In this paper, we investigate *how* a non-software-founded company who develop robots embed UX in robot development and discuss whether legacy plays an enabling or impeding role in how practitioners work with UX. We investigate this through a case study of mechanical and software teams involved in a large-scale robot development project. The following section presents related work on the need for UX in robot development followed by barriers and enablers of UX in industry development contexts. Then we introduce our method and empirical setting. Next, findings are presented and subsequently discussed in relation to existing research on UX integration in industry. Finally, we conclude our study.

## 2  Related Work

There is a growing need to ensure robots are designed to enter social contexts as they are increasingly deployed in our daily lives. This section presents related work on the need for UX in robot development and how robots pose unique challenges compared to other technologies. Next, we provide a brief overview of extant research on barriers and enablers of UX in industry development contexts.

### 2.1  UX in Robot Development

Integrating UX in design and development of robots has been advocated by several researchers [11,24,27,38], who also recognize current means may not account for robots' unique qualities. Physical embodiment combined with autonomous abilities are two prominent ways robots differ substantially from other technologies [37]. Autonomous abilities enable robots to influence social structures and evoke a sense of agency through robots' dynamic, socially situated, and multifaceted presence in real-world settings [45]. Additionally, people tend to treat robots differently from other technologies by ascribing robots life-like qualities (e.g., names, gender, and personalities) even to robots not specifically designed to evoke such social responses [13,19]. Tonkin et al. [38] argue designing robots' interactive behavior may be the most complicated part of robot development, as it relies on multimodal behavioral patterns accounting for both non-verbal (e.g., gestures, gaze, body rotation and orientation, lights, and sounds) and verbal (e.g., speech recognition and synthetic voice capabilities [9]) behaviors. These behaviors must be complementary to create coherent and fluent experiences at every point of interaction [38]. This critical stage of robot development–as we see it–relies on contributions from mechanical and industrial design, UX and UI design, and software and hardware and these domains must be able to collaborate and coordinate. According to Alenljung et al. [1], we need to better support developers by enabling them to design robots that are accepted and experienced in desirable ways. Particularly since developers seem inclined to "cook up" their own UX assessment tools, methods, and user studies with limited knowledge of established practices [6]. Tonkin et al.'s [38] UX of robots methodology includes phases deliberately oriented towards designing robot behavior, personality, and choosing the robot's identity principles which ideally align with company values and branding. This is not–to our knowledge–considered in software development but it is crucial for robots deployed in social contexts because people tend to assign agency, social qualities, and attribute personality to robots.

In spite of researchers' justification of UX in robot development, there does not yet exist an extensive research-knowledge base of how robotics companies develop robots designed to interact with specific people [33], while sharing the space with people referred to as *Incidentally Co-present Persons* (InCoPs) [29]. This case study therefore contributes an empirical investigation of how technical teams involved in robot development embed UX in the development process.

## 2.2   Barriers and Enablers of UX in Industry Development Contexts

Existing research on UX integration in industry primarily focus on barriers faced by UX specialists and how UX can become more influential, e.g. by teaming up with software developers and teach them UX (see e.g., [4,8]), and less so on how technical practitioners manage and embed UX in development, when UX specialists are not involved. In these cases, delegating responsibility of UX becomes more critical [8]. Frequently mentioned barriers relate to practitioners having different and sometimes conflicting understanding of what constitutes UX [14,30], seeing UX as mainly consisting of usability aspects [4], as well as developers being skeptical about importance and value of UX [8,40] or consider UX a "black-box" before development [28]. Organizational factors, such as corporate culture, also influence UX integration. That is, senior and executive managers (i.e., C-suite) may verbally endorse UX and expect development teams to work with UX, but developers do not view UX as something they can just do without support and practice [4]. Developers may also encourage UX but it tends to remain at an intentional level rather than being practiced during development cycles [40].

Various strategies have been proposed to overcome these barriers. Training and educating developers seem to be the first go to strategy despite researchers acknowledging perhaps this should merely be treated as a way to get started with the UX integration process [4,8]. Successful UX integration does not rely entirely on UX specialists but should be treated as a team effort. This means, practitioners must be prepared to compromise [40], for example, by delegating and scaling UX activities to match colleagues' skills, resources, and needs. Prior research moreover demonstrates practitioners have different opinions regarding when to include UX in development. Bang et al. [4] observed practitioners were inclined to consider UX late in the process, rather than in initial phases. Contrarily, Persson et al. [28], amongst others, found a lot of UX work was carried out before development. This is referred to as upfront design, i.e., activities taking place before development begins which focus on user and context understanding, defining preliminary user requirements, and producing initial sketches and wireframes of a *potential* solution [40]. Upfront design enabled developers to *"be proactive about changes in the system's architectural design by anticipating development risks"* [28]. A common artifact produced in upfront design is user stories. Practitioners likely define numerous user stories which, according to Kuusinen [23], have to be prioritized, and this prioritization typically does not favor authentic users. Instead, user stories are prioritized according to business value which is often informed by the most important customer's interests, followed by an assessment of required development efforts (i.e., cost of implementation) [23]. Ananjeva et al. [2] found that the way practitioners' use user stories indicate how well UX is integrated in agile development. That is, concise user stories are indicators of good integration, while verbose user stories are manifestations of underlying collaboration and communication issues within the team. Furthermore, practitioners occasionally invalidate user stories and undermine user needs because they fall in love with the product, rather than the problem [2]. Upfront design can also take place during development. This can be achieved by introducing a sprint 0 for UX work to be carried out ahead of or in parallel to development sprints [28,40]. However, this might be complicated in practice, since unforeseen things may happen during sprints, which can lead to loss of overview of UX activities down to smaller aspects (e.g., designing wireframes) [28]. These studies share focus on software development within agile teams somewhat accustomed to UX. This case study thus builds on extant research by concentrating on UX integration within technical teams with distinct development traditions.

## 3   Method

In order to understand *how* a non-software-founded company embed UX in robot development, the case study methodology was deemed most appropriate [44]. We find the case study approach particularly fitting because it allows us to study a contemporary phenomenon in its real-world context [18,44] to develop insights into our *how* question [44]. Case studies have previously been used to study, e.g., software developers' experiences of being involved in usability engineering [8] and UX in agile software development [28]. Additionally, we view this case as an extreme case [18], as it seeks to understand the deeper causes and consequences of how software and mechanical teams embed UX in a *shared* robot development project. Thus, this case provides new perspectives in HCI research, which traditionally explores UX integration predominantly from the perspective of UX specialists and software developers. In this section, we introduce the case company, robots, and stakeholders in as much detail as we can given the company's request for anonymity and describe the data collection and analysis.

### 3.1   Case Company

The company was founded in the early 1900s s and in 2015, the company started building their own professional service robots. According to the project manager: *"This firmware development has traditionally taken place within the Electrical Team, and the developers have always had an electrical engineering background as opposed to a software development background (i.e. electrical engineers became software developers, not the other way around)"*. This case study focuses on teams responsible for developing these mobile robots meant for facility management tasks in airports, malls, grocery stores, and hotels. The robots differ in size to optimize operational efficiency depending on context of use. Operators can operate the robots in manual mode using steering wheel and throttle knob or initiate autonomous mode. The robots' touchscreen and physical buttons allow operators to define basic settings (e.g., language), select pre-defined settings, initiate new or existing operational routines, and access machine history (e.g., errors). Robots are equipped with sensors and safety systems and use light and sound signals to alert people in the environment that it is operating.

**Team Constellation.** The project has 40+ domain experts, who span project, product, and supply chain management as well as mechanical, electrical, software, hardware, and test engineers along with autonomous teams and systems designers. Several external partners are responsible for delivering technological components, UI, and software management (same partner as for UI). According to the project manager: *"[...] the current project is the first time an explicit software development team was implemented in a cross-functional machine development project"*. Figure 1 offers a simplified overview of the internal practitioners. The mechanical team is responsible for robots' mechanical and aesthetic design, and integrating modules and parts such as touchscreen, physical interactive elements, and sensing capabilities, whereas the software team is responsible for developing UI displayed on the touchscreen and integrating it with the robots' other systems. Practitioners in supporting functions assist both teams.

UX/UI consultants have senior level UX and UI expertise working primarily with software solutions; however, they are tasked exclusively with UI design

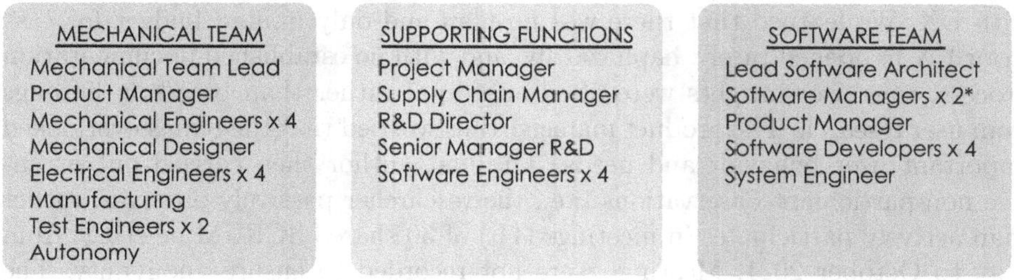

| MECHANICAL TEAM | SUPPORTING FUNCTIONS | SOFTWARE TEAM |
|---|---|---|
| Mechanical Team Lead | Project Manager | Lead Software Architect |
| Product Manager | Supply Chain Manager | Software Managers x 2* |
| Mechanical Engineers x 4 | R&D Director | Product Manager |
| Mechanical Designer | Senior Manager R&D | Software Developers x 4 |
| Electrical Engineers x 4 | Software Engineers x 4 | System Engineer |
| Manufacturing | | |
| Test Engineers x 2 | | |
| Autonomy | | |

**Fig. 1.** Practitioners in the mechanical and software teams as well as practitioners supporting the teams. *One of the software managers is the lead software architect.*

based on pre-defined requirements. None of the internal team members has any formal UX expertise and no one has experience working with UX of robots. The mechanical team's product manager is responsible for robots' physical appearance and interactions users (i.e., operators, supervisors, and service technicians) can have with robots, which are not screen-based. The product manager from the software team is responsible for UX and UI design of screen-based interactions. The two product managers are both in charge of UX and thus responsible for gathering, communicating, and evaluating requirements, defining use cases and user stories, evaluating designs, and creating sketches of the solution.

**Project Management.** The project manager organizes 2–3 weekly SCRUM meetings for the whole project team, while teams run separate SCRUM meetings and sprint planning, review, and retrospectives. The mechanical team did this from the beginning, while the software team gradually implemented it as the project progressed. This project adopts a stage-gate approach to New Product Development which comprises idea, preliminary assessment, concept, development, testing, trial, and launch [16], and practitioners experimented with adopting agile. The project is managed through the commercial platform: Jira, where teams plan, assign, and track tasks. It lets teams create backlogs with tasks they can assign to different sprints. If a task has not been completed in a sprint, Jira asks whether to move the task to the next sprint. Tasks are created as "tickets" which are assigned to developers as part of a sprint. Sprints lasted two workweeks unless, e.g., supply chain issues forced an extension of an ongoing sprint.

## 3.2   Data Collection and Analysis

The objective of this case study is to examine *how* technical teams embed UX in the underexplored intersection of physical product and software development. We do not attempt intervention through, e.g., action research [25], but extend previous research by studying how practitioners from an established robotics company work with UX. During the 12+ months collaboration with the company, the first author was first onboarded to the project by the software team's product manager, which enabled a preliminary inquiry of how both teams worked with UX. We learned that there was no plan and only limited budget for UX. Prior UX happened rarely, haphazardly, and with no established documentation process, thus user insights were often anecdotal rather than based on findings from user research. The product manager thus worried that the teams overlooked important user behavior and needs. The first author then carried out extensive non-participant observations (i.e., the researcher passively observes, rather than actively participates in meetings [44]) of 30 shared SCRUM meetings from May to October 2021. Meetings were not recorded to ensure anonymity. The researcher therefore took meticulous notes capturing as accurately as possible practitioners' behavior, what they said, and how they said it (e.g., jokingly). Additionally, date, duration, who participated, and central topics brought up by practitioners were captured. We followed up with product managers to clarify cases of doubt, e.g., how teams were affected by immediate problems such as material availability. We applied an open observation protocol to stay open to the possibility that issues raised by practitioners, which initially appeared not to affect UX, could evolve and impact UX over time. We treat our observations as our primary data. Supplementary data comprise of presentation slides, documents (e.g., user stories), practitioners' email correspondence, and access to Jira, which provided insights into coordination of, e.g., implementation tasks. This data was collected throughout the entire collaboration.

Our data analysis is inspired by Simoneÿ et al. [36] who base their analytical approach on Riceoeur-thinking where *"the lived experiences and recognition of being in the world are expressed through language"* [36]. Practically, this mean we take both the experiences of practitioners (what is said) and of the researcher (what is observed) into account. Researchers from HCI participated in the analysis, which followed a three-level structure. First, naïve reading of data as a whole meant that the first author read and re-read observational notes and consolidated aforementioned supplementary data to gain overview of relevant units of meaning (i.e., what is said and observed). Second, the first author and two senior HCI researchers conducted structural analysis alternating between what was said and observed (i.e., units of meaning) and what practitioners talked about and what observations were about (i.e., units of significance) to generate initial themes as well as developed and refined themes. Third, together we critically interpreted and discussed themes in relation to existing research.

## 4   Findings

We carried out an extreme case study to explore *how* mechanical and software teams involved in a *shared*, large-scale robot development project embed UX in the development of robots. We found that UX was not a shared responsibility within the project and because of this separated coordination of UX, we further examined how teams accounted for UX in development. This section presents our identified themes: 1) the role of UX in robot development; 2) workarounds in design evaluation; 3) listening to authentic users when dealing with requirements; and 4) coordination through ceremonies and artifacts.

## 4.1   The Role of UX in Robot Development

This theme illustrates how practitioners (who come from distinct disciplines with different traditions for managing development) fused technical development with UX. The theme additionally incorporates the extent to which UX was allowed impact on development and depicts individual teams' UX processes.

Practitioners frequently asked what the process was for implementing UI, factoring in user insights, evaluating, and analyzing whether a design satisfied user stories. Thus, the UX process and progress seemed unclear to nearly everyone. The software team spent months working on building consensus and establishing UX processes, and a software manager commented that they had not solved coordination of UX between–who the software manager referred to as–"UX/UI people" and software developers. Some in the software team saw UX was something that should be rushed and not get in the way of developers. In effort to have UX inform development, product managers sought to coordinate user involved activities ahead of software developers' implementation. The software team's product manager and lead software architect explained the intention was to have wireframes ready at least two sprints before execution ensuring what gets implemented had been vetted by customers and users. Moreover, the product manager tried to increase impact of UX by *"mak[ing] a proposal for a maturity-road map that will be highly user-driven based on what I think is most important, what is technically feasible to implement, and what is more risky such that we can track how far we are deviating from user needs"* (product manager, ST). Although the team encouraged user testing and claimed that it could help find surprises early and inform design decisions, this sentiment did not translate in actual practice. We also did not observe a UX sprint with follow-up user evaluations of software implementations during this study. Instead, the software team went from the product manager's rough ideas and PowerPoint sketches, to Figma wireframes, to internal reviews, to simulation, and finally implementation.

The mechanical team had a more iterative and experimental process. They organized brainstorming sessions to generate viable ideas that would improve the design and consolidated earlier designs and ideas for inspiration. Whenever a new design was pursued, it was reviewed by mechanical engineers, prototyped, subjected to experimentation, and presented in major reviews before committing to a design that would progress to implementation (where the design was tested and refined). Although the mechanical team did not have UX competences, they accounted for 1) how users and InCoPs deliberately or accidentally could misuse and damage the robots; 2) how to prevent unauthorized usages; and 3) how operating, maintaining, and servicing the robots could be easier and more user friendly for operators and service technicians in their design process. Furthermore, the new robot design required a lot of customization, which the mechanical team managed by running parallel design tracks and creating roadmaps which visualized how far along they were with respect to experimenting and iterating. Managing the design process in this way was, according to mechanical engineers, necessary to avoid deploying robots just to call them back for fixing bugs. It additionally allowed the team to discover and resolve design weaknesses.

## 4.2   Workarounds in Design Evaluation

Observations showed authentic users were not involved in design evaluations. The software team dealt with UX in parallel to internal reviews, but user insights were often considered less relevant and less valuable. While the mechanical team ran experiments to uncover design weaknesses, neither of these experiments involved authentic users. This theme focuses on teams' workarounds, i.e., what teams did to compensate for lack of user involvement in design evaluations. Evaluations based on internal reviews are included in the third theme.

To compensate for not involving authentic users in design evaluations, the mechanical team acted as proxies, i.e., pretending to be actual operators. They were able to utilize this approach as they had extensive personal experience operating the robots and in training supervisors and operators to operate the robots. Also, the autonomy team tried to evaluate their design based on the user stories, whereas test engineers experimented with misuse of robots caused deliberately or accidentally by users and InCoPs. To include some UX-related aspects, the mechanical team took inspiration from the software team's UX work and created drawings based on wireframes. The mechanical team saw this as a way to get closer to a "real-life" experience. However, a majority of this team's experiments were conducted in simulated environments and laboratories and focused on: reliability, durability, robustness (e.g., from slamming the hood), vibrations (e.g., shock loading from normal operation), and (mis)use over time. These experiments were conducted using various prototypes mentioned by mechanical engineers, ranging from 3D models to full-size robots made of spare and scraped parts from old machines and cardboard boxes. The team additionally experimented with membranes, springs, molding techniques, materials (e.g., silicone), 3D printing, and screen materials (e.g., glass with different properties). Limited access to robots was arguably the main reason why only few experiments were carried out in the field. Mechanical engineers explained that external partners were responsible for several experiments and therefore had more experience with the robots compared to the mechanical team. However, *"testing shouldn't rely on others [i.e., external partners] doing it, but we should be able to do it ourselves"* (mechanical team lead) and they worried experimental results would be less trustworthy, which was why the team wanted access to robots. Lack of access to robots additionally meant user testing could not be conducted with robots neither in controlled settings nor in the field. Consequently, user studies carried out by the software team were conducted in meeting rooms on laptops.

Both the autonomy team and test engineers collaborated with mechanical engineers to define the scope and set up experiments which provided necessary knowledge to iterate and improve designs. This was not the case in the software team, where it was the sole responsibility of the product manager. The two product managers teamed up with colleagues known to have direct customer contact and access to authentic users, which resulted in some user tests being carried out by these colleagues. Even so, the product managers, project manager, and software team kept raising issues of not having processes in place for systematically involving users, evaluating designs with users, or implementing changes based on user insights. Consequently, design evaluations were made chiefly by internal stakeholders or based on external UX/UI consultants' personal expertise. At some point, the software team's product manager asked what the plan was for validating what developers had made, because the product manager wanted authentic users to evaluate implemented designs. A software manager replied: "*demos*". When the product manager pressed the issue and asked questions such as "*now that we finally have developed something what should then be the criteria for evaluating this?*" (product manager, ST), the software manager explained this was something they should deal with internally in the software team. To the best of our knowledge, this was not handled within the software team.

## 4.3 Listening to Authentic Users When Dealing with Requirements

Our observations revealed that teams had different sensitivity towards listening to authentic users and dealing with customer and user requirements. This theme therefore zooms in on how requirements were dealt with and how this reflected teams' sensitivity towards listening to authentic users.

The mechanical team had an established process for handling requirements. They relied on upfront requirements defined in customer meetings and specified in preliminary technical drawings, where customers outlined demands for the mechanical design and specific components. The team proactively managed risks through regular check-ins with their product manager and customers. According to mechanical engineers, check-ins served two purposes: 1) being informed of changing customer requirements and 2) evaluating whether requirements were meet satisfactorily. In some cases, the mechanical team effectively blocked development until they had the necessary information regarding customer requirements. Mechanical engineers explained that changes affecting robots' operational reliability and robustness were subject to experimentation, as previously outlined, whereas changes influencing aesthetics or adding to product price were discussed with product managers and C-suite. Implemented changes were documented in technical drawings, which were returned to customers for approval. Based on our observations, the mechanical team was vocal about not committing to a design before it had been fully vetted from technical-mechanical and usages perspectives, as well as from a customer requirement perspective. They opted for knowing customer requirements immediately and up front and if anything changed, the team prototyped and conducted experiments to ensure that the change did not negatively impact robots' operational capabilities. By continuously adjusting to changing requirements, the mechanical team reduced waste of materials (some of which are expensive, difficult to manufacture, and difficult to get) and development time. However, requirements tied directly to the user experience neither came from nor were evaluated with authentic users.

The software team also relied on upfront requirements. Their requirements were captured in use cases and user stories based on historic interviews, informal conversations with sales and customer support, in-house knowledge, and gut feeling, while some came from customer meetings. In contrast to the mechanical team, the software team had an ad-hoc approach to changing requirements. We observed that users were given less priority compared to upfront requirements, use cases, user stories, and others' opinions. The lead software architect declared changes could not be too big and only be about reducing scope, not extending scope by adding features users wanted if it had been decided such feature should not be part of the UI. Furthermore, the lead software architect advocated for "locking" and "freezing"–i.e., having clearly defined screen designs from visual and interactive perspectives which developers could implement–screens such that software developers would not be interrupted or required to deal with incoming changes unless minimal (e.g., changing size, color, and labels). The mechanical team's product manager and a mechanical engineer objected to this approach and stressed the importance of not "locking" or "freezing" anything until it had been user tested and that authentic users should be the ones making final decisions, not developers. The two product managers called attention to the risk that the final product would deviate from delivering a design which satisfies users' needs. They reasoned that this was due to the lack of a clear UX process. What seemed to amplify this risk was that the software team based *user* requirements on potentially outdated and questionable data (i.e., when it is not possible to separate authentic user insights from colleagues' personal interpretations and agendas) without proactively assessing the legitimacy of requirements, seeking to continuously adjusting requirements, or evaluating designs with authentic users. Substantial changes were, however, allowed if product managers insisted and had it approved by software managers and a Change Committee, but there was no mention of such decisions having to be based on user insights.

### 4.4   Coordination Through Ceremonies and Artifacts

Our findings have revealed the two teams' distinct processes regarding development, design evaluation, and handling requirements as well as ways of dealing with UX. This theme therefore uncovers how teams managed coordination and collaboration concentrating on how practitioners shared design progress, immediate design problems, and user insights within and across project teams.

   We focus on two coordination mechanisms, which we observed that teams relied on: 1) ceremonies and 2) artifacts capturing implementation tasks. Teams organized ceremonies to share design progress, immediate challenges, and user insights. These ceremonies served as a formal venue for brainstorming, gaining internal feedback, and handling stakeholders' opinions. Some ceremonies were included in the project plan from the beginning, while others were planned ad-hoc within teams or with stakeholders outside the project. According to practitioners, ad-hoc reviews did not follow standardized structures. We, therefore, concentrate on *Design Reviews*, which the mechanical team organized for the entire project team presenting concepts or prototypes. Design reviews lasted from 1h 30m to 3h (no breaks) and were facilitated according to an established structure presented at the beginning of each ceremony. As a minimum, design reviews addressed the *purpose* and scope of the design review and the intended *outcomes*, which refer to feedback (e.g., on design direction) and reaching alignment between design, requirements, and goals. These two items furthermore concerned:

- **Purpose:** Weighing pros and cons, benefits and compromises of concepts, components, assemblies, and systems in order to identify high risk areas of the design and potential alternatives.
- **Outcomes:** Action list capturing subsequent decisions made by the team on solutions: act on feedback, reject feedback, or initiate alternative directions.

Knowledge sharing from software to project teams regarding UX was considered inadequate by the project manager, who recommended that the software team organized UX/UI reviews in the same way other design reviews were run. This started a discussion amongst practitioners, as it was unclear whose responsibility it was to organize UX/UI design reviews and who would be responsible for creating, assigning, monitoring, and evaluating tickets generated from the review. We observed one UX/UI design review. The lead software architect explained the plan was to rush through the UI and have external consultants facilitate the design review. Afterwards, the lead software architect would collect inputs from colleagues and prioritize them with the software team's product manager before coordinating with external consultants. Organizing design reviews in this way imposed extra coordination steps and did not provide the same opportunity for internal stakeholders to share concerns and ideas compared to design reviews organized by the mechanical team, where attendees shared feedback immediately.

The most used and discussed artifact capturing implementation tasks and user insights was Jira tickets. The content of tickets could come from feedback obtained in design reviews, which practitioners had translated into implementation tasks. Given that the feedback was provided by developers who knew it had to go into Jira and there was a chance they would be in charge of implementation; it is likely they formulated feedback to simplify translation. Both teams used tickets and while it seemed uncomplicated for practitioners to work with tickets consisting of technical implementation tasks, UX/UI tickets posed problems. Throughout the project, the software team struggled to communicate use cases, user stories, and user insights through tickets. Different suggestions were made, and initiatives were tried to improve coordination and collaboration. An early suggestion, for example, made by the lead software architect was to include all tickets related to UX/UI in Jira, followed by an internal evaluation of value to the user, risks, and development efforts. Trying to start this process and find a way that would work for developers where they would both understand UX/UI tickets and be able to proceed with implementation, the product manager asked: *"If you, [lead software architect], approve of the format, then I'll do the same for the other flows [i.e., flows in the UI]. For me it is not important how that format would look like, so whatever works for you"* (product manager, ST). Having experienced that communicating use cases, user stories, and user insights in excel files and PowerPoints shared via email or shared folders was inefficient and that *"Jira tickets are the golden book [for developers]"* (product manager, ST), the product manager frequently brought up this topic in SCRUM meetings. Likewise, the lead software architect several times stressed the importance of quickly establishing this process and that it had the potential to become a company-wide standard. However, neither the lead software architect nor the team provided feedback on the product manager's proposed formats.

We also identified artifacts that influenced coordination of mechanical development and collaboration between the mechanical team and partners. The mechanical team expressed how deeply reliant they were on physical samples as well as inbound (i.e., from external stakeholders such as customers, technical partners, and suppliers to the mechanical team) and outbound (i.e., from the mechanical team to external stakeholders, including manufacturing and production) documentation. These artifacts were essential for integrating new parts and modules with robots' existing ones as well as for manufacturing and assembling robots. Timely delivery and access to artifacts were considered imperative by the mechanical team but prone to risks. Based on observed coordination issues, we identified two risks: 1) *delays* effectively blocking the mechanical team from completing tasks due to missing documentation or supply chain issues, consequently affecting the team's ability to meet deadlines, and 2) *forced design modifications* imposed by unavailable artifacts, as physical design decisions, to some extent, relied on documentation and physical samples. Forced design modifications affected the mechanical team, external partners, suppliers, production, project planning, as well as the final robot design, which ultimately affects UX.

## 5   Discussion

We discuss central aspects from our findings in relation to extant literature. We additionally present recommendations and discuss limitations.

### 5.1   Coordination and Collaboration in Robot Development Teams

We found that the lack of a collective strategy for dealing with UX in this robot development project was a combination of at least two factors. First, this was the first time the case company involved a dedicated software development team in a cross-functional development project of a physical robot. Second, the case company is unaccustomed to managing robot development projects where authentic users and UX are prioritized and allowed to influence design decisions. We discuss implications of these two factors on coordination and collaboration.

Developing robots require competencies not necessarily present in ordinary software teams. This increases complexity in robot development, because different professions have their own theories, methods, tools, and terminology [39] as well as design representations (e.g., artifacts) [17]. For example, we found evidence of New Product Development fused with agile worked well for the mechanical team who continuously adjusted to changing customer requirements, ran parallel design tracks, experimented, and iterated while remaining vigilant to the New Product Development process, which they are accustomed to. Adopting agile at team level thus reduced project complexity, and this might have contributed to successful integration of agile in New Product Development as seen in, e.g., [15]. Contrarily, the software team struggled with fusing agile with

New Product Development, which manifested in several coordination and collaboration issues within the project. Examples of these issues are lack of standardized ceremonies, progress documentation, and agreement on deliverables. The mechanical team is accustomed to coordinating through standardization of outputs, which is something the software team aspires to do. Although teams aimed to streamline coordination, it seemed like each team wanted coordination to be based on individual domain preferences. For example, the software team used user stories, which the mechanical team seemed unaccustomed to. Even so, teams achieved some integration through coordination by mutual adjustment, which, according to Persson et al. [28], preserves teams' different practices yet make them mutually complementary. This was achieved with design reviews.

It is not uncommon issues occur for teams trying to integrate UX at the same time they initiate agile transformation. Past research found developers refused to make changes because they saw it as "wasteful work" and seemed to distrust the team responsible for UX [2]. In this case, it manifested in software developers pushing and rushing UX activities, and increased protectiveness of developers and their time. Despite some UX being carried out in parallel to development, UX did not inform development, nor was it used to evaluate implementations. We observed that software developers overly focused on the outcomes of upfront design activities and perceived outcomes (i.e., preliminary wireframes and user stories) as "set in stone", resulting in developers being less open and willing to adjust to changing user requirements. This is different from previous findings, where software developers, managers, and UX designers saw these wireframes as preliminary and likely to change, which led Persson et al. [28] to conclude *"upfront design helps software developers be proactive about changes in the system's architectural design by anticipating development risks"*. Being proactive about changing requirements and not committing to development before prototypes have been thoroughly tested and vetted by customers and from a user perspective is exactly what we observed the mechanical team did. Such approach is crucial for mechanical teams because they rely on access to material and depend on suppliers to deliver, which ultimately influence mechanical design. This has practical issues, because doing something "wrong" is costly and mechanical engineers cannot as easily as software developers remedy mistakes or make major design changes through subsequent launches. To mitigate these risks, we saw the mechanical team adopted experimental and iterative design approaches with parallel design tracks, which resembles several mainstream UX approaches and Lean methodologies [31]. Our findings further showed that UX was compartmentalized across teams and assigned specifically to product managers, rather than being a shared responsibility across teams as is often the case in software development [21]. Product managers repeatedly called attention to the lack of established processes for communicating user stories, tracking progress, and evaluating implemented designs against user stories, and asked developers to get involved in finding a solution, which would be meaningful to them. Thus, product managers saw it as a shared responsibility to find solutions for embedding UX, yet developers did not make it their priority. Consequently, preventing UX from being a shared responsibility where developers participate in UX activities, rather than being passive consumers of information, as was also the case in [46]. Because of this apparent lack of involvement, coordination and communication remained a challenge which reduced attention to UX as well as user needs and values.

Integrating UX in robot development is, however, not only about overcoming collaboration and coordination issues related to processes and mindsets which are not conducive to UX, there are practical barriers too. For example, access to robots, which in this case was split between external partners and mechanical engineers. Not having access to robots had considerable implications for product managers' ability to involve authentic users in the design process as it resulted in UX activities not being carried out in the actual context of use with robots.

## 5.2    Treating "Robot UX" as "Software UX"

Wallström and Lindblom [41] argue that integrating UX in robot development *"would require substantial changes in the existing robot development processes, which also poses changes in existing mindsets"*. Our findings showed that teams dealt with UX in their own ways and only focused on specific parts of the robots' design, rather than treating it as a cross-team effort. The software team, for example, did not work with UX in a substantially different way compared to what we see in existing literature studying companies who embed UX in software development. However, designing for positive, coherent experiences of users and InCoPs requires companies to consider that robots pose unique design challenges due to their physical embodiment, autonomous abilities, and socially situated presence [13,19,37,45]. These are qualities that digital solutions and products typically do not possess, and which are generally not considered in mainstream UX practices. Neither the mechanical nor the software team accounted for these qualities in the robot design except from the robots' autonomous abilities, which were only considered from technical and safety perspectives. It is because of these unique robot characteristics that Young et al. [45] stress UX should not be compartmentalized in robot development as it leads to shallow and potentially wrong understanding of how the robot affects people. Instead, UX should be treated holistically and without detaching it from the situated, social context encounters and interactions are bound to take place in. While there might be reasons for this compartmentalization of UX–a consequence of legacy with respect to the company's habitual practices and low UX maturity—it poses major risks to the holistic experience of authentic users interacting with robots [1] and InCoPs being within robots' vicinity [32]. For example, sound signals robots could produce were only briefly talked about in connection to designing robot interactions, whereas lights and robots' expressive behavior were overlooked. It is well demonstrated that robots' non-verbal behavior and factors like appearance influence how people perceive, experience, and ascribe agency to robots, which help people make sense of and interact with robots [6,9,22,45]. If UX is not appropriately considered in robot development, it can result in reluctance towards accepting and using robots as well as erroneous handling of robots [1]. We fully agree with these authors and the importance of designing robots from a holistic UX perspective. Even so, these studies do not seem to consider autonomous robots operating in human populated environments are heavily regulated which influence what companies are actually allowed to do. For example, with respect to light and sound design of robots as well as robots' movements. Therefore, even if companies increasingly integrate UX in robot development, we might not see holistically designed robots in these contexts until regulations allow companies more freedom to design for good UX.

## 5.3   Practical Recommendations for Robot Development Teams

Based on our findings, we propose five practical recommendations for closer integration of UX in robot development:

1. Apply frameworks, such as the one proposed in [28], to identify main coordination mechanism for each team to improve UX in robot development.
2. Align coordination mechanism when developing physical, mechanical products as design decisions are difficult to change post hoc.
3. Align stage-gate transition outputs critical for mechanical development following New Product Development:
   – Establish software and UX design reviews similar to concept and prototype design reviews currently organized by the mechanical team and seen as gate deliverables.
   – Define software and UX outputs to be designed for each gate transition.
4. Ensure easy and equal access to physical, robot prototypes for mechanical and software teams to support UX evaluation practices with authentic users.
5. Establish up front UX goals and metrics using, e.g., robot design canvases [3, 26] and metrics developed specifically to assess UX of robots [41].

We found no shared coordination mechanism between teams (Theme 1, 3, and 4). For example, the mechanical team expects coordination based on standardization of outputs; the software team expects mutual adjustment. The stakes and risks are higher for mechanical teams, because doing something "wrong" is costly, while software developers can push updates in subsequent releases making them less vulnerable to changing requirements. To circumvent issues arising from this, we recommend that project managers, product managers, and team leaders consider implementing our recommendations 1 to 3. The quality of teams' UX work suffered considerably due to the lack of user involvement and because practitioners had limited or no access to physical robots, which necessitated workarounds (Theme 2). We therefore recommend that project managers, product managers, team leaders, and external partners strive to enforce recommendation 4. We see an opportunity for UX specialists to create impact beyond screen-based interactions–which was how UX was predominantly considered in this project–by engaging with mechanical teams. That is, screen-based UX and UI might be the way in, but it should not stop there. In robot development, we need a more holistic view on UX design [1, 38] since screen-based interaction is not the only way nor necessarily the dominant way authentic users and InCoPs interact and engage with robots. Development teams may overlook this important aspect and instead compartmentalize UX. We acknowledge that in large cross-disciplinary robot development projects it may be necessary to split the workload across multiple teams, who would then work on separate parts of the robots' UX. Recommendation 5 therefore encourage project and product managers, as well as UX specialists and design teams (if such exists in the project) to establish UX goals and metrics specifically for the robot(s) they develop. HCI researchers can support the transition towards more holistically designed robots by collaborating with practitioners on creating, implementing, and evaluating (new) design tools and guidelines specifically for integrating UX in robot development, which several researchers [5, 7, 20] argue is needed.

### 5.4 Limitations

Changing work practices and mindsets requires long-term engagement and investment of researchers and practitioners [2, 4, 8]. In prior cases, researchers appeared to be the main drivers behind integrating UX in both software development [2, 4] and robot development [3, 38]. However, researchers recognize that intervention research concerning UX integration struggle with establishing long-term or permanent impact [2, 4] as well as ensuring interventions are reinforced in practice [2] and that acquired skills are maintained [8]. Because robot development is an underexplored area, we did not pursue intervention. Instead, our objective was to examine and gain a contextualized understanding of *how* a non-software-founded company embeds UX in robot development. We achieved this through a case study of a single extreme case of mechanical and software teams involved in a *shared* large-scale robot development within a well-established company. Our case study's trustworthiness is ensured through credibility, transferability, dependability, and confirmability [34]. Credibility of our study was accomplished through extended engagement with practitioners [18], which enabled us to obtain tacit knowledge as well as observe transformation and practitioners' own integration of UX over time. Member-checking and conversations with practitioners also contributed to credibility. We do not claim our findings are generalizable; even so, they might be transferable because the case study reflects real practices in natural surroundings, but this requires additional research, e.g., in other robotics companies. Dependability was established by ensuring confidentiality of practitioners and through regular meetings with independent researchers ensuring inquiry audit during data collection and analysis. Lastly, the researcher involved with the company kept meticulous order of the detailed observations from every interaction with practitioners as well as of shared documents and artifacts to ensure confirmability.

## 6   Conclusion and Future Work

We conducted an extreme case study of mechanical and software teams involved in a *shared* large-scale robot development project within a non-software-founded company. We extend the work in, e.g., [2, 4, 8, 28] by emphasizing particularities of UX in physical robot development by hybrid mechanical/software teams over companies that deal exclusively with software products. We carried out extensive non-participant observations of 30 project SCRUM meetings from where four themes were identified: 1) the role of UX in robot development; 2) workarounds in design evaluations; 3) listening to authentic users when dealing with requirements; and 4) coordination through ceremonies and artifacts. Our findings reveal that although practitioners aspire to let UX impact robot development, UX played an inferior role. Practitioners did not account for robots' unique qualities in designing for coherent and positive experiences authentic users and InCoPs can have with their robots. The project also suffered from lack of common coordination and collaboration mechanisms between teams coming from distinct disciplines and development traditions. Based on these findings, we propose five practical recommendations encouraging robot development teams to 1) identify coordination mechanisms to improve UX in robot development; 2) align coordination mechanisms to avoid changing design decisions post hoc; 3) align, establish, and define stage-gate transition outputs critical for UX, mechanical, and software development; 4) ensure easy and equal access to physical, robot prototypes to support UX evaluation with authentic users; and 5) establish UX goals and metrics using robot design canvases [3,26] and metrics developed to assess UX of robots [41]. We recommend the research community to further engage with practitioners and support *their* transition towards long-lasting UX integration in robot development. Furthermore, we believe legacy could play an enabling role in integrating UX in robot development. Our observations revealed that the mechanical team's established practices and orientation towards experimentation, proactively adjusting to customer (and user) requirements, iteration, and parallel design tracks did not transfer to the software team. Considering the dominant role of mechanical design in the company's history, we did expect those practices to transfer to the software team. Further studies are therefore needed to examine mechanisms enabling and impeding transfer of practices from mechanical to software teams involved in *shared* robot development projects.

**Acknowledgments.** We like to thank the case company and practitioners involved for providing an interesting setting for our research. Additionally, we thank Aleksandra Kaszowska for proofreading the final manuscript.

# References

1. Alenljung, B., Lindblom, J., Andreasson, R., Ziemke, T.: User experience in social human-robot interaction. Int. J. Ambient Comput. Intell. (IJACI) 8(2), 12–31. IGI Global (2017). https://doi.org/10.4018/IJACI.2017040102
2. Ananjeva, A., Persson, J.S., Bruun, A.: Integrating UX work with agile development through user stories: an action research study in a small software company. J. Syst. Softw. **170**. Elsevier Inc (2020). https://doi.org/10.1016/j.jss.2020.110785
3. Axelsson, M., Oliveira, R., Racca, M., Kyrki, V.: Social robot co-design canvases: a participatory design framework. ACM Trans. Hum.-Robot Interact. **11**(1), 3–39. Association for Computing Machinery, New York, NY, USA (2021). https://doi.org/10.1145/3472225

4. Bang, K., Kanstrup, M.A., Kjems, A., Stage, J.: Adoption of UX evaluation in practice: an action research study in a software organization. In: Bernhaupt, R., Dalvi, G., Joshi, A., K. Balkrishan, D., O'Neill, J., Winckler, M. (eds.) INTERACT 2017. LNCS, vol. 10516, pp. 169–188. Springer, Cham (2017). https://doi.org/10.1007/978-3-319-68059-0_11

5. Barattini, P., Virk, G.S., Mirnig, N., Giannaccini, M.E., Tapus, A., Bonsignorio, F.: Experimenting in HRI for priming real world set-ups, innovations and products. In: Proceedings of the 2014 ACM/IEEE International Conference on Human-Robot Interaction, pp. 511–512. Association for Computing Machinery, New York, NY, USA (2014). https://doi.org/10.1145/2559636.2560030

6. Bartneck, C., Kulić, D., Croft, E., Zoghbi, S.: Measurement instruments for the anthropomorphism, animacy, likeability, perceived intelligence, and perceived safety of robots. Int. J. Soc. Robot. 71–81. Springer (2009). https://doi.org/10.1007/s12369-008-0001-3

7. Bethel, C.L., Henkel, Z., Baugus, K.: Conducting studies in human-robot interaction. In: Jost, C., et al. (eds.) Human-Robot Interaction. SSBN, vol. 12, pp. 91–124. Springer, Cham (2020). https://doi.org/10.1007/978-3-030-42307-0_4

8. Bornoe, N., Stage, J.: Active involvement of software developers in usability engineering: two small-scale case studies. In: Bernhaupt, R., Dalvi, G., Joshi, A., K. Balkrishan, D., O'Neill, J., Winckler, M. (eds.) INTERACT 2017. LNCS, vol. 10516, pp. 159–168. Springer, Cham (2017). https://doi.org/10.1007/978-3-319-68059-0_10

9. Breazeal, C.: Toward sociable robots. Robot. Auton. Syst. **42**(3–4), 167–175. Elsevier Science (2003). https://doi.org/10.1016/S0921-8890(02)00373-1

10. Bruun, A., Larusdottir, M.K., Nielsen, L., Nielsen, P.A., Persson, J.S.: The role of ux professionals in agile development: a case study from industry. In: Proceedings of the 10th Nordic Conference on Human-Computer Interaction, pp. 352–363. Association for Computing Machinery, New York, NY, USA (2018). https://doi.org/10.1145/3240167.3240213

11. Buchner, R., Mirnig, N., Weiss, A., Tscheligi, M.: Evaluating in real life robotic environment: bringing together research and practice. In: 2012 IEEE RO-MAN: The 21st IEEE International Symposium on Robot and Human Interactive Communication, pp. 602–607. IEEE, Paris, France (2012). https://doi.org/10.1109/ROMAN.2012.6343817

12. Cheon, E., Su, N.M.: Integrating roboticist values into a value sensitive design framework for humanoid robots. In: 2016 11th ACM/IEEE International Conference on Human-Robot Interaction (HRI), pp. 375–382. IEEE, Christchurch, New Zealand (2016). https://doi.org/10.1109/HRI.2016.7451775

13. Chun, B., Knight, H.: The robot makers: an ethnography of anthropomorphism at a robotics company. J. Hum.-Robot Interact. **9**(3). Association for Computing Machinery, New York, NY, USA (2020). https://doi.org/10.1145/3377343

14. Clemmensen, T., Hertzum, M., Yang, J., Chen, Y.: Do usability professionals think about user experience in the same way as users and developers do? In: Kotzé, P., Marsden, G., Lindgaard, G., Wesson, J., Winckler, M. (eds.) INTERACT 2013. LNCS, vol. 8118, pp. 461–478. Springer, Heidelberg (2013). https://doi.org/10.1007/978-3-642-40480-1_31

15. Conforto, E.C., Amaral, D.C.: Agile project management and stage-gate model - a hybrid framework for technology-based companies. J. Eng. Technol. Manag. **40**, 1–14. Elsevier (2016). https://doi.org/10.1016/j.jengtecman.2016.02.003

16. Cooper, Robert, G.: A process model for industrial new product development. IEEE Trans. Eng. Manag. **30**(1), 2–11. IEEE (1983). https://doi.org/10.1109/TEM.1983.6448637

17. Dittmar, A., Forbig, P.: Integrating personas and use case models. In: Lamas, D., Loizides, F., Nacke, L., Petrie, H., Winckler, M., Zaphiris, P. (eds.) Human-Computer Interaction – INTERACT 2019. LNCS, vol. 11746, pp. 666–686. Springer, Cham (2019). https://doi.org/10.1007/978-3-030-29381-9_40

18. Flyvbjerg, B.: Five misunderstandings about case-study research. Qual. Inquiry **12**(2). Sage Publications (2006). https://doi.org/10.1177/1077800405284363

19. Forlizzi, J.: How robotic products become social products: an ethnographic study of cleaning in the home. In: Proceedings of the ACM/IEEE International Conference on Human-Robot Interaction, pp. 129–136. Association for Computing Machinery, New York, NY, USA (2007). https://doi.org/10.1145/1228716.1228734

20. Frederiks, A.D., Octavia, J.R., Vandevelde, C., Saldien, J.: Towards participatory design of social robots. In: Lamas, D., Loizides, F., Nacke, L., Petrie, H., Winckler, M., Zaphiris, P. (eds.) INTERACT 2019. LNCS, vol. 11747, pp. 527–535. Springer, Cham (2019). https://doi.org/10.1007/978-3-030-29384-0_32

21. Garcia, A., da Silva, T.S., Silveira, M.S.: Artifact-facilitated communication in agile user-centered design. In: Kruchten, P., Fraser, S., Coallier, F. (eds.) XP 2019. LNBIP, vol. 355, pp. 102–118. Springer, Cham (2019). https://doi.org/10.1007/978-3-030-19034-7_7

22. Jochum, E., Derks, J.: Tonight we improvise!: real-time tracking for human-robot improvisational dance. In: Proceedings of the 6th International Conference on Movement and Computing, p. 11. Association for Computing Machinery, New York, NY, USA (2019). https://doi.org/10.1145/3347122.3347129

23. Kuusinen, K.: Value creation and delivery in agile software development: overcoming stakeholder conflicts. In: Clemmensen, T., Rajamanickam, V., Dannenmann, P., Petrie, H., Winckler, M. (eds.) INTERACT 2017. LNCS, vol. 10774, pp. 123–129. Springer, Cham (2018). https://doi.org/10.1007/978-3-319-92081-8_12

24. Lindblom, J., Andreasson, R.: Current challenges for UX evaluation of human-robot interaction. In: Schlick, C., Trzcieliński, S. (eds.) Advances in Ergonomics of Manufacturing: Managing the Enterprise of the Future. AISC. vol. 490, pp. 267–277. Springer, Cham (2016). https://doi.org/10.1007/978-3-319-41697-7_24

25. McKay, J., Marshall, P.: The dual imperatives of action research. Inf. Technol. People, **14**(1), p46–59 (2001). https://doi.org/10.1108/09593840110384771

26. Nielsen, S., Ordoñez, R., Hansen, K.D., Skov, M.B., Jochum, E.: RODECA: a canvas for designing robots. In: Companion of the 2021 ACM/IEEE International Conference on Human-Robot Interaction, pp. 266–270. Association for Computing Machinery, Boulder, CO, USA (2021). https://doi.org/10.1145/3434074.3447173

27. Obaid, M., Ahtinen, A., Kaipainen, K., Ocnarescu, I.: Designing for experiences with socially interactive robots. In: Proceedings of the 10th Nordic Conference on Human-Computer Interaction, pp. 948–951. Association for Computing Machinery, Oslo, Norway (2018). https://doi.org/10.1145/3240167.3240257

28. Persson, J.S., Bruun, A., Lárusdóttir, M.K., Nielsen, P.A.: Agile software development and UX design: A case study of integration by mutual adjustment. J. Inf. Softw. Technol. **152**. Elsevier (2022). https://doi.org/10.1016/j.infsof.2022.107059

29. Rosenthal-von der Puetten, A., Sirkin, D., Abrams, A., Platte, L.: The forgotten in HRI: incidental encounters with robots in public spaces. In: Proceedings of the 2020 ACM/IEEE International Conference on Human-Robot Interaction, pp. 656–657. Association for Computing Machinery, New York, NY, USA (2020). https://doi.org/10.1145/3371382.3374852

30. Rajanen, D., et al.: UX professionals' definitions of usability and UX – a comparison between Turkey, Finland, Denmark, France and Malaysia. In: Bernhaupt, R., Dalvi, G., Joshi, A., K. Balkrishan, D., O'Neill, J., Winckler, M. (eds.) INTERACT 2017. LNCS, vol. 10516, pp. 218–239. Springer, Cham (2017). https://doi.org/10.1007/978-3-319-68059-0_14

31. Ries, E.: The Lean Startup - How Today's Entrepreneurs Use Continuous Innovation to Create Radically Successful Businesses. Currency, Crown Publishing Group, New York, NY, USA, First International edn (2017)

32. Rossi, S., Rossi, A., Dautenhahn, K.: The secret life of robots: perspectives and challenges for robot's behaviours during non-interactive tasks. Int. J. Soc. Robot. **12**(6), 1265–1278 (2020). https://doi.org/10.1007/s12369-020-00650-z

33. Sandoval, E.B., Brown, S., Velonaki, M.: How the inclusion of design principles contribute to the development of social robots. In: Proceedings of the 30th Australian Conference on Computer-Human Interaction, pp. 535–538. Association for Computing Machinery, New York, NY, USA (2018). https://doi.org/10.1145/3292147.3292239

34. Shah, S.K., Corley, K.G.: Building better theory by bridging the quantitative-qualitative divide. J. Manag. Stud. **43**(8), 1821–1835. Blackwell Publishing Ltd. (2006). https://doi.org/10.1111/j.1467-6486.2006.00662.x

35. Sheppard, B., Kouyoumjian, G., Sarrazin, H., Dore, F.: The business value of design. Mckinsey quarterly report (2018). https://www.mckinsey.com/capabilities/mckinsey-design/our-insights/the-business-value-of-design

36. Simonÿ, C., Specht, K., Andersen, I.C., Johansen, K.K., Nielsen, C., Agerskov, H.: A Ricoeur-inspired approach to interpret participant observations and interviews. Glob. Qual. Nurs. Rese. **5**, 1–10. SAGE Publications (2018). https://doi.org/10.1177/233339361880739

37. Thrun, S.: Toward a framework for human-robot interaction. Hum.-Comput. Interact. **19**, 9–24. Lawrence Erlbaum Associates, Inc. (2004). https://doi.org/10.1207/s15327051hci1901%262_2

38. Tonkin, M., Vitale, J., Herse, S., Williams, M.A., Judge, W., Wang, X.: Design methodology for the UX of HRI: a field study of a commercial social robot at an airport. In: Proceedings of the 2018 ACM/IEEE International Conference on Human-Robot Interaction, pp. 407–415. Association for Computing Machinery, New York, NY, USA (2018). https://doi.org/10.1145/3171221.3171270

39. Šabanović, S., Michalowski, M.P., Caporael, L.R.: Making friends: Building social robots through interdisciplinary collaboration. In: Multidisciplinary Collaboration for Socially Assistive Robotics. Papers from the 2007 AAAI Spring Symposium, pp. 71–77. Association for the Advancement of Artificial Intelligence, Stanford, California, USA (2007)

40. Wale-Kolade, A., Nielsen, P.A., Päivärinta, T.: Usability work in agile systems development practice: a systematic review. In: Linger, H., Fisher, J., Barnden, A., Barry, C., Lang, M., Schneider, C. (eds.) Building Sustainable Information Systems, pp. 569–582. Springer, Boston, MA (2013). https://doi.org/10.1007/978-1-4614-7540-8_44

41. Wallström, J., Lindblom, J.: Design and development of the USUS goals evaluation framework. In: Jost, C., et al. (eds.) Human-Robot Interaction. SSBN, vol. 12, pp. 177–201. Springer, Cham (2020). https://doi.org/10.1007/978-3-030-42307-0_7

42. Weiss, A., Spiel, K.: Robots beyond science fiction: mutual learning in human-robot interaction on the way to participatory approaches. AI Soc. (6), 1–15 (2021). https://doi.org/10.1007/s00146-021-01209-w

43. Yigitbas, E., Jovanovikj, I., Engels, G.: Simplifying robot programming using augmented reality and end-user development. In: Ardito, C., et al. (eds.) INTERACT 2021. LNCS, vol. 12932, pp. 631–651. Springer, Cham (2021). https://doi.org/10.1007/978-3-030-85623-6_36

44. Yin, R.K.: Case Study Research and Applications: Design and Methods, 6th edn. SAGE Publications Inc, Los Angeles (2018)

45. Young, J.E., Sung, J., Voida, A., Sharlin, E., Igarashi, T., Christensen, H.I., Grinter, R.E.: Evaluating human-robot interaction. Int. J. Soc. Robot. **3**, 53–67. Springer (2011). https://doi.org/10.1007/s12369-010-0081-8

46. Zaina, L.A.M., Sharp, H., Barroca, L.: UX information in the daily work of an agile team: a distributed cognition analysis. In: Brumby, D.P. (ed.) Int. J. Hum.-Comput. Stud. **147**. Elsevier Ltd (2021). https://doi.org/10.1016/j.ijhcs.2020.102574

# Information Visualization

# BiVis: Interactive and Progressive Visualization of Billions (and Counting) Items

Renaud Blanch[✉]

Univ. Grenoble Alpes, CNRS, Grenoble-INP, LIG, 38000 Grenoble, France
blanch@imag.fr

**Abstract.** Recent advances in information visualization have shown that building proper structures to allow efficient lookup in the data can reduce significantly the time to build graphical representation of very large data sets, when compared to the linear scanning of the data. We present BiVis, a visualization technique that shows how such techniques can be further improved to reach a rendering time compatible with continuous interaction. To do so, we turn the lookup into an *anytime* algorithm compatible with a progressive visualization: a visualization presenting an approximation of the data and an estimation of the error can be displayed almost instantaneously and refined in successive frames until the error converges to zero. We also leverage the *spatial coherency* of the navigation: during the interaction, the state of the (possibly partial) lookup for the previous frames is reused to bootstrap the lookup for the next frame despite the view change. We show that those techniques allow the interactive exploration of *out-of-core* time series consisting of billions of events on commodity computers.

**Keywords:** Anytime visualization · progressive visualization

## 1 Introduction

Interactive visualization of large data sets has always been a challenge. The advances in hardware and software technologies keep on redefining what scale should be considered *large*. Twenty years ago, a million items was a large data set and its mere visualization was a challenge [13]. Five years later, such a data set could easily fit in RAM, and be explored with continuous interaction, i.e., rendered at interactive frame rates [4]. In the era of cheap SDRAM and solid-state drives, the size of the data sets are no longer capped by the technology: the most common USB stick can hold 8 GiB of data, i.e., a billion of numerical values encoded using 8 bytes (e.g., double precision floats, or 64 bit integers). However, allowing the exploration at *interactive frame rates* of such a data set is still a challenge despite recent advances, and BiVis shows a way to reach this goal.

Conceptually, the way tools that produce visualizations work is to iterate through the data, and to project each data point onto the screen, encoding some of its attributes with visual variables [7]. This makes sense as long as the number of data points is not larger than the number of pixels on screen. At some point though, the size of the data and the size of the screens become comparable, and the idea of *pixel-oriented* techniques, that

**Supplementary Information** The online version contains supplementary material available at https://doi.org/10.1007/978-3-031-42283-6_4.

© The Author(s), under exclusive license to Springer Nature Switzerland AG 2023
J. Abdelnour Nocera et al. (Eds.): INTERACT 2023, LNCS 14143, pp. 65–85, 2023.
https://doi.org/10.1007/978-3-031-42283-6_4

assigns a single pixel per data point comes-up [30]. Now that the size of the data is much larger than the number of pixels on screen, people realized it is more efficient to switch to a model that does not scan the data to produce the visualization, but rather scans the pixels of the view and lookup the corresponding data to produce a visualization. This path, dubbed *pixel-based* or image order rendering, has been followed for some time in the Scientific Visualization domain for volumetric data: that is the main idea behind volume ray casting [31]; and some recent techniques in the field of Information Visualization drew inspiration from there (e.g., [33,35,39]).

During the same period, the idea of presenting aggregations computed over partial data, proposed more than twenty-five years ago in the field of databases [23], was tested in visualizations. Various terms have been coined to denote visualization techniques that first present a coarse view of the data, and then make subsequent refinements so that the user can start to make judgements without waiting for the information to be complete. Initially dubbed *incremental visualization* [42], such techniques have later been included as a key part of the *progressive visual analytics* field [2] because of the impact they have on the whole analysis process; and with an even broader view, they are considered as a stone to build a *progressive data science* [47].

In this paper we present BiVis, a visualization technique that shows a way to make interactive exploration of very large data sets possible by turning a *pixel-based* technique into an *progressive visualization*. The key here is to turn the lookup into the data, which is performed for each pixel of the visualization, into an *anytime algorithm* [11]: the lookup is interruptible and resumable at will, and the information present in a partially-completed lookup allows to build a visualization that makes sense.

To demonstrate how this is possible, we use a simple *pixel-based* technique for which the lookup is easy to describe. We consider a time series of events, i.e., a sequence of timestamps at which the event occurred, sorted in chronological order. Since they are sorted, looking up a particular time can be done using a binary search. The size considered is billions of events, i.e., several orders of magnitude larger than the size of screens, and also larger than the RAM of a typical desktop computer.

After reviewing related works, we present in Sect. 3 the details of the BiVis technique. In Sect. 4, we show that the technique can be extended, first to handle more general time series, and then to 2D data sets. We also show that BiVis is compatible with many existing visualization and interaction techniques: it makes them scale up to very large data sets. Section 5 gives details about the implementation of BiVis and some optimizations, and also provides an evaluation of the performance of the technique. Finally, we conclude in Sect. 6 by discussing how this approach could be applied to other lookup-based techniques and by giving some potential extensions of this work.

## 2    Previous Work

**Pixel-Based Binning.** Handling large data sets has always been a relevant challenge for the information visualization community. The definition of *large* has yet to be updated regularly: in this paper, we consider as large a data set that does not fit into the RAM of a commodity computer at the time of writing. As this limit has grown quickly through the time, the size available on screen did not follow the same exponential growth. When the size of data sets became comparable with those of screens, this discrepancy led to the

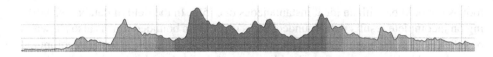

**Fig. 1.** BiVis showing a tweets data set (abscissa encodes time; ordinate the tweet rate, hue encodes approximation error, see Sect. 3.2).

proposition of *pixel-oriented* techniques by Keim et al. [29,30]. Relying on the advance in graphical processors, exploring interactively million items data sets (the number of pixels found on a typical screen at that time) became possible more than ten years ago [4,13].

However, now that data sets are commonly several orders of magnitude larger than the size of the screen, each pixel can only present an aggregation of the underlying data. When visualizing a billion items time series on a visualization about 1000 pixels wide as shown on Fig. 1, each pixel is, on average, the aggregation of a million data points. In the field of databases, this problem of approximating accurate histograms has been studied for a long time as the distribution of the values present in the tables can be decisive to choose an execution plan [26,27,40]. The strategies that have been proposed to perform this binning, like those aimed at commodity computers (e.g., the *Bin-summarise-smooth* framework provided for the R language [49]) are not interactive. Being able to provide interactive visualization of data sets at this scale requires dedicated infrastructure, e.g., to prefetch the data in the case of the *ATLAS* system [8], or to use Big Data infrastructures that are able to handle the *volume* and the *velocity* of the data at this scale [5,20,25].

**Scalability.** The scalability that we aim for is a combination of visual and software scalability, as defined by Thomas and Cook in their Visual Analytics agenda [45]. More recently, Liu et al. proposed two kinds of scalability that refine the previous ones: *perceptual* scalability (the fact that there are far more data than pixels) and *interactive* scalability (the fact that visualizations should be updated interactively) [35]. They come to the conclusion that building a histogram of the data using the pixels as bins is the way to address perceptual scalability. This path was proved effective in the past, e.g., by Munzner and Slack et al. in their TreeJuxtaposer tool and PRISAD system [38,43] for trees and sequences. As for addressing the interactive scalability, Liu et al.'s *imMens* system relies on precomputed levels of detail (LoDs) in the data space as are doing Ferreira et al. in their different works [14,15]. Other systems, especially the *\*cubes* family [33,39,48], address this scalability by precomputing data structures allowing efficient aggregations. Here, we use a simpler alternative that does not require heavy pre-computations nor fixed arbitrary LoDs (for the 1D case of time series). This approach is also proved valid by the Falcon system [36] that builds on similar ideas to get interactive brushing across linked histogram visualizations. While less sophisticated and probably less efficient, its simplicity allows us to show how to turn lookup-based technique into progressive visualization, and this result can probably be generalized to more complex lookup schemes such as the ones used in the *\*cubes* family techniques.

This approach to interactive scalability is backed up by studies that show that latency is detrimental to analysts [34], but that they are able to make judgments using progressive visualizations [16], and that exploration is as efficient with a progressive tool as it would be with an ideal instantaneous one [50]. In the field of databases, working on incomplete results with bounded errors returned in bounded time is also shown to be efficient [1]. The use of progressive visualizations in conjunction with precomputed LoDs has also been experimented with success for web-based systems or distributed infrastructure, where the network can introduce a bottleneck not present on desktop applications [21, 25]. The idea of using anytime algorithms to build progressive visualizations (i.e., visualizations that refine during interaction) is also at the heart of a visualization toolkit [12]. Ultimately, the BiVis technique could be included in such toolkit as a binning algorithm that scales with the logarithm of the data set size rather than linearly, so that systems that support progressive visual analytics (like InsightsFeed [3]) could be build more easily.

Finally, BiVis borrows ideas widely used by the Scientific Visualization community. The *pixel-based* nature of our technique is a variation on ray casting [31]. This technique is known to reduce the complexity to the size of the screen rather than to the size of the data set, and has been extensively used for efficient volume rendering (e.g., [17] or [9]). We also benefit from their experience of handling data sets larger than the computer RAM to work *out-of-core*, and thus to rely on efficient I/O [18].

## 3   BiVis Technique

BiVis operates on time series of events: each event is characterized by the time of its occurrence. The data sets are then just a list of timestamps (e.g., the number of seconds elapsed since a given origin) sorted in increasing order. This ordering is inherent to most data sets: time series are acquired as the values are produced, thus their timestamps naturally increase. The fact that the data set is ordered is crucial: it will enable lookups in the data without performing linear scans.

At its heart, BiVis mainly computes a histogram of the data: for the time period displayed by the visualization, the events occurring during the span covered by each pixel are counted, and then shown as a smoothed line chart. This rendering is performed at interactive frame rate: an approximation of the exact counts is computed using the time budget fixed by the program. This approximation is then refined in subsequent frames. Finally, during interactive exploration, BiVis is able to reuse as much information as possible from the previous view to bootstrap the rendering of the new visualization with a good approximation. Those steps are detailed below.

### 3.1   Image-Based Rendering

The first principle that makes BiVis able to visualize a data set consisting of billions of events is that it never scans the data set linearly as traditional visualization tools usually do. The classical approach in visualization is to project the data onto the screen. BiVis takes the opposite approach: it looks up the pixels into the data set. The difference is the same as the one found for 3D rendering between rasterization (where geometry is projected on screen) vs. raytracing (where pixels are projected in the geometry). This difference matters because the size of the visualization (its width because time is 1D) is bounded by the size of the screen (a few thousand pixels for the width of current largest screens) which is 5 or 6 orders of magnitude smaller than a billion events data set.

To display the time interval $[t_{min}, t_{max}]$ of a time series consisting of the $N$ time-stamps of the events $\{ts_0, \ldots, ts_i, \ldots, ts_{N-1}\}$ with $i \in [0, N-1]$ on a $W$ pixels wide visualization, BiVis first computes the $W+1$ borders of the pixels (Fig. 2):

$$t_0 = t_{min}, \ldots, t_k = t_{min} + k \times dt, \ldots, t_W = t_{max} \tag{1}$$

where $dt = (t_{max} - t_{min})/W$ is the time span of a pixel and $k \in [0, W]$ is the position of the pixel border. Those borders are then looked up in the data set. This lookup can be performed efficiently (e.g., with a binary search) since the timestamps are sorted. It returns the indices of the events that occurred just before each pixel border, i.e.:

$$i_k \in [0, N-1] \text{ such that } ts_{i_k} \le t_k < ts_{i_{k+1}}, \quad k \in [0, W]. \tag{2}$$

The density of events is then computed, giving the histogram:

$$h_k = \frac{i_{k+1} - i_k}{t_{k+1} - t_k}, \quad k \in [0, W-1] \tag{3}$$

where, given Eq. 2, $i_{k+1} - i_k$ is the number of events that occurred in the $[t_k, t_{k+1}[$ time frame, i.e., that are located under the $k^{\text{th}}$ pixel. Dividing this count by the duration of the time frame $t_{k+1} - t_k$ turns the units of the histogram into event per second rather than event per pixel. With this technique, we can count the events without the need of processing them individually: the differences between the ranks $i_{k+1}$ and $i_k$ provides a direct access to an aggregation of the events.

The computation needed to build this histogram scales linearly with the width of the visualization since each step is performed for each pixel. The most demanding computation is the lookup in the time series: the time needed depends on the size of the data set. Since the lookup is performed using a binary search, the time needed scales with $\log_2 N$ on average. Thus the time needed for the construction of the histogram roughly grows like $W \times \log_2 N$. With $N \approx 10^9$ and $W \approx 10^3$, this gives about $3.2 \times 10^4$ lookups in the data. Those lookups are not cheap: for data sets that can not fit in the computer's RAM, they involve accessing the permanent storage at random offsets. For a given machine (see the more thorough discussion in Sect. 5), and a 4.3 billion timestamps (i.e., 32 GiB) data set that does not fit in its RAM, the linear scan of the data takes about 50 s. With this view-based rendering, the computation of a 5120 pixel wide histogram takes less than 4 s. This time is still too long to explore such a data set interactively.

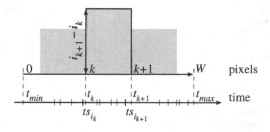

**Fig. 2.** Histogram: the borders $t_k$ and $t_{k+1}$ of the $k^{\text{th}}$ pixel are looked up, leading to timestamps $ts_{i_k}$ and $ts_{i_{k+1}}$; the number of events is then the difference between their ranks: $i_{k+1} - i_k$.

## 3.2  Anytime Rendering

To improve the user experience while computing the rendering, BiVis turns the lookup into an anytime algorithm. This allows the visualization to become progressive: an approximate presentation is proposed to the user, and it is refined at interactive frame rates. To do so, each iteration of the binary search is applied on every pixel before stepping to the next bisection. This outside loop is interrupted as soon as the computation exceeds a given time budget compatible with an interactive rendering, i.e., typically 15 ms ($\approx$ 60 fps). In practice, two arrays, *lo* and *hi*, keep the lower and higher bounds of the interval in which the indices $i$ defined by Eq. 2 are known to be, i.e.:

$$lo_k \leq i_k \leq hi_k \iff ts_{lo_k} \leq ts_{i_k} \leq ts_{hi_k}, \quad k \in [0, W]. \tag{4}$$

Algorithm 1 shows the BISECT function that refines those bounds as much as possible in the given time budget *max_time*. It uses a classical bisection, but with aa additional halting condition based on a measure of the elapsed time.

Instead of returning the exact indices $i$ which may not have been reached yet, the midpoints *mid* of last known bounds *lo* and *hi* are returned as their best approximations for now. The widths of the intervals in which the indices are known to be, *width*, are also returned. DISPLAY_HISTOGRAM can then be called to compute an approximated *histogram* using *mid* (instead of the exacts $i$ as in Eq. 3) with:

$$histogram_k = \frac{mid_{k+1} - mid_k}{t_{k+1} - t_k}, \quad k \in [0, W-1];$$

and *width* to compute an estimate of the *error* per pixel by averaging the errors on the pixel borders with:

$$error_k = (width_{k+1} + width_k)/2, \quad k \in [0, W-1].$$

---

**Algorithm 1.** Anytime bisection

**function** BISECT(*t, lo, hi, max_time*)                    ▷ *t, lo, hi* are arrays indexed by $k \in [0, W]$
  *start_time* ← NOW                                 ▷ anytime stop
  **while** NOW − *start_time* ≤ *max_time* **and** ANY(*lo < hi*) **do**
    *mid* ← (*lo + hi*) ÷ 2                   ▷ integer division
    **for all** $k \in [0, W]$ **do**           ▷ bisection for each pixel border
      **if** $t_k < ts_{mid_k}$ **then**
        $hi_k \leftarrow mid_k$
      **else**
        $lo_k \leftarrow mid_k + 1$
  *mid* ← (*lo + hi*) ÷ 2
  *width* ← *hi − lo*
  **return** *mid, width*

**procedure** DISPLAY_HISTOGRAM(*t, mid, width*)
  *histogram* ← $(mid_{k+1} - mid_k)/(t_{k+1} - t_k)$, $k \in [0, W-1]$
  *error* ← $(width_{k+1} + width_k)/2$, $k \in [0, W-1]$
  DRAW_FRAME(*histogram, error*)

---

**Fig. 3.** Anytime rendering: some steps of the binary search refinement (hue encode the error, see below for the mapping used).

Algorithm 2 shows how this bisection is used. First, the BOOTSTRAP_BOUNDS function computes $t$ according to the current period of time and to the width of the visualization using Eq. 1. It also initializes $lo$ and $hi$ with the indices of the first and last events, the most pessimistic estimates for the bounds of any timestamp. After this bootstrapping, the DISPLAY_LOOP procedure passes those values to the anytime BISECT function. The result of the anytime binary search is then passed for display to DIS-PLAY_HISTOGRAM. Finally, *mid* and *width* are used to update the $lo$ and $hi$ bounds before looping back to the bisection.

Figure 3 shows successive frames of a progressive refinement. In practice, only few frames are rendered: the time budget is often large enough to perform many steps of the bisection. Here, the DRAW_FRAME procedure encodes the distance to the exact histogram using the hue. The reciprocal of the number of steps needed to reach the result, $1/\log_2(error + 2)$, is used: it varies from 0 (encoded using red) when the number of steps is large, to 1 (encoded using green) when it reaches 0, i.e., when the histogram is exact. Of course, other visual encodings of this error could be used, e.g., any of the existing techniques aimed at representing uncertainty in data.

At the beginning of the bisection, many pixels share their midpoints and thus the events are accumulated at the borders where midpoints are not shared, leading to the spikes observed on the first frames. When the bisection proceeds further, those accumulation are distributed more and more precisely over their actual positions.

---

**Algorithm 2.** Anytime histogram

---

**function** COMPUTE_BORDERS($t_{min}$, $t_{max}$)    ▷ Compute pixel borders for a given screen width
    **return** $t_{min} + k \times (t_{max} - t_{min})/W$, $k \in [0, W]$

**function** BOOTSTRAP_BOUNDS($t_{min}$, $t_{max}$)    ▷ Compute pixel borders and initial search bounds
    $t \leftarrow$ COMPUTE_BORDERS($t_{min}$, $t_{max}$)
    $lo, hi \leftarrow 0, N-1$, $k \in [0, W]$
    **return** $t$, $lo$, $hi$

**procedure** DISPLAY_LOOP
    $t, lo, hi \leftarrow$ BOOTSTRAP_BOUNDS($t_{min}$, $t_{max}$)
    **while** True **do**
        $mid, width \leftarrow$ BISECT($t$, $lo$, $hi$, 15 ms)
        DISPLAY_HISTOGRAM($t$, $mid$, $width$)
        $lo \leftarrow mid - width \div 2$
        $hi \leftarrow lo + width$

---

## 3.3  Interactive Rendering

The goal is now to make the visualization interactive, and a first stage for the interaction is to allow the user to change the view, e.g., by panning and zooming. The other stages would be to allow the manipulation of higher steps of the visualization pipeline (e.g., brushing or filtering the data), but allowing the exploration of the data by navigating inside the data set is a first challenge to tackle with such large datasets.

To do so, any interaction technique can be used, as they all boil down to update $t_{min}$ and $t_{max}$ between two frames. This update invalidates the pixel borders $t$, and thus also $lo$ and $hi$. BOOTSTRAP could be used to recompute those arrays, but then the bisection would start again to scan the whole data set for the pixel borders. Instead of this naive solution, BiVis exploits the spatial coherence of the continuous interaction: the new pixel borders may not be too far from the previous ones, so the information from the previous bounds may be reused to compute the new bounds.

Algorithm 3 shows how this can be done. The general idea implemented by UPDATE_BOUNDS is to lookup the new pixel borders $t^n$ into the previous ones $t^p$, and then to reuse the knowledge about the previous bounds $lo^p$ and $hi^p$ to compute good candidates for the new bounds $lo^n$ and $hi^n$.

---

**Algorithm 3.** Reusing previous pixel border approximation

---

**function** UPDATE_BOUNDS($t^n, t^p, lo^p, hi^p$)

  **if** $t_0^n < t_0^p$ **then**            ▷ ensure previous interval includes new one

    $lo_0^p \leftarrow$ EXPSEARCH_LO($ts, t_0^n, lo_0^p$)

    $t_0^p \leftarrow ts_{lo_0^p}$

  **if** $t_{-1}^p < t_{-1}^n$ **then**

    $hi_{-1}^p \leftarrow$ EXPSEARCH_HI($ts, t_{-1}^n, hi_{-1}^p$)

    $t_{-1}^p \leftarrow ts_{hi_{-1}^p}$

  $l, h \leftarrow 0, 0$                ▷ new bounds for each pixel border

  **for all** $k \in [0, W^n]$ **do**

    **while** $h < W^p$ and $t_h^p < t_k^n$ **do**

      $h \leftarrow h + 1$

    **while** $l < W^p$ and $t_l^p \leq t_k^n$ **do**

      $l \leftarrow l + 1$

    $lo_k^n, hi_k^n \leftarrow lo_{l-1}^p, hi_h^p$

  **return** $t^n, lo^n, hi^n$

**procedure** INTERACTIVE_DISPLAY_LOOP

  $t, lo, hi \leftarrow \{ts_0, ts_{N-1}\}, \{0, 0\}, \{N-1, N-1\}$

  **while** True **do**

    $t^n \leftarrow$ COMPUTE_BORDERS($t_{min}, t_{max}$)

    $t, lo, hi \leftarrow$ UPDATE_BOUNDS($t^n, t, lo, hi$)

    $mid, width \leftarrow$ BISECT($t, lo, hi, 15\,\text{ms}$)

    DISPLAY_HISTOGRAM($t, mid, width$)

    $lo \leftarrow mid - width \div 2$

    $hi \leftarrow lo + width$

---

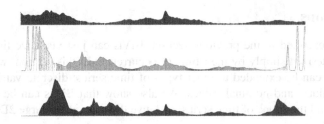

**Fig. 4.** Interactive rendering: starting from an exact view (top); zooming out while keeping known information (second line), the center of the histograms is more precise than peripheral regions which were not present in previous frames; and finally refining the histogram (last line).

So, for each new pixel border $t_k^n$, we look into the previous borders $t^p$ for the closest values. Since those borders are sorted, the lookups can be performed efficiently by iterating over the $t^n$ and $t^p$ simultaneously, avoiding the need for an extra binary search. We then find the largest $l \in [0, W^p]$ such that $t_{l-1}^p \leq t_k^n$ and the smallest $h \in [0, W^p]$ such that $t_k^n \leq t_h^p$. We then know from Eqs. 2 and 4 that:

$$ts_{lo_{l-1}^p} \leq ts_{i_{l-1}} \leq t_{l-1}^p \leq t_k^n \quad \text{and} \quad t_k^n \leq t_h^p < ts_{i_h} \leq ts_{hi_h^p}.$$

Those relations give:

$$ts_{lo_{l-1}^p} \leq t_k^n < ts_{hi_h^p}$$

and the two bounds we are looking for: $lo_k^n = lo_{l-1}^p$ and $hi_k^n = hi_h^p$.

Before performing those lookups of $t^n$ in $t^p$, we have to be sure that they will be found. To ensure that, if the new lower pixel border $t_0^n$ is before the previous one $t_0^p$, BiVis updates $t_0^p$ and $lo_0^p$ by looking up a lower bound for $t_0^n$ in the whole data set. Similarly, if the new higher pixel border $t_{-1}^n$ is after the previous one $t_{-1}^p$, $t_{-1}^p$ and $hi_{-1}^p$ are updated by looking up an higher bound for $t_{-1}^n$ in the data set[1]. Those lookups are performed using exponential searches since we know in which direction to look and since the bounds we are looking for are likely to be not far from the previous bounds.

By doing so, we keep all the available information present in $t^p$, $lo^p$ and $hi^p$, while ensuring $t_0^p \leq t_0^n$ and $t_{-1}^n \leq t_{-1}^p$.

Finally, we can plug the UPDATE_BOUNDS function into our DISPLAY_LOOP procedure from Algorithm 2 and get the INTERACTIVE_DISPLAY_LOOP from Algorithm 3. It should be noted that the bootstrapping of $t$, $lo$ and $hi$ can be reduced to a simpler form, since they will be updated to match the actual pixel borders by COMPUTE_BORDERS at the start of each iteration of the INTERACTIVE_DISPLAY_LOOP.

Figure 4 shows Algorithm 3 at work, step by step, while zooming out from a histogram that is exact (top) to a larger view (bottom). We can see that during the zooming out interaction, the central region, which was present in the previous frames, is quite close to the exact histogram, while the peripheral regions do not benefit from previous estimates of their upper and lower bounds, and thus need to be computed from scratch.

---

[1] Because of a resizing of the visualization by the user, $W$ may have changed between the previous and next steps. UPDATE_BOUNDS use the $-1$ index to denote the last element in the $t$ or $hi$ arrays, be it at index $W^p$ or $W^n$.

## 4  Extensions

In the form described in the previous section, BiVis can just visualize time series of events characterized simply by their time of occurrence. In this section, we show that the technique can be extended to other types of time series: discrete values, sampled continuous values, and nominal values. We also show that BiVis can be extended to data sets beyond the scope of time series, and give the example of large 2D data sets.

### 4.1  Extensions to Other Types of Time Series

To be able to build the histogram, BiVis needs to have a direct access to an aggregation of the events for any time span. In the case of event time series, this aggregation is the count of events associated with each pixel. This count is provided by the difference between the ranks of the events at their borders (Eq. 3). But the rank of an event is in fact the count of events between the beginning of the time series and the event considered. The count below the pixel is then computed using the difference between two counts running from the beginning.

For other forms of time series, the count of events is not sufficient, we need to access their value. We can generalize the way the count is computed to other aggregations: we just need to replace the index of the event by the aggregation of the values since the beginning of the time series. Thus, provided an aggregate $a_k$ of the value from $ts_0$ to $t_k$ is known, the general form of $histogram$, can be expressed as:

$$histogram_k = \frac{a_{k+1} - a_k}{t_{k+1} - t_k}, \quad k \in [0, W-1].$$

In the case of events time series, the aggregate $a_k$ is the number of events between $ts_0$ and $t_k$, i.e., $a_k = i_k$ (the index such that $ts_{i_k} \leq t_k < ts_{i_k+1}$) and we are back to Eq. 3. We do not have to store this aggregate since it is exactly the index of the timestamp, which is given directly by the bisection. For other time series, other aggregates have to be constructed. The general idea is to store alongside with the timestamps a sequence of partial sums of the values instead of the values themselves, as it is done with summed-area tables [10]. We show below which aggregate makes sense depending on the type of values considered.

**Discrete Values.** Discrete values are an extension of events time series: the events are characterized by their time $ts_i$ but also by a value $v_i$. This kind of data is commonly found for event data aggregated at specific time granularities, e.g., the number of requests handled by a server every second (or minute, etc.) In this case, if we store the partial sums $s_i$:

$$s_i = \sum_{j \leq i} v_j, \quad i \in [0, N-1]$$

with the timestamps $ts_i$, we will be able to reconstruct any partial sum by accessing only the data at the borders of the pixels. The aggregate $a_k$ needed at each pixel border to construct the histogram is then:

$$a_k = s_{i_k}, \quad k \in [0, W-1]$$

with the $i_k$ defined as in Eq. 2.

**Continuous Values.** Continuous values can also be represented using BiVis: the data is then characterized by its value $v_i$ sampled at various timestamps $ts_i$. To construct the graph of such a series, the meaningful aggregation for the value over a given time period is its mean, i.e., its integral divided by the duration of the interval. To be able to construct such aggregation for any time period, we will store the sequence of partial integrals $s_i$ of the value at each timestamp. For values that are constant during intervals between two timestamps (e.g., stock prices), an exact sum can be used:

$$s_i = \sum_{j \leq i} v_j \times \left( ts_{j+1} - ts_j \right), \quad i \in [0, N-1], \tag{5}$$

whereas for values that are really continuous, a trapeze approximation may be more suited:

$$s_i = \sum_{j \leq i} \frac{v_j + v_{j+1}}{2} \times \left( ts_{j+1} - ts_j \right), \quad i \in [0, N-1]. \tag{6}$$

To rebuild the aggregation at pixel borders, we have to interpolate between those known partial integrals. So for the aggregate $a_k$ at $t_k$, we can do a linear interpolation between $s_{i_{k+1}}$ and $s_{i_k}$:

$$a_k = s_{i_k} + \left( s_{i_{k+1}} - s_{i_k} \right) \times \frac{t_k - ts_{i_k}}{ts_{i_{k+1}} - ts_{i_k}}, \quad k \in [0, W-1].$$

**Nominal Values.** The previous extensions all involve quantitative values. But some time series consist of nominal values (e.g., the state of a process switching over the time between *waiting*, *running*, and *blocked*). Since it is not possible to aggregates such values using arithmetic mean, we can not simply assign different quantitative values to each state and use one of the previous aggregation (spending half of the time *waiting* and the other half *blocked* is not the same as spending all the time *running*).

Thus, the way we handle nominal values is to store a time series for each state. Each time series encodes the fact of being in the given state with the value 1 and of not being in this state with the value 0. By doing so, aggregation has a meaning: if the aggregated value is .5 over a specific time span, it means that this state was active half of the time during this period. The time series are then handled as continuous values as seen previously using the partial sum $s_i$ from Eq. 5.

### 4.2 Extension to Spatial Data

The BiVis technique can be applied to data sets other than time series. The only assumption on which it relies is that the data is sorted, so that a bisection algorithm can be used to efficiently find pixel borders. To show how versatile BiVis is, we have applied the technique to 2D spatial data. Since there is no natural order in 2D, we first have to encode the 2D positions into 1D coordinates that can be used to sort and search the points. Once done, the data can be searched for pixel borders, assuming those borders are also expressed in the 1D coordinate system.

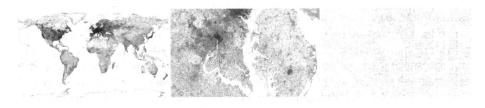

**Fig. 5.** OpenStreetMap planet data set (2 863 152 191 nodes) rasterized as a 1280 × 800 bitmap, 1 px ≈ (left) 32 km, (center) 256 m, and (right) 2 m (Scales are given along the equator).

**1D Geospatial Data Hashing.** To encode spatial data along a single dimension, we use a hashing: the two spatial coordinates are combined into a single coordinate. Various schemes exist to do such a hashing, the most popular one being the Lebesgue curve

In our case we have a strong requirement on continuity: two points that are close in the 1D space should also be close in the 2D space. This property is needed because BiVis computes aggregations along this 1D axis, and for geospatial information, aggregation is likely to make sense only for nearby areas. A better hashing scheme is then the curvilinear abscissa along the space-filling Hilbert curve [24] since it has good locality properties [22] (close points in 2D can be distant on this 1D axis, but they will still end up aggregated in nearby pixels), while being easy to compute.

2D data sets are thus preprocessed so that BiVis can apply. The coordinates of the points are normalized with respect to a bounding box. Then they are hashed with a precision of 64 bit (32 bit per coordinate, which gives for example a precision of 2.4 m along the 40 000 km of the equator) using their 1D Hilbert hash. Those hashes are then sorted so that the bisection method can be applied. Those preprocessing steps took several days to complete for the OSM planet data set used below.

**2D Bitmap Rasterization.** To produce a 2D bitmap from the hashed data, the coordinates of the center of the pixels are projected into the coordinate system defined by the bounding box used to normalize the data. The centers are then hashed using the Hilbert hash. The pixels are then sorted according to their hashes, and the midpoints separating them are used as pixel borders. The BiVis algorithm can then be applied without modification to compute the anytime aggregation of the data. To produce the final image, the histogram has to be permuted back to invert the sorting performed on the pixels centers so that each bucket finds its place in the final image.

Figure 5 shows the result of this process for the 2 863 152 191 nodes (2D points) used to define all the geometries (buildings, roads, coasts, borders, etc.) present in the OSM planet data set. The coordinates are normalized to fit the latitude and longitude into [0, 1] intervals, and rasterized at various scales in a 1280 × 800 bitmap. The density of nodes is encoded by the luminance channel using a non-linear mapping: first it is normalized, and then raised to an adjustable exponent (here .5) to allow for some interactive contrast adjustment. The error is encoded per pixel using a superimposed red layer whose pixel's opacity grows with the distance to the exact image.

## 4.3   Compatibility with Existing Techniques

A nice property of BiVis is that it introduces no incompatibility with other visualization or interaction techniques common for time series. The fact that the visualization is generated at the pixel level is even an interesting properties for some of them.

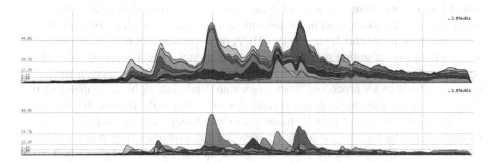

**Fig. 6.** Multiple series: 148571 tweets sent during the State of The Union 2014 speech of the president of the USA classified by topics, shown as (top) stacked graphs, and (bottom) braided graphs(data from <twitter.github.io/interactive/sotu2014>).

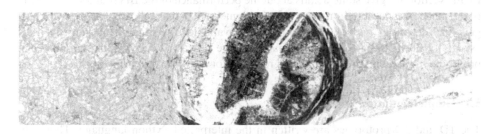

**Fig. 7.** Non-linear projection: a 2D fisheye lens magnifying 4 times its circular focus region centered on Manhattan island.

**Multiple Series.** Many variants of time series visualization can be used as is with BiVis: generally it is just a matter of applying them per pixel once the histograms of each time series have been computed. There is a choice that still has to be made by the developer when working with multiple time series: the timestamps can be shared by all the time series, and then a single bisection is needed to compute the pixels borders. But in this case, the column storing the cumulative sums of the values may contain redundant values. The alternative is to store a timestamps column per series which in return gets shorter, but this solution leads to multiple bisections. Depending on the size of the data, and on the distributions of the timestamps, one of the approaches may perform better and/or need more storage than the other.

Figure 6 shows 10 time series representing the 10 main topics of tweets sent during State of The Union 2014 speech of the president of the USA. At the top, they are combined using the well known stacked graph technique [6]. Each time series is processed by the bisection algorithm, and the values are stacked for each pixel without needing further computation. At the bottom of Fig. 6, the same data set is shown using the braided graph visualization technique [28], the braiding being computed per pixel.

**Non-Linear Projections.** Non-linear projections are often used in information visualization: they are widespread in focus+context techniques. They have been used for a long time, both in 1D and 2D (e.g., [19,41]). A recent example of non-linear projection applied to the visualization of time series is the ChronoLenses system where multiple scales can coexist on a same timeline [51]. To implement such system with BiVis, the COMPUTE_BORDERS procedure from Algorithm 2 has just to be specialized so that pixel borders are distributed along the time axis according to the desired distribution.

Figure 7 shows a non-linear 2D transformation: a fisheye lens that magnifies 4 times its central circular focus region and compress 2.5 times its outer ring to connect to the context region. The fact that the pixels are looked-up into the data makes any part of the visualization pixel-precise, whatever the deformation is.

## 5    Implementation and Performance Evaluation

In this section we give some details about the performance of the BiVis algorithms. This performance is measured on a specific implementation that relies on many technologies that, despite being advanced, are widely available. The implementation specifics, especially how out-of-core data is managed, are described below for reference. The prototype implementation evaluated is released for anyone to experiment[2].

### 5.1    Implementation

The 1D and 2D prototypes are written in the interpreted Python language. They rely on the NumPy package, which provides compiled extensions to Python for handling raw arrays of data with the performance of native compiled code. The graphical display and the interaction are managed using the OpenGL library and the GLUT toolkit, and their standard Python bindings: PyOpenGL (the BiVis algorithms do not depend on the graphical stack, any graphical backend would do).

**Using Static Typing for Efficiency.** Both 1D and 2D prototypes rely on our *bivis* module, which implements the critical parts of the BiVis algorithms: the BISECT (Algorithm 1) and UPDATE_BOUNDS (Algorithm 3) functions. This module is written in Python, but the code is annotated with type information, which makes it suitable for translation in C using the Cython static compiler.

---

[2] BiVis, <iihm.imag.fr/blanch/projects/bivis/>.

**Handling of Out-of-Core Data Sets.** The data sets are seen by the program as normal arrays, but they are in fact memory-mapped files, using the NumPy *memmap* function (which in turns typically relies on the standard *mmap* system call). It means that the data sets are kept on-disk, but when they are randomly accessed, a page of the file is loaded into the RAM, and is subsequently available if another random access needs it. This whole caching mechanism is handled efficiently by the operating system, provided the access pattern exhibits some regularity and some coherency. The advent of solid state drive (SSD) makes this mechanism even more efficient, since they exhibit negligible latency, even for random access. And indeed the *bivis* functions do not access the time series *ts* sequentially, they only need to perform random access to compute their results, and the access pattern is very coherent.

## 5.2 Parallelizations

The overall performance of BiVis relies also on taking advantage of the multi-core processors that are ubiquitous nowadays to parallelize some workloads. The obvious candidate for parallelization is the inner loop of the BISECT function (Algorithm 1) that refines the border bounds for each pixel. This loop is easy to distribute among multiple CPU cores since there is no dependency between the pixels: the iterations of the loop can be computed in any order. To parallelize this loop, we rely on the OpenMP API which provides a standardized interface to parallelize loops with threads by simply annotating their code with pragma directives handled through compiler support. In the best case, i.e., when all the needed data is present in RAM, the workload is CPU-bound, and the speedup is exactly the number of cores (typically 4 or 8 on current computers). In the worst case, i.e., when none of the data is present in RAM, the workload would become I/O-bound, but in practice it is rarely the case: the coherency of the access pattern makes it very unlikely that successive iterations of the loop hit totally different pages. And even in this case, a speedup is observed, which may be due to the fact that SSDs support some concurrency.

Another level of parallelism is implemented by the prototypes: multiple instances can be launched on the same or different machines. They are synchronized by sharing their interaction state through broadcasting over the network. This capability is especially useful for large screens composed of multiple monitors. One process per monitor can be used, and they can be distributed amongst any number of computers.

Other parallelizations mentioned earlier are specific to the 2D prototype: first, the Hilbert hash is parallelized using the OpenCL API and its PyOpenCL Python binding to leverage the computing power of GPUs. The sorting step performed on the pixel hashes is parallelized on the CPU using a parallel merge sort.

## 5.3 Performance

The first *performance* of BiVis is to be able to handle data sets containing several billion of items. The only systems that can handle such data sets are those from the *\*cubes* family, but we do not aim at overpassing their performances, but rather at showing that such systems could benefit from this progressive approach.

The overall performance of BiVis is the result of the combination of the techniques described above, which are focussed on the main bottlenecks present between the data and the visualization shown on screen. It is also impacted by mechanisms beyond the control of a program operating in user space, e.g., the policy used by the operating system to manage the memory-mapped files and to keep pages in cache. When the BISECT function performs a lookup in the data set to refine its estimates of a border, the value could be stored anywhere from the various CPU cache levels, to the RAM, to the cache of the SSD, to the actual SSD.

**Computers.** We have run our tests on two computers: *desktop* is a 27-inch iMac with Retina 5K display from 2015 with a 4.0 GHz quad-core i7 processor, 32 GB of 1600 MHz DDR3 SDRAM, a 1 TB SSD, and an AMD Radeon R9 M295X graphics card with 4096 Mbit of memory; while *laptop* is a 13-inch MacBook Pro Retina from 2015 with a 2.9 GHz dual-core i5 processor, 16 GB of 1867 MHz DDR3 SDRAM, a 500 GB SSD, and an Intel Iris Graphics 6100 graphics card with 1536 Mbit of memory.

**Data Sets.** We have used two kinds of data sets to measure the performance of BiVis. First, we have synthesized events time series of various lengths. The events are generated using a Poisson process model: the delays between successive events follow an exponential distribution. Each of those data sets has a number of event that is a power of two. We have explored sizes from $2^{24} \approx 16.8$ million events for the *poisson-24* data set up to $2^{32} \approx 4.3$ billion events for the *poisson-32* data set. Since each timestamp is stored using a double precision float that needs 8 bytes of storage, the largest data set is 32 GiB, i.e., $\approx 34.36$ GB, which is big enough to overflow the RAM available on both computers used for the tests.

We have also used real data sets, which present distributions that are less uniform. The first, *tweet*, is a collection of 3 193 047 170 ($\approx 2^{31.5}$) timestamps from tweets collected over one year. It needs 25.55 GB to be stored. The second, *planet*, is the OSM planet data set, i.e., 2 863 152 191 ($\approx 2^{31.4}$) nodes, hashed and sorted in 1D along the Hilbert curve. Each node is stored using a double precision float, and thus the data set needs 22.91 GB to be stored.

As mentioned earlier, the linear scanning of the data is often not possible. Table 1 shows the time needed to read the data sets without performing any operation on it (i.e., the time needed for the execution of the command *cat poisson-XX > /dev/null*). For each computer and data set, two times are given: *cold* is the time for the first run of the command, with the cache emptied, and *hot* is the time for the subsequent runs of the same command, with the cache used by the operating system. Beyond the billion of items (i.e., $2^{30}$), the time is on the order of 10 s for a cold scanning. When the size of the file exceeds the size of the RAM (with poisson-32 here), there is no cache effect. The laptop, which has less powerful components than the desktop, benefits from a faster SSD.

**Timing of First Exact Histogram.** Figure 8 (left) shows the time needed to build histograms of width 640, 1280, 2560 and 5120 px (each width is the double of the previous one, 2560 and 5120 being the actual width of the laptop and desktop screens) for the Poisson data sets when they are not present in cache. As we can see, those timings are far from interactive time, but they behave nicely with respect to the size of the data: they do not quadruple from one data set to the next as the size does. Figure 8 (right) shows the effect of cache: the timings fall below 100 ms which is the limit to build interactive visualization.

**Table 1.** Time (s) to read sequentially the poisson data sets. Ranges give the variability of the timings amongst repeated runs.

| cold / hot cache | $2^{24}$ | $2^{26}$ | $2^{28}$ | $2^{30}$ | $2^{32}$ |
|---|---|---|---|---|---|
| laptop | 0/0 | 0/0 | 2/0–1 | 8/1–2 | 29–30/29–30 |
| desktop | 0/0 | 0/0 | 1/0 | 13/ 1 | 51–52/51–52 |

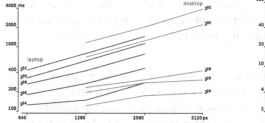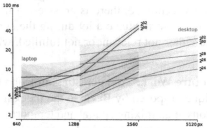

**Fig. 8.** Time (ms) to build exact histograms, for each Poisson data set, starting with cold cache (left) and hot cache (right, areas showing the variability of the timings introduced by the cache).

**Table 2.** Time (ms) to achieve exact histograms of various width, on beyond billion events time series, while taking advantage of the spatial coherency of interaction.

| time (ms) | 640 px | 1280 px | 2560 px | 5120 px |
|---|---|---|---|---|
| laptop | 6.3 ± 13 | 7.4 ± 10.5 | 8.5 ± 11.9 | |
| desktop | 0.8 ± 1.1 | 1.9 ± 1.4 | 2.0 ± 1.6 | 2.5 ± 2.2 |

**Timing During Exploration.** The timings above do not exploit the spatial coherency of the interactions upon which UPDATE_BOUNDS is built. To show its effect, we scripted an interaction aimed at reproducing a typical drill-down: 100 zooming steps scaling the visualization by 5% towards the center are interleaved with 100 panning step translating the visualization by 5 px towards the right. This scenario is repeated with the *poisson-32*, the *tweet* and the *planet* data sets which are of comparable sizes. Table 2 reports the timings by giving the average time and its standard deviation in ms for those $200 \times 3$ steps for each histogram width. Timings are now below 10 ms on average, even when the data sets are out-of-core. This leaves more than 20 ms to do the actual rendering while being able to keep a frame rate above 30 fps. To do the measurements reported here, the bisection is allowed to run until it reaches the exact histogram. By fixing the time budget at 15 ms, we can guarantee this frame rate, at the expense of an approximated histogram on some frames.

# 6  Future Work and Conclusion

Even if the BiVis technique has not been tested as a part of a complete system dedicated to visual analytics, its properties can be considered from the angle of the various requirements for progressive visual analytics gathered by Angelini et al. [2] from various sources, esp. from Stolper et al. [44], Mühlbacher et al. [37] and Turkay et al. [46]. The main requirements that BiVis may help address are the consequence of its ability to quickly provide meaningful results that improve over the time. In that way BiVis follows the first recommendation of Angelini et al.: "provide early partial results, first processing results should be delivered promptly, while maintaining their significance and interactivity". The fact that BiVis provides an estimation of the error for each pixel at each step of the interaction also makes it compliant with the second and third recommendations: the uncertainty of the results and the state of the process can be observed (provided a good visual encoding is chosen to display this information). However in the BiVis technique, there is no steering involved from the user, and the distribution displayed can fluctuate a lot during the converging phase, so the other recommendations are either not relevant or not fulfilled, which gives directions for future works.

**Future Work.** An interesting direction to explore is how to adapt the progressive technique proposed by BiVis to the indexing of massive data sets through multiple dimensions, e.g., mixing spatial and temporal exploration of a single data set as performed by the *cubes* family or the Falcon techniques to further improve them. While those data structures are superior than the one used in BiVis, they do not provide yet an *anytime* lookup, which is key to building progressive visualisations.

The key to this adaptation is to externalize the state of the lookup (the *lo* and *hi* indices in the case of the simple bisection) from the lookup algorithm itself. Once the lookup algorithm is stateless, it can be interrupted and resumed at will, becoming an anytime algorithm. The techniques from the *cubes* family use lookups based on trees which are very similar in essence to a bisection, thus their states are mostly the current node of the index tree. The second step to build a progressive visualization is to compute an approximation of the data (and ideally of the error made) from this lookup state. The nodes of the index should contain enough information to build this approximation, but this remains to be investigated.

In the future, we also would like to explore the idea of computing the histogram with buckets of adaptative widths when the interactive frame rate requirement can not be met, especially in the 2D case or to use knowledge of the data distribution to drive locally the refinements like Li et al. do [32]. We will also investigate the adaptation of BiVis to distributed architectures. Running the binning on a server, and managing the rendering and the interaction state in a web browser is easy to achieve: the size of the data to exchange (e.g., on a web socket) and the complexity of the rendering is limited to the number of pixels. And since the inner loop of BiVis is parallelized, the main challenge to distributing the technique on a computer cluster is the handling of the data, which is a well studied problem.

**Conclusion.** We have presented BiVis, a technique that allow the interactive exploration of very large time series. It can be generalized to several types of data (at the expense of some complex preprocessing step when not in 1D). BiVis leverages several technologies and algorithms to allow the progressive computation of a histogram with a complexity that scales linearly with the size of the view and logarithmically with the size of the data. This *pixel-based* approach, together with the *anytime* nature of the core algorithm, makes it suitable to explore *out-of-core* data sets at interactive frame rates with a progressive visualization. We have shown that BiVis is compatible with many visualization and interaction techniques already existing.

**Acknowledgements.** Figure 5 contains information from OpenStreetMap, which is made available under the Open Database License (ODbL).

# References

1. Agarwal, S., Mozafari, B., Panda, A., Milner, H., Madden, S., Stoica, I.: BlinkDB: queries with bounded errors and bounded response times on very large data. In: Proceedings of the 8th ACM European Conference on Computer Systems, pp. 29–42 (2013)
2. Angelini, M., Santucci, G., Schumann, H., Schulz, H.J.: A review and characterization of progressive visual analytics. Informatics **5**(3), 31 (2018)
3. Badam, S.K., Elmqvist, N., Fekete, J.D.: Steering the craft: UI elements and visualizations for supporting progressive visual analytics. Comput. Graph. Forum (Proc. EuroVis 2017) **36**(3), 491–502 (2017)
4. Blanch, R., Lecolinet, É.: Browsing zoomable treemaps: structure-aware multi-scale navigation techniques. IEEE Trans. Visual. Comput. Graph. (Proc. InfoVis 2007) **13**(6), 1248–1253 (2007)
5. Budiu, M., et al.: Interacting with large distributed datasets using sketch. In: Proceedings of the Eurographics Symposium on Parallel Graphics and Visualization (EGPGV 2016), pp. 31–43 (2016)
6. Byron, L., Wattenberg, M.: Stacked graphs: geometry & aesthetics. IEEE Trans. Visual Comput. Graphics **14**, 1245–1252 (2008)
7. Card, S.K., Mackinlay, J.: The structure of the information visualization design space. In: Proceedings of the IEEE Symposium on Information Visualization (InfoVis 1997), pp. 92–99 (1997)
8. Chan, S.M., Xiao, L., Gerth, J., Hanrahan, P.: Maintaining interactivity while exploring massive time series. In: Proceedings of the IEEE Symposium on Visual Analytics Science and Technology (VAST 2008), pp. 59–66 (2008)
9. Crassin, C., Neyret, F., Sainz, M., Green, S., Eisemann, E.: Interactive indirect illumination using voxel cone tracing. Comput. Graph. Forum (Proc. Pacific Graphics 2011) **30**(7), 1921–1930 (2011)
10. Crow, F.: Summed-area tables for texture mapping. In: Proceedings of the 11th Annual Conference on Computer Graphics and Interactive Techniques (SIGGRAPH 1984), pp. 207–212 (1984)
11. Dean, T., Boddy, M.: An analysis of time-dependent planning. In: Proceedings of the Seventh National Conference on Artificial Intelligence. pp. 49–54 (1998)
12. Fekete, J.D.: ProgressiVis: a toolkit for steerable progressive analytics and visualization. In: Proceedings of the 1st Workshop on Data Systems for Interactive Analysis (2015), p. 5 (2015)

13. Fekete, J.D., Plaisant, C.: Interactive information visualization of a million items. In: Proceedings of the IEEE Symposium on Information Visualization (InfoVis 2002), pp. 117–124 (2002)
14. Ferreira, N., et al.: BirdVis: visualizing and understanding bird populations. IEEE Trans. Visual Comput. Graphics 17(12), 2374–2383 (2011)
15. Ferreira, N., Poco, J., Vo, H.T., Freire, J., Silva, C.T.: Visual exploration of big spatio-temporal urban data: a study of New York city taxi trips. IEEE Trans. Visual Comput. Graphics 19(12), 2149–2158 (2013)
16. Fisher, D., Popov, I., Drucker, S.M., Schraefel, M.: Trust me, i'm partially right: incremental visualization lets analysts explore large datasets faster. In: Proceedings of the ACM Conference on Human Factors in Computing Systems (CHI 2012), pp. 1673–1682 (2012)
17. Fogal, T., Krüger, J.: Tuvok, an architecture for large scale volume rendering. In: Proceedings of the 15th International Workshop on Vision, Modeling, and Visualization, pp. 139–146 (2010)
18. Fogal, T., Krüger, J.: Efficient I/O for parallel visualization. In: Eurographics Symposium on Parallel Graphics and Visualization, pp. 81–90 (2011)
19. Furnas, G.W.: Generalized fisheye views. In: Proceedings of the ACM Conference on Human Factors in Computing Systems (CHI 1986), pp. 16–23 (1986)
20. García, I., Casado, R., Bouchachia, A.: An incremental approach for real-time big data visual analytics. In: Proceedings of the IEEE 4th International Conference on Future Internet of Things and Cloud Workshops (FiCloudW), pp. 177–182 (2016)
21. Glueck, M., Khan, A., Wigdor, D.: Dive in! enabling progressive loading for real-time navigation of data visualizations. In: Proceedings of the ACM Conference on Human Factors in Computing Systems (CHI 2014), pp. 561–570 (2014)
22. Haverkort, H., van Walderveen, F.: Locality and bounding-box quality of two-dimensional space-filling curves. Comput. Geom. 43(2), 131–147 (2010)
23. Hellerstein, J.M., Haas, P.J., Wang, H.J.: Online aggregation. In: ACM SIGMOD Record, vol. 26, pp. 171–182. ACM (1997)
24. Hilbert, D.: Ueber die stetige abbildung einer line auf ein flächenstück. In: Mathematische Annalen, vol. 38, pp. 459–460 (1891)
25. Im, J.F., Villegas, F.G., McGuffin, M.J.: VisReduce: fast and responsive incremental information visualization of large datasets. In: Proceedings of the IEEE International Conference on Big Data, pp. 25–32 (2013)
26. Ioannidis, Y.E., Poosala, V.: Balancing histogram optimality and practicality for query result size estimation. In: Proceedings of the ACM International Conference on Management of Data (SIGMOD 1995), pp. 233–244 (1995)
27. Jagadish, H.V., Koudas, N., Muthukrishnan, S., Poosala, V., Sevcik, K.C., Suel, T.: Optimal histograms with quality guarantees. In: Proceedings of the 24rd International Conference on Very Large Data Bases (VLDB1998), pp. 275–286 (1998)
28. Javed, W., McDonnel, B., Elmqvist, N.: Graphical perception of multiple time series. IEEE Trans. Visual Comput. Graphics 16, 927–934 (2010)
29. Keim, D.A.: Designing pixel-oriented visualization techniques: theory and applications. IEEE Trans. Visual Comput. Graphics 6(1), 59–78 (2000)
30. Keim, D.A., Kriegel, H.P., Ankerst, M.: Recursive pattern: a technique for visualizing very large amounts of data. In: Proceedings of the IEEE Conference on Visualization, pp. 279–286 (1995)
31. Levoy, M.: Display of surfaces from volume data. IEEE Comput. Graphics Appl. 8(3), 29–37 (1988)
32. Li, J., et al.: A hybrid prediction and search approach for flexible and efficient exploration of big data. J. Visualization 26(2), 457–475 (2023)

33. Lins, L., Klosowski, J.T., Scheidegger, C.: Nanocubes for real-time exploration of spatiotemporal datasets. IEEE Trans. Visual Comput. Graphics 19(12), 2456–2465 (2013)
34. Liu, Z., Heer, J.: The effects of interactive latency on exploratory visual analysis. IEEE Trans. Visualiz. Comput. Graph. (Proc. InfoVis 2014) 20(12), 2122–2131 (2014)
35. Liu, Z., Jiang, B., Heer, J.: imMens: real-time visual querying of big data. Comput. Graph. Forum (Proc. EuroVis 2013) 32(3), 421–430 (2013)
36. Moritz, D., Howe, B., Heer, J.: Falcon: balancing interactive latency and resolution sensitivity for scalable linked visualizations. In: Proceedings of the ACM Conference on Human Factors in Computing Systems (CHI 2019), pp. 1–11 (2019)
37. Mühlbacher, T., Piringer, H., Gratzl, S., Sedlmair, M., Streit, M.: Opening the black box: Strategies for increased user involvement in existing algorithm implementations. IEEE Transactions on Visualization and Computer Graphics (Proc. VAST 2014) 20(12), 1643–1652 (2014)
38. Munzner, T., Guimbretière, F., Tasiran, S., Zhang, L., Zhou, Y.: TreeJuxtaposer: scalable tree comparison using focus+context with guaranteed visibility. Trans. on Graphics (Proc. SIGGRAPH 03) 22(3), 453–462 (2003)
39. Pahins, C.A.L., Stephens, S., Scheidegger, C., Comba, J.: Hashedcubes: simple, low memory, real-time visual exploration of big data. IEEE Trans. Visual. Comput. Graph. (Proc. InfoVis 2016) 23(1), 671–680 (2017)
40. Poosala, V., Haas, P.J., Ioannidis, Y.E., Shekita, E.J.: Improved histograms for selectivity estimation of range predicates. In: Proceedings of the ACM International Conference on Management of Data (SIGMOD 1996), pp. 294–305 (1996)
41. Sarkar, M., Brown, M.H.: Graphical fisheye views. CACM 37(12), 73–83 (1994)
42. Schulz, H.J., Angelini, M., Santucci, G., Schumann, H.: An enhanced visualization process model for incremental visualization. IEEE Trans. Visual Comput. Graphics 22(7), 1830–1842 (2016)
43. Slack, J., Hildebrand, K., Munzner, T.: PRISAD: a partitioned rendering infrastructure for scalable accordion drawing (extended version). Inf. Vis. 5(2), 137–151 (2006)
44. Stolper, C.D., Perer, A., Gotz, D.: Progressive visual analytics: user-driven visual exploration of in-progress analytics. IEEE Trans. Visual. Comput. Graph. (Proc. VAST 2014) 20(12), 1653–1662 (2014)
45. Thomas, J.J., Cook, K.A.: Illuminating the Path: the R&D Agenda for Visual Analytics, chap. Grand Challenges. United States, Department of Homeland Security (2005)
46. Turkay, C., Kaya, E., Balcisoy, S., Hauser, H.: Designing progressive and interactive analytics processes for high-dimensional data analysis. IEEE Trans. Visual. Comput. Graph. (Proc. VAST 2016) 23(1), 131–140 (2017)
47. Turkay, C., et al.: Progressive data science: potential and challenges (2018). arXiv:1812.08032
48. Wang, Z., Ferreira, N., Wei, Y., Bhaskar, A.S., Scheidegger, C.: Gaussian cubes: real-time modeling for visual exploration of large multidimensional datasets. IEEE Trans. Visual. Comput. Graph. (Proc. InfoVis 2016) 23(1), 681–690 (2017)
49. Wickham, H.: Bin-summarise-smooth: a framework for visualising large data, p. 9 (2013). http://vita.had.co.nz/papers/bigvis.html
50. Zgraggen, E., Galakatos, A., Crotty, A., Fekete, J.D., Kraska, T.: How progressive visualizations affect exploratory analysis. IEEE Trans. Visual Comput. Graphics 23(8), 1977–1987 (2017)
51. Zhao, J., Chevalier, F., Pietriga, E., Balakrishnan, R.: Exploratory analysis of time-series with chronolenses. IEEE Trans. Visual. Comput. Graph. (Proc. InfoVis 2011) 17(12), 2422–2431 (2011)

# Modeling and Assessing User Interaction in Big Data Visualization Systems

Dario Benvenuti[✉], Matteo Filosa, Tiziana Catarci, and Marco Angelini

Sapienza, University of Rome, Rome, Italy
{dario.benvenuti,matteo.filosa,tiziana.catarci,
marco.angelini}@uniroma1.it

**Abstract.** When users interact with large data through a visualization system, its response time is crucial in keeping engagement and efficacy as high as possible, and latencies as low as 500 ms can be detrimental to the correct execution of the analysis. This can be due to several causes: *(i)* for large data or high query rates, database management systems (DBMS) may fail to meet the performance needs; *(ii)* modeling all the interactions with a visualization system is challenging due to their exploratory nature, where not all of them are equally demanding in terms of computation time; *(iii)* there is a lack of models for integrating optimizations in a holistic way, hampering consistent evaluation across systems. In response to these problems, we propose a conceptual *interaction-driven framework* that enhances the visualization pipeline by adding a new *Translation layer* between the *Data-, Visualization- and Interaction-* layers, leveraging the modeling of interactions with augmented statecharts. This new layer aims to collect information about queries and rendering computations, linking such values to interactions in the statechart. To make the Translation layer actionable, we contribute a software component to automatically model the user interactions for a generic web-based visualization system through augmented statecharts, in which each interaction is labeled with its latency threshold. We first demonstrate its generality on ten state-of-the-art visualization systems. Then we perform a user study (n = 50), collecting traces by asking users to perform already established exploratory tasks on the well-known Crossfilter interface. Finally, we replay those traces over its generated statechart, assessing the capability to model the user interactions correctly and describing violations in the latency thresholds.

**Keywords:** Visualization Systems · Visualization Pipeline · User Interaction Modeling.

## 1 Introduction

Big Data analysis and exploration is in today's world a common activity in many domains. Due to the characteristics of Exploratory Data Analysis, data visualization became a good solution for supporting this type of analysis. At the

© The Author(s), under exclusive license to Springer Nature Switzerland AG 2023
J. Abdelnour Nocera et al. (Eds.): INTERACT 2023, LNCS 14143, pp. 86–109, 2023.
https://doi.org/10.1007/978-3-031-42283-6_5

same time, designing an effective visualization system can be difficult, and must take into account the continuous involvement of the stakeholders. For this reason, among several design methodologies emerging over the years, User Centred Design (UCD) [56] became more and more adopted. During the UCD process of a visualization system, there are two main types of users involved: *(VSD)* the visualization system designer, aiming at developing the system itself and *(EU)* the end user for whom the system is designed, and who are meant to provide accurate feedback on its development and intermediate artifacts. A key aspect of this process is the capability of VSDs, during the continuous evaluation and optimization activities that they must conduct with the end users, to correctly capture their feedback. This activity usually requires multiple interactions and the design of user studies to assess the quality of the produced artifacts. Three problems arise from this scenario: *(i)* the designer would like to minimize possible confounding factors in those evaluation activities, to have them as much effective as possible. Latency is the worst factor, being not dependent on the specific application domain of the system under design, and capable of producing negative effects (e.g., incorrect evaluation of proposed design choices, disruption of mental model, drop-out from the system); *(ii)* the end users provide "general feedback", not being able to identify the specific interactions or elements hindering their experience or being capable of identify specific latency problems. *(iii)* Those activities are time-consuming, require a lot of effort during their design, and cannot easily be repeated multiple times without lowering their effect (e.g., memory effects, etc.). Additionally, VSDs may struggle to manually build a complete model of the user interaction space and to accurately interpret the feedback obtained from EUs to understand which portion of that interaction space is generating issues and what is causing them. For EUs, even latencies as low as 500 ms can be detrimental [36,57], potentially leading to drop-outs from the system usage, or acting as a confounding factor during the evaluation phase of the UCD process, causing them to give biased feedback.

Looking at the problem from the system perspective, this can be due to several causes: *(i)* for large data or high query rates database management systems (DBMS) may fail to meet the performance required to maintain response times below the desired threshold, as demonstrated by Battle et al. [12]; *(ii)* modeling all the interactions with a visualization system is challenging due to their exploratory nature, where not all of them are equally demanding in terms of computation time; *(iii)* while there exists a variety of optimization techniques to handle this issue in specific scenarios, there is a lack of models for integrating them in a holistic way, hampering consistent evaluation across systems. Furthermore, although effective models exist for optimizing the data and rendering computations (e.g., BIRCH [62], DEVise [37]), to the best of the authors' knowledge no formal approach exists to connect known performance models in the visualization and HCI communities with optimization strategies at the data management level. To support VSDs in mitigating these problems, being more efficient during the evaluation phase of the UCD process, and overall being able to design better visualization systems, we contribute a conceptual interaction-driven framework that enhances the basic visualization pipeline [41] by introducing a new layer, the *Translation layer*, and by automatically modeling interactions using *augmented statecharts* [31]. This layer allows the automatic collection of user traces, the translation from low-level events into high-level user interactions, and from them to database queries and rendering information annotated in the statechart. The augmented statechart can be automatically computed and explored by VSDs to identify which interactions suffer from excessive latency and hypothesize how to fix them. By exploiting the proposed conceptual framework, it becomes possible for the VSDs to *(i)* automatically get a complete model of how EUs interact with the visualization system. It can be annotated with helpful information for optimization (e.g., *latency thresholds*); *(ii)* know in advance the SQL queries that could be triggered from the current interaction state and *(iii)* derive through them the optimized computations needed to render the results. This information can be used to optimize the system at the required layer and in the specific portion of the interaction space during the evaluation phase of UCD. The optimization leads to a reduced response time that cascades into a better user experience for EUs. Moreover, by removing the confounding factor caused by excessive latency during the interaction, EUs will be able to provide more accurate feedback on the system, thus improving the overall outcome of subsequent iterations of the UCD process.

To make the framework actionable, our second contribution is a software component for the Translation layer, the *Statechart Generator*, that automatically models the user interaction for a generic web-based visualization system. We first demonstrate its generality on ten state-of-the-art visualization systems. Then, we perform a user study (n = 50) with the goal of collecting user traces by asking users to perform already established exploratory tasks on the well-known Crossfilter interface. Finally, we replay those traces over the generated statechart, assessing its capability to model the user interactions completely (capturing all user interactions) and identifying violations in the latency thresholds.

## 2   Motivating Scenario

We use in our motivating scenario the Crossfilter interface (see Fig. 1) for exploring airline data (similar to Falcon [42]) using the Flights dataset, containing nearly 120 million tuples. Changing the selection of the flight distance, by brushing the histogram in the upper row, causes all other histograms to update in real-time. Battle et al. proposed a benchmark [12] for evaluating how DBMSs support real-time interactive querying of large data. They report that interactions with a Crossfilter interface can generate hundreds of queries per second, with high latencies introduced while users expect near-immediate results. This makes it a fitting example to motivate our proposal.

Jessie, the VSD working on the design of this system following the UCD approach, lets EUs explore data about flights during the first evaluation phase. To evaluate and optimize the first version of the system and prepare it for the next iteration, she needs to collect feedback about its usage from EUs. To do

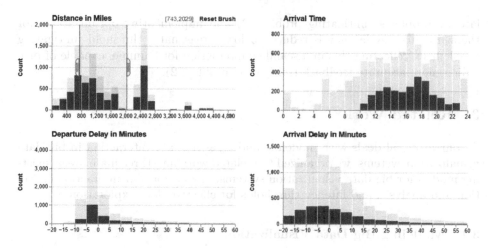

**Fig. 1.** An end user exploring flight performance data via a Crossfilter interface. Brushing on one bar chart filters the others in real-time.

so, she chooses to use an *exploratory task* retrieved from the benchmark, which requires EUs to explore all columns to respond to the following question: "Which factors appear to have the greatest impact on departure delays?". Sammie, an EU performing such a task, brushes several times on each histogram of the interface, to observe the effect on the departure delays, using the well-known brushing and linking technique [11]. Furthermore, Sammie needs more than one iteration to explore the data and verify which data feature (e.g., Arrival Delay in Minutes) has the greatest impact, generating a huge number of queries. Because of this, while Sammie interacts with the interface exploring the data, the system fails to maintain a fast response time, beginning to lag heavily. Experiencing such a high level of latency from the system, Sammie rapidly loses interest in the task and drops out from the system usage due to frustration (**problem 1**). She reports on the generic lag experienced and the impossibility of fulfilling the task. Jessie ends up with inaccurate feedback about the system, more focused on its latency problems than on the visual design choices or its efficacy. This is due to Sammie's poor experience because latency exceeds the threshold levels (**problem 2**). Furthermore, Jessie is interested in analyzing the actual sequence of analysis steps triggered by Sammie through interactors, since the effectiveness of an action on the system can vary depending on what happened before it. To do so, she would need to model the entire user interaction space of the system and collect logs from its usage at the same granularity level (**problem 3**). In the end, Jessie does not get any insight on where to focus the optimization activities, nor does the generic feedback received help her. She spent time and resources designing a test that proved not to be effective in informing her for the second iteration.

Our conceptual framework is then aimed at assisting Jessie by automatically modeling the entire user interaction space and then by capturing the specific latency problems (mitigating problem 3) and implementing optimizations for them. In this way latency is reduced below a reasonable threshold (mitigating problem 1), reflecting this in a seamless interaction for Sammie, capable of providing more accurate feedback (mitigating problem 2).

# 3 Related Work

As our proposal deals with modeling and assessing user interaction in big data visualization systems, we organized the related work into three main areas: existing models for big data visualization systems, models for user interaction collection and analysis, and latency thresholds for effective data exploration.

## 3.1 Modeling Big Data Visualization

An interactive visualization system is designed following state-of-the-art guidelines for information visualization [18,53,60] and Visual Analytics [34,50]. It can be modeled with three main blocks: a data management block, a visualization (visual rendering) block, and an interaction block. Visualization systems managing small data implement each part in an ad-hoc way, storing everything in memory without worrying about optimizations. For big data visualization systems, data cannot be assumed to fit in memory instead. Several works have analyzed the literature at different stages to provide an overview of Big Data Visualization [1,35,40,49], but only a few coped with proposing frameworks for its modeling and management. Conner et al. [20] provide an analysis of how the visualization aspects of Big Data Visualization have been coped with from the born of the Information Visualization discipline to the present day and how this term and related solutions evolved. Qin et al. [48] propose DeepEye, an automatic big data visualization framework for recommending the best suitable visualizations for the data at hand, a set of automatic analyses on these data coupled with preservation of interactivity through database optimization techniques. While sharing with our proposal the goal of modeling the entire pipeline, they do not have a specific focus on the user interaction as we propose, and they do not consider exploiting user interaction for optimizations. Similar considerations are valid for Erraissi et al. [24] and Golfarelli and Rizzi [29]. Both works try to model Big Data Visualization, with the former focused on proposing a meta-modeling for the visualization block and the latter augmenting it with automated visualization recommendations. Galletta et al. [28] cope with requirements coming from users in modeling Big Data Visualization. However, they target a specific domain, telemedicine, and focus on the interpretability and ease of use of the visualizations by physicians, not on capturing and modeling user interactions to support the identification of latency problems. Finally, a new branch of Visual Analytics, named *Progressive Visual Analytics* [10] or *Progressive Data Analysis and Visualization* [25], proposed models for managing latency through the continuous visualization of intermediate partial results computed on data samples or approximated versions of highly costly algorithms, capable of keeping the visual rendering and user interaction below latency constraints. Although providing sound solutions, none of the contributions in this field considers user interaction modeling as a driving factor to produce the intermediate partial results, limiting their intervention on the data, the algorithms, or the visualization rendering separately.

## 3.2 Modeling Interaction

Interactions are used for various tasks in visualization systems, modeled in a range that covers from low-level description [2] to high-level user intent [22,55]. High-level tasks are abstract, and their concrete implementation can take radically different forms. For example, selection can be done by mouse-clicking, using a lasso, or typing in a search box. A popular method for modeling interactions consists in using *widgets* that encapsulate a visual representation and interactive behavior (e.g., [5]). These widgets are connected to the main application through callbacks or other communication mechanisms. A significant issue with widgets is that they encapsulate both a graphical representation and a behavior, making it hard to modify one aspect independently of the other [15,23,32,46]. To address this limitation and provide more structure to interactions, Meyers introduces Interactors [43], using state machines to specify and implement the interactions. While using Interactors allows for separating the visual appearance of interaction components from their behavior, the actions performed during interactions are open-ended and cannot be fully modeled in general. However, in visualization, the roles of interactions are more specific, so modeling them is possible in most cases. In addition to the work of Meyers [43], other works modeled interactions as state machines [26,27,33,47]. For our framework, we rely on statecharts [31], allowing us to run interactions while reasoning about them simultaneously. Statecharts are high-level specifications translated into a simple state machine through standardized semantics. Furthermore, they are mature, standardized, well-documented, and implemented by several libraries in multiple languages. Also, since their syntax is declarative, it can be easily extended.

A statechart is (conceptually) a simple state machine, equivalent to a directed graph with nodes denoting states, directed edges labeled with a triggering event and pointing to a target state. Running the state machine consists in navigating its directed graph. It starts from a specified state $A$. When an event $Y$ occurs in that state, it searches for an edge labeled with event $Y$ having a guarding condition that is true. When it finds one, it then runs its transition action and moves to target state $B$ which becomes the current state. Statecharts can also manage a *data model*, that can be tested and updated during transitions. We use this feature to manage the data model and internal states of interactions' statecharts.

## 3.3 Latency Thresholds

Big data exploration makes it hard to guarantee that latency will remain under well-specified thresholds. The latency threshold is the maximum system response time before the user's cognition starts degrading. Latency thresholds are defined by studying threshold values of response time in various contexts. During the interaction, if the system does not show any result before the latency threshold, users could lose attention, be surprised, and feel that the system is unresponsive. While many latency thresholds have been proposed, it is still unclear which values should be considered for specific interactions, making it difficult to determine how and when to optimize interactions for big data exploration. The initial works of Miller [39], Shneiderman [52], and Nielsen [45] are not directly supported by empirical studies. Dabrowski and Munson [21] conducted an experiment with the aim of discovering new latency thresholds supported by empirical results but tied these thresholds to entire widgets (e.g., button, menu, dialog). Nah [44] conducted a State-of-The-Art analysis by gathering information from Miller [39], Nielsen [45], and Shneiderman [52], concluding that delay of 2 s for type 1 latency is not acceptable. Shneiderman et al. [54] introduce an additional threshold of 3 s for *"common tasks"* that is useful to determine the effect that waiting has on end users. After 3 s, end users feel like the system is slow, and start losing focus on their task. Waloszek and Kreichgauer [57] revisited Nielsen's thresholds by relaxing them into ranges, introducing the 3 s category from Shneiderman et al. [54] and extending the upper threshold to 15 s. We will refer to the categories from this work as four latency levels, which can be seen in Table 1, of which we will mainly use *"level 0: 0.2s"* and *"level 1: 1s"*. Liu and Heer [36] show the impact that the 800 ms gap between level 0 and level 1 latency has on the end user by providing an empirical study on macro interaction types, which they call *operations*: brush & link, select, pan & zoom. Zgraggen et al. [61] show the same impact but on the gap between level 1 and level 2 latency types through an empirical study that contained two exploratory interfaces, exploiting progressive data computation and visualization, with a simulated delay of 6 s and 12 s.

**Table 1.** Revised version of latency levels.

| Level | Latency Threshold | Description |
|---|---|---|
| Level 0 | 0.1 (0–0.2) seconds | Perceptual Level: feedback after UI input involving direct manipulation/hand-eye coordination (e.g., mouse click, mouse movement, keypress). |
| Level 1 | 1.0 (0.2–2) seconds | Dialog Level: finishing simple tasks (e.g., opening a window or dialog box, closing a window, completing a simple search). |
| Level 2 | 3.0 (2–5) seconds | Cognitive Level: finishing common tasks, such as logging in to a system. |
| Level 3 | 10 (5–15) seconds | Cognitive Level: completing complex tasks, or a complex search or calculation. |
| Level 4 | >15 seconds | |

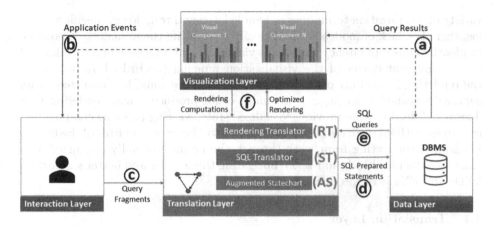

**Fig. 2.** High-level description of how the conceptual interaction-driven framework enhances the classical visualization pipeline by introducing the Translation layer.

# 4  Conceptual Interaction-Driven Framework

The proposed conceptual framework, visible in Fig. 2, is targeted at Big Data exploration. The main user task it supports is the exploratory task [17], where the user explores the visualized data through interactive means looking to formulate a new hypothesis that will then be tested. This task is the most demanding in terms of latency constraints, as well expressed by Liu and Heer [36]. The conceptual framework is built on the basic visualization pipeline described by Moreland [41], modeled into three different layers: *(i)* a *data layer*, which collects the relevant data through selection and applies optional binning and aggregation operations (*source*); *(ii)* a *rendering layer* that uses the binned and aggregated data (*filter*) to generate visualization components and computes the extent of each rendered column to produce axes and scales (*sink*) (Fig. 2.a). Due to its interactive nature, the basic visualization pipeline is generally extended with an *(iii) interaction layer*, in charge of issuing queries either from dynamic query widgets or direct manipulation of the visualization components (Fig. 2.b). Big data exploration is made possible through the cooperation of these layers. At the same time, each of these layers, taken in isolation, can introduce problems. Concerning the data layer, for large data or high query rates DBMSs may fail to meet the performance needs required to maintain response times below the desired threshold, introducing latency and violating near real-time or real-time interaction (**technical issue 1**). Looking at the interaction layer, it usually simply captures the user interactions at a low level (e.g., events of a browser) and directly passes them to the data layer, creating high query rates even for simple interactions (e.g., brushing operation) (**technical issue 2**). Additionally, modeling all the interactions with a visualization system is challenging due to their exploratory nature, where not all of them are equally demanding in terms of computation time and latency (**technical issue 3**). Finally, while there exists a variety of optimization techniques to handle latency thresholds in specific scenarios, there is a lack of models for holistically integrating them, making it possible to identify causes of latency thresholds violations and intervene in a coordinated way at different stages of the visualization pipeline (**technical issue 4**). At the rendering layer, fully optimized query results that must be visualized by an aggregate visualization (e.g., a heatmap) could produce a new rendering that does not differ from the previous visualized state, wasting precious computation resources without providing any advantage to the user (**technical issue 5**). Without a connecting framework through the layers (normally organized as a stack, see the blue blocks in Fig. 2), mitigating these issues and better supporting VSDs and EUs becomes difficult.

### 4.1   Translation Layer

One of the key ideas behind the proposed framework is the addition of a fourth layer, Translation layer, to integrate critical information coming from the other three and effectively connect them. In this section, we provide a general overview of its high-level functions and interplay with the layers of the basic visualization pipeline. The Translation layer is managed during the visualization system design, providing benefits that the other system layers cannot offer in isolation. It is formed by three components: *(i)* an augmented statechart (AS), *(ii)* an SQL translator (ST), and *(iii)* a rendering translator (RT).

Through AS, the interaction between users and the system is modeled with a statechart in which nodes represent the set of possible contexts (i.e., the state of the visual component during the interaction, like the cursor position or HTML focus) and edges represent transitions between states caused by events triggered on the visual components by the EU. Furthermore, AS labels the edges of the statechart with desired latency thresholds. Then, ST communicates with the data layer to translate user interactions into the corresponding queries to be performed on the DBMS and adds this information to the labels in the statechart, allowing it to describe the relation between user interactions and DBMS queries furtherly. Finally, RT translates those queries into rendering computations by communicating with the visualization layer.

As can be seen in Fig. 2, once the augmented statechart is built, the Translation layer can receive in input a high-level query fragment generated by the interaction layer, representing a user interaction on the visualization system (e.g., the selection of a set of points in a scatterplot) (Fig. 2.c). Then, the fragment is used to fetch from AS an SQL-prepared statement, representing a parametrized query that should be instantiated and then performed on the DBMS when such an activity is performed. The statement is then sent to the data layer to execute the actual SQL queries (Fig. 2.d,  2.e). Knowing those queries, the Translation layer can finally apply the rendering optimizations for the visualization layer through RT (Fig. 2.f). In this way, our conceptual framework enables more versatile management of query load driven by user actions. It provides a centralized layer that leverages and orchestrates, rather than modify, the existing data, visualization, and interaction layers. This property makes it adaptable to any existing visualization system designed using the basic visualization pipeline and its derivatives. Additionally, it can be used to design a new system (effectively providing optimization capabilities) or put on top of an existing one (working only as a descriptor/detector of what happens in the implemented system).

## 4.2  Benefits

A key aspect of the Translation layer is its modular nature. The process carried out is strictly bound only to the presence of AS, making its implementation mandatory to exploit the framework's benefits. While ST and RT can be used to build additional layers of exploitable information on the edges of the statechart for implementing query or rendering optimization, AS can be used in isolation to model the interaction between the user and the system and link it to latency thresholds. Overall, AS is central in supporting the evaluation phase of UCD. We refer to this configuration as the *evaluation configuration*, capable of describing the user interaction space and identifying violations of latency thresholds, both locally (i.e., subparts of the statechart) or globally (i.e., global efficacy score). This configuration provides mitigations for technical issues 3 and 4. It also allows a VSD to exploit AS during the UCD process to automatically get the augmented statechart modeling the entire user interaction space, solving problem 3. Then, AS can be exploited during the evaluation phase to *(i)* fix the level of granularity to be used while collecting logs from the activity of users and *(ii)* use such logs to get measures related to the user experience with the system (e.g., the frequency with which each path in the statechart is visited or the specific interactions that effectively suffered from excessive latency), not biased by the impressions of EUs potentially affected by latency, mitigating problem 2. More details about how AS mitigates this issue are given in Sect. 6.

Moving a step forward, ST can be used for translating user interactions into queries and applying optimization on the DBMS based on the SQL-prepared statements. It is possible, for example, to count the frequency of similar or equal statements and prioritize them in the DBMS or cache their answers, or use them as inputs for classic DBMS optimization techniques. This step allows an interaction-driven optimization on the data layer. We refer to this configuration as the *data optimization configuration*. This configuration additionally mitigates technical issues 1 and 2, inheriting the previous mitigations for technical issues 3 and 4. Finally, the data optimization configuration would not consider the inefficiency that even an optimized query could produce on the visualization layer. To mitigate this problem, RT provides optimizations considering the query result from ST and the information from AS. In this way, it could exploit the first to manage the rendering efficiently and the second to prioritize rendering in specific areas more used by the EUs or prone to stronger latency violations in cases in which multiple areas of the visualization must be updated. We refer to this configuration as the *full optimization configuration*. This is the best configuration possible, in which also technical issue 5 got mitigated, providing solutions for all the reported issues. The data optimization and full optimization configurations can be exploited by VSDs during the evaluation phase of UCD to improve the experience of EUs with the system drastically, solving problem 1. By reducing excessive latency during system usage, EUs can better focus and understand their interaction with it and provide more accurate feedback. The conceptual framework then improves the efficacy of the evaluation phase of UCD and the quality of the corrective actions leading to the next iteration of the design phase.

Having introduced the main concepts, working, configurations, and benefits of the whole conceptual framework, from this point on we will consider as the reference configuration of this paper the evaluation configuration, leaving to future works the optimization configurations.

## 5   The Statechart Generator

The first step to make the Translation layer actionable is building a component to automatically model the interaction space of a visualization system, so generating AS. Such a component must be applicable to a generic visualization system to be useful for VSDs without limiting their designs or requiring complex procedures to be used. At the same time, it must be trustable by the VSD, effectively modeling the entire interaction space that the visualization system allows. AS was implemented through a software component, namely the Statechart Generator, which is described in the following. We refer to *interaction path* as the sequence of transitions in the statechart starting and ending in the rest state, and with *user trace* as the collection of interaction paths performed by the same EU. After a thorough investigation of the possible implementation solutions and deep state-of-the-art analysis, we ended up targeting visualization systems with the following characteristics: *(i)* designed for desktop devices; *(ii)* working properly on web browsers with Chromium command line interface (CLI), thus including all the major browsers except Mozilla Firefox; *(iii)* implemented through event-based techniques (the best results can be achieved with the JQuery or D3.js libraries). Those characteristics are very common for web-based visualization systems, making the Statechart Generator component general.

The final design of the Statechart Generator, visible in Fig. 3, revolves around capturing the interaction events, avoiding the case in which some of them could be masked by high-level frameworks or libraries used by the visualization system. This goal has been achieved by instrumenting a module that, through the Chromium CLI, retrieves all non-masked interaction information for a specified document object model (DOM) object from the running visualization system. Given an object of the DOM as input, it will output a list of the event listeners registered on it, alongside their description and properties (e.g., event functions). Thus, it can be exploited by calling it on each object of the starting DOM to get the contextless *Root Statechart*, modeling all the states reachable from the root, which we call *Rest State* (e.g., when the visualization system has just been started). Then, exploiting the *Puppeteer* Node.js library (for the automatic simulation of human actions with a web application), a modified depth-first-search (DFS) exploration of the visualization system interactions is started by automatically triggering each detected event on the web browser and checking which

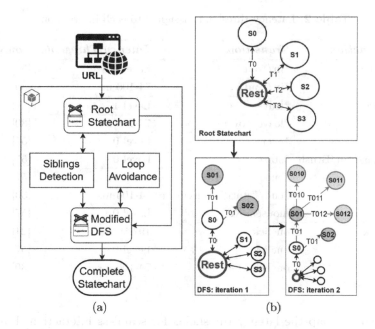

**Fig. 3.** (a) Architecture of the Statechart Generator. (b) During execution, the Root Statechart is expanded by triggering events and looking for new states in a DFS fashion.

events can be triggered from the new context (e.g., cursor position), to reconstruct all the possible interaction paths in the application. To avoid infinite loops (e.g., selecting the same bar of a histogram over and over) the *getEventListeners* function can be invoked after triggering each event, and by comparing the new result with the last one it is possible to understand if new information has been discovered (e.g., if there are different numbers of listeners) or if the exploration reached a leaf and should backtrack to a new branch. Furthermore, to avoid the explosion of states that can be caused by specific implementations of some visualization components (e.g., a scatterplot with thousands of selectable dots), a mechanism to cluster together objects sharing the same interaction behavior and parents, which we call *Siblings*, has been implemented. The inner working of the Statechart Generator is resumed in Fig. 3: *(i)* the URL of the visualization system is given in input to a Node.js module; *(ii)* the Root Statechart is built exploiting Puppeteer and a siblings detection mechanism; *(iii)* the Root Statechart is used to perform a customized DFS that outputs the *Complete Statechart* exploiting both the siblings detection and a loop avoidance mechanisms. Leveraging on the literature analysis (see Sect. 3.3) on latency thresholds, we propose a mapping between each atomic interaction and a latency threshold, which can be seen in Table 2. In this way, whenever a new transition is added to the statechart, it is automatically labeled with its mapped latency level. This design of the Statechart Generator allows for drastically reducing the time required to build a complete representation of the interaction space. It presents on this

**Table 2.** Latency thresholds assigned to each interaction.

| Interaction | Transition | Latency Threshold | Source |
|---|---|---|---|
| *Zoom | *in/*out | Level 1 | [57] |
| | *in/*out | 74-106 ms | [30] |
| *Hover | *leave | Level 1 | [57] |
| | *leave/*over | 74-106 ms | [30] |
| | *over | Level 0 | [57] |
| *Drag/Pan/Brush | *start | Level 0 | [57] |
| | *end | Level 1 | [57] |
| | *end/*start/mousemove | 74-106 ms | [30] |
| | mousemove | Level 0 | [57] |
| *Click | onclick | 197.56 ms | [21] |
| | onclick | Level 0 | [57] |
| | onclick | 74-106 ms | [30] |

comprehensive map the latency thresholds for seamless interaction. Finally, it represents the statechart in an easier-to-read form with respect to classic interaction logs, by showing only semantically different states. In this way, the VSD can obtain a comprehensible map of the interaction space of the designed visualization system. At the same time, this inner complexity is masked to the VSD, who needs to pass to the component only the URL of the visualization system to make it work.

The source code and documentation of AS, alongside a detailed description of validation activities and instructions on how to replicate the experiments, are available in an OSF project[1].

## 6   Validation

In this section, we validate the effectiveness of the proposed conceptual framework in its evaluation configuration. We remember that the framework is composed only of the Statechart Generator component in this configuration. We first resume its characteristics as follows:

**Claim C1 - Generality:** The Statechart Generator can be executed on a generic web-based visualization system.

**Claim C2 - Completeness:** The output of the Statechart Generator models the entire interaction space of the visualization system in input.

**Claim C3 - Efficacy:** The statechart obtained through the Statechart Generator can be exploited to detect latency violations during the user interaction with a visualization system, with a fine grain down to single user interactions.

---

[1] https://osf.io/79hsw/?view_only=be4e5107a18145e6b86a7eaf6109cb60

In the following, we validate C1 by applying the Statechart Generator to ten web-based visualization systems from the Information Visualization and Visual Analytics literature. Then, we show how we performed a user study to collect 50 interaction traces directly from EUs with the most challenging system, Crossfilter, to validate C2 and C3.

## 6.1   Generality

To validate the capability of the Statechart Generator to be executed on a generic web-based visualization system, a set of ten systems was collected from the Information Visualization and Visual Analytics literature to be used as input to the software component. These ten systems were subjected to formal scrutiny from four experts (two among the authors of this paper, two external), which took both intrinsic and extrinsic information to estimate the level of complexity of the candidate visualization system. This information was then used to ensure the systems were chosen to spread equally across the complexity spectrum and cover the range of existing visualization systems. An additional constraint was for the chosen systems to be publicly available. Overall, the experts considered the richness of the visual encodings used (number of visualizations and number of visual elements per visualization) and the richness of interactions available (in terms of single interactions and interaction paths). The detailed list of considered factors to assign a level of complexity to a visualization system can be seen in Table 4. The software ran on a virtual machine on the cloud with an eight-core i7 CPU, 32 Gb of RAM, an HDD, and Ubuntu 22.04 (Jammy Jellyfish). The ten chosen visualization systems with the associated level of complexity and time required to execute the Statechart Generator can be seen in Table 3. Finally, to assess a potential correlation between the time required to build the Complete Statechart and the factors that we used to assess their complexity level, we computed the Pearson correlation coefficient. From the result of this process, visible in Table 4, we highlight a strong correlation between computation time and *(i)* the number of states in the Complete Statechart and *(ii)* the number of events in the visualization system.

To summarize, having not encountered any major problems in the generation of the statecharts for the ten representative visualization systems, we conclude that claim C1 is verified.

**Table 3.** List of the ten visualization systems selected to validate the Statechart Generator, with details about their level of complexity and the execution time required to obtain the Complete Statechart.

| Visualization System | Complexity | Time (minutes) |
|---|---|---|
| DataVis [58] | 568 | 30 |
| Crumbs [9] | 889 | 65 |
| CrossWidget [5] | 2532 | 100 |
| Ivan [8] | 2649 | 420 |
| Nemesis [3] | 5052 | 90 |
| IDMVis [63] | 5168 | 705 |
| W4sp [7] | 5918 | 1140 |
| Radviz [4] | 6458 | 1860 |
| InfluenceMap [51] | 8581 | 420 |
| Summit [19] | 16427 | 30 |

**Table 4.** Factors making up the complexity level of the ten candidate visualization systems alongside their Pearson correlation coefficient with respect to execution time.

| Intrinsic | | Extrinsic | |
|---|---|---|---|
| Factor | Pearson | Factor | Pearson |
| #Elements | -0.205 | #Siblings | -0.045 |
| #Events | 0.858 | Execution Time | - |
| #Attributes and Data Fields | 0.439 | #Generated States | 0.892 |
| #Peculiar Events | -0.281 | #Generated Edges | 0.645 |
| #Peculiar Contexts | 0.636 | | |

## 6.2   User Study

To validate claims C2 and C3, we performed a user study to collect real user traces from the end users of a target visualization system and replay them over the generated statechart to find potential discrepancies (e.g., missing states or transitions, illegal paths) highlighting, in the process, response times exceeding the thresholds. In the following, we discuss how we designed the user study.

**Participants.** We recruited a pool of 50 participants. 27 were in the age range 18-24, 17 between 25-34, 3 in the range 35-44, and 3 ranging from 45 to 54. The majority of the pool consisted of males, with 34 participants, while 14 were females, 1 answered "Prefer not to say", and 1 answered "Other". With respect to education, three had a PhD, 23 had a master degree, 14 had a Bachelor degree, and 10 had a high-school degree. Knowledge about the IT field was distributed with 11 having advanced knowledge, 14 participants having good knowledge, 8 having intermediate one, 9 with low knowledge, and 8 with no knowledge at all in the field.

**Procedure.** The study was designed to be completed within a 1-hour session. The users were first presented with an informative page on the study and its goals. After providing informed consent, the users were first asked to answer demographic questions, then they were asked to perform a simple tutorial on an example task, to familiarize themselves with the Crossfilter interface and the modality to submit a response. Finally, they were asked to solve four exploratory tasks on the system. The chosen visualization system is the Crossfilter interface shown in Sect. 2, since it is the most challenging scenario for latency and comes with exploratory tasks. We instrumented it with the flight dataset sized at 7M entries. The rationale behind this choice is to make sure that the system configuration is managing a high quantity of data in real-time while taking into account the remote nature of the experiment, which did not give us control over the computer capabilities used by the participants.

**Experimental Setup.** Since the main goal of the study was to collect user traces, we opted for a remote setup, requiring the user to just use a web browser. To implement the study we exploited *Stein* [6], a framework that makes it possible to execute task-based evaluations on visualization systems with users, collecting their interaction logs. To host the experiment online and collect the results, we used *PythonAnywhere*. At the end of the experiment, the user traces were automatically uploaded to a remote repository.

**Tasks.** The following four exploratory tasks were retrieved by the work of Battle et al. [12]: (***T1***): "How many flights were longer than four and less than six hours?"; (***T2***): "Which two-hour window (during time of day) contains more flights with longer arrival delays?"; (***T3***): "Which factors appear to have the greatest effect on the length of departure delays?" and (***T4***): "How do distance, departure delays, and both distance and departure delays together appear to affect arrival delays?". They were chosen for their complexity and exploratory nature, which required the user to explore all the dimensions of the dataset under analysis and the relations that could potentially exist among them in order to fulfill each task.

**Objectives.** The objectives of this user study were to collect user traces to validate claims C2 and C3. To validate *C2*, we *(i)* compute the statechart of a candidate web-based visualization system through the Statechart Generator; *(ii)* collect the traces of the user interaction with the chosen system and *(iii)* replay the collected traces over the statechart to check their compliance [13,38] (e.g., missing states, illegal paths). To validate *C3*, we *(i)* collect the system response time for each interaction while replaying user traces; *(ii)* compare such measures with the latency thresholds labeled on the statechart and *(iii)* identify and quantify violations. Concerning the replay of the collected traces, this step has been conducted to eliminate potential latency introduced by the internet connection of each participant. We have automatically replayed traces on the statechart using *Selenium*, that: *(i)* counted how many times each edge of the statechart has been traversed; *(ii)* recorded how much time was required to reproduce each interaction; *(iii)* labeled latency violations. Finally, the violations have been counted and classified, both in total and split for each exploratory task. In particular, we assigned to each violation a severity, *Level Distance (LD)*, defined as follows: **$LD$** = *measured latency level - latency threshold.*

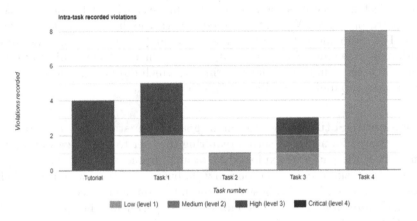

**Fig. 4.** Stacked bar chart showing how many violations were highlighted by the user study, divided by task and by Level Distance.

**Results.** Concerning claim **$C2$**, we evaluated it with the following formula: *completeness = (# replayed interactions included in the statechart)/(# total replayed interactions).* Results show that no missing states/transitions or illegal paths were encountered while replaying the 8481 collected user interactions contained in the user traces on the statechart (completeness = 1).

This result validates claim **$C2$**. Joining it with the result for claim **$C1$** allows us to conclude that the contributed Statechart Generator can model the user interaction space of a generic web-based visualization system completely. Concerning claim **$C3$**, we evaluated it with the following formula: *efficacy = 1 - [(# recorded violations)/(# total interactions)].*

The rationale of this formula is to quantify the saving in the number of interactions to analyze for the VSD with respect to the entire user trace from an EU. We report the results averaged for all the participants. A participant on average executed 169.62 interactions and evidenced in the worst case as many as 5 latency violations. Applying the formula results in an efficacy equal to 97.05%. The VSDs experience a strong reduction in the number of interactions to analyze (violations, and) to provide optimization for, with respect to the full user traces. Preliminary results on perceived latency show similar efficacy: for example, participant P49 declared a perceived high level of latency for all the tasks while executing a total of 199 interactions. Without using our framework, the VSD should have looked at all of them. By using our framework, the VSD must focus only on the 5 identified violations resulting in a saving of 97.49% in interactions to analyze. In this case, the EU feedback was too broad and not accurate, while the proposed framework helped in identifying correctly only the true latency violations. Focusing on the Level Distance, Fig. 4 shows the violations in latency thresholds found while replaying the user traces, split by task. We highlight that task T4 introduced the majority of violations, while the tutorial introduced the most critical ones. This was expected, since it was the most difficult task, making users explore data deeper than in the others, while in the tutorial not having a clear goal made the users freely interact with the system in a highly variable way (e.g., rapidly brushing back and forth). All the recorded violations were only caused by two types of interaction: *mousemove* and *brush mousemove*. This is easily explainable by the nature of the Crossfilter interface, which exploits brush for selections and mouseover for inspection of precise values. As can be seen in Table 5, the *Departure Time* and *Airtime in Minutes* visual components were the ones that introduced the most violations, with six each. In contrast, the *Flights Selected* visual component did not present any violation, as it is the only non-brushable visual component of the entire system. Finally, Fig. 5 highlights which paths in the statechart produced more violations while replaying the user traces *(a)*, and how many times each interaction was performed *(b)*. Interestingly, the grey portion of the statechart identifies paths never taken by any user. We explained this result as a consequence of the task formulation, which asked to focus on visual components outside the grey area. This information can be helpful to a VSD to better comprehend how EUs interact with the system and for optimization strategies that can prioritize the other areas of the statechart. In particular, three cases can be identified: *(case 1)* in which latency violations with medium LD were discovered in an interaction path not frequently taken by participants; *(case 2)* in which violations were discovered in a path frequently taken and *(case 3)* in which no violations were discovered in a path frequently taken. Paths belonging to *(case 2)* should be prioritized for the VSD inspection, followed by paths belonging to *(case 1)*. Paths belonging to *(case 3)* allow quantifying a visualization system's effectiveness in supporting the intended EUs. Quantitative measures computed on these path sets can prove helpful for the VSD in comprehending the results of the evaluation phase of UCD.

This thorough analysis of latency violations clearly shows that by labeling the statechart with latency thresholds, it is possible to easily highlight violations when replaying user traces, thus supporting claim **C3**.

**Table 5.** The violations found while replaying the user traces over the Complete Statechart, divided by triggering event and visual component.

| Visual component | mousemove | brush mousemove |
|---|---|---|
| Departure Time | 4 | 2 |
| Distance in Miles | 1 | 1 |
| Arrival Time | 0 | 2 |
| Airtime in Minutes | 1 | 5 |
| Arrival/Departure Delay | 2 | 3 |
| Flights Selected | 0 | 0 |

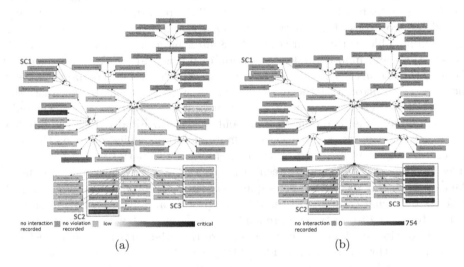

(a)                                                    (b)

**Fig. 5.** The Complete Statechart (rectangles are edge labels) of the Crossfilter interface mapped with: (a) discovered latency violations; (b) paths frequency. Three scenarios are highlighted: SC1, in which there are medium violations in a path not so frequently taken; SC2, in which violations were discovered in a path frequently taken; SC3, in which there are no violations in a path frequently taken.

## 7    Discussion and Conclusions

In this paper, we presented a novel conceptual interaction-driven framework enhancing the basic visualization pipeline through the addition of the Translation Layer. This layer allows for modeling the user interaction space of a generic visualization, collects data about experienced latencies, and identifies latency violations for future optimization. We made the conceptual framework actionable, in its evaluation configuration, through the implementation of the Statechart Generator component. It was initially tested for generality on a set of ten representative visualization systems. A user study ($n = 50$) demonstrated the capability to automatically model the entire user interaction space of a visualization system (mitigating problem 3) and to correctly identify and describe violations in latency thresholds when a user trace is replayed on top of it (mitigating problem 2). Applying optimizations for these specific violations, the VSD obtains a more responsive visualization system, improving the experience of the EU (mitigating problem 1). By using the proposed conceptual framework, we identify as the first benefit for the VSD the *easy automatic modeling of the interaction space*, which does not depend on low-level implementation details, through the statechart description. The VSD can comprehend the interaction paths present and their characteristics. The generated statechart can be used for statistical analysis of post-hoc event-based traces to understand which parts of the visualization system are the most traversed and for which tasks so to optimize the design accordingly. By exploiting the annotated latency thresholds, it is also possible to distinguish between latency-sensitive and latency-insensitive interactions automatically. In this way, the VSD can focus on applying optimizations only for the interactions that truly need it. The EUs inherit benefits from the reduced latency by experiencing a responsive system. In this way, they are supported in expressing more focused feedback on the effective support of the visualization system to the intended exploratory task.

Looking at the limitations, while the Statechart Generator showed general support for any web-based visualization design that can be specified using existing visualization languages such as D3.js [16] , we experienced from our testing activities some minor incompatibilities with HTML Canvas, moving objects (e.g., Origraph [14]), the native Javascript apparatus alert and Vega, that will be further investigated in future activities. Some interesting insights come from a recent work on this matter [59]. Additionally, in the current state the identification of violations can happen only during the usage of a system by EUs. We are working on an automatic violations detector to allow the simulation of user behavior, trained by the traces collected during the user study, to relax this limitation. We also plan to conduct dedicated evaluation activities with VSDs, to collect quantitative feedback on the benefits this conceptual framework enables for them, and with EUs, to measure gain in usability and perceived smoothness during the usage of visualization systems. Finally, we intend to continue working on the remaining components, ST and RT, to include optimizations that will allow the conceptual framework to express its full potential, providing support to the VSD even for optimization.

**Acknowledgements.** We thank Dr. Leilani Battle and Dr. Jean-Daniel Fekete for the initial discussion and precious suggestions on this work. This study was carried out within the MICS (Made in Italy - Circular and Sustainable) Extended Partnership and received funding from the European Union Next-GenerationEU (PIANO NAZIONALE DI RIPRESA E RESILIENZA (PNRR) - MISSIONE 4 COMPONENTE 2, INVESTIMENTO 1.3 - D.D. 1551.11- 10-2022, PE00000004).

The work of Dario Benvenuti is supported by the H2020 project DataCloud (Grant number: 101016835)

# References

1. Ali, S.M., Gupta, N., Nayak, G.K., Lenka, R.K.: Big data visualization: tools and challenges. In: 2016 2nd International Conference on Contemporary Computing and Informatics (IC3I), pp. 656–660 (2016). https://doi.org/10.1109/IC3I.2016.7918044

2. Amar, R.A., Eagan, J., Stasko, J.T.: Low-level components of analytic activity in information visualization, pp. 111–117. IEEE (2005). https://doi.org/10.1109/INFVIS.2005.1532136

3. Angelini, M., Blasilli, G., Farina, L., Lenti, S., Santucci, G.: Nemesis (network medicine analysis): Towards visual exploration of network medicine data (2019)

4. Angelini, M., Blasilli, G., Lenti, S., Palleschi, A., Santucci, G.: Towards enhancing radviz analysis and interpretation. In: 2019 IEEE Visualization Conference (VIS), pp. 226–230 (2019). https://doi.org/10.1109/VISUAL.2019.8933775

5. Angelini, M., Blasilli, G., Lenti, S., Palleschi, A., Santucci, G.: CrossWidgets: enhancing complex data selections through modular multi attribute selectors (2020). https://doi.org/10.1145/3399715.3399918

6. Angelini, M., Blasilli, G., Lenti, S., Santucci, G.: STEIN: speeding up evaluation activities with a seamless testing environment INtegrator. In: Johansson, J., Sadlo, F., Schreck, T. (eds.) EuroVis 2018 - Short Papers. The Eurographics Association (2018). https://doi.org/10.2312/eurovisshort.20181083

7. Angelini, M., Blasilli, G., Lenti, S., Santucci, G.: A visual analytics conceptual framework for explorable and steerable partial dependence analysis. IEEE Trans. Visual. Comput. Graph. 1–16 (2023)

8. Angelini, M., Catarci, T., Santucci, G.: Ivan: an interactive Herlofson's nomogram visualizer for local weather forecast. Computers **8**(3) (2019). https://doi.org/10.3390/computers8030053

9. Angelini, M., Lenti, S., Santucci, G.: Crumbs: a cyber security framework browser. In: 2017 IEEE Symposium on Visualization for Cyber Security (VizSec), pp. 1–8 (2017). https://doi.org/10.1109/VIZSEC.2017.8062194

10. Angelini, M., Santucci, G., Schumann, H., Schulz, H.J.: A review and characterization of progressive visual analytics. Informatics **5**(3) (2018). https://doi.org/10.3390/informatics5030031

11. Baeza-Yates, R., Ribeiro-Neto, B., et al.: Modern Information Retrieval, vol. 463. ACM Press, New York (1999)

12. Battle, L., et al.: Database benchmarking for supporting real-time interactive querying of large data. In: SIGMOD '20, New York, NY, USA, pp. 1571–1587, June 2020. https://doi.org/10.1145/3318464.3389732

13. Benvenuti, D., Buda, E., Fraioli, F., Marrella, A., Catarci, T.: Detecting and explaining usability issues of consumer electronic products. In: Ardito, C., et al. (eds.) INTERACT 2021. LNCS, vol. 12935, pp. 298–319. Springer, Cham (2021). https://doi.org/10.1007/978-3-030-85610-6_18

14. Bigelow, A., Nobre, C., Meyer, M., Lex, A.: Origraph: interactive network wrangling. In: 2019 IEEE Conference on Visual Analytics Science and Technology (VAST), pp. 81–92. IEEE (2019)

15. Blanch, R., Beaudouin-Lafon, M.: Programming rich interactions using the hierarchical state machine toolkit. In: AVI '06, pp. 51–58. ACM, New York, NY, USA (2006). https://doi.org/10.1145/1133265.1133275

16. Bostock, M., Ogievetsky, V., Heer, J.: $D^3$ data-driven documents. IEEE Trans. Vis. Comput. Graph. **17**(12), 2301–2309 (2011). https://doi.org/10.1109/TVCG.2011.185

17. Brehmer, M., Munzner, T.: A multi-level typology of abstract visualization tasks. IEEE Trans. Visual Comput. Graph. **19**(12), 2376–2385 (2013). https://doi.org/10.1109/TVCG.2013.124
18. Card, S., Mackinlay, J.: The structure of the information visualization design space. In: Proceedings of VIZ '97: Visualization Conference, Information Visualization Symposium and Parallel Rendering Symposium, pp. 92–99 (1997). https://doi.org/10.1109/INFVIS.1997.636792
19. Class, B.: Summit: scaling deep learning interpretability by visualizing activation and attribution summarizations
20. Conner, C., Samuel, J., Garvey, M., Samuel, Y., Kretinin, A.: Conceptual frameworks for big data visualization: discussion of models, methods, and artificial intelligence for graphical representations of data. In: Handbook of Research for Big Data, pp. 197–234. Apple Academic Press (2021)
21. Dabrowski, J.R., Munson, E.V.: Is 100 milliseconds too fast? In: CHI'01 Extended Abstracts on Human Factors in Computing Systems, pp. 317–318 (2001)
22. Desolda, G., Esposito, A., Lanzilotti, R., Costabile, M.F.: Detecting emotions through machine learning for automatic UX evaluation. In: Ardito, C., et al. (eds.) INTERACT 2021. LNCS, vol. 12934, pp. 270–279. Springer, Cham (2021). https://doi.org/10.1007/978-3-030-85613-7_19
23. Edwards, M., Aspinall, D.: The synthesis of digital systems using ASM design techniques. In: Computer Hardware Description Languages and their Applications, pp. 55–64 (1983)
24. Erraissi, A., Mouad, B., Belangour, A.: A big data visualization layer meta-model proposition. In: 2019 8th International Conference on Modeling Simulation and Applied Optimization (ICMSAO), pp. 1–5 (2019). https://doi.org/10.1109/ICMSAO.2019.8880276
25. Fekete, J.D., Fisher, D., Nandi, A., Sedlmair, M.: Progressive data analysis and visualization (Dagstuhl Seminar 18411). Dagstuhl Rep. **8**(10), 1–40 (2019). https://doi.org/10.4230/DagRep.8.10.1, http://drops.dagstuhl.de/opus/volltexte/2019/10346
26. Ferrentino, A., AB, F.: State machines and their semantics in software engineering (1977)
27. Feyock, S.: Transition diagram-based cai/help systems. Int. J. Man Mach. Stud. **9**(4), 399–413 (1977)
28. Galletta, A., Carnevale, L., Bramanti, A., Fazio, M.: An innovative methodology for big data visualization for telemedicine. IEEE Trans. Industr. Inf. **15**(1), 490–497 (2019). https://doi.org/10.1109/TII.2018.2842234
29. Golfarelli, M., Rizzi, S.: A model-driven approach to automate data visualization in big data analytics. Inf. Visual. **19**(1), 24–47 (2020). https://doi.org/10.1177/1473871619858933, https://doi.org/10.1177/1473871619858933
30. Han, F., Xu, T., Tian, C., Hou, Z.: Investigation on human visual response latency. In: 2010 International Conference On Computer Design and Applications, vol. 1, pp. V1–602. IEEE (2010)
31. Harel, D.: Statecharts: a visual formalism for complex systems. Sci. Comput. Program. **8**(3), 231–274 (1987)
32. Huot, S., Dumas, C., Dragicevic, P., Fekete, J.D., Hégron, G.: The MaggLite post-WIMP toolkit: draw it, connect it and run it. In: Proceedings of ACM Symposium on User Interface Software and Technology. UIST '04, pp. 257–266. ACM, New York, NY, USA (2004)
33. Jacob, R.J.: Using formal specifications in the design of a human-computer interface. Commun. ACM **26**(4), 259–264 (1983)

34. Keim, D., Andrienko, G., Fekete, J.-D., Görg, C., Kohlhammer, J., Melançon, G.: Visual analytics: definition, process, and challenges. In: Kerren, A., Stasko, J.T., Fekete, J.-D., North, C. (eds.) Information Visualization. LNCS, vol. 4950, pp. 154–175. Springer, Heidelberg (2008). https://doi.org/10.1007/978-3-540-70956-5_7

35. Keim, D., Qu, H., Ma, K.L.: Big-data visualization. IEEE Comput. Graph. Appl. **33**(4), 20–21 (2013). https://doi.org/10.1109/MCG.2013.54

36. Liu, Z., Heer, J.: The effects of interactive latency on exploratory visual analysis. IEEE Trans. Vis. Comput. Graph. **20**(12), 2122–2131 (2014). https://doi.org/10.1109/TVCG.2014.2346452

37. Livny, M., et al.: Devise: integrated querying and visual exploration of large datasets. In: SIGMOD '97, pp. 301–312. Association for Computing Machinery, New York, NY, USA (1997)

38. Marrella, A., Catarci, T.: Measuring the learnability of interactive systems using a petri net based approach. In: Proceedings of the 2018 Designing Interactive Systems Conference. In: DIS '18, pp. 1309–1319 (2018). https://doi.org/10.1145/3196709.3196744

39. Miller, R.B.: Response time in man-computer conversational transactions. In: Proceedings of the December 9–11, 1968, Fall Joint Computer Conference, Part I, pp. 267–277 (1968)

40. Mohammed, L.T., AlHabshy, A.A., ElDahshan, K.A.: Big data visualization: a survey, In: 2022 International Congress on Human-Computer Interaction, Optimization and Robotic Applications (HORA), pp. 1–12 (2022). https://doi.org/10.1109/HORA55278.2022.9799819

41. Moreland, K.: A survey of visualization pipelines. IEEE Trans. Vis. Comput. Graph. **19**(3), 367–378 (2013). https://doi.org/10.1109/TVCG.2012.133

42. Moritz, D., Howe, B., Heer, J.: Falcon: balancing interactive latency and resolution sensitivity for scalable linked visualizations. In: CHI '19. ACM, New York, NY, USA (2019). https://doi.org/10.1145/3290605.3300924

43. Myers, B.A.: Separating application code from toolkits: eliminating the spaghetti of call-backs. In: Proceedings of the 4th Annual ACM Symposium on User Interface Software and Technology. UIST '91, pp. 211–220. ACM, New York, NY, USA (1991)

44. Nah, F.F.H.: A study on tolerable waiting time: how long are web users willing to wait? Behav. Inf. Technol. **23**(3), 153–163 (2004)

45. Nielsen, J.: Usability Engineering. Morgan Kaufmann, Burlington (1993)

46. Oney, S., Myers, B., Brandt, J.: Interstate: a language and environment for expressing interface behavior. In: Proceedings of ACM Symposium on User Interface Software and Technology. UIST '14, pp. 263–272. ACM, New York, NY, USA (2014)

47. Parnas, D.L.: On the use of transition diagrams in the design of a user interface for an interactive computer system. In: Proceedings of the 1969 24th National Conference, pp. 379–385 (1969)

48. Qin, X., Luo, Y., Tang, N., Li, G.: Deepeye: an automatic big data visualization framework. Big Data Min. Anal. **1**(1), 75–82 (2018). https://doi.org/10.26599/BDMA.2018.9020007

49. Raghav, R.S., Pothula, S., Vengattaraman, T., Ponnurangam, D.: A survey of data visualization tools for analyzing large volume of data in big data platform. In: 2016 International Conference on Communication and Electronics Systems (ICCES), pp. 1–6 (2016). https://doi.org/10.1109/CESYS.2016.7889976

50. Sacha, D., Stoffel, A., Stoffel, F., Kwon, B.C., Ellis, G., Keim, D.A.: Knowledge generation model for visual analytics. IEEE Trans. Visual Comput. Graph. **20**(12), 1604–1613 (2014). https://doi.org/10.1109/TVCG.2014.2346481

51. Shin, M., Soen, A., Readshaw, B.T., Blackburn, S.M., Whitelaw, M., Xie, L.: Influence flowers of academic entities. In: 2019 IEEE Conference on Visual Analytics Science and Technology (VAST), pp. 1–10. IEEE (2019)

52. Shneiderman, B.: Response time and display rate in human performance with computers. ACM Comput. Surv. (CSUR) **16**(3), 265–285 (1984)

53. Shneiderman, B.: The eyes have it: a task by data type taxonomy for information visualizations, pp. 364–371. Interactive Technologies (2003). https://doi.org/10.1016/B978-155860915-0/50046-9

54. Shneiderman, B., Plaisant, C., Cohen, M., Jacobs, S., Elmqvist, N., Diakopoulos, N.: Designing the User Interface: Strategies for Effective Human-Computer Interaction, 6th edn. Pearson, London (2016)

55. Strahl, J., Peltonen, J., Floréen, P.: Directing and combining multiple queries for exploratory search by visual interactive intent modeling. In: Ardito, C., et al. (eds.) INTERACT 2021. LNCS, vol. 12934, pp. 514–535. Springer, Cham (2021). https://doi.org/10.1007/978-3-030-85613-7_34

56. Vredenburg, K., Mao, J.Y., Smith, P.W., Carey, T.: A survey of user-centered design practice. In: Proceedings of the SIGCHI Conference on Human Factors in Computing Systems. CHI '02, pp. 471–478. Association for Computing Machinery, New York, NY, USA (2002)

57. Waloszek, G., Kreichgauer, U.: User-centered evaluation of the responsiveness of applications. In: Gross, T., et al. (eds.) INTERACT 2009. LNCS, vol. 5726, pp. 239–242. Springer, Heidelberg (2009). https://doi.org/10.1007/978-3-642-03655-2_29

58. Woodburn, L., Yang, Y., Marriott, K.: Interactive visualisation of hierarchical quantitative data: an evaluation. In: 2019 IEEE Visualization Conference (VIS), pp. 96–100. IEEE (2019)

59. Yang, J., Bäuerle, A., Moritz, D., Çağatay Demiralp: Vegaprof: Profiling vega visualizations (2022)

60. Yi, J.S., ah Kang, Y., Stasko, J.T., Jacko, J.A.: Toward a deeper understanding of the role of interaction in information visualization. IEEE Trans. Vis. Comput. Graph. (2007)

61. Zgraggen, E., Galakatos, A., Crotty, A., Fekete, J.D., Kraska, T.: How progressive visualizations affect exploratory analysis. IEEE Trans. Vis. Comput. Graph. **23**(8), 1977–1987 (2017). https://doi.org/10.1109/TVCG.2016.2607714

62. Zhang, T., Ramakrishnan, R., Livny, M.: Birch: an efficient data clustering method for very large databases. SIGMOD '96, pp. 103–114. Association for Computing Machinery, New York, NY, USA (1996)

63. Zhang, Y., Chanana, K., Dunne, C.: IDMVis: temporal event sequence visualization for type 1 diabetes treatment decision support. IEEE Trans. Visual Comput. Graph. **25**(1), 512–522 (2018)

# The Effect of Teleporting Versus Room-Scale Walking for Interacting with Immersive Visualizations

Alejandro Rey[✉][iD], Andrea Bellucci[✉][iD], Paloma Díaz[✉][iD], and Ignacio Aedo[✉][iD]

Universidad Carlos III de Madrid, Madrid, Spain
alejandro.rey@uc3m.es, {abellucc,pdp}@inf.uc3m.es, aedo@ia.uc3m.es

**Abstract.** The use of different locomotion techniques such as walking or teleportation affects the way people explore and build an understanding of complex data in immersive visualizations. We report results from a quantitative user study (14 participants) comparing the effect of room-scale real walking versus teleportation on information search and task performance in a word-cloud immersive visualization. Participants performed an ordering task and we measured performance, post-task recall, workload and flow. Results suggest that room-scale real walking favors interaction and short-term recall but could imply higher workload.

**Keywords:** locomotion · data visualization · virtual reality · information search · information foraging

## 1 Introduction

The way we move in the world plays an important role on how we process information and generate knowledge [14]. Likewise, the use of different locomotion mechanisms to explore immersive data visualizations [22] affects people's ability to access, interact and make sense of complex information spaces [1]. While many locomotion techniques have been proposed for moving in immersive environments [9], only a few have been studied in the context of Immersive Analytics (IA henceforth) [12,18], i.e., the use of MR technology to aid data-powered understanding and decision making [22].

Teleportation is the most widespread locomotion scheme in Virtual Reality (VR) applications [4] due to its simplicity and the flexibility it offers to virtual environment designers. However, previous work has shown multiple benefits of embodied VR locomotion mechanisms such as real walking (e.g., spatial orientation [8], search tasks performance [27] and mental map building [28]). Advances in HMDs and tracking technologies have enabled the creation of room-scale immersive experiences in which walking can be used without imposing hard

**Supplementary Information** The online version contains supplementary material available at https://doi.org/10.1007/978-3-031-42283-6_6.

J. Abdelnour Nocera et al. (Eds.): INTERACT 2023, LNCS 14143, pp. 110–119, 2023.
https://doi.org/10.1007/978-3-031-42283-6_6

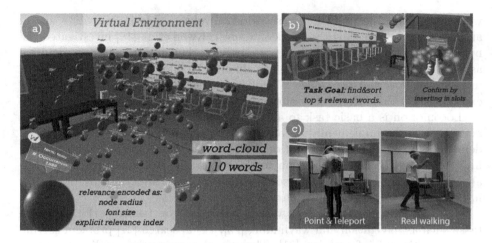

**Fig. 1.** Summary of the experiment. a) The word-cloud visualization and the virtual environment. In the bottom left corner a sphere accompanied by a floating UI represents a word in the word-cloud. Relevance is encoded through node radius, font size and a numeric value that increases linearly with relevance. b) Task: find the four most relevant words and order them in decreasing order using the slots. c) Participants moved using either point-and-teleport or real walking within the boundaries of a floor tracked area.

design constraints for the virtual environment [28], and many solutions to support space-constrained real walking have been proposed [6].

Being IA an incipient research area [10, 29], it is still unclear to what extent the benefits of more embodied locomotion mechanisms can be leveraged for the design of effective immersive exploration of data visualizations that adapt to the (different) bodily and cognitive abilities of the users [29]. To this end, we conducted a user study comparing the effect of two common locomotion techniques in VR (room-scale real walking and teleportation) in relation to information search and task performance. The study required participants to perform a searching and ordering task while immersed in a word-cloud visualization. Results suggest that room-scale walking can foster immediate recall and engage users in exploration and interaction. Task workload was higher for unconstrained room-scale walking, even thought it was the preferred modality.

## 2   Related Work

In IA systems, users seek to derive conclusions from a dataset presented as an immersive visualization. The process starts by determining relevant data for the task at hand (information foraging), and then a more holistic understanding is gained analysing such data in what is known as the sensemaking loop [24].

Most of the empirical studies in IA have addressed the sensemaking loop [11], including research to enhance the clarity of data representations [19], explore the impact on insights generation [25], and identify sensemaking strategies [21]. Our work focuses on the previous phase, which involves exploring the data space, and filtering and selecting the items of interest. Kwon et al. [19] investigated the benefits provided by different data representation layouts letting aside cognitive aspects. Reski and Alissandrakis [25] evaluated the information foraging process in terms of flow and workload. We followed a similar approach in our study, exploring how the different locomotion mechanisms may impact this process.

Locomotion is a basic task to allow the exploration of virtual environments and requires the implementation of mechanisms to move the user viewport on demand [30]. While many locomotion techniques have been proposed for moving in VR (e.g., [4]), their application to the exploration of immersive data visualizations is still underinvestigated, especially when comparing joystick-based interfaces and physical room-scale walking.

Many studies show that real walking can result on better performance on tasks such as navigation and wayfinding [23], visual search [27] problem solving and evaluation of information [31]. There exist comparative studies regarding locomotion techniques applied to various kinds of immersive visualizations, some of which involve physical locomotion (e.g., 3d biological structures [20], scatterplots [31]) or teleportation (graphs [10]), but these two widespread locomotion techniques have not been compared directly in a room-scale IA task.

Our study is the first comparing real walking and teleportation in room-scale virtual environments for an Immersive Analytics task. Additionally, while previous work on locomotion techniques in IA has focused on assessing the task performance in the data analysis process [21], we explore the impact of locomotion on information lookup search factors such as recall, flow or workload.

## 3    User Study

We designed an experiment to compare room-scale real walking ($W$) and point-and-teleport teleportation ($TP$) [5] for an immersive lookup and ordering task. The main goal was to explore the effects of embodied versus non-embodied locomotion techniques in a room-scale word-cloud visualization in terms of both task performance and reportedly sensemaking-related metrics.

### 3.1    Research Questions

We designed the study to address the following research questions:

*RQ1* **Does the use of a specific locomotion technique in VR (walking/teleportation) yield benefits in terms of recall, flow or workload?**

$H_1$ Scores for the Flow subscale of the FSS Questionnaire are significantly higher for the real walking experimental condition: $TP_{flow} < W_{flow}$ (see [15]).
$H_2$ Participants remember a significantly higher number of words of the word cloud when they are exposed to the real walking experimental condition: $TP_{recall} < W_{recall}$ (see [3]).

$H_3$ The NASA-TLX score for participants is significantly lower in the teleportation experimental condition: $TP_{wkload} < W_{wkload}$ (see [20]).

**RQ2 Does the use of different locomotion techniques lead to significant differences in task performance (e.g., accuracy, completion time) for a immersive analytics lookup and ordering task?**

$H_4$ Task performance differs across conditions: $TP_{tskP} \neq W_{tskP}$ (see [23]).

## 3.2  Virtual Environment and Immersive Visualization

We developed an immersive word-cloud visualization, designed to mimic 2D word-clouds [17]. Instead of relying on 3D text rendering, we combined 2D text and a 3D spherical element to represent datapoints (words) as well as their features in the visualization. Figure 1a shows an overview of the visualization, where a set of spherical nodes (each of which is accompanied by a floating UI), display a word and a numeric value. The visualization is composed of 110 words or concepts, where each concept is represented in space by a sphere placed in a given position within a virtual room, accompanied by a panel displaying its associated label. The visualization was built on top of a dataset about the 2017 Catalonia conflict [7]. The word-cloud was designed ad-hoc (no clustering, no displayed semantic relationships) and words were scattered around the environment in order to provide participants with an egocentric view of the raw data space that required its exploration. We carried out a pilot study to calibrate the difficulty of the task, control the distance between the most important words to prevent them influencing performance, and determine whether participants could both read the words comfortably and manipulate them without jumping or crouching heavily. Distinct words within the system differ from one another in terms of: (1) the radius of its linked sphere, (2) the size of their label and (3) the number accompanying the word label. All of these visual features encode the relevance of a word within the dataset, where larger means more relevant. Relevance matches the number of occurrences of each word in the corpus of documents.

## 3.3  Experimental Task Description

Participants were asked to locate the *top 4* words (in terms of relevance criteria) and order them in decreasing order by placing them within a set of reserved hollow boxes we refer to as *ordering slots*, located in a wall of the virtual environment (see Fig. 1b). The pilot study allowed us to choose the number of words to order so that the task was not too time consuming yet not trivial.

The study comprises two experimental conditions: real walking versus teleport. In the walking condition, participants could physically move around using real walking. In the teleport condition, a raycast-based teleporting mechanism [5] allowed participants to move around the environment while staying stationary in the real world. Each participant was exposed to a single experimental condition (between-subjects design).

Participants were introduced to the visualization before carrying out the task. They were informed about the theme of the dataset ("politics"), as well as the fact that words differed in terms of an objective relevance metric. Participants were explicitly told to perform the task as accurately as possible (no hard time constraints were imposed). All participants were immersed in the same exact word visualization and started the experiment at a fixed position in the scene.

### 3.4  Apparatus and Materials

The experiment took place in a laboratory equipped with an Antilatency floor tracking area (3 m × 4.8 m) within whose boundaries participants were instructed to carry out the task (see Fig. 1c). A Meta Quest 2 headset was used to present the virtual environment to participants.

### 3.5  Participants

A total of 14 participants successfully carried out the experiment (3 female) age range 24–55 years (M = 31.4, SD = 9.76). Most of the participants (11) had technical backgrounds (e.g., engineering). Only 5 participants had a moderate to high level of experience with VR. Half of the participants wore prescription lenses during the experiment. Recruitment was made by means of social network advertising and physical notice advertising in our university campus. After completion, each participant was awarded a 10 euro gift card. The experiment was approved by the university's research ethics board.

### 3.6  Procedure

Each full session took around 30 min to complete and comprised 4 phases.

**Informed consent and pre-experiment questions**: a researcher explained the purpose of the experiment and asked the participant to fill an informed consent form and a short demographic questionnaire along with information regarding possible confounding variables.

**Training**: The researcher presented the VR headset and controller devices to be used during the session. The participant was also informed about the safe boundaries. The researcher helped the participant to put the headset on and enter the virtual environment. The participant went through a tutorial in the virtual environment, which showed how to perform the basic interactions enabled (namely grabbing nodes, inserting them in slots, moving around, and toggling contextual information) according to the experimental condition (W or TP).

**Task execution**: Once feeling confident with the controls in VR, the participant was introduced to the lookup and ordering task: finding the 4 most relevant words in an immersive word-cloud representation and placing them in decreasing order in the ordering slots. The participant explored the virtual space and wandered around, interacting with nodes to generate the final ordering, while articulating what she was doing. The experiment ended once the participant was satisfied with the ordering (see avg. completion times in Table 1).

**Post-experiment questionnaires**: After the task, three questionnaires were handed over to the participant in order to extract information about words recalled, task load and flow.

## 3.7 Interaction Methods

All interactions in the immersive application were performed using the Meta Touch controllers. Holding down the LH joystick allowed teleportation via pointing towards a destination and releasing the joystick. Participants could also grab words and toggle extra information about an element in the virtual world. Both could be achieved by pressing both triggers on the controllers (i.e., closing the fist) on a virtual element.

## 3.8 Data Collection and Measures

We collected quantitative and qualitative data before, during and after the task execution phase. Gathered data includes the English level of participants, their academic level, their business area and their experience with VR. We collected the following metrics during task execution: travelled distance, number of interactions performed (manipulations and toggles), task completion time, ordering errors, and number of slots left empty. In the post-task phase, participants were asked to fill out three questionnaires: (1) a custom short-term recall questionnaire (we asked for most relevant and also any recalled word), (2) the NASA TLX [16] (workload) and (3) the Flow Short Scale that aims to measure the cognitive flow of the participants [26].

**Table 1.** Summary of results. Avg. values and standard deviations are listed for all measured variables and experimental conditions. Statistically significant differences for a variable are marked with an asterisk (*) $p \leq 0.05$ with $\alpha = 0.05$.

| | | TP (N=6) | | RW (N=8) | | | | |
|---|---|---|---|---|---|---|---|---|
| | Variable | μ | σ | μ | σ | t-value | p-value | Stat. Test |
| Workload (NASA-TLX) | **Overall*** | 29.056 | 18.344 | 49.667 | 16.445 | 1.807 | **0.035** | WRS |
| | Physical Demand | 1.500 | 1.329 | 1.458 | 1.754 | -0.051 | 0.520 | TSTT (dof=12) |
| | Temporal demand | 1.444 | 1.377 | 4.501 | 5.080 | 1.162 | 0.123 | WRS |
| | **Performance*** | 4.111 | 3.942 | 9.458 | 5.623 | 2.091 | **0.029** | TSTT (dof=12) |
| | Effort | 5.833 | 7.083 | 6.875 | 2.845 | 1.356 | 0.088 | WRS |
| | Frustration | 7.111 | 5.536 | 11.020 | 9.483 | 0.962 | 0.178 | TSTT (dof=12) |
| Task Performance | Exp Duration | 4.849 | 1.658 | 6.916 | 4.101 | 1.291 | 0.098 | WRS |
| | correct(max4) | 3.833 | 0.408 | 3.750 | 0.463 | -0.258 | 0.602 | WRS |
| | #t aps | 3.333 | 8.165 | 14.625 | 37.428 | 0.827 | 0.216 | TSTT (dof=12) |
| | **travelled VR world distance*** | 54.683 | 23.839 | 87.498 | 38.365 | 1.966 | **0.037** | TSTT (dof=12) |
| | # manipulations* | 11.500 | 5.683 | 28.250 | 19.718 | 2.066 | **0.019** | WRS |
| Flow | Flowscore(FSS) | 5.833 | 0.463 | 5.112 | 1.134 | -1.626 | 0.932 | TSTT (dof=12) |
| | Anxiety(FSS) | 4.278 | 1.583 | 4.167 | 1.008 | -0.151 | 0.558 | TSTT (dof=12) |
| | **Challenge(FSS)*** | 3.500 | 0.548 | 4.500 | 0.535 | 2.324 | **0.010** | WRS |
| Recall (Custom Questionnaire) | **#wordsrecalled*** | 3.000 | 2.098 | 6.875 | 3.944 | 2.368 | **0.019** | TSTT (dof=12) |
| | #Top words(in order) | 0.667 | 0.516 | 0.500 | 0.535 | -0.516 | 0.697 | WRS |
| | #Top words recalled (unordered) | 1.167 | 0.753 | 1.125 | 0.991 | -0.258 | 0.602 | WRS |
| Background info | Previous VR experience | 3.667 | 2.805 | 2.500 | 1.309 | -0.516 | 0.697 | WRS |
| | English level | 2.667 | 0.516 | 2.500 | 0.756 | -0.258 | 0.602 | WRS |
| | Age | 30.833 | 8.377 | 33.500 | 10.461 | 0.323 | 0.373 | WRS |

## 4   Results

To tackle RQ1, we performed hypothesis testing to analyze the differences in questionnaire scores across experimental conditions. To address RQ2 we analyzed the performance metrics captured during the task execution phase of the experiment. The Shapiro-Wilk method was used to assess the normality of values for each set of measures. We performed a two sample t-test (dof = 12) for data that satisfied the assumption of normality or a Wilcoxon rank-sum test otherwise. Spearman's correlation was used to support relationships among measured variables. Table 1 depicts the results of all quantitative analyses performed.

*Information Search and Locomotion Technique:* Regarding the FSS questionnaire metrics, we found that Reported Challenge level was significantly higher in the $W$ condition using a Wilcoxon Rank-sum test (t = 2.324, p = 0.01). No significant differences were found for any other subscale.

Regarding short-term word recall, we found statistically significant differences in the number of recalled words out of the whole word-cloud, with results of a t-test supporting our hypothesis of higher recall in the W condition (t = 2.368, p = 0.0186). No significant differences were found across experimental conditions for words recalled in the *top 4*, neither ordered nor unordered.

With regard to task workload, we found statistically significant differences across experimental conditions, with teleportation showing lower workload after a Wilcoxon Rank-sum test (t = 1.81, p = 0.035). Moreover, we found a statistically significant difference in Performance using a t-test (t = 2.091, p = 0.029). No other NASA-TLX subscale score difference was found to be statistically significant.

*Locomotion Technique and Task Performance:* The number of manipulation gestures performed by participants in the W condition was found to be notably larger than the number of interactions in the TP condition (t = 2.066, p = 0.019). No significant differences were found regarding number of toggle interactions. We found no statistically significant differences regarding task completion time across conditions. Eleven participants were able to complete without errors, while the remaining 3 made a single error (when deciding the word in fourth place). Additionally, users of the W condition were found to travel a longer virtual distance according to the results of a t-test (t = 1.966, p = 0.037).

## 5   Discussion

Contrary to what we expected, no statistically significant differences were found in terms of flow between the experimental conditions, therefore, there is no evidence to support $H_1$. Participants were reported to feel significantly more challenged in the W condition, however this did not seem to lead to increased flow. We argue that, while the challenge level contribute to flow [15], our lookup task might not provide a sufficient challenge-skill balance that could have lead

to observe significant differences. Anxiety levels were very similar in both experimental conditions and correlated positively to errors in the task (C = 0.604),
which aligns with previous work regarding attention [13].

Results support $H_2$ and suggest that the use of physical locomotion (i.e., real
walking) is a better fit for activities involving immediate recall. We argue that
these differences in terms of recall might be due to teleportation inducing disorientation in users, often associated to a lack of optical flow [2]. On the contrary,
participants performance dropped when asked to recall the top 4 words (order
and unordered). We argue this is due to the fact that most word acquisition
happened during the initial exploration of the environment. To further quantify
the benefits of real walking, future designs shall focus on comparing navigation
schemes for tasks whose main goal involves recall.

The W condition led to higher workload, which supports $H_3$, consistently
with previous work [20]. It may be explained by the fact that participants
performed more interactions with data in the walking condition. Results on
self-reported performance scores suggest that participants were more confident
about their actions in the W condition. We found a positive correlation between
the number manipulations gestures participants performed and reported performance (C = 0.656), all of which suggests that walking seems to foster interaction
which seems to influence recall at the expense of a higher workload.

We found two significant differences on task performance ($H_4$): travelled
virtual distance and manipulation count. Travelled distance was higher in the
W condition, which aligns with previous work [32]. Distance positively correlate
to the self-reported performance (C = 0.615), so participants seem to feel more
accomplished in the walking condition because (1) they exploit free navigation
and cover a larger data space in a similar amount of time and (2) they leverage
manipulation more. This is analogous to the results reported in [31].

The results come with limitations. We handed over the NASA TLX questionnaire right after the recall questionnaire, which may have introduced noise in the
workload scores, even though we reminded participants to reflect only about the
ordering task performance. Participants had mostly an engineering background,
which limits generalisation.

## 6   Conclusions and Future Work

We compared room-scale real walking and teleportation with respect to information search in an immersive word-cloud visualization. Results suggest that
walking affords users to recall more words immediately after the task. Participants seemed more willing to interact with data when they walk around and
workload was found to be lower whenever they made use of teleportation. Our
study constitutes a step towards the development of benchmarks to evaluate IA
interfaces not only in terms of performance but also regarding aspects such as
information search and exploration.

**Acknowledgements.** This work is supported by the Spanish State Research Agency (AEI) under grant Sense2MakeSense (PID2019-109388GB-I00) and CrossColab (PGC2018-101884-B-I00).

# References

1. Andrews, C., Endert, A., North, C.: Space to think: large high-resolution displays for sensemaking. In: Proceedings of the SIGCHI Conference on Human Factors in Computing Systems, pp. 55–64 (2010)
2. Bakker, N.H., Passenier, P.O., Werkhoven, P.J.: Effects of head-slaved navigation and the use of teleports on spatial orientation in virtual environments. Hum. Factors **45**(1), 160–169 (2003)
3. Ball, R., North, C.: The effects of peripheral vision and physical navigation on large scale visualization. In: Proceedings of Graphics Interface 2008, pp. 9–16 (2008)
4. Boletsis, C.: The new era of virtual reality locomotion: a systematic literature review of techniques and a proposed typology. Multimodal Technol. Interact. **1**(4), 24 (2017)
5. Bozgeyikli, E., Raij, A., Katkoori, S., Dubey, R.: Point & teleport locomotion technique for virtual reality. In: Proceedings of the 2016 Annual Symposium on Computer-Human Interaction in Play, pp. 205–216 (2016)
6. Cardoso, J.C., Perrotta, A.: A survey of real locomotion techniques for immersive virtual reality applications on head-mounted displays. Comput. Graph. **85**, 55–73 (2019)
7. Carrion, B., Onorati, T., Díaz, P., Triga, V.: A taxonomy generation tool for semantic visual analysis of large corpus of documents. Multimed. Tools Appl. **78**(23), 32919–32937 (2019). https://doi.org/10.1007/s11042-019-07880-y
8. Chance, S.S., Gaunet, F., Beall, A.C., Loomis, J.M.: Locomotion mode affects the updating of objects encountered during travel: The contribution of vestibular and proprioceptive inputs to path integration. Presence **7**(2), 168–178 (1998)
9. Di Luca, M., Seifi, H., Egan, S., Gonzalez-Franco, M.: Locomotion vault: the extra mile in analyzing VR locomotion techniques. In: Proceedings of the 2021 CHI Conference on Human Factors in Computing Systems, pp. 1–10 (2021)
10. Drogemuller, A., Cunningham, A., Walsh, J., Cordeil, M., Ross, W., Thomas, B.: Evaluating navigation techniques for 3d graph visualizations in virtual reality. In: 2018 International Symposium on Big Data Visual and Immersive Analytics (BDVA), pp. 1–10. IEEE (2018)
11. Endert, A., et al.: The state of the art in integrating machine learning into visual analytics. In: Computer Graphics Forum, vol. 36, pp. 458–486. Wiley Online Library (2017)
12. Ens, B., et al.: Grand challenges in immersive analytics. In: Proceedings of the 2021 CHI Conference on Human Factors in Computing Systems. CHI '21, Association for Computing Machinery, New York (2021). https://doi.org/10.1145/3411764.3446866
13. Eysenck, M.W.: Anxiety and attention. Anxiety Res. **1**(1), 9–15 (1988)
14. Gibson, E.J.: Exploratory behavior in the development of perceiving, acting, and the acquiring of knowledge. Annu. Rev. Psychol. **39**(1), 1–42 (1988)
15. Hamari, J., Shernoff, D.J., Rowe, E., Coller, B., Asbell-Clarke, J., Edwards, T.: Challenging games help students learn: an empirical study on engagement, flow and immersion in game-based learning. Comput. Hum. Behav. **54**, 170–179 (2016)

16. Hart, S.G., Staveland, L.E.: Development of nasa-tlx (task load index): results of empirical and theoretical research. Adv. Psychol. **52**, 139–183 (1988)
17. Heimerl, F., Lohmann, S., Lange, S., Ertl, T.: Word cloud explorer: text analytics based on word clouds. In: 2014 47th Hawaii International Conference on System Sciences, pp. 1833–1842 (2014). https://doi.org/10.1109/HICSS.2014.231
18. Kraus, M., et al.: Immersive analytics with abstract 3d visualizations: a survey. In: Computer Graphics Forum, vol. 41, pp. 201–229. Wiley Online Library (2022)
19. Kwon, O.H., Muelder, C., Lee, K., Ma, K.L.: A study of layout, rendering, and interaction methods for immersive graph visualization. IEEE Trans. Visual Comput. Graphics **22**(7), 1802–1815 (2016)
20. Lages, W.S., Bowman, D.A.: Move the object or move myself? walking vs. manipulation for the examination of 3d scientific data. Frontiers in ICT 5, 15 (2018)
21. Lisle, L., Davidson, K., Gitre, E.J., North, C., Bowman, D.A.: Sensemaking strategies with immersive space to think. In: 2021 IEEE Virtual Reality and 3D User Interfaces (VR), pp. 529–537. IEEE (2021)
22. Marriott, K., et al.: Immersive analytics, vol. 11190. Springer (2018)
23. Peck, T.C., Fuchs, H., Whitton, M.C.: An evaluation of navigational ability comparing redirected free exploration with distractors to walking-in-place and joystick locomotio interfaces. In: 2011 IEEE Virtual Reality Conference, pp. 55–62. IEEE (2011)
24. Pirolli, P., Card, S.: The sensemaking process and leverage points for analyst technology as identified through cognitive task analysis. In: Proceedings of International Conference on Intelligence Analysis, vol. 5, pp. 2–4. McLean, VA, USA (2005)
25. Reski, N., Alissandrakis, A.: Open data exploration in virtual reality: a comparative study of input technology. Virtual Reality **24**(1), 1–22 (2020)
26. Rheinberg, F., Vollmeyer, R., Engeser, S.: Flow short scale. PsycTESTS Dataset (2003)
27. Ruddle, R.A., Lessels, S.: The benefits of using a walking interface to navigate virtual environments. ACM Trans. Comput.-Hum. Interact. (TOCHI) **16**(1), 1–18 (2009)
28. Sayyad, E., Sra, M., Höllerer, T.: Walking and teleportation in wide-area virtual reality experiences. In: 2020 IEEE International Symposium on Mixed and Augmented Reality (ISMAR), pp. 608–617 (2020). https://doi.org/10.1109/ISMAR50242.2020.00088
29. Skarbez, R., Polys, N.F., Ogle, J.T., North, C., Bowman, D.A.: Immersive analytics: theory and research agenda. Front. Robot. AI **6**, 82 (2019)
30. Suma, E.A., Finkelstein, S.L., Reid, M., Ulinski, A., Hodges, L.F.: Real walking increases simulator sickness in navigationally complex virtual environments. In: 2009 IEEE Virtual Reality Conference, pp. 245–246. IEEE (2009)
31. Whitlock, M., Smart, S., Szafir, D.A.: Graphical perception for immersive analytics. In: 2020 IEEE Conference on Virtual Reality and 3D User Interfaces (VR), pp. 616–625. IEEE (2020)
32. Zanbaka, C.A., Lok, B.C., Babu, S.V., Ulinski, A.C., Hodges, L.F.: Comparison of path visualizations and cognitive measures relative to travel technique in a virtual environment. IEEE Trans. Visual Comput. Graphics **11**(6), 694–705 (2005)

# Information Visualization and 3D Interaction

# Playing with Data: An Augmented Reality Approach to Interact with Visualizations of Industrial Process Tomography

Yuchong Zhang[1]([✉])(iD), Yueming Xuan[1], Rahul Yadav[2](iD), Adel Omrani[3](iD), and Morten Fjeld[1,4](iD)

[1] Chalmers University of Technology, Gothenburg, Sweden
{yuchong,fjeld}@chalmers.se
[2] University of Eastern Finland, Kuopio, Finland
[3] Karlsruhe Institute of Technology, Karlsruhe, Germany
[4] University of Bergen, Bergen, Norway
Morten.Fjeld@uib.no

**Abstract.** Industrial process tomography (IPT) is a specialized imaging technique widely used in industrial scenarios for process supervision and control. Today, augmented/mixed reality (AR/MR) is increasingly being adopted in many industrial occasions, even though there is still an obvious gap when it comes to IPT. To bridge this gap, we propose the first systematic AR approach using optical see-through (OST) head mounted displays (HMDs) with comparative evaluation for domain users towards IPT visualization analysis. The proof-of-concept was demonstrated by a within-subject user study ($n = 20$) with counterbalancing design. Both qualitative and quantitative measurements were investigated. The results showed that our AR approach outperformed conventional settings for IPT data visualization analysis in bringing higher understandability, reduced task completion time, lower error rates for domain tasks, increased usability with enhanced user experience, and a better recommendation level. We summarize the findings and suggest future research directions for benefiting IPT users with AR/MR.

**Keywords:** Augmented Reality · Industrial Process Tomography · Optical See-through Head Mounted Display · User Study

## 1 Introduction

Industrial process tomography (IPT) (Fig. 1.$a$) is a dedicated and non-invasive imaging technique which is pervasively used in manufacturing scenarios for process monitoring or integrated control [23,35,42–44,52,56,57]. It is an effective mechanism to extract complex data, visualize it and interpret it for domain users [5,20,44,54,58]. Due to the speciality and professionality of IPT, some rising technologies are therefore harnessed for both experts and laymen to perform complex tomographic data analysis to improve their productivity and efficiency.

J. Abdelnour Nocera et al. (Eds.): INTERACT 2023, LNCS 14143, pp. 123–144, 2023.
https://doi.org/10.1007/978-3-031-42283-6_7

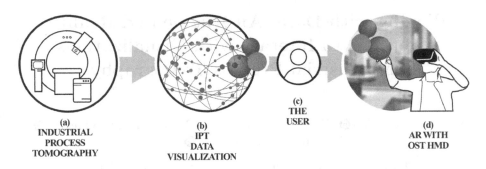

**Fig. 1.** Conceptualization of our proposed AR approach for IPT visualization analysis. *a*): The specialized IPT controlled industrial process is implemented in a confined environment. *b*): The IPT data visualizations originated from different processes are imported and displayed in OST HMD AR. *c*): Users engage with relevant data analysis. *d*): User equipped with the proposed AR environment by an OST HMD interacting with the visualizations for further analysis.

Through augmented reality/mixed reality (AR/MR) [49], a now highly popular technique which superposes virtual objected into the real world [29,30,51,60], it is possible to provide the digital information extracted from intricate tomographic data to the front view of users. As a representative human computer interaction technology, AR consolidates the interplay between digital objects and human subjects with immersion based on a powerful and interactive AR visualization modality [26,41,53]. Such usage has still not become mainstream in most industries but a moderate number of research projects have successfully demonstrated its value [48]. Yet, wide adoption of AR within IPT is scarce due to the lack of technology fusion, and challenges such as hardware limitation and ease of use [59].

AR features an exceptional characteristic that establishes immersive experiences where users intimately interact with the virtual object floating in front of their field of view [3,7,61]. With the rapid development of hardware technology, Wearable head-mounted display (HMD) AR has become widespread in many contexts since it enables interaction between physical objects coupled with digital information using human hands [25]. Under this circumstance, manipulation tasks that require interaction with the virtual objects can be achieved more accurately and quickly than when using conventional tangible interfaces [6,28]. Optical see-through (OST) HMDs occupy the majority of contemporary AR contexts due to their ability to use optical elements to superimpose the real world with virtual augmentation [40]. This differs from video see-though AR where the camera calibrating is realized by handling the captured image: in an OST AR system, the final camera is the human eye, and thus there is no captured camera imagery to process [27]. With the ability of displaying manifold data in a more perceivable and interactive way [14,21], applying AR to generate interactive visualizations for user-oriented tasks is often the preferred choice, and not only for industrial applications [1,19,33,34,39]. More specifically, it has been proven that OST AR can insert virtual information into the physical environment with visual enhancement for human observers to control, thus improving the performance of information-dense domain tasks and further adding to its appeal to industrial practitioners [15, 22].

While industrial AR has attracted considerable attention among researchers and engineers, the gap between this emerging technique and actual IPT scenarios still remains [59, 63]. Recently, some practitioners have acknowledged the high value and potential of AR to be adopted in a variety of IPT-related situations. The combination of IPT and AR is seen as a thriving methodology since AR has the capacity to handle sophisticated 2D/3D data in an immersive, interactive manner, under the premise that IPT is used for monitoring and controlling confined processes. When combined, AR and IPT have a strong potential for visualization and interpretation of complex raw data [12, 36, 37]. The visualization supportablity and interactivity of AR is well justified in some IPT-controlled processes, including visualizing fluid mixture for stirred chemical reactors [32] and providing in-situ collaborative analysis in remote locations regarding numerical data [36]. Nonetheless, even though plenty of mobility has been brought about, there is no research into the essential interaction between IPT data visualizations and domain related users with the aid of OST AR.

In this paper, we offer a novel AR approach which concentrates on the interaction between data visualization from IPT (Fig. 1.*b*) and pertinent users (Fig. 1.*c*) to allow them to easily observe and manipulate the visualizations with high immersion. The target domain users are those who are in need of getting involved with IPT to any extent. We propose deploying AR/MR applications to tackle the practical problems stemming from the specific area (interactive IPT visualization analysis). The main advantage of the proposed methodology is that it initiates, to our knowledge, the first mechanism for furnishing IPT users with OST HMD AR with comparative evaluation to communicate with informative visualizations for better comprehension of industrial processes. The AR system employs Microsoft HoloLens 2; one of the representative OST HMDs (Fig. 1.*d*), as the fundamental supplying equipment to create the AR/MR environments. The source data derived from the IPT supported industrial processes is always formidable to understand, so needs straightforward and precise patterns to be visualized and interpreted. Our proposed approach provides a systematic framework which adopts accurate 2D/3D IPT data visualizations and supplies interactive analysis that is comprehensible to domain users regardless of their IPT experience. We carried out a comparative study to demonstrate the superiority of our AR approach on bringing interactive visualization surroundings as well as eliciting better contextual awareness. We envision our AR approach to benefit any areas where users deal with IPT visualization analysis. The main contributions of this paper are as follows:

– Proposing a novel AR approach for domain users to perform contextual IPT data visualization analysis using OST HMDs, with better understandability, task performance and user experience.

– Designing and implementing a comparative study with user testing to prove
the effectiveness of our proposed AR approach compared to the conventional
method and acquiring early-stage feedback.

The structure of this paper is as follows: The background and motivation
are narrated Sect. 1. Section 2 presents state-of-the-art related works of using
AR with IPT for interactive visualization in related contexts. Section 3 comprehensively presents of the proposed AR approach, including system overview,
contextual stimulus, and the apparatuses. Section 4 offers experimental design
and implementation for evaluation. Section 5 discusses insights and limitations.
Finally, Sect. 6 draws concluding remarks and future work.

## 2    Related Work

AR/MR and derivative techniques are gradually appearing in more industrial
contexts [8,45] due to AR offering computer-generated virtual and context/task
related information in-situ for users [24]. The interactivity derived from AR technology regarding virtual visualizations in various industrial application scenes
has particularly been advocated by researchers over the past few years.

### 2.1    Augmented Reality Visualizations for Industry

Over a decade ago, Bruno et al. [10] developed an AR application named
VTK4AR, featuring that functionality which uses AR to scientifically visualize
industrial engineering data for potential manipulation of the dataset. The many
requirements of applying AR within industrial applications have been summarized by Lorenz et al. [31] as they enumerate the user, technical, and environmental requirements. Mourtzis et al. [34] proposed a methodology to visualize and
display the industrial production scheduling and monitoring data by using AR,
empowering people to supervise and interact with the incorporated components.
In industrial manufacturing, a comparative study conducted by Alves et al. [1],
demonstrated that users who replied on AR based visualizations obtained better
results in physical and mental demand in production assembly procedures. Even
more specifically, Büttner et al. [11] identified that using in-situ projection based
spatial AR resulted in a significantly shorter task completion time in industrial
manual assembly. They designed two assisting systems and proved that the projection based AR outperformed HMD based AR in ease of use and helpfulness in
their context. Avalle et al. [2] proposed an adaptive AR system to visualize the
industrial robotic faults through the HMD devices. They developed an adaptive
modality where virtual metaphors were used for evoking robot faults, obtaining
high effectiveness in empowering users to recognize contextual faults in less time.
Satkowski et al. [46] investigated the influence of the physical environments on
the 2D visualizations in AR, suggesting that the real world has no noticeable
impact on the perception of AR visualizations.

**Fig. 2.** The block diagram of our proposed AR approach. The user starts the procedure by wearing the OST HMD. The immersive experience is then created, which accommodates the multiple IPT data visualizations for supporting interactive analysis. The user feedback is then obtained.

## 2.2    Augmented Reality for Industrial Process Tomography

Even though the volume of intersection research between AR and IPT is not substantial, other researchers have been investigating diverse pipelines of applying AR to generate interactive and effective visualizations for complex tomographic process data. Dating back to 2001, Mann et al. [32] exploited an AR application to visualize the solid-fluid mixture in a 5D way in stirred chemical reactors operated by one breed of IPT–electrical resistivity tomography (ERT). A few years later, Stanley et al. [50] directed the first study of applying ERT to a precipitation reaction process by using AR visualization to display images shown in a suitable format. Zhang et al. [59] conducted a need-finding study investigating the current status and prospective challenges of AR in IPT. They pointed out that there is a great potential of deploying cutting-edge AR technique among IPT practitioners. A new solution to visualize IPT data, leading to collaborative analysis in remote locations, was proposed by Nowak et al. [36]. More specifically, their team also explored a more in-depth AR system with a more advanced but still preliminary prototype which created an entire 3D environment for users to interact with the information visualizations characterizing the workflow of IPT with better immersion [37]. The OST HMD AR was satisfactorily adopted in the experiment they conducted but there were no specific interaction and evaluation included. Later, Zhang et al. [62] formulated a novel system to generalize IPT within the context of mobile AR, and directed a proof-of-concept implementation where an AR framework was developed to support volumetric visualization of IPT, especially to yield high mobility for users but without involving any practical user testing. Sobiech et al. [47] conducted an exploratory study on user gestural interactions with general IPT 3D data by involving HMD AR, affirming the initial adoption of AR in interacting with IPT data, however, no comparison to conventional tools and no structured user study were engaged either. At present, there is to our knowledge no systematic research into framing the use of OST HMD AR for IPT data visualization analysis and comparing it with the conventional tools through constructive user studies.

## 3    Methodology

### 3.1    System Overview

Our AR system is designed as an interactive approach to accommodate users with immersion to interact with different visualizations originated from IPT monitored contexts. A schematic diagram of the system is shown in Fig. 2. The practical embodiment of our approach is an AR application with switchable options for different modalities of visualizations being placed accurately in front of human eyes for desired immersion [17]. Users launch the AR app after putting on the OST HMD. This enables them to manipulate visualizations, generated from IPT supervised processes, with their hands. As displayed in Fig. 3, the IPT visualization is cast as a floating object in our AR context, while users are supported to intimately drag (grabbing the visualization to force the motion as it deviates from the original position), rotate (grabbing the edges of the visualization to turn or spin it around its central point), zoom in/out (grabbing the edges of the visualization to adjust it's level of magnification), and execute other physical manipulations (moving, flipping, aligning, etc.) in order to get deeper understanding of the data and perform further analysis. The virtual objects in front of the users' eyes are at a proper distance and completely visible within the field of view of the OST HMD, so they can view all the content shown. The provided AR interaction formulated for users towards these intricate tomographic data visualizations is deemed to be the most striking attribute, and has not been indicated in any previous IPT scenarios. Furthermore, a user feedback component is involved in this approach to appropriately appraise this AR system. We designed and implemented a comparative user study to evaluate our proposed methodology and gain early-stage feedback, which is presented in Sect. 4.

### 3.2    Stimulus

The contextual data used in this study was acquired from a microwave drying process for polymer materials monitored by a specific genre of IPT – microwave tomography (MWT). This imaging modality was applied to detect the moisture levels and distribution of the polymer material through specific tomography imaging algorithms [38]. Three different visualizations were employed in this study, obtained from three dissimilar MWT drying processes including two in 3D and one in 2D, as 3D figures incorporate more information regarding the polymer materials used in the process. The three visualizations were positioned individually in three interchangeable interfaces with three virtual buttons arranged on the right-hand side to switch to another. An example including one 3D visualization and the buttons are shown in Fig. 3. As displayed, different moisture levels are rendered with distinct colors and marked A, B, C and D, denoting low moisture area, moderate moisture, the dry part, and the high moisture area respectively. The annotations were created based on the physical understanding by the domain expert tightly correlated to the process. Nevertheless, it is critical

**Fig. 3.** An example scene of the user interacting with one of the three visualizations derived from IPT in AR environment. Different colors and the annotations represent different moisture levels of the polymer material after the microwave drying process. Virtual buttons [6] for switching to alternative visualizations are located on the right side. ([6] The darker background and white grid lines were only visible during the app activation and the screenshot capture process, but not visible during the experiment.)

for users who intend to deal with IPT related analysis, regardless of their expertise, to fully understand the contextual information for in-depth visualization analysis.

### 3.3 Apparatus

For the environmental configuration of our AR system, we used Microsoft HoloLens 2 glasses; the specialized OST HMD with one dedicated application developed on it. This HMD weighs 566 grams with a built-in battery, and has see-through holographic lenses, a SoC Qualcomm Snapdragon 850, and a second-generation custom-built holographic processing unit. All of these characteristics enable the user to wear it freely and comfortably. The AR application was developed with Unity3D 2020.3.20f1 and Mixed Reality Toolkit 2.7 (MRTK). MRTK is an open-source development kit for creating MR applications for Microsoft HoloLens and Windows MR devices. It provides a number of fundamental components to build user interfaces and interactions in mixed reality settings. The MRTK components "NearInteractionTouchable" and "NearInteractionGrabbable" were combined in this application to provide hand tracking and touch input on the visualization figures. Additionally, the offered "ObjectManipulator" component was utilized to allow users to grab and move the figures with their hands, with gestures like translation, rotation, and scale enabled. Furthermore, three virtual buttons were created for switching between visualization figures using the "PressableRoundButton" component. For the conventional visualization analysis settings, a 16-in. MacBook Pro (3072 * 1920) with the operating system macOS Monterey version 12.3.1 was used to conduct the comparison study. The actual tool used for users to observe and manipulate the data visualizations in the conventional setting was Matlab_R2021_a (the common tool used in IPT related visualization and analysis [38]) with visualization window.

## 4   Experiment Design

A user study was conducted to find out whether our proposed AR approach, offering interactive and immersive experience for communicating with IPT visualizations, was superior to customary in-situ data analysis pertaining to supporting users' understandability and user experience. The main realization of this study was two different scenarios where the engaged participants encountered two different environments; our proposed AR approach to interact with the data representations with the aid of OST HMD; and the conventional setting using an ordinary computer with 2D screen and Matlab (only the visualization window was utilized for the experiment). Three tasks were designed towards IPT contextual visualization analysis for the participants to implement. We selected the within-subjects principle and examined all the participants in both scenarios, and their performance when dealing with the data visualizations by means of several specific domain tasks. To precisely investigate the feedback as well as mitigate the order effect from the displacement of the two environmental settings, we followed the counterbalancing design principle [9]. We divided the participants into two groups (AR-first group equipped with the AR approach and baseline-first group equipped with conventional computer involving a 2D screen at the beginning) with ten people in each. The AR-first group was first equipped with our AR system to complete the tasks, then they were shifted to the conventional computer with 2D screen for the same tasks while the baseline-first group was treated in the reverse order. After task completion, each participant was directed to fill in a post-study questionnaire followed by a short interview session. The total study duration was 12–18 min. As aforementioned, the ultimate goal of the designed system was to assist domain users for better in-depth comprehension of the IPT data, allowing better visualization analysis through the AR technique. Therefore, the following hypotheses were made in our study regarding IPT contextual data visualization and task performing:

- **H1:** Our proposed AR approach can obtain better understandability for users compared to using the conventional setting.
- **H2:** Our proposed AR approach can contribute to a lower task completion time and fewer task errors.
- **H3:** Our proposed AR approach has better usability for users to interact with IPT data visualizations.
- **H4:** Our proposed AR approach has a greater recommendation level than the conventional setting.

### 4.1   Participants

Twenty participants ($n = 20$, 12 self-identified male and 8 self-identified female) aged between 24 and 41 ($M = 30.1$, $SD = 4.78$) were recruited by either e-mail or personal invitations at a local university. All the participants were proficient in dealing with most of the computer operations within the MacOS system. They were first asked about their familiarity and prior experience with AR in general as well as any previous exposure to IPT. Only two reported occasional experience with AR while four had previous experience with IPT. The proficiency of Matlab was not considered since the participants were merely required to conduct the tasks within the Matlab visualization window through simple operations without any coding procedures or data creation. Participants were then evenly and randomly divided into the AR-first group ($n = 10$) and baseline-first group ($n = 10$). None reported any kind of discomfort when wearing the HMD while each completely finished the whole study procedure, and none reported circumstances of mis-seeing any virtual objects through HoloLens 2. The study was conducted in a bright and spacious function room without any other distractors. We acted in strict accordance with the Covid-19 rules in each step of the study. Each participant was rewarded with a small gift for helping with the study. All the data collection conformed with the ethical guidelines of the local university where the study was carried out.

## 4.2   Procedure

All participants signed an informed consent at the beginning of each session, which stated that there would be no personal information collected and that they could quit the study at any time. They were also told that the sessions would be audio-recorded, but all recordings would be treated confidentially, and references would only be made in a purely anonymized form for scientific analysis. All participants had sufficient time to read the consent form and ask questions before signing it. Due to the high professionality and complexity of IPT, the data generated is usually difficult to interpret by outsiders, even some experts. Hence, we started our study with a concise but detailed introduction about the study background, including the fundamental schematic of IPT, the source of the data visualizations, and the basic information about the visualizations used in this study. Before we began with the actual study sessions, we calibrated the Microsoft HoloLens glasses for each participant by helping them follow the instructions from the built-in calibration functional module. A short pre-training session was implemented to get the participants familiarized and adapted to the HMD and the AR application used.

The entire study procedure is displayed in Fig. 4. Participants were required to complete three micro tasks regarding three selected figures to become familiarized with the IPT data visualizations as well as interacting with them in-situ. Each person had the identical opportunity to use both our AR system and the conventional tools to complete the tasks. Figure 5 shows an example scene of a participant being equipped with the two different environmental settings. They were also told they could convey real-time feedback in any form during the task implementation. The first task was called Observation, in which the participants were required to inspect the three visualizations (one 2D and two 3D figures), reading the introduction for five minutes but free to move to the next task of they felt ready. This was to familiarize them with IPT and also consolidate the information. After that they went onto the second task – Manipulation. This required them to interact with the visualizations by dragging, rotating, and

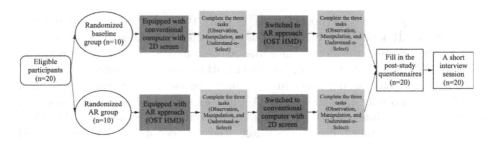

**Fig. 4.** Flowchart of our user study with counterbalancing design.

zooming in/out with either the AR context in the OST HMD or Matlab visualization window in the conventional computer. When manipulating with the AR glasses, they were free to walk around the visualizations to carry out the designated interactions. The last task was Understand-n-Select, where they were required to select four from a number of annotated pre-marked areas representing different moisture levels of the polymer materials on the three figures. The "Understand" component referred to that the participants had to understand the questions given related to IPT and annotations marked on the visualizations. The "Select" component implied that participants commenced doing practical tasks after understanding. All figures (2D and 3D) were shown identically in each environmental setting but the participants had to select four different areas by switching from one environment setting to another (they informed the authors the answers after the selection). The questions presented to the two settings are listed below.

### AR Approach:

- For Visualization 1, select the one area of moderate moisture level.
- For Visualization 2, the two areas of high and low moisture levels.
- For Visualization 3, select the one area of low moisture level.

### Conventional Setting:

- For Visualization 1, select the two areas of high moisture level and dry area.
- For Visualization 2, select the one area of moderate moisture level.
- For Visualization 3, select the one area of dry area.

Participants were not allowed to refer to previous information when doing the tasks. We measured the task completion time (TCT) and the error rate of Understand-n-Select merely, since we believed it sufficient that it represented the hands-on task performance of the IPT visualization analysis. After task completion in both of the settings, a post-study questionnaire containing a few questions with quantitative scales to rate was completed. Finally, everyone was asked to attend a short interview session.

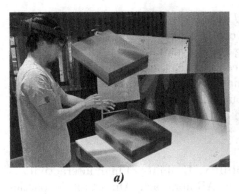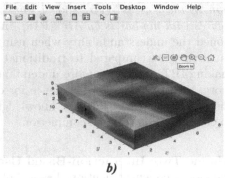

a)                                        b)

**Fig. 5.** User study example scene of the two environmental settings. *a*: AR approach–the participant equipped with the OST HMD is interacting with the three IPT visualizations studied in this paper for data analysis. **Note:** the three visualizations are not placed together in one scene as the figure shows; they are placed individually in three different switchable interfaces in the AR app. *b*: Conventional computer with 2D screen–the IPT visualization is placed in a Matlab visualization window for participants to interact with. The 2D figure represents the surface information while 3D figures represent the volumetric information of the polymer materials used in the study.

## 4.3  Qualitative Results

We compiled the results collected from the post interview sessions and real-time feedback of the participants during the study. The qualitative measurements generalized by a thematic analysis are presented in this section. The real-time feedback was conveyed spontaneously by the participants and recorded by the authors. For the post study interview, we asked the participants several subjective questions regarding what they liked and disliked about the tasks regarding our AR approach as well as the comparison between the two tested environmental settings. Concerning privacy and anonymity, we denoted the participants as P1 to P20 when recording the real-time feedback and encoding the interview answers. Based on the codes, we derived three themes: in-task understandability, interaction-based usability, and user experience.

**Theme One: In-Task Understandability.** It became apparent that the AR approach contributed to the understandability of the tasks' complex IPT data. Nearly half of the participants reported that the AR approach assisted in their understanding of the tasks, as it enabled convenient observation and offered useful information. For instance, when doing the tasks in the AR setting, P7 commented: *"Now I understand the introduction better when playing with these [the figures] in AR"* and P15 remarked: *"It's really helpful for me to understand the IPT by observing the visualizations in a 3D space"*. For similar reasons, P8 reported: *"It was convenient to manipulate the visualizations near me, which was good for tasks"*. Furthermore, some owed their preference for the AR approach over conventional computers by articulating *"3D objects present more informa-*

*tion in the glasses"* (P5) and *"I think I can see more content by rotating the figures with my hands by AR"* (P18). In contrast, none of the participants mentioned the understandability when using the conventional computer. This indicates that, as compared to traditional computers, the AR approach excels at making IPT data tasks more understandable, which supports our **H1**. Furthermore, a certain degree of evidence for our **H2** is shown by the fact that when the participants had a better knowledge of the IPT data, they were less likely to commit errors in task completion.

**Theme Two: Interaction-Based Usability.** Usability of high interactivity is the most frequently mentioned aspect of the AR approach. Almost all the participants commented that the approach presented high usability in an immersive, interactive manner, whereas they deemed the interactivity of the conventional interface undesirable: e.g., *"it was difficult to rotate and amplify them [the figures] in Matlab window especially when I wanted deeper observation, but it was very convenient to observe them [the figures] in AR"* (P3), and *"It was nearly impossible to manipulate the figures in the computer. It felt nice to interact with an object in 3D"* (P5). Such remarks pointed out the manipulation of quality enabled by the AR approach. In essence, they helped confirm **H3** by acknowledging the approach's better usability for user interaction with the data visualizations than conventional computers. Moreover, the participants provided further explanations for the high usability perceived, as they gave credit to intuitive hand gestures and immersive 3D space distance. As for hand gestures, for example, P4 reported: *"To use my hands to manipulate the figures in 3D is preferable"*. P9 reported: *"It felt very intuitive to move the objects [the figures], and zoom in becomes easier"*. In addition, some who had visualization-related experience in Matlab discovered: *"It was easy to switch to another figure in AR by my hands. There is no need to generate different codes as I usually did in Matlab"* (P10). When it comes to space distance, some found that the close distance from the 3D objects to them contributed to the interaction and usability, and remarked that *"In AR, it was amazing to see the figures can be manipulated in desired way. I could make them [the figures] closer to me and see them more clearly"* (P4), and that *"The interaction is really nice. It was cool to closely interact with the figures"* (P8). Comparatively, P14 affirmed: *"It's super hard to zoom in the figures and it's impossible to move them in Matlab visualization window since the positions are fixed"*. To summarize, the AR approach achieved its satisfying usability mainly by allowing for immersive interaction, which enabled participants to manipulate the data visualizations in the 3D space using their hands.

**Theme Three: User Experience.** Finally comes the theme of user experience offered by the AR approach, which most participants found to be favorable. Some described their use experience as pleasant: e.g., *"The interaction with the figures in AR was adorable. It made me feel pleasant"* (P2), *"It felt nice to interact with them [the figures] in 3D"* (P8), and *"It was amazing to see AR with interaction"* (P9). Some discovered that *"The immersion was really nice"* (P7), and that *"The*

*3D visualizations made me feel real"* (P3). In addition, some deemed the task completion process enjoyable, because they *"had fun exploring 3D space"* (P1), *"The interaction in AR was interesting"* (P5), and *"The interactive method in AR was easy to use. I enjoyed exploring the objects [the figures] there."* (P9). It can be seen that most participants gained good user experience when interacting with and explore the data visualizations immersively. Conversely, most participants expressed negative attitudes towards performing the tasks in the conventional computer. For example, P1 reported that *"I could not do it properly in Matlab, but AR gave me gunny experience"*, P4 reported that *"It was nearly impossible to manipulate the figures in the computer"*, and P8 reported that *"It was horrible to interact with the figures in the computer"*. In other words, the AR approach has the potential to provide more enjoyable experiences than those frustrating ones experienced with conventional computers, which addresses **H3** to some extent.

### 4.4    Quantitative Results

We present our quantitative measurements here. The independent variables were identified as the two different environmental settings. From the study process and post-study questionnaire, five metrics – TCT, understandability, error rate, usability, and recommendation level employed as dependent variables were investigated. The TCT was merely measured from Understand-n-Select since this task is representative for practical IPT visualization analysis. To test the understandability, a 7-point Likert scale was adopted for participants to rate the level of the two environmental settings helping with understanding complex IPT data. The error was also exclusively collected from the third task when users were supposed to select the designated areas. The largest number of errors was four in each environmental setting. Every error, if one occurred, was noted during the study and the error rate was thereby calculated by the authors. The system usability scale (SUS) [4] was harnessed to quantify the usability. We uniquely investigated the recommendation level by asking the participants the extent (the 7-point Likert scale) of recommending the two environmental settings. We statistically analyzed the collected results to identify any significance among the four metrics evaluated. Normality was checked as a prerequisite.

**Understandability.** This metric was targeted to justify **H1** which states that the proposed AR approach has a better impact in facilitating IPT visualization analysis. Since the requirement of normality of the collected data did not suffice, a Wilcoxon signed-rank test (non-parametric dependent t-test, confidence interval (CI) 95%) was then implemented to verify the statistical significance. The result showed that the understandability of the AR approach ($M = 5.75$; $SD = 1.36$) elicits a statistically significant lead over the conventional setting ($M = 3.00$, $SD = 1.41$) in IPT contextual understanding ($Z = -2.290, p = 0.022$). Actually, the median understandability levels were rated as 6 and 3 for AR approach and conventional setting respectively as shown in Fig. 6.a. Also, it shows most of the participants perceived a much higher understandability level with the aid of OST HMD AR in contrast to the conventional settings.

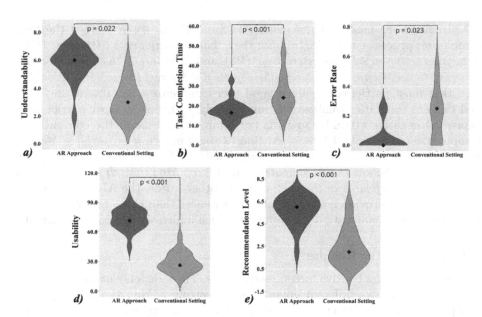

**Fig. 6.** Statistical results between the AR approach and the conventional setting. *a*: The distribution of the understandability levels (1 to 7) rated by participants. *b*: The distribution of task completion time (s). *c*: The distribution of the error rate (0.00 to 1.00). *d*: The distribution of the SUS scores representing usability (0 to 100). *e*: The distribution of the recommendation levels (1 to 7).

**Task Completion Time (TCT).** The TCTs in the Understand-n-Select task verified **H2**. As we elaborated, the reason we only measured the time periods generated from this micro-task was due to them representing the practical IPT visualization task solving. Since the normality of the data was confirmed, a dependent t-test (95% CI) was implemented which determined that the mean TCT used with the AR approach ($M = 17.56$, $SD = 5.31$) possessed a statistically significant decline compared to that consumed by the conventional setting ($M = 25.66$; $SD = 9.49$), ($t(19) = -3.967$, $p < 0.001$), as shown in Fig. 6.*b*. The median TCT with the use of AR was 16.47 while that of the conventional setting (24.05) had a noticeable lead (nearly 8s). In other words, participants obtained an obvious performance improvement with our proposed AR approach when conducting IPT related visualization analysis.

**Error Rate.** The numbers of errors were gathered to investigate **H2** as well. After the error rate was calculated, we conducted the normality test but it did not show normal distribution on both of the groups. Likewise, we implemented a Wilcoxon signed-rank test with 95% CI to measure the significance of the two tested scenarios. The result indicated a significant difference between the error rate of the AR approach ($M = 0.02$; $SD = 0.07$) and that of conventional setting ($M = 0.19$; $SD = 0.19$) with $Z = -2.271$, $p = 0.023$. As shown in Fig. 6.*c*, the distribution plot shows that participants with AR equipment tended to generate much lower error rates when conducting the IPT domain tasks in comparison to being placed in front of the conventional computers. Noteworthily, most of the participants committed 0 errors during the task completion in AR.

**Usability. H3** was designed for examining the usability of our methodology. The fiducial SUS questionnaire was engaged to evaluate the practical usability of the proposed AR approach in helping with IPT visualization analysis. The individual scale values were collected and then calculated to obtain a final SUS score for each participant. A pre-requisite normality testing was implemented and the SUS scores showed normal distribution over the two group conditions. Here, a dependent t-test (95% CI) determined that the mean usability in the AR approach ($M = 72.71$, $SD = 13.12$) differed statistically from the usability in the conventional setting ($M = 29.38$; $SD = 11.03$), ($t(11) = 6.614$, $p < 0.001$). As illustrated in Fig. 6.$d$, the median SUS score achieved by the AR approach had an evident lead to conventional setting, implying that satisfactory usability of the proposed AR approach is fully disclosed. In fact, the majority of the participants admitted a substantial exceeding in usability and user experience of the AR method, compared to the conventional settings when tackling IPT contextual visualization analysis.

**Recommendation Level.** This metric was harnessed to demonstrate **H4**. During the study, each participant was asked to rate how likely they would recommend the two different approaches. As the normality of the collected data was not exhibited, we used a Wilcoxon signed-rank test to identify the statistical significance of the recommendation level. The result indicated that the reported recommendation level from the AR approach ($M = 5.70$; $SD = 1.30$) elicits a statistically significant superiority to the conventional setting ($M = 2.45$, $SD = 1.61$) in IPT contextual visualization tasks ($Z = -3.366$, $p < 0.001$). As Fig. 6.$e$ shows, the median values of the recommendation level were calculated as 6 and 2 for the AR approach and conventional computer with 2D screen respectively as shown in Fig. 6. This shows that most of the participants were willing to recommend the OST HMD AR in contrast to the conventional setting regarding IPT related visualization analysis.

## 5   Discussion

### 5.1   Findings

Through the qualitative and quantitative measurements, we rephrase our main findings as follows. When it refers to IPT related visualization and analysis:

- The proposed AR approach with OST HMD can provide better understandability compared to conventional computers with 2D screen.

- The proposed AR approach helps users obtain a lower task completion time and fewer domain task errors.
- The proposed AR approach can provide better user experience with higher usability regarding interactions.
- The proposed AR approach is preferred by users.

## 5.2  Reflections

In this study we proposed a framed AR approach to benefit users in the context of IPT visualization analysis. Due the reason that we intended to bring portable AR devices with virtual IPT data visualizations while having the capacity to monitor the ongoing industrial processes in reality, we embraced the AR technique instead of virtual reality (VR). The proof-of-concept of the AR framework was achieved in HoloLens 2 and the evaluation of a within-subject user study with counterbalancing design was implemented based on the 20 recruited participants to verify the four raised hypotheses. The qualitative and quantitative resolution demonstrated better understandability for users facing complex IPT data, a lower error rate in related IPT domain task performing, and advanced usability for offering exceptional user experience compared to the conventional setting.

The total duration of the study fluctuated around 15 min, which was advisable and did not cause tiredness of participants in line with our observation. Following [18,55], the "Gorilla arm" effect of fatiguing arms might occur if interacting with tangible/virtual displays for too long, especially in XR environments. We did not consider this as a drawback since our study lasted for an appropriate duration and the effect of the time period on analytical tasks was beyond the scope. However, this factor should be considered as an inspiration for future study design.

Generally, the raw data derived from specialized IPT monitored industrial processes are difficult to interpret [37], requiring more advanced tools and techniques for users to conduct in-depth visualization analysis. Our approach offers a complete conceptualization with the realization of an immersive AR method with the aid of OST HMD towards IPT. Our participants were highly favorable towards its interactive features. In particular, the convenient and immersive interactions were highlighted by them to facilitate better comprehension on IPT data, since the conventional settings did not provide the corresponding functions. While no previous work emphasized this, we structured a systematic AR framework with high interaction capabilities for IPT users. In addition, this attribute further facilitated our users' understanding of IPT which resulted in better task performing. Especially, according to Beheiry et al. [16], the immersive experience of VR which makes people feel spatially realistic of 3D data can lead to a "wow" effect by users. We believe that our AR approach brings similar immersion and "wow" effect to users, contributing to high user satisfaction, which is deemed to be an advantage of the proposed methodology since few IPT practitioners have been exposed to AR. Applied to the industrial world, we see the approach enhancing the user experience of a related tooling environment.

Another important property to be realized is the ubiquity and knowledge transferability of the proposed AR approach. It is noteworthy that most of the participants praised the effect of our AR approach of enabling them to understand the context of IPT which resulted in favorable domain task performance. As most of the participants had little experience in IPT, we are therefore encouraged about the potential for our method to bring outsiders to this specialized technique for domain supporting. Additionally, although the data used in this study was generated from a specific IPT – MWT, the diverse genres of IPT have high transferability since they comply with similar mechanisms and imaging principles [62]. It is fair to say that the superiority revealed in our AR approach is highly transferable to different genres of IPT.

## 5.3 Limitations

Even though we obtained early-stage satisfactory results, we have to acknowledge that there still exist some shortcomings. Foremost, the virtual buttons for switching different figures in the AR application were reported as not sensitive enough even if they worked well in this study, particularly due to the limitations of the AR device's distance detecting technology. This could require users to press for longer than they would with physical buttons, causing fatigue and affecting task performance. Additionally, the buttons were designed to be medium in size and positioned on the lower right side of the participants' field of view so that they did not interfere with their manipulation of 3D figures. This could cause the buttons to be relatively small, far, and inconvenient for users to touch. Finally, the lack of haptic feedback may cause confusion when interacting with the virtual buttons, even though visual and aural feedback was provided by the buttons to show whether users had hovered and pressed the button or not.

To address these issues, future editions of the application could experiment with other button positions, sizes, and feedback mechanisms, as well as incorporate advanced hand gesture recognition technologies. Larger buttons, for example, might be shifted to users' top right side while allowing flexibility for movement by users. Incorporating haptic cues would also improve the user experience when interacting with virtual buttons.

Although hand gestures in AR space are intuitive and highly close to what people commonly do in physical reality, some participants reported a tiny difficulty when the app was initiated. There could be a brief tutorial about basic operation gestures when the participants activate the app, for instance, a short guided video where a pair of virtual hands show how to seize and rotate the virtual objects by pinching fingers and moving arms could be instructive.

Nonetheless, even though the obtained results were satisfying as early-stage feedback, we admit that the experiment itself and the contextual IPT data were monotonous and small scale. To rectify this, the number of participants engaged could be enlarged and more types of experimental design for evaluation could be added. The stimuli in this paper had only three visualizations derived from different industrial processes supervised by the specific MWT, which lacks diversity. More manifold data from other genres of IPT could be examined to make the results more robust.

## 6   Conclusions and Future Work

In this paper, we proposed a novel AR approach with OST HMD for users to immersively interact with the specific IPT data visualizations for contextual understanding and task performing. As the first mechanism of furnishing IPT related users with OST HMD AR, three key findings were explored from our proposed approach. The early-stage advantageous understandability, reduced TCT, lower error rate, greater usability, and higher recommendation level of the methodology were reflected through a within-subject user study. We brought this technique to traditional industrial surroundings, filling the gap between AR developers and IPT domain users. We observed its superiority over the current standard IPT visualization analytical environment, indicating that the immersion in 3D AR outperforms conventional 2D screen computers in enhancing contextual understanding and user experience.

In future, we will firstly concentrate on upgrading the AR app by improving the design of the virtual buttons on the interface, especially focusing on the size design, the touch sensitivity, and the design of the haptic feedback of the buttons as aforementioned. Correspondingly, we will give more early guidance for users to get better adaptation with the app. In addition, another concern will be increasing the experimental diversity by, for instance, involving a larger number of participants including both experts and outsiders and adding more nonidentical experiments with distinct design principles (e.g., between-subject). Promoting inclusivity and diversity of domain users across all races and genders (e.g., engaging non-binary participants) will be at the forefront of our endeavors. Our work benchmarks the intersection between OST HMD AR and IPT to highlight the future direction of bringing more related and advanced techniques into different industrial scenarios. We hope it will lead to better strategic design within this context and bring more interdisciplinary novelty to Industry 4.0 [13].

**Acknowledgements.** This project has received funding from the European Union's Horizon 2020 research and innovation programme under the Marie Sklodowska-Curie grant agreement No. 764902. This work was also partly supported by the Norges Forskningsrad (309339, 314578), MediaFutures user partners and Universitetet i Bergen.

## References

1. Alves, J.B., Marques, B., Ferreira, C., Dias, P., Santos, B.S.: Comparing augmented reality visualization methods for assembly procedures. Virtual Reality **26**(1), 235–248 (2022)
2. Avalle, G., De Pace, F., Fornaro, C., Manuri, F., Sanna, A.: An augmented reality system to support fault visualization in industrial robotic tasks. IEEE Access **7**, 132343–132359 (2019)
3. Azuma, R.T.: A survey of augmented reality. Teleop. Virtual Environ. **6**(4), 355–385 (1997)
4. Bangor, A., Kortum, P.T., Miller, J.T.: An empirical evaluation of the system usability scale. Int. J. Hum.-Comput. Interact. **24**(6), 574–594 (2008)

5. Beck, M.S., et al.: Process Tomography: Principles, Techniques and Applications. Butterworth-Heinemann (2012)
6. Besançon, L., Issartel, P., Ammi, M., Isenberg, T.: Mouse, tactile, and tangible input for 3D manipulation. In: Proceedings of the 2017 CHI Conference on Human Factors in Computing Systems, pp. 4727–4740 (2017)
7. Billinghurst, M., Clark, A., Lee, G., et al.: A survey of augmented reality. Found. Trends® Hum.–Comput. Interact. **8**(2–3), 73–272 (2015)
8. Bottani, E., Vignali, G.: Augmented reality technology in the manufacturing industry: a review of the last decade. IISE Trans. **51**(3), 284–310 (2019)
9. Bradley, J.V.: Complete counterbalancing of immediate sequential effects in a Latin square design. J. Am. Stat. Assoc. **53**(282), 525–528 (1958)
10. Bruno, F., Caruso, F., De Napoli, L., Muzzupappa, M.: Visualization of industrial engineering data visualization of industrial engineering data in augmented reality. J. Visual. **9**(3), 319–329 (2006)
11. Büttner, S., Funk, M., Sand, O., Röcker, C.: Using head-mounted displays and in-situ projection for assistive systems: a comparison. In: Proceedings of the 9th ACM International Conference on Pervasive Technologies Related to Assistive Environments, pp. 1–8 (2016)
12. Chen, C., et al.: Using crowdsourcing for scientific analysis of industrial tomographic images. ACM Trans. Intell. Syst. Technol. (TIST) **7**(4), 1–25 (2016)
13. De Pace, F., Manuri, F., Sanna, A.: Augmented reality in industry 4.0. Am. J. ComptSci. Inform. Technol. **6**(1), 17 (2018)
14. Dubois, E., Nigay, L., Troccaz, J.: Consistency in augmented reality systems. In: Little, M.R., Nigay, L. (eds.) EHCI 2001. LNCS, vol. 2254, pp. 111–122. Springer, Heidelberg (2001). https://doi.org/10.1007/3-540-45348-2_13
15. Dunn, D., Tursun, O., Yu, H., Didyk, P., Myszkowski, K., Fuchs, H.: Stimulating the human visual system beyond real world performance in future augmented reality displays. In: 2020 IEEE International Symposium on Mixed and Augmented Reality (ISMAR), pp. 90–100. IEEE (2020)
16. El Beheiry, M., Doutreligne, S., Caporal, C., Ostertag, C., Dahan, M., Masson, J.B.: Virtual reality: beyond visualization. J. Mol. Biol. **431**(7), 1315–1321 (2019)
17. Ens, B., et al.: Grand challenges in immersive analytics. In: Proceedings of the 2021 CHI Conference on Human Factors in Computing Systems, pp. 1–17 (2021)
18. Feuchtner, T., Müller, J.: Ownershift: facilitating overhead interaction in virtual reality with an ownership-preserving hand space shift. In: Proceedings of the 31st Annual ACM Symposium on User Interface Software and Technology, pp. 31–43 (2018)
19. Fite-Georgel, P.: Is there a reality in industrial augmented reality? In: 2011 10th IEEE International Symposium on Mixed and Augmented Reality, pp. 201–210. IEEE (2011)
20. Hampel, U., et al.: A review on fast tomographic imaging techniques and their potential application in industrial process control. Sensors **22**(6), 2309 (2022)
21. Heemsbergen, L., Bowtell, G., Vincent, J.: Conceptualising augmented reality: from virtual divides to mediated dynamics. Convergence **27**(3), 830–846 (2021)
22. Henderson, S.J., Feiner, S.K.: Augmented reality in the psychomotor phase of a procedural task. In: 2011 10th IEEE International Symposium on Mixed and Augmented Reality, pp. 191–200. IEEE (2011)
23. Ismail, I., Gamio, J., Bukhari, S.A., Yang, W.: Tomography for multi-phase flow measurement in the oil industry. Flow Meas. Instrum. **16**(2–3), 145–155 (2005)

24. Jasche, F., Hoffmann, S., Ludwig, T., Wulf, V.: Comparison of different types of augmented reality visualizations for instructions. In: Proceedings of the 2021 CHI Conference on Human Factors in Computing Systems, pp. 1–13 (2021)

25. Kahl, D., Ruble, M., Krüger, A.: Investigation of size variations in optical see-through tangible augmented reality. In: 2021 IEEE International Symposium on Mixed and Augmented Reality (ISMAR), pp. 147–155. IEEE (2021)

26. Kalkofen, D., Mendez, E., Schmalstieg, D.: Comprehensible visualization for augmented reality. IEEE Trans. Visual Comput. Graph. 15(2), 193–204 (2008)

27. Khan, F.A., et al.: Measuring the perceived three-dimensional location of virtual objects in optical see-through augmented reality. In: 2021 IEEE International Symposium on Mixed and Augmented Reality (ISMAR), pp. 109–117. IEEE (2021)

28. Kress, B., Saeedi, E., Brac-de-la Perriere, V.: The segmentation of the HMD market: optics for smart glasses, smart eyewear, AR and VR headsets. Photon. Appl. Aviat. Aerosp. Commercial Harsh Environ. V 9202, 107–120 (2014)

29. Leebmann, J.: An augmented reality system for earthquake disaster response. Int. Arch. Photogram. Remote Sens. Spatial Inf. Sci. 34(Part XXX) (2004)

30. Liu11, X., Sohn, Y.H., Park, D.W.: Application development with augmented reality technique using unity 3D and Vuforia. Int. J. Appl. Eng. Res. 13(21), 15068–15071 (2018)

31. Lorenz, M., Knopp, S., Klimant, P.: Industrial augmented reality: requirements for an augmented reality maintenance worker support system. In: 2018 IEEE International Symposium on Mixed and Augmented Reality Adjunct (ISMAR-Adjunct), pp. 151–153. IEEE (2018)

32. Mann, R., Stanley, S., Vlaev, D., Wabo, E., Primrose, K.: Augmented-reality visualization of fluid mixing in stirred chemical reactors using electrical resistance tomography. J. Electron. Imaging 10(3), 620–630 (2001)

33. Masood, T., Egger, J.: Adopting augmented reality in the age of industrial digitalisation. Comput. Ind. 115, 103112 (2020)

34. Mourtzis, D., Siatras, V., Zogopoulos, V.: Augmented reality visualization of production scheduling and monitoring. Procedia CIRP 88, 151–156 (2020)

35. Nolet, G.: Seismic tomography: with Applications in Global Seismology and Exploration Geophysics, vol. 5. Springer, Heidelberg (2012). https://doi.org/10.1007/978-94-009-3899-1

36. Nowak, A., Woźniak, M., Rowińska, Z., Grudzień, K., Romanowski, A.: Towards in-situ process tomography data processing using augmented reality technology. In: Adjunct Proceedings of the 2019 ACM International Joint Conference on Pervasive and Ubiquitous Computing and Proceedings of the 2019 ACM International Symposium on Wearable Computers, pp. 168–171 (2019)

37. Nowak, A., Zhang, Y., Romanowski, A., Fjeld, M.: Augmented reality with industrial process tomography: to support complex data analysis in 3D space. In: Adjunct Proceedings of the 2021 ACM International Joint Conference on Pervasive and Ubiquitous Computing and Proceedings of the 2021 ACM International Symposium on Wearable Computers, pp. 56–58 (2021)

38. Omrani, A., Yadav, R., Link, G., Jelonnek, J.: A multistatic uniform diffraction tomography algorithm for microwave imaging in multilayered media for microwave drying. IEEE Trans. Antennas Propag. (2022)

39. Ong, S.K., Nee, A.Y.C.: Virtual and Augmented Reality Applications in Manufacturing. Springer, Dordrecht (2013). https://doi.org/10.1007/978-94-009-3899-1

40. Peillard, E., Itoh, Y., Moreau, G., Normand, J.M., Lécuyer, A., Argelaguet, F.: Can retinal projection displays improve spatial perception in augmented reality? In: 2020 IEEE International Symposium on Mixed and Augmented Reality (ISMAR), pp. 80–89. IEEE (2020)
41. Pierdicca, R., Frontoni, E., Zingaretti, P., Malinverni, E.S., Colosi, F., Orazi, R.: Making visible the invisible. Augmented reality visualization for 3D reconstructions of archaeological sites. In: De Paolis, L.T., Mongelli, A. (eds.) AVR 2015. LNCS, vol. 9254, pp. 25–37. Springer, Cham (2015). https://doi.org/10.1007/978-3-319-22888-4_3
42. Plaskowski, A., Beck, M., Thorn, R., Dyakowski, T.: Imaging Industrial Flows: Applications of Electrical Process Tomography. CRC Press, Boca Raton (1995)
43. Primrose, K.: Application of process tomography in nuclear waste processing. In: Industrial Tomography, pp. 713–725. Elsevier, Amsterdam (2015)
44. Rao, G., Aghajanian, S., Zhang, Y., Strumillo, L.J., Koiranen, T., Fjeld, M.: Monitoring and visualization of crystallization processes using electrical resistance tomography: Caco3 and sucrose crystallization case studies (2022)
45. Regenbrecht, H., Baratoff, G., Wilke, W.: Augmented reality projects in the automotive and aerospace industries. IEEE Comput. Graph. Appl. **25**(6), 48–56 (2005)
46. Satkowski, M., Dachselt, R.: Investigating the impact of real-world environments on the perception of 2D visualizations in augmented reality. In: Proceedings of the 2021 CHI Conference on Human Factors in Computing Systems, pp. 1–15 (2021)
47. Sobiech, F., et al.: Exploratory analysis of users' interactions with AR data visualisation in industrial and neutral environments (2022)
48. de Souza Cardoso, L.F., Mariano, F.C.M.Q., Zorzal, E.R.: A survey of industrial augmented reality. Comput. Ind. Eng. **139**, 106159 (2020)
49. Speicher, M., Hall, B.D., Nebeling, M.: What is mixed reality? In: Proceedings of the 2019 CHI Conference on Human Factors in Computing Systems, pp. 1–15 (2019)
50. Stanley, S., Mann, R., Primrose, K.: Interrogation of a precipitation reaction by electrical resistance tomography (ERT). AIChE J. **51**(2), 607–614 (2005)
51. Tainaka, K., et al.: Guideline and tool for designing an assembly task support system using augmented reality. In: 2020 IEEE International Symposium on Mixed and Augmented Reality (ISMAR), pp. 486–497. IEEE (2020)
52. Tapp, H., Peyton, A., Kemsley, E., Wilson, R.: Chemical engineering applications of electrical process tomography. Sens. Actuators, B Chem. **92**(1–2), 17–24 (2003)
53. Tonnis, M., Sandor, C., Klinker, G., Lange, C., Bubb, H.: Experimental evaluation of an augmented reality visualization for directing a car driver's attention. In: Fourth IEEE and ACM International Symposium on Mixed and Augmented Reality (ISMAR'05), pp. 56–59. IEEE (2005)
54. Yao, J., Takei, M.: Application of process tomography to multiphase flow measurement in industrial and biomedical fields: a review. IEEE Sens. J. **17**(24), 8196–8205 (2017)
55. Zenner, A., Krüger, A.: Estimating detection thresholds for desktop-scale hand redirection in virtual reality. In: 2019 IEEE Conference on Virtual Reality and 3D User Interfaces (VR), pp. 47–55. IEEE (2019)
56. Zhang, Y., Ma, Y., Omrani, A., et al.: Automated microwave tomography (MWT) image segmentation: state-of-the-art implementation and evaluation. J. WSCG **2020**, 126–136 (2020)
57. Zhang, Y., Fjeld, M.: Condition monitoring for confined industrial process based on infrared images by using deep neural network and variants. In: Proceedings of

the 2020 2nd International Conference on Image, Video and Signal Processing, pp. 99–106 (2020)

58. Zhang, Y., Fjeld, M., Fratarcangeli, M., Said, A., Zhao, S.: Affective colormap design for accurate visual comprehension in industrial tomography. Sensors **21**(14), 4766 (2021)

59. Zhang, Y., Nowak, A., Rao, G., Romanowski, A., Fjeld, M.: Is industrial tomography ready for augmented reality? In: Chen, J.Y.C., Fragomeni, G. (eds.) HCII 2023. LNCS, vol. 14027, pp. 523–535. Springer, Cham (2023). https://doi.org/10.1007/978-3-031-35634-6_37

60. Zhang, Y., Nowak, A., Romanowski, A., Fjeld, M.: An initial exploration of visual cues in head-mounted display augmented reality for book searching. In: Proceedings of the 21st International Conference on Mobile and Ubiquitous Multimedia, p p. 273–275 (2022)

61. Zhang, Y., Nowak, A., Romanowski, A., Fjeld, M.: On-site or remote working?: An initial solution on how COVID-19 pandemic may impact augmented reality users. In: Proceedings of the 2022 International Conference on Advanced Visual Interfaces, pp. 1–3 (2022)

62. Zhang, Y., Omrani, A., Yadav, R., Fjeld, M.: Supporting visualization analysis in industrial process tomography by using augmented reality—a case study of an industrial microwave drying system. Sensors **21**(19), 6515 (2021)

63. Zhang, Y., Yadav, R., Omrani, A., Fjeld, M.: A novel augmented reality system to support volumetric visualization in industrial process tomography. In: Proceedings of the 2021 Conference on Interfaces and Human Computer Interaction, pp. 3–9 (2021)

# Supporting Construction and Architectural Visualization Through BIM and AR/VR: A Systematic Literature Review

Enes Yigitbas[✉], Alexander Nowosad, and Gregor Engels

Paderborn University, Zukunftsmeile 2, 33102 Paderborn, Germany
{enes.yigitbas,alexander.nowosad,gregor.engels}@upb.de

**Abstract.** The Architecture, Engineering, Construction, and Facility Management (AEC/FM) industry deals with the design, construction, and operation of complex buildings. Today, Building Information Modeling (BIM) is used to represent information about a building in a single, non-redundant representation. Here, Augmented Reality (AR) and Virtual Reality (VR) can improve the visualization and interaction with the resulting model by augmenting the real world with information from the BIM model or allowing a user to immerse in a virtual world generated from the BIM model. This can improve the design, construction, and operation of buildings. While an increasing number of studies in HCI, construction, or engineering have shown the potential of using AR and VR technology together with BIM, often research remains focused on individual explorations and key design strategies. In addition to that, a systematic overview and discussion of recent works combining AR/VR with BIM are not yet fully covered. Therefore, this paper systematically reviews recent approaches combining AR/VR with BIM and categorizes the literature by the building's lifecycle phase while systematically describing relevant use cases. In total, 32 out of 447 papers between 2017 and 2022 were categorized. The categorization shows that most approaches focus on the construction phase and the use case of review and quality assurance. In the design phase, most approaches use VR, while in the construction and operation phases, AR is prevalent.

**Keywords:** Design · Construction · Operation · BIM · AR · VR

## 1 Introduction

The Architecture, Engineering, and Construction (AEC) industry is essential for a country's economy [40]. For example, in Germany in 2021, the investments into construction were 416.700 billion euros, 11:6% of the Gross Domestic Product (GDP) [50]. Construction projects are complex, especially in organizational and technological aspects [34]. Thus, stakeholders in the industry need to be supported with tools to increase their performance. In the past, information about

J. Abdelnour Nocera et al. (Eds.): INTERACT 2023, LNCS 14143, pp. 145–166, 2023.
https://doi.org/10.1007/978-3-031-42283-6_8

the project has been separated into different paper documents, CAD models, and other tools, leading to inconsistencies and inefficient communication [18].

Here, Building Information Modeling (BIM) is a technology that avoids this fragmentation and prevents inconsistencies by combining the information into a non-redundant representation that can be viewed from different views [18]. This supports the entire lifecycle of a building, from the design phase over the construction up to the operation and maintenance leading to improvements for the Architecture, Engineering, Construction, and Facility Management (AEC/FM) industry [18]. The advantages of BIM are, for example, precise visualization of a building in the design phase and simulation of the construction process by adding time as a fourth dimension to the model [18]. Currently, printed 2D plans, computers, and tablets are used to show 2D or 3D models of a building. This brings many disadvantages and challenges. For example, a customer cannot see the real sizes of geometries on a computer screen, leading to wrong design decisions. Furthermore, a project manager has to manually map aspects displayed on a computer to structures in the real world to check the progress of a building, which is time-consuming. A facility manager has to orient via a 2D plan of a building and use a 2D plan of assets to repair them.

Virtual Reality (VR) and Augmented Reality (AR) have been a topic of intense research in the last decades [9, 15]. In the past few years, massive advances in affordable consumer hardware and accessible software frameworks are now bringing these technologies to the masses. While VR is a technology that allows a user to immerse in a virtual world, AR adds virtual objects to the real world [37]. These technologies can overcome the visualization issues of BIM models in different phases of the building's lifecycle. For example, a customer could experience different designs of a building through VR in an immersive way [3, 41], a project manager can use AR to check the progress of a building and the building structures are augmented with information about their progress [36, 43]. A facility manager can leverage AR to find failed assets in a building and get step-by-step guides on how to repair the assets [12, 57].

While an increasing number of such approaches and studies in HCI, construction, or engineering have shown the potential of using AR and VR technology together with BIM, often research remains focused on individual explorations and key design strategies. In addition to that, a systematic overview and discussion of recent works combining AR/VR with BIM are not yet fully covered. Therefore, this paper investigates recent developments in the field of using AR and VR as visualization tools for BIM models in all phases of a building's lifecycle with a focus on use cases and answers the following research questions (RQs):

*RQ1: What are the current use cases for using AR and VR together with BIM in the AEC/FM industry?*

*RQ2: For which use cases is AR and for which use cases is VR used and why?*

To answer the research questions, we have conducted a systematic literature review where we review recent approaches combining AR/VR with BIM. The main goal of this literature review is to categorize the literature by the building's lifecycle phase while systematically describing relevant use cases.

The remainder of this paper is as follows. Section 2 gives background information about important aspects of the research topic. Section 3 shows other surveys that have already dealt with the topic. Section 4 describes the methodology used to gather literature. Section 5 presents the results from the literature review. Section 6 sketches gaps in the literature that have the potential for further research. Section 7 shows the limitations of this work. Finally, Sect. 8 summarizes this paper and shows potential for future work.

## 2    Background

In this section, we briefly describe essential concepts from the AEC/FM industry focusing on the lifecycle phases of a building and the BIM.

### 2.1    Lifecycle Phases of a Building

The lifecycle phases of a building are essential to categorize applications based on the building's lifecycle phase in which they are used. The lifecycle of a building can be broken down into different phases. Multiple options exist, e.g., Eadie et al. [17] split the field into feasibility, design, preconstruction, construction, and operation and management, while Arditi and Gunaydin [4] use the three phases of planning and design, construction, and maintenance and operation. This paper uses the phases of *Design*, *Construction*, and *Operation*.

Here, the *Design* phase includes the feasibility and actual design of a building. Feasibility is the initial planning of a building by defining the main goals, a broad schedule, and a budget [16]. Then, the actual design of a building is done by creating detailed construction documents that define the building [16].

The *Construction* phase includes all tasks necessary for the construction, which are pre-construction and actual construction. Pre-construction is the organization of the construction works [16]. This includes detailed planning of the construction works and planning of the construction site layout, e.g., where machines and materials are placed [16]. After pre-construction, the actual construction works start where construction workers are constructing the building [16].

The *Operation* phase includes all maintenance and operation tasks after the building is finished. Here, this is taking care of the repairing of parts of the building to retain the expected functionality [2]. This can also include monitoring the building via sensor values [57].

### 2.2    BIM

Building Information Modeling (BIM) technology allows the precise construction of a digital virtual model of a building [18]. Here, this model can be viewed in different views, for example, as a 2D plan or 3D model, that are all consistent with each other [18]. Furthermore, BIM is not only the model but also has linked processes to create, communicate, and evaluate this model [18]. These processes are supported by the model, which itself is not only 3D geometric data but consists of so-called parametric objects that contain the geometry and are associated with additional data and rules [18]. Additionally, it is possible to add behavioral data to objects to allow evaluations and simulations [18]. Here, consistency plays an important role and is achieved by the non-redundant representation of geometries in the BIM model [18]. Moreover, if a parametric object in a BIM model is changed, all related objects are updated, too [18].

Through this, BIM technology can enhance the whole lifecycle of a building [18]. In the design phase, there is always one consistent representation of the building [18]. This representation allows for early visualizations in 3D, and the exports, e.g., for 2D plans, in any stage are always consistent [18]. Additionally, design changes are automatically reflected in all building parts [18]. The BIM model can also be used for early automatic evaluations, for example, to check energy efficiency [18].

In the construction phase, BIM allows for the simulation of the construction process by associating a construction plan with the parametric objects in the BIM model [18]. This simulation can reveal on-site conflicts and safety issues [18]. Additionally, it supports scheduling material orders and deliveries [6]. Furthermore, design changes in this phase are automatically updated in the BIM model, and all consequences of the change are visible [18]. Finally, the operation phase is supported by the precise and up-to-date BIM model through the knowledge of all spaces and systems in the building [18].

## 3  Related Work

Augmented Reality (AR) and Virtual Reality (VR) have been a topic of intense research in the last decades. While VR interfaces support the interaction in an immersive computer-generated 3D world and have been used in different application domains such as training [61], education [64], modeling [58], prototyping [62], or evaluation [29], AR enables the augmentation of real-world physical objects with virtual elements and has been also applied in various application domains such as product configuration (e.g., [21,22]), prototyping [27], planning and measurements [63], robot programming (e.g., [32,59]), or for realizing smart interfaces (e.g., [31,60]).

In the following, we especially focus on and present other surveys that deal with the combination of BIM and AR or VR. Additionally, we describe what makes this paper different from the related work and why a novel and updated literature review is required on this topic.

Calderon-Hernandez and Brioso [8] survey papers that use AR and BIM together in the design and construction phases. Here, they focus on the last five years from 2018 backward and main journals in the field of construction planning neglecting HCI, especially AR/VR relevant venues.

Wu et al. [55] conduct an application-focused literature review. They show gaps, challenges, and future work in the field. Furthermore, they classify the papers by their application category. The application categories, which they defined, are task guidance and information retrieval, design and refinement, process planning and control, and upskilling of the AEC workforce.

Sidani et al. [49] perform a survey of BIM-based VR. They classify the approaches by the research field, the BIM dimensions, construction stages, and target groups. Here, the research field can be collaboration, construction design, construction management, construction safety, education, or facility management.

Salem et al. [46] show different use cases for AR and VR. They state that VR is used for visualization and AR in broader applications. However, they do not provide a classification and also do not have a concrete methodology.

Wang et al. [54] develop a classification framework for AR in the built environment. Their classification framework consists of multiple parts. One of them categorizes the application area. They come up with the following areas: architecture and design, landscape and urban planning, engineering-related, construction, facility management, life cycle integration, and training and education. The literature that is reviewed is from 2005 to 2011.

Compared to the above-mentioned works, this paper considers both, AR and VR approaches combined with BIM. Additionally, all building's lifecycle phases are considered, and the surveyed literature is categorized by the building's lifecycle phase and the use case category. With this regard, our work contributes a systematic and holistic overview of recent approaches where AR and VR technologies are combined with BIM.

## 4   Methodology

In this section, we describe the methodology of the research.

To answer the research questions, which are defined in Sect. 1, we conducted a systematic literature review based on [56] focusing on concrete use cases in the AEC/FM industry that combine AR/VR with BIM. An overview of the review methodology is shown in Fig. 1. To find literature, we used Scopus[1]. Here, we used the following search terms: *bim AND ar* (87 results), *bim AND vr* (101 results), *bim AND "augmented reality"* (99 results), and *bim AND "virtual reality"* (160 results). For all search terms, the search fields were set to article title, abstract, and keywords. Additionally, the search was limited to open-access articles. Furthermore, only articles between 2017 and 2022 were considered, the language was set to English, and the document type was restricted to article or conference paper.

After exporting the results from Scopus, duplicates were removed, resulting in 251 unique results. Then, papers that were less than ten times cited according to Scopus were removed to only consider established and impactful papers with a certain relevance, resulting in 64 remaining papers. After that, irrelevant papers were removed. Here, five were removed because they are not part of the AEC/FM industry, and nine were removed because they use neither AR nor VR. Ten were

[1] www.scopus.com.

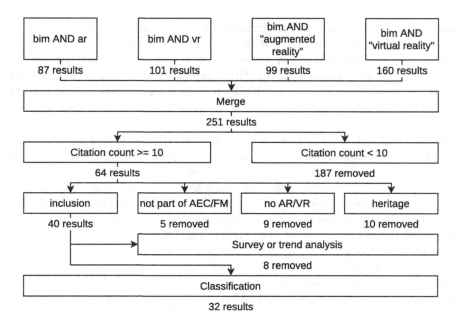

**Fig. 1.** Methodology of the conducted systematic literature review

removed because they focused on heritage and not on the design, construction, or operation of current buildings. Eight of the remaining 40 papers were removed because they are surveys or trend analyses and do not present a concrete use case that could be analyzed. After these filtering steps, 32 papers remain.

The remaining papers were categorized by whether they use AR or VR or both, which device they use, in which building's lifecycle phase the approach they present is used, and whether they present a prototype or only sketch the solution. Additionally, the use case they present was categorized.

## 5   Results

In this section, we present the results of the literature review. An overview of the categorization of the 32 papers is shown in Table 1.

The approaches are categorized by whether they use AR or VR. For AR, the definition of Azuma [7] is used. Here, already the navigation in the AR environment is counted as real-time interactivity. For VR, fully and partly immersive solutions are considered. This means it is enough for a solution to use a 3D screen. If an approach uses AR and VR, both cells are marked. It is also possible that an approach uses AR and VR for different use cases. These cases are not visible in the table but in the detailed descriptions below.

The devices are classified into different groups. The group *HMD* contains all consumer Head-Mounted Displays (HMDs) developed for AR or VR, e.g., a

**Table 1.** Categorization of identified approaches related to AR/VR and BIM

| Publication | Year | AR | VR | Device | Phase | | | | Use Case | | | | | |
|---|---|---|---|---|---|---|---|---|---|---|---|---|---|---|
| | | | | | Design | Construction | Operation | Prototype | Planning | Review & Quality Assurance | Task guidance | Safety | Education | Localization & Tracking |
| Afzal, M. et al. [1] | 2021 | | • | HMD | | • | • | | | | | • | • | |
| Azhar, S. [5] | 2017 | | • | HMD | | • | • | | | | | • | • | |
| Chalhoub, J. and Ayer, S. K. [10] | 2018 | • | | HMD | | • | • | | | | • | | | |
| Chalhoub, J. et al. [11] | 2021 | • | | HMD | | • | • | | • | | | | | |
| Chew, M. Y. L. et al. [12] | 2020 | • | • | – | | | • | | | | • | | | • |
| Dallasega, P. et al. [13] | 2020 | • | • | HMD | | • | • | • | • | | | | | |
| Diao, P.-H. and Shih, N.-J. [14] | 2019 | • | | Mobile | | | • | • | | | | • | • | |
| Garbett, J. et al. [19] | 2021 | • | | Mobile | • | • | | • | • | | | | | |
| Gomez-Jauregui, V. et al. [20] | 2019 | • | | Mobile | | • | • | | | | | | | • |
| Hasan, S. M. et al. [23] | 2022 | • | | Mobile | | • | • | | | | | • | | |
| Herbers, P. and König, M. [24] | 2019 | • | | HMD | | • | • | • | | | | | | • |
| Hernández, J. L. et al. [25] | 2018 | • | | Mobile | | • | • | | • | | | | | |
| Hübner, P. et al. [26] | 2018 | • | | HMD | | • | • | | | | | | | • |
| Kamari, A. et al. [28] | 2021 | | • | M.-HMD | • | | • | | • | | | | | |
| Khalek, I. A. et al. [30] | 2019 | • | | HMD | • | | • | | • | | | | | |
| Lou, J. et al. [33] | 2017 | • | | – | | • | | | • | | | | | |
| Mahmood, B. et al. [35] | 2020 | • | | HMD | | • | • | | | | | | | • |
| Mirshokraei, M. et al. [38] | 2019 | • | | Mobile | | • | • | | • | | | | | |
| Natephra, W. et al. [39] | 2017 | | • | HMD | • | | • | | • | | | | | |
| Pour Rahimian, F. et al. [41] | 2019 | | • | HMD | • | | • | | • | | | | | |
| Pour Rahimian, F. et al. [42] | 2020 | | • | HMD | | • | • | | • | | | | | |
| Ratajczak, J. et al. [43] | 2019 | • | | Mobile | | • | • | | | | • | | | |
| Riexinger, G. et al. [44] | 2018 | • | | Mobile&HMD | | • | • | | • | • | | | | |
| Saar, C. C. et al. [45] | 2019 | • | | Mobile | | • | • | • | • | • | | | • | |
| Schranz, C. et al. [47] | 2021 | • | | Mobile&HMD | • | | | | • | | | | | |
| Schweigkofler, A. et al. [48] | 2018 | • | | Mobile | | • | • | | • | • | | | | |
| Vasilevski, N. and Birt, J. [51] | 2020 | | • | M.-HMD | • | | • | | | | | | • | |
| Ventura, S. M. et al. [52] | 2020 | | • | Other | • | | • | | • | | | | | |
| Vincke, S. et al. [53] | 2019 | | • | HMD | | • | • | | • | | | | | |
| Xie, X. et al. [57] | 2020 | • | | HMD | | | • | • | | | • | | | |
| Zaher, M. et al. [65] | 2018 | • | | Mobile | • | | • | | • | | | | | |
| Zaker, R. and Coloma, E. [66] | 2018 | | • | HMD | • | | • | | • | | | | | |

Microsoft HoloLens[2] for AR or a Valve Index[3] for VR. Further, *M.-HMD* stands for mobile HMD and contains low-cost devices where a smartphone is mounted

---

[2] https://www.microsoft.com/en-us/hololens.

[3] https://store.steampowered.com/valveindex.

as an HMD, e.g., Google Cardboard[4]. *Mobile* contains all handheld devices, like smartphones or tablets, and *Other* contains all devices that do not fit into this classification. Additionally, if an approach uses multiple devices, they are connected by an and (&), and if they are using different devices for AR and VR, the device for AR is separated from the device for VR via a slash (/).

The building's lifecycle phases used for the categorization are *Design, Construction*, and *Operation*, as described in Sect. 2.1. If an approach is used in multiple phases, both are marked.

If a paper also presents a prototype to show the approach, the mark in the *Prototype* column is set. Otherwise, the approach is only described in the paper. If an approach is only described and does not present a prototype, the device column might be empty if a concrete device type is not mentioned.

The use cases are grouped into *Planning, Review & Quality Assurance, Task guidance, Safety*, and *Education*. A detailed description of these use case categories is given in Sect. 5.1. If an approach supports multiple use cases, all categories that can be applied are marked. Here, the table does not show which use cases are used in which building's lifecycle phases if multiple use case categories are marked. This interrelation is only visible in the detailed description below. Additionally, there is the category *Localization & Tracking* for approaches that do not focus on concrete use cases but on localization and tracking improvements on-site.

General statistics about the reviewed approaches show that AR is used by most approaches with 69%, and VR is only used by 31% of the approaches. Over half of the approaches use an HMD as a device to achieve VR or AR, followed by mobile devices with 38%. Only two approaches use a mobile HMD, and only one approach uses another device, in this case, a special 3D screen [52].

The prevalent phase in which AR or VR are used with BIM is the *Construction* phase, with 56% of the approaches. Only 28% of the approaches are used in the *Design* phase and 16% in the *Operation* phase. Almost all papers present a prototype of their approach.

The remainder of this section is as follows. Section 5.1 focuses on the first research question by defining a classification for the use cases and describing them. Section 5.2 deals with the second research question by showing when AR is preferred and when VR is preferred and giving reasons for this. Section 5.3 sums up the results to answer the research questions.

## 5.1 Use Cases for Combining BIM with AR/VR

Based on the elicited literature, five use case categories for combining AR or VR with BIM are defined. The use case categories are independent of the building's lifecycle phase in which they are used.

The first category is *Planning*. It is given whenever the BIM model is used for planning purposes, e.g., to plan the design of a building, to plan the construction, or to plan maintenance tasks. The second category is *Review & Quality*

---

[4] https://arvr.google.com/cardboard/.

*Assurance*. It includes all use cases where the BIM model is used for reviewing tasks, e.g., to review the design represented as a BIM model, to review the construction works based on the planning in a BIM model, or to review maintenance tasks. *Task guidance* groups use cases that help a user to complete a task, e.g., by giving them information about the task, concrete steps to complete it, or visualizing the task or asset to work on. The *Safety* use case is given if an approach increases the safety of workers or facility managers on-site. The last use case, *Education*, includes all approaches that can be used to educate stakeholders prior to the actual design, on-site work, or maintenance.

Additionally, there is the category *Localization & Tracking*, which is not directly a use case, but groups approaches that focus on the technical aspects of AR on-site. These approaches do not present concrete use cases but based on their findings, multiple other use cases on-site become feasible. They make them feasible by allowing the localization of the user on-site and the improvement of the tracking of the device to allow precise positioning of virtual objects in an AR environment.

In the following, the different use cases in the different building's lifecycle phases are described.

**Design.** Nine approaches reside in the design phase [19, 28, 30, 39, 41, 47, 51, 52, 66]. Most of them either focus on the *Planning* or the *Review & Quality Assurance* use case.

For the *Planning* use case category in the design phase [19, 39, 41], the user is provided with tools to edit the BIM model of a building in an AR/VR environment. The simplest realization of this is a system where the users can collaboratively add annotations to the BIM model [19]. The two other approaches focus on interior design. Here, one approach [41] shows the possibility of designing the painting of the walls and allows the customization of the furniture. This approach is shown in Fig. 2a. Here, the user has the possibility to change the material and color of a sofa [41]. The second approach [39] deals with the more specialized topic of indoor lighting design. It allows the user to add different light bulbs to the room and simulate the resulting lighting situation.

The *Review & Quality Assurance* use case category in the design phase [28, 30, 47, 52, 66] allows the user to view a BIM model in an AR/VR environment to review the design. Here, the focus can be on general architecture review [66] and can also be structured through a concrete protocol [52]. One approach [47] describes the potential of this architecture review to be used for the regulatory process of checking a building for compliance with legal rules. Here, instead of submitting printed plans, the BIM model is submitted and can be viewed in an AR environment by the building authority to check the model for compliance. This is shown in Fig. 2b. Here, a user can see the building next to the surrounding buildings to check whether it fits into the environment [47].

It is also possible to focus on more specialized topics. Here, one approach [28] deals with the sustainability of a building's façade design by showing the user different design alternatives in a VR environment and letting them choose one

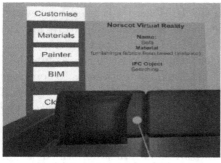

(a) Interior design [41]                (b) Placement in the real world [47]

**Fig. 2.** Design-related approaches in the area of AR/VR and BIM

based on the costs and sustainability. In this approach, the virtual environment is only used to show the design to the user. The costs and sustainability are shown in an analog form. The BIM model is used to generate the VR environment and also to calculate the costs and sustainability. Two other approaches [30,66] use an AR respectively a VR environment to let the user test a design for maintainability. This testing is done by doing the maintenance steps in the AR/VR environment and thus finding flaws in the design that hinder maintenance.

Only one approach [51] resides in the *Education* use case category in the design phase. Here, a BIM model is explored in a VR environment to teach students. The approach allows the user to change the time in the simulation to see the model at different daytimes. Additionally, the approach supports collaboration with other students to explore the model collaboratively.

The use case categories *Task guidance* and *Safety* are not used in the Design phase.

**Construction.** There are 21 approaches that reside in the construction phase [1,5,10,11,13,19,20,23–26,33,35,38,42–45,48,53,65]. Over half of them focus on the *Review & Quality Assurance* use case category.

In the construction phase, the *Planning* use case category deals with the actual planning of the construction works [13,19]. Here, this can be viewing the BIM model in VR prior to construction to get an overview of the necessary construction steps [13] or the possibility of annotating the BIM model off-site [19].

The *Review & Quality Assurance* use case category in the construction phase [11,25,33,38,42–45,48,53,65] allows the user to check the construction progress and identify potential flaws. Lou et al. [33] describe different potentials for using AR for on-site quality management. The potentials presented by them are the coordination through the information provided by the new applications, the possibility to adapt the BIM model on-site to collect data and to account for rapid changes, and construction quality inspection.

One approach to support quality management is an information management system [48]. Here, users can select different objects on-site via an AR interface and retrieve information, e.g., quality checklists [48]. Additionally, they can add information to the objects [48]. It is also possible to build a specialized system for quality assurance that allows users to use an AR app on-site to go through the checklists and upload the inspection results to the BIM model [38].

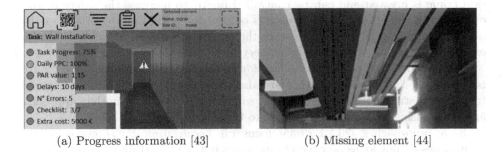

(a) Progress information [43]    (b) Missing element [44]

**Fig. 3.** AR-related approaches that amend the real world with BIM information

Additionally, such a system can be extended to show the progress information by adding colored virtual elements to the real world and amending them with progress, costs, time, and quality information [43]. In this approach, site managers do not have to study 2D plans and other artifacts in their offices but can directly walk through the building under construction and check the progress, quality, and next steps [43]. The approach is shown in Fig. 3a. Here, different progress information about the highlighted wall structure is visualized [43].

Another approach is to give this possibility directly to the workers to allow them to self-inspect their work [25, 44, 45]. In these approaches, the real world is compared with the as-planned BIM model in AR. This comparison allows users to find deviations [11]. Figure 3b shows an example of how a missing element in the real world could be visualized via an AR virtual object. Furthermore, there is the possibility to do this remotely via VR solutions to monitor the current construction progress or to show the current progress to clients [42, 53]. For this, there is the need for measurements on-site either by combining different sensors [53] or by using depth images [42].

Another approach [65] focuses on monitoring the time and costs. It shows them in an AR environment, where the user sees the building visualized, e.g., on a table as a miniature model.

Applications of the *Task guidance* use case category in the construction phase [10, 13, 44, 48] help construction workers complete their construction tasks. This guidance can be done by simply showing the planned model to the worker, so the worker can start replicating it in the real world [10, 13]. An extension to such approaches is adding an information system to also show the workers the tasks that need to be done by amending the task information to the object via AR [48]. A more enhanced method is visualizing each task step-by-step with animations and information to guide the worker [44].

Approaches of the *Safety* use case category in the construction phase [1,5, 23] assure the safety of stakeholders at the construction site. This is done by simulating the construction works in a VR environment prior to on-site work [1, 5]. Based on this, safety plans can be created and refined, and potential hazards can be detected and mitigated [1,5]. In addition, in case of an accident, these simulations can later be used to recreate and investigate it [5].

Another approach [23] is used on-site. Here, a digital twin of a construction crane is created and can be controlled in AR to increase the safety of the operation of the crane. The approach is only tested with a model of a crane in a laboratory setup. The authors state that the usage of digital twins could be extended to other construction machinery too.

The last use case category is *Education* in the construction phase [1,5,45]. It is mainly used by approaches that are also part of the *Safety* use case category to train construction workers to avoid safety hazards [1,5]. Another approach argues for using archived BIM models to train novices [45].

Some approaches [20,24,26,35] focus on *Localization & Tracking*. These approaches do not focus on concrete use cases but make certain use cases on-site possible by increasing the precision of localization and tracking on-site. Here, it is possible to use GPS and device sensors [20], to use one-time marker-based localization and then to rely on the device sensors [26], or to match the observed data from the device sensors with the BIM model to localize the user [24,35].

**Operation.** Five approaches have been identified in the operation phase [12, 14,24,45,57]. In this phase, most of the approaches focus on *Task guidance*.

Here, *Task guidance* in the maintenance phase [12,14,45,57] helps facility managers or other maintenance staff to complete maintenance tasks. This assistance can start with a system that automatically detects anomalies via sensors and uses the BIM model to find the failed asset [57]. Then, AR can be used to highlight the failed asset that might be hidden behind a wall [14,45,57]. It is also possible to extend this by showing maintenance workers a path in AR that guides them to the failed asset [14]. This navigation is shown in Fig. 4a, where the red arrows show the maintenance worker a safe path [14]. Some approaches [12,14] also support maintenance workers by showing them information and animations for a step-by-step guide on how to do their tasks. This guidance is shown in Fig. 4b, where red arrows are used to indicate the direction in which the valve needs to be turned [14].

(a) Navigation [14]               (b) Task guidance [14]

**Fig. 4.** Operation-related approaches in the area of AR/VR and BIM

One approach [14] is also part of the *Safety* use case category as it guides the maintenance workers via a safe path to a failed asset in a dark environment, thus increasing safety. Another approach is part of the *Education* use case category by using the step-by-step guide for training novice maintenance workers [12]. This approach is also used to introduce maintenance workers to facility management basics [12]. Finally, one of the *Localization & Tracking* approaches [24] also states that it can be used in the *Operation* phase to localize a maintenance worker in the building.

## 5.2   Comparison of AR and VR for Different Use Cases

In this section, an analysis is done based on whether a use case can be realized with AR or VR and the reasons for using AR or VR for a specific use case. To achieve this, the reasons for selecting AR or VR are elicited from the surveyed approaches.

**Design.** In the *Design* phase, three approaches use AR [19,30,47], and six use VR [28,39,41,51,52,66]. Thus, VR is prevalent in this phase.

For the *Planning* use case category, one approach uses AR [19], and two use VR [39,41]. The AR approach combines AR with a touch table at which users collaborate [19]. Here, AR allows more intuitive collaboration between the users and allows to combine 3D models in AR with 2D models shown on the touch table or 2D printed plans, as the users can still see the real world when using AR [19]. The first VR approach needs to use VR because the user should design the indoor lighting situation [39]. This design task is only possible with VR because the user needs to immerse in the virtual world to experience the different possibilities for lighting in the room [39].

The second VR approach [41] claims to use AR and VR with a mobile device for AR and an HMD for VR. Here, it is crucial to notice that the real world is not visible on the mobile device, and only an entirely virtual world is shown. This AR usage is contrary to the definition used in this paper, and thus it is not counted as an AR approach in this paper. The advantage of using VR for interior design is that it allows the users to immerse in the environment, and thus make better design decisions [41]. The main disadvantage of VR is that it is prone to motion sickness, which needs to be avoided [41].

For the *Review & Quality Assurance* use case category, two approaches use AR [30,47], and three use VR [28,52,66]. The first AR approach selects AR to check a building for building regulations because it allows showing the planned building on the plot of land on which it is to be built [47]. This visualization allows the users to check whether it fits the neighboring buildings [47]. Additionally, when multiple people discuss the planned building, an AR approach allows for better collaboration [47]. Here, AR allows showing the planned house as a model on a table together with the neighboring buildings, and the discussants sit around the table all equipped with an AR device [47].

Another approach, which allows a user to compare different façade designs, selects VR as a medium because a user is more immersed in it [28]. The immersion is also mentioned by Zaker and Coloma [66], who highlight the advantage that VR allows users to see the actual dimensions of the building. All of these approaches [28,47,66] emphasize that novices that do not understand complicated 2D plans, like clients and owners, profit from the usage of AR/VR in the review process. Also, in this use case, the disadvantage of the VR approaches is the potential for motion sickness [52,66]. Here, Ventura et al. [52] mention that novice users should not be trained before the actual review in VR to avoid prior motion sickness. Additionally, they add breaks to their design review protocol to allow users to recover from potential motion sickness.

One of the two approaches that review the design's maintainability uses AR [30], and the other one uses VR [66]. The VR approach reports that joysticks, which are used by many VR devices today, are not that easy to use for the simulation of the maintenance task, and participants needed some training [66]. In this context, the authors report that they selected AR because users can see their own bodies and can do the same tasks a facility manager would need to do [30]. This also enables novices to find design flaws that lead to poor maintainability [30].

For the *Education* use case category, only a VR approach is used [51]. Here, a significant aspect is an ability to change the time of day to see the design in different lighting situations, which is only possible to experience in VR. Still, also in this approach, motion sickness is reported by a few of the participants [51].

**Construction.** In the construction phase, 17 approaches use AR [8,10,11,13, 19,20,23,24,26,33,35,38,43–45,48,65], and five approaches use VR [1,5,13,42, 53]. Thus, AR is prevalent in this building's lifecycle phase.

In the *Planning* use case category, one approach uses AR [19], and one uses VR [13]. The participants in the VR approach reported that the VR environment is too complicated without prior training [13]. The AR approach [19] is the same approach used for planning in the design phase. Thus, the same reasons for the selection of AR apply, which are intuitive collaboration, combination with other 2D screens, and the possibility to include analog artifacts [19].

Nine approaches [8,11,33,38,43–45,48,65] use AR, and two use VR [42,53] in the *Review & Quality Assurance* use case category. Thus, AR is prevalent in this use case category in the construction phase. Here, all AR approaches can be used on-site, which is not possible with immersive VR as users must see the real world on-site. One approach also mentions the advantage for site managers to be able to walk through the building and see the physical construction objects amended with the necessary information [43]. Additionally, it is only possible with AR to compare the as-planned and as-built state on-site by amending the real world with the as-planned objects to see deviations [11]. Still, the issue is that only large deviations or missing parts are easily detectable via AR [11].

Additionally, the tracking of AR is imperfect, and thus, the model can have an offset or starts to drift [11,38,43]. This imperfection even leads to the fact that measurements are imprecise if done in AR [38]. Furthermore, there is the issue of occlusions, that some objects are displayed in front of real-world objects although they should be displayed behind [38]. This occlusion is even safety critical for on-site usage as the user's vision could be hindered [38].

Another possibility is to do the quality assurance and deficit detection remotely in an office with VR [42,53]. Here, the advantages are the possibility to easily show the progress to the client without going to the construction site, and the construction works are not interrupted [42]. Additionally, it does not rely on the imprecise tracking and localization of AR and can provide more accurate results [42,53]. These accurate results allow for more fine-grained quality control [53]. The disadvantages of this approach are that the monitoring does not happen in real-time, and sensors must be used beforehand to get a representation of the current on-site status [42,53].

One approach [65] uses AR in another way. Here, instead of overlaying the real world with the as-planned state, a virtual model of the building is presented in AR, for example, standing on a table. For this approach, it is also necessary to acquire the current state on-site beforehand [65]. However, compared to the VR applications, this approach can also be used on-site, as the user is not immersed in the model [65]. On the other side, the approach only allows for an overview of the progress of the construction works and not detailed deficit detection [65].

All approaches [10,13,44,45,48] of the *Task guidance* use case category use AR. As already mentioned in the previous sections, the usage of VR on-site is not possible, and thus, as *Task guidance* has to be done on-site, the usage of AR is required. Additionally, AR is felt intuitive by users for *Task guidance* [13]. Here, already significant performance improvements of workers were shown in laboratory setups [10,13]. To provide the user with visualized task guidance, a 3D model of the to-be-constructed part of the building must exist, and thus the BIM model must contain these details [10].

In the *Safety* use case category, one approach [23] uses AR, and the other two [1,5] use VR. The AR approach supports the workers on-site to enhance their safety there [23]. The VR approaches are used off-site to plan and review safety [1,5]. Here, the communication of safety to the construction workers is increased, as they can immerse in the on-site situation without being there [1]. Through this, they are able to get to know the on-site environment and experience safety-critical situations without danger to their lives [1]. The problems are the need for precise BIM models that include not only the building but also the different construction stages with the machines and tools used there [1]. This modeling task can lead to increased costs [5]. Additionally, users of the system can suffer from motion sickness [5].

In the *Education* use case category, one approach uses AR [45], and two use VR [1,5]. The AR approach [45] only states to use AR. Here, the prototype presented does not use AR yet but should include the real world in newer versions, and thus we count the approach as AR. They do not mention specific reasons why AR should be used instead of VR for education. The two VR approaches [1,5] are the two mentioned in the *Safety* use case category. They also use the VR system to train workers, and thus the same reasons mentioned in the last paragraph apply.

**Operation.** In the operation phase, four approaches use AR [14,24,45,57], and one uses both AR and VR for different use cases [12]. Thus, AR is prevalent in this phase.

All approaches [12,14,45,57] of the *Task guidance* use case category in the operation phase use AR. Obviously, VR is not possible in this phase, as the maintenance workers must do their tasks on-site and need to do the tasks in the real world. AR supports them in finding the failed asset by guiding them toward it with a path shown in AR [14]. Here, this is also part of the *Safety* use case category as it improves the safety of the maintenance workers to find a safe path in a dark environment [14]. Additionally, AR allows highlighting the asset, which might be hidden behind a wall [14,57], and can give them instructions on how to fix the failed asset by highlighting different parts of it and showing animations of what they need to do [12,14]. Again, the potential model drift of AR systems is a problem [14].

One approach [12] uses AR and VR for the *Education* use case category. Here, the approach uses AR to support novices while doing maintenance work [12]. Additionally, VR is used to teach them the basics of facility management in an immersive environment [12]. Here, the advantage is that the participants do not need to be in the same physical location and can still experience an interactive 3D world to learn together [12].

### 5.3   Discussion

In this section, the results are concluded to answer the research questions.

The first research question deals with the use cases in which AR and VR are used together with BIM. Here, the five use case categories *Planning*, *Review & Quality Assurance*, *Task guidance*, *Safety*, and *Education* are defined. Additionally, some papers deal with the technical detail of on-site localization and tracking. The results show that the most supported use case category is *Review & Quality Assurance*, especially in the *Construction* phase, followed by *Task guidance* in the *Construction* and *Operation* phases. Only a few papers focus on the other three use case categories.

The second research question deals with the reasons why AR or VR should be used for a use case. In the *Design* phase, the results show that AR and VR support novices that do not understand complicated 2D plans. AR is used in this phase for rough planning and collaborative tasks, for tasks that involve visualizing the building in the real world, or for tasks that require the simulation of physical work. VR is used for detailed planning tasks, where a user benefits from the immersive environment.

In the *Construction* phase, the usage of AR and VR depends more on the use case. Here, for the *Planning* use case category, the same arguments as for the *Design* phase are valid. For all use cases that need to be done on-site, the usage of AR is mandatory, as it is impossible to use VR on-site. Thus, for *Task guidance*, only AR is used. For *Review & Quality Assurance*, AR is often used to allow for on-site usage, but it is also possible to use VR, which allows for more precise results but also needs prior measurements. In the *Safety* use case category, VR is used for planning steps, and AR is used to support the safety on-site. For *Education*, AR or VR might be used.

In the *Operation* phase, for all use case categories, AR is used, because maintenance is a task that needs to be done on-site, and thus only AR is possible. The only exception is the *Education* use case category. Here, AR is still used if novices are trained on-site, but VR can be used for off-site education.

# 6 Further Research

Most approaches focus on the *Construction* phase, second most on the *Design* phase. This fits the findings of earlier surveys that also see the construction and design phase as the dominant research subject [49,54]. Thus, one open issue is to have more studies in the *Operation* phase. Additionally, most of the approaches in the *Operation* phase focus on maintenance tasks. Only one uses sensors that are placed in the building to monitor the building. Here, more research is possible in the domain of connecting smart Internet of Things (IoT) devices, AR/VR, and BIM not only for maintenance but also for the operation of a building, like controlling light and heating systems.

None of the surveyed approaches does a direct comparison between AR and VR solutions. Especially for use cases where both technologies could be used, e.g., in the *Design* phase and *Review & Quality Assurance* in the *Construction* phase, this would be beneficial to get a deeper insight into the usability of such approaches in direct comparison.

Only a few approaches focus on the *Safety* use case category. Especially in the *Construction* phase, only one approach is used directly on-site to increase safety. Here, more research in this area would be beneficial to bring the simulation features that BIM provides for the *Construction* phase directly on-site. Furthermore, in the *Operation* phase, only one approach increases safety. Also, here, more research is possible. Additionally, research is needed on how AR devices can be used safely on-site.

Many of the surveyed papers focus on the *Review & Quality Assurance* use case category. Here, a shift towards allowing workers to use such approaches and directly supporting them with *Task guidance* would be beneficial. Through this, errors could be avoided and found in the early stages and easily resolved.

From the classified literature, only two approaches deal with the *Planning* use case category in the *Construction* phase. Here, more research to leverage the simulation features of BIM for detailed planning of the on-site environment is required. Currently, BIM is only used to look at the model or add some information to objects in the BIM model. Additionally, this planned model of the on-site environment could then be used on-site to place materials, machines, and other equipment in the correct position on-site.

# 7 Limitations

First of all, there are limitations to the literature selection progress. Here, papers could be missed through the selected literature database and search terms.

Additionally, only open-access papers and papers with a citation count of ten or more citations were examined. This could affect the results in three aspects. First, the given statistics about the lifecycle phases, use cases, used technology, devices, and combination of these categories could differ. Second, use case categories could be missing due to missing papers.

Still, the statement that there is missing research should be valid. If an approach is not in the surveyed literature, either it is not open-access, or it is not cited often enough. Thus, if a topic is already researched in detail, it is unlikely that all papers in that research field are not open access. Additionally, if there is much research in a field, the papers of the field cite each other leading to many citations on some papers, which should then be included in this survey.

## 8  Conclusion

While an increasing number of studies in HCI, construction, or engineering have shown the potential of using AR and VR technology together with BIM, often research remains focused on individual explorations and key design strategies. In addition to that, a systematic overview and discussion of recent approaches are missing. Therefore, we have systematically reviewed recent approaches combining AR/VR with BIM and categorized the literature by the building's lifecycle phase while systematically describing relevant use cases.

Future work should examine approaches of specific lifecycle phases or use case categories in more detail. Additionally, it would be helpful to analyze the surveyed literature based on other categories. Here, especially aspects such as usability, UX as well as safety, and security could be investigated in more detail to provide further insights about the applicability of AR/VR and BIM in the AEC/FM industry.

## References

1. Afzal, M., Shafiq, M.T.: Evaluating 4D-BIM and VR for effective safety communication and training: a case study of multilingual construction job-site crew. Buildings 11(8) (2021)
2. Allen, D.: What is building maintenance? Facilities 11(3), 7–12 (1993)
3. Anthes, C., García-Hernández, R.J., Wiedemann, M., Kranzlmuller, D.: State of the art of virtual reality technology. In: 2016 IEEE Aerospace Conference. IEEE, Big Sky, MT (2016)
4. Arditi, D., Gunaydin, H.M.: Total quality management in the construction process. Int. J. Project Manag. 15(4), 235–243 (1997)
5. Azhar, S.: Role of visualization technologies in safety planning and management at construction jobsites. Procedia Eng. 171, 215–226 (2017)
6. Azhar, S.: Building information modeling (BIM): trends, benefits, risks, and challenges for the AEC industry. Leadersh. Manag. Eng. 11(3), 241–252 (2011)
7. Azuma, R.T.: A survey of augmented reality. Teleoper. Virtual Environ. 6(4), 355–385 (1997)

8. Calderon-Hernandez, C., Brioso, X.: Lean, BIM and augmented reality applied in the design and construction phase: a literature review. Int. J. Innov. Manag. Technol. **9**(1), 60–63 (2018)

9. Carmigniani, J., Furht, B., Anisetti, M., Ceravolo, P., Damiani, E., Ivkovic, M.: Augmented reality technologies, systems and applications. Multimedia Tools Appl. **51**, 341–377 (2011)

10. Chalhoub, J., Ayer, S.K.: Using mixed reality for electrical construction design communication. Autom. Constr. **86** (2018)

11. Chalhoub, J., Ayer, S.K., McCord, K.H.: Augmented reality to enable users to identify deviations for model reconciliation. Buildings **11**(2) (2021)

12. Chew, M.Y.L., Teo, E.A.L., Shah, K.W., Kumar, V., Hussein, G.F.: Evaluating the roadmap of 5G technology implementation for smart building and facilities management in Singapore. Sustainability **12**(24) (2020)

13. Dallasega, P., Revolti, A., Sauer, P.C., Schulze, F., Rauch, E.: BIM, augmented and virtual reality empowering lean construction management: a project simulation game. Procedia Manuf. **45**, 49–54 (2020)

14. Diao, P.H., Shih, N.J.: BIM-based ar maintenance system (BARMS) as an intelligent instruction platform for complex plumbing facilities. Appl. Sci. **9**(8) (2019)

15. Doerner, R., Broll, W., Grimm, P., Jung, B. (eds.): Virtual and Augmented Reality (VR/AR): Foundations and Methods of Extended Realities (XR). Springer, Cham (2022). https://doi.org/10.1007/978-3-030-79062-2

16. Dykstra, A.: Construction Project Management: A Complete Introduction. Kirshner Publishing Company, San Francisco (2018)

17. Eadie, R., Browne, M., Odeyinka, H., McKeown, C., McNiff, S.: BIM implementation throughout the UK construction project lifecycle: an analysis. Autom. Constr. **36**, 145–151 (2013)

18. Eastman, C., Teicholz, P., Sacks, R., Liston, K.: BIM Handbook: A Guide to Building Information Modeling for Owners, Managers, Designers, Engineers, and Contractors. Wiley, Hoboken (2008)

19. Garbett, J., Hartley, T., Heesom, D.: A multi-user collaborative BIM-AR system to support design and construction. Autom. Constr. **122** (2021)

20. Gomez-Jauregui, V., Manchado, C., Del-Castillo-igareda, J., Otero, C.: Quantitative evaluation of overlaying discrepancies in mobile augmented reality applications for AEC/FM. Adv. Eng. Softw. **127**, 124–140 (2019)

21. Gottschalk, S., Yigitbas, E., Schmidt, E., Engels, G.: Model-based product configuration in augmented reality applications. In: Bernhaupt, R., Ardito, C., Sauer, S. (eds.) HCSE 2020. LNCS, vol. 12481, pp. 84–104. Springer, Cham (2020). https://doi.org/10.1007/978-3-030-64266-2_5

22. Gottschalk, S., Yigitbas, E., Schmidt, E., Engels, G.: ProConAR: a tool support for model-based AR product configuration. In: Bernhaupt, R., Ardito, C., Sauer, S. (eds.) HCSE 2020. LNCS, vol. 12481, pp. 207–215. Springer, Cham (2020). https://doi.org/10.1007/978-3-030-64266-2_14

23. Hasan, S.M., Lee, K., Moon, D., Kwon, S., Jinwoo, S., Lee, S.: Augmented reality and digital twin system for interaction with construction machinery. J. Asian Archit. Build. Eng. **21**(2), 564–574 (2022)

24. Herbers, P., König, M.: Indoor localization for augmented reality devices using BIM, point clouds, and template matching. Appl. Sci. **9**(20) (2019)

25. Hernández, J.L., Lerones, P.M., Bonsma, P., van Delft, A., Deighton, R., Braun, J.D.: An IFC interoperability framework for self-inspection process in buildings. Buildings **8**(2) (2018)

26. Hübner, P., Weinmann, M., Wursthorn, S.: Marker-based localization of the Microsoft Hololens in building models. Int. Arch. Photogramm., Remote Sens. Spat. Inf. Sci. - ISPRS Arch. **42**. International Society for Photogrammetry and Remote Sensing (2018)
27. Jovanovikj, I., Yigitbas, E., Sauer, S., Engels, G.: Augmented and virtual reality object repository for rapid prototyping. In: Bernhaupt, R., Ardito, C., Sauer, S. (eds.) HCSE 2020. LNCS, vol. 12481, pp. 216–224. Springer, Cham (2020). https://doi.org/10.1007/978-3-030-64266-2_15
28. Kamari, A., Paari, A., Torvund, H.: BIM-enabled virtual reality (VR) for sustainability life cycle and cost assessment. Sustainability **13**(1) (2021)
29. Karakaya, K., Yigitbas, E., Engels, G.: Automated UX evaluation for user-centered design of VR interfaces. In: Ardito, C., Sauer, S. (eds.) HCSE 2022. LNCS, vol. 13482, pp. 140–149. Springer, Cham (2022). https://doi.org/10.1007/978-3-031-14785-2_9
30. Khalek, I., Chalhoub, J., Ayer, S.: Augmented reality for identifying maintainability concerns during design. Adv. Civil Eng. **2019** (2019)
31. Krings, S., Yigitbas, E., Jovanovikj, I., Sauer, S., Engels, G.: Development framework for context-aware augmented reality applications. In: EICS '20, pp. 9:1–9:6. ACM (2020)
32. Krings, S.C., Yigitbas, E., Biermeier, K., Engels, G.: Design and evaluation of AR-assisted end-user robot path planning strategies. In: EICS '22, pp. 14–18. ACM (2022)
33. Lou, J., Xu, J., Wang, K.: Study on construction quality control of urban complex project based on BIM. Procedia Eng. **174**, 668–676. Elsevier Ltd (2017)
34. Luo, L., He, Q., Jaselskis, E.J., Xie, J.: Construction project complexity: research trends and implications. J. Constr. Eng. Manag. **143**(7) (2017)
35. Mahmood, B., Han, S., Lee, D.E.: BIM-based registration and localization of 3D point clouds of indoor scenes using geometric features for augmented reality. Remote Sens. **12**(14) (2020)
36. Meža, S., Turk, Ž., Dolenc, M.: Component based engineering of a mobile BIM-based augmented reality system. Autom. Constr. **42** (2014)
37. Milgram, P., Kishino, F.: A taxonomy of mixed reality visual displays. IEICE Trans. Inf. Syst. **77**(12), 1321–1329 (1994)
38. Mirshokraei, M., De Gaetani, C.I., Migliaccio, F.: A web-based BIM-AR quality management system for structural elements. Appl. Sci. **9**(19) (2019)
39. Natephra, W., Motamedi, A., Fukuda, T., Yabuki, N.: Integrating building information modeling and virtual reality development engines for building indoor lighting design. Visual. Eng. **5**(1) (2017)
40. Pheng, L.S., Hou, L.S.: The economy and the construction industry. In: Construction Quality and the Economy. MBE, pp. 21–54. Springer, Singapore (2019). https://doi.org/10.1007/978-981-13-5847-0_2
41. Pour Rahimian, F., Chavdarova, V., Oliver, S., Chamo, F.: OpenBIM-Tango integrated virtual showroom for offsite manufactured production of self-build housing. Autom. Constr. **102** (2019)
42. Pour Rahimian, F., Seyedzadeh, S., Oliver, S., Rodriguez, S., Dawood, N.: On-demand monitoring of construction projects through a game-like hybrid application of BIM and machine learning. Autom. Constr. **110** (2020)
43. Ratajczak, J., Riedl, M., Matt, D.: BIM-based and AR application combined with location-based management system for the improvement of the construction performance. Buildings **9**(5), 118 (2019)

44. Riexinger, G., Kluth, A., Olbrich, M., Braun, J.D., Bauernhansl, T.: Mixed reality for on-site self-instruction and self-inspection with building information models. In: Procedia CIRP, vol. 72, pp. 1124–1129. Elsevier B.V. (2018)
45. Saar, C., Klufallah, M., Kuppusamy, S., Yusof, A., Shien, L., Han, W.: BIM integration in augmented reality model. Int. J. Technol. **10**(7), 1266–1275 (2019)
46. Salem, O., Samuel, I.J., He, S.: BIM and VR/AR technologies: from project development to lifecycle asset management. Proc. Int. Struct. Eng. Constr. **7**(1) (2020)
47. Schranz, C., Urban, H., Gerger, A.: Potentials of augmented reality in a BIM based building submission process. J. Inf. Technol. Constr. **26**, 441–457 (2021)
48. Schweigkofler, A., et al.: Development of a digital platform based on the integration of augmented reality and BIM for the management of information in construction processes. IFIP Adv. Inf. Commun. Technol. **540**, 46–55 (2018)
49. Sidani, A., et al.: Recent tools and techniques of BIM-based virtual reality: a systematic review. Arch. Comput. Methods Eng. **28**(2), 449–462 (2021)
50. Statistisches Bundesamt (Destatis): Volkswirtschaftliche Gesamtrechnungen - Arbeitsunterlage Investitionen. Technical report (2022)
51. Vasilevski, N., Birt, J.: Analysing construction student experiences of mobile mixed reality enhanced learning in virtual and augmented reality environments. Res. Learn. Technol. **28** (2020)
52. Ventura, S., Castronovo, F., Ciribini, A.: A design review session protocol for the implementation of immersive virtual reality in usability-focused analysis. J. Inf. Technol. Constr. **25**, 233–253 (2020)
53. Vincke, S., Hernandez, R., Bassier, M., Vergauwen, M.: Immersive visualisation of construction site point cloud data, meshes and BIM models in a VR environment using a gaming engine. Int. Arch. Photogramm., Remote Sens. Spat. Inf. Sci. - ISPRS Arch. **42**, 77–83. International Society for Photogrammetry and Remote Sensing (2019)
54. Wang, X., Kim, M.J., Love, P.E., Kang, S.C.: Augmented Reality in built environment: classification and implications for future research. Autom. Constr. **32**, 1–13 (2013)
55. Wu, S., Hou, L., Zhang, G.K.: Integrated application of BIM and eXtended reality technology: a review, classification and outlook. In: Toledo Santos, E., Scheer, S. (eds.) ICCCBE 2020. LNCE, vol. 98, pp. 1227–1236. Springer, Cham (2021). https://doi.org/10.1007/978-3-030-51295-8_86
56. Xiao, Y., Watson, M.: Guidance on conducting a systematic literature review. J. Plan. Educ. Res. **39**(1), 93–112 (2019)
57. Xie, X., Lu, Q., Rodenas-Herraiz, D., Parlikad, A., Schooling, J.: Visualised inspection system for monitoring environmental anomalies during daily operation and maintenance. Eng. Constr. Archit. Manag. **27**(8), 1835–1852 (2020)
58. Yigitbas, E., Gorissen, S., Weidmann, N., Engels, G.: Collaborative software modeling in virtual reality. In: 24th International Conference on Model Driven Engineering Languages and Systems, pp. 261–272. IEEE (2021)
59. Yigitbas, E., Jovanovikj, I., Engels, G.: Simplifying robot programming using augmented reality and end-user development. In: Ardito, C., et al. (eds.) INTERACT 2021. LNCS, vol. 12932, pp. 631–651. Springer, Cham (2021). https://doi.org/10.1007/978-3-030-85623-6_36
60. Yigitbas, E., Jovanovikj, I., Sauer, S., Engels, G.: On the development of context-aware augmented reality applications. In: Abdelnour Nocera, J., et al. (eds.) INTERACT 2019. LNCS, vol. 11930, pp. 107–120. Springer, Cham (2020). https://doi.org/10.1007/978-3-030-46540-7_11

61. Yigitbas, E., Jovanovikj, I., Scholand, J., Engels, G.: VR training for warehouse management. In: VRST '20: 26th ACM Symposium on Virtual Reality Software and Technology, pp. 78:1–78:3. ACM (2020)
62. Yigitbas, E., Klauke, J., Gottschalk, S., Engels, G.: VREUD - an end-user development tool to simplify the creation of interactive VR scenes. In: IEEE Symposium on Visual Languages and Human-Centric Computing, VL/HCC, pp. 1–10. IEEE (2021)
63. Yigitbas, E., Sauer, S., Engels, G.: Using augmented reality for enhancing planning and measurements in the scaffolding business. In: EICS '21. ACM (2021)
64. Yigitbas, E., Tejedor, C.B., Engels, G.: Experiencing and programming the ENIAC in VR. In: Mensch und Computer 2020, pp. 505–506. ACM (2020)
65. Zaher, M., Greenwood, D., Marzouk, M.: Mobile augmented reality applications for construction projects. Constr. Innov. **18**(2), 152–166 (2018)
66. Zaker, R., Coloma, E.: Virtual reality-integrated workflow in BIM-enabled projects collaboration and design review: a case study. Visual. Eng. **6**(1) (2018)

# Through Space and Time: Spatio-Temporal Visualization of MOBA Matches

Adam Šufliarsky[1], Günter Wallner[2], and Simone Kriglstein[1,3]

[1] Masaryk University, Brno, Czech Republic
asufliarsky@gmail.com, kriglstein@mail.muni.cz
[2] Johannes Kepler University, Linz, Austria
guenter.wallner@jku.at
[3] AIT Austrian Institute of Technology GmbH, Vienna, Austria

**Abstract.** With data about in-game behavior becoming more easily accessible, data-driven tools and websites that allow players to review their performance have emerged. Among the many different visualizations used as part of these systems, spatio-temporal visualizations which do not rely on animations have received little attention. In this paper, we explore if the established space-time cube (STC) visualization is a suitable means for simultaneously conveying information about space and time to players. Towards this end, we have created a STC visualization for reviewing matches, focusing on *Heroes of the Storm* as a use case, and conducted a study among 30 Multiplayer Online Battle Arena (MOBA) players to establish how successfully various tasks can be performed and how this kind of 3D representation is received. Our results indicate that such a visualization, despite its complexity, can be usefully applied for match analysis if the design and interaction possibilities are well chosen.

**Keywords:** Gameplay visualization · Space-time cube · Replay analysis

## 1  Introduction

Understanding player behaviour in video games through data-driven methods often requires suitable visualizations to facilitate sense-making of the collected data. As such, various visual representations of behavioral in-game data have been proposed to date [53]. Initially, such gameplay visualizations were primarily targeting game developers to assist in games user research activities. However, over time efforts have also been directed towards creating visualizations for players to visually review their own gameplay and those of others to foster skill development [55]. This development has been further spurred by the increased popularity of competitive gaming and esports. This, in turn, has spawned a range of community-driven efforts directed towards visualizing in-game data and performance as evidenced by a variety of websites and tools [30] and increased academic discourse on this subject (e.g., [30,36,55]).

J. Abdelnour Nocera et al. (Eds.): INTERACT 2023, LNCS 14143, pp. 167–189, 2023.
https://doi.org/10.1007/978-3-031-42283-6_9

However, expressive gameplay visualizations are not straightforward to design as play is complex, regularly resulting in spatio-temporal datasets (e.g., movement over time) that are difficult to visualize. Consequently, visualizations of in-game data often resort to presenting a temporal (e.g., [2, 43]) or spatial slice (e.g., [14, 54]) of the data to reduce visual complexity which, however, can be insufficient for analyzing spatio-temporal patterns (cf. [18]). Current spatio-temporal gameplay visualizations that show both dimensions simultaneously (e.g., [1, 36]; see Sect. 2) primarily rely on multiple views using different visualization types or on animations. As such they may impose additional cognitive load, e.g., for context switching and drawing comparisons between the views or frames (cf. [23, 26]) or require extra time to run through the animation.

In this paper, we propose and explore the usefulness of a space-time cube (STC) representation of player movement and event data to avoid using animations to communicate temporal information. In a STC two axis form the spatial space and the third axis represents the time. Originally proposed by Hägerstrand [22] in 1970, the concept has since then been applied in a variety of domains as it enables a *clear observation of various features in time and space* [17]. In addition, various studies have confirmed analytic benefits of the STC compared to other representations (e.g., [5, 35, 37]). As such we consider a STC to also be an appropriate visualization of in-game data to observe spatio-temporal gameplay patterns. As use case we employ a STC to help players review the course of multiplayer online battle arena (MOBA) matches, specifically from *Heroes of the Storm* [8] (*HotS*). Towards this end, an interactive online tool that presents match data extracted from replay files has been developed.

However, while having several benefits, STCs have also shown to be potentially difficult to interpret [20] and to be affected by visual clutter [17, 37]. As such the effectiveness of STCs may vary across different target groups which makes it essential to assess its value based on domain and target audience. Therefore, we evaluated our STC implementation through an online user study involving 30 MOBA players to establish a) how correctly the data in the STC can be interpreted and b) how this kind of visualization is perceived by the community. For this purpose, the study followed a predominantly task-based approach – following established practices in visualization research to ascertain its effectiveness – but also included a lightweight insight-based evaluation to probe into how the visualization promotes insights [19] as well as qualitative feedback questions.

Our results indicate that players can, by and large, successfully deduct facts from the STC and take a positive stance towards such kind of representation. Yet, visual clutter and interactions have to be carefully considered to counteract misreadings of the data. Based on our results, we discuss potential implications to help spark further research on 3D visualizations in the games analytics field.

## 2   Related Work

In the following we briefly review works concerned with the visualization of in-game data in general, visualizations particularly targeting players for reviewing gameplay, and previous work on spatio-temporal visualization, with particular attention towards STC visualizations.

*Gameplay Visualization:* Heatmaps that show the density of observations (e.g., kills) across space through color coding are one of the most frequently used visualizations in game analytics but they usually do not work well if more than one variable needs to be analyzed (cf. [34]). To address this issue other distribution maps such as hexbin maps in combination with glyphs [54] have been proposed to show multiple in-game metrics simultaneously. Like heatmaps, these are, however, two-dimensional and do not consider the temporal dimension. They also do not lend themselves well to displaying player trajectories which are often, as in our case, of key interest. Trajectories are frequently visualized using connected line segments, either within the games environment itself (e.g., [15]) or projected onto a two-dimensional map of it (e.g., [51]) but without consideration of timings. Such approaches are useful for studying overall navigation patterns or unexpected paths but they do not allow for temporal analysis. Hoobler et al. [24], for instance, therefore addressed this by encoding the passing of time in the width of the lines while Dixit and Youngblood [13] used color coding. Others have used animation to show how movement unfolds over time. For instance, *ECHO* [40] allows to playback positional information through a time slider. Goncalves et al. [21] animated player icons over a 2D map. Wallner and Kriglstein [52] took a different spatio-temporal approach, abstracting game states into nodes and showing temporal progression through animating transitions between the nodes. While animation over time seems a natural choice to convey temporal information, literature is not conclusive about its effectiveness (e.g., [23]). Tversky et al. [50], for instance, surveying literature on animation found that in many cases animation did not have benefits over static representations. In contrast, a STC allows to observe space-time paths without the need to rely on animations.

Purely temporal approaches, except basic charts, to visualize sequences of actions are less common in game analytics. Some, such as Li et al. [38], have proposed visualizations of sequences of actions without taking the timings between them into account which, however, can sometimes be of interest as well. Agarwal et al. [2] proposed a timeline-based visualization to help explore dependencies between interactions of multiple players. Interactions of a player are shown along individual rows and interactions between entities through vertical lines. *Stratmapper* [3], in contrast, juxtaposes a map visualization and a timeline showing in-game events to achieve a spatio-temporal perspective on gameplay. The timeline can be used to filter the information visible on the map. As such time and space are represented through two different visualizations which need to be related to match the spatial with the temporal information and may thus require additional cognitive demand. In contrast, a STC displays both space and time within a single representation. Multiple views provide different perspectives on the STC, thus showing the same visualization rather than different ones.

*Player-Facing Analytics:* While visualizations of in-game data have historically emerged from a need to facilitate sense-making of collected player data, players too have developed an increased interest in reviewing play data to improve their gaming skills. However, as Kleinman and Seif El-Nasr [30] argue, research currently lacks an understanding of how players use their data to gain expertise. Wallner et al. [55] studied the information needs of players particularly with respect to post-play visualizations, focusing on three popular competitive genres. Among others, information about movement and positioning of units has shown to be highly relevant for players. Kleinman et al. [31] started to develop a taxonomy of user interactions with spatio-temporal gameplay visualizations using *Defense of the Ancients 2 (DotA 2)* as a use case. Being able to study movement and positioning and consequently *form hypothesis of context and behavior that evolves over time* [31] have shown to be critical user activities. A STC visualization (see below) can facilitate these goals. As such we contribute to current research on player-centric visualizations. Previous systems in this space mostly relied on 2D map-based solutions such as *VisuaLeague* [1] which depicts player trajectories using animated maps or the system by Kuan et al. [36] which combines a global view, showing summarized troop movements, and a local view of individual unit movements using animations. In contrast, our proposed approach is 3D-based, integrating space and time without a need to resort to animations.

*Spatio-temporal Visualization and Space-Time Cubes:* Spatio-temporal visualization is a rich and active research field with numerous techniques having been published over the years. An extensive review goes beyond the scope of this paper but commonly used techniques in this space include animations and multiple views but also single view approaches (see also [6]). Animations may require higher cognitive load and time and complicate comparisons as discussed above. As such multiple views, each showing different aspects of the data, are frequently employed. These are then usually linked together to provide a coherent picture of the data [6], e.g., often through linking a map and a timeline view. For instance, Ferreira et al. [16] used such a combination to represent taxi trips, while Slingsby and van Loon [47] employed it for the analysis of animal movement.

In contrast, the STC attempts to convey the data within a single three-dimensional view. The STC was initially described by Hägerstrand [22] in 1970. With computer technology making 3D visualizations much easier to produce, interest in the approach has revived [18]. Consequently, the STC visualization technique has been used in many different settings. For example as a narrative tool to revisit a historical event [42], in the context of geospatial visualization [18,27,33], to visualize eye movement [39] or the movement of animals [32], in sports [45], and recently for conveying spatio-temporal patterns of *COVID-19* [44]. In addition, the STC visualization technique has also been applied in mixed [49] and virtual reality [17] settings. STCs usually use lines to display the individual trajectories but for the sake of completeness it should also be mentioned that variants of it exists. For instance, Demšar and Virrantaus [12] used a kernel density technique to visualize the density of movement rather than the individual trajectories to address the issue of clutter. We were, however, interested in showing the details of the individual trajectories.

Various studies have compared the STC to different 2D representations. Among them, Kristensson et al. [35] have shown that a STC visualization resulted in faster response times when users had to solve complex spatio-temporal questions compared to a 2D map. Likewise, Amini et al. [5] found that the STC is beneficial in instances where users have to inspect sequences of events in order to identify complex behaviour in movement data. Kveladze et al. [37], studying a geo-visualization environment with multiple coordinated views using three different graphical representations (including a STC), observed that domain as well as non-domain experts mostly used the STC for all involved tasks. However, STCs also have drawbacks such as being prone to visual clutter [17,37], being potentially difficult to interpret [20], and having a steep learning curve [37].

Nevertheless, given the many benefits, it is surprising that the STC representation has not been studied more extensively in the context of gameplay visualization where spatio-temporal movement data is also ubiquitous. In fact, we are only aware of a single paper which utilized a STC for visualizing player behaviour, namely the work of Coultan et al. [10] who used a STC to visualize movement of players in a location-based game. However, in their paper the STC was used to facilitate their own analysis of the data. In contrast, we report on a user study assessing the effectiveness of the STC for analyzing play by players.

# 3   Use Case: Heroes of the Storm

*Heroes of the Storm* (*HotS*) [8] is a MOBA game in which two teams of five players each compete against each other. The team who first destroys the opponent's main building, the so-called 'King's Core', wins. In contrast to other MOBA's, *HotS* offers a wide range of maps which have different secondary objectives, which when achieved provide an advantage to the respective team. Each map has multiple so-called lanes, i.e. direct pathways connecting the bases of the teams and in which typically the majority of combat takes place. Controlling them gives an advantage to the team and they thus form important geographic features of the maps. In addition, defensive structures such as towers and forts are placed across the maps which attack enemies within their range. Destroying these structures can also bring additional benefits to the team. Players can choose from a variety of heroes, each one having unique abilities and talents. These heroes are divided into different categories, e.g., tank, healer, assassin.

*HotS* allows players to record replays of matches that contain all events and actions necessary to reconstruct a match. These replays were parsed using the *Heroes.ReplayParser* library [7] to extract information about player movement and events. In particular, we extracted the players' positions on a per-second interval. In case no position data was available for a specific time interval, the

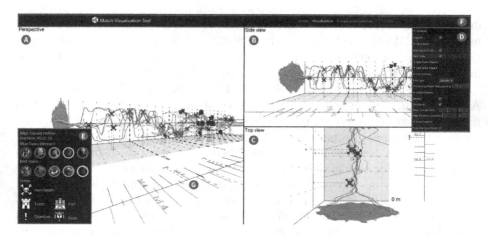

**Fig. 1.** Interface of the visualization, consisting of perspective, side, and top view (A-C), controls and filters (D), legend (E), menu bar (F), and auxiliary time axis (G). The legends and controls can be collapsed.

position was linearly interpolated. Apart from the positions of the players each second, we also extracted match specific data (map, game length), player deaths, team levels, map objectives, destroyed structures, and major camp captures. This data is stored in a JSON file that serves as input to the visualization.

## 4    Visualization Approach

The visualization was developed as a web-based application using the *Three.js* library [48]. It uses *WebGL* to enable 3D GPU-accelerated graphics and is broadly supported by web browsers. Some GUI elements were implemented using the *lil-gui* library [9]. The visualization is shown in Fig. 1. The landing page of the visualization lists the supported and tested web browsers and gives a brief introduction to the visualization approach and the navigation controls. At the top of the visualization itself, a menu (Fig. 1, F) allows to access a number of pre-uploaded matches but also to upload one own's replays that have been processed with our parser beforehand.

*Space-Time Cube:* The extracted data from the replay file is displayed in the form of a STC [22]. A STC is a visual representation that shows how spatial data changes over time. Two-dimensions of the cube form the geographical space and the third axis the temporal dimension. Spatio-temporal data (in our case player movement and events) can then be visualized within the coordinate system defined by the cube. Traditionally, the height of the cube represents the time axis. However, in our implementation time progresses along the depth axis as traditional time diagrams usually depict time along the $x$-axis, which is better resembled using this configuration.

Movements of players are visualized as lines connecting the recorded positions. The paths of the players are color coded to distinguish between the 10 players. Since *HotS* uses the colors blue and red for the two teams we used cold colors, shades of blue and green, for one team and warm colors, i.e. shades of red and yellow for the other. In this way players of different teams should be more easily distinguishable from each other.

In addition two major types of events are depicted through icons: player deaths and the destruction of structures. Player deaths are shown using color-coded skull icons (using the same colors as the paths). Likewise, the destruction of buildings (towers and forts) is indicated with icons. Since structures belong to a team, the icons are either colored in blue or red. Blue icons represent a structure destroyed by the blue team, red icons structures destroyed by the red team. As the icons are two-dimensional objects, billboarding (cf. [29]) is used to ensure that they always face the camera. To avoid icons being heavily occluded by the players' paths they are always rendered on top of them. These events are also projected onto the ground and back plane (indicated with dashed lines) to help identify patterns more easily than in 3D where the depth could be misleading. However, we refrained from projecting them onto the basemap since a) the map can be moved and b) the dashed lines would have followed the principal direction of the trajectories which would have increased clutter. Circles indicate deaths and use the same color coding as used for the players' paths. Squares denote destroyed structures colored according to the team who destroyed them.

The ground plane is further divided into two halves which are colored based on the teams to convey in which team's territory the game events have happened. The time axis ($z$-axis) is divided into one minute intervals represented by dashed lines. Every fifth minute is accentuated by using a thicker line and is additionally labelled. Level milestones, achieved map objectives, and major camp captures are not shown within the STC itself to reduce visual clutter. Instead these are visualized along an auxiliary time axis to the right of the STC and placed on the ground plane (Fig. 1, G). Level milestones are depicted as lines with talent-unlocking milestones (i.e. levels 4, 7, 10, 13, 16, and 20) also having a label. Map objectives are visualized as team-colored exclamation marks connected to the time axis using dashed lines. In the same manner but using different icons, major boss camps and achieved map objectives are indicated.

Three panels provide a perspective, side, and top view of the STC (see Fig. 1, A-C). The perspective can be freely rotated (left mouse button), translated (right mouse button), and zoomed in and out (mouse wheel). The top and side view can be zoomed in and out as well as translated along one axis.

*Legend & Control Panel.* A legend located in the bottom left corner (Fig. 1, E) contains the name of the map, the match duration, and an explanation of the icons. In addition, it shows the heroes of each team surrounded by a circle matching the color used to encode the hero in the STC. The winning team is also marked. The legend can be expanded or collapsed by the user.

The control panel (Fig. 1, D) provides means to filter the data shown in the STC and to adjust the appearance and the view navigation. In particular, the paths of the players can be toggled on or off on a per-team basis or for individual players. Lines can either be displayed using the raw coordinates extracted from

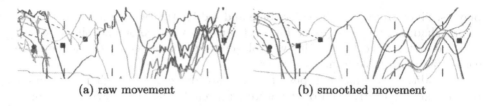

(a) raw movement                    (b) smoothed movement

**Fig. 2.** Comparison of player trajectories using the raw position data (left) and path interpolation (right).

the replay or can be interpolated (default setting). Interpolation was added to help reduce visual noise and clutter and to abstract from fine-grained movement details as the goal of the visualization is to provide an overview of movement rather than showing its intricacies (see Fig. 2 for a comparison). In addition, the transparency of the lines of filtered players can be changed which allows to display them semi-transparently to enable comparisons. Icons representing hero deaths and destroyed structures can also be toggled on and off. The position of the map can be moved along the time axis which eases contextualization of the data at later time points within the map. Lastly, the views can be synchronized to link them. If enabled, translations performed in one view are automatically performed in the others as well. As the legend, the controls can be collapsed.

## 5    User Study

To evaluate the visualization, we conducted an online survey to

a) assess how correctly the visualization is interpreted by players, and
b) understand how this kind of visualization is perceived by the players.

For the former we followed a task-based methodology using tasks which inquiry about different aspects of the data. For the latter we included qualitative feedback questions as well as an open-task asking about gained insights.

Participants were sourced via *Reddit*, *Discord*, and *Facebook* communities associated with *HotS* and other MOBAs as well as through the first author's network. Participants had to have some previous experience with MOBAs, either by actively playing or passively watching matches. We recruited players of *HotS* as well as players of other MOBA games to see if the visualization is also understandable for players who prefer related games within the same genre.

### 5.1    Survey Design

The first part of the survey provided a short introduction to the purpose of the study and consent information. Next, the survey gathered demographic data about age and gender (female, male, non-binary, prefer not to disclose, other) and inquired into participants interest and experience with post-match game analysis as well as experience with gameplay visualizations. Both interest and

Table 1. Task types used in the evaluation.

| Type | Description | Tasks |
|------|-------------|-------|
| Events | Analyzing which events happened during a specified time interval | T-1, T-2, T-3, T-19 |
| Counts | Analyzing how many events of a certain kind happened within a specified time interval | T-10, T-11, T-12, T-13 |
| Location | Analyzing the locations at which certain events happened | T-6, T-7, T-8, T-14 |
| Time | Identifying when specific events happened | T-18, T-21, T-22 |
| Comparison | Comparing which team achieved more | T-9, T-15, T-16 |
| Basic | Reading basic variables | T-5, T-17, T-20, T-23 |

experience were measured on a 7-point scale anchored by *1 = not at all interested/experienced* and *7 = very interested/experienced*. In addition, participants were asked about their preferred MOBA game (*League of Legends, DotA 2, HotS*, Other). This was included because we hypothesized that – despite MOBAs sharing the basic gameplay rules – players preferring other MOBAs than *HotS* might not be as knowledgeable about the used maps which might impact the ability to solve the tasks, especially when they referred to locations (e.g., lanes) on the maps. Lastly, we inquired about their experience with their preferred MOBA game, e.g., rank, average hours spent playing per week. The answer options for the latter varied based on the selected game.

Next, the participants were instructed to open the visualization, read the overview provided on the webpage, and familiarize themselves with the user interface and controls. When ready the participant had to click the 'Next' button of the survey to proceed to the main part. This part consisted of 23 tasks (see Table 2). For the tasks (T), we took into account existing task taxonomies, specifically the triad framework by Peuquet [46] which distinguishes between three components of spatio-temporal data: *what, where,* and *when*. Several of the tasks related directly to these individual elements as their proper identification is essential for more complex tasks. Some, such as T-6 or T-14, however also required the simultaneous consideration of two components. The triad framework also formed the foundation for the task typology of Andrienko et al. [6] which extended it in various ways, amongst others, by distinguishing between identification and comparison tasks with respect to the three components, an aspect which we also took into account in our tasks. In addition, our tasks should also relate to the different types of game-related information shown and vary in difficulty. These tasks were categorized into six task types (see Table 1).

In addition, to probe into which insights about gameplay participants can gain from the visualization, we included an open task (T-4) asking *Which are the three main insights you can get when analyzing this match with the visualization?*

The tasks were posed with respect to four predefined matches taking place on four different maps (Blackheart's Bay, Battlefield of Eternity, Towers of Doom, and Cursed Hollow). This was done to reduce potential bias caused by using only one specific replay or map. Table 2 shows which tasks were performed on which map. T-4 was conducted on Blackheart's Bay. The upload of personal replays was turned off for the study. Once all tasks were completed, the survey asked participants to rate the usefulness of the three different views (perspective, top, side), the legend, and of the control panel on a 7-point scale anchored by *1 = not useful at all* and *7 = very useful*. Open-text questions further asked for three aspects participants liked about the visualization, three weaknesses of it, suggestions for improvements, and additional features which would be desirable. Participants could also share additional feedback. In total, the survey took about 20 to 30 min and fulfilled Masaryk University's ethical guidelines.

## 5.2   Participants

In total, 30 participants took part in the study. The age ranged from 18 to 40 years (M = 27, SD = 4.9). The gender ratio was skewed towards males, with 26 participants indicating to be male and 4 to be female, reflecting the overall general gender split observed in MOBA games [56]. The sample consisted of three players whose preferred MOBA game is *DotA 2*, 13 who preferred *League of Legends*, and 14 who preferred *HotS*. Participants expressed rather high interest in post-match game analysis (All: M = 5.6, SD = 1.1; *HotS*: M = 6.1, SD = 0.9; Other MOBAs: M = 5.1, SD = 1.1) while experience with post-match game analysis (All: M = 4.5, SD = 1.7; *HotS*: M = 4.4, SD = 1.7; Other MOBAs: M = 4.6, SD = 1.8) and gameplay visualization (All: M = 4.1, SD = 1.9; *HotS*: M = 3.9, SD = 2.0; Other MOBAs: M = 4.4, SD = 1.9) where both slightly above the scale's midpoint. In terms of experience with their selected MOBA game, participants indicated to spend 8.4 h on average per week (SD = 5.1) playing them. *HotS* players mainly had ranks of Gold (2), Platinum (5), and Diamond (4) and can thus be considered as highly skilled in the game. One player was at Masters rank and hence extremely skilled while the other two indicated a rank of Bronze and no rank (but having more than 12,000 games of quick match). In case of *League of Legends* ranks were a bit more distributed but the majority as well had a rank of Gold (2), Platinum (3), and Diamond (1). Three had a rank below Gold and three reported no rank. The three *DotA 2* players indicated ranks of Guardian, Crusader, and Archon, which can be considered low to middle ranks.

## 6   Results

Open-ended questions (e.g., insights reported during T-4, feedback questions) were analyzed individually using an inductive qualitative content analysis approach (cf. [41]). First, responses were coded by two of the authors individually to derive a set of keywords which were then grouped into categories. Participants' statements (or parts of them) were then assigned to these categories. Discrepancies in the assignment to the categories were resolved in discussion with a third researcher and the naming of the categories was adjusted. Below we only report categories that have been mentioned by at least 10% (N=3) of the participants.

Correctness of the tasks was established as follows. Tasks with a single answer (e.g., T-6, T-10) counted as correct if exactly this answer was provided. Tasks with multiple answers (e.g., T-1, T-2) only counted as correct if all correct answers (and only these) were given. Times of events had to be reported in minutes and were counted as correct if they referred to one of the 1-minute-bounds within the event took place. For instance, if an event took place at 7:30 min, both 7 and 8 min counted as correct.

## 6.1   Task Correctness

To asses if there are differences in terms of the number of correctly solved tasks between *HotS* players and players of other MOBA games (*DotA 2* and *League of Legends*) in our sample, we conducted – after confirming normality of the data using Shapiro-Wilk – an independent samples t-test. No statistically significant differences were observed ($t(28) = -.378$, $p = .708$). Additionally, we conducted Fisher exact tests (due to sparse contingency tables in the majority of cases, i.e. tables with expected cell frequencies less than five) to compare the correctness of the individual tasks. For all tasks, no significant differences were found with $p > .05$. As such we will not differentiate between them in the following.

Table 2 gives an overview of how many participants correctly solved the different tasks. Across all tasks, average correctness is 74.1%. Next, we discuss the results based on the task types specified in Table 1.

With respect to analyzing EVENTS that occurred during a certain time span, the two tasks (T-2, T-3) asking about which champions died within a certain interval were more successfully solved than tasks requiring to check different types of events (T-1, T-19). As these were only counted as correct if all correct answer options were checked, we more closely inspected these. Correct answer options for T-1 where selected with 70.0% to 93.33% correctness and those for task T-19 with 76.67% to 93.33%, suggesting that participants either missed a correct answer or selected an additional false one.

COUNTS related questions showed quite some variation in correctness. T-13, asking about the number of deaths about a certain champion, was solved correctly most frequently, likely because the task only involves counting the number of death icons of a particular color. Only about two-thirds could, however, solve T-11 correctly. This is likely caused by the fact that the user has to either rotate the perspective view or additionally refer to the side and top views to check if the paths are really adjacent (Fig. 3a,b). Likewise, T-12 was only solved correctly by slightly more than half of the participants. While the asked for information can also be extracted from the projected circles in addition to the 3D view, these circles may overlap too, causing participants to miss a certain death. However, T-10 was the least correct answered one in this group. As we could see from the feedback, participants thought that respawns were less obvious than other events (see Sect. 6.3). This is likely because respawns were only indirectly depicted through lines restarting at the location of the team's base (Fig. 3c).

**Table 2.** Tasks and percentage of participants correctly solving them. Tasks within each task type are sorted in ascending order according to correctness. (BB = Blackheart's Bay, BE = Battlefield of Eternity, CH = Cursed Hollow, TD = Towers of Doom)

| | ID | Map | Question | | Correctness |
|---|---|---|---|---|---|
| **Events** | 19 | CH | Check everything that also happened in the given time frame, you entered above. ($\rightarrow$ T-18) | | 13.33% |
| | 1 | BB | Check all correct statements that describe what happened between 6 - 7 minutes of the match. | | 46.67% |
| | 3 | BB | Check member(s) of the RED team that died between 6 - 7 minutes of the match. | | 73.33% |
| | 2 | BB | Check member(s) of the BLUE team that died between 6 - 7 minutes of the match. | | 80.00% |
| **Counts** | 10 | BE | How many RED team players respawned between 9 - 11 minutes? | | 46.67% |
| | 12 | BE | At 15 minute a team fight happened. How many players were involved? | | 56.67% |
| | 11 | BE | Analyze the gameplay between 14 - 15 minutes. How many players moved together in the biggest group? | | 63.33% |
| | 13 | TD | How many times the player, who played CASSIA, died? | | 83.33% |
| **Location** | 8 | BE | In which lane did the final push happen? | | 73.33% |
| | 6 | BE | In which lane did the first death happen? | | 90.00% |
| | 7 | BE | In which lane was the first structure destroyed? | | 90.00% |
| | 14 | TD | In which lane did the last death of the player, who played CASSIA, happen? | | 90.00% |
| **Time** | 18 | CH | Identify the time frame when the large number (3+) of structures was destroyed by the BLUE team. | | 80.00% |
| | 22 | CH | Time (in minutes) when the first structure was destroyed. | | 80.00% |
| | 21 | CH | Time (in minutes) when both teams reached level 10. | | 96.67% |
| **Comp.** | 9 | BE | How many RED team members were dead when BLUE team destroyed the first structure? | | 6.67% |
| | 16 | TD | Which team finished the game with more levels? | | 80.00% |
| | 15 | TD | Which team managed to reach more objectives? | | 100.00% |
| **Basic** | 5 | BE | Check the correct statement about the map. | | 93.33% |
| | 17 | TD | Was the boss captured in this match? | | 93.33% |
| | 20 | CH | Identify the game length in minutes. | | 93.33% |
| | 23 | CH | First destroyed structure type? | | 100.00% |

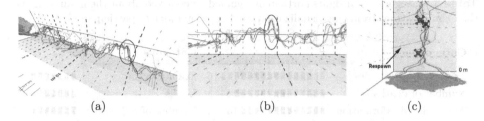

(a)                              (b)                              (c)

**Fig. 3.** Examples of visual representation issues causing difficulties with interpretation. (a & b) Estimating distances and visual depths can be difficult in a 3D perspective and thus may cause uncertainties when judging the proximity of heroes as required by T-11. (a) suggests that all except one player moved together between 14 and 15 min. Rotating the view (b) or observing other views is required to resolve this ambiguity. (c) Respawns were not explicitly marked in the visualization. Rather they had to be inferred from the paths originating at the base, potentially impacting T-9 and T-10.

Tasks requiring to infer the rough LOCATION of specific events where generally answered with very high correctness of 90%, except T-8 which has shown to be a bit more difficult. While the other tasks focused on events represented by icons, this task required to check the paths of the players and relate them to the map. Tasks dealing with when (TIME) certain events were happening were also answered with overall high correctness, independent of whether the information had be read from the STC itself or the auxiliary time axis.

However, COMPARISON tasks appear to have been considerable more difficult if they had to be solved using the STC itself (T-9) compared to when the information was depicted along the auxiliary time axis (T-15, T-16). However, it should be mentioned that T-9 was rather complex because it involved observing the death icons as well as the respawns within the proximity of the destruction event. If we neglect the respawn shortly before the event, 40% provided the correct answer. This again, indicates that respawns are not clearly visualized. In addition, participants also found the color coding of the structures unclear (see Sect. 6.3). The BASIC tasks were, as expected, solved without major issues.

## 6.2   Insights

In addition to the specific tasks above, we also included an open task (T-4) asking participants about the insights they can extract from the visualization. The derived categories of insights are summarized in Table 3. As we can see from the table, a bit less than half of the participants (N = 13) gained insights related to time such as when somebody died or a structure was destroyed.

The focus on time confirms the value of the STC for depicting temporal in-game data. Related to the spatio-temporal nature of the STC, participants also commented on spatial aspects (N = 7), notably on the positioning of players (e.g., closeness of players, positioning over time) and the spatial distribution of events.

**Table 3.** Categories of insights participants gained when asked about the main insights they could extract from the visualization (T-4, # = number of participants).

| Category | # | Category | # |
|---|---|---|---|
| Tactics and strategies | ▮▮▮▮▮▮▮▮▮▮▮▮▮▮▮▮ 16 | Team Advantage | ▮▮▮▮▮▮▮ 7 |
| Number of deaths | ▮▮▮▮▮▮▮▮▮▮▮▮▮▮ 14 | Levels | ▮▮▮▮▮▮ 6 |
| Time-related information | ▮▮▮▮▮▮▮▮▮▮▮▮▮ 13 | Number of objectives | ▮▮▮▮▮▮ 6 |
| Positions | ▮▮▮▮▮▮▮ 7 | Win/Loss | ▮▮▮ 3 |

Slightly more than half of the participants (N = 16) also reflected upon the different general tactics and strategies which might have been used by the teams. P12 was particularly detailed in this respect as the following quote illustrates:

*Blue was more consistent about objective, but Red primarily turned in after kills. Probably blue was hanging back farming camps more aggressively, but would push in to Red's territory too far and lose their stockpiled coins to a team fight. In a more general sense, Red team didn't throw the game, but capitalized on their advantage when they had it. Blue team played consistently well, but did not have enough of an advantage late game to avoid a decisive, opportunistic blow from Red. I'd say 'the comeback is real', but while that may have been the interpretation of the players in the match, Red never slipped too far behind on XP [experience points] despite losing significantly more structures and having fewer turn ins. Essentially, Blue team's lead was an illusion. They were doing more but not pulling far enough head in the process.* [P12]

Related to this, participants discussed instances of how teams compared to each other (N = 7), particularly which team had an advantage over the other, often also related to time aspects. Apart from higher-level inferences regarding strategies, participants also commented on the visualizations ability to gain insights about particular aspects such as the number of deaths (N = 14), level gains (N = 6), number of objectives (N = 6), and who ultimately won or lost the match (N=3).

### 6.3  Feedback

In terms of usefulness of the different parts of the visualization, the perspective view (M = 5.31, SD = 2.00), the legend (M = 5.31, SD = 1.99), as well as the control panel (M = 6.00, SD = 1.69) were rated to be similarly useful with all scoring at the higher end of the scale. The top (M = 3.79, SD 1.72) and side view (M = 4.07, SD = 1.73) scored lower around the midpoint of the scale.

The categories developed with respect to the benefits and weaknesses of the visualization as well as regarding suggestions for improvements and additional data to include are summarized in Table 4 and will be further discussed next.

**Table 4.** Categories of participants' feedback regarding benefits, drawbacks, and potential improvements (# = number of participants).

| Category | # |
| --- | --- |
| **Benefits** | |
| Filters and controls | ∎∎∎∎∎∎∎∎∎∎ 10 |
| Design and usability (e.g., color coding, icons, lines) | ∎∎∎∎∎∎∎∎∎ 9 |
| Overall approach | ∎∎∎∎∎∎∎∎ 8 |
| Overview | ∎∎∎∎∎∎∎∎ 8 |
| Timeline | ∎∎∎∎∎∎ 6 |
| Navigation | ∎∎∎∎ 4 |
| Visualization of movement | ∎∎∎ 3 |
| **Weaknesses** | |
| Color coding of players can be hard to distinguish | ∎∎∎∎∎∎∎∎∎∎∎∎∎ 13 |
| Lack of interaction possibilities (e.g., filter options) | ∎∎∎∎∎∎ 6 |
| Visual clutter | ∎∎∎∎∎ 5 |
| Respawns of the players are poorly visualized | ∎∎∎∎ 4 |
| Movement is sometimes not clear | ∎∎∎ 3 |
| **Suggestions for improvement** | |
| Graphical representation (e.g., display of respawns, colors) | ∎∎∎∎∎∎∎∎∎∎∎∎∎∎ 14 |
| Interactions (e.g., more filter options, highlighting of players) | ∎∎∎∎∎∎∎∎∎∎∎∎ 12 |
| Strictly orthogonal top and side view | ∎∎∎∎∎ 5 |
| **Suggestions for additional data to include** | |
| Additional statistics (e.g., gold, damage, precision, healing) | ∎∎∎∎∎∎∎∎∎∎∎∎∎∎ 14 |
| Information about camps | ∎∎∎∎ 4 |
| Talent choices | ∎∎∎ 3 |

*Benefits:* The filter possibilities and the control options received the most positive comments (N = 10). Related to this, four participants highlighted the intuitive navigation in the views themselves. Participants also made general comments about the design and usability of the system (N = 9), e.g., mentioning the well-chosen color coding, the descriptive icons, and the interpolation of lines.

The approach in general was also received positively, with eight participants commenting about the novelty of the visualization in this particular application domain. Three also specifically mentioned the 3D aspect. For instance, P22 who was initially not convinced commented: *While I initially thought the 3D view wasn't that interesting, I think it can bring a very interesting insight at a short glance.* Eight participants also appreciated the overview of the data (i.e. of the different aspects of a match) which comes with the STC approach. Three participants specifically lauded the visualization of movement. For example, P22 thought that it *provides a very clear view of the match, with movement of players across the map. It is easy to track the main events.* Lastly, the temporal perspective the visualization provides was also appreciated by six participants.

*Weaknesses:* While some people mentioned the color coding as benefit, it was also the most mentioned drawback of the visualization (N = 13). While participants thought that the players of the red and blue team could be well-distinguished, players within a team were less differentiable due to the color hues sometimes being too similar. Three of them also found the color coding of the destroyed buildings confusing since it was not exactly clear if the color indicates the team who destroyed it or the team the building belonged to.

Participants also commented about a lack of interaction possibilities (N = 6) such as missing options to filter the data and to be able to turn off the grid. Five participants considered the visualization to be crowded which, in turn, caused the displayed information to overlap, especially in places with high activity. This sometimes made it difficult to infer information, as P3 commented: *Deaths can overlap, making it hard to be sure who exactly died.*

As reported by four participants, respawns were not well recognizable in the visualization which made it difficult to find them. As discussed previously in Sect. 6.1 this is likely due to them not being explicitly encoded (see Fig. 3c). Indeed, one participant suggested to use icons to make them more obvious.

Lastly, while three participants liked the visualization of movement, an equal number of participants found it unclear. We assume that the clutter mentioned by other participants could be a reason for this.

*Suggestions for Improvements and Additional Data:* Made suggestions for improving the visualization are partly in line with the identified drawbacks and include changes to the graphical representation (N=14), particularly with respect to the encoding of respawns and adjusting the colors within the teams. Likewise, participants proposed additional interactions (N=12) such as more filter options and ways to navigate the views and customize their arrangement. Lastly, participants suggested to use a strictly 2D orthographic top and side view instead of having a perspective camera viewpoint from the top and side as in our case. We conclude that this is due to the slight perspective effect which was caused by this choice and which causes small displacements of the viewed data based on the position of the camera.

When asked about additional features, participants only reflected which additional data would be useful for their analyses. Primarily, participants (N = 14) suggested to include further statistics such as about gold, damage dealt, precision in team fights, healing done, and more. Four participants suggested to add information about camps which were currently not considered at all. Lastly, talent choices were also thought worthwhile to include by three participants.

# 7  Discussion

While various visualization types have been employed for visually representing in-game data, a substantial number uses 2D representations. If three dimensions have been used for depicting behavioral in-game data these are mostly concerned with visualizing trajectories in the actual 3D game environment (e.g., [11, 15, 28]). In this work, we thus adapted the established STC representation to explore its value in the context of spatio-temporal match review and if the added complexity poses difficulties for players. With respect to our two study goals we can conclude that a) facts about the data can on overall be well retrieved from the STC and b) that it was generally well received.

With respect to the correct interpretation of the data, we can summarize that across all tasks overall correctness was rather high with participants on average solving 74% of the tasks correctly (regardless of the preferred game). However, correctness also varied between the tasks from about 7% (T-9) to 100% (T-15 and T-23). This is, however, in line with findings from other studies in other domains. For instance, Filho et al. [17] reported task success rates in a similar range. Lower performance on certain tasks can usually be attributed to visual clutter (i.e. occlusions) or to a lack of depth cues which made it difficult to estimate the proximity of graphical elements (e.g., lines, icons) inside the STC. Both are well-known drawbacks of the STC representation as reported in the literature (cf. [12, 17]). For icons we attempted to address this, by projecting them onto the bottom and back plane of the STC which, however, could only solve this issue partially as occlusions may still occur. The issue with the proximity of lines could potentially be addressed by automatically detecting co-located champions and visually encoding them (e.g., through the transparency of the lines).

The 3D representation and the complexity arising through it can be a disadvantage (e.g., [5]) but this did not appear to cause issues in our study. On the contrary, participants appreciated this approach (see Table 4, Benefits), taking a positive stance towards the 3D representation. We assume that this is because players are in general familiar with navigating 3D environments and adjusting camera perspectives. Previous work such as [5, 18] has highlighted the importance of interactions to manipulate the STC. Although we supported already various ways for navigating the camera and filtering the data – and this was appreciated by the participants – they also called for further interaction possibilities such as additional filters. As such, if 3D visualizations are used for gameplay analysis an appropriate set of interactions should be provided to support data inference. Another opportunity could be to offer a set of pre-defined configurations of the display that align with commonly performed analysis tasks.

Another issue was mainly caused by a particular design choice we made: respawns were only visible through the players' paths. This made them less obvious to detect in the STC, also because the visibility depends on the perspective from which the cube is viewed. This could be resolved by, as proposed, marking those respawns explicitly with icons. Related to this, participants also made suggestions for including further game-related information. However, this will add further visual elements to the STC which, in turn, can contribute to visual clutter. An interesting observation in this regard is that albeit participants reported visual clutter as a drawback of the STC they, at the same time, requested to display further information. As such it is important to carefully weight the importance of different gameplay aspects to be shown within the STC. Another possibility could be to show specific information only on demand, for instance, when hovering over lines and icons. In conclusion, we can say that the drawbacks mainly revolved around specific design aspects (e.g., colors, respawns) and a lack of interaction possibilities but less about the actual 3D representation.

Displaying space and time simultaneously has shown to be valuable to the players as our participants reported insights related to both spatial and temporal aspects. At this point it is, however, important to note that our evaluation was mainly task-based to assess if the data can be correctly inferred from the visualization. This is an important prerequisite to construct higher-level insights [4]. While we probed briefly into the types of insights players can derive, further studies will be necessary to evaluate the STC for higher-level analytical tasks. However, even if only touched upon this briefly, we could see that participants were reflecting about the tactics and strategies used by the different teams.

On the other hand, the STC does not seem an appropriate choice for all games. As we could see from our results, even when only showing the data of ten players visual clutter already caused difficulties when interpreting the data in case of certain tasks (e.g., group movements, overlapping of icons). Results from the field of geographic information sciences [12] also do not recommend STCs for a larger number of movers. As such we consider the STC more helpful in games with a small number of actors. A possible direction forward could also be to combine individual space-time paths with a density-based approach (e.g., [12]) to aggregate movement, for instance, to allow players compare their own with the average behaviour of others. It should also be noted that a STC is only suitable for games where movement can be reasonable described in two dimensions, as the third axis is used to represent time. As such it may have limited use for games in which 3D movement patterns are important.

Lastly, we would like to acknowledge some limitations arising from the study itself. First, our sample was composed of players who indicated to have an above-average interest in and experience with post-match game analysis. It should also be kept in mind, that our sample mostly consisted of intermediate to more highly experienced players. Previous work such as [20] has shown that STCs can potentially be difficult to interpret. Hence, it would be interesting to expand the demographics to players with less pre-knowledge and skill to investigate in more depth if novice players can interpret and benefit from the visualization in the same way. Secondly, due to the online setup we did refrain from measuring timings for the individual tasks as those may be unreliable and focused only on task correctness. Future work should thus further investigate the effectiveness of the visualization by not only considering correctness but also factors such as mental effort and time spent on the task (see [25]). Lastly, we used multiple matches to avoid potential bias caused by using only a single match. While we visually picked matches of similar complexity, some impact on the results caused by the different particularities of each match cannot be completely ruled out.

While our results showed that the tasks, with some exceptions, were well performed we need to highlight that many tasks were rather elementary and spatial tasks were few. Nevertheless, the findings still provide a promising path forward as elementary tasks are important for higher-level inferences. Related to this, future work also needs to look into comparative evaluations to assess whether the STC is more or less helpful compared to existing gameplay visualization methods such as animated maps. This was outside the scope of this study.

## 8 Conclusions

Visualizations of in-game data are an increasingly important asset of data-driven tools that allow players to review their in-game performance. However, spatio-temporal visualisations that provide an integrated perspective of both space and time in a single view found little attention in games-related literature. Such visualizations are often realized in 3D, which adds additional complexity and may thus not be suitable for all user groups. In this paper, we focused on the established STC visualization to study how it is received by players and if they can observe the displayed data correctly. Our results show that such representations do have potential for this application scenario with players being able to extract data with comparatively high overall correctness and responding positively to this kind of approach. However, it also shows that interaction- and design choices need to be made with care to provide adequate means to adapt and manipulate the visualization. Given our findings, we would advocate for further research in this direction to explore the prospects of 3D visualizations for gameplay analysis.

## References

1. Afonso, A.P., Carmo, M.B., Gonçalves, T., Vieira, P.: Visualeague: player performance analysis using spatial-temporal data. Multimed. Tools Appl. **78**(23), 33069–33090 (2019)
2. Agarwal, S., Wallner, G., Beck, F.: Bombalytics: visualization of competition and collaboration strategies of players in a bomb laying game. Comput. Graph. Forum **39**(3), 89–100 (2020). https://doi.org/10.1111/cgf.13965
3. Ahmad, S., Bryant, A., Kleinman, E., Teng, Z., Nguyen, T.H.D., Seif El-Nasr, M.: Modeling individual and team behavior through spatio-temporal analysis. In: Proceedings of the Annual Symposium on Computer-Human Interaction in Play, pp. 601–612. Association for Computing Machinery, New York (2019). https://doi.org/10.1145/3311350.3347188
4. Amar, R., Eagan, J., Stasko, J.: Low-level components of analytic activity in information visualization. In: IEEE Symposium on Information Visualization, pp. 111–117 (2005). https://doi.org/10.1109/INFVIS.2005.1532136
5. Amini, F., Rufiange, S., Hossain, Z., Ventura, Q., Irani, P., McGuffin, M.J.: The impact of interactivity on comprehending 2d and 3d visualizations of movement data. IEEE Trans. Visual Comput. Graphics **21**(1), 122–135 (2015). https://doi.org/10.1109/TVCG.2014.2329308
6. Andrienko, N., Andrienko, G., Gatalsky, P.: Exploratory spatio-temporal visualization: an analytical review. J. Visual Lang. Comput. **14**(6), 503–541 (2003). https://doi.org/10.1016/S1045-926X(03)00046-6, visual Data Mining

7. Barrett, B.: Heroes. ReplayParser (2020). https://github.com/barrett777/Heroes. ReplayParser. Accessed May 2023
8. Blizzard Entertainment: Heroes of the Storm. Game [PC] (Juni: Blizzard Entertainment. Irvine, California, USA (2015)
9. Brower, G.M.: lil-gui (2022), https://github.com/georgealways/lil-gui Accessed: May, 2023
10. Coulton, P., Bamford, W., Cheverst, K., Rashid, O.: 3d space-time visualization of player behaviour in pervasive location-based games. International Journal of Computer Games Technology 2008 (2008)
11. Dankoff, J.: Game telemetry with DNA tracking on assassin's creed (2014). https://www.gamedeveloper.com/design/game-telemetry-with-dna-tracking-on-assassin-s-creed. Accessed May 2023
12. Demšar, U., Virrantaus, K.: Space-time density of trajectories: exploring spatio-temporal patterns in movement data. Int. J. Geogr. Inf. Sci. 24(10), 1527–1542 (2010). https://doi.org/10.1080/13658816.2010.511223
13. Dixit, P.N., Youngblood, G.M.: Understanding playtest data through visual data mining in interactive 3d environments. In: 12th International Conference on Computer Games: AI, Animation, Mobile, Interactive Multimedia and Serious Games, pp. 34–42 (2008)
14. Drachen, A., Canossa, A.: Analyzing spatial user behavior in computer games using geographic information systems. In: Proceedings of the 13th International MindTrek Conference: Everyday Life in the Ubiquitous Era, pp. 182–189. Association for Computing Machinery, New York (2009). https://doi.org/10.1145/1621841.1621875
15. Drenikow, B., Mirza-Babaei, P.: Vixen: interactive visualization of gameplay experiences. In: Proceedings of the 12th International Conference on the Foundations of Digital Games. Association for Computing Machinery, New York (2017). https://doi.org/10.1145/3102071.3102089
16. Ferreira, N., Poco, J., Vo, H.T., Freire, J., Silva, C.T.: Visual exploration of big spatio-temporal urban data: a study of New York city taxi trips. IEEE Trans. Visual Comput. Graphics 19(12), 2149–2158 (2013). https://doi.org/10.1109/TVCG.2013.226
17. Filho, J.A.W., Stuerzlinger, W., Nedel, L.: Evaluating an immersive space-time cube geovisualization for intuitive trajectory data exploration. IEEE Trans. Visual Comput. Graphics 26(1), 514–524 (2020). https://doi.org/10.1109/TVCG.2019.2934415
18. Gatalsky, P., Andrienko, N., Andrienko, G.: Interactive analysis of event data using space-time cube. In: Proceedings. Eighth International Conference on Information Visualisation, pp. 145–152. IEEE, Washington, DC (2004). https://doi.org/10.1109/IV.2004.1320137
19. Gomez, S.R., Guo, H., Ziemkiewicz, C., Laidlaw, D.H.: An insight- and task-based methodology for evaluating spatiotemporal visual analytics. In: IEEE Conference on Visual Analytics Science and Technology (VAST), pp. 63–72. IEEE, Washington, DC (2014). https://doi.org/10.1109/VAST.2014.7042482
20. Gonçalves, T., Afonso, A.P., Martins, B.: Why not both? - combining 2D maps and 3D space-time cubes for human trajectory data visualization. In: Proceedings of the 30th International BCS Human Computer Interaction Conference, pp. 1–10. BCS Learning and Development Ltd., Swindon (2016). https://doi.org/10.14236/ewic/HCI2016.22

21. Gonçalves, T., Vieira, P., Afonso, A.P., Carmo, M.B., Moucho, T.: Analysing player performance with animated maps. In: 22nd International Conference Information Visualisation (IV), pp. 103–109. IEEE, Washington, DC (2018). https://doi.org/10.1109/iV.2018.00028

22. Hägerstrand, T.: What about people in regional science? In: European Congress of The Regional Science Association Copenhagen, vol. 69 (1970)

23. Harrower, M., Fabrikant, S.: The Role of Map Animation for Geographic Visualization, chap. 4, pp. 49–65. John Wiley & Sons, Ltd (2008). https://doi.org/10.1002/9780470987643.ch4

24. Hoobler, N., Humphreys, G., Agrawala, M.: Visualizing competitive behaviors in multi-user virtual environments. In: IEEE Visualization 2004, pp. 163–170. IEEE, Washington, DC (2004). https://doi.org/10.1109/VISUAL.2004.120

25. Huang, W., Eades, P., Hong, S.H.: Measuring effectiveness of graph visualizations: a cognitive load perspective. Inf. Vis. 8(3), 139–152 (2009). https://doi.org/10.1057/ivs.2009.10

26. Jun, E., Landry, S., Salvendy, G.: Exploring the cognitive costs and benefits of using multiple-view visualisations. Behav. Inf. Technol. 32(8), 824–835 (2013). https://doi.org/10.1080/0144929X.2011.630420

27. Kapler, T., Wright, W.: Geotime information visualization. Inf. Vis. 4(2), 136–146 (2005)

28. Kepplinger, D., Wallner, G., Kriglstein, S., Lankes, M.: See, feel, move: Player behaviour analysis through combined visualization of gaze, emotions, and movement. In: Proceedings of the 2020 CHI Conference on Human Factors in Computing Systems, CHI 2020, pp. 1–14. Association for Computing Machinery, New York (2020). https://doi.org/10.1145/3313831.3376401

29. Kessenich, J., Sellers, G., Shreiner, D.: OpenGL Programming Guide: The Official Guide to Learning OpenGL, 9th edn. Addison Wesley, Boston (2016)

30. Kleinman, E., El-Nasr, M.S.: Using data to "git gud": a push for a player-centric approach to the use of data in esports (2021). https://doi.org/10.31219/osf.io/v3g79, oSF Preprints

31. Kleinman, E., Preetham, N., Teng, Z., Bryant, A., Seif El-Nasr, M.: "What happened here!?" a taxonomy for user interaction with spatio-temporal game data visualization. Proc. ACM Hum.-Comput. Interact. 5(CHI PLAY), October 2021. https://doi.org/10.1145/3474687

32. de Koning, R.: Visualization of Animal Behaviour Within the Space-Time Cube: A Transformation Framework to Improve Legibility. Master's thesis, Wageningen University and Research Centre (2016). https://edepot.wur.nl/410205

33. Kraak, M.J.: The space-time cube revisited from a geovisualization perspective. In: ICC 2003: Proceedings of the 21st International Cartographic Conference, pp. 1988–1996. International Cartographic Association, New Zealand (2003)

34. Kriglstein, S., Wallner, G., Pohl, M.: A user study of different gameplay visualizations. In: Proceedings of the SIGCHI Conference on Human Factors in Computing Systems, CHI 2014, pp. 361–370. Association for Computing Machinery, New York (2014). https://doi.org/10.1145/2556288.2557317

35. Kristensson, P.O., Dahlback, N., Anundi, D., Bjornstad, M., Gillberg, H., Haraldsson, J., Martensson, I., Nordvall, M., Stahl, J.: An evaluation of space time cube representation of spatiotemporal patterns. IEEE Trans. Visual Comput. Graphics 15(4), 696–702 (2009). https://doi.org/10.1109/TVCG.2008.194

36. Kuan, Y.T., Wang, Y.S., Chuang, J.H.: Visualizing real-time strategy games: the example of starcraft ii. In: 2017 IEEE Conference on Visual Analytics Science and Technology (VAST), pp. 71–80. IEEE, Washington, DC (2017). https://doi.org/10.1109/VAST.2017.8585594

37. Kveladze, I., Kraak, M.J., Elzakker, C.P.V.: The space-time cube as part of a geovisual analytics environment to support the understanding of movement data. Int. J. Geogr. Inf. Sci. **29**(11), 2001–2016 (2015). https://doi.org/10.1080/13658816.2015.1058386

38. Li, W., Funk, M., Li, Q., Brombacher, A.: Visualizing event sequence game data to understand player's skill growth through behavior complexity. J. Visualization **22**(4), 833–850 (2019)

39. Li, X., Çöltekin, A., Kraak, M.J.: Visual exploration of eye movement data using the space-time-cube. In: Fabrikant, S.I., Reichenbacher, T., van Kreveld, M., Schlieder, C. (eds.) Geographic Information Science, pp. 295–309. Springer, Heidelberg (2010). https://doi.org/10.1007/978-3-642-15300-6_21

40. MacCormick, D., Zaman, L.: Echo: Analyzing Gameplay Sessions by Reconstructing Them From Recorded Data, pp. 281–293. Association for Computing Machinery, New York (2020)

41. Mayring, P.: Qualitative Content Analysis: Theoretical Background and Procedures, pp. 365–380. Springer, Netherlands (2015). https://doi.org/10.1007/978-94-017-9181-6_13

42. Menno-Jan Kraak, I.K.: Narrative of the annotated space-time cube - revisiting a historical event. J. Maps **13**(1), 56–61 (2017). https://doi.org/10.1080/17445647.2017.1323034

43. Mirza-Babaei, P., Nacke, L.E., Gregory, J., Collins, N., Fitzpatrick, G.: How does it play better? exploring user testing and biometric storyboards in games user research. In: Proceedings of the SIGCHI Conference on Human Factors in Computing Systems, pp. 1499–1508. Association for Computing Machinery, New York (2013). https://doi.org/10.1145/2470654.2466200

44. Mo, C., et al.: An analysis of spatiotemporal pattern for coivd-19 in china based on space-time cube. J. Med. Virology **92**, 1587–1595 (2020). https://doi.org/10.1002/jmv.25834

45. Moore, A., Whigham, P., Holt, A., Aldridge, C., Hodge, K.: A time geography approach to the visualisation of sport. In: Proceedings of the 7th International Conference on GeoComputation. University of Southampton, Southampton, UK, May 2022

46. Peuquet, D.J.: It's about time: A conceptual framework for the representation of temporal dynamics in geographic information systems. Ann. Assoc. Am. Geogr. **84**(3), 441–461 (1994). https://doi.org/10.1111/j.1467-8306.1994.tb01869.x

47. Slingsby, A., van Loon, E.: Exploratory visual analysis for animal movement ecology. Comput. Graph. Forum **35**(3), 471–480 (2016). https://doi.org/10.1111/cgf.12923

48. three.js authors: ThreeJs (2022). https://github.com/mrdoob/three.js/. Accessed May (2023)

49. Turchenko, M.: Space-Time Cube Visualization in a Mixed Reality Environment. Masterarbeit, Technische Universität München, 80333 München, September 2018

50. Tversky, B., Bauer Morrisony, J., Betrancourt, M.: Animation: can it facilitate? Int. J. Hum. Comput. Stud. **57**(4), 247–262 (2002). https://doi.org/10.1006/ijhc.2002.1017

51. Wallner, G., Halabi, N., Mirza-Babaei, P.: Aggregated visualization of playtesting data. In: Proceedings of the 2019 CHI Conference on Human Factors in Computing Systems, pp. 1–12. Association for Computing Machinery, New York (2019). https://doi.org/10.1145/3290605.3300593

52. Wallner, G., Kriglstein, S.: A spatiotemporal visualization approach for the analysis of gameplay data. In: Proceedings of the SIGCHI Conference on Human Factors in Computing Systems, pp. 1115–1124. Association for Computing Machinery, New York (2012). https://doi.org/10.1145/2207676.2208558

53. Wallner, G., Kriglstein, S.: Visualization-based analysis of gameplay data - a review of literature. Entertainment Comput. 4(3), 143–155 (2013). https://doi.org/10.1016/j.entcom.2013.02.002

54. Wallner, G., Kriglstein, S.: Multivariate visualization of game metrics: an evaluation of hexbin maps. In: Proceedings of the Annual Symposium on Computer-Human Interaction in Play, pp. 572–584. Association for Computing Machinery, New York (2020). https://doi.org/10.1145/3410404.3414233

55. Wallner, G., van Wijland, M., Bernhaupt, R., Kriglstein, S.: What players want: information needs of players on post-game visualizations. In: Proceedings of the 2021 CHI Conference on Human Factors in Computing Systems, CHI 2021. Association for Computing Machinery, New York (2021). https://doi.org/10.1145/3411764.3445174

56. Yee, N.: Beyond 50/50: Breaking down the percentage of female gamers by genre (2017). https://quanticfoundry.com/2017/01/19/female-gamers-by-genre/. Accessed May 2023

# Interacting with Children

# Awayvirus: A Playful and Tangible Approach to Improve Children's Hygiene Habits in Family Education

Xiang Qi[1], Yaxiong Lei[2(✉)], Shijing He[3(✉)], and Shuxin Cheng[4]

[1] Hong Kong Polytechnic University, Hung Hom, Hong Kong SAR, China
xiang.qi@connect.polyu.hk
[2] University of St Andrews, St Andrews, UK
yl212@st-andrews.ac.uk
[3] King's College London, London, UK
shijing.he@kcl.ac.uk
[4] Central Academy of Fine Arts, Beijing, China
shuxincheng@cafa.edu.cn

**Abstract.** Despite various playful and educational tools have been developed to support children's learning abilities, limited work focuses on tangible toys designed to improve and maintain children's hygiene perception, habits and awareness, as well as fostering their collaboration and social abilities in home education contexts. We developed **Awayvirus** to address this research and design gap, aiming to help children gain hygiene habits knowledge through tangible blocks. Our findings indicate that a playful tangible interaction method can effectively increase children's interest in learning and encourage parents to become actively involved in their children's hygiene and health education. Additionally, Awayvirus seeks to build a collaborative bridge between children and parents, promoting communication strategies while mitigating the adverse effects of the challenging the post-pandemic period.

**Keywords:** Playful Learning · Tangible · Children Hygiene Habits

## 1 Introduction

The COVID-19 pandemic has highlighted the significance of overall health and well-being, emphasising the necessity of effective hygiene practices within family units, such as handwashing. This needs for additional measures is particularly crucial during resettlement periods, given the heightened risk of viral infections. Moreover, the pandemic has disrupted conventional education and socialisation methods for children, resulting in elevated levels of stress, and anxiety, reduced

**Supplementary Information** The online version contains supplementary material available at https://doi.org/10.1007/978-3-031-42283-6_10.

interest in learning [20], and ineffective communication strategies [3]. Consequently, health literacy assumes a substantial role in shaping health behaviours, especially among preschool children.

Playfulness has been recognised as an effective approach for children's education [11]. However, parents faced challenges in teaching their children proper hygiene habits using engaging and playful strategies. To address such challenges, we aim to investigate the potential of gamified educational tools with tangible interactions to enhance children's interest in learning about hygiene protection and to promote parent-child interaction during the learning process. To guide our research, we have formulated the following research questions: **RQ1:** Can the incorporation of gamified elements increase children's interest in learning about hygiene and improve the acceptance of the educational design? **RQ2:** How can a gamified design effectively facilitate children's learning of hand washing and good hygiene habits? **RQ3:** In what ways can a gamified design enhance communication about hygiene between parents and children?

Our findings indicate that children's interest in learning hygiene knowledge increased after engaging with Awayvirus. We also observed that parental encouragement positively impacted children's emotions during play. Children demonstrated enthusiasm and voluntarily assisted their parents in completing collaborative educational tasks. Additionally, the power imbalance between child and parent tended to shift towards a more balanced relationship during interaction and negotiation processes.

Our main contributions are: 1) exploring how gamified educational tools with tangible interactions can increase children's learning about hygiene protection knowledge and promote parent-child communication; and 2) highlighting the challenges and findings surrounding tangible interaction in learning about hygiene protection knowledge and parent-child interaction.

## 2   Related Work

### 2.1   Gamification in Health Professions Education

Human-computer interaction (HCI) has shown that gamification holds significant potential within health and educational research spheres [10,23]. This potential is largely due to its capacity to enhance learning outcomes and modify children's behaviour [5,6]. Examples of such applications can be seen in efforts to alleviate stress in paediatric patients within healthcare settings [17,27], as well as to bolster digital health literacy and health awareness among children [28]. Gamification has even been used to encourage physical activity and social interaction [19]. However, its use in fostering hygiene habits and promoting hygiene education among children remains under-explored, presenting an opportunity for further research in this domain.

### 2.2   Educational Tangible Interaction

A growing body of research highlights the extensive applicability of tangible user interfaces (TUI) in diverse environments and fields [22,29]. The transformative potential of TUI lies in its capacity to revolutionise traditional teaching methods, enhance student engagement, and facilitate informal learning experiences [14, 18,25]. Furthermore, the incorporation of tactile interactions in TUI has been found to support learning [7]. The integration of gamified elements within TUI represents an engaging design approach, enabling children to develop essential skills through play [1,9].

### 2.3 Parent-Child Interactions in Home Learning Activities

The crucial role of parent-child interactions in children's growth and development is well-established, particularly when it comes to enhancing learning interest through positive reinforcement [15]. Recently, researchers have started to investigate the influence of various media, such as tablets [4] and artificial intelligence [8], on these interactions. They serve as vehicles for conveying family values and beliefs to children, shaping their perceptions and interpretations of the world around them [13,24].

Despite these insights, research on tangible interactions specifically designed to educate early childhood learners about hygiene, with a special emphasis on parent-child interaction, remains scarce. Our design aims to bridge this gap, providing parents with a tool that captivates children's attention during home-based learning, while simultaneously stimulating their interest and fostering their communication abilities.

## 3    Methodology

Our research aims to comprehend children's perspective of hygiene habits and investigate how parental support can enhance their learning in this area. To achieve this, we employed a design thinking process [21] to underscore the significance of understanding adoption, usage, preference, and family health education strategies. Our multifaceted research methodology included surveys, semi-structured interviews with parents and professionals, and field trials [2], designed to gauge collaboration, children's comprehension, and behaviours. Our study has received the ethics approval from the university's ethics committee.

### 3.1    Survey

We conducted two surveys on wjx.com, we applied social media and snowball sampling for participant recruitment. The first survey delved into the nature of parent-child interactions during game-playing, toy preferences, and educational necessities. The second survey aimed to understand parents' concerns about family education during the pandemic. We obtained 36 responses for the hygiene education strategy survey and 43 responses for the purchasing preferences survey. The results indicated a prevalent pattern among parents regarding hygiene knowledge learning and application. 24.9% of parents expressed apprehension about their child's health protection and individual personality development within the context of home education. A majority of parents (66%) employed varied educational tools such as animated videos (63.9%), picture books (55.6%), mobile games (27.8%), and toys (47.2%) to educate their children about hygiene and raise awareness. Yet, a significant challenge remained in effectively engaging their children in comprehending hygiene knowledge. These survey findings offered critical insights for designing educational tools that facilitate more effective children's learning about hygiene habits and knowledge.

## 3.2    Interview

We organised semi-structured interviews with two families, a 35-year-old father and his 5-year-old son, and a 30-year-old mother and her 6 years old son. We also conducted a semi-structured interview with a paediatrician from a public hospital. We inquired about their experiences, focusing on the challenges encountered in promoting family hygiene education. A shared difficulty was maintaining a balance of parental involvement across varied contexts. One father highlighted the struggle of effective communication and education during home quarantine, pointing to challenges in hygiene learning and managing distractions. Despite her nursing expertise, one mother confessed to resorting to corporal punishment due to a lack of effective educational approaches. She recognised the potential benefits of game-playing and role-playing but was concerned about excessive screen exposure. The paediatrician underscored the need to captivate preschool children's interest and cater to their inclination for hands-on learning, advocating entertaining learning methods like assembly activities, and emphasising the essential role of parental support and effective communication strategies.

The interviews revealed common issues faced by parents in promoting home hygiene education, such as limited parental experience, ineffective pedagogical approaches, power imbalance, limited child interest, and distractions. The increased shared time during home quarantine underscored the need for effective communication strategies. To overcome these challenges, the proposed design focuses on incorporating tangible and gamified design elements to increase children's engagement with hygiene knowledge, support family education, encourage parent-child communication, and enhance hygiene learning outcomes.

## 3.3    Design Process

We brainstormed and developed design concepts based on insights gleaned from previous investigations. We used a solution chart with four axes: usability, playfulness, metaphor comprehension, and prototyping practices. Subsequently, we amalgamated the four concepts into three novel product solutions and assessed each for their strengths and weaknesses. From a human-centred design perspective, we proposed tangible blocks of various geometric shapes that provide different assembly challenges and are made of natural materials [30]. Our design aims to enhance children's understanding and promote their auditory and spatial language abilities [26], as well as foster practical cooperation skills.

*Gamification Elements.* We integrated gamification elements based on the recommendations of Hamari [12] and Lessel [16]. We incorporated principles including "Establishing objectives", "Capacity to overcome challenges", "Offering feedback on achievements", "Encouragement & motivation", "Assessing & tracking progress", "Fostering social connections" and "Fun & playfulness". However, to prioritise parent-child interaction and learning effectiveness, we excluded competitive mechanisms and point allocation. The design solution focuses on utilising gamification elements to encourage parents and children to engage in activities such as assembling and discussing hygiene knowledge, enhancing interest and effectiveness in learning within the family context.

*Prototype.* Our prototype, as depicted in Fig. 1, consists of an assembly block prototype, an Arduino motion sensor module, and learning cards. The blocks represent objects susceptible to virus attachment, and assembling them conveys the metaphor of virus transmission, such as the assembly of virus stingers onto a doorknob block. An interactive voice module with a wearable detection device prompts hand-washing by notifying the child of unhygienic behaviour. The primary objectives of Awayvirus are to raise awareness of virus attachment, emphasise timely handwashing, and facilitate learning and practice of proper handwashing techniques with parental involvement. Learning cards supplement children's understanding of basic hygiene knowledge.

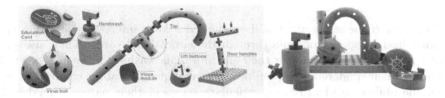

**Fig. 1.** Prototype of Awayvirus, made of different shapes and wooden materials, including tap, doorknob, handrail, and hand sanitiser. Stingers on virus blocks can be assembled onto other blocks

*Pilot Study and Results.* We conducted a pilot test involving a mother and her 6-year-old son in a home context, which lasted approximately 2 h. We obtained recorded consent from the participants. The overall feedback from the tests indicated positive attitudes towards usability. However, challenges were identified, including low interest in voice interaction reminders and limited acceptance of wearable devices. For example, children displayed reluctance to wear the devices and demonstrated decreased enthusiasm. Parents also expressed concerns about small parts posing a potential choking hazard. Based on the pilot study results, we removed the voice model and wearable detection features, while the wooden building blocks and card learning components were retained.

## 4    Findings

Our findings are categorised under three main headings: Playful Learning, Learning Hygiene Habits, and Parent-Child Communication.

*Playful Learning.* Tests yielded positive responses, with children showing strong enthusiasm towards the learning blocks. We observed that children demonstrated their autonomous engagement for active participation during the cooperative learning process, such as paper cutting and simulating handwashing (see Fig. 2). The gamification elements successfully instigated intrinsic motivation and creativity, as exemplified by children modifying the learning materials based on their own ideas and activities involving adults in the handwashing process.

**Fig. 2.** Pilot Test in Home Context (a): Engagement for paper cutting and cooperative interaction

*Learning Hygiene Habits.* Children showed a keen interest in listening and learning basic hygiene concepts through the educational cards. They also presented a propensity to imitate their parents' handwashing movements, which enhanced their understanding of proper technique. Notably, children showcased the ability to identify and articulate errors in their parents' handwashing behaviour, exemplifying their grasp of hygiene principles. While occasional difficulties in recalling specific vocabulary were observed, as shown in Fig. 3, children exhibited a solid comprehension of the association between the building blocks and real-life hygiene items, showcasing their autonomy and critical thinking skills.

*Parent-Child Communication.* Incorporating playful design elements positively influenced parent-child communication and engagement. Parents observed increased eagerness and reduced distractions in their children during educational activities. The interaction during paper cutting and block assembly tasks positioned parents as guides, motivating their children (Fig. 2) and fostering the parent-child bond. Children actively participated in collaborative learning, suggesting ideas and rectifying their parents' mistakes (Fig. 3). These actions contribute to equalising power dynamics in home education. Additionally, children independently initiated further activities such as simulating handwashing and reminding parents to use hand sanitiser.

Our findings also pinpoint areas for potential improvement in the prototype design, particularly concerning safety and materials. For instance, the lack of ventilation holes in the extended parts of the virus spikes raised concerns

**Fig. 3.** Pilot Test in Home Context (b): The upper part shows children rectifying their parents' mistakes, and the lower part illustrates learning outcomes after playing

about accidental swallowing. Adult participants stressed the importance of long-term safety considerations in selecting materials. Moreover, children exhibited a greater preference for parental interaction compared to the interactive sound and showed limited interest in the wearable device.

## 5   Discussion

In the home context, the gamified learning method stimulates children's learning interests, proactive learning attitudes, and imitating behaviours. Parents further reported that their children has been increased focus and engagement in learning about hygienic habits (e.g., handwashing), they actively involve their parents and offer feedback. However, equipping children with wearable devices led to negative emotional outbursts, which could be alleviated through parental encouragement and support. We emphasise the importance of addressing children's emotional fluctuations during learning and underscore the significant impact of parent-child relationships on children's emotional development.

We further demonstrate the efficacy of employing a playful learning approach to teach children about hygiene habits and facilitate positive parent-child communication. Future research will focus on addressing identified areas of improvement in the prototype design and refining teaching aids to enhance children's understanding and engagement. We also highlight the potential of gamification and interactive learning tools in effectively teaching essential hygiene habits to young children, fostering autonomy, and critical thinking skills, and strengthening parent-child relationships.

Our research findings highlight the role of parents in fostering collaboration with their children during joint learning activities. Awayvirus effectively maintains children's engagement and encourages them to express their ideas, seek cooperation, and address parents' improper hygiene behaviours or raise questions. The gamified design of Awayvirus promotes mutual assistance between parents and children, creates opportunities for open and equal dialogue, and mitigates parental blame and power during the learning and negotiation process. It establishes new channels for parent-child communication and enhances the overall family learning experience.

### 5.1   Design Implications

We highlight two key design insights: 1) addressing children's hands-on practice needs, and 2) fostering parent-child communication with parents as scaffolding. We also show that tangible interaction is an effective approach for early childhood educational tools, promoting interaction and collaboration.

*Hands-on Requirements.* Tangible interactions facilitate practical knowledge application and self-expression, aiding young children in understanding content and minimising distractions. It is essential to integrate features that accommodate children's hands-on learning needs and ensure ease of use.

*Communication Requirements.* Playful designs should emphasise parental involvement and cooperative processes, encouraging children's active participation and expression. The design needs to enhance parent-child communication and contributes to stronger emotional bonds and improved learning experiences.

### 5.2   Limitations

We acknowledge certain limitations in the present study. Firstly, the study was conducted during the quarantine period in China and involved a limited number of participants from a specific demographic group. Therefore, the results may not fully represent the diverse experiences and perspectives of families across different cultural, social, and economic backgrounds. Secondly, we did not investigate the long-term impact of the intervention on children's hygiene habits, behaviour, or sustainability of the observed positive outcomes. Thirdly, we did not compare the effectiveness of our prototype with other educational interventions for teaching children about hygiene protection. Future research comparing the design with other approaches could provide valuable insights into the most effective strategies for promoting hygiene habits education in early childhood.

## 6   Conclusion

Our study introduces a playful educational block approach for teaching hygiene habits to children, with the goal of stimulating their interest in learning, providing age-appropriate hygiene education, and facilitating communication between children and parents in a home-based educational context. We demonstrate the potential of the playful approach in teaching young children about hygiene habits, balancing the power differential in home-based education contexts, and promoting positive parent-child communication. Furthermore, we emphasise the importance of designing educational tools that consider children's developmental needs, engage parents, and address the emotional facets of the learning process. Moving forward, we will continue to refine and enhance our design to create an engaging, effective, and emotionally supportive learning environment for children and their families. We hope that such interventions will not only promote better hygiene habits among young children but also contribute to their overall learning development and the strengthening of familial bonds.

# References

1. Alexander, B., et al.: Educause horizon report: 2019 higher education edition. Educause (2019)
2. Brown, B., Reeves, S., Sherwood, S.: Into the wild: challenges and opportunities for field trial methods. In: Proceedings of the SIGCHI Conference on Human Factors in Computing Systems, pp. 1657–1666 (2011)
3. Cherry, K.: Characteristics and Effects of an Uninvolved Parenting Style (3 2023), https://www.verywellmind.com/what-is-uninvolved-parenting-2794958
4. Cingel, D., Piper, A.M.: How parents engage children in tablet-based reading experiences: an exploration of haptic feedback. In: Proceedings of the 2017 ACM Conference on Computer Supported Cooperative Work and Social Computing, pp. 505–510 (2017)
5. Deterding, S.: The lens of intrinsic skill atoms: a method for gameful design. Human-Comput. Interact. 30(3–4), 294–335 (2015)
6. Deterding, S., Sicart, M., Nacke, L., O'Hara, K., Dixon, D.: Gamification. using game-design elements in non-gaming contexts. In: CHI'11 Extended Abstracts on Human Factors in Computing Systems, pp. 2425–2428 (2011)
7. Devi, S., Deb, S.: Augmenting non-verbal communication using a tangible user interface. In: Smart Computing and Informatics: Proceedings of the First International Conference on SCI 2016, vol. 1, pp. 613–620. Springer (2018)
8. Druga, S., Christoph, F.L., Ko, A.J.: Family as a third space for AI literacies: how do children and parents learn about ai together? In: Proceedings of the 2022 CHI Conference on Human Factors in Computing Systems, pp. 1–17 (2022)
9. Faber, J.P., Van Den Hoven, E.: Marbowl: increasing the fun experience of shooting marbles. Pers. Ubiquit. Comput. 16, 391–404 (2012)
10. van Gaalen, A.E., Brouwer, J., Schönrock-Adema, J., Bouwkamp-Timmer, T., Jaarsma, A.D.C., Georgiadis, J.R.: Gamification of health professions education: a systematic review. Adv. Health Sci. Educ. 26(2), 683–711 (2021)
11. Ginsburg, K.R., on Psychosocial Aspects of Child, C., Health, F., et al.: The importance of play in promoting healthy child development and maintaining strong parent-child bonds. Pediatrics 119(1), 182–191 (2007)
12. Hamari, J., Koivisto, J., Sarsa, H.: Does gamification work?-a literature review of empirical studies on gamification. In: 2014 47th Hawaii International Conference on System Sciences, pp. 3025–3034. Ieee (2014)
13. Hiniker, A., Lee, B., Kientz, J.A., Radesky, J.S.: Let's play! digital and analog play between preschoolers and parents. In: Proceedings of the 2018 CHI Conference on Human Factors in Computing Systems, pp. 1–13 (2018)
14. Horn, M.S.: Tangible interaction and cultural forms: supporting learning in informal environments. J. Learn. Sci. 27(4), 632–665 (2018)
15. Leseman, P.P., De Jong, P.F.: Home literacy: opportunity, instruction, cooperation and social-emotional quality predicting early reading achievement. Read. Res. Q. 33(3), 294–318 (1998)

16. Lessel, P., Altmeyer, M., Krüger, A.: Users as game designers: analyzing gamification concepts in a "bottom-up" setting. In: Proceedings of the 22nd International Academic Mindtrek Conference, pp. 1–10 (2018)

17. Liszio, S., Graf, L., Basu, O., Masuch, M.: Pengunaut trainer: a playful VR app to prepare children for MRI examinations: in-depth game design analysis. In: Proceedings of the Interaction Design and Children Conference, pp. 470–482 (2020)

18. Marshall, P., Rogers, Y., Hornecker, E.: Are tangible interfaces really any better than other kinds of interfaces? (2007)

19. Montero, C.S., Kärnä, E., Ng, K.: Digipack pro: revamping social interactions and supporting physical activity. In: Proceedings of the 18th ACM International Conference on Interaction Design and Children, pp. 751–754 (2019)

20. Patel, K., Palo, S.K., Kanungo, S., Mishra, B.K., Pati, S.: Health literacy on hygiene and sanitation, nutrition, and diseases among rural secondary school children-findings from a qualitative study in odisha, india. J. Family Med. Primary Care **11**(9), 5430–5436 (2022)

21. Razzouk, R., Shute, V.: What is design thinking and why is it important? Rev. Educ. Res. **82**(3), 330–348 (2012)

22. Sadka, O., Erel, H., Grishko, A., Zuckerman, O.: Tangible interaction in parent-child collaboration: encouraging awareness and reflection. In: Proceedings of the 17th ACM Conference on Interaction Design and Children, pp. 157–169 (2018)

23. Sardi, L., Idri, A., Fernández-Alemán, J.L.: A systematic review of gamification in e-health. J. Biomed. Inform. **71**, 31–48 (2017)

24. Sheehan, K.J., Pila, S., Lauricella, A.R., Wartella, E.A.: Parent-child interaction and children's learning from a coding application. Computers & Education **140**, 103601 (2019)

25. Starčič, A.I., Turk, Ž., Zajc, M.: Transforming pedagogical approaches using tangible user interface enabled computer assisted learning. Int. J. Emerging Technol. Learn. **10**(6) (2015)

26. Verdine, B.N., Zimmermann, L., Foster, L., Marzouk, M.A., Golinkoff, R.M., Hirsh-Pasek, K., Newcombe, N.: Effects of geometric toy design on parent-child interactions and spatial language. Early Childhood Res. Quarterly **46**, 126–141 (2019)

27. Vonach, E., Ternek, M., Gerstweiler, G., Kaufmann, H.: Design of a health monitoring toy for children. In: Proceedings of the The 15th International Conference on Interaction Design and Children, pp. 58–67 (2016)

28. Wang, C., Chen, G., Yang, Z., Song, Q.: Development of a gamified intervention for children with autism to enhance emotional understanding abilities. In: Proceedings of the 6th International Conference on Digital Technology in Education, pp. 47–51 (2022)

29. Warren, J.L.: Exploring the potential for tangible social technologies for childhood cancer patients within the hospital. In: Proceedings of the Thirteenth International Conference on Tangible, Embedded, and Embodied Interaction, pp. 733–736 (2019)

30. Yazgin, E.: Toys and creativity. J. Educ. Gifted Young Sci. **9**(3), 215–222 (2021)

# "Money from the Queen": Exploring Children's Ideas for Monetization in Free-to-Play Mobile Games

Dan Fitton<sup>(⊠)</sup> and Janet C. Read

Child-Computer Interaction Research Group, University of Central Lancashire, Preston, UK
{dbfitton,jcread}@uclan.ac.uk

**Abstract.** Over 95% of mobile games found on the Android Play Store are free to download and play which typically means that income for the publishers is generated through monetization mechanisms included within the gameplay. It is already established that monetization within mobile games often makes use of deceptive design (sometimes called 'dark design') in relation to aspects such as advertising and game-related purchasing. The limited spending power of young people often means that children and teenagers play these 'free' games extensively and are therefore regularly experiencing in-game monetization attempts developed by adults to target adult players. Monetization typically plays a key role in gameplay and associated gameplay experience in free games. We asked young people (n = 62) aged 12–13 years how they thought developers should monetize free mobile games. Findings show that participants were able to suggest novel mechanisms for monetization, new monetization possibilities developers could consider, and ways in which the experience of monetization mechanisms for players could be improved. We hope this work can help prompt discussion around participatory approaches for monetization and focus attention on the user experience of monetization techniques within mobile games.

**Keywords:** Children · Adolescents · Teenagers · Mobile Games · Deceptive Design · Dark Design · Deceptive Design Patterns · Monetization

## 1 Introduction

Children and teenagers are prolific users of mobile phone and tablet devices along with the apps and games they provide access to. For example, in the UK, 97% of children aged 12–15 have their own mobile phone and 63% play games on their phones [1]. Due to the limited spending power of this demographic the games they play are often free-to-play i.e., with no upfront cost for downloading and installing. Regardless of spending power, data from the Android play store shows that over 96% of mobile apps (including games) are in fact free-to-play [2]. Clearly the cost of developing and marketing mobile games is substantial and, to generate revenue, monetization mechanisms are built into these 'free' games. Monetization within free mobile games appears to be very effective and despite the extremely high proportion of free-to-play games revenue from the mobile games sector is forecast to exceed $172 billion in 2023 [3]. Monetization can typically be divided into two distinct approaches, the first being where a user makes small payments (microtransactions) with actual currency (for example, through purchasing a subscription or purchasing items within the game which may be through an intermediate currency), and the second being where the attention of the user is engaged in ways which generate income for the game publisher (referred to as the Attention Economy [4] and usually involving advertising). Monetization tactics deployed within mobile games are often categorised as deceptive design pattens in themselves or are enhanced using deceptive design. Deceptive design (sometimes called 'dark design' or referred to as 'dark patterns') is typically defined as an attempt to trick a user into action that that user would not normally choose to engage in [5]. A common tactic is the use of interstitial (full screen) adverts within the game, the efficacy of which may be 'enhanced' by deceptive design such as having an extremely small dismiss or skip button which, when the player tries and likely fails to tap it accurately enough, will inadvertently lead the player into visiting the content associated with the advert.

Whatever monetization strategy is employed by a game publisher, whether it contains deceptive design or not, this is unlikely to be a desirable or positive part of the gameplay experience for the player. This is because monetization strategies introduce an 'annoyance' [6, 7] which must either interrupt the game to engage the user's attention (e.g., with advertising), or be annoying to such an extent that the user would be prepared to pay to remove it (e.g., subscribe to remove adverts). Crucially the monetization model and associated tactics are chosen by the developer; if the player wishes to engage with the game, they have little or no choice in how they participate in income generation for the publisher. Outside of mobile games other innovative mechanisms for monetization exist where contributors are given choices such as Crowdfunding, Pay What you Want (/Pay What you Can), Membership platforms (such as Patreon), and appeals for donations (e.g., as used by Wikipedia).

Within this work we sought to gather ideas from young people about how they thought 'free' apps should be paid for by asking directly for their ideas. The ideas collected were then thematically analysed to give four themes of Status Quo, Novel Mechanisms, Developer Possibilities, and Improving Experience. The contributions of this paper are twofold, firstly the findings show the potentially valuable insights young people can provide in participatory activities related to mobile game monetization, and secondly findings highlight areas for future work focused on the impact of monetization techniques within mobile games on the player experience. These issues are important due to the prevalence of mobile gaming among young people and pervasiveness of monetization in free-to-play mobile games.

## 2   Related Literature

While historically, mobile developers faced a choice between free or paid (or multiple) offerings [8], most mobile games are now free to download and play (termed 'free-to-play' or 'freemium') meaning that monetization mechanisms (to earn revenue for the developer) are built into the game. Commonly, monetization is achieved through advertising using Ad (Advertising) Networks which provide APIs for developers to integrate into products to display adverts to users, for which they receive remuneration from the Ad Network. The appearance of the advert to the player is largely dependent on the Ad Network's and developer's choices but five basic types exist: Offerwall, Popup, Notification, Floating and Embedded [9]. Additionally, there are typically five different ways the remuneration to the developer is calculated which is also dependent on the Ad Network's and developer's choices:

- Cost Per Mile (CPM): Per 1000 views of the advert.
- Cost Per View (CPV): Per view of a video advert.
- Cost Per Click (CPC): Per click on the advert.
- Cost Per Install (CPI): Per download/install of the app/game being advertised.
- Cost Per Action (CPA): Per action a user carries out based on the advert.

As early as 2015, the use of Ad Networks was known to increase data usage, device energy consumption, and make mobile apps more annoying [10]. There is a growing body of work on deceptive design within the HCI research community focussing on adults which includes practitioner perspectives [11], ecommerce web sites [12], mobile apps [13], cookie consent banners [14, 15, 16], recognition and experience of deceptive design [17, 18], along with deceptive design within video stream services [19] and voice interfaces [20]. Very few examples currently exist which focus on monetization within games or mobile games specifically. Zagal et al. [21] were the first to identify and classify deceptive design patterns within games: "pattern[s] used intentionally by a game creator to cause negative experiences for players which are against their best interests and likely to happen without their consent". While Zagal et al., do not reference advertising they do identify grinding (repetitive in-game tasks) as a "way of coercing the player into needlessly spending time in a game for the sole purpose of extending the game's duration" which would expose the player to more advertising and increase revenue.

Zagal et al., also describe "Monetary Dark Patterns" as designs in which "players [are] being deceived into spending more money than they expected or anticipated". This points to the potentially problematic use of microtransactions which is also highlighted King and Delfabbro's explanation of predatory monetization: "purchasing systems that disguise or withhold the long-term cost of the activity until players are already financially and psychologically committed" [22]. Fitton and Read [7] explored deceptive design in free-to-play games with children and identified six separate types of Monetary deceptive design patterns specific to mobile games (Pay for Permanent Enhancements, Pay for Expendable Updates, Pay to Skip/Progress, Pay to Win, Subscriptions, Intermediate Currencies). In the same paper they also introduced the categories of 'Disguised Ads' and 'Sneaky Ads' (the example used in the introduction of adverts with extremely small dismiss or skip button aligns with this latter category). Another example of questionable monetization practices is the Loot Box [23] which is effectively a form of gambling which has been incorporated in many popular mobile and desktop games.

The experience of players who come across these designs has been studied with adult users, for example Zendle and Petrovskaya [24] who surveyed player's experiences (mobile and desktop platforms) and found participants considered many of their monetary transactions within games "misleading, aggressive or unfair". There is overlap between the survey findings from [24] and the classifications within [21] and [7] such as grinding, pay to win and in-game currency.

Regularity bodies (such as Ofcom in the UK and FTC in the USA) along with policies provided to developers by App Stores should mitigate problematic use of monetization by developers, but existing literature would suggest these are not yet sufficiently effective [7, 23–25]. Presently it seems there are no compelling alternatives to the Free-to-Play monetization model in the mobile gaming context (unlike the more innovate approaches used in other popular technologies such as YouTube [26]). To-date only a small number of studies have focussed on deceptive design within the context of mobile games for younger users [7, 25], and no work we have found takes a participatory approach to identifying new or innovative monetization possibilities.

## 3   The Study

### 3.1   Method

The data analysed in this study was part of a larger data set collected when two high school in the North-West of the UK visited our university to participate in research studies and STEM activities as part of a MESS (Mad Evaluation Session with Schoolchildren) Day session [27]. Within a MESS Day session, a group of pupils and teachers visit our university and circulate between different activities and research studies, each approximately 20 min in length, in small groups. All pupils participate in all activities and research studies on the day. Participant information and parental consent sheets were provided to the participating schools who dealt with distribution and collection of such consent; only pupils with consent confirmed attended. The participants were aged 12–13 years with 62 participants in total (23 male, 35 female, 4 chose not to disclose a gender). Pupils worked in small groups (typically pairs) to respond to questions about their experiences of mobile games by writing answers on Post-it notes and placing them on a large sheet of paper (1 sheet per group). This approach to collecting data is known to work with adolescents and has successfully been used previously [7]. In this paper we focus on answers to the question of "How should developers of free apps/games make money?". Figure 1 shows a completed question sheet. A facilitator introduced and explained the activity and a class teacher was always present. The groups worked independently for approximately five minutes answering the question, all data was collected anonymously, and groups were told that they did not have to allow their data to be collected.

### 3.2   Analysis

Thematic analysis was used to code the data using an inductive and semantic approach as we were most interested in understanding the raw ideas from the participants. Two coders familiarised themselves with the data by reading through the answers on the Post-it notes; the Post-it notes were then removed from the answer sheets and organised into initial codes which were labelled (and re-labelled) during the coding process. The coding was completed collaboratively, with both coders considering each Post-it note in turn. There was no disagreement when assigning codes, and only a single code was necessary for each idea. In total, 98 Post-it notes/ideas were gathered from the answer sheets; of these, 14 were unclear/irrelevant and excluded from the analysis. Codes and associated examples from the data are shown in Table 1. The final stage of analysis involved both coders considering the codes and organising them into themes, this resulted in four themes which are discussed in the following section.

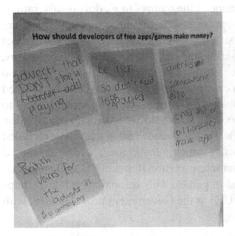

**Fig. 1.** Completed question sheet.

**Fig. 2.** Data from Improving Experience theme.

### 3.3 Results

The following subsections describe the four themes which emerged from the analysis and associated codes (from Table 1) within them.

**Status Quo Theme:** This theme included monetization techniques which are already widely used in free-to-play games. These included unspecific references to advertising (from the *In-Game Advertising* code), and references to in-game purchasing (from the *In-Game Purchases* code) which were either unspecific or mentioned in-game currency (typically 'coins'). The third code subsumed into this category was *Player Pays*; this code primarily included references to paying for the game 'up front', which had three examples making it clear that the paid for version had no advertising. Also included in this category were two examples of 'subscription' which implied continual cost instead of initial cost. Interestingly the *Player Pays* code had the largest number of occurrences in the data (18) and the *Status Quo* theme overall accounted for 46% (45/98) of the total data. This may be because participants were already familiar with these examples and assume they are effective.

**Novel Mechanisms Theme:** This theme included funding mechanisms which do not yet exist and that can provide external sources of funding for developers of games. The first code in this theme, *App stores pay*, implies reversing the role of app store, where the app stores would pay for games to be included (we assume this would mean that monetization within games would not be necessary) rather than app stores being vehicles for developers to distribute and sell their products to consumers. While this is an interesting idea is not clear how the money to pay the developers would be generated. The next code, *Popularity*, appears to be a variation on the previous theme where a mechanism is proposed to pay developers based on the number of downloads or users of a game. These two codes highlight the relatively sophisticated understandings of app stores that participants had, they had likely noticed the metrics (e.g., downloads, ratings etc.) provided on the user interfaces in the app stores, and realised that app stores are associated with large, and very financially successful, companies (Google and Apple) which could potentially renumerate developers somehow. The next code, *Philanthropy*, hinted primarily at wealthy 'others' who would be able to pay for mobile games so they would be free to players. In addition to charity events, data in this code also hinted that only very wealthy people should be developing games who, participants seem to assume, would not need additional income, and so would not include monetization (e.g., 'Be Rich so don't need to get paid'). The final code, *State Funding*, included examples which specified that the Government (or monarchy in the UK context) should pay the developers of mobile games, again our interpretation is that this would mean that monetization would not need to be included in games. This reasoning should perhaps seem logical to participants (children in the UK) as the Government provides them with free education and healthcare.

**Developer Possibilities Theme:**  This theme contained ideas for possibilities that game developers could explore to generate income outside of traditional in-game monetization techniques. The first code within this theme, *Change Business Model,* suggested ideas not related to the mobile games specifically that would be potentially relevant to any business. The theme also included the code *Dark Income* which included ideas which hinted at changes to games which, while potentially illegal or unethical, could generate additional income for the developer. The code that aligned with the most data within this theme was *Other Advertising* which included ideas for advertising outside of mobile games which included 'posters', 'email marketing', 'tv adverts' and 'celebrity promotions'. The participants in this case had potentially not fully understood the nuances of how advertising within games is used for monetization; as the coders took a semantic approach to analysis, we accepted the implied premise that advertising generates income and included it within this theme. The next code within this theme, *Sponsorship*, made unspecific references to 'sponsorship' and 'get a sponsor', we interpreted this to imply arrangements analogous to commercial sponsorship within sport teams, players, events etc. where the income from the sponsor would change the monetization mechanism used. Similar to the previous code, the participants perhaps did not fully consider that a sponsorship arrangement within a mobile game would still likely mean the game included extensive advertising (as seen previous when a level on Rovio Entertainment Corporation's Angry Birds 2 was sponsored by Honey Nut Cheerios). The final code included in this theme was the *WhatsApp Model* where the ideas specified that mobile games could be 'like WhatsApp'. Participants seemed to be aware that WhatsApp did not include any kind of advertising or monetization (for them) and implied that would like mobile games to be similar. There was no evidence that participants fully understood that the income within WhatsApp is generated through charging business customers.

**Table 1.** Codebook from analysis of responses to 'How should developers make money?'

| Code | n | Description | Example |
|---|---|---|---|
| In-Game Advertising | 15 | Refers to existing examples of advertising within gameplay for monetization | 'Have ads within the game' |
| In-Game Purchases | 12 | Refers to existing examples of purchasing possibilities within gameplay for monetization | 'In game purchases' |
| Player Pays | 18 | Refers to the player paying for the game, so no further monetization is necessary | 'Pay for the game up front' |
| App Stores Pay | 3 | Refers to app stores paying game developers | 'App store pay to have apps on their store' |
| Popularity | 2 | Refers to income being based on popularity with players | 'How many people download it' |
| Philanthropy | 4 | Refers to wealthy benefactors or charitable activities as a means for monetization | 'Charity Events' |
| State Funding | 3 | Refers to income from state sources | 'Money from the queen' |
| Change Business Model | 3 | Refers to the publishers of games changing their business model to generate additional income | 'Get Investors' |
| Dark income | 2 | Refers to generating income via unethical methods | 'Add a gambling aspect to the game' |
| Other Advertising | 6 | Refers to advertising possibilities outside of the game | 'Normal TV Adverts' |
| Sponsorship | 5 | Refers to the use of sponsorship as a means for income | 'Get a sponsor' |
| WhatsApp model | 2 | Refers to a business model like that used by WhatsApp (i.e., no monetization within the app) | 'Like WhatsApp don't make money but worth money' |
| Less Annoying | 9 | Refers to ideas about how to improve current in-game monetization mechanisms for the player | 'Adverts that don't stop you playing' |

**Improving Experience Theme:** Data in this theme was related to altering the experience of existing in-game advertising primarily to improve the experience for the player when encountering advertising within a game. This theme was solely built from the *Less Annoying* code as the coders considered this data to be the most relevant to the HCI community as it focusses on the experience of child users. The theme is also novel as, while monetization strategies are known to be annoying for the user (e.g., [6, 7]), work to-date has not yet explored how this situation can be addressed. As discussed earlier in the related work section, the experience of in-game advertising is dictated to a large extent by the Ad Network API chosen by the developer and (maximising revenue from) the monetization metrics used, so the developer may ultimately have limited control over player experience. All nine examples for this theme were shown earlier in Fig. 2. Eight of the ideas specially referenced 'Ads' and several included specific and practical ideas for improvement: 'British voices for the adverts…', 'Bottom of the screen ads'. Other ideas implied addressing the interstitial nature of advertising within mobile games: 'Adverts that DONT stop u playing', 'non interrupting ADS', '…more skippable', and one proposed an alternative way for players to access adverts 'make a page on the game which you can look at ads'. These suggestions appear to refer to interstitial adverts (which typically take up the entire screen and therefore interrupt all possibility for gameplay) which are presumably used to ensure CPM/CPV returns are maximised, and which may potentially lead to high returns on other metrics (e.g., CPC). While developers may be unwilling to make changes that could directly reduce their income, other suggestions, such as the altering the voice-overs on adverts to be country-specific, could potentially increase both gameplay experience and effectiveness of the advert [28].

# 4   Conclusion

The free-to-play business model is widely used and extremely lucrative within the mobile games development industry, however the associated monetization techniques necessary to generative income for developers are known to be problematic, having been identified as 'predatory' [22], 'misleading, aggressive or unfair' [24] and often including deceptive design [7]. This situation is particularly concerning for younger users who are prolific users of mobiles games and are likely being exposed to a range of these problematic monetization techniques on a regular basis. While there is a growing body of work on deceptive design and monetization with adult users, there are presently far fewer examples of studies focussing on younger users.

This work sought to explore young peoples' ideas for how developers should make money within free-to-play mobile games and gathered 84 usable ideas from 62 participants (aged 12–13) which yielded 14 codes organised into four top-level themes of Status Quo, Novel Mechanisms, Developer Possibilities and Improving Experience. The theme of Improving Experience of monetization is perhaps the most relevant to the HCI community and highlights aspects of mobile game monetization which could be explored in future work. In this theme participants were highlighting the negative impact of existing monetization techniques and suggesting ideas for improvement. While the implementation of some of these ideas (such not using interstitial adverts) may have a negative impact on advertising effectiveness and monetization metrics discussed in the related literature section, other ideas may improve the effectiveness of the adverts in addition to improving the experience of encountering them (such as 'British voices for the adverts'). The other themes highlighted interesting ideas around income for developers which, while not necessarily practical, highlight the potential value in taking a participatory approach to exploring monetization. For example, it was surprising to the authors that participants had identified the business model used by WhatsApp as a positive example that games developers may be able to follow, even though it was clear they did not fully understand the specifics of that model. We see this dichotomy, participants thinking being both sophisticated and unsophisticated, as valuable in providing new insights.

Within this work the context of the participants should be considered carefully. We would argue that the wide range of interesting responses within the data implied that participants understood the importance of income for mobile game developers; for example, there were no responses stating that monetization should be removed entirely, only ideas for solutions. Younger participants, less able to empathise with the financial needs of the developers, may have been less sympathetic, which may have influenced ideas generated. The context of this study was the UK (where services such as education and healthcare are free for children) which may have influenced ideas from participants (especially those aligning with the code 'State funding'); it would be interesting future work to conduct similar studies in countries with different approaches to funding of the key services that young people encounter.

We hope the findings from this paper will help promote discussion around new, and potentially participatory, approaches for monetization within the technologies that young people use, and specifically focus attention and further study on the user experience of monetization techniques used within mainstream mobile games.

# References

1. Ofcom: Children and parents: media use and attitudes report (2022). https://www.ofcom.org. uk/__data/assets/pdf_file/0024/234609/childrens-media-use-and-attitudes-report-2022.pdf. Accessed 14 June 2023
2. Number of available Android applications I AppBrain. https://www.appbrain.com/stats/free-and-paid-android-applications. Accessed 24 Jan 2023
3. Mobile Games - Worldwide I Statista Market Forecast. https://www.statista.com/outlook/dmo/digital-media/video-games/mobile-games/worldwide. Accessed 24 Jan 2023
4. Davenport, T.H., Beck, J.C.: The attention economy. Ubiquity **6** (2001)
5. Brignull, H.: Types of deceptive pattern. https://www.deceptive.design/types. Accessed 14 June 2023
6. Appel, G., Libai, B., Muller, E., Shachar, R.: On the monetization of mobile apps. Int. J. Res. Mark. **37**, 93–107 (2020). https://doi.org/10.1016/J.IJRESMAR.2019.07.007
7. Fitton, D., Read, J.C.: Creating a framework to support the critical consideration of dark design aspects in free-to-play apps. In: Proceedings of the 18th ACM International Conference on Interaction Design and Children, pp. 407–418, IDC 2019 (2019). https://doi.org/10.1145/331 1927.3323136
8. Lee, Y.-J., Ghasemkhani, H., Xie, K., Tan, Y.: Switching decision, timing, and app performance: an empirical analysis of mobile app developers' switching behavior between monetarization strategies. SSRN Electron. J. (2019). https://doi.org/10.2139/SSRN.3345988

9. He, B., Xu, H., Jin, L., Guo, G., Chen, Y., Weng, G.: An investigation into android in-app ad practice: implications for app developers. In: IEEE INFOCOM 2018 - IEEE Conference on Computer Communications, pp. 2465–2473. https://doi.org/10.1109/INFOCOM.2018.848 6010

10. Gui, J., Mcilroy, S., Nagappan, M., Halfond, W.G.J.: Truth in advertising: the hidden cost of mobile ads for software developers. In: 2015 IEEE/ACM 37th IEEE International Conference on Software Engineering, pp. 100–110 (2015). https://doi.org/10.1109/ICSE.2015.32

11. Gray, C.M., Kou, Y., Battles, B., Hoggatt, J., Toombs, A.L.: The dark (patterns) side of UX design. In: Proceedings of the 2018 CHI Conference on Human Factors in Computing Systems, pp. 534:1–534:14. ACM, New York (2018). https://doi.org/10.1145/3173574.317 4108

12. Mathur, A., et al.: Dark patterns at scale. Proc. ACM Hum. Comput. Interact. **3** (2019). https://doi.org/10.1145/3359183

13. di Geronimo, L., Braz, L., Fregnan, E., Palomba, F., Bacchelli, A.: UI dark patterns and where to find them: a study on mobile applications and user perception. In: Conference on Human Factors in Computing Systems - Proceedings (2020). https://doi.org/10.1145/3313831.337 6600

14. Nouwens, M., Liccardi, I., Veale, M., Karger, D., Kagal, L.: Dark patterns after the GDPR: scraping consent pop-ups and demonstrating their influence. In: Conference on Human Factors in Computing Systems - Proceedings (2020). https://doi.org/10.1145/3313831.3376321

15. Habib, H., Li, M., Young, E., Cranor, L.: Okay, whatever: an evaluation of cookie consent interfaces. In: Conference on Human Factors in Computing Systems - Proceedings **27** (2022). https://doi.org/10.1145/3491102.3501985

16. Krisam, C., Dietmann, H., Volkamer, M., Kulyk, O.: Dark patterns in the wild: review of cookie disclaimer designs on top 500 german websites. In: ACM International Conference Proceeding Series, pp. 1–8 (2021). https://doi.org/10.1145/3481357.3481516

17. Bongard-Blanchy, K., et al.: I am definitely manipulated, even when i am aware of it. it's ridiculous! - Dark patterns from the end-user perspective. In: DIS 2021 - Proceedings of the 2021 ACM Designing Interactive Systems Conference: Nowhere and Everywhere, pp. 763–776 (2021). https://doi.org/10.1145/3461778.3462086

18. Gray, C.M., Chen, J., Chivukula, S.S., Qu, L.: End user accounts of dark patterns as felt manipulation. Proc. ACM Hum. Comput. Interact. **5** (2021). https://doi.org/10.1145/3479516

19. Chaudhary, A., Saroha, J., Monteiro, K., Forbes, A.G., Parnami, A.: Are you still watching?": exploring unintended user behaviors and dark patterns on video streaming platforms. In: DIS 2022 - Proceedings of the 2022 ACM Designing Interactive Systems Conference: Digital Wellbeing, pp. 776–791 (2022). https://doi.org/10.1145/3532106.3533562

20. Owens, K., Gunawan, J., Choffnes, D., Emami-Naeini, P., Kohno, T., Roesner, F.: Exploring deceptive design patterns in voice interfaces. In: ACM International Conference Proceeding Series, pp. 64–78 (2022). https://doi.org/10.1145/3549015.3554213

21. Zagal, J.P., Björk, S., Lewis, C.: Dark patterns in the design of games (2013). http://dblp.uni-trier.de/db/conf/fdg/fdg2013.html#ZagalBO13

22. King, D.L., Delfabbro, P.H.: Predatory monetization schemes in video games (e.g. 'loot boxes') and internet gaming disorder. Addiction **113**, 1967–1969 (2018). https://doi.org/10.1111/ADD.14286

23. Zendle, D., Meyer, R., Cairns, P., Waters, S., Ballou, N.: The prevalence of loot boxes in mobile and desktop games. Addiction **115**, 1768–1772 (2020). https://doi.org/10.1111/ADD.14973

24. Petrovskaya, E., Zendle, D.: Predatory monetisation? A categorisation of unfair, misleading and aggressive monetisation techniques in digital games from the player perspective. J. Bus. Ethics **181**, 1065–1081 (2021). https://doi.org/10.1007/S10551-021-04970-6/TABLES/1

25. Fitton, D., Bell, B.T., Read, J.C.: Integrating dark patterns into the 4Cs of online risk in the context of young people and mobile gaming apps. In: Ardito, C., et al. (eds.) INTERACT 2021. LNCS, vol. 12935, pp. 701–711. Springer, Cham (2021). https://doi.org/10.1007/978-3-030-85610-6_40
26. Hua, Y., Horta Ribeiro, M., Ristenpart, T., West, R., Naaman, M.: Characterizing alternative monetization strategies on YouTube. Proc. ACM Hum. Comput. Interact. **6**, 1–30 (2022). https://doi.org/10.1145/3555174
27. Horton, M., Read, J.C., Mazzone, E., Sim, G., Fitton, D.: School friendly participatory research activities with children. In: Conference on Human Factors in Computing Systems – Proceedings, January 2012, pp. 2099–2104 (2012). https://doi.org/10.1145/2212776.2223759
28. Moriuchi, E.: English accent variations in YouTube voice-over ads and the role of perceptions on attitude and purchase intentions. J. Interact. Advert. **21**, 191–208 (2021). https://doi.org/10.1080/15252019.2021.1973620

# Motivating Children's Engagement with Sleep Diaries Through Storytelling

Hannah C. van Iterson[✉], Panos Markopoulos[✉], and Leonardo E. Gerritsen

Eindhoven University of Technology, 5612 AZ Eindhoven, The Netherlands
`h.c.v.iterson@student.tue.nl`, `P.Markopoulos@tue.nl`

**Abstract.** Children often experience sleep problems that can negatively impact their well-being and development. Clinicians ask parents to record in a journal information about their child's sleep, but such parental reports can be biased. Sleep diaries suitable for children can triangulate parental reports and allow children to be actively involved in their treatment. Earlier attempts at sleep diaries for children rely on written text input, which is not suitable for younger children. We designed EP-Sleepy, an interactive console that allows children aged six to eight to report on their sleep experience. EP-Sleepy was designed in two iterations, which explored different interaction mechanisms for keeping children engaged for the required by clinicians period of two weeks. We evaluated the appliance with parents and children demonstrating the feasibility of self-reporting for children six to eight, and how storytelling can motivate children to adhere to a daily self-reporting regime.

**Keywords:** Sleep diary · Self-tracking · Children

## 1 Introduction

Lack of sleep is detrimental to the brain and body and negatively impacts children, causing behavioural and cognitive problems, and can decrease motivation for social activities [2,3,13,17,25]. To treat sleeping problems and assess potential environmental influences, clinicians ask parents to fill out diaries that typically cover a one- or two-week period to complement what parents and children can recall during consultations. However, parental reports can be incomplete or biased [11], so the need arises for methods to provide children with a way to report on their sleep independently.

Earlier research in child-computer interaction has demonstrated the feasibility of interactive diaries for children, that rely on text in- and output with a chatbot [1]. However, for younger children who cannot yet read and write well, different interaction mechanisms are required. Here, we present the design and evaluation of an interactive diary targeting children six to eight. Following a research-through-design approach, we examine how to enable children this young to keep a sleep diary and how to keep them engaged for a period of two weeks, which is roughly what is needed by clinicians. In the following sections,

J. Abdelnour Nocera et al. (Eds.): INTERACT 2023, LNCS 14143, pp. 214–223, 2023.
https://doi.org/10.1007/978-3-031-42283-6_12

we report on a participatory design of the children's diary that proceeded in two main iterations. First, Sleep o' Meter, a physical user interface inspired by advent calendars, was designed and evaluated. We conclude with EP-Sleepy, an interactive appliance that uses storytelling to enhance children's engagement with the self-reporting regime.

## 2   Related Work/Background

Through monitoring sleep, clinical practitioners can identify maladaptive sleep practices or disorders [28]. and help determine factors that might be causing or worsening symptoms [8]. The subjective assessment of sleep is a critical component in understanding sleep behaviour [10]. Adults are the main reporters when their child has sleep problems, monitoring their child's sleep-wake schedule and any changes in behaviour or mood over two weeks [8, 18, 27].

Parental report is valuable for children aged six to twelve, but get increasingly biased as children grow older and more independent of their parents [11, 19]. This makes it important to find ways for children to self-report their sleep experience to complement parental reports [21, 22, 26]. Meltzer et al. [18] showed that children aged eight to twelve can provide more reliable and richer information than their parents when reporting on their sleep. Younger children, six to eight years old, have more difficulty providing such information, as they are not old enough to fully grasp the concept of time or sleep, and therefore cannot estimate times or duration of sleep [14, 24, 29]. However, their additional insights are valuable to clinicians and has been found to be reliable, as their subjective sleep experience is correlated with objective sleep measures, such as sleep quality [7].

Few methods have been developed for children under twelve years to track their sleep independently [18]. The Consensus Sleep Diary is frequently used for adults; it's a standardized sleep diary in English, written at a level to be understandable for most of the English-speaking population [5]. If used for children, it is via parental report. The same applies to the Child Sleep Habit Questionnaire (CSHQ) [20] which is for parents of children aged four to ten. The only questionnaire designed specifically for children is the Children's Report of Sleep Patterns (CRSP) [18], a self-report measure for children aged eight to twelve for recording sleep patterns, sleep hygiene, and sleep disturbances.

These latter questionnaires can support clinical interviews but may suffer from recall bias, for which we look at developing diary methods for triangulation, to capture experiences day by day, and allow contextual influences and fluctuations over different days to be captured.

Pina et al. [23], created Dreamcatcher, a probe to test the tracking of sleep in a family. The interactive shared display uses data from wrist-worn sleep sensors and self-reported mood. They found that children can be active contributors and that tracking sleep together as a family encourages collaboration. However, there were moments when members felt uncomfortable sharing things.

Aarts et al. followed a participatory approach to design an experience sampling chatbot [1] to allow children aged eight to twelve years to report on sleep-related experiences. The chatbot presented an engaging dialogue with fun elements, providing children a non-invasive way to share information with their doctor. The user experience with the diary was positively evaluated, and a one-week field test confirmed the feasibility of the approach. Their research encouraged further development of tools and investigation of interaction design patterns to collect subjective sleep reports from children to complement parental reports.

## 3    Initial Design Concept: The Sleep o' Meter

To involve children in the design of the sleep diary, we collaborated with 14 children aged six to eight, who were in the same class at a school in Italy. For ethical reasons, we did not seek to directly involve children with sleep problems, as this could interfere with their treatment and because health professionals require that patients should be exposed to prototypes and discussions cautiously and when a device is unlikely to interfere with their sleep health. Ethical approval was granted by the Eindhoven University of Technology for all interventions in this article. Co-design activities, suitable for this age group, were conducted in the classroom twice a week for six weeks. Parents provided informed consent and the children assented at the start, while it was made clear to them that they could stop at any time they wanted. All activities were designed with the children's teachers to ensure they would be fun and educational, so the burden of participation could be justified. The children's role evolved through the design process, initially as testers of simple mock-ups, then as informants. Eventually, we concluded with children again as testers to test the designed prototype.

In the first meeting, children tested three low-fidelity paper prototypes of sleep diaries, that were modelled after familiar artefacts: the snakes and ladder game, a card game with questions and answers relating to sleep (the set of questions was developed with a child psychologist we consulted), an emotion-wheel inspired by the Pixar [6] animation studios motion picture "Inside Out" for reporting their mood when going to sleep and when waking up, and a stuffed animal that would ask questions to their children about their sleep and record spoken answers. These mock-ups were adapted between meetings based on suggestions by the children and aspects we found were creating difficulties for them.

The children experienced interaction with low-fidelity mock-ups of these design concepts and then participated in co-design workshops. While the typical format for such workshops involves very active and engaging activities with designers and children sitting in circles on the floor [31], the format had to be adapted to the social-distancing and mask-wearing restrictions that were active in April and May 2021. Children provided feedback on these ideas in group discussions with seven at a time. Regarding the cards, we found that the children could answer simple questions about their sleep using rating scales, which we did not take for granted at the beginning. For the wheel of emotions, they proposed a transparent wheel for ease of use and a daily schedule for reporting. Experiences were mixed with the stuffed animal, which seemed more effective in soliciting comments from girls than for boys, but succeeded in collecting richer qualitative sleep-related information than the other methods. Children varied regarding the extent to which they provided qualitative data regarding their sleep, or whether they could answer using numeric scales.

The third author invited parents for a discussion in case they wanted to know more about the research their child was involved in, and they could also, if they wanted, join as informants in the study. Six parents took up the invitation. They were positive about self-reporting between consultations with clinicians but found it difficult to inject this reporting into their daily routines, e.g. it can be busy in the mornings, while there is more time for such interactions in the evening. Most parents thought that their children would not use the suggested devices unless parents reminded them to do so.

We concluded that we needed to develop interaction mechanisms that would trigger children to self-report daily. Options considered were a story delivered in daily instalments, a puzzle, or a Lego set obtained in pieces day by day. Twelve children took part in a co-discovery interview [12] wherein a single session they simulated the reporting for four days. After this, we asked the children about their level of interest and motivation to engage with the system. Our conclusion about storytelling was that it needed to be tailored to the child, and that the daily part of the story should end with cliffhangers to increase the child's motivation to return to the device the next day. The participants thought the puzzle should be personalized, but did not find it as motivating as Lego pieces.

The Sleep o' Meter prototype combined elements of these three directions and the initial mock-ups (Fig. 1). It presents questions to children via audio output, and children respond on a five-point scale using big buttons on the device. The questions were based on a paediatric questionnaire [27] regarding what a child thinks could interfere with their sleep. Children's responses are stored on a secure digital card. This interaction is offered in the centre of a $46 \times 59x7cm$ wooden box housing the computing hardware and a speaker, and features an advent calendar-like appearance around its perimeter. Each day in the reporting period, the child hears a story about an animal and can open a box to find Lego pieces for creating a model of it. It was thought that the anticipation and reward of opening the calendar box would draw children to interact with the device daily. The advent calendar and centre decorations are printed on paper, offering options tailored to different children's age and interests. Stories can be customized by providing suitable audio files for each calendar box.

## 3.1   Initial Evaluation of Sleep o' Meter

An interactive prototype was evaluated in October '21, with a class of Dutch children (N = 12), at an after-school care group, who had not been involved in the earlier stages of the design. All text and questionnaire items were translated with the help of native speakers of Italian and Dutch. Finally, one seven-year-old child took the device home to try it out for a week. Interviews with the child and the parent were held at the beginning and the end of this week. It turned out that the child and the mother understood well how to use the device, and

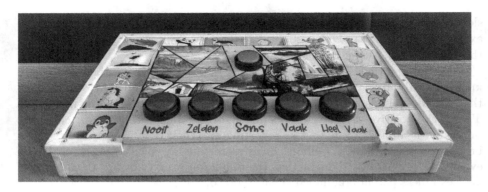

**Fig. 1.** The Sleep o' Meter: an advent calendar-like perimeter with Lego pieces to be collected and big buttons in the centre for answering questions

thought that if a clinician would offer such a device to them, they should provide instructions and tailor content to the specific child.

To capture the parent's perspective on Sleep o' Meter we interviewed ten parents of eleven children aged six to eight years, with no sleep problems. The semi-structured interviews lasted 30–60 min and focused on their experiences with tracking sleep, their family dynamics and routines at home, and the children's hobbies and interests. Additionally, we interviewed two clinicians with expertise in treating children and three who work in a multidisciplinary centre for treating parasomnia about the Sleep o' Meter and how they currently assess children's sleep problems, the reliability of those methods, what conclusions they wished to be able to draw from a child's self-report, and important questions to include. All interviews were in Dutch. Notes were made during the interview.

### 3.2   Results of Initial Evaluation

Inductive thematic analysis [4] of interviews with parents and children resulted in two categories of interest: One-on activities performed by the children, with sub-categories around activities done alone, with the family, or with siblings/friends; Favourite things for children, with subcategories: hobbies, sports, and toys. Both categories pointed to the need for an adaptable system.

The themes emerging from the expert interviews were: the usage of rewards, problems in the process, the process itself, common causes of bad sleep, contact with children, the age range of questionnaires, and ideas and tips concerning the design process. Reactions to the prototype varied. The data gathered were found useful. However, experts suggested improvements to the questions asked and the choice of answers that a child can choose from, and simplifications of the language. They found rewarding children with Lego pieces excessive for their task and not consistent with their practice.

From this design process and especially from the evaluation session, we concluded that younger children can understand questions about sleep and respond on five-point rating scales, rather than open questions as in the Snoozy system [1]. We also concluded that tailoring the appearance and the Lego construction activity would work, but the Lego pieces as a reward incurs costs and can cause satisficing behaviours in children trying to earn the reward [9,30]. We were concerned that children might hesitate to answer questions truthfully as these are read out loud, and it is difficult to respond privately. Privacy is crucial when self-reporting in diaries [15,16], so we considered this a necessary improvement. Further, we wished to encourage children to fill in Sleep o' Meter in the morning, when the memory of the night is fresh, and there is less risk of recall bias (Fig. 2).

**Fig. 2.** Research prototypes LtR: analogue questionnaire booklet, digital questionnaire, the website of the digitized Sleep o' Meter

### 3.3   Field-Testing of Physical and Digital Versions of Sleep o' Meter

To evaluate the necessity of a physical design and non-material rewards, we created a digital version of Sleep o' Meter and compared its use to the physical prototype in two field tests. In the first user test, children aged six to eight (N = 8) and their parents (N = 13) were asked to complete the questionnaires, with or without a reward in the form of a story, for five days each. After ten days, participants shared their experiences in a semi-structured interview. Further, a digital version was created and tested following the same reward setup. For the digital version, two children (age seven) in the same family, used either version of Sleep o' Meter for ten days. Participants were recruited through a social media post. It was made clear in the information about the study that the intention was to study the impact of storytelling on children's motivation, not to provide a solution to existing or potential sleeping problems. Informed consent was obtained from the parents. Participants were informed they could stop at any point during the study.

### 3.4   Results of the Field-Test

The digital and physical versions of Sleep o' Meter were used very similarly. The reward did not make a difference in completion rates. Opinions about it were spread; two children liked it, one was indifferent, and another asked for a different reward. Seven children preferred listening over reading the questions as it was easier, they could do other things simultaneously, and they preferred the audio story. All but one, filled out the questionnaires in the morning because this fitted the family's daily schedule better. Two children mentioned that the stories motivated them to follow through with the questions. Some would have liked spookier stories (N = 1), or a daily short story (N = 1). Parents and children both mentioned that the physical device provided a visual reminder (N = 7). The field test revealed practical limitations, with the prototype crashing and showing wear. Participants found it difficult to carry and store the prototype. One child using the digital version was annoyed at spending their 'online time' for the study, so their parents gave additional time to compensate for the lost time.

## 4  Improved Design: EP-Sleepy

Based on user tests, we iterated the design concept and developed EP-Sleepy, a dedicated handheld device that can be easily stored and carried. The child can listen to the questions with headphones for privacy and to help focus on the questions in noisy situations. A button-based rating scale helps answer questions without having to read and write. Lighting feedback in the buttons guides the user along with the audio, blinking to signal which buttons can be pressed.

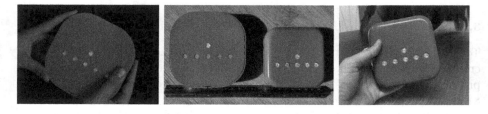

**Fig. 3.** LtR: EP-Sleepy v1, a comparison between v1 and v2, EP-sleepy v2

## 5  Comparative Evaluation

In this user test, both the Sleep o' Meter and EP-Sleepy were deployed. We aimed to compare the devices regarding completion rate and experience. We asked participants to use both devices for five days. At the end of the ten-day test, we asked parents (N = 4) and children aged seven to eight (N = 3) questions about their experience using the device in a semi-structured 30'–45' interview. Participants were recruited through a social media post. Informed consent was obtained from the parent(s). Children could give assent and were informed they could stop at any point during the study.

## 5.1   Results

The completion rate of EP-Sleepy was 4/5 (N = 1) and 5/5 (N = 2). The Sleep o' Meter showed large differences in completion rate between the three participants. The reason for this was a system crash. EP-Sleepy performed more reliably through the test, and was better appreciated for its size, which suits children's hands, the clarity of the questions, and the guidance to the child through the interaction. The smaller size and improved portability seemed to make a difference, as children stated bringing the device to sleepovers (N = 1), and parents praised the ease of storing (N = 3). Parents stated that children could use these devices independently (N = 3) whereas they needed help with the Sleep o' Meter (N = 4). On the other hand, Sleep o' Meter appealed to them more visually as it is colourful and visually interesting, (N = 2). The visual appeal, and the physical rewards, caused younger siblings to want to interfere in using the device. The audio quality of the Sleep o Meter was preferred, as children (N = 3) mentioned the voice of EP-Sleepy was too soft to hear through headphones. Consequently, an improved version of EP-Sleepy was created to address audio quality.

# 6   Conclusions

We set out to investigate how children could self-report on their subjective sleep experiences. This article has demonstrated the feasibility of self-report diaries on sleep quality using purpose-made interactive devices for children six to eight, who cannot yet read and write. This study contributes an exploration of the design space which is characterized by cognitive, contextual, and motivational barriers to allowing children in this age group to keep diaries in order to inform treating clinicians regarding sleep problems. We have contributed two design concepts and prototypes for interactive appliances serving subjective sleep quality reporting for children, that explore different mechanisms for motivating children. We have found that storytelling, which continues in parts throughout the diary-keeping period, can motivate children to adhere to a daily self-reporting regime. Further research is needed to provide further empirical evidence in different contexts and to explore the validity of the reporting and how it is utilized in clinical consultations. For research in child-computer interaction, sleep diaries are an interesting design case as they require sustained engagement with young children. This article documents an exploration of different design solutions, with their failings and successes. We explored storytelling, advent calendars, and construction activities as possible ways to enhance engagement. Further exploration of design solutions and metaphors to encourage children to perform routine tasks or tasks that span days and weeks is needed. These design options, we explored, may be extended or can be found to be differently suited in other contexts. Building up experience with such cases can hopefully consolidate design knowledge for sustaining children's engagement with tasks that while beneficial for the children are not intrinsically motivating.

**Acknowledgments.** We are grateful to the children and their guardians for their effort and cooperation during our studies. We deeply appreciate S. Pillen, L. Quadackers and R. Kurvers for their insights and expertise. We thank the staff and children of the Convitto Nazionale G. Leopardi School in Macerata, Italy, and the Korein after-school child-care centre in Eindhoven, the Netherlands.

# References

1. Aarts, T.: Optimizing Data Collection of Sleep Self-reporting for Children Aged 8–12, by means of an Experience Sampling Chatbot Created through Informant Design. Technical report (2018)
2. Astill, R.G., Van der Heijden, K.B., Van IJzendoorn, M.H., Van Someren, E.J.W.: Sleep, cognition, and behavioral problems in school-age children: a century of research meta-analyzed. Psychol. Bull. **138**(6), 1109–1138 (2012). https://doi.org/10.1037/a0028204
3. Bates, J.E., Viken, R.J., Alexander, D.B., Beyers, J., Stockton, L.: Sleep and adjustment in preschool children: sleep diary reports by mothers relate to behavior reports by teachers. Child Dev. **73**(1), 62–75 (2002). https://doi.org/10.1111/1467-8624.00392
4. Braun, V., Clarke, V.: Using thematic analysis in psychology. Qual. Res. Psychol. **3**(2), 77–101 (2006)
5. Carney, C.E., et al.: The consensus sleep diary: standardizing prospective sleep self-monitoring. Sleep **35**(2), 287–302 (2012). https://doi.org/10.5665/sleep.1642
6. Criscuolo, I.: What colors mean, with the characters from the film inside out: Blog, June 2021. https://www.domestika.org/en/blog/4814-what-colors-mean-with-the-characters-from-the-film-inside-out
7. Gaina, A., Sekine, M., Chen, X., Hamanishi, S., Kagamimori, S.: Validity of child sleep diary questionnaire among junior high school children. J. Epidemiol. **14**(1), 1–4 (2004). https://doi.org/10.2188/jea.14.1
8. Gerber, L.: Sleep deprivation in children. Nurs. Manage. **45**(8), 22–28 (2014). https://doi.org/10.1097/01.numa.0000451997.95978.2f
9. Hoogendoorn, A.: A questionnaire design for dependent interviewing that addresses the problem of cognitive satisficing. J. Official Stat. Stockh. **20**(2), 219 (2004). https://www.proquest.com/scholarly-journals/questionnaire-design-dependent-interviewing-that/docview/1266794169/se-2
10. Ibáñez, V., Silva, J., Cauli, O.: A survey on sleep assessment methods. PeerJ **6**, e4849 (2018). https://doi.org/10.7717/peerj.4849
11. Infante-Rivard, C.: Empirical study of parental recall bias. Am. J. Epidemiol. **152**(5), 480–486 (2000). https://doi.org/10.1093/aje/152.5.480
12. Markopoulos, P., Read, J.C., MacFarlane, S., Hoysniemi, J.: Evaluating children's interactive products: principles&practices for interaction designers. Elsevier (2008)
13. Maski, K.P., Kothare, S.V.: Sleep deprivation and neurobehavioral functioning in children. Int. J. Psychophysiol. **89**(2), 259–264 (2013). https://doi.org/10.1016/j.ijpsycho.2013.06.019
14. Matricciani, L.: Subjective reports of children's sleep duration: Does the question matter? A literature review. Sleep Med. **14**(4), 303–311 (2013). https://doi.org/10.1016/j.sleep.2013.01.002
15. Matthews, M., Doherty, G., Coyle, D., Sharry, J.: Designing mobile applications to support mental health interventions. In: Handbook of Research on User Interface Design and Evaluation for Mobile Technology, pp. 635–656 (2008). https://doi.org/10.4018/978-1-59904-871-0.ch038

16. Matthews, M., Doherty, G., Sharry, J., Fitzpatrick, C.: Mobile phone mood charting for adolescents. Br. J. Guid. Couns. **36**(2), 113–129 (2008). https://doi.org/10.1080/03069880801926400
17. Meijer, Habekothé, Wittenboer, V.D.: Time in bed, quality of sleep and school functioning of children. J. Sleep Res. **9**(2), 145–153 (2000). https://doi.org/10.1046/j.1365-2869.2000.00198.x
18. Meltzer, L.J., Avis, K.T., Biggs, S., Reynolds, A.C., Crabtree, V.M., Bevans, K.B.: The Children's Report of Sleep Patterns (CRSP): a self-report measure of sleep for school-aged children. J. Clin. Sleep Med. **09**(03), 235–245 (2013). https://doi.org/10.5664/jcsm.2486
19. Minde, K., et al.: The evaluation and treatment of sleep disturbances in young children. J. Child Psychol. Psychiatry **34**(4), 521–533 (1993). https://doi.org/10.1111/j.1469-7610.1993.tb01033.x
20. Owens, J.A., Spirito, A., McGuinn, M.: The Children's Sleep Habits Questionnaire (CSHQ): psychometric properties of a survey instrument for school-aged children. Sleep **23**(8), 1–9 (2000). https://doi.org/10.1093/sleep/23.8.1d
21. Owens, J.A., Spirito, A., McGuinn, M., Nobile, C.: Sleep habits & sleep disturbance in elementary school-aged children. J. Dev. Behav. Pediatr. **21**(1), 27–36 (2000). https://doi.org/10.1097/00004703-200002000-00005
22. Paavonen, E., Aronen, E., Moilanen, I., Piha, J., Räsänen, E., Tamminen, T., Almqvist, F.: Sleep problems of school-aged children: a complementary view. Acta Paediatr. **89**(2), 223–228 (2000). https://doi.org/10.1111/j.1651-2227.2000.tb01220.x
23. Pina, L., Sien, S.W., Song, C., Ward, T.M., Fogarty, J., Munson, S.A., Kientz, J.A.: DreamCatcher: exploring how parents and school-age children can track and review sleep information together. Proceedings of the ACM on Human-Computer Interaction **4**(CSCW1), 1–25 (2020). https://doi.org/10.1145/3392882
24. Riley, A.W.: Evidence that school-age children can self-report on their health. Ambul. Pediatr. **4**(4), 371–376 (2004). https://doi.org/10.1367/a03-178r.1
25. Sadeh, A.: Consequences of sleep loss or sleep disruption in children. Sleep Med. Clin. **2**(3), 513–520 (2007). https://doi.org/10.1016/j.jsmc.2007.05.012
26. Sonne, T., Müller, J., Marshall, P., Obel, C., Grønbæk, K.: Changing family practices with assistive technology. In: Proceedings of the 2016 CHI Conference on Human Factors in Computing Systems (2016). https://doi.org/10.1145/2858036.2858157
27. Spruyt, K., Gozal, D.: Pediatric sleep questionnaires as diagnostic or epidemiological tools: a review of currently available instruments. Sleep Med. Rev. **15**(1), 19–32 (2011). https://doi.org/10.1016/j.smrv.2010.07.005
28. Taylor, D.J., Roane, B.M.: Treatment of insomnia in adults and children: a practice-friendly review of research. J. Clin. Psychol. **66**(11), 1137–1147 (2010). https://doi.org/10.1002/jclp.20733
29. Varni, J., Limbers, C., Burwinkle, T.: How young can children reliably and validly self-report their health-related quality of life?: An analysis of 8,591 children across age subgroups with the PedsQL™ 4.0 Generic Core Scales. Health Qual Life Outcomes **5**(1) (2007). https://doi.org/10.1186/1477-7525-5-1
30. Vriesema, C.C., Gehlbach, H.: Assessing survey satisficing: the impact of unmotivated questionnaire responding on data quality. Educ. Res. **50**(9), 618–627 (2021). https://doi.org/10.3102/0013189x211040054
31. Yip, J.C., et al.: Children initiating and leading cooperative inquiry sessions. In: Proceedings of the 12th International Conference on Interaction Design and Children, pp. 293–296 (2013)

# The Peer Data Labelling System (PDLS). A Participatory Approach to Classifying Engagement in the Classroom

Graham Parsonage[1,2]([✉]), Matthew Horton[1], and Janet Read[1]

[1] University of Central Lancashire, Preston, UK
{mplhorton,jcread}@uclan.ac.uk
[2] University of the West of Scotland, Paisley, UK
gbparsonage1@uclan.ac.uk, graham.parsonage@uws.ac.uk
https://chici.org/

**Abstract.** The paper introduces a novel and extensible approach to generating labelled data called the Peer Data Labelling System (PDLS), suitable for training supervised Machine Learning algorithms for use in CCI research and development. The novelty is in classifying one child's engagement using peer observation by another child, thus reducing the two-stage process of detection and inference common in emotion recognition to a single phase. In doing so, this technique preserves context at the point of inference, reducing the time and cost of labelling data retrospectively and stays true to the CCI principle of keeping child-participation central to the design process. We evaluate the approach using the usability metrics of effectiveness, efficiency, and satisfaction. PDLS is judged to be both efficient and satisfactory. Further work is required to judge its effectiveness, but initial indications are encouraging and indicate that the children were consistent in their perceptions of engagement and disengagement.

**Keywords:** data labelling · artificial intelligence · engagement

## 1 Introduction

Learning is a complex process which relies on many factors, not least the skill of the teacher in maintaining pupils' attention to their learning activities so that they complete any set tasks. As children use more technology in the classroom, it becomes enticing to consider what an intelligent system might be able to do independently to keep a child engaged on a task. In this study we explore the extent to which pupils can assist in the design of such a system and their acceptance of its judgments.

In Child Computer Interaction (CCI) it is common to engage children in design activities. In our study we "employ" children as labellers of data by using their expertise to decide if a peer is engaged on task or not. We consider this to be a novel approach to assist in training a recogniser. Our contributions

J. Abdelnour Nocera et al. (Eds.): INTERACT 2023, LNCS 14143, pp. 224–233, 2023.
https://doi.org/10.1007/978-3-031-42283-6_13

include reflections on the approach taken, survey findings indicating pupils' level of acceptance of such a method and a data set that others in the CCI community can use and develop. Validation of the children's judgments is currently ongoing and is not included in this study.

The paper proposes a novel and extensible approach to generating labelled data suitable for training supervised Machine Learning (ML) algorithms for use in CCI research and development called the Peer Data Labelling System (PDLS). The novelty is in classifying one child's engagement using peer observation by another child. This reduces the two stage process of detection, (the capture of the data) and inference, (the latter coding of the data) common in emotion recognition to a single synchronous phase. In doing so, this technique preserves context at the point of inference, reduces the time and cost of labelling data retrospectively and stays true to the CCI principle of keeping child-participation central to the design process. We evaluate the approach using the usability metrics of effectiveness, efficiency and satisfaction.

## 1.1 Learning and Engagement

Pupil engagement is widely considered to be a positive factor in, and an important driver of, pupil attainment [3]. Multiple definitions of engagement exist [12] but for the purpose of this study, we consider engagement on task, namely a pupil's interaction with a computerised learning activity completed within a school classroom. Whilst school age education in the UK has largely returned to the physical classroom, the Covid-19 pandemic fast-forwarded the development and adoption of hybrid and blended learning pedagogical approaches [30]. This created new requirements for tools and techniques that can aid teachers in monitoring and interpreting pupils' level of engagement with academic tasks both online and in the classroom.

## 1.2 Approaches to Recognising Children's Engagement

The study of children's understanding of emotions based on facial expressions and other stimuli is well researched [13,29]. Children start to be able to discern emotion from an early age [9] and are also able to differentiate between contexts of expressions, for example they can understand that a parent crying at a TV drama is not the same as one crying following an injury [23]. Hence we argue that context is an important factor on the accuracy of children's recognition and classification of emotion [28].

A popular and established system for emotion recognition is the Facial Action Coding System (FACS) [11]. One drawback to FACS is the considerable training required which at the time of writing is estimated by the Paul Ekman Group to be between 50 and 100 h [10]. An alternative approach commonly used both in academia and commercially is to automate the emotion classification process using algorithms such as AFFDEX [1,20] or FACET [19]. Whilst the algorithmic approach has the potential to save considerable time, there is concern that current emotion recognition systems are less accurate than their human counterparts when employed on children [2].

### 1.3  Existing Data Sets for Machine Learning that Include Children

Specialised child-centered data sets are relatively scarce. Princeton University Library have curated a directory of databases containing face stimulus sets available for use in behavioural studies of which just four are specific to children [24]. This lack of material restricts the options for CCI researchers looking for data as a starting point on which to train their models.

### 1.4  Machine Learning and Child Computer Interaction

There is a rich vein of work within the CCI Community enshrining child participation as core to a child-centered design process [8,15,25,27]. Hourcade [14] organises the key principles of CCI research into ten pillars, the second of which, "Deeply engage with stakeholders" enshrines the principle of child participation as the core of a child-centred design process. At a time where a growing number of academic studies are exploring ML based systems and intelligent interfaces both within the CCI community [7,22,26] and the wider HCI community [4,6,17]. We propose an approach to data labelling that makes child participation intrinsic not only to the development of the system but also core to the system's outputs.

## 2  Studies

Two studies were conducted at a single UK secondary school (ages 11–16). The aim of the first study was to generate video data that captured the engagement status of children while they completed a computerised task in a classroom. Values for the engagement status of the child completing the task were recorded synchronously by peer observation effectively reducing the two stage operation of detection and inference to a single stage operation while maintaining context during inference and in a time and resource effective manner. The second study assessed the children's experience of, and confidence in, the data labelling process and a theoretical system based on its output.

### 2.1  Participants

Forty-five pupils took part in the studies. Twenty-two children, (12 boys and 10 girls) aged between 11 and 15 took part in the first study and a further twenty-three children, (10 boys, 13 girls) aged between 11 and 12 took part in the second study. Prior to the study commencing, written consent was obtained from the school, parents or carers, and the pupils. The pupils were also advised that they could withdraw their data after completing the task regardless of any previous consent given by themselves or third parties. No incentives or rewards were offered to the children who took part in the study.

## 2.2 Apparatus

Three artefacts were prepared for the studies, the first was a website of material about cryptography. The material was designed to support at least 15 min of activity which was the time allocated for each child to interact with the cryptography webpage and was deemed, by the teachers, to be suitable for children within an eleven to fifteen year age range.

The second artefact was an online form with a drop-down list that allowed the (child) observer to log the engagement level of the pupil completing the cryptography task. Using the form, the observer recorded the engagement level as; engaged (interested and working) or disengaged (disinterested or distracted). When the observer felt that the learner had changed engagement category they then logged the updated value.

The final artefact used only in the second study was a short paper based questionnaire. Pupils completed the questionnaire to gauge their feelings about the logging process. Pupils were asked:

1. How accurately they thought their classmate had judged their engagement level whilst completing the task
2. How accurately they thought they had judged their classmate's engagement level whilst completing the task
3. How accepting they would be if a system was utilised in the classroom to monitor their engagement level
4. To what degree would they trust the system to identify disengagement

A Likert scale ranging from 1–10 was used to rate the pupils' responses where 1 equated to low and 10 equated to high. For instance for Question 1, a recorded score of 1 would indicate that the pupil thought the accuracy of their classmate's judgement of their engagement level was low whilst a score of 10 would indicate a perceived high accuracy of judgment.

## 2.3 Procedure

The children worked in pairs each taking turns at being the learner and the observer switching roles half way through the study. The learner completed the online task on their laptop. The observer was positioned so that they could watch the learner completing the task but could not see their laptop screen and logged the learner's engagement status. The importance of the logging process was emphasised to the children as having equal importance to the computerised task.

For the second study, after completing the online task, the children were asked to complete the questions and record any other observations about the study.

# 3 Results

The first set of studies produced 22 videos of which 17 were usable. 2 videos were discarded as they had audio but no image frames and 3 videos were complete but had no engagement statuses recorded. The 17 usable videos and engagement logs yielded 2 h, 33 min and 48 s of video of which 2 h, 27 min and 32 s has labels generated from the pupil logs. This resulted in 221,300 labelled JPEG images. The observers logged 57 instances of an engaged status totalling 2 h, 12 min and 33 s yielding 198,825 labelled images. Forty-four instances of a disengaged status were logged totalling 14 min and 59 s yielding 22,475 images. The average duration of an instance of learner engagement was 2 min and 20 s and the average duration of learner disengagement was 20 s. The frequency of the logged data ranged from a single recording of engaged through to 26 recorded statuses (M = 3.35, SD = 3.6).

Time spent on the task ranged from 2 min and 24 s to 20 min and 13 s (M = 09:03, SD = 05:26). The logged duration ranged in time from 2 min and 8 s to 19 min and 52 s (M = 08:41, SD = 05:28). Six minutes and 16 s of video were discarded as they had no logging status. The majority of the discarded data occurred at the beginning of the videos in the period after the learner had started the video camera generating the starting timestamp and before the observer recorded their first engagement status.

In addition 22 questionnaires were completed from the second study the results of which are presented in Table 1. For a discussion see Sect. 4.1 Satisfaction.

## 4    Discussion

### 4.1    Evaluating the Usability of the Process

The stated aims of this paper were to introduce a novel and extensible approach to generating labelled data suitable for training supervised ML algorithms for use in CCI research and development which were then evaluated using the usability metrics effectiveness, efficiency and satisfaction outlined in ISO 9241-11 [16].

**Efficiency.** We judge PDLS to be both a time and cost efficient system that compares favourably against the options considered. FACS coding by human experts requires both extensive training and a has a considerable time and cost overhead. PDLS labels the data at the point of capture using peer judgments thus avoiding these pitfalls. Algorithmic implementations such as AFFDEX and products that implement them such as iMotions can be configured to perform evaluations in real time but are considerably more costly than PDLS which requires no specialist equipment other than a laptop and a camera both of which are relatively low cost and freely available. PDLS is extensible and suitable for gathering and labelling data concurrently.

**Satisfaction.** Children indicated their satisfaction with both their own and their peers effectiveness in reaching a classification and the potential of a system built upon data from the study to make effective judgments. They expressed confidence in their own ability to accurately measure the engagement level of

**Table 1.** Children's Responses to Survey Questions (scale 1–10)

| Classmate's Judgment | Own Judgment | Acceptance of System | Trust in System |
| --- | --- | --- | --- |
| 9 | 9 | 7 | 10 |
| 8 | 9 | 7 | 10 |
| 9 | 10 | 8 | 7 |
| 10 | 10 | 10 | 10 |
| 9 | 9 | 5 | 5 |
| 6 | 9 | 8 | 7 |
| 3 | 8 | 7 | 3 |
| 5 | 5 | 3 | 3 |
| 8 | 9 | 4 | 5 |
| 5 | 8 | 4 | 4 |
| 8 | 10 | 5 | 4 |
| 8 | 6 | 4 | 4 |
| 8 | 10 | 9 | 9 |
| 8 | 7 | 4 | 6 |
| 9 | 9 | 9 | 9 |
| 10 | 10 | 8 | 6 |
| 9 | 9 | 9 | 9 |
| 9 | 10 | 9 | 9 |
| 6 | 5 | 4 | 4 |
| 10 | 10 | 6 | 8 |
| 10 | – | – | – |
| 10 | 10 | 7 | 8 |

their classmate (R2). When asked to rate the accuracy of their judgements on a Likert scale of 1 to 10 where 1 is not accurate and 10 is very accurate, the average recorded score was 8.667 (SD = 1.623). They were marginally less positive about the ability of their classmate to assess their own engagement levels whilst still expressing confidence (M = 8.045, SD = 1.914) (R1). The children were also asked how accepting they would be if a system were deployed to monitor their level of engagement in the classroom and how trusting they would be in the accuracy of its judgements. The children were neutral to accepting of the proposed system (M = 6.523, SD = 2.159) (R3) and its predictions (M = 6.666, SD = 2.456) (R4) with both scores lower than their confidence in their own and their peers ability.

**Effectiveness.** Evaluating the effectiveness of PDLS is challenging and requires further work, however the initial signs are promising. The children's judgments appear to be consistent and there are few outliers in the data indicating that the classifications are cohesive and the children are measuring the same phenomena.

Whilst we can't say with certainty that the children's judgments are correct, a random sample of ten of the 44 videos that were classified as disengaged indicates that in the majority of cases the learner is exhibiting behaviour which may show disengagement or distraction from the task (Table 2). Certainly their focus often appears to be elsewhere. The exception may be video 212 where although the learner appeared amused by something there is no obvious indication that they were not engaged. Study 212 had the most statuses recorded across both categories, (26 for a logged duration of 11 min and 18 s), or one every 26 s on average with an average duration of $\approx 7$ s for each logging of disengagement. As such it is feasible that the observer's judgements were not in line with the other children.

**Table 2.** Characteristics of Children's observations of disengagement

| Study ID clip | Observation of Behaviour |
| --- | --- |
| 171_2 | The learner appears distracted and looks away from the screen |
| 172_4 | The learner is laughing |
| 173_4 | The learner is talking and hits out at someone off camera |
| 196_2 | The learner is laughing and appears distracted |
| 212_12 | The learner is smiling and scratching their head |
| 212_24 | The learner is smiling but appears to be working |
| 213_6 | The learner is smiling and scratching their ear |
| 213_10 | The learner is smiling and looks away from the screen in parts but appears to be working |
| 219_1 | The learner is talking and looking away from the screen |
| 237_2 | The learner appears to be working but is holding a conversation unrelated to the task |

### 4.2    A Child-Centred Process

Our final stated objective was to stay true to the CCI principle of keeping child-participation central to the design process. In using the children's own classifications to generate the data set, they become central not just to the design process but also to the operation of a system built using that data set. They are in effect judging themselves. Firstly, they classify each others level of engagement in the classroom using the PDLS method. The labelled data is then used by the system to learn about engagement, this learning process is entirely dependent on the children's classifications. Once operational the system monitors the children in the classroom and uses what it has learnt from them to classify their engagement level. As such, PDLS not only uses the children's judgment to label the data but by the very nature of the supervised machine learning process their participation and input will form the basis of future system development and deployment.

### 4.3   Data Bias, Authenticity and Future Work

Data bias is a recurrent theme in ML literature [18, 21] and beyond. In the UK in 2020 there was uproar that the algorithm designed to predict exam results was unfair and disadvantaged students from certain demographics resulting in teachers predicting grades [5]. As Intelligent systems become increasingly embedded into society it is an inherent responsibility of designers and developers to ensure that the decisions made by the technology are fair. When making this point we note that the data collected for this study is produced from a single computerised task in one school and the output from any ML model built based on this data will reflect these limitations.

To address these limitations further studies should reflect children's diverse backgrounds increasing the scope of the data set and therefore the quality of the judgments produced by ML models trained upon it. In addition, the scope and circumstance of the observed tasks can be extended to provide new context to the observations. Whilst the work to date has involved a computerised task and webcam it is feasible that judgments could be recorded of children completing more tradition activities which do not involve computers.

## 5   Conclusion

This paper presents PDLS, a peer observation approach to generating a labelled data set suitable for use in CCI research. The system is evaluated against the usability metrics, effectiveness, efficiency and satisfaction and is judged to be both efficient and satisfactory. Further work is ongoing to judge its effectiveness but initial indications are encouraging and indicate that the children were consistent in their perceptions of engagement and disengagement. The CCI principle of Child Participation is central to the PDLS process which generates labelled data in both a time and cost effective manner. Children were surveyed for their feelings on the accuracy of both their own and their peers' judgment of engagement status after completing the task and expressed their confidence in both these aspects.

**Acknowledgments.** We would like to thank the Head Teacher, staff and pupils of Ribblesdale High School and in particular the Head of Computer Science, Mr Steven Kay for their invaluable assistance and participation in this study.

## References

1. Bishay, M., Preston, K., Strafuss, M., Page, G., Turcot, J., Mavadati, M.: Affdex 2.0: a real-time facial expression analysis toolkit. arXiv preprint arXiv:2202.12059 (2022)
2. Bryant, D., Howard, A.: A comparative analysis of emotion-detecting AI systems with respect to algorithm performance and dataset diversity. In: Proceedings of the 2019 AAAI/ACM Conference on AI, Ethics, and Society, pp. 377–382 (2019)

3. Christenson, S., Reschly, A.L., Wylie, C., et al.: Handbook of research on student engagement, vol. 840. Springer (2012)

4. Chromik, M., Butz, A.: Human-XAI interaction: a review and design principles for explanation user interfaces. In: Ardito, C., Lanzilotti, R., Malizia, A., Petrie, H., Piccinno, A., Desolda, G., Inkpen, K. (eds.) INTERACT 2021. LNCS, vol. 12933, pp. 619–640. Springer, Cham (2021). https://doi.org/10.1007/978-3-030-85616-8_36

5. Coughlan, S.: Why did the a-level algorithm say no? August 2020. https://www.bbc.co.uk/news/education-53787203. Accessed on 06.01.2023

6. Desolda, G., Esposito, A., Lanzilotti, R., Costabile, M.F.: Detecting emotions through machine learning for automatic UX evaluation. In: Ardito, C., Lanzilotti, R., Malizia, A., Petrie, H., Piccinno, A., Desolda, G., Inkpen, K. (eds.) INTER-ACT 2021. LNCS, vol. 12934, pp. 270–279. Springer, Cham (2021). https://doi.org/10.1007/978-3-030-85613-7_19

7. Dietz, G., King Chen, J., Beason, J., Tarrow, M., Hilliard, A., Shapiro, R.B.: Artonomous: introducing middle school students to reinforcement learning through virtual robotics. In: Interaction Design and Children, IDC 2022, pp. 430–441. Association for Computing Machinery, New York (2022). https://doi.org/10.1145/3501712.3529736

8. Druin, A.: The role of children in the design of new technology. Behav. Inf. Technol. **21**(1), 1–25 (2002)

9. Durand, K., Gallay, M., Seigneuric, A., Robichon, F., Baudouin, J.Y.: The development of facial emotion recognition: the role of configural information. J. Exp. Child Psychol. **97**(1), 14–27 (2007)

10. Ekman, P.: Facial action coding system, January 2020. https://www.paulekman.com/facial-action-coding-system/

11. Ekman, P., Friesen, W.V.: Facial action coding system. Environmental Psychology & Nonverbal Behavior (1978)

12. Groccia, J.E.: What is student engagement? New Dir. Teach. Learn. **2018**(154), 11–20 (2018)

13. Gross, A.L., Ballif, B.: Children's understanding of emotion from facial expressions and situations: a review. Dev. Rev. **11**(4), 368–398 (1991)

14. Hourcade, J.P.: Child-computer interaction. Self, Iowa City, Iowa (2015)

15. Inkpen, K.: Three important research agendas for educational multimedia: learning, children, and gender. In: AACE World Conference on Educational Multimedia and Hypermedia, vol. 97, pp. 521–526. Citeseer (1997)

16. Iso - international organization for standardization. iso 9241–11:2018(en) ergonomics of human-system interaction - part 11: Usability: Definitions and concepts (2018). https://www.iso.org/obp/ui/. Accessed 18 Jan 2023

17. Jasim, M., Collins, C., Sarvghad, A., Mahyar, N.: Supporting serendipitous discovery and balanced analysis of online product reviews with interaction-driven metrics and bias-mitigating suggestions. In: Proceedings of the 2022 CHI Conference on Human Factors in Computing Systems, CHI 2022. Association for Computing Machinery, New York (2022). https://doi.org/10.1145/3491102.3517649

18. Jiang, H., Nachum, O.: Identifying and correcting label bias in machine learning. In: International Conference on Artificial Intelligence and Statistics, pp. 702–712. PMLR (2020)

19. Littlewort, G., et al.: The computer expression recognition toolbox (cert). In: 2011 IEEE International Conference on Automatic Face & Gesture Recognition (FG), pp. 298–305. IEEE (2011)

20. McDuff, D., Mahmoud, A., Mavadati, M., Amr, M., Turcot, J., Kaliouby, R.e.: Affdex SDK: a cross-platform real-time multi-face expression recognition toolkit. In: Proceedings of the 2016 CHI Conference Extended Abstracts on Human Factors in Computing Systems, pp. 3723–3726 (2016)
21. Mehrabi, N., Morstatter, F., Saxena, N., Lerman, K., Galstyan, A.: A survey on bias and fairness in machine learning. ACM Comput. Surv. (CSUR) 54(6), 1–35 (2021)
22. Nguyen, H.: Examining teenagers' perceptions of conversational agents in learning settings. In: Interaction Design and Children, IDC 2022, pp. 374–381. Association for Computing Machinery, New York (2022). https://doi.org/10.1145/3501712.3529740
23. Pollak, S.D., Messner, M., Kistler, D.J., Cohn, J.F.: Development of perceptual expertise in emotion recognition. Cognition 110(2), 242–247 (2009)
24. Databases (a-z) - face image databases - research guides at Princeton university January 2022. https://libguides.princeton.edu/facedatabases. Accessed 18 January 2023
25. Read, J.C., Horton, M., Fitton, D., Sim, G.: Empowered and informed: participation of children in HCI. In: Bernhaupt, R., Dalvi, G., Joshi, A., Balkrishan, D.K., O'Neill, J., Winckler, M. (eds.) INTERACT 2017. LNCS, vol. 10514, pp. 431–446. Springer, Cham (2017). https://doi.org/10.1007/978-3-319-67684-5_27
26. Rubegni, E., Malinverni, L., Yip, J.: "Don't let the robots walk our dogs, but it's ok for them to do our homework": children's perceptions, fears, and hopes in social robots. In: Interaction Design and Children, IDC 2022, pp. 352–361. Association for Computing Machinery, New York (2022). https://doi.org/10.1145/3501712.3529726
27. Scaife, M., Rogers, Y., Aldrich, F., Davies, M.: Designing for or designing with? informant design for interactive learning environments. In: Proceedings of the ACM SIGCHI Conference on Human Factors in Computing Systems, pp. 343–350 (1997)
28. Theurel, A., Witt, A., Malsert, J., Lejeune, F., Fiorentini, C., Barisnikov, K., Gentaz, E.: The integration of visual context information in facial emotion recognition in 5-to 15-year-olds. J. Exp. Child Psychol. 150, 252–271 (2016)
29. Widen, S.C.: Children's interpretation of facial expressions: the long path from valence-based to specific discrete categories. Emot. Rev. 5(1), 72–77 (2013)
30. Zhao, Y., Watterston, J.: The changes we need: education post covid-19. J. Educ. Change 22(1), 3–12 (2021)

# WashWall: An Interactive Smart Mirror for Motivating Handwashing Among Primary School Children

Dees B.W. Postma$^{(\boxtimes)}$ (ID), Champika M. Ranasinghe (ID),
Christos Constantinou (ID), Vincent P.G. Diks (ID), Younghun Rhee (ID),
Willem H.P. van Dijk (ID), Amir Sassanian, and Dennis Reidsma (ID)

University of Twente, Enschede, The Netherlands
d.b.w.postma@utwente.nl

**Abstract.** Hand hygiene became one of the key measures to prevent COVID-19 infection and the spread of the virus. This, however, is challenging with young children (e.g., primary school). Primary school teachers spend a lot of time supervising and helping children to wash their hands and making sure they wash their hands regularly and correctly. Educating children of the need for handwashing and training them to wash hands for 20 s alone does not motivate young children enough to wash their hands without supervision. We developed WashWall, an interactive smart mirror that uses gamification to motivate young children to wash their hands in an engaging way. We deployed WashWall in a primary school and conducted a user study (N = 14) to evaluate its practicality, effectiveness, and user experience. Results show that children engaged in the activity for a significantly longer duration, enjoyed playing WashWall, and learned the game easily and fast.

**Keywords:** Infections · COVID-19 · Handwashing · Children · Gamification

## 1 Introduction

Handwashing is one of the key infection control measures used to control the spread of infections during recent pandemics (e.g. COVID-19 pandemic and the pandemic influenza) [9]. Not only COVID-19 but also the impact of other potential future viruses as well as common infections such as gastrointestinal illnesses and respiratory illnesses which are common in tropical countries can be mitigated by practising proper handwashing and making it a habit among school children [13]. Although, children are less affected by COVID-19 infections compared to other age groups, they are one of the main contributors to spearheading the virus to other vulnerable groups. Therefore, controlling the infections among children is considered key to mitigate the impact of common viruses, COVID-19, and future viruses [23]. However, motivating and persuading children to wash

J. Abdelnour Nocera et al. (Eds.): INTERACT 2023, LNCS 14143, pp. 234–253, 2023.
https://doi.org/10.1007/978-3-031-42283-6_14

their hands properly and regularly, without supervision and help still remains a challenge especially with primary school children [34].

Current hand hygiene interventions in schools mainly aim at improving the knowledge and awareness of handwashing [9], for example through persuasive messaging using posters, videos, leaflets, games [10,41] and educational activities in schools. However, increased awareness alone might not be sufficient to incentivise children to wash their hands. Song and colleagues, for example, found that while education on handwashing benefits handwashing technique, it does not affect handwashing compliance among primary school children [42]. In fact, teaching complex multi-stage handwashing directives may have a negative impact on handwashing compliance [2]. Moreover, the importance of handwashing may not be sufficiently clear to many primary school children as they are not yet able to associate *"the probability of unhealthiness with invisible dirt"* [34]. Finally, it is difficult to implement hand hygiene interventions in school settings, especially with primary school children [18,29,41]. For example, since the COVID-19 pandemic emerged, kindergarten and school teachers and their assistants spend a lot of time helping and supervising handwashing [38]. Therefore, there is a need for developing creative approaches that can steer or nudge children to wash their hands regularly. To address this challenge, we explored the following research question: *"How might we design an interactive system that incentivises elementary school children to practice proper handwashing procedures, both in terms of technique and duration, without the help of caregivers?"*

In this research, we introduce WashWall (Fig. 1), a creative innovation that does not primarily focus on improving the knowledge and awareness of handwashing or supervision of handwashing by adults but on making handwashing an interactive, enjoyable, and engaging activity for children. WashWall gamifies the act of handwashing by implementing a *Space-Invader* style video game on an interactive mirror. The game is controlled by handwashing motions that are tracked by an integrated video camera at the base of the mirror. With WashWall, children wash their hands to control an interactive video game.

To study the effectiveness of WashWall to positively influence handwashing behaviour, we evaluated the system in a primary school setting with fourteen children. Using a within-subjects design, we contrasted the handwashing behaviours of children in two conditions: 'mirror mode' where WashWall functioned like a regular mirror and 'game mode' where WashWall could be used to play the Space-Invader style game. The study results show a significant increase in handwashing duration in favour of the 'game mode' condition. Furthermore, it was found that in 'game mode' children prioritised handwashing motions that contributed towards successful game-play (e.g. the rubbing and scrubbing of the hands and frequently exposing the palms of the hands to the running faucet). This suggests that the implemented game mechanics provide a meaningful way to steer behaviour towards better (hand) hygiene. Overall, WashWall was considered to be fun, engaging, and non-disruptive to ongoing class activities. In this paper, we present the details of WashWall and the empirical, in-the-wild, user study and our findings.

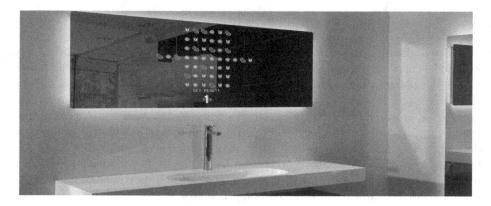

**Fig. 1.** WashWall: an interactive smart mirror that gamifies the act of handwashing for primary school children.

Our contributions in this work are two fold. First, we offer an interactive smart mirror that aims to promote handwashing practices among elementary school children. We illustrate how key-performance metrics can be recognised from (complex) motor behaviour and be translated to controls for gamified systems for health and hygiene. Second, we carried out an empirical evaluation of the artefact using an in-the-wild user study to evaluate its effectiveness and user experience.

## 2    Related Work

With WashWall, we wish to turn the act of handwashing into an engaging experience for primary school children, thereby promoting their hand hygiene. In this section, we will explore the state-of-the-art and investigate how WashWall is situated within this solution space. First, we will consider non-technical, non-interactive approaches to improving hand hygiene among (primary school) children. Second, we will discuss interactive solutions, specifically focusing on social robots, smart mirrors and the potential of gamification.

### 2.1    Raising Awareness

Raising awareness and knowledge about handwashing through education and training in schools is the most widely used method for motivating and practising handwashing behaviour among school children [18]. This is usually done using posters, leaflets, games, and videos [9,10,13], see also: [5]. While such approaches have shown effective in raising awareness and in improving handwashing practice, they are less effective in persuading and motivating *children*; they are difficult to implement in school settings especially with primary school children; and often require supervision by adults (teachers or teaching assistants) [38]. The HCI-community has taken a rising interest in exploring more technical, interactive and persuasive solutions to promote hand hygiene (among children) – each taking their own unique approach, for example: [4,6,13,30,32]. Mondol and colleagues, for instance, employ smartwatches to monitor and inform users about proper handwashing technique [32], whereas Deshmukh and colleagues explored the use of (low-cost) social robots to promote hand hygiene among elementary school children [12,13,46]. We will discuss the most relevant HCI-powered handwashing innovations below.

## 2.2  Monitoring Systems

Currently existing systems that are concerned with hand hygiene range widely in their level of interactivity. Minimally interactive systems focus on tracking and monitoring handwashing compliance. Monitoring handwashing compliance is especially useful in settings where hand hygiene is of critical importance, such as in hospital settings. Rabeek and colleagues for instance developed the 'automated hand hygiene and documentation system' to monitor handwashing compliance in hospitals [39,40]. Using ultrasonic technology, they were able to track the movements of clinicians between 'washing zones' and 'bed zones', inferring handwashing compliance from such movements. As such, the system is agnostic to handwashing quality or duration. In contrast, Llorca and colleagues designed a computer vision system that could reliably classify six different handwashing poses [30] that were deemed essential to proper handwashing technique. Using this system, automatic handwashing quality measurement could be performed.

## 2.3  Prompting and Signalling Systems

Beyond mere tracking and monitoring, systems have been developed that proactively prompt the user to wash their hands [4] or re-actively signal the user when handwashing protocol was not followed (properly). One such example stems from the work of Edmond and colleagues [19]. Driven by the high number of healthcare-associated infections that occur annually, they developed a system that could recognise whether nurses (and potentially other hospital personnel) adhered to the disinfection protocols by sensing alcohol vapour. Nurses wore tags that were sensitive to alcohol vapour. The tag would be activated once a nurse entered a room. If alcohol vapour was detected after activation, a tag-light would glow green and a 'ping' sound would be emitted. If no alcohol vapour was detected after activation, a tag-light would glow red and a 'beeping' sound would be emitted. Mondol and Stankovic developed a similar system for a hospital setting, but with the use of smartwatches [32]. Using the gyroscopes from the smartwatch, handwashing gestures could be recognised. Upon entering a 'critical zone', the smartwatch would signal the user whether hand washing was performed at all and whether handwashing was of sufficient duration and quality. Both systems were found to significantly increase adherence to hand hygiene protocols. Also, both systems make use of prompts to alert the user of their handwashing compliance. Through auditory and vibratory signals, users are persuaded to act according to protocol. However, interaction remains minimal and while the level of incentivisation might be enough to prompt health-care professionals towards handwashing compliance, more might be needed to incentivise children to wash their hands.

## 2.4   Interactive Systems

Recently, there is a rising interest for exploring more interactive and persuasive solutions that can motivate children to wash their hands. Three systems are of particular interest to the current case: WallBo [12,13,46]; smart mirror [38]; and Germ Destroyer [1]. We will briefly introduce each of these systems and discuss the pros and cons of each for aiding handwashing procedures in elementary school children.

Deshmukh and colleagues [12,13,46] developed WallBo, a low-cost, social robot that is expected to act as a persuasive agent in changing the handwashing behaviour of children. WallBo has the shape of a hand to associate it with handwashing, has two eyes to imply a sense of being watched and can be mounted on a wall (so that it can be deployed closer to a handwashing sink). WallBo is controlled by a remote researcher, using the Wizard-of-Oz technique to communicate handwashing instructions to the children. It displays handwashing instructions on a small screen together with audio (using childlike voice) instructions. WallBo was deployed and empirically evaluated in an in-the-wild setting and was found to increase handwashing compliance, technique, and knowledge during a 5-day intervention [13]. While the results of the system are promising, at current, WallBo cannot run autonomously. A remote researcher is needed to interact with the children through the interface of the robot. This renders the implementation of the system time intensive and limits its broader application as it still requires supervision by adults.

Rabben and Mikkelsplass [38] explored the use of smart mirrors to encourage children to wash their hands independently (without requiring the supervision of adults - teachers and teaching assistants). They proposed to use smart mirrors to convey handwashing instructions and feedback about handwashing progress in a way that more appealing to young children (from grade one to four). They explored two design options for presenting step-by-step instructions and feedback. The first option shows a series of images displaying step-by-step instructions on handwashing. These images were taken from common handwashing awareness posters used in the school. A progress bar shows the progress of handwashing and fills up in 40 s. After 40 s (i.e. when the progress bar is filled completely), the screen shows balloons to indicate the successful completion of handwashing and is meant to give the children a sense of achievement. The second design option uses videos, rather than still images, for presenting handwashing instructions. Similar to design option 1, the progress bar fills up over the course of 40 s and shows a smiley face after completion. The concept was evaluated using a tablet (placed on the sink) that displayed the content for design option 1 and 2. Interview data from the teacher learns that 'smart mirror' was well received by the children. The children found it engaging to work with the smart mirror and were observed to spent more time washing their hands than they used to. Unfortunately, no quantitative data are presented to support these claims.

Finally, Altmeyer and colleagues [1] developed 'Germ Destroyer' to encourage people to wash their hands to meet the recommended duration (20 s). Germ Destroyer achieves this by gamifying the handwashing activity. The system consists of two parts, a sensor device attached to the tap to detect water flow and the presence of hands and a gameful mobile application running on a tablet. The screen shows cartoon-like germs when the faucet is running, then when the user holds their hands under the tap, a soap animation is displayed and the germs will disappear at a constant rate. After 20 s the screen displays a clean hand to indicate successful handwashing. If the user stops washing their hands earlier than that, detected by the sensor device attached to the tap, the faces of the germ are converted to angry faces to redirect users to wash their hands. Germ Destroyer was empirically evaluated both in a lab setting and in-the-wild and was shown to enhance the enjoyment of hand washing, reduce the perceived hand washing duration and increase (doubled) the actual hand washing duration. Clearly, Germ Destroyer could be a game-changer for promoting hand hygiene in shared bathrooms. However, Germ Destroyer (as well as many other systems) focus only on handwashing quantity (i.e. duration) and not on handwashing quality (i.e. technique). It has been shown that both duration as well as technique are of key-importance when it comes to handwashing effectiveness [34]. With Wash-Wall, we aim to bridge this gap by gamifying the handwashing experience for elementary school children, explicitly focusing both on handwashing duration *and* technique.

# 3   WashWall System

The objective of WashWall is to make handwashing a fun and engaging activity while also ensuring proper handwashing protocol. What makes WashWall stand out from existing technologies is that it focuses both on handwashing duration *and* technique (cf. [1]). Towards motivating young children, WashWall uses gamification as a persuasive technique (cf. [38]). Gamification is defined as *"the use of game design elements in non-game contexts"* [15] to motivate and increase user activity and engagement. It a is a well known persuasive technique and is used in a wide range of domains and contexts to motivate users [14]. WashWall is designed to run autonomously (cf. [12,13,46]). Below, we will give a brief overview of the design process that led up to the creation of WashWall and we will discuss the system design and game design of WashWall.

## 3.1   Design Process

For the design of WashWall, we followed a design thinking approach, iteratively cycling through the various stages of the design thinking process (i.e., empathise, define, ideate, prototype, test) to arrive at meaningful designs that would incentivise primary school children to follow proper handwashing procedures without the help of caregivers. In doing so, we organised interviews, observations, and play-testing sessions with ten children aged 6–11 ($M = 6.7$; $SD = 1.9$). During the interviews, we asked them about their pass-time activities and their knowledge and habits regarding handwashing. For the observations and play-testing sessions, we asked them to engage with a number of lofi prototypes (images, videos, presentations, and paper prototypes) and show and tell us how our designs would impact their handwashing behaviour.

For the lofi prototypes, we explored different concepts, which can be summarised as: informing, guiding, and gamifying. The inform-concepts were meant to educate the children on the need for handwashing and give them information about their own handwashing behaviour and practices. The guiding-concepts were meant to guide the children through the handwashing procedures and the gamification-concepts explored the use of (simple) game mechanics to trigger the right handwashing motions. Maybe unsurprisingly, it was found that the children were most enthusiastic about the concepts that included some form of gamification. When asked about their favourite (mobile) games, two children indicated that they liked 'Space Invaders' best. Another arcade-game classic that got mentioned was 'Tetris', while also more modern games were mentioned such as 'Call of Duty'.

Based on the insights that were derived from the interviews, observations, and play-testing sessions, we designed a Space-Invaders style game that children could play simply by washing their hands. To tune our final design, we recruited five children aged 6–8 ($M = 6.4$; $SD = 0.9$) for a pilot-test. This allowed us to study the game control mapping (physical movements to in-game movements) as well as the number of targets that would be needed to ensure proper handwashing durations. The pilot test also enabled us to tailor the computer vision algorithms to the hands of primary school children. The insights that were derived from this pilot test were incorporated in the final system design, which we will describe in detail, below.

### 3.2    System Design

WashWall is an interactive smart mirror that features a Space-Invaders style shooter game. User can play the game by washing their hands. Handwashing movements are recognised and translated to easy-to-understand game controls (see Sect. 3.3). The main interface of WashWall is a smart mirror constructed using a Raspberry pi4 microcontroller (8 GB RAM), a two-way mirror and a TV (32 in. Philips 32PFS6805/12) that acts as the display. A webcam (K&L Webcam - 2K Quad HD - microphone - 4 megapixels), attached to the base of the mirror, is used to track the hands of the user (cf. Fig. 2, panel A and B).

The Raspberry pi is connected to the webcam via a USB cable and to the TV via an HDMI (Fig. 2, panel A). The two-way mirror and the TV are mounted above the sink, facing towards the person who is using the sink (Fig. 2, panel B). The Raspberry pi is mounted to the back side of the mirror. The webcam is oriented downwards, such that only the tap and the hands are in view.

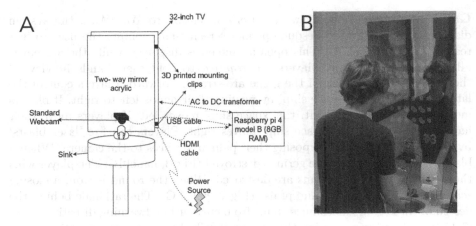

**Fig. 2.** Overview of the WashWall system: (A) System architecture diagram, (B) Wash-Wall in 'game mode'

## 3.3   Game Design and Rationale

The game for the WashWall installation was modelled after 'Space Invaders': An arcade-game classic that is lauded for its simplicity and attraction. In 'Space Invaders', players control the lateral movement of a space craft, while shooting alien invaders. In our game, participants shoot germs instead. In what follows we give a brief outline of the main game-mechanics (Sect. 3.3) and discuss the design rationale behind these (Sect. 3.3).

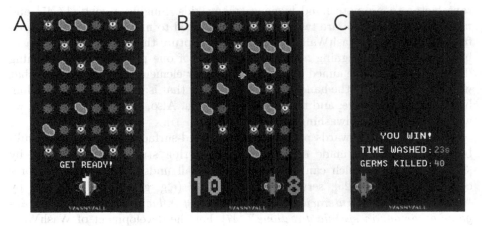

**Fig. 3.** The shooter game that the user sees on the mirror above the sink. Three typical stages of the game: (A) Opening screen of the shooter game, (B) mid-way through the game, (C) Closing screen of the shooter game

**Game Mechanics.** To draw the user's attention to WashWall, the system displays a 'Space Invader'-esque opening screen that prompts the user to 'get ready!' (Fig. 3, panel A). This opening screen is displayed while the system is idle. To start the game, players are *required* to hold their hands in view of the camera. The controls of the game are straight-forward. Players control the lateral motion of the 'space ship' by moving their hands left to right. If players move their hands to the left, the 'space ship' moves left; if players move their hands to the right, the 'space ship' moves right. Players can fire 'laser blasts' by opening their hands – exposing their palmar surfaces to the camera. When a blaster-shot hits a germ, the germ is destroyed (Fig. 3, panel B). The player wins the round when all the germs are destroyed. When the round is won, a closing screen is shown with stats and praise (Fig. 3, panel C). The rationale behind the design of these game mechanics stems from current handwashing directives, e.g.: [7,17,28,45] and game-design theory, specifically *behaviour steering* [47].

**Design Rationale.** To steer players towards effective handwashing rituals, we studied several handwashing guidelines [7,16,17,28,45] and translated their key-components to game mechanics. With slight variation in focus [34], most hand-washing directives underline the importance of handwashing duration (20 s) and proper technique. Especially the latter is communicated with ranging levels of detail. For example, the *Center for Disease Control and Prevention* provide a 5-step handwashing procedure [17], whereas the *World Health Organisation* describes a 12-step procedure [7]. While more elaborate and complex handwashing directives might lead to better results, it has been suggested that the number of steps involved might also adversely affect handwashing compliance [2]. Interestingly, besides technique and duration, 'fun' gets mentioned as an important factor to promote hand hygiene among kids. Singing a song [17,45] and using a 'fun' soap [45] are two examples mentioned to make handwashing more fun for kids. With WashWall, we intended to capture the essence of handwashing, rather than designing a 1-to-1 translation of one particular handwashing directive. As such, we aimed to embody three key-elements to handwashing that were shared between the handwashing guidelines, that is: handwashing duration, hand-surface exposure, and the scrubbing motion. Also, in line with [17,45], we wanted to make handwashing fun.

To guide users towards proper duration, hand-surface exposure, and scrubbing behaviour, we made explicit use of 'steering strategies' as framed by [37,47]. Steering, which can be considered to fall under the umbrella of procedural persuasion [25], serves goal attainment (e.g. good hand hygiene) by *"carefully designing interactions that deliberately influence or guide player in-game behaviour in specific directions."* [47]. For the development of WashWall, we specifically made use of three steering strategies, that is: require, insist, and entice. With *require*, players of a game are quite simply required to act in a certain way for the game to run as intended. With *insist*, players are incentivised to act in a certain way through the provisioning of game-outcome related rewards (e.g. power-ups). And with *entice*, players are seduced to act in a certain way through the provisioning of *non* game-outcome related rewards (e.g. upgrades in avatar appearance). The require-strategy is typically considered the most forceful and effective, while the entice-strategy is typically considered to be more gentle [37].

Taken together, the current handwashing directives and steering strategies inspired the design of our game mechanics. To *entice* children to wash their hands for at least 20 s, we experimented with the number of germs that had to be defeated. Through play-testing and pilot-testing we found that with 42 germs, players would be engaged for long enough to reach the intended target duration. Further, to incentivise children to focus on the palmar surfaces of the hands [34], we *insisted* that players expose their hand palms to the running faucet. Doing so would result in the 'space ship' firing laser blasts. Finally, to promote an even exposure of both hands to the running faucet and to promote left-to-right scrubbing behaviours, we coupled the location of the centroid of the hands to the lateral (on-screen) position of the 'space ship'. We distributed the germs such that users need to expose both of their hands to the running faucet to kill all germs. This can also be considered a form of 'insisting' – players are steered by granting them game-outcome related rewards (i.e. the killing of germs and thus a higher score).

## 4   User Study

To investigate the potential of the WashWall system to improve the handwashing routine of primary school children as well as their engagement in doing so, we conducted an in-the-wild user study with 14 participants. For the study, we created a two-condition within-subjects design. Participants interacted with the WashWall system under two conditions. In the first condition, the interactive mirror was set to 'mirror mode'. In this mode the smart mirror was not powered on and looked and functioned just like a regular mirror. In the second condition, the interactive mirror was set to 'game mode'. In this mode the interactive capabilities of the mirror were activated to show an interactive shooter game (Fig. 2, panel B). All children washed their hands under both conditions. The sessions were organised around existing collective handwashing moments in the class routine. In between conditions, there was a 90-minute break. We performed both quantitative and qualitative research methods to investigate the merits of WashWall. The specifics of the experiment, along with the results, are given below.

### 4.1   Selection and Participation of Children

For the experimental study, we recruited 14 children from a primary school in the Netherlands. All children were between the age of 6 and 7. For recruitment, we contacted the principal of an elementary school from our professional network. The research protocols were designed in consultation with the ethics board of our institution; the elementary school principal; and with the class-room teacher.

Internally, we informed about best practice examples and adhered to those. In consultation with the principal, we designed the research procedure such that the research would not interfere with the classes or would otherwise be a nuisance. Before reaching out to the children and their parents, we checked the final research procedure with the principal and the teachers involved. We reached out to 24 parents, of which 14 gave their written informed consent. Parents were given an information letter that was endorsed by the school principal, an information brochure about the research, and an informed consent form. Children that did not receive their parents' consent to partake in the study were *not* excluded from playing with the installation. All children were free to interact with the system. Only the children with consent were researched upon. This means that only the children with consent were interviewed/observed/measured during the research. The researchers kept a (private) list of the children that enrolled in the research. Finally, the interactive mirror was mounted in the classroom and the camera only recorded the sink area – no other parts than the sink were visible. The study was reviewed and approved by the ethical committee of the Electrical Engineering Mathematics and Computer Science faculty of the University of Twente.

## 4.2   Session Design

All participants interacted with WashWall in both conditions (i.e. 'mirror mode' and 'game mode'). The sessions were organised around existing collective handwashing moments, as also described in: [9]. The first session was when participants entered the classroom in the morning, the second session was when participants re-entered the classroom after their midday (play) break. In the first session, participants interacted with WashWall with the system in 'mirror mode'. In the second session, participants interacted with WashWall in 'game mode'. No specific instructions were given to the children prior to using Wash-Wall in either condition. The order of the conditions was not randomised as the practical context and the teaching schedule did not allow the group of children to be divided in two without them sharing information about the two conditions.

## 4.3   Setup and Procedure

The experimental system setup of WashWall was as described in Sect. 3. Handwashing movement and duration in both conditions were recorded using the integrated high-resolution webcam. To also learn about the experiential aspects of WashWall in both conditions, we employed three qualitative research methods. First, we took observational notes of the handwashing routines of the participants for both conditions. Second, we employed the Draw-Write-Tell method [3] to interview the children about their experiences using WashWall. The Draw-Write-Tell method is an effective method to gain insights from children on their experiences. With this method, participants are asked to draw out their experiences and write and/or tell about their experiences on the basis of their drawing. This method typically results in rich data sets, consisting of drawings, writings, and recorded conversation. Finally, we performed a semi-structured interview with the supervising teacher, asking her to reflect on what she observed during the day.

## 4.4 Data Analysis

*Handwashing duration* was automatically tracked and written to a txt-file for each handwashing session. Time was recorded in seconds. Data on handwashing duration were analysed using a two-tailed Wilcoxon signed-rank test ($\alpha = 0.05$). To analyse *handwashing technique*, video footage from the integrated webcam was written to AVI-files and stored for each handwashing session. Using OpenCV, we intended to quantify and contrast handwashing technique for 'mirror mode' and 'game mode' by deriving relevant performance-metrics from the video footage (e.g. 'exposed hand-surface area'). Unfortunately, the video-files obtained from the 'mirror condition' turned out to be corrupt, precluding such quantitative comparisons. As such, we analysed handwashing technique qualitatively by contrasting the observational notes of the 'mirror mode' condition with those of the 'game mode' condition. We complemented the observational notes of the 'game mode' condition by reviewing the non-corrupted video-footage of that condition.

*User experience* was investigated by analysing the data from the observational notes; the semi structured interview; and the Draw-Write-Tell methodology. Data from the Draw-Write-Tell method (i.e. the drawings and the verbally shared experiences) were analysed using a grounded theory approach [8,21,33,43] – subsequently coding the data with open codes, axial codes and selective codes. To make a fair comparison between the two conditions; participants were only interviewed once, either after using the interactive mirror in 'mirror mode' or after using the mirror in 'game mode'. Resulting in two distinct 'sets' of data. Each data set was analysed by a different pair of researchers (VD & YR and WD & CC). Each pair of researchers was agnostic to which data set they were analysing. The final step of analysing the data from the Draw-Write-Tell method consisted of contrasting the emergent themes from both data sets. This final step was performed by all researchers involved.

## 5 Results

WashWall livened up the classroom. The children were eager to interact with the system in 'game mode' and were excited to play the space invader-esque game. Below, we will present the results from our quantitative and qualitative analyses.

### 5.1 Handwashing Duration and Technique

**Handwashing Duration:** A significant difference in handwashing duration ($p < 0.001$) was apparent between 'mirror mode' and 'game mode'. On average, participants spent 11.3 s (SD = 5.4) washing their hands in 'mirror mode' while spending an average of 45.9 s (SD = 9.1) in game mode. When comparing these results to the recommended handwashing duration of 20 s, it can be concluded that our participants washed their hands too briefly in a normal setting, while washing their hands longer than the recommended duration in 'game mode'.

**Handwashing Technique:** To analyse handwashing technique, we made a qualitative comparison of the observational notes that were taken for both conditions. In the 'mirror mode' condition it was observed that the children displayed quite sophisticated handwashing techniques, also taking into account the wrists as well as the areas between the fingers. After about five seconds, children started rushing the handwashing procedure and generally finished the session about five seconds later. Children were aware that viruses, such as COVID-19, spread via hand contamination and noted that handwashing was more effective if washing duration was increased. In the 'game mode' condition, participants were found to focus comparatively more on washing their hand palms. Participants frequently rubbed their hands together and exposed their hand palms more to the running faucet. The spaces in between the fingers received comparatively less attention, just as the wrists and the back of the hands. Finally, in the 'game mode' condition, we observed some inexpedient handwashing behaviours. One participant, for example, was observed to 'slap the water stream' while another participant nearly moved their hands outside of the sink-area while playing the game. Besides these occurrences, no further inexpedient handwashing behaviours were observed.

## 5.2   User Experience

**General Observations:** The very first children that interacted with the smart mirror in 'game mode' required some time to get the hang of the game controls. They needed about 30 s to understand the game mechanics and how they related to handwashing. Interestingly, a collective learning showed: Children later in line were aware of how the game should be played within several seconds. This can be considered a good indication of the system's learnability. After washing their hands, children stuck around to observe other children play.

**Draw-Write-Tell:** Using the Draw-Write-Tell method [3], we interviewed participants about their user experience with WashWall. Children were asked to make drawings about the experience and were invited to talk about their drawings in relation to the experience (see Fig. 4 for some exemplary drawings). Nine participants were asked about their experience with WashWall in 'mirror mode' and five participants were asked about their experience with WashWall in 'game mode'[1]. The results from the Draw-Write-Tell method between these two

---

[1] Ideally, we would have had an equal number of interviewees for both conditions, however the teaching schedule did not allow for this.

groups were contrasted. It was found that participants, in 'mirror mode', were very descriptive of the handwashing procedures and had a pronounced focus on handwashing duration. Participants referred little to the experiential aspects of handwashing. One participant was anxious about germs and expressed that as a concern related to handwashing. In contrast, participants that interacted with WashWall in 'game mode', were less descriptive of the handwashing process and referred more to experiential aspects. Enjoyment and fun were strongly represented in their drawings and oral reflections. Interestingly, the thematic presence of 'hands', 'water' and 'soap' was more pronounced in 'game mode' than in 'mirror mode'. So while being less descriptive of the process, children interacting with the system in 'game mode' appeared to be more aware of the constituent elements that are relevant to the handwashing process.

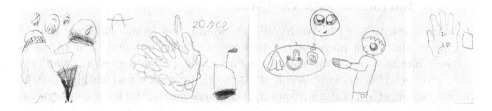

**Fig. 4.** Exemplary output from the Draw-Write-Tell methodology

**Teacher Interviews:** Finally, we interviewed the teacher to learn about her role in the handwashing rituals of the kids and how WashWall might be supportive to this. The teacher mentioned that she felt that good hand hygiene was important; first because she felt that hand hygiene is an essential part of *personal* hygiene and second because proper hand hygiene might mitigate the spread of the Corona-virus. The teacher felt that the WashWall system speaks to the intrinsic motivation that her pupils feel to wash their hands. She remarked that the kids were much more engaged in the handwashing process than they would otherwise have been. Interestingly, the teacher also remarked that the system sparked conversation and inspired a setting where children learnt from one another in an informal way. The system was not considered disruptive to ongoing or planned teaching activities. Finally, it was mentioned that the system should be very robust – teachers would not feel comfortable updating or maintaining the system or its software.

## 6   Discussion

With this research, we set out to investigate a novel approach for incentivizing elementary school children to practice proper handwashing procedures without the help of caregivers. Following an iterative design thinking cycle, we developed

WashWall – an interactive smart mirror that promotes handwashing behaviour among elementary school children. It is novel in the way it invites children to engage in proper handwashing procedures. It was found that the interaction with WashWall was intuitive and that the game was easy to understand. Children picked up the controls quickly and were engaged in the handwashing process. Handwashing duration increased significantly compared to the use of a regular mirror. A qualitative comparative analysis on handwashing technique revealed that children prioritised the washing of the palms and the scrubbing of the hands in 'game mode' and focused less on the spaces between their fingers, the back of their hands, and their wrists as compared to 'mirror mode'. Finally, WashWall sparked conversation about handwashing and inspired a setting where children learnt from one another in an informal way.

## 6.1    The Interaction with WashWall

In their interaction with WashWall, we found that some children showed behaviours that were more geared towards winning the game than to washing their hands. One of the children for example, was observed to 'slap' the water stream. This is reminiscent of the work by Pasch and colleagues who studied (amongst others) 'motivation and movement strategies' in movement-based games. They found that some players do not perform the intended bodily expressions, but rather resort to a movement strategy that "*maximises scoring ability*" [35]. While such behavioural artefacts are not uncommon in designing interactive technologies, it *is* something that needs to be dealt with (for some nice examples see e.g.: [26,27]). Furthermore, we found that children spend an average of *45.9* seconds washing their hands in 'game mode'. This is more than twice the duration advised in authoritative handwashing directives [7,17,28,45] and also more than we had expected from play testing (see Sect. 3.3). For this group of children, the number of 'germs' (N = 42) was too much. Lowering the number of 'germs' will limit play time and prevent water wastage.

With our current research, we have shown how game design strategies [25,37,47], can effectively be leveraged to steer player behaviour, improving focal aspects of handwashing technique such as palmar exposure, scrubbing behaviour, and handwashing duration. Yet, the washing of hands, a seemingly simple act, is in actuality an intricate and multidimensional motor movement that requires complex coordinative patterns [22]. The next step would be to implement computer vision techniques that are appreciative of this complexity and can reward users accordingly. Llorca and colleagues for example, have made promising strides towards automatic handwashing quality assessment [30]. They were able to recognise six different handwashing poses that were elemental to proper handwashing technique. Implementing their work into the WashWall architecture might allow us to steer user behaviour on the basis of these six poses, leading to a more comprehensive interaction-scheme.

Still, the act of washing ones hands is more than the six poses identified by Llorca and colleagues [30]. Handwashing is a multi-segmental, nested, motion pattern that consists of different activities. Getting soap is one of them. Expressly including this activity in the design of the game could allow for exciting new opportunities. For example, pressing the soap dispenser could provide users with unique benefits, like getting power-ups or 1-ups [47]. The use of the soap dispenser could be limited to a desired number so no new inexpedient behaviour would occur.

Finally, washing hands is an activity that is embedded in a broader (social-cultural and behavioural) context. As in our case, washing hands can be part of entering/returning to class. In future research, we aim to explore how WashWall might impact the social-behavioural context of which it is part [9]. Interactive smart mirrors offer unique opportunities to kids and teachers, inspiring novel interactions that extend beyond its intended design [24]. In future research we aim to explore how we can highlight some of those possibilities in a meaningful manner.

## 6.2   The User Experience of WashWall

WashWall was positively received both by the children and by the teacher. The kids were excited to play the 'Space Invader'-esque game and to engage in the handwashing behaviour that it required. Kids quickly learned to control the game. Interestingly, a collective and informal learning emerged during the use of WashWall. Finally, WashWall was not disruptive to ongoing or planned teaching activities. The teacher noticed that the kids were much more engaged with washing their hands and all that surrounds it. Still, kids are easily persuaded when it comes to playing video games. The question is, will the introduction of WashWall cause *persistent* change on handwashing behaviour? The current findings might well be subject to the novelty effect, i.e. *"the first responses to a technology, not the patterns of usage that will persist over time as the product ceases to be new."* [44] To investigate the long-term patterns of usage, both in terms of user experience and in terms of handwashing behaviours, a longitudinal study design is needed – implementing WashWall at more schools, targeting a wider range of class grades, for an extended period of time. The findings from such a study could be used to also reflect on the generalizability of the present findings; as the sample size in this study is limited, caution should be exercised in making any definitive statements about the (long-term) adoption and effects of WashWall. To promote long-term adoption, future design efforts should also be geared towards the development of a 'suite of games', so that the system can offer different games for ranging age groups (for examples see: [11, 20, 31]).

## 6.3   Limitations

While WashWall shows promising in its potential to steer handwashing behaviour and in engaging its users, its use of optical sensors presents a barrier to wide-spread implementation. In the current context, WashWall was implemented in the classroom. Children wash their hands there when they first enter the class or when they dirtied their hands crafting or playing outside. However, most sinks are *not* installed in the classroom, but rather in (public) washrooms.

Using a camera for tracking the hands can be considered a major threat to the privacy of users [1,32]. For the further development of WashWall or similar such systems, future research should focus the use of non-optical alternatives for sensing handwashing gestures (e.g. [19,32,39,40]) to protect the privacy of its users. Finally, in further development of the system, costs should be kept at a minimum. Elementary schools are often on a tight budget for buying school supplies. To promote the adoption of WashWall and encourage further research, we have shared the system diagrams and accompanying code in the supplementary materials.

## 7    Conclusion

With this work, we explored the potential of steering [47] and gamification [14] to incentivise proper handwashing procedures among elementary school children. Our results indicate that steering can be a powerful technique for eliciting tangible changes in motor behaviour *and* that steering mechanics need to be designed carefully to avoid inexpedient or exploitative behaviours. With Wash-Wall, handwashing duration significantly increased and handwashing technique changed to focus more on the palmar surfaces of the hands. The overall experience with WashWall was positive – children quickly picked up on the controls of the game and were engaged in the process of washing their hands. The findings of the present study open up new ways of looking at the gamification of personal hygiene and health. Where extant methods are more focused on raising awareness [36], WashWall explores the use of in-situ gamification mechanics to directly impact the focal behaviour. Allowing daily routines, such as washing the body and brushing the teeth to be transformed in fun and engaging experiences.

## References

1. Altmeyer, M., Lessel, P., Schubhan, M., Hnatovskiy, V., Krüger, A.: Germ destroyer-a gamified system to increase the hand washing duration in shared bathrooms. In: Proceedings of the Annual Symposium on Computer-Human Interaction in Play, pp. 509–519 (2019)
2. Amin, N., et al.: Effects of complexity of handwashing instructions on handwashing procedure replication in low-income urban slums in bangladesh: a randomized non-inferiority field trial. J. Water Sanitation Hygiene Dev. **9**(3), 416–428 (2019)
3. Angell, R.J., Angell, C.: More than just "snap, crackle, and pop": "draw, write, and tell": an innovative research method with young children. J. Advertising Res. **53**(4), 377–390 (2013)
4. Asai, T., Kanazawa, A., Hayashi, H., Minazuki, A.: Development of a system to raise awareness of hand hygiene in various environments. In: 2013 International Conference on Signal-Image Technology & Internet-Based Systems, pp. 924–931. IEEE (2013)
5. Biran, A., et al.: Effect of a behaviour-change intervention on handwashing with soap in India (superamma): a cluster-randomised trial. Lancet Glob. Health **2**(3), e145–e154 (2014)

6. Bonanni, L., Arroyo, E., Lee, C.H., Selker, T.: Exploring feedback and persuasive techniques at the sink. Interactions **12**(4), 25–28 (2005)
7. Challenge, F.G.P.S.: Who guidelines on hand hygiene in health care: a summary. Geneva: World Health Organ. **119**(14), 1977–2016 (2009)
8. Charmaz, K.: Constructing grounded theory: A practical guide through qualitative analysis. sage (2006)
9. Chittleborough, C.R., Nicholson, A.L., Basker, E., Bell, S., Campbell, R.: Factors influencing hand washing behaviour in primary schools: process evaluation within a randomized controlled trial. Health Educ. Res. **27**(6), 1055–1068 (2012)
10. Curtis, V., Schmidt, W., Luby, S., Florez, R., Touré, O., Biran, A.: Hygiene: new hopes, new horizons. Lancet. Infect. Dis **11**(4), 312–321 (2011)
11. van Delden, R.W., et al.: Personalization of gait rehabilitation games on a pressure sensitive interactive LED floor. In: Proceedings of the International Workshop on Personalization in Persuasive Technology co-located with the 11th International Conference on Persuasive Technology (PT 2016), pp. 60–73, April 2016
12. Deshmukh, A., Babu, S.K., Unnikrishnan, R., Ramesh, S., Anitha, P., Bhavani, R.R.: Influencing hand-washing behaviour with a social robot: Hri study with school children in rural India. In: 2019 28th IEEE International Conference on Robot and Human Interactive Communication (RO-MAN), pp. 1–6. IEEE (2019)
13. Deshmukh, A., Riddoch, K., Cross, E.S.: Assessing children's first impressions of "wallbo"-a robotic handwashing buddy. In: Interaction Design and Children, pp. 521–526 (2021)
14. Deterding, S.: Gamification: designing for motivation. Interactions **19**(4), 14–17 (2012)
15. Deterding, S., Dixon, D., Khaled, R., Nacke, L.: From game design elements to gamefulness: defining "gamification". In: Proceedings of the 15th International Academic MindTrek Conference: Envisioning Future Media Environments, pp. 9–15 (2011)
16. for Disease Control, C., Prevention: Hand hygiene at school (Januari 2022). https://www.cdc.gov/handwashing/handwashing-school.html
17. for Disease Control, C., Prevention: When and how to wash your hands (Januari 2022). https://www.cdc.gov/handwashing/when-how-handwashing.html
18. Dreibelbis, R., Kroeger, A., Hossain, K., Venkatesh, M., Ram, P.K.: Behavior change without behavior change communication: nudging handwashing among primary school students in bangladesh. Int. J. Environ. Res. Public Health **13**(1), 129 (2016)
19. Edmond, M., Goodell, A., Zuelzer, W., Sanogo, K., Elam, K., Bearman, G., et al.: Successful use of alcohol sensor technology to monitor and report hand hygiene compliance. J. Hosp. Infect. **76**(4), 364–365 (2010)
20. Fogtmann, M.H., Grønbæk, K., Ludvigsen, M.K.: Interaction technology for collective and psychomotor training in sports. In: Proceedings of the 8th International Conference on Advances in Computer Entertainment Technology, pp. 1–8 (2011)
21. Glaser, B.G., Strauss, A.L.: The Discovery of Grounded Theory: Strategies for Qualitative Research. Sociology Press, Mill Valley (1967)
22. Gløersen, Ø., Myklebust, H., Hallén, J., Federolf, P.: Technique analysis in elite athletes using principal component analysis. J. Sports Sci. **36**(2), 229–237 (2018)
23. Gurdasani, D., et al.: School reopening without robust covid-19 mitigation risks accelerating the pandemic. The Lancet **397**(10280), 1177–1178 (2021)
24. Hafermalz, E., Hovorka, D., Riemer, K.: Shared secret places: social media and affordances. arXiv preprint arXiv:1606.02478 (2016)

25. de la Hera Conde-Pumpido, T.: A conceptual model for the study of persuasive games. In: Proceedings of DiGRA 2013: DeFragging Game Studies (2013)
26. Jensen, M.M., Rasmussen, M.K., Mueller, F.F., Grønbæk, K.: Designing training games for soccer. Interactions **22**(2), 36–39 (2015)
27. Kajastila, R., Hämäläinen, P.: Motion games in real sports environments. Interactions **22**(2), 44–47 (2015)
28. KidsHealth, N.: Hand washing: Why it's so important (Januari 2022). https://kidshealth.org/en/parents/hand-washing.html
29. Lendrum, A., Humphrey, N.: The importance of studying the implementation of interventions in school settings. Oxf. Rev. Educ. **38**(5), 635–652 (2012)
30. Llorca, D.F., Parra, I., Sotelo, M.Á., Lacey, G.: A vision-based system for automatic hand washing quality assessment. Mach. Vis. Appl. **22**(2), 219–234 (2011)
31. Ludvigsen, M.K., Fogtmann, M.H., Grønbæk, K.: Tactowers: an interactive training equipment for elite athletes. In: Proceedings of the 8th ACM Conference on Designing Interactive Systems, pp. 412–415 (2010)
32. Mondol, M.A.S., Stankovic, J.A.: Harmony: A hand wash monitoring and reminder system using smart watches. In: Proceedings of the 12th EAI International Conference on Mobile and Ubiquitous Systems: Computing, Networking and Services, pp. 11–20 (2015)
33. Muller, M.J., Kogan, S.: Grounded theory method in HCI and CSCW. Cambridge: IBM Center for Social Software, pp. 1–46 (2010)
34. Öncü, E., Vayısoğlu, S.K.: Duration or technique to improve the effectiveness of children' hand hygiene: a randomized controlled trial. Am. J. Infect. Control **49**(11), 1395–1401 (2021)
35. Pasch, M., Bianchi-Berthouze, N., van Dijk, B., Nijholt, A.: Movement-based sports video games: investigating motivation and gaming experience. Entertainment Comput. **1**(2), 49–61 (2009)
36. Pereira, P., Duarte, E., Rebelo, F., Noriega, P.: A review of gamification for health-related contexts. In: Marcus, A. (ed.) DUXU 2014. LNCS, vol. 8518, pp. 742–753. Springer, Cham (2014). https://doi.org/10.1007/978-3-319-07626-3_70
37. Postma, D., ten Brinke, S., van Delden, R., Reidsma, D.: Coaxing: An empirical exploration of a novel way to nudge athletic performance in sports. Persuasive Technology (2022 - in press)
38. Rabben, N., Mikkelsplass, S.: A smart mirror to encourage independent hand washing for children. In: 4th International Conference on Human Interaction and Emerging Technologies: Future Applications, IHIET-AI 2021, pp. 447–456 (2021)
39. Mohamed Rabeek, S., Norman, A., Je, M., Kumarasamy Raja, M., Peh, R.F., Dempsey, M.K.: A reliable handwash detector for automated hand hygiene documentation and reminder system in hospitals. In: Goh, J. (ed.) The 15th International Conference on Biomedical Engineering. IP, vol. 43, pp. 892–895. Springer, Cham (2014). https://doi.org/10.1007/978-3-319-02913-9_230
40. Rabeek, S.M., Raja, M.K., Schiefen, S., Dempsey, M.K., Peh, R.F., et al.: Wireless tag and reader module design for automated hand hygiene documentation and reminder system in hospitals. Int. J. Comput. Electr. Eng. **4**(5), 637 (2012)
41. Rutter, S., Stones, C., Macduff, C.: Communicating handwashing to children, as told by children. Health communication (2019)
42. Song, I.H., Kim, S.A., Park, W.S.: Family factors associated with children's handwashing hygiene behavior. J. Child Health Care **17**(2), 164–173 (2013)
43. Strauss, A.L., Corbin, J.: Basics of Qualitative Research: Grounded Theory Procedures and Techniques. Sage Publications Inc., Thousand Oaks (1990)

44. Sung, J., Christensen, H.I., Grinter, R.E.: Robots in the wild: understanding long-term use. In: Proceedings of the 4th ACM/IEEE International Conference on Human Robot Interaction, pp. 45–52 (2009)
45. UNICEF: Everything you need to know about washing your hands to protect against coronavirus (covid-19) (Januari 2022). https://www.unicef.org/coronavirus/everything-you-need-know-about-washing-your-hands-protect-against-coronavirus-covid-19
46. Unnikrishnan, R., Deshmukh, A., Ramesh, S., Babu, S.K., Anitha, P., Bhavani, R.R.: Design and perception of a social robot to promote hand washing among children in a rural Indian school. In: 2019 28th IEEE International Conference on Robot and Human Interactive Communication (RO-MAN), pp. 1–6. IEEE (2019)
47. Van Delden, R., Moreno, A., Poppe, R., Reidsma, D., Heylen, D.: A thing of beauty: Steering behavior in an interactive playground. In: Proceedings of the 2017 CHI Conference on Human Factors in Computing Systems, pp. 2462–2472 (2017)

# Interaction with Conversational Agents
# I and II

# Beyond Browser Online Shopping: Experience Attitude Towards Online 3D Shopping with Conversational Agents

Pedro Valente[✉], Tiago Fornelos, Rafael Ferreira, Diogo Silva, Diogo Tavares, Nuno Correia, João Magalhães, and Rui Nóbrega

NOVA LINCS, NOVA School of Science and Technology, Caparica, Portugal
{pm.valente,rah.ferreira,dmgc.silva,dc.tavares}@campus.fct.unl.pt,
{nmc,jmag,rui.nobrega}@fct.unl.pt

**Abstract.** With the growing interest in recreating live and realistic outside experiences within the confines of our homes, the online shopping industry has also been impacted. However, traditional modes of interaction with online storefronts have remained mainly unchanged. This paper studies the factors influencing user experience and interaction in 3D virtual stores. We created a prototype that uses a 3D virtual environment for users to navigate, purchase items, and communicate with a conversational agent. The designed interface was tested by studying a set of variables, including the user's interaction medium with the conversational agent, the movement method within the store, the user's perception of the conversational agent, the conversational agent's usability, and the store items' visual representation. Through the user study, we gained insights into the factors that guide the user's experience in 3D virtual stores. We concluded that 80% of users preferred less intrusive conversational agents and 75% preferred agents that did not hide visual elements. Additionally, 80% of the participants favored combining 2D and 3D visualization techniques.

**Keywords:** 3D Interaction · ChatBot · Avatars · Online Shopping

## 1 Introduction

There is a growing desire to replicate outdoor experiences within the comfort of our own homes. This pursuit of enhancing the online living experience has also impacted the online shopping industry [32]. Some research has begun to explore different methods of interacting with these storefronts, from virtual reality [23] to other non-traditional approaches such as 3D virtual environments [12]. By contrast, we have well-defined guidelines for developing browser interfaces for commerce [20]. Additionally, conversational agents have become an integral part of the online shopping experience [1], providing customers with 24/7 assistance as they interact with storefronts.

---

https://nova-lincs.di.fct.unl.pt/.

J. Abdelnour Nocera et al. (Eds.): INTERACT 2023, LNCS 14143, pp. 257–276, 2023.
https://doi.org/10.1007/978-3-031-42283-6_15

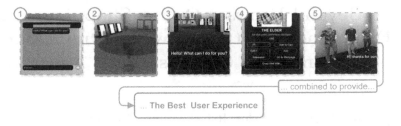

**Fig. 1.** The studied factors: **(1)** the dialogue interface; **(2)** the locomotion system; **(3)** the agent's visual presentation; **(4)** the agent's functionality; **(5)** the product visualization;

To this end, our goal was to thoroughly examine the factors influencing user experience and interaction in 3D virtual stores with conversational agents. Furthermore, we aim to make online shopping more accessible and convenient for consumers and summarize our findings into design guidelines. Considering this, we conducted a two-part user study, starting with formative interviews that gave us insight into the most relevant features users look for in online and physical stores. These interviews enabled us to create a 3D shopping application that uses the online store catalog from Farfetch, our project's partner, and compile five variables that guide the user's interaction.

Two of the variables cover the design of the virtual store, and three, the user's interaction with the conversational agent in the virtual store environment: **(V1)** the preferred method of interaction for users with a conversational agent: textbox or voice interface; **(V2)** the most effective method for users to navigate a virtual store using keyboard and mouse controls or teleport to specific points; **(V3)** the most effective representation of the conversational agent, a humanoid avatar, or a text-based representation; **(V4)** the conversational agent's capacity to substitute parts of the visual interface, a dialogue based interface compared to a visual interface; **(V5)** the Visual representation of the items in the store, a context window or a 3D model. These variables represent the factors we identified as crucial transition points from conventional browser interfaces to 3D virtual environments (Fig. 1).

By studying these factors, we wanted to answer the following research questions: **(RQ1)** How should these factors drive the UX design of virtual stores with conversational agents? **(RQ2)** How do these variables rank by their importance regarding the design of Virtual Stores with conversational agents?

Through this research, we sought insights into which of the selected variables should be prioritized to improve the user's experience when designing 3D Virtual Stores with conversational agents and what impact these variables have on the UX design of these interfaces.

We start this article with a review of the related work (Sect. 2), followed by an examination of the formative interviews (Sect. 3). Next, we introduce the interface we developed (Sect. 4) and discuss the results of a subsequent user study (Sect. 5). Finally, we analyze our findings (Sect. 6) and present our conclusions (Sect. 7).

## 2  Related Work

Online shopping has followed a steady browser-based 2D interface recipe in recent years. To change this paradigm, some companies have recently attempted to create 3D virtual environments for their online marketplaces [19,32]. This has prompted researchers to consider the most effective methods for designing virtual social environments, specifically virtual simulated stores [7].

This field has seen considerable progress since the early 1990s,s, as evidenced by works such as Burke et al.'s [5] original publication, where the authors used a simulated environment to study consumer behavior. Recent studies have demonstrated that users feel more comfortable navigating virtual stores through VR [27], indicating the potential for researching this area.

Despite the advancements in these applications' immersive and interactive features, there has been limited progress in providing task-specific assistance to users. However, conversational agents can offer users additional support in completing tasks such as purchasing products [30]. Additionally, conversational agents have proven valuable in providing systems with intelligence and natural language capabilities [15]. These tools can process natural language inputs and give innate responses, enabling a conversation with the user [9]. Furthermore, this technology can automate interactions between a company and its customers, creating the illusion of conversation with a human being [6].

The traditional chatbox is often the first consideration when discussing conversational agent user interfaces [24]. However, alternative forms of interaction may be more beneficial in some cases. One example is an interface developed by Quarteroni et al. [26]. This interface enlarged the chat window into two sections: a text box on the left and a panel on the right to present additional information about the conversation context, such as links to web pages or more informative answers to user questions.

Vaddadi et al.'s [31] conducted a similar research project. They developed a wrapper for an online shopping assistant on mobile devices that incorporates buttons, cards, and text messages. The researchers found that buttons helped select product sizes, as it is more convenient for the conversational agent to display the available sizes as buttons for the user to choose, rather than requiring the user to type in the size. The cards show images or videos of requested products, links, and text.

Likewise, Pricilla et al. [25] also researched this field and developed a mobile chatbot interface for online fashion shopping. This team took a user-centered approach to the conversational agent's development and proposed a swiping list of messages containing various products presented by the agent. Each item includes the product image, information about the product, and a link to the web page or a more informative view.

Another critical question surrounding the presence of conversational agents in virtual spaces is how we present this type of interaction in 3D environments. The most common way is using an embodied virtual agent (EVA) [14]. EVAs are an interface where an Avatar[1] physically represents the agent in the virtual space. This avatar is usually presented as a human to create a more empathetic experience.

There have been multiple attempts to implement EVAs before, with one of the first attempts by Nijholt et al. [21], where the authors experimented with blemishing traditional dialog with a virtual environment populated with the avatar of the agent. The authors observed the possible potential for these interfaces to be used in helping people with disabilities. Another study by Martin Holzwarth et al. [11] showed that using an avatar in web-based information increased the customer's satisfaction with the retailer, attitude toward the product, and purchase intention.

Some recent research has focused on whether these interfaces can provide a better experience than regular dialog interfaces. For example, Jessica et al. [28] focused on questioning parents about how the agent's interface presentation could affect the parent's perception of a specific agent and whether the interface was a toy. They did this by questioning parents about their attitude toward multiple interfaces, including toys with chatbot functionalities. Further research has been done on the usefulness of this type of interface. Yet, in Li et al.'s [13] research, the authors conclude that the physical embodiment alone does not provide a better social presence when interacting with chatbots.

A major problem with these interfaces is that many of the used avatars fall into the uncanny valley [18]. In Nowak et al.'s [22] work, the authors observed that when EVAs try to have a more anthropomorphic design, they fall short of being realistic because they create higher expectations, making them more challenging to meet without complex technological features. Similar results can be seen in Groom et al.'s [10] research. Furthermore, in Ben Mimoun et al.'s [2] work, the authors identified another problem: many EVAs fail to meet the user's expectations when providing a realistic interaction, leading to a more frustrating interaction.

Another critical question is how we should show shopping items in the context of a 3D virtual world. In most cases, in online stores, items are shown in a 2D view with no additional 3D information, so most catalogs only contain information about the 2D representation of the items. A common technique is to have the 2D images of the items mapped onto a 3D model. This was what Aymen Mir et al. [17] did in *Pix2Surf*. Their open-source algorithm was implemented to handle input images of t-shirts, shorts, and pants, being able to render 3D models of mannequins with different poses.

---

[1] Avatar in this context is used to refer to the virtual representation of the interactable agent in the virtual world.

**Fig. 2.** Dialog graph for a common interaction with the conversational agent, where we can see all the tasks the agent has to complete

## 3  On the Design of Virtual Stores with Conversational Agents

Our focus was on the fashion domain. In this context, creating a conversational agent primarily consists of creating a dialog interaction that can assist the user in finding and buying items in the store. The conversational agent should be able to perform tasks grouped in the following categories:(**1**) store assistance, meaning assisting with tasks related to the main interface, (**2**) product recommendations, (**3**) product question-answering (QA), this is, answering questions about the characteristics of a particular product, and (**4**) finding products in the store. Figure 2 shows an example of a dialog graph from a conversation.

Furthermore, we designed the interface in such a way that users could simulate the purchase of items, navigate the store, and interact with the conversational agent. A major part of designing this interface is understanding the user's expectations. To achieve this, **we conducted formative interviews with six participants**. We deliberately sought participants with previous experience buying clothes online.

All the study participants were female and bought clothes online at least four times per year, with one of the users buying 24 items per year. Furthermore, all the participants had had previous experience interacting with a conversational agent. The participants also varied in age. Three participants were between 21 and 27, one was less than 21, and the other two were above 27.

In the interview, we showed users three distinct scenarios. ($1^{st}$) The first scenario was focused on buying clothes in a browser store, ($2^{nd}$) the second was buying clothes in a physical store, ($3^{rd}$) and the third was purchasing clothes with the assistance of a voice agent. In each scenario, users were asked what their main buying habits were when shopping for clothes and what information they expected to be available in the described scenario. Furthermore, the interviewees were also asked what advantages they could identify in buying clothes online and in physical stores.

Some noteworthy findings were the following. When asked about their online practices in the first scenario, a common answer was looking first at sales and discounted items. When asked what information the users found relevant, two participants answered that shipping information was the most important. Two others said they wished that stores had better recommendation systems. For instance, a user said that they valued "(...) *showing me relevant items that have a similar style or are similar to the ones I've been searching* (...)".

In the second scenario, when describing their practices, four users said they usually go around the store looking for interesting items. Regarding what information they found relevant, three users said they do not seek additional information when buying clothes in physical stores. One said they usually avoid interacting with store assistants. For instance, a user said, *"I don't usually ask for anything from the retail worker besides when I want a clothing item in a different size, and cannot find it. (...)"*.

When shown the third scenario and asked what information they expected from the conversational agent, three participants said they would ask for specific details regarding the product they were trying to buy, either shipping information or specific features. Two participants also said they would ask for recommendations or items that go well with what they previously saw or bought, *"I'd like to ask for possible suggestions based on the things that I've previously seen, or the articles of clothing we've talked about. (...)"*.

When asked about the benefits of buying clothes in physical stores, all users answered unanimously that the only benefit is that they can try the items immediately without waiting for them, for instance, *"Definitely seeing how the clothes fit me. That's the only downside of buying them online. Sometimes an item looks really good on the model but doesn't fit properly on my body. (...)"*.

When asked about the benefits of buying clothes online, four participants answered that a major advantage is avoiding interacting with other people, the assistants or other people in the store, *"I like the convenience of being able to shop from home, not having to deal with queues and other people. (...)"*.

The interviews were a valuable tool in formulating our research questions. Through the interviews, we identified some critical factors, which later informed the design of our ranking tasks in the user study. Furthermore, we also saw that users avoid interacting with store assistants in the real world.

Therefore, when studying conversational agents within a virtual store environment, we aimed to test various levels of interactivity and the use of different representations, each with varying levels of presence and multimodality. Three of our research variables explored the extent to which the conversational agent's interaction should be hidden or revealed. The study also included a task that evaluates the store's usability and the effectiveness of product visualization, two other concerns raised during the interviewing process.

## 4   System Description of the 3D Shopping Experience

The conceived interface is a 3D virtual store where the user navigates in the first person. We created a 3D store environment (Sect. 4.1) and implemented multiple methods of locomotion (Sect. 4.2), different dialog interfaces (Sect. 4.3), and multiple visualization techniques (Sect. 4.4). In the sections below, we will cover every element of the developed interface.

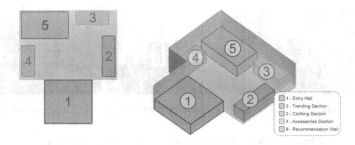

**Fig. 3.** The store's overall layout, with a top-down view on the **left** an isometric view on the **right**

## 4.1  Virtual Store Environment

The virtual environment can be divided into multiple sections. A section is an area of the store. Each section can contain a variable number of display screens, including none, that show a preview of the available items. These areas are organized based on the type of items they contain and what activities can be performed in that section. The store has five sections (Fig. 3):

- **Entry Hall** (Red zone - 1 in Fig. 3): This section corresponds to the store's starting area. From here, they can see every other section of the store. It is also the only section that does not contain any article of clothing;
- **Trending Section** (Green zone - 2 in Fig. 3): In this section, users can visualize a set of premade outfits that correspond to the trending outfits (Fig. 4a);
- **Clothing Section** (Purple zone - 3 in Fig. 3): This section of the store corresponds to the place where users can visualize multiple clothing items, with every article category mixed in the same display window (Fig. 4b);
- **Accessories Section** (Yellow zone - 4 in Fig. 3): Here, users can find items that do not fit in the clothing item category, such as bags and watches (Fig. 4c);
- **Recommendation Wall** (Orange zone - 5 in Fig. 3): In this section, users can use a set of three mannequins to preview outfits with a three-dimensional presentation.

## 4.2  Virtual Store Navigation

To navigate the store, the user can use a mouse or touchscreen. To facilitate navigation, we created a point-of-interest (PoI) system. Every section of the store has its point of interest. To navigate to a specific PoI, the user must select one of the 3D arrows in the interface by pressing it with their finger or the mouse cursor (Fig. 5a).

Each PoI also defines a focus point, so the camera rotates to shift the user's attention toward a specific position when traveling to a PoI. The camera is

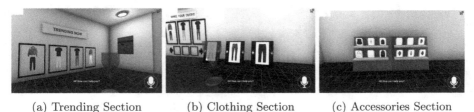

(a) Trending Section          (b) Clothing Section          (c) Accessories Section

**Fig. 4.** Some of the multiple sections of the 3D store

controlled by clicking and dragging the mouse. To smooth the navigation around the store's geometry, we used a pathfinding algorithm to find the shortest path between two points of interest. Then we smoothed the navigation along the track with a bezier curve (Fig. 5b).

We have incorporated an alternative locomotion system within our study, namely a conventional first-person control scheme utilizing a keyboard and mouse. In this system, the camera turns using a mouse, while navigation uses the arrow keys on the keyboard. This solution is an ideal benchmark due to its extensive adoption in video games over the course of several decades. As a result, users who are familiar with this scheme may have developed ingrained motor skills or muscle memory and perform better [16,29].

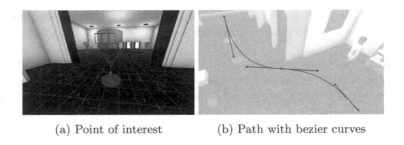

(a) Point of interest          (b) Path with bezier curves

**Fig. 5.** The various components that make the point of interest system

### 4.3   The Conversational Agent

The conversational agent was designed to effectively understand and respond to the user's intent using Automated Speech Recognizers and multiple Natural Language Processing (NLP) algorithms [7]. To interact with the conversational agent, we implemented a chatbox that contains the history of the conversation between the user and the agent located in the bottom right corner of the screen.

When designing the dialog interface, we had to present the agent's responses to the user. These responses are a mixture of text, actions to be performed in the interface, and product recommendations. Therefore, we implemented three interfaces (Fig. 6). The first one uses the chatbox interface. Here the text is presented as a dialog bubble in the chat window that sometimes contains a preview of specific products (Fig. 6a).

We also implemented a speech interface using the Cortana voice API[2]. Users can activate this interface by pressing the microphone icon in the screen's bottom right corner, which will bring up a window displaying the system's detected voice input. This interface aims to provide a more multimodal interaction while removing the necessity for an on-screen chatbox. This speech interface uses a visual representation we called the *subtitle interface*, where text is presented at the bottom of the screen, similar to a movie's subtitles, and recommendations are shown in a context window above the text (Fig. 6b).

Lastly, we experimented with having a fully embodied conversational agent represented by a hologram (Fig. 6c). Each section of the store has its point. At runtime, the system deciphers the closest visible point to the user's camera and instantiates the avatar. When the system receives or sends a message, the assistant does an animation to give the user feedback. The conversational agent's text is shown as a speech bubble floating over the avatar in the screen space. The recommendations are offered inside the bubble.

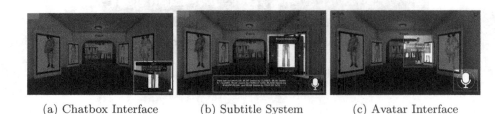

(a) Chatbox Interface        (b) Subtitle System        (c) Avatar Interface

**Fig. 6.** The multiple dialog interfaces

## 4.4   Product Visualization

A problem with migrating from a traditional 2D viewport to 3D is how we should display the products available around the store and what product information should be presented to the user. The items around the store combine items from an online fashion store catalog with manually selected items. As a result, we can see a representative mix of each type of clothing.

Multiple display screens around the store show the available items, as seen in Fig. 7a. Each section of the store has its own set of displays. Objects are displayed in frames with a 2D image of the product. Clicking on one of these frames opens a context window containing information about the selected item. Here we display the product's brand, price, available sizes, and a short description.

---

[2] Cortana Speech detection, Unity API, https://learn.microsoft.com/en-us/windows/mixed-reality/develop/unity/voice-input, Last Access 2023.

An alternative approach to presenting these items is to show them in a 3D viewport. To achieve this, we mapped the images of our 2D catalog to a 3D mannequin. We did this using Pix2Surf[3] [17]. To work with this model, we had to restrict our catalog further, as it only works with short-sleeved t-shirts, trousers, and shorts.

To see an item in a mannequin, one has to select the item they want to preview and mark it as "*Interested.*" This will add that item to the recommendation tab. After that, in the Recommendation Section, one can drag and drop an item from one frame to another, updating the mannequin's clothes. Furthermore, depending on the interface, recommendations are shown as a special message with arrows and cards, where every card has the item's preview and name. Alternatively, recommendations can be displayed in a context window with arrows and information about the articles (Fig. 7b).

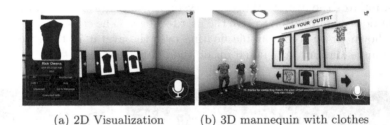

(a) 2D Visualization          (b) 3D mannequin with clothes

**Fig. 7.** The multiple visualization interfaces

## 5   Evaluation

Considering the described interface, we tested the variables stated in Sect. 1. To do so, we conducted a user study with multiple interfaces, two for each variable, interfaces A and B. The variables can be seen in Table 1.

Our study focused on whether these variables could affect the user's experience while interacting with the 3D virtual store and how they stack against each other to improve their experience.

### 5.1   Protocol

When designing the questionnaire for our user study, we based many of our questions on existing literature [3,4] and the interviews that we previously conducted (Sect. 3). The data collected from the users was anonymized, and users were informed that they could leave at any point during the test.

The experience was composed of five tasks (T1, T2, T3, T4, and T5) with a climatization task (T0). T1 through 5 were meant to evaluate each of the

---

[3] Pix2Surf, repository, https://github.com/aymenmir1/pix2surf, Last Access: 2023.

**Table 1.** The variables being studied and their respective interfaces

| Variable | Interface A | Interface B |
|---|---|---|
| **V1**: The medium that the user employs to communicate with the conversational agent | **1A**: Speech Interface | **1B**: Chatbox |
| **V2**: The most effective method of locomotion in the store | **2A**: Mouse and Keyboard | **2B**: Points of Interest |
| **V3**: The way the user visualizes the agent | **3A**: Humanoid Avatar | **3B**: Text-based Representation |
| **V4**: The conversational agent's capacity to substitute parts of the visual interface | **4A**: Dialogue Based Interface | **4B**: Visual Interface |
| **V5**: The Visual representation of the items in the store | **5A**: Context Window | **5B**: 3D Model |

corresponding variables. For each of the five main tasks, users had to test two interfaces, A and B. The order was alternated in a Latin Square order to reduce learning bias. For the context of every task, A differed from B, and every task was independent of the other.

After every task, the user answered ten questions, some regarding Interface A or B and some about both interfaces. Questions comprised Likert scale evaluations (1 to 5) and ranking questions. At the end of the questionnaire, users would evaluate both interfaces using a Likert scale (1 to 5) and are asked what was their favorite. For the fifth task, users had to rank the features of both interfaces. At the end of the test, users responded to some questions about a complete version of the interface, including the System Usability Scale (SUS) [4].

For every task, we annotated whether the user could finish the task (if they finished the task in less than 4 min) and if they asked for guidance. For T1 and T2, we recorded the time it took for participants to finish.

The setup for the experience was comprised of a computer where the user would test the multiple interfaces. Every user also used a microphone to communicate with the conversational agent. Users were also given paper instructions containing all the tasks they had to perform and a map of the store with every section labeled. Users could consult this map at any time during testing.

## 5.2 The Population

Users were selected by surveying college students. All the participants had at least a K12 education level and were fluent in English. The study was conducted with 20 users, 11 female (55%) and 9 male users (45%). Users were between the ages of 19 and 49. Many users had rarely interacted with a conversational agent before (30%) or interacted yearly (25%). The rest of the participants interacted monthly (20%) or weekly (25%). Most users played video games, with only 1 (5%) saying they rarely played. 75% said they played games daily or weekly, and the rest played monthly or yearly. We further questioned the users about how frequently they play FPS games. Although 35% users still played FPS games weekly, 25% said they didn't play FPS games.

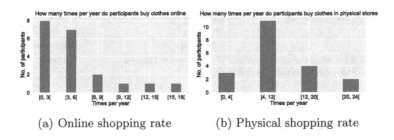

(a) Online shopping rate          (b) Physical shopping rate

**Fig. 8.** How many times do users buy items in online (a) and physical (b) stores?

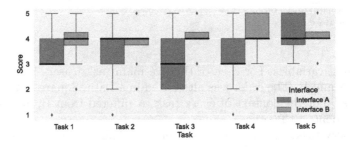

**Fig. 9.** Interface ratings for every task (median in bold)

Furthermore, when asked if they follow the most influential trends in fashion, 85% of the users answered no. Following this trend, 5 users said they do not buy clothes in online stores. Still, the rest of the users said they buy at least one clothing item per year online, with a user even they buy around 15 clothing items per year in online stores (Fig. 8a). Moreover, when asked how frequently users bought clothes in physical stores, the most common answer (45%) was between 4 and 11 times per year (Fig. 8b).

## 5.3   Results

As previously mentioned, users completed five tasks while freely interacting with the virtual store. Starting with **T1**, users had to interact with the conversational agent using a voice interface (1A) and a chatbox (1B). When observing the overall scores of both interfaces, 55% of users said they preferred interface 1B. We can see this reflected in the general scores of the two interfaces, where we could see that users rated 1B higher but without having a notable enough statistical significance ($p=0.176$) (Fig. 9). Furthermore, on average, users took more time to complete the task using 1B. Yet, this difference was not major at a 5% significance level. See Table 2.

An observation where we saw a major difference was the number of times the users had to repeat commands. In 1A, 90% of users had to repeat utterances, while in 1B, only 35% had to repeat. Repeated commands happened either when the agent didn't understand the user's intent or when the voice detection algorithm didn't correctly pick up the user's utterance.

Regarding **T2**, users had to perform the task using traditional FPS controls (2A) and the PoI system (2B). Although a larger number of users preferred 2B (55%), it was not a large difference. This was reflected in the data where 2B had marginally better results than 2A (Fig. 9). Furthermore, observing the times in Table 2 we can see that 2A and 2B had similar times. When analyzing this data, we must remember that many users are familiar with this interface type, as seen in Sect. 5.2.

On task **T3**, we tested the presence of the agent's avatar in the store, where one interface had the avatar (3A) while the other didn't (3B). 80% of the users said they preferred 3B to 3A. This is observed in the rest of the collected data (Fig. 9). One such example is seen in the scores of each interface, where users rated 3B much higher than 3A ($p$=0.007). The preference for 3B is further verified by the users' responses to questions about readability and uncanniness. See the first two rows in Table 3.

When looking at these values, we can infer that users felt more comfortable interacting with 3B than with 3A, yet they didn't feel as if the dialog was disconnected from the store. During testing, users even commented on the presence of the avatar in the store being weird or uncomfortable. When we observe the boxplots for Q6 (I liked the presence of the avatar in the store) and Q7 (The avatar contributed to the experience of interacting with the chatbot) (Fig. 10), we can see that users did not enjoy the presence of the avatar in the store.

In **T4**, users were asked to complete the task with the assistance of the conversational agent (4A) and without (4B). When users were asked what their favorite interface was, most said they preferred 4B to 4A (75%). This answer is well represented in the rating given by the users, where we verified a significant difference between the scores of both interfaces ($p$=0.006). 4A had a median score of three, while 4B had a median score of four (Table 4).

Although we saw this significant difference in the ratings, this did not extend to the answers users gave in questions about frequency of use and cumbersomeness of the interface (see the first two rows of Table 4). Furthermore, when the users were asked whether they agreed with "I found the interaction with the agent unnecessary," they answered with a mode of 4 and a median of 3.5. This indicates that when presented with the option of utilizing the conversational agent, the participants preferred not utilizing it.

**Table 2.** Average time it took for users to finish each task (T1 and T2), the standard deviation, and the t-test p-value for every interface

| # | time (m) | mean | Std. Dev. | t-test |
|---|----------|------|-----------|--------|
| T1 : 1A | Complete T1 with 1A | **02:12,9** | 00:51,6 | $p = 0,099$ |
| T1 : 1B | Complete T1 with 1B | 02:55,5 | 00:57,9 | $p > 0,05$ |
| T2 : 2A | Complete T2 with 2A | **00:46,9** | 00:23,4 | $p = 0,147$ |
| T2 : 2B | Complete T2 with 2B | 01:05,5 | 00:31,0 | $p > 0,05$ |

**Table 3.** Median, first quartile ($Q1$), third quartile ($Q3$), and chi-square test p-value ($X^2$) of the scores of both interfaces in questions about readability, uncanniness, frequency of use and consistency in Task 3

| Interface | Question | median | Q1 | Q3 | $X^2$ |
|---|---|---|---|---|---|
| 3A | I could read the text well. | 4 | 3 | 5 | $p = 0,015$ |
| 3B | | **5** | 4 | 5 | $p < 0,05$ |
| 3A | I found the experience unnatural. | 3 | 2 | 4,25 | $p = 0,014$ |
| 3B | | **2** | 1 | 3 | $p < 0,05$ |
| 3A | I want to use the chatbot more often. | 3 | 2 | 3,25 | $p = 0,053$ |
| 3B | | **3.5** | 3 | 4 | $p > 0,05$ |
| 3A | The dialog felt disconnected. | 2 | 1 | 3 | $p = 0,825$ |
| 3B | | 2 | 1 | 3 | $p > 0,05$ |

**Table 4.** Median, first quartile ($Q1$), third quartile ($Q3$), and chi-square test p-value ($X^2$) of the scores of both interfaces in questions about frequency, cumbersomeness, and the ratings in Task 4

| Interface | Question | median | Q1 | Q3 | $X^2$ |
|---|---|---|---|---|---|
| 4A | I would use this interface frequently. | 3,5 | 3 | 4 | $p = 0,372$ |
| 4B | | **4** | 3 | 5 | $p > 0,05$ |
| 4A | I found the interface cumbersome. | 2 | 1,75 | 3 | $p = 0,470$ |
| 4B | | **1,5** | 1 | 3 | $p > 0,05$ |
| 4A | How would you rate this interface? | 3 | 3 | 4 | $p = 0,006$ |
| 4B | | **4** | 4 | 5 | $p < 0,05$ |

In **T5**, the participants were presented with two distinct interfaces for visualizing clothing items, a traditional visualization interface (5A) and a 3D item visualization interface using a mannequin (5B). When asked to indicate their preferred interface, participants had the option to select 5A, 5B, or both interfaces simultaneously. Results of the study revealed that 80% of the participants preferred utilizing both 5A and 5B simultaneously.

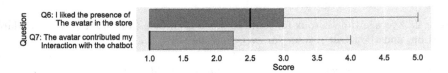

**Fig. 10.** Data for presence and interaction in T3 (median in bold)

Furthermore, the participants were requested to rank various features from 5A and 5B (Fig. 11). These features were product information and visualization techniques. About 5A, 70% of the participants considered the price the most crucial feature to be shown on the user interface. At the same time, the material used was considered the least important feature (35%) to be shown. The participants were also asked about which features they would include in the visualization of the product. Some examples of the mentioned features were the brand of the product and a size guide.

Concerning 5B, the participants deemed that the most salient features were the ability to map the clothes directly onto an image of themselves (25%) and a 360-degree view of the mannequin with the clothes (25%). However, unlike 5A, there was no consensus among the participants as to which feature was the most desirable, as illustrated in Fig. 11b. Additionally, features such as having a 360-degree view of the mannequin and the ability to adjust the clothes according to the users' size were not rated as the least important feature. In contrast, 35% of the participants stated that having multiple lighting options in the mannequin was the least important feature.

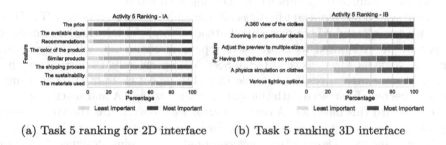

(a) Task 5 ranking for 2D interface       (b) Task 5 ranking 3D interface

**Fig. 11.** Task 5 rankings, for 2D and 3D product visualization

After the questionnaire, the participants were instructed to rank every task they performed during the study. The results of this ranking can be observed in Fig. 12. Upon examination of this graph, we can see that the participants prioritized the visualization of items over all other factors. Additionally, although it elicited the strongest reaction from the participants, the agent's avatar was primarily considered the least important feature, with 75% of the participants rating it as the least important.

The SUS score was calculated at the end of the test. We obtained an average SUS score of 70.625 with a standard deviation of 9,516. The lowest score we obtained was 45, and the highest was 82,5. For reference, a study by Debjyoti Ghosh et al. [8] found that Siri had a SUS mean value of 54,167.

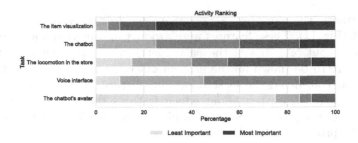

**Fig. 12.** Ranking of each task

## 6    Discussion

Our objective was to determine which factors are crucial when designing and developing 3D virtual stores and which can be ignored. By examining the data collected from the study, we will gain insights into the most effective solutions for enhancing the user experience in 3D virtual stores and how to prioritize the importance of different factors when planning such interfaces.

We observed no significant findings after examining the results from **T1**. However, we saw a trend where participants tended to prefer the chatbox interface. This may be attributed to many users repeating commands when interacting with the voice interface, as reported in Sect. 5.3. Specifically, 18 participants had to repeat their utterances in 1A, while 13 had to repeat them in 1B. This caused users to become frustrated with the system while testing 1A and react more negatively toward this interface. A common error we observed was the voice-to-text algorithm misreading the user's words, for example, interpreting "Nike shorts" as "knight shorts". Despite the conversational agent being designed to handle this type of error, when users saw their utterances misspelled, they still felt the need to repeat their command, even when the system responded correctly. This suggests that, in future designs, hiding the user's utterance from them might improve the user experience and reduce frustration.

In **T2**, participants, after answering the questionnaire, were asked a follow-up question regarding their preference of interface if 2B (the Point of Interest system) were to be on a tablet device. In response, 80% of users said they prefer 2B to 2A. This represents a major difference from the results obtained when tested on a laptop, where 55% preferred 2B over 2A.

Given the increasing impact of tablet interfaces on e-commerce, as noted in previous studies [33], this large difference in user preference is noteworthy and merits further investigation. We posit that the improved reception of 2B as a tablet interface may be due to its reduced degrees of freedom. When using touchscreen devices, users are limited to controlling the camera's orientation with virtual inputs. Additional degrees of freedom for user locomotion would require additional clutter in the user interface. This explanation may also be applied to the voice interface tested in **T1**, as the inclusion of a chatbox would imply the presence of a virtual keyboard on the screen.

A notable finding in our study was that participants in **T3** did not appreciate the avatar's presence in the store, as outlined in Sect. 5.3. We attribute this adverse reaction to two factors. First, the avatar used to represent the conversational agent in the store employed a semi-realistic, anthropomorphic model that attempted to mimic a hologram. This model made participants uneasy, as they felt the chosen representation was unnatural, which is consistent with the findings of Nowak et al.'s [22] work on the uncanny valley applied to avatars.

In addition, the avatar's non-interactive nature and inability to create empathy with users contributed to its negative reception. Looking at Sect. 5.3, we obtained a negative response when participants were asked if the avatar had a positive effect on their interaction (Fig. 10). Furthermore, when considering this result in conjunction with the participants rating this aspect of the interface as the least important (Fig. 12), we can infer that users found the avatar unnatural and unnecessary. With this in mind, we can conclude that when designing this type of interface, this aspect should not be the development focus if we cannot ensure a realistic and meaningful interaction.

Another noteworthy finding was in **T4**, where users expressed a preference for the interaction where they didn't have to use the conversational agent, in contrast to the one in which they did (Table 4). Users performed a recommendation task, they either asked the agent for clothing items that would complement a selected product or clicked a button on the visual UI. We posit that this outcome resulted from users perceiving the interaction as unnecessarily complex for a task that could be accomplished by simply pressing a button. Although some studies [6] have shown the benefit of using chatbox interfaces to aid users, they should not be seen as alternatives to traditional interfaces.

In **T5**, participants still considered the visualization of the product the most important feature (Fig. 12). Additionally, users demonstrated a high receptivity to using a three-dimensional representation of the item they were seeking to purchase, indicating that this type of visualization may offer a superior solution to traditional visualization methods.

Information was gathered during the data collection process to divide the study population into sub-groups. However, upon analysis of the data, we observed no statistically meaningful differences among the sub-groups based on variables such as age, gender, frequency of interaction with games and chatbots, and frequency of usage of online stores.

# 7   Conclusion

With the valuable insights we gained from our research on creating 3D virtual stores with conversational agents, we identified several domains that require further inquiry. Primarily, while our study encompassed a broad range of variables, other factors may require investigation in this field, for example, the capacity of the conversational agent to interrupt the user's interaction. Furthermore, we acknowledge that delving deeper into 3D visualization techniques can reveal the complete advantages of utilizing this interface.

We studied the impact of several variables on the user's experience when interacting with a 3D virtual store with conversational agents in the fashion domain. The study found that the interface type, either a chatbox or a speech interface, impacted the user experience. Participants preferred the chatbox interface, possibly due to the repetition of commands in the voice interface. The study also revealed that the point-of-interest system was helpful for users (Fig. 9). The study also found that intrusive agents negatively impacted the user's experience (Fig. 10). The study also suggested that conversational agents should be unobtrusive in their visual representation and not hide any features of the visual interface (Fig. 9) (**RQ1**).

Our research also revealed that 3D visualization techniques in a virtual store environment significantly impact the user's shopping experience (Fig. 12). This feature is perceived as crucial by participants when shopping for clothes online and should be prioritized in designing a 3D virtual store. Furthermore, our study suggests that the point-of-interest system benefits users (Fig. 9). In addition, we observed that users generally prefer the chatbox interface over the speech interface (Fig. 9), and it was considered one of the least important features (Fig. 12). Beyond this, our study showed that the agent's presentation should not be prioritized as it could harm the user's experience. Also, hiding the visual elements of the interface can lead to a more frustrating interaction (Fig. 9). However, users still value using the conversational agent as an alternative to the main interface (Fig. 12) (**RQ2**). We can summarize our findings into the following **guidelines**:

1. We recommend using a chatbox instead of a speech interface for user interaction, as the latter may elicit a higher frequency of utterance repetition and subsequent user frustration.
2. Implement a point-of-interest system for navigating the virtual store. Users often prefer this system, and it's more suitable for touchscreens.
3. It is crucial to refrain from using intrusive agents, as users strongly rejected them and found them irrelevant to their interaction.
4. Conversational agents must not obscure visual interface features through dialogue. It will adversely affect the user's experience.
5. Emphasize 3D visualization techniques, such as mapping clothes to 3D models that allow you to rotate and zoom in on particular details, allowing for meticulous examination of specific details.

In conclusion, we highlight the preference for a chatbox interface over a voice interface, the importance of a point-of-interest system, the negative effect of intrusive agents, the need to avoid obscuring visual interface features, and the significance of emphasizing 3D visualization techniques.

**Acknowledgements.** This work has been partially funded by the CMU-Portugal research project iFetch, reference - LISBOA-01-0247-FEDER-045920, and by the NOVA LINCS project Ref. UIDP/04516/2020. We also gratefully acknowledge the support of the NVIDIA Corporation regarding the GPUs used for this research. This work is supported by NOVA LINCS (UIDB/04516/2020) with the financial support of FCT.IP.

# References

1. Bavaresco, R., et al.: Conversational agents in business: a systematic literature review and future research directions. Comput. Sci. Rev. **36**, 100239 (2020)
2. Ben Mimoun, M.S., Poncin, I., Garnier, M.: Case study-embodied virtual agents: an analysis on reasons for failure. J. Retailing Consum. Serv. **19**(6), 605–612 (2012). https://doi.org/10.1016/j.jretconser.2012.07.006
3. Borsci, S., et al.: The chatbot usability scale: the design and pilot of a usability scale for interaction with AI-based conversational agents. Personal Ubiquitous Comput. **26**(1), 95–119 (2022)
4. Brooke, J., et al.: SUS-a quick and dirty usability scale. Usability Eval. Indust. **189**(194), 4–7 (1996)
5. Burke, R.R., Harlam, B.A., Kahn, B.E., Lodish, L.M.: Comparing Dynamic Consumer Choice in Real and Computer-simulated Environments. J. Consum. Res. **19**(1), 71–82 (1992). https://doi.org/10.1086/209287
6. van Eeuwen, M.: Mobile conversational commerce: messenger chatbots as the next interface between businesses and consumers (2017). www.essay.utwente.nl/71706/
7. Fornelos, T., et al.: A conversational shopping assistant for online virtual stores. Association for Computing Machinery. https://doi.org/10.1145/3503161.3547738
8. Ghosh, D., Foong, P.S., Zhang, S., Zhao, S.: Assessing the utility of the system usability scale for evaluating voice-based user interfaces. In: Proceedings of the Sixth International Symposium of Chinese CHI (2018)
9. Griol, D., Carbó, J., Molina, J.M.: An automatic dialog simulation technique to develop and evaluate interactive conversational agents. Appl. Artif. Intell. **27**(9), 759–780 (2013). https://doi.org/10.1080/08839514.2013.835230
10. Groom, V., Nass, C., Chen, T., Nielsen, A., Scarborough, J.K., Robles, E.: Evaluating the effects of behavioral realism in embodied agents. Int. J. Human-Comput. Stud. **67**(10), 842–849 (2009)
11. Holzwarth, M., Janiszewski, C., Neumann, M.M.: The influence of avatars on online consumer shopping behavior. J. Market. **70**(4), 19–36 (2006). https://doi.org/10.1509/jmkg.70.4.019
12. Kang, H.J., Shin, J.h., Ponto, K.: How 3D virtual reality stores can shape consumer purchase decisions: the roles of informativeness and playfulness. J. Interact. Market. **49**, 70–85 (2020)
13. Li, J.: The benefit of being physically present: a survey of experimental works comparing copresent robots, telepresent robots and virtual agents. Int. J. Human-Comput. Stud. **77**, 23–37 (2015)
14. Lugrin, B., Pelachaud, C., Traum, D.: The handbook on socially interactive agents: 20 years of research on embodied conversational agents, intelligent virtual agents, and social robotics, volume 2: Interactivity, platforms, application (2022)
15. Luo, B., Lau, R.Y., Li, C., Si, Y.W.: A critical review of state-of-the-art chatbot designs and applications. Wiley Interdiscip. Rev. Data Mining Knowl. Disc. **12**(1), e1434 (2022)
16. McClymont, J., Shuralyov, D., Stuerzlinger, W.: Comparison of 3d navigation interfaces. In: 2011 IEEE International Conference on Virtual Environments, Human-Computer Interfaces and Measurement Systems Proceedings, pp. 1–6 (2011). https://doi.org/10.1109/VECIMS.2011.6053842
17. Mir, A., Alldieck, T., Pons-Moll, G.: Learning to transfer texture from clothing images to 3D humans (2020). https://doi.org/10.48550/ARXIV.2003.02050

18. Mori, M., MacDorman, K.F., Kageki, N.: The uncanny valley [from the field]. IEEE Robot. Autom. Mag. **19**(2), 98–100 (2012)
19. Mystakidis, S.: Metaverse. Encyclopedia **2**(1), 486–497 (2022). https://doi.org/10. 3390/encyclopedia2010031
20. Nah, F.F.H., Davis, S.: HCI research issues in e-commerce. J. Electron. Comm. Res. **3**(3), 98–113 (2002)
21. Nijholt, A., Heylen, D., Vertegaal, R.: Inhabited interfaces: attentive conversational agents that help. In: Proceedings 3rd International Conference on Disability, Virtual Reality and Associated Technologies (2000)
22. Nowak, K.L., Rauh, C.: Choose your "buddy icon" carefully: the influence of avatar androgyny, anthropomorphism and credibility in online interactions. Comput. Human Behav. **24**(4), 1473–1493 (2008)
23. Peukert, C., Pfeiffer, J., Meißner, M., Pfeiffer, T., Weinhardt, C.: Shopping in virtual reality stores: the influence of immersion on system adoption. J. Manage. Inform. Syst. **36**(3), 755–788 (2019)
24. Piro, L., Desolda, G., Matera, M., Lanzilotti, R., Mosca, S., Pucci, E.: An interactive paradigm for the end-user development of chatbots for data exploration. In: Ardito, C., et al. (eds.) Human-Computer Interaction - INTERACT 2021–18th IFIP TC 13 International Conference, Bari, Italy, 30 August–3 September 2021, Proceedings, Part IV. Lecture Notes in Computer Science, vol. 12935, pp. 177–186 (2021). https://doi.org/10.1007/978-3-030-85610-6_11
25. Pricilla, C., Lestari, D.P., Dharma, D.: Designing interaction for chatbot-based conversational commerce with user-centered design. In: 2018 5th International Conference on Advanced Informatics: Concept Theory and Applications (ICAICTA), pp. 244–249 (2018). https://doi.org/10.1109/ICAICTA.2018.8541320
26. Quarteroni, S., Manandhar, S.: A chatbot-based interactive question answering system. Decalog **2007**, 83 (2007)
27. Schnack, A., Wright, M.J., Holdershaw, J.L.: Immersive virtual reality technology in a three-dimensional virtual simulated store: Investigating telepresence and usability. Food Res. Int. **117**, 40–49 (2019), special issue on "Virtual reality and food: Applications in sensory and consumer science". https://doi.org/10.1016/j. foodres.2018.01.028
28. Szczuka, J.M., Güzelbey, H.S., Krämer, N.C.: Someone or something to play with? an empirical study on how parents evaluate the social appropriateness of interactions between children and differently embodied artificial interaction partners. In: Proceedings of the 21st ACM International Conference on Intelligent Virtual Agents, pp. 191–194. IVA 2021. Association for Computing Machinery, New York (2021). https://doi.org/10.1145/3472306.3478349
29. Tan, D.S., Robertson, G.G., Czerwinski, M.: Exploring 3D navigation: combining speed-coupled flying with orbiting, pp. 418–425. CHI 2001. Association for Computing Machinery, New York (2001). https://doi.org/10.1145/365024.365307
30. Tan, S.M., Liew, T.W.: Designing embodied virtual agents as product specialists in a multi-product category e-commerce: the roles of source credibility and social presence. Int. J. Hum.-Comput. Interact. **36**(12), 1136–1149 (2020). https://doi. org/10.1080/10447318.2020.1722399
31. Vaddadi, S., Asri, S., Ghemi, Y., Aytha, R.: Developing chatbot wrapper for online shopping: a case study of using generic mobile messaging system (2020)
32. Xi, N., Hamari, J.: Shopping in virtual reality: a literature review and future agenda. J. Bus. Res. **134**, 37–58 (2021)
33. Xu, K., Chan, J., Ghose, A., Han, S.P.: Battle of the channels: the impact of tablets on digital commerce. Manage. Sci. **63**(5), 1469–1492 (2017)

# Effects of Prior Experience, Gender, and Age on Trust in a Banking Chatbot With(Out) Breakdown and Repair

Effie Lai-Chong Law[1]([✉]), Nena van As[2], and Asbjørn Følstad[3]

[1] Department of Computer Science, Durham University, Durham DH1 3LE, UK
lai-chong.law@durham.ac.uk
[2] Boost.ai, Grenseveien 21, 4313 Sandnes, Norway
nena.van.as@boost.ai
[3] SINTEF, Forskningsveien 1, 0373 Oslo, Norway
Asbjorn.Folstad@sintef.no

**Abstract.** Trust is an attitudinal construct that can be sensitive to prior experience, gender, and age. In our study, we explored how trust in a banking chatbot might be shaped by these user characteristics. Statistical analysis of 251 participants, who interacted with one of six chatbots defined by humanlikeness (high/low) and conversational performance (no breakdown, breakdown with repaired, breakdown without repair), showed that the user characteristics of gender and age did not significantly impact trust, but prior experience did. Trust resilience was found across the gender and age groups. The effect of users' prior experience on their trust in a chatbot which they have never used holds implications for research and practice. Future studies on the effect of cultural context, longer interaction episodes, and more diverse application contexts on trust in chatbots are recommended.

**Keywords:** Chatbot · Artificial Intelligence (AI) · Trust · Age · Gender · Prior experience · Breakdown · Repair

## 1 Introduction

Chatbots, text-based conversational agents powered by artificial intelligence (AI), are gaining inroads in an ever-expanding scope of sectors. People from all walks of life with different demographic backgrounds interact with chatbots, albeit to different extents, for banking, shopping, healthcare consultancy, and other online services [12]. Despite the increasing sophistication of the technologies underpinning the design and development of chatbots, including natural language processing, machine learning algorithms, human-robot interaction, and speech emotion recognition [30], communication breakdowns with chatbots still happen frequently [3]. Some attempts to repair breakdowns succeed, for instance, by asking users to rephrase requests so that their intents can better be identified, but some fail. Such failure to repair leads to frustration and confusion in users, whose trust in the chatbot of interest can be so severely undermined that they reject the chatbot altogether.

© The Author(s), under exclusive license to Springer Nature Switzerland AG 2023
J. Abdelnour Nocera et al. (Eds.): INTERACT 2023, LNCS 14143, pp. 277–296, 2023.
https://doi.org/10.1007/978-3-031-42283-6_16

Two significant factors influencing trust in chatbots are *humanlikeness* and *conversational performance*. While several empirical studies have recently been conducted to investigate how trust could vary with these two factors (Sect. 2.2 and Sect. 2.3), other non-technological factors have captured less research effort. Impressions formed in previous interactions with fellow humans, products, and services, be they technology-based or not, can shape people's attitudes and behaviours in subsequent encounters with entities having some similar traits. This phenomenon, from the psychological research perspective, is generally referred to as *cognitive bias* [13]. Specifically, positive and negative transfer of opinions and perceptions built upon experiences in previous events to a current one can be known as *halo effect* and *horn effect*, respectively [34, 39]. In the field of Human-Computer Interaction (HCI), the halo effect of beauty to usability in different products was systematically studied and confirmed (e.g. [20]). However, to the best of our knowledge, little research on the halo (or horn) effect of trust across computing products/services has been conducted.

Apart from prior interaction experience, demographic variables, especially *gender* and *age*, can play a significant role in influencing the level of trust in people as well as technology. For instance, based on some neuropsychological and behavioural data, it was found that male trusted interaction objects (human or nonhuman entity) more than female who were more risk aversive, as observed in the context of trust-sensitive games (e.g., [6, 45]). This corroborates the arguments pertinent to gender difference in predisposition to trust [47]. Specifically, based on their analysis of the neuroimaging data on eleven heterosexual dyads playing a multi-round binary trust game, Wu and colleagues [45] found that men trusted their partner more than women, that the payoff level moderated the effect of gender on trust, and that women were more sensitive to social risk while trusting. Furthermore, in understanding the motivation underlying behaviours in an investment game exhibited by the two genders, Buchan and colleagues [6] found that men trusted interacting entities more than women; men than women emphasized more the relationship between expected return and trusting behaviour; women felt more obligated both to trust and reciprocate.

In addition, Haselhuhn and colleagues [19] had intriguing findings on gender difference in *trust dynamics*. The authors reported that following a trust violation, women were both less likely to lose trust and more likely to restore trust in a transgressor than men. Toader and colleagues [44] examined the impact of chatbot error on trust with gender as a moderating factor, which was manipulated in terms of avatar's gender but not user's gender. They found that the chatbot with a female avatar was much more forgiven when committing errors compared to one with a male avatar. In contrast, two other studies did *not* find any gender differences in trust in functional chatbots, one for online shopping [23] and the other for student support [33].

The effect of users' age on their attitudes towards chatbots has been examined in a small number of studies. Terblanche and Kidd [43], based on the adapted Technology Acceptance Model (TAM) questionnaire, found that age did *not* play a significant role in determining the level of perceived risk for deploying non-directive reflective coaching chatbot. They further reported that older adults' intention to use the chatbot was influenced by the effort expected to invest in using it whereas younger adults valued more the usefulness and level of enjoyment of the chatbot. Goot and Pilgrim [15], based on the intriguing socioemotional selectivity theory, conducted interviews with older adults and younger ones on attitudes towards customer service chatbots. They found that the motivation for the chatbot use was contrasting. While older adults would appreciate chatbots with "human touch", their younger counterparts intended to use chatbots that enable them to avoid human contact.

Based on the literature reviewed, we were motivated to explore the following research question as part of a larger empirical study investigating the issue of trust in customer service chatbots [26]:

*What is the respective effect of (a) prior experience, (b) gender, (c) age on the perceived trust and interaction qualities of the chatbots characterised by humanlikeness and conversational performance?*

## 2 Related Work and Hypotheses

In this section, we first present an overview on the work related to the design and development of chatbots, especially on the two attributes – *Humanlikeness* and *Conversational Performance*. Note that the effects of these two attributes on the fluctuation of trust levels are published in a conference paper [26]. Nonetheless, it is necessary to present the relevant descriptions in this paper to contextualise the analyses to be reported subsequently. It is also important to point out that the data and results included here are *not* covered in [26] where the analysis results on demographic variables are *not* reported to keep it more focused. Towards the end of this section, we delineate the three main hypotheses of our study.

### 2.1 Trust in Chatbots

Trust is typically understood as the willingness of a trustor to "accept vulnerability based on positive expectations of the intentions or behaviour of the other" [37]. Several models of trust in technology exist (e.g. [8, 18, 25, 28, 29]). They typically consider trust as determined by a set of underlying factors representing beliefs about the trustworthiness of the trustee. In a review of trust-building factors in embodied conversational agents, [36] identified social intelligence, communication style, performance and humanlikeness as among the factors impacting agent trustworthiness. [22] also found that chatbot humanlikeness leads to increased trust and adoption, contributing to customer loyalty. Research on cognitive agents and social robots has studied how humanlikeness may lead to 'trust resilience', that is, upkeep of trust in spite of undesirable system outcomes [9]. Similarly, [17] found that humanlike design cues conveyed by social robots can strengthen user trust and positively impact user preference regardless of operation failure. Nonetheless, findings on the relative effects of humanlikeness and conversational performance on trust in chatbots remain inconsistent (e.g., [31, 46]).

### 2.2 Humanlikeness of Chatbots

Many AI-powered systems are designed to mimic human behaviour, verbal as well as non-verbal. The extent to which a chatbot is perceived to be humanlike shapes the user experience [21], intention to use [42], and goal attainment that the chatbot is aimed to enable [4]. The phenomena of the Turing test [27] and uncanny valley effect [7] are associated with the humanlikeness of such AI-based conversational interactions. In fact, Rapp and colleagues, in their review of chatbot research [35], found that more than 25% of the studies addressed the topic of humanness. Furthermore, several design features of chatbots have been found influencing the perceived level of humanlikeness (i.e., anthropomorphism), including conversational style [21], visual representation and initial self-presentation [2, 14], informal language [2], and features hinting at chatbot intelligence such as backchanneling [14] and conversational relevance [40].

### 2.3 Conversational Performance of Chatbots

In the context of customer service, we define '*conversational performance*' as the chatbot's ability to provide relevant and helpful responses to users' requests. This interpretation is supported by certain industry reports. Accordingly, efficient and effective access to help can motivate users to engage with chatbots [10] whereas getting stuck in a conversation without progress or receiving irrelevant responses can undermine the chatbot use [12]. Despite the advances of machine learning methods, especially large language models deployed in GPT-3 and BERT, human-chatbot interactions involve breakdowns [12], which often occur even in human-human interactions [38]. Conversational breakdown in chatbots may happen when the chatbot fails to predict any user intent for the user request. It typically triggers a fallback response as a common attempt to conversational repair where the chatbot states that it has not understood and asks the user to rephrase [11, 16, 31].

### 2.4 Chatbots for Customer Service

One of the rapidly growing application areas of chatbots is customer service [35]. The banking chatbot we created for our empirical study (Sect. 3) is a typical example. Basically, customer service chatbots are deployed to respond to frequently asked questions (FAQs) posed by customers [41] and integrated into customer websites as alternative text-based information source [1]. User interactions with customer service chatbots are generally short. Technically, chatbots can be rule-based or AI-based. The former relies on pre-defined decision trees whereas the latter utilises statistical data-driven methods to infer user intents based on prediction models. Specifically, a user enters a request in a chatbot in free text from which an intent is predicted [21]. The chatbot responds according to the intent inferred by conveying to the user one or more messages that may meet the request. The user may refine the chatbot's response through selecting one of answer options, presented as buttons or menu items. The content and prediction models of customer service chatbots can be complex, especially when the scope of user intents is diverse [48].

### 2.5 Research Hypotheses

In this subsection, first we reiterate the three key insights discussed in Introduction, corresponding to the three parts of the main research question:

(a) The halo and horn effects have not been applied to analyse the phenomenon of people's trust in chatbots.
(b) Results of some studies of trust in interpersonal relationships and technologies, including chatbots, suggest that some gender-specific patterns could be observed. In general, male tend to trust interacting objects, be they animate or inanimate, more than their female.
(c) There seem age-dependent factors influencing people's trust in chatbots with older adults relying more on the perceived humanness of chatbots.

However, as the number of the related studies is limited, the observed patterns and factors remain inconclusive and more empirical research is required.

We integrate the insights to formulate the following *null* hypotheses (H), indicating the non-conclusive directions as derived from our analysis of the related work.

Hypothesis 1: There are no significant differences between users with different prior chatbot experience in their overall trust in the banking chatbots characterised by specific levels of humanlikeness and conversational performance.
Hypothesis 2: There are no significant differences between male and female in their overall trust in the banking chatbots characterised by specific levels of humanlikeness and conversational performance.
Hypothesis 3: There are no significant differences between younger and older users in their overall trust in the banking chatbots characterised by specific levels of humanlikeness and conversational performance.

## 3    Methods

Our empirical study employed a 2 × 3 factorial design with Humanlikeness (yes/no) and Conversational Performance (no breakdown, breakdown with repair, breakdown without repair) as IVs. This resulted in six groups of participants of which two did not experience breakdown (Table 1). We go into details on the operationalization of each IV level below.

**Table 1.** Six variants of chatbots tested with six groups of participants

|                       | No Breakdown | Breakdown with Repair | Breakdown without Repair |
|-----------------------|--------------|-----------------------|--------------------------|
| Humanlikeness: Yes    | Group 1      | Group 2               | Group 3                  |
| Humanlikeness: No     | Group 4      | Group 5               | Group 6                  |

### 3.1   Instrument – Customer Service Chatbot Variants

For our study, we developed a customer service chatbot representing a fictitious bank called "Boost Bank", using a dedicated platform for virtual agents [26] where user messages are processed by an AI-powered intent prediction model. The chatbot was modified into six variants characterised by the combination of two attributes. Each version of the chatbot deployed an equal number of open-ended as well as button-based answer options for the participants.

*Conversational performance* was operationalized in terms of the presence (or absence) of *breakdown* and *repair* for one of the three tasks as shown in Fig. 1. Breakdown and repair followed the 'repeat' pattern of [3] where breakdown involved the chatbot failing to understand the user request and asking the user to reformulate, and repair involved the chatbot understanding the users' reformulated request and providing a relevant response. Each version was evaluated by different groups of participants.

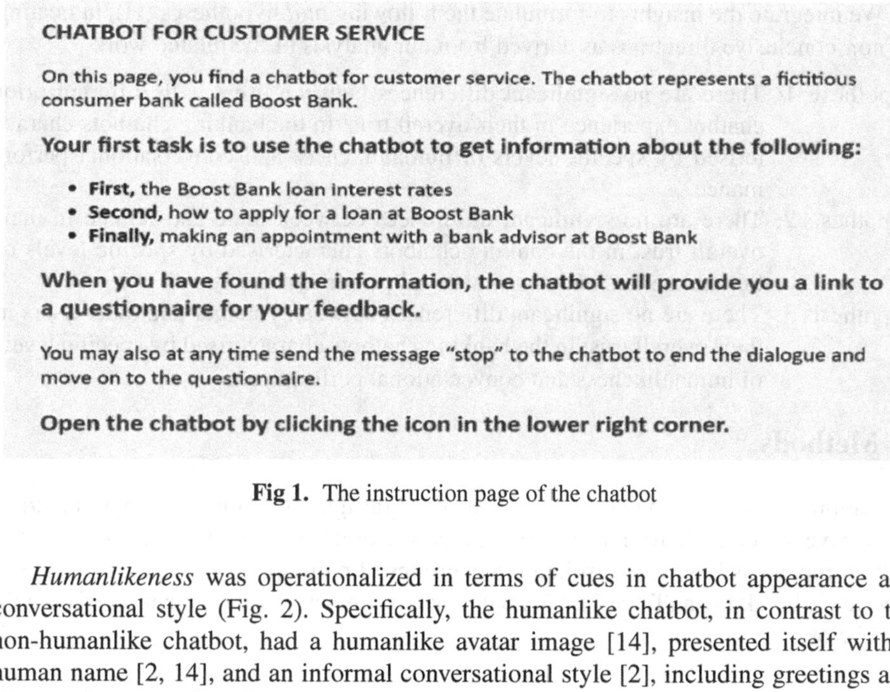

**CHATBOT FOR CUSTOMER SERVICE**

On this page, you find a chatbot for customer service. The chatbot represents a fictitious consumer bank called Boost Bank.

**Your first task is to use the chatbot to get information about the following:**

- **First,** the Boost Bank loan interest rates
- **Second,** how to apply for a loan at Boost Bank
- **Finally,** making an appointment with a bank advisor at Boost Bank

**When you have found the information, the chatbot will provide you a link to a questionnaire for your feedback.**

You may also at any time send the message "stop" to the chatbot to end the dialogue and move on to the questionnaire.

**Open the chatbot by clicking the icon in the lower right corner.**

**Fig 1.** The instruction page of the chatbot

*Humanlikeness* was operationalized in terms of cues in chatbot appearance and conversational style (Fig. 2). Specifically, the humanlike chatbot, in contrast to the non-humanlike chatbot, had a humanlike avatar image [14], presented itself with a human name [2, 14], and an informal conversational style [2], including greetings and pleasantries. as well as first and second person pronouns.

## 3.2  Measurement: Post-intervention Questionnaire

After completing the tasks with the chatbot, participants were asked to complete a questionnaire with four parts: Part 1 on measuring trust in the chatbots, overall as well as task-specific; Part 2 on qualitative feedback on trust in the chatbots; Part 3 on reliability, anthropomorphism, and social presence; Part 4 on demographics and prior chatbot experience. Each item, where applicable, is measured with a 7-point Likert scale with 1 (Strongly disagree) and 7 (Strongly agreed). Table 2 shows the items that are relevant to this paper.

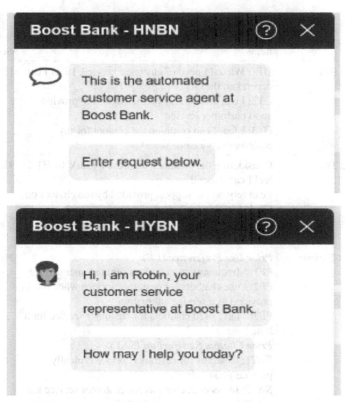

**Fig. 2.** Chatbot humanlikeness implementation with different greeting styles. Upper (abstract icon, impersonal style; Humanlikeness - No); Lower (avatar with name, personal conversational style; Humanlikeness - Yes). HYBN = Humanlikeness No Breakdown No; HYBN = Humanlikeness Yes Breakdown No

### 3.3  Participants

Altogether 251 participants were recruited via the crowdsourcing platform Prolific. Among them, 178 were female, 69 male and 4 preferred not to say. For country of residence, the distribution was: 128 UK, 106 US, 5 Canada, 5 Ireland, 4 South Africa, and 1 from Australia, Hungary, and Mexico each. Most of the participants (n = 226) had higher education level and the rest had high school level. The average age was 35.7 years old (SD = 12.1, range: 18–68). The majority (n = 112) of participants were under 30 years old (Table 3).

Each participant was randomly assigned to one of the six groups and given a unique code to log into the website where they carried out the tasks with the chatbot (Fig. 1). On the cover page, participants were informed about the study's tasks, that data collection was fully anonymous, that data would be used for research purposes, and that they would agree to participate and enter the study by clicking the 'next' button. On average, they spent 5.8 min (SD = 4.0, range: 2.8–23.9) in completing the three tasks.

**Table 2.** Post-intervention questionnaire items

| Variable | Items | Source |
|---|---|---|
| Overall Trust (OT) | OT1: When in need of customer service, I feel I can depend on the chatbot<br>OT2: I can always rely on the chatbot to provide good customer service<br>OT3: I feel I can count on the chatbot for my customer service needs | [25] |
| Task-specific Trust TT1, TT2, TT3 | Considering the chatbot's answer on [Task 1/2/3], I feel I can depend on it<br>I can rely on the support provided by the chatbot on [Task 1/2/3]<br>I feel I can count on the chatbot for questions on [Task 1/2/3] | Home-grown |
| Prior Chatbot Experience | *Prior Use Preference (PF)*<br>PF1: I frequently use chatbots for customer service<br>PF2: I use chatbots for customer service when this is provided as a service alternative<br>PF3: I have used chatbots for customer service for a long time<br>*Prior Chatbot Satisfaction* (SAT)<br>SAT1: Chatbots for customer service typically provide good help<br>SAT2: In general, chatbots for customer service are an efficient way to get support<br>SAT3: I usually find chatbots for customer service pleasant to use<br>*Prior Use Frequency (FQ)*<br>Five options:<br>• More than 10 times<br>• 5–10 times<br>• 3–4 times<br>• 1–2 times<br>• Never | Home-grown |
| Demographic | Gender (female, male, prefer not to say)<br>Age (free text)<br>Country of residence (free text)<br>Education (three options) | Home-grown |

**Table 3.** Distribution of participant ages

| Age Range | 18–20 | 21–30 | 31–40 | 41–50 | 51–60 | 61–68 |
|---|---|---|---|---|---|---|
| Frequency | 17 | 95 | 72 | 34 | 23 | 10 |

# 4   Results

In this section, we present our empirical findings in the order of the three hypotheses (Sect. 2.5), which correspond to the three parts of the main research question: effects of *Prior Experience* first, then those of *Gender*, and end with effects of *Age*.

## 4.1   Effects of Humanlikeness and Conversational Performance on Trust: A Synopsis

As mentioned earlier, results on the effects of the two factors – humanlikeness and conversational performance – on trust are published elsewhere [26]. Nonetheless, when presenting and discussing the effects of prior experience, gender, and age on trust, it is relevant to contextualise them with reference to these factors.

Results of between-group analysis showed that for the task with seeded breakdowns there were significant differences in trust across the six groups with the lowest ratings for the two groups experiencing breakdowns without repair, and that humanlikeness did not impact the extent to which the trust level changed. Results of within-group analysis showed significant differences in trust across the three tasks (Fig. 1). These observations challenge the effect of humanlikeness on trust while supporting the notion of trust resilience as the participants did not spill the impaired trust over the subsequent task (for details see [26]).

## 4.2   Effect of Prior Experience on Trust (Hypothesis 1)

The participants' prior experience with chatbots was measured through three variables: *Prior Use Preference*, *Prior Use Frequency*, and *Prior Chatbot Satisfaction* (Table 2). The variables were measured with 7-point Likert scales. To investigate the effect of these variables on the participants' trust, it was beneficial to conceptualise these as different grouping variables rather than scales. We applied the same analysis approach for the effect of *Gender* and *Age* (Sect. 4.3 and Sect. 4.4). To this end, we regrouped participants into three ranges for each of these variables: Low, Middle, and High. The ranges were based on the 33rd and 66th percentiles of the ratings (see Tables 4, 5 and 6 for details).

Specifically, 3 * 2 * 3 ANOVAs ([*Prior variables*]*Humanlikeness*Conversational Performance*) were performed, where [*Prior variables*] include *Prior Use Preference*, *Prior Use Frequency* or *Prior Chatbot Satisfaction* (Table 2). The DV was Overall Trust.

Results showed that *Prior Use Preference* significantly impacted the participants' Overall Trust ($F_{(2,233)} = 21.920, p < .001, \eta^2 = .158$). However, no significant interaction effects were observed. Means and standard deviations for Overall Trust across the three ranges of participants' ratings for *Prior Use Preference* are shown in Table 4.

Furthermore, results showed that *Prior Use Frequency* did not have any significant impact on the participants' Overall Trust ($F_{(2,233)} = 1.917, p = .149, \eta^2 = .016$). No significant interaction effects were observed here either. Means and standard deviations for the Overall Trust across the three ranges of participant's ratings for *Prior Use Frequency* are presented in Table 5.

**Table 4.** Mean (SD) of Overall Trust across the three rating ranges of *Prior Use Preference*

| Group | Range | n | Overall Trust |
|---|---|---|---|
| Low | 1.00–3.67 | 91 | 3.71 (.16) |
| Middle | 3.68–5.33 | 74 | 4.08 (.17) |
| High | 5.34–7.00 | 86 | 5.13 (.14) |

**Table 5.** Mean (SD) of Overall Trust across the three rating ranges of *Prior Use Frequency*

| Group | Range | n | Overall Trust |
|---|---|---|---|
| Low | <5 times | 64 | 3.95 (0.19) |
| Middle | 5–10 times | 90 | 4.44 (0.16) |
| High | >10 times | 97 | 4.44 (0.16) |

Finally, results showed that *Prior Chatbot Satisfaction* significantly impacted the participants' levels of Overall Trust ($F_{(2,233)} = 65.456$, $p < .001$, $\eta^2 = .360$). No significant interaction effects were observed. Means and standard deviations for Overall Trust across the three ranges of participants' ratings for *Prior Chatbot Satisfaction* are presented in Table 6.

**Table 6.** Mean (SD) of Overall Trust across the three rating ranges of *Prior Chatbot Satisfaction*

| Group | Range | n | Overall Trust |
|---|---|---|---|
| Low | 1.00–3.67 | 91 | 3.28 (0.14) |
| Middle | 3.68–5.33 | 74 | 4.32 (0.13) |
| High | 5.34–7,00 | 86 | 5.41 (0.14) |

To further investigate why out of the three measures on prior experience only *Prior Use Frequency* did not have a significant impact on Overall Trust, bivariate Spearman correlations among the three components, factored by gender and age, were computed. Some intriguing findings were obtained.

Significant *positive* correlations between *Prior Use Preference* and *Prior Chatbot Satisfaction* were found, irrespective of gender or age groups (Table 7). In other words, the results suggested that participants who tended to choose to use customer service chatbots when available, were satisfied with the experience. At the same time, a significant *negative* correlation was found between *Prior Chatbot Satisfaction* and *Prior Use Frequency*, i.e., the more participants used such chatbots the less satisfied they became. Interestingly, for male participants this correlation was not significant; nor was it significant for the younger or middle age group (Table 7).

**Table 7.** Bivariate correlations among the three components of prior experience: *Prior Chatbot Satisfaction* (Satisfaction), *Prior Use Preference* (Preference) and *Prior Use Frequency* (Frequency) by *Gender* and *Age* groups.

|  | All N = 251 | Female N=178 | Male N=69 | Younger N=112 | Middle N=72 | Older N=67 |
|---|---|---|---|---|---|---|
| **Satisfaction vs. Preference** | 0.64 $p<.001$ | 0.640 $p<.001$ | 0.624 $p<.001$ | 0.677 $p<.001$ | 0.607 $p<.001$ | 0.611 $p<.001$ |
| **Satisfaction vs. Frequency** | -0.195 $p=.002$ | -0.230 $p=.002$ | -0.083 $p=.496$ | -0.168 $p=.076$ | -0.210 $p=.076$ | -0.251 $p=.041$ |

## 4.3 Effect of Gender on Perceived Trust (Hypothesis 2)

To analyse the main effect of *Gender* (female, male - participants who reported "prefer not to say" were excluded for this analysis) and its interaction effects with *Humanlikeness* (no, yes) and *Conversational Performance* (no breakdown, breakdown with repair, breakdown without repair) of the chatbots, a 2 * 2 * 3 ANOVA was performed with Overall Trust as DV.

Results showed that the main effects of the three IVs were not significant for Overall Trust. The interaction effects were also non-significant.

Concerning the notion of gender-related "trust dynamics" or "trust resilience" (Sect. 1 and 2), we examined how the level of trust varied with the tasks and gender. When breakdown occurred, the impact on the task-specific trust (i.e., TT2; Trust in Task 2) was obvious (Table 8). Interestingly, while there were obvious drops in TT2, the level of trust bounced back for TT3 for both genders, albeit to a slightly larger extent for male. We performed 2 * 2 * 3 ANOVAs on TT1-TT2 (i.e., trust difference between Task 1 and Task 2) and TT2-TT3 (i.e. trust difference between Task 2 and Task 3). The main effect of *Conversational Performance* was significant, but non-significant for *Humanlikeness* or *Gender*. None of the interaction effects were significant. This suggested both female and male demonstrated trust resilience.

## 4.4 Effect of Age on Perceived Trust (Hypothesis 3)

As indicated in Table 3, the distribution of ages was skewed towards the younger ones. To address this issue, we regrouped participants into three age brackets: Younger (18–30 years old, n = 112), Middle (31–40 years old, n = 72), Older (41–68 years old, n = 67). Similar to the analysis on the effect of *Gender* (Sect. 4.3), a 3 * 2 * 3 ANOVA (*Age*Humanlikeness*Conversational Performance*) was performed with Overall Trust as a DV.

Results showed that *Age* did not play any significant role in influencing Overall Trust ($F_{(2,231)} = .759, p = .469$). None of the interaction effects among the three IVs were significant. Regardless of age brackets, participants had lowest trust when they experienced breakdowns in both human-like and non-humanlike conditions.

Table 9 illustrates the observation that the three age groups gave similar ratings for Overall Trust with the means leaning towards neutrality (i.e., 4 out of 7). We also applied

**Table 8.** Mean Task-specific Trust (TT) per task for two genders under different conditions

| | Female | | | | | |
| | Humanlike | | | Non-humanlike | | |
| Conversational Performance | TT1 | TT2 | TT3 | TT1 | TT2 | TT3 |
|---|---|---|---|---|---|---|
| No Breakdown | 6.01 | *5.77* | 5.74 | 5.15 | *4.91* | 5.35 |
| Breakdown with Repair | 5.27 | *4.76* | 5.31 | 5.37 | *4.66* | 5.32 |
| Breakdown without Repair | 6.08 | *1.45* | 5.22 | 5.06 | *1.1* | 4.94 |
| | Male | | | | | |
| | Humanlike | | | Non-humanlike | | |
| Conversational Performance | TT1 | TT2 | TT3 | TT1 | TT2 | TT3 |
| No Breakdown | 5.86 | *5.05* | 5 | 5.4 | *4.53* | 5.2 |
| Breakdown with Repair | 5.69 | *5.21* | 5.59 | 5.21 | *4.31* | 0.31 |
| Breakdown without Repair | 5.5 | *1.38* | 5.07 | 5.52 | *2.09* | 5.45 |

the same analysis of trust dynamics to the three age groups (cf. Sect. 4.3 for *Gender*). Table 10 displays the descriptive statistics. Results of 3 * 3 * 2 ANOVAs showed that the only significant main effect was *Conversational Performance*.

**Table 9.** Mean (SD) of the four variables across three age groups

| Group | Range (years) | N | Overall Trust |
|---|---|---|---|
| Younger | 18–30 | 112 | 4.21 (1.61) |
| Middle | 31–40 | 72 | 4.39 (1.50) |
| Older | 41–68 | 67 | 4.41 (1.55) |

However, the three-way interaction effects (*Age*Conversational Performance *Humanlikeness*) for both TT1-TT2 ($F_{(4,233)} = 3.57, p = 0.008$) and TT2-TT3 ($F_{(4,233)} = 2.49, p = .044$) trust differences were significant (Fig. 3a; Fig. 3b). These suggested that the three age groups changed the level of trust from task to task significantly under different chatbot conditions. For instance, for the Middle age group, the TT2-TT3 value of 4.47 for the group 'breakdown without repair and humanlike' was higher than the corresponding values of 4.09 and 2.6 for the Younger and Older age groups.

**Table 10.** Mean Task-specific Trust (TT) per task for three age groups under different conditions of the chatbot *Conversational Performance*

| | Younger | | | | | |
| --- | --- | --- | --- | --- | --- | --- |
| | Humanlike | | | Non-humanlike | | |
| Conversational Performance | TT1 | TT2 | TT3 | TT1 | TT2 | TT3 |
| No Breakdown | 5.87 | *5.56* | 5.69 | 4.88 | *4.59* | 4.90 |
| Breakdown with Repair | 5.15 | *4.75* | 5.32 | 5.20 | *3.8* | 4.98 |
| Breakdown without Repair | 5.96 | *1.23* | 5.32 | 4.85 | *1.24* | 4.85 |
| | Middle | | | | | |
| | Humanlike | | | Non-humanlike | | |
| Conversational Performance | TT1 | TT2 | TT3 | TT1 | TT2 | TT3 |
| No Breakdown | 6.03 | *5.93* | 5.73 | 5.34 | *4.79* | 5.49 |
| Breakdown with Repair | 5.89 | *4.83* | 5.39 | 5.54 | *5.28* | 5.72 |
| Breakdown without Repair | 6.00 | *1.17* | 5.64 | 5.25 | *1.52* | 5.00 |
| | Older | | | | | |
| | Humanlike | | | Non-humanlike | | |
| Conversational Performance | TT1 | TT2 | TT3 | TT1 | TT2 | TT3 |
| No Breakdown | 6.13 | *5.47* | 5.33 | 5.83 | *5.13* | 5.5 |
| Breakdown with Repair | 5.48 | *5.10* | 5.48 | 5.24 | *4.97* | 5.42 |
| Breakdown without Repair | 5.42 | *1.97* | 4.57 | 5.49 | *1.23* | 5.44 |

## 5 Discussion

Based on the analysis results, we can address the main research question of this work (Sect. 1). Of the three components of prior chatbot experience, both *Prior Use Preference* and *Prior Chatbot Satisfaction* had a significant effect on Overall Trust whereas *Prior Use Frequency* had no significant effect. Hence, we can only partially accept the null Hypothesis 1. *Gender* and *Age* did not have any significant effect on Overall Trust. Hence, we accept the two null Hypothesis 2 and Hypothesis 3.

### 5.1 Hypothesis 1: Prior Experience

Concerning the effect of prior experience on trust in chatbots for customer service, we found that both *Prior Use Preference* and *Prior Chatbot Satisfaction* significantly impacted trust. There are some interesting things to note about these variables, however. The measures were taken after the participants had interacted with the chatbots of this study, in a post-intervention questionnaire. Note that it was a procedural arrangement rather than any intentional experimental manipulation. Nevertheless, it was plausible that the positive or negative user experience the participants had in this study influenced

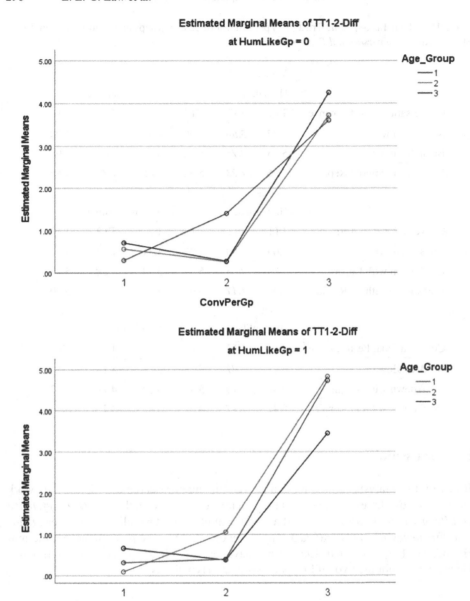

**Fig. 3. (a):** Significant three-way interaction effects. The upper graph shows the trust difference between Task 1 and Task 2 (TT1-2-Diff) under the condition of *Humanlikeness* = No. The lower graph shows the trust difference between Task 1 and Task 2 (TT1–2 Diff) under the condition of *Humanlikeness* = Yes. *ConvPerGp* = Conversational Performance (1 = No breakdown; 2 = Breakdown without repair; 3 = Breakdown with repair)

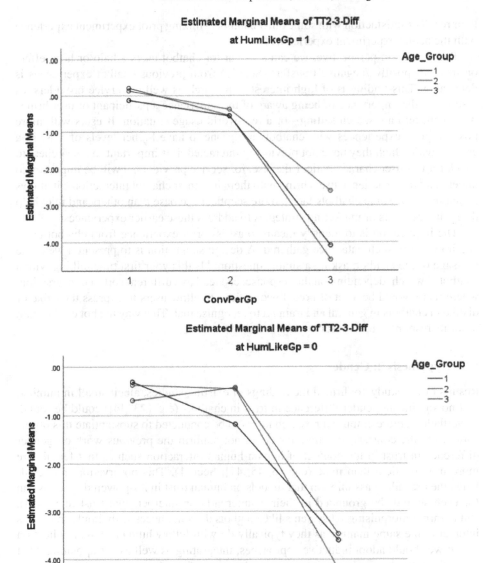

**Fig. 3. (b):** Significant three-way interaction effects. The upper graph shows the trust difference between Task 2 and Task 3 (TT2-3-Diff) under the condition of *Humanlikeness* = No. The lower graph shows the trust difference between Task 2 and Task 3 (TT2–3-Diff) under the condition of *Humanlikeness* = Yes. *ConvPerGp* = Conversational Performance (1 = No breakdown; 2 = Breakdown without repair; 3 = Breakdown with repair)

their recall of satisfaction with some other chatbots - mixing prior experiment experience with the actual experiment experience.

Putting this in perspective, we can say that for chatbot users a halo or horn effect on trust (of positive/negative transfer) (Sect. 1) from previous chatbot experiences is detectable. This finding is of high interest to research as well as service providers, as it suggests the importance of being aware of the experience a participant or user brings with them into a research setting - or a real-world usage situation. If users with more positive prior experiences with chatbots are prone to have higher levels of trust in a chatbot with which they have not previously interacted, it is important to researchers to check for this user characteristic. Likewise, for service providers, it will be important to understand the experience users bring with them into their chatbot interactions: it allows explaining why some chatbots face a more sceptical use base than others and may help designing prompts or marketing strategies to address these earlier experiences.

The implication is to identify means to assess prior experience from chatbot users and how to use such data once gathered. A design suggestion is to present a welcome message of the chatbot, asking a simple question: "Is this your first time talking with a chatbot?" which, depending on the response, can lead to a different sort of conversation, where there would be a set of predefined options to allow users to express their like or dislike in chatbots in general and train AI to recognise that. That way the bot could again tailor its responses to the user.

### 5.2 Hypothesis 2: Gender

Results of our study confirmed the findings of existing studies, albeit small in number, that no significant gender difference in trust in chatbots (e.g. [23, 44]) could be found. Nevertheless, more empirical research needs to be conducted to substantiate this observation. On the contrary, our findings could not confirm the previous work on gender difference in trust in the context of human-human interaction such as that female are more trust resilient than male (e.g. [6, 45, 47]; Sect. 1). This observation may challenge the prevailing assumption that models on human trust in AI-powered systems can (or even should) be grounded in their counterparts on interpersonal trust (e.g. [18]). But anthropomorphising AI systems like chatbots does not necessarily imply that users interact in the same manner as they typically do with fellow humans. One implication is that we should adopt inductive approaches, integrating as well as extrapolating what is empirically observed to inform the development of an alternative model of trust in human-AI interaction.

### 5.3 Hypothesis 3: Age

Concerning the effect of *Age* on the level of trust in chatbots, our findings confirmed the work of [43] that age did not play a significant role in the form of any main effects. Nevertheless, the coaching chatbot examined in [43] did not impart any knowledge to users but rather gave them space to reflect through conversational stimulation whereas the chatbot used in this study was directive by conveying specific information requested to users. Clearly, more research on different types of chatbots is needed, especially given the observed interaction effects due to age differences. Furthermore, the analyses of [18, 43] on the different motivations underpinning younger and older adults for their acceptance and intention to use chatbots are intriguing. While older adults may appreciate more emotional than practical value from chatbot interactions, which may be appreciated more by their young counterparts [18], it is critical that trustworthy AI-powered chatbots can convey a strong sense of fairness, respect, and transparency to users, irrespective of their ages or gender.

### 5.4 Limitations

There are some limitations of our work. Trust is a culture-sensitive construct. People's propensity to (dis)trust objects, human or non-human objects, can be shaped by the sociocultural environment where they grow up. While potentially interesting to explore the effect of culture or social environment on trust, our data collection did not consider including this as demographic variables, given the concern that it would be difficult to get a balanced distribution of relevant subgroups with the sample size of 200–300. This can be addressed in our future work. Another limitation is that the three tasks could be completed in a relatively short period of time, which is rather common in chatbot interaction (e.g., a comparable duration in [42]). Nonetheless, the effect of gender, age and prior use experience on trust might be more detectable with longer interaction episodes. In the same vein, the application context and associated tasks, which are online banking services, can have a strong impact on trust. In our future work, we aim to explore other contexts such as healthcare and education.

## 6 Conclusion

AI-powered systems like chatbots are increasingly prevalent in many sectors. It is critical to ensure the trustworthiness of the systems, which should be developed with effective algorithms and human-centred design approaches. Prospective users of a trustworthy system can only benefit if they accept and adopt the system. Hence, it is deemed important to examine systematically factors influencing trust in AI-powered systems. Trust is an attitudinal construct that can be sensitive to demographic variables such as gender, age, and prior experience interacting with similar entities, human as well as non-human. Based on the results of our empirical study on the effect of different characteristics of customer service chatbots, these demographic variables did not play any significant role in influencing trust in the chatbots. This observation lent further evidence to the conclusion of some existing work while defying the others. Overall, the landscape of trust in AI is evolving as well as diversifying. To state the obvious: more research needs to be conducted to gain insights into the design of AI-powered systems that improve the quality of huma lives in a fair and safe manner.

# References

1. Adam, M., Wessel, M., Benlian, A.: AI-based chatbots in customer service and their effects on user compliance. Electron. Mark. **31**(2), 427–445 (2021)
2. Araujo, T.: Living up to the chatbot hype: the influence of anthropomorphic design cues and communicative agency framing on conversational agent and company perceptions. Comput. Hum. Behav. **85**, 183–189 (2018)
3. Ashktorab, Z., Jain, M., Liao, Q.V., Weisz, J.D.: Resilient chat- bots: repair strategy preferences for conversational breakdowns. In: Proceedings of the 2019 CHI Conference on Human Factors in Computing Systems, pp. 1–12 (2019)
4. Blut, M., Wang, C., Wünderlich, N.V., Brock, C.: Understanding anthropomorphism in service provision: a meta-analysis of physical robots, chatbots, and other AI. J. Acad. Mark. Sci. **49**(4), 632–658 (2021)
5. Brzowski, M., Nathan-Roberts, D.: Trust measurement in human– automation interaction: a systematic review. In: Proceedings of the Human Factors and Ergonomics Society Annual Meeting, vol. 63, pp. 1595–1599. SAGE, Los Angeles (2019)
6. Buchan, N.R., Croson, R.T.A., Solnick, S.: Trust and gender: an examination of behavior and beliefs in the investment game. J. Econ. Behav. Organ. **68**(3–4), 466–476 (2008)
7. Ciechanowski, L., Przegalinska, A., Magnuski, M., Gloor, P.: In the shades of the uncanny valley: an experimental study of human–chatbot interaction. Future Gener. Comput. Syst. **92**, 539–548 (2019)
8. Corritore, C.L., Kracher, B., Wiedenbeck, S.: On-line trust: concepts, evolving themes, a model. Int. J. Hum. Comput. Stud. **58**(6), 737–758 (2003)
9. De Visser, E.J., et al.: Almost human: anthropomorphism increases trust resilience in cognitive agents. J. Exp. Psychol. Appl. **22**(3), 331 (2016)
10. Drift: The 2018 State of Chatbots Report. Technical report (2018). https://www.drift.com/blog/chatbots-report/
11. Følstad, A., Taylor, C.: Conversational repair in chatbots for customer service: the effect of expressing uncertainty and suggesting alternatives. In: Følstad, A., et al. (eds.) CONVERSATIONS 2019. LNCS, vol. 11970, pp. 201–214. Springer, Cham (2020). https://doi.org/10.1007/978-3-030-39540-7_14
12. Følstad, A., Taylor, C.: Investigating the user experience of customer service chatbot interaction: a framework for qualitative analysis of chatbot dialogues. Qual. User Exp. **6**(1), 1–17 (2021). https://doi.org/10.1007/s41233-021-00046-5
13. Forgas, J.P., Laham, S.M.: Halo effects. In: Pohl, R.F. (ed.) Cognitive Illusions: Intriguing Phenomena in Thinking, Judgment and Memory, pp. 276–290. Taylor & Francis Group, Routledge (2017)
14. Go, E., Shyam Sundar, S.: Humanizing chatbots: the effects of visual, identity and conversational cues on humanness perceptions. Comput. Hum. Behav. **97**, 304–316 (2019)
15. van der Goot, M.J., Pilgrim, T.: Exploring age differences in motivations for and acceptance of chatbot communication in a customer service context. In: Følstad, A., et al. (eds.) CONVERSATIONS 2019. LNCS, vol. 11970, pp. 173–186. Springer, Cham (2020). https://doi.org/10.1007/978-3-030-39540-7_12
16. Hall, E.: Conversational Design. A Book Apart New York (2018)
17. Hamacher, A., Bianchi-Berthouze, N., Pipe, A.G., Eder, K.: Believing in BERT: using expressive communication to enhance trust and counteract operational error in physical human-robot interaction. In: Proceedings of 25th IEEE International Symposium on Robot and Human Interactive Communication (RO-MAN), pp. 493–500 (2016)
18. Hancock, P.A., Kessler, T.T., Kaplan, A.D., Brill, J.C., Szalma, J.L.: Evolving trust in robots: specification through sequential and comparative meta-analyses. Hum. Factors **63**(7), 1196–1229 (2021)

19. Haselhuhn, M.P., Kennedy, J.A., Kray, L.J., Van Zant, A.B., Schweitzer, M.E.: Gender differences in trust dynamics: women trust more than men following a trust violation. J. Exp. Soc. Psychol. **56**, 104–109 (2015)
20. Hassenzahl, M.: The interplay of beauty, goodness, and usability in interactive products. Hum. Comput. Interact. **19**(4), 319–349 (2004)
21. Haugeland, I.K.F., Følstad, A., Taylor, C., Bjørkli, C.A.: Understanding the user experience of customer service chatbots: an experimental study of chatbot interaction design. Int. J. Hum. Comput. Stud. **161**, 102788 (2022)
22. Jenneboer, L., Herrando, C., Constantinides, E.: The impact of chatbots on customer loyalty: a systematic literature review. J. Theor. Appl. Electron. Commer. Res. **17**(1), 212–229 (2022)
23. Kasilingam, D.L.: Understanding the attitude and intention to use smartphone chatbots for shopping. Technol. Soc. **62**, 101280 (2020)
24. Laban, G., Araujo, T.: Working together with conversational agents: the relationship of perceived cooperation with service performance evaluations. In: Følstad, A., et al. (eds.) CONVERSATIONS 2019. LNCS, vol. 11970, pp. 215–228. Springer, Cham (2020). https://doi.org/10.1007/978-3-030-39540-7_15
25. Lankton, N.K., Harrison McKnight, D., Tripp, J.: Technology, humanness, and trust: rethinking trust in technology. J. Assoc. Inf. Syst. **16**(10), 1 (2015)
26. Law, E.L.-C., Følstad, A., van As, N.: Effects of humanlikeness and conversational breakdown on trust in chatbots for customer service. In: Proceedings of Nordic Human-Computer Interaction Conference (NordiCHI 2022), Aarhus, Denmark. ACM (2022)
27. Lortie, C.L., Guitton, M.J.: Judgment of the humanness of an interlocutor is in the eye of the beholder. PLoS ONE **6**(9), e25085 (2011)
28. Mayer, R.C., Davis, J.H., David Schoorman, F.: An integrative model of organizational trust. Acad. Manag. Rev. **20**(3), 709–734 (1995)
29. Harrison Mcknight, D., Carter, M., Thatcher, J.B., Clay, P.F.: Trust in a specific technology: An investigation of its components and measures. ACM Trans. Manag. Inf. Syst. (TMIS) **2**(2), 1–25 (2011)
30. McTear, M.: Conversational AI: dialogue systems, conversational agents, and chatbots. Synth. Lect. Hum. Lang. Technol. **13**(3), 1–251 (2020)
31. Myers, C.M., Pardo, L.F.L., Acosta-Ruiz, A., Canossa, A., Zhu, J.: Try, try, try again:" sequence analysis of user interaction data with a voice user interface. In: Proceedings of the 3rd Conference on Conversational User Interfaces (CUI 2021), pp. 1–8, Article no. 18. ACM, New York (2021)
32. Nordheim, C.B., Følstad, A., Bjørkli, C.A.: An initial model of trust in chatbots for customer service—findings from a questionnaire study. Interact. Comput. **31**(3), 317–335 (2019)
33. Pesonen, J.A.: Are you ok?' Students' trust in a chatbot providing support opportunities. In: Zaphiris, P., Ioannou, A. (eds.) HCII 2021. LNCS, vol. 12785, pp. 199–215. Springer, Cham (2021). https://doi.org/10.1007/978-3-030-77943-6_13
34. Radeke, M.K., Stahelski, A.J.: Altering age and gender stereotypes by creating the Halo and Horns effects with facial expressions. Humanit. Soc. Sci. Commun. **7**(1), 1–11 (2020)
35. Rapp, A., Curti, L., Boldi, A.: The human side of human - chatbot interaction: a systematic literature review of ten years of research on text-based chatbots. Int. J. Hum. Comput. Stud. **151**, 102630 (2021)
36. Rheu, M., Shin, J.Y., Peng, W., Huh-Yoo, J.: Systematic re- view: trust-building factors and implications for conversational agent design. Int. J. Hum. Comput. Interact. **37**(1), 81–96 (2021)
37. Rousseau, D.M., Sitkin, S.B., Burt, R.S., Camerer, C.: Not so different after all: a cross-discipline view of trust. Acad. Manag. Rev. **23**(3), 393–404 (1998)

38. Schegloff, E.A.: Conversation analysis and socially shared cognition. In: Resnick, L.B., Levine, J.M., Teasley, S.D. (eds.) Socially Shared Cognition. American Psychological Association, Washington, DC, US, pp. 150–171 (1991)
39. Schönitz, M.-S.: The horn effect in relationship marketing: a systematic literature review. In: Proceedings of the 48th European Marketing Academy, pp. 8378 (2019)
40. Schuetzler, R.M., Giboney, J.S., Mark Grimes, G., Nunamaker Jr, J.F.: The influence of conversational agent embodiment and conversational relevance on socially desirable responding. Decis. Support Syst. **114**, 94–102 (2018)
41. Shevat, A.: Designing Bots: Creating Conversational Experiences. O'Reilly Media Inc., Boston (2017)
42. Taylor, M.P., Jacobs, K., Subrahmanyam, K.V.J., et al.: Smart talk: how organizations and consumers are embracing voice and chat assistants. Technical report. Capgemini SE (2019)
43. Terblanche, N., Kidd, M.: Adoption factors and moderating effects of age and gender that influence the intention to use a non-directive reflective coaching chatbot. SAGE Open **12**(2), 21582440221096136 (2022)
44. Toader, D.-C., et al.: The effect of social presence and chatbot errors on trust. Sustainability **12**(1), 256 (2019)
45. Yan, W., Hall, A.S.M., Siehl, S., Grafman, J., Krueger, F.: Neural signatures of gender differences in interpersonal trust. Front. Hum. Neurosci. **14**, 225 (2020)
46. Yuksel, B.F., Collisson, P., Czerwinski, M.: Brains or beauty: how to engender trust in user-agent interactions. ACM Trans. Internet Technol. (TOIT) **17**(1), 1–20 (2017)
47. Zeffane, R.: Gender, individualism–collectivism and individuals' propensity to trust: a comparative exploratory study. J. Manag. Organ. **26**(4), 445–459 (2020)
48. Zhang, J.J.Y., Følstad, A., Bjørkli, C.A.: Organizational factors affecting successful implementation of chatbots for customer service. J. Internet Commer., 1–35 (2021)

# EaseOut: A Cross-Cultural Study of the Impact of a Conversation Agent on Leaving Video Meetings Early

Eureka Foong[1], Jack Jamieson[2]([⊠]), Hideaki Kuzuoka[1],
Naomi Yamashita[2], and Tomoki Nishida[1]

[1] University of Tokyo, Tokyo, Japan
eureka.foong@gmail.com, {kuzuoka,nishida}@cyber.t.u-tokyo.ac.jp
[2] NTT Communication Science Labs, Kyoto, Japan
jack@jackjamieson.net, naomiy@ieee.org

**Abstract.** Designing ways for people to engage in social interactions during remote work has become more critical than ever, but few CSCW researchers have studied how to support people in disengaging from these interactions. This could be challenging in online video meetings, where users must interrupt while maintaining a positive self-image. We evaluate the potential of a conversation agent to support leaving video meetings early through a system called EaseOut. In an experiment with 162 Japanese and US-based participants on Zoom, an agent interrupting online discussions improved perceptions of leaving participants, but did not significantly improve ease of leaving early. We highlight potential cultural differences–US-based users felt more annoyed by the agent and found its attempts to include the leaving participant as less effective. We contribute recommendations for future tools, including shifting the burden of interruption from the user to technology and providing legitimacy to users' reasons for leaving.

**Keywords:** video meetings · culture · conversation agent · leaving meetings

## 1 Introduction

Understanding and innovating ways for people to connect during remote work has become more critical than ever as more and more people participate in remote work [35]. While CSCW scholars have contributed ways to "engage" people in remote social activities through engaging content and well-timed notifications (e.g., [15,44]), relatively few have studied how to support people in disengaging from such activities. Research on text-based communication suggests that disengaging can be challenging, as people feel the need to project a

**Supplementary Information** The online version contains supplementary material available at https://doi.org/10.1007/978-3-031-42283-6_17.

positive self-image, for example by lying when they leave a conversation early [18]. Disengaging from online video meetings may pose an even bigger challenge. An industry survey showed that people across the globe use excuses, such as having a poor internet connection, to leave online video meetings early [49], and some users have designed software [13] and physical products [12] to help people "escape" online video meetings. Having control over when to participate in an online space is important for supporting privacy and autonomy in remote work (e.g., [6,32]), and at a broader level, people who are better able to manage boundaries between different activities in their work and personal lives experience better outcomes, such as reduced stress [25].

Recent research [11] suggests that a conversation agent (CA) can impact group dynamics to assist people who are hesitant to interrupt an ongoing discussion. However, we lack an understanding of how to design such agents to support disengaging from online meetings. Leveraging social strategies [47] such as offering a new perspective or asking a question could make it easier for people to interrupt, but we lack evidence about whether this would improve the effectiveness of a CA. Moreover, there may be cross-cultural differences in how CAs are perceived. For example, people in Japan have demonstrated more positive attitudes towards social robots than in the UK or US [34]. It is currently unclear how users across cultures would experience leaving an online video meeting early with the help of a conversation agent.

To better understand the impact of a conversation agent on ease and impressions of a person leaving an online video meeting early, we conducted an experiment with triads of US-based and Japanese participants ($N = 162$) using Ease-Out, a system that displays a conversation agent that makes an announcement when a participant needs to leave (Fig. 1). We compare US and Japan residents due to reported differences in their degree of collectivism and attitude toward virtual agents [17,34,36]. To begin, we conducted an informal, formative survey with 200 US-based and Japanese internet users, who reported that leaving formal video meetings with fewer than five participants was the most challenging, compared to larger or informal meetings. Therefore, we decided to study small groups completing a formal problem-solving task.

We invited ad-hoc triads to participate in an online remote study on Zoom, where they were asked to solve two fictitious survival scenarios (e.g., [26,40,46,52]) for 15 min each. To simulate the need to leave early, we asked

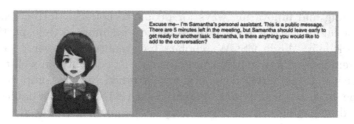

**Fig. 1.** The conversation agent that appeared at the top of participants' Instructions pages to notify that the leaving participant was needed for another task.

one random member of the group (the "leaving participant") to leave both discussions five minutes early to complete a separate task, while the remaining participants ("non-leaving participants") continued the discussion. At this time, the agent would appear, announcing aloud that the leaving participant needed to leave early. We manipulated whether the agent was publicly shown to the group or only privately shown to the leaving participant, and when it was publicly shown, we manipulated whether the agent used a social strategy [47] to ask the leaving participant to offer their perspective before leaving (Table 1). We hypothesized that this would not only increase positive perceptions of the agent but also improve ease and comfort of leaving and others' impressions of the leaving participant.

We asked the following research questions within the above context: **RQ 1:** How does a publicly visible agent that uses a social strategy to interrupt a discussion impact (A) a leaving participant's ease and comfort of leaving an online video meeting early, and (B) non-leaving participants' perceptions of the leaving participant? **RQ 2:** How might these features (publicly visible agent and social strategy use) impact US-based and Japanese users differently? To address these questions, we test 4 agents with different configurations, described in Sect. 3.1

Contrary to our expectations, the agent improved perceptions of the leaving participant (e.g., "The way the person left the meeting was appropriate"), but did not have a significant impact on ease or comfort of leaving for both Japanese and US-based participants. The agent achieved this by "taking the blame" for leaving participants and by providing a clear reason for their leaving. We also found evidence of cultural differences in how users experienced the agent's social strategy (i.e., inviting leaving participants in the conversation). Although the agent using the social strategy improved perceptions of the Japanese leaving participants, only the agent without the social strategy improved the perceptions of the US-based leaving participants.

Our work is the first of its kind to compare US-based and Japanese users' social dynamics of disengaging from online video meetings with the support of a conversation agent. Consistent with Grudin's [16] work on holistic collaborative systems, we show that different groups of users in online video meetings (i.e., leaving and non-leaving participants; users across cultures) perceive different benefits and drawbacks from using an agent. We recommend that future systems balance these competing needs, such as by lowering disruptiveness by limiting interruptions to one modality (e.g., visual or audio). Finally, we contribute a methodology for studying time-sensitive group dynamics (i.e., leaving a meeting on time) with online, ad-hoc groups.

## 2 Background

### 2.1 Supporting Remote Social Interactions

The Pew Research Center in 2020 estimated that the number of working professionals who would want to work remotely more than doubled from before to after the COVID-19 pandemic [35]. For decades, researchers in CSCW and human-computer interaction have designed ways to support people in engaging in remote social interactions in professional and personal settings (e.g., [9,48,51]). Researchers have studied various methods for encouraging remote social interactions in professional settings, such as representations of remote coworkers [29,50] and tools to indicate availability [42]. More recently, Song and colleagues [44] developed Minglr, an online platform for mediating informal conversations between virtual conference attendees, and others have built systems for prompting remote social interactions between relatives and friends [15,48,51]. As remote work becomes increasingly prevalent, innovative ways to interact with each other over distance will continue to proliferate.

While ample research has investigated ways to help people engage in remote social interactions, relatively little has helped us understand ways to support disengaging from remote social interactions.

Prior work in CSCW suggests users may find disengaging from remote social interactions challenging as they are motivated to project a positive self-image with conversation partners. Hancock et al. [18] found that people routinely deceive text-messaging partners for the sake of their self-image and that more than 40% of deceptive text messages are about leaving a conversation early. The authors demonstrated how the limited modality of text messaging creates enough ambiguity to allow users to "lie" and save face. In contrast, we know little about how to support users in disengaging from online video meetings, an increasingly common feature of remote work [49]. People across cultures deceive colleagues when leaving online video meetings, as demonstrated by a survey of 3,100 people in 10 countries [49], which reported that between 16–19% of respondents had ever faked a poor internet connection to leave a video meeting early. Additionally, there are several user-made interventions that use deception to support leaving online video meetings early, such as *Zoom Escaper* [13], which self-sabotages one's audio stream with disruptive sound effects (e.g., a crying baby) and *Yomicomu* [12], which places a physical "buffering" symbol in front of one's face to insinuate a poor internet connection. These examples illustrate some existing challenges and solutions for disengaging from online video meetings while maintaining a positive self-image.

Another challenging aspect of leaving online video meetings is finding opportunities to interrupt an ongoing conversation. Seminal work by Abigail Sellen [41] suggests that people find it more difficult to interrupt and gain control of a conversation in online video-mediated spaces compared to face-to-face conversations. These findings echo broader research in CSCW, which suggests that there may be fewer social, non-verbal cues, such as turning one's body away, to facilitate shifts in a conversation (e.g., media richness theory [10]).

More broadly, researchers beyond the CSCW domain have found that interrupting an ongoing conversation is a challenging process that involves the use of various social strategies, including "reactive" and "proactive" speech. Scholars recommend various ways to appropriately interrupt, which include being direct when wanting to change the topic of a discussion [28,37]. Thomas and colleagues [47] found support that certain types of speech, such as offering consent (i.e., agreeing or endorsing what another person has said) and requesting information (i.e., asking a question), are "reactive" types of speech that relinquish one's turn to speak in a conversation. On the other hand, offering new information, replying to another speaker, and creating dissent are "proactive" types of speech that allow one to gain a turn to speak. We speculate that interrupting to leave an online video meeting early would also require one to balance the use of these strategies, by first "proactively" gaining control of a conversation, and then "reactively" relinquishing control to leave the meeting.

Adding to these challenges are several potential confounding factors, such as culture, psychological collectivism, and group conformity (e.g., [21]); gender, age, and race [5,33,43], personality [22,37], and experience with online video conferencing. For example, leaving a meeting early by interrupting an ongoing conversation could be more challenging for people with a higher level of psychological collectivism (i.e., regard for in-group norms and goals). This is particularly important for understanding people in the United States and Japan, which strongly differ in terms of individualism/collectivism, according to Hofstede's cultural dimensions [19].

## 3  Method

To answer our research questions, we conducted an online experiment. We took a multi-faceted approach to understanding participants' experiences in this study. This included capturing behavioral and attitudinal measures, such as: 1) survey measures taken during and after the experiment, 2) semi-structured interviews after the experiment, and 3) coding video recordings of participants' reactions to the agent.

### 3.1  Experimental Study Design

We conducted a $2 \times 2$ between- and within-subjects online experiment with Japanese and US-based participants who participated in two online video discussions in groups of three, where one participant was asked to leave both discussions five minutes early. Participants viewed an online meeting using Zoom on the left side of their screen and viewed an "instructions" page on the right side of their screen. To simulate a group problem-solving discussion, we asked participants to decide as a group the ranking of different items for two survival scenarios [26,40,46], see Supplementary Materials for full details.

We designed EaseOut, a web app that displays a simple conversation agent and announces when the leaving participant should leave the meeting. This agent appeared on the "Instructions" page, which was visible to participants throughout the group discussions (see Fig. 1. We chose to display an anthropomorphic agent to increase user familiarity with the agent and make it seem more like a part of the group. We designed an anthropomorphic agent that appeared feminine, as prior work suggests that these features are more likely to be accepted by online users (e.g., [7,8]).

To understand the impact of the conversational agent's visibility, all groups took part in a discussion where an agent was publicly visible to everyone in the group (public) and a discussion where the agent was only shown to the leaving participant (private; see Agent Design section below). This was our within-subjects comparison variable. To prevent possible sequence effects [1], we counterbalanced these conditions so that half of the participants were shown the private condition first, while the other half were shown the public condition first.

Additionally, we manipulated whether different groups saw an agent with or without a social strategy (i.e., saying to the group: "[Leaving participant's name], is there anything you would like to add to the conversation?"). Because this social strategy is directed toward the group, we used it only when the public, and not the private agent, was shown (Table 1). This was our between-subjects variable.

To reduce the likelihood that participants would miss the agent's message, the agent played an audio cue in both private and public conditions, and the message was also displayed on the screen. In the public condition, the agent additionally read the message aloud. The agent did not read the message aloud to the leaving participant in the private condition. The agent was automatically activated five minutes before the end of each discussion.

## 3.2   Survey Design

Participants were asked to rate on a scale of 1 (strongly disagree) to 5 (strongly agree) how much they agreed or disagreed with several statements. We measured several factors, including *leaving participants' perceptions of the process of leaving* (e.g., "I felt awkward to leave the meeting early"); *non-leaving participants' perceptions of the leaving participant* (e.g., "'The way the person-people left the meeting was appropriate"); and all participants' perceptions of the agent, in line with prior work [11] (e.g., "The agent's behavior was appropriate" and "The agent interrupted my thoughts,"). In most cases, these factors were measured across multiple survey items. The full survey is included in the supplementary materials.

**Table 1.** The four study conditions used in this study. In the first two conditions, participants saw the privately displayed agent first, followed by the public agent with or without social strategy. In the last two conditions, participants saw the public agent with or without social strategy first, followed by the private agent.

| First discussion | | Second discussion |
|---|---|---|
| Private | → | Public with social strategy |
| Private | → | Public (no social strategy) |
| Public with social strategy | → | Private |
| Public (no social strategy) | → | Private |

In addition to demographic variables such as education and ethnicity, we accounted for several potential confounding variables based on cultural and other differences among participants. For example, individual differences in group conformity or psychological collectivism can impact how group members are perceived by other members (e.g., [43]). Therefore, we adapted Jackson and colleagues' [21] measure of psychological collectivism, which asked for participants' agreement with four statements (e.g., "I followed the norms of that group"). We also accounted for gender; age; and baseline comfort with and acceptability of leaving video meetings early. Finally, since extraversion and agreeableness are associated with assertiveness during social interactions [22], we included measures of these factors, using an abridged version of the Big Five personality scale [14].

## 3.3    Procedure

We used two popular freelancing platforms–Lancers[1] and Prolific[2]–to recruit participants based in Japan and the US, respectively. Participants were told that they would be taking part in a study to develop better group problem-solving tools. After filling out a screening survey, eligible participants were scheduled to attend a group session with two other anonymous participants. To control for possible effects of time, we held study sessions via Zoom almost every weekday for 12 weeks between June and August 2021 at 5:00 PM Pacific Time and either 5:00 PM or 7:00 PM Japan Time in each participant's local time zone.

Three team members (two English-speaking and one Japanese-speaking) conducted the study sessions. At the beginning of each session, the experiment confirmed that all participants could see and hear through their headphones, and everyone had their camera on and displayed a first name. Next, the experimenter introduced the study as one related to understanding group collaboration in online meetings. Participants then read and signed a consent form in either Japanese or English. At the end of this consent form, we also asked participants about their favorite digital writing tool for a separate study task. We asked this because the leaving participant would later be asked to leave each discussion early to help with this separate task, and we wanted to make the need to leave convincing. The experimenter then made sure that participants could enter and leave the virtual "breakout room" where the experimenter would remain during the group's discussion. As a way to heighten status differences in the group and potentially increase the difficulty of leaving the discussion early, the experimenter then asked one participant to volunteer to be the group leader. Then, the experimenter surreptitiously used a random number generator to assign one of the remaining participants as the "leaving participant."

Next, the experimenter sent each participant a unique link to a video describing the study procedure, which they were asked to watch quietly on their own. The videos were identical except that the leaving participant's video included an instruction that the experimenter needed their help with an additional task,

---

[1]  https://lancers.co.jp/en/.
[2]  https://prolific.co.

so they were to leave the discussion and enter the breakout room five minutes before the end of each discussion. While the non-leaving participants were not explicitly told that the leaving participant would need to leave early, the leaving participant was free to tell the rest of the group if they wished.

In each discussion, participants were asked to complete a 15-minute group ranking task [26,40,46,53], during which they kept both their zoom window and an instructions page visible on their screen. A 15-minute timer was visible on all participants' instructions pages.

The experimenter waited in the breakout room and noted if and when the leaving participant joined the breakout room. The leaving participant was asked to answer an open-ended question about the digital writing tool they mentioned earlier in the study, writing as much as possible within the remaining discussion time. At the end of the 15-minute discussion time, both the experimenter and the leaving participant returned to the main room to the rest of the group. Participants were then asked to complete a survey about the discussion (see Sect. 3.2). After the first session, there was a short break, and then the second discussion followed the same procedure. The survey after the second discussion included additional questions to measure demographic and other potential confounding variables. Finally, the experimenter briefly interviewed participants about what they thought the study was about and then debriefed them on the true purpose. The leaving participant was interviewed separately from the non-leaving participants and was asked additional questions about their perception of the agent and their experience leaving the discussions early.

Each session took 1.5 h and participants were compensated with $30 USD or 3000 Japanese yen. All procedures were approved by our institutions' ethical review boards.

### 3.4 Participants

We recruited 180 participants (90 Japanese and 90 US-based) in 60 groups, out of which 162 participants (78 Japanese and 84 US-based) were included in our final analysis. We aimed to recruit about 15 groups in each of the four conditions, based on recommendations from prior work [3,4]. We excluded six groups due to recruitment and technical errors (e.g., where participants reported they could not see or hear the agent, one group where two participants knew each other, etc.)

Among participants, women were a majority (Japan: 60% women, 40% men; US: 62% women, 1% non-binary, 37% men). On average, Japanese participants were 34 years old (range = 19–68 years old), while US-based participants were 30 years old (range = 20–57 years old). The majority had at least a bachelor's degree (Japan: 77% US: 80%). All Japanese participants were Asian, and US participants were 60% white, 26% Asian, 7% Black or African American, 1% Middle Eastern, and 1% American Indian or Alaska Native, and <5% identified as multi-racial. Overall, Japanese (median = 3, $M = 2.98$, $SD = 0.65$) and US-based (median = 2.6, $M = 2.61$, $SD = 0.83$) participants reported being moderately extraverted. Similarly, Japanese (median = 4.0, $M = 3.75$, $SD = 0.71$) and

US-based participants (median = 4.25, $M$ = 4.14, $SD$ = 0.66) reported being highly agreeable.

## 3.5  Data Analyses

To reduce dimensionality and improve the interpretability of the survey results, we combined items into larger factors where appropriate, such as "ease and comfort of leaving," "group conformity," "agreeableness," "extraversion," and "baseline ease and comfort of leaving meetings early." To determine suitability for dimension reduction, evaluated each factor's model fit using confirmatory factor analysis and reliability using Cronbach's $\alpha$. We dropped low-loading items from each factor to achieve acceptable levels[3] (model fit: CFI > 0.95, TFI > 0.95, RMSEA < 0.05 [23]; reliability: $\alpha$ >= 0.5   [39]. We expected reliability to be moderate given the small number of survey items [39]. We report on the validity and reliability of all our final factors in the Supplementary Materials.

We reduced two survey items into binary variables: 1) frequency of observing others leave video meetings early, and 2) frequency of leaving video meetings early. Half of the participants reported that their frequency of observing others leaving video meetings early was "never" or "less than once a month" (45.1%). Hence, we recoded this survey item from a categorical to a binary variable, with '0' representing less than once a month and '1' representing more than once a month. We repeated this process for participants' frequency of leaving video meetings early, for which we observed nearly half (38%) of participants answering "never." Therefore, we recoded this variable, with '0' representing never, and '1' representing at least less than once a month.

To provide detail about participants' reactions to the agent, two independent coders on our team (one native English and one native Japanese speaker) coded participants' reactions to the agent [45]. The coders developed a coding scheme by first viewing the recording of each group's estimated moment of experiencing the agent in their native language. After open coding and memoing separately [45], the coders discussed their results to develop an initial coding scheme, which measured: 1) Did the leaving participant leave? 2) Did the leaving participant mention or explain needing to leave? 3) Did the leaving participant contribute to the discussion after the agent appeared, and if so, which group member initiated their participation? 4) Had the group already completed the discussion prior to the agent appearing?

The coders then coded a random sample of 10% (n = 12) of the recordings, and then discussed and resolved differences to refine the coding scheme until they achieved moderate to high inter-rater reliability measured by Cohen's Kappa. Prior to analysis, we excluded an additional two discussions from the US-based data, in which the leaving participants had left before the agent appeared.

The three experimenters also wrote memos during and after the interviews with participants. They discussed these together and found considerable overlap.

---

[3] We removed two factors with poor model fit and reliability, "baseline motivation to contribute to the group" and "baseline motivation to appear polite.".

The first author collated memos into themes such as "perceptions of the agent," "benefits and drawbacks of the agent," and "benefits and drawbacks of the social strategy content."

## 4 Results

### 4.1 Manipulation and Confound Checks

Most participants could see and hear the agent clearly during the study ($M = 4.5$, mode $= 5.0$) on a scale of $1 =$ strongly disagree, $5 =$ strongly agree). Due to a technical limitation with the automated voice tool powering the agent, some participants may have heard a male rather than a female voice. However, a manipulation check showed that the majority (on average 80.5% in both discussions) heard a female voice. At the time of our debriefing interviews, 62% of participants (55% Japanese, 69% US-based) expressed awareness or suspicions about the true purpose of the study (i.e., understanding experiences around leaving meetings). During the experiment itself, we observed that all participants reacted authentically to the agent when it appeared, only discerning the true purpose of the study toward the end of the experiment, which we confirmed during the debriefing interviews. Besides that, using Chi-square and Kruskall-Wallis H tests, we did not find evidence that participants across study conditions differed significantly on any of the demographic or potential confounding variables listed in Sect. 3.2 (in all cases, p > .05).

### 4.2 Baseline Behaviors and Attitudes

Participants' baseline view of the ease and comfort of leaving video meetings early was slightly negative, rated on a scale from 1 to 5. Japanese participants (median $= 2.0$) reported less comfort than US participants (median $= 2.5$), U $= 2348$, p $= 0.005$. However, the perceived acceptability of other people leaving a meeting early was higher for Japanese participants (median $= 4.0$) than for US participants (median $= 3.0$), U $= 4143$, p $= .003$. Most participants reported having video meetings at least once a week (Japanese: 53%; US-based: 79%). Most US-based participants (42%) reported leaving video meetings early less than once a month, while most Japanese participants (56%) had never done this before, $\chi^2(1, 4) = 29.44$, $p < .001$. About 71% of US participants and 37% of Japanese participants had seen someone else leave a meeting early at least once a month, $\chi^2(1, 4) = 30.86$, $p < .001$.

### 4.3 RQ 1: Impact Across Japanese and US-Based Participants

**Leaving Participant's Ease and Comfort.** Table 2 indicates that the public and private agents both led to similar levels of ease and comfort for the leaving participant, with or without the social strategy. Furthermore, comparing the two public agents (across all participants), we did not find a significant difference in ease and comfort of leaving based on whether there was a social strategy (median = 3.5 or no social strategy (median = 3.25), U = 403, p = .50.

However, qualitative results suggest that the public agent seemed to benefit users by helping them find a time to raise the issue of leaving and feel less rude to interrupt the discussion themselves. For example, some participants described that the public agent helped them prioritize other tasks without having to focus on announcing their departure: "[in the private condition] It somewhat took my focus away from the whole discussion" (US-based leaving participant, Group 32, with social strategy). Another benefit to the public condition was its perceived consideration for the other discussion members: "The [private agent] just felt rude. I don't know if the others saw the same message, and I told the participants of the reason I was leaving, since they couldn't see what I saw" (US-based leaving participant, Group 14, with social strategy).

In short, while neither the public agent nor the social strategy led to a statistically significant difference in leaving participants' comfort, some felt that the public agent allowed them to be less rude and to pay more attention to the discussion at hand.

**Perceptions of Leaving Participants.** Evaluating the Japanese and US-based groups together (*group = all*), Fig. 2 shows that, in conditions where the agent used a social strategy, impressions about the leaving participant were more positive with the public agent than with the private agent. However, there was no difference in the groups with no social strategy.

Our findings suggest that the public agent in general may have supported more positive impressions toward the leaving participant by providing non-leaving participants with a clear reason for their early exit. Participants were less likely to provide their own reason for leaving with the public agent than with the private agent (US: $\chi^2(1, 1) = 7.64$, $p < .01$; Japan: $\chi^2(1, 1) = 8.21$, $p < .01$), suggesting that the public agent took on that burden. As one Japanese participant said about the public agent: "The [public agent] increased awareness that it was not the person's fault [for leaving early]" (Japanese non-leaving participant, Group 48, with social strategy).

Adding to this, one non-leaving participant described being confused in the private agent condition when it appeared that another participant had sud-

**Table 2.** Median scores and Wilcoxon signed-rank tests comparing the conditions, grouped into all participants, only Japanese participants, and only US participants. There was no difference between the public and private conditions regarding *comfort and ease of leaving*.

| | Group | Public social strategy | Private | W | p | Public no social strategy | Private | W | p |
|---|---|---|---|---|---|---|---|---|---|
| Comfort + | All | 3.50 | 3.25 | 128 | .35 | 3.25 | 3.38 | 145.5 | .44 |
| ease of | JP | 3.75 | 3.00 | 14.0 | .05 | 3.50 | 3.75 | 40 | .74 |
| leaving | US | 3.50 | 3.25 | 37.5 | .57 | 3.00 | 2.75 | 24.5 | .17 |

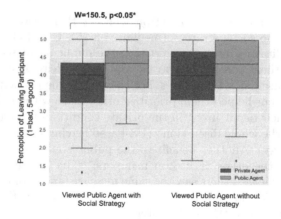

**Fig. 2.** A box plot of the ratings of the perceptions of the leaving participant across all participants. Ratings were significantly higher when the agent was public than when it was private for groups who were shown the public agent that used a social strategy. We did not find a significant difference between ratings with the public and private agent for groups who were shown the public agent that did not use a social strategy.

denly left the discussion without justifying their departure. Hence, knowing why a group member needs to leave could help maintain the leaving participant's impressions in the group: "When [the leaving participant] just left, most people wouldn't know if he got disconnected, whether or not they should continue, whether we should just stop and wait for him... [it caused] a little bit of confusion." (US-based non-leaving participant, Group 4, without social strategy)

**Impressions of the Agent.** Table 3 shows that both leaving and non-leaving participants had a somewhat favorable impression of the agent's behavior, requests, and timing, but felt that the agent had moderately interrupted their thoughts. Mann-Whitney U-tests reported in that table indicate that leaving participants had more positive impressions that the agent's request made sense and that the timing of those requests was appropriate.

**Table 3.** A table describing differences between the median of leaving and non-leaving participants' perceptions of the public agent. Leaving and non-leaving participants' perceptions of the agents' requests and timing were significantly different.

| Survey Statement | Leaving | Non-leaving | $U$ | $p$ |
|---|---|---|---|---|
| Agent's behavior was appropriate | 4.0 | 4.0 | 3286 | .17 |
| Agent's requests made sense | 5.0 | 4.0 | 3686 | .00*** |
| Timing of agent's requests was appropriate | 5.0 | 4.0 | 3690 | .00*** |
| Agent interrupted my thoughts | 3.0 | 3.0 | 2925.5 | .97 |
| I was annoyed by the agent | 1.5 | 2.0 | 2506.5 | .13 |

We also examined whether impressions of the agent were different based on whether there was a social strategy, and found no statistically significant differences (in Wilcoxon sign-rank tests across all impression variables, p > .05).

The effectiveness of the agent appears to have been negatively impacted by perceptions that it was "loud," "intrusive," and spoke too slowly. For example, one participant explained, "I feel [like I am being] blunt [to the group] when there is an agent. The discussion stopped while the agent was speaking" (Japanese leaving participant, Group 33, without social strategy). Another participant described the agent as speaking too slowly: "I wanted to get out early because the agent talks lazily" (Japanese leaving participant, Group 53, without social strategy).

## 4.4   RQ 2: Comparing Japanese and US-Based Participants

Comparing the *US* and *JP* groups in Table 2 shows that both Japanese and US-based leaving participants experienced similar levels of ease and comfort with leaving the discussions early, with no statistically significant differences between groups. However, there were some differences between Japanese and US-based participants regarding non-leaving participants' perceptions of the leaving participant. Figure 3 shows that, for Japanese participants, the public agent that used a social strategy significantly improved perceptions of the leaving participant relative to the private agent. However, for US-based participants, the public agent that did *not* use a social strategy significantly improved perceptions of the leaving participant relative to the private agent.

We speculate that the agent with a social strategy may have heightened expectations to contribute to the discussion before leaving, especially for US-based participants. Through our qualitative coding, we found that US-based leaving participants were significantly more likely to attempt to participate in the discussion before leaving when the public agent used a social strategy, $\chi^2(1, 1) = 4.21$, $p < .05$, whereas Japanese leaving participants attempted to participate at the same rate, regardless of whether the public agent had used a social strategy or not, $\chi^2(1, 1) = 0.18$, $p = .67$.

We observed another behavioral difference between Japanese and US-based that may have influenced perceptions around leaving. In both groups, some leaving participants informed the rest of their group that they needed to leave early in the discussion. Japanese leaving participants (37%, n = 19 discussions) were significantly more likely than US-based leaving participants (7%, n = 4 discussions) to do this, $\chi^2(1, 1) = 12.83$, $p < .001$. This difference could be important because knowing that a member of the group needs to leave early could lead to better time management. For example, some groups structured the discussion to accommodate the leaving member. This was more common for the second discussion of each session, e.g., "The second time [the experimenter] did that to us, we had a game plan. We had a lot of time with [the leaving participant], to suss out [her opinions]" (US-based non-leaving participant, Group 17, with social strategy).

310    E. Foong et al.

**Impressions of the Agent.** To better understand Japanese and US-based participants' perceptions of the public agent with and without the social strategy, we first ran a series of Wilcoxon and Mann-Whitney U tests to compare participants' ratings across study conditions. In general, we did not find that the study conditions led to differences in either Japanese or US-based participants' impressions of the agent, with one exception. US-based leaving participants were more likely to find the agent with social strategy's behavior appropriate in the private (median = 5.0, $M = 4.87$, $SD = 0.35$) compared to the public (median = 5.0, $M = 4.27$, $SD = 1.1$) condition, $W = 0.0$, $p<.05$. Nevertheless, the magnitude of that difference was small. (See supplementary materials for full results.)

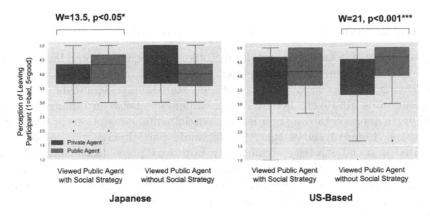

**Fig. 3.** For Japanese participants, the public agent that used a social strategy significantly improved the impressions of the leaving participant relative to the private agent. In contrast, for US-based participants, the public agent that did not use a social strategy significantly improved the impressions of the leaving participant.

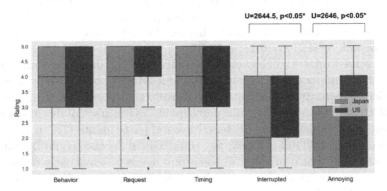

**Fig. 4.** US-based participants were significantly more likely to report having their thoughts interrupted by the agent and finding the agent annoying than Japanese participants.

Next, we proceeded to compare Japanese and US-based participants' perceptions of the public agent, regardless of social strategy content, using Mann-Whitney U tests. The results, shown in Fig. 4, indicate that US-based participants were more likely to agree that the agent "interrupted their thoughts" and that they were "annoyed by the agent" than were Japanese participants. Therefore, we find some evidence of cultural differences, showing that Japanese participants were more accepting of the agent.

Of note, we also noticed in our debriefing interviews that at least four (13%) of the US-based groups, but no Japanese groups, described the assistant agent (with or without the social strategy) as making the leaving participant seem "pretentious" or having a higher status than the rest. For example, as one US-based participant described: "[The agent]...sounded a little intrusive and demanding. Maybe instead of saying he needs to attend another meeting, the robot or assistant could say, 'You may need to excuse [the leaving participants'] presence.' 'Personal assistant' is a little pretentious. He should tell us himself [if he needs to leave]..." (US-based non-leaving participant, Group 9, with social strategy) Other US-based group members also described the leaving participant's higher status in sarcastic terms: "Oh, it's hard to have a personal assistant and be so important, my goodness. Millionaire [leaving participant's name]," (US-based non-leaving participant, Group 14, with social strategy). In contrast, no Japanese participants described the leaving participants in this way when the agent arrived.

## 5    Discussion

Compared to the private agent, the public agent helped improve impressions of the leaving participant among the rest of the group. Our interviews suggest that the agent was able to do this by providing a clear reason why participants needed to leave early. In contrast, the public agent was unable to significantly improve the ease and comfort of leaving early compared to the private agent, as hypothesized. As in prior work with conversation agents (e.g., [11]), the automatically triggered agent may have been seen as too disruptive to the ongoing conversation. Moreover, the public agent's influence on perceptions of the leaving participant was affected by the social strategy. Taking both groups together, these perceptions were only improved by the public agent when the agent used the social strategy. When looking at the groups separately, this pattern was only pronounced for Japanese participants. When isolating US-based participants, by contrast, the public agent only improved perceptions of the leaving participant when it did *not* use a social strategy. This suggests that conversation agents could be improved using social strategies from psychological research (e.g., [47]). However, this should be approached judiciously, with consideration for cultural differences such as attitudes toward conversational agents in general, and attitudes among some that employing a virtual assistant could be "pretentious."

Below, we further describe positive insights from this study, including design implications, the implications for different user groups, and opportunities to extend this work to other contexts.

## 5.1   Design Implications

**Managing Disruptiveness.** In line with prior work [11], participants shared in the interviews that they sometimes felt interrupted or annoyed by the automatic agent's dialogue, due largely to its volume, speed, and perceived intrusiveness. There are several ways to address this, such as using non-audio cues or non-speech sounds or shortening the length of the agent's message. Additionally, designers could draw on social robotics research to design an agent that uses human gestures [20] or adapts its timing [27] to interrupt more naturally. Related to timing, our results show the promise of using alternative social strategies to facilitate leaving video meetings early, such as setting expectations about leaving early at the beginning of a meeting. In our study, leaving participants in about 21% of the individual discussions mentioned needing to leave early at the beginning of or during the meeting. In addition, some of our participants in the interviews also mentioned changing the structure of their meeting to better facilitate the leaving participant when these expectations had been set early on. Hence, although participants did not specify if this strategy could have replaced the use of an agent, we speculate that modifying the timing of the agent's notification to earlier in a meeting may provide additional benefits.

We also see opportunities to draw on research about conversation-aware video-conferencing systems to reduce disruptiveness; for example, Schmitt and colleagues [38] suggest ways to amplify visual "back channels" in video conferencing systems, such as by changing the color of the background to symbolize participants who are in agreement. These more subtle background cues might help participants recognize when a group member needs to leave early. However, care must be taken as these subtle cues require group members to have a mutually understood set of conventions.

**One Design Does Not Fit All.** We found that users' cultural backgrounds affected their acceptance of system features for leaving video meetings early. For example, perceptions of Japanese leaving participants significantly improved when the agent used a social strategy, but the perceptions of the US-based leaving participants only improved when the agent did not use a social strategy. Based on the interviews, we speculate that the agent may have heightened expectations for the US-based to participate and contribute to the group before leaving, but with limited time to gather their thoughts once the agent interrupted, US-based leaving participants may have left a more negative impression in their group. This may resonate with broader cultural differences in work meetings. Meetings in US work culture are often defined by substantial contributions from all members of the group, while Japanese meetings often only take place after most decisions have already been made in smaller "pre-meetings" [24]. Hence, in Japanese culture, it is common to end a discussion by asking if anyone has any questions, even though group members are not expected to contribute anything further to the discussion. The agent with the social strategy may have implicitly activated this script for Japanese participants, making the scenario seem more relatable and transferring these positive impressions onto perceptions of the leaving participant. On the other hand, it may have had the opposite impact on leaving participants in the US-based groups, who may have felt unprepared to summarize their thoughts when the public agent appeared.

These results show that using an agent to interrupt a video meeting may impact users from different cultures differently, and we urge scholars to evaluate future social interaction tools within these larger social contexts.

**Supporting Small Group, Ad-Hoc Meetings and Beyond.** This study focused on supporting remote social interactions in small, ad-hoc groups. Therefore, we expect these findings will be most applicable in settings where groups of strangers interact in a professional context. For instance, we can imagine people using this tool during virtual conferences, virtual community deliberations (e.g., to gather opinions on public policy), or virtual civic hackathons [30]. We imagine that this kind of system could be built into existing tools, such as Minglr [44] and CoasterMe [42], to help more users feel comfortable engaging and disengaging from remote social interactions. We see future opportunities to study expectations for leaving video meetings in different settings, such as with familiar or unfamiliar peers and in larger or smaller groups.

# 6    Limitations and Future Work

We recognize the potential harms of using a stereotypically female agent. We acknowledge that our choice of presenting the agent as an assistant and as female plays into stereotypical and often harmful perceptions of women through AI-driven virtual assistants (e.g., [2,31]). Through this work and our other research as gender and equity HCI scholars, we do not condone the notion that virtual agents should be women by default. Our findings provide avenues for replacing such an agent in the future. For example, participants suggested that more subtle visual cues, such as a changing color or message, and including a reason for why the user needs to leave, may be more effective for signaling when a person needs to leave. Hence, we believe the potential harm of this study is limited to the experimental context itself, whereas the knowledge provided by this study outweighs these potential harms and contributes valuable information about how to design future systems better.

An important limitation is that the study design did not include a condition with no agent, which could have served as a control condition. Thus, while we can compare public and private conditions, we cannot compare our results to what would have happened without any agent. For example, differences between US and Japanese participants may have occurred even without the agent.

Another limitation is that leaving participants were not aware of how the agent appeared to other group members, which could have influenced their behavior (e.g., if they incorrectly thought others had seen the message in the private condition, they might not have felt a need to announce their departure). Additionally, the study design did not control whether participants told the other members about their departure in advance. Future research could control this by providing more specific instructions to participants and programming the agent to provide advance notice.

As this was an online experiment, the study duration was relatively short and may not have accurately captured the dynamics of real online video meetings. Nevertheless, given the benefits of doing a within-subjects comparison and wanting to ensure participants were engaged throughout the study, we felt it was necessary to keep the discussions as short as possible. Even with discussions limited to a 15-min duration, the overall length of the study was approximately 90 min due to the extra time needed for study instructions and surveys, potential latecomers, participant questions, and troubleshooting internet and audio connections. Again, we urge researchers to explore longitudinal study designs to overcome these limitations.

Additionally, while we strove to capture multiple measures in this study (e.g., interviews, surveys, qualitative coding of video recordings), there are other ways we could have identified even more positive insights from this research. For example, we could have allowed leaving participants to observe others leaving so that they could compare their experiences both as leaving and non-leaving participants. In future research with fewer time constraints, we would encourage researchers to explore the possibility of letting participants compare both experiences.

## 7  Conclusion

Maintaining a positive impression when leaving a remote social interaction is no simple feat, yet little research to date has examined the design of systems to support this key part of remote interaction. Through an experiment with Japanese and US-based participants, we are the first to show that a conversation agent can help improve the impressions of users who need to leave a video meeting early. Nevertheless, scholars and designers must carefully consider the design of such agents in future systems to reduce the disruptiveness of the agent, particularly for US-based users who may be more sensitive to the interruption. Our work also points to key ways the agent benefits different types of users and offers opportunities to expand the design space of these tools beyond conversation agents. As more and more people turn to remote work around the world, we show that it is not enough to encourage participation in remote social interactions but also help users manage impressions when they need to leave.

## References

1. Acheson, A.: Sequence effects. In: Encyclopedia of Research Design. SAGE Publications Inc, 2455 Teller Road, Thousand Oaks California 91320 United States (2010). https://doi.org/10.4135/9781412961288.n411
2. Adams, R., Loideáin, N.N.: Addressing indirect discrimination and gender stereotypes in AI virtual personal assistants: the role of international human rights law. Cambridge Int. Law J., 241–257 (2019). https://doi.org/10.4337/cilj.2019.02.04

3. Axtell, P.: The most productive meetings have fewer than 8 people. Harvard Bus. Rev., June 2018. https://hbr.org/2018/06/the-most-productive-meetings-have-fewer-than-8-people, section: Meetings

4. Barcikowski, R.S.: Statistical power with group mean as the unit of analysis. J. Educ. Stat. **6**(3), 267–285 (1981). https://doi.org/10.2307/1164877

5. Berger, J., Cohen, B.P., Zelditch, M.: Status characteristics and social interaction. Am. Sociol. Rev. **37**(3), 241–255 (1972). https://doi.org/10.2307/2093465

6. Boyle, M., Greenberg, S.: The language of privacy: learning from video media space analysis and design. ACM Trans. Comput.-Hum. Interact. **12**(2), 328–370 (2005). https://doi.org/10.1145/1067860.1067868

7. Cambre, J., Kulkarni, C.: One voice fits all? social implications and research challenges of designing voices for smart devices. In: Proceedings of the ACM on Human-Computer Interaction 3(CSCW), pp. 223:1–223:19, November 2019. https://doi.org/10.1145/3359325

8. Chang, R.C.S., Lu, H.P., Yang, P.: Stereotypes or golden rules? exploring likable voice traits of social robots as active aging companions for tech-savvy baby boomers in Taiwan. Comput. Hum. Behav. **84**, 194–210 (2018). https://doi.org/10.1016/j.chb.2018.02.025

9. Churchill, E., Nelson, L., Denoue, L., Murphy, P., Helfman, J.: The plasma poster network. In: O'Hara, K., Perry, M., Churchill, E., Russell, D. (eds.) Public and Situated Displays: Social and Interactional Aspects of Shared Display Technologies, pp. 233–260. The Kluwer International series on Computer Supported Cooperative Work. Springer, Netherlands (2003). https://doi.org/10.1007/978-94-017-2813-3_10

10. Daft, R.L., Lengel, R.H.: Organizational information requirements, media richness and structural design. Manage. Sci. **32**(5), 554–571 (1986). https://doi.org/10.1287/mnsc.32.5.554

11. Duan, W., Yamashita, N., Shirai, Y., Fussell, S.R.: Bridging fluency disparity between native and nonnative speakers in multilingual multiparty collaboration using a clarification agent. In: Proceedings of the ACM on Human-Computer Interaction 5(CSCW2), pp. 435:1–435:31, October 2021. https://doi.org/10.1145/3479579

12. Fujiwara, M.: Yomicomu / Online Drinking Party Escape Machine — Making Waste, August 2020. https://fujiwaram.com/archives/689

13. Gault, M.: Escape Zoom Meetings by Faking Technical Issues and Crying With This App. VICE, March 2021. https://www.vice.com/en/article/pkdnkz/escape-zoom-meetings-by-faking-technical-issues-and-crying-with-this-app

14. Goldberg, L.R.: The development of markers for the Big-Five factor structure. Psychol. Assess. **4**(1), 26–42 (1992). https://doi.org/10.1037/1040-3590.4.1.26

15. Grevet, C., Tang, A., Mynatt, E.: Eating alone, together: new forms of commensality. In: Proceedings of the 17th ACM International Conference on Supporting Group Work, GROUP 2012, , pp. 103–106. Association for Computing Machinery, New York, October 2012. https://doi.org/10.1145/2389176.2389192

16. Grudin, J.: Why CSCW applications fail: problems in the design and evaluation of organizational interfaces. In: Proceedings of the 1988 ACM conference on Computer-supported cooperative work, CSCW 88, pp. 85–93. Association for Computing Machinery, Portland, January 1988. https://doi.org/10.1145/62266.62273

17. Hamamura, T.: Are cultures becoming individualistic? a cross-temporal comparison of individualism-collectivism in the United States and Japan. Pers. Soc. Psychol. Rev. **16**(1), 3–24 (2012). https://doi.org/10.1177/1088868311411587

18. Hancock, J., Birnholtz, J., Bazarova, N., Guillory, J., Perlin, J., Amos, B.: Butler lies: awareness, deception and design. In: Proceedings of the SIGCHI Conference on Human Factors in Computing Systems, CHI 2009, pp. 517–526. Association for Computing Machinery, New York, April 2009. https://doi.org/10.1145/1518701. 1518782

19. Hofstede, G., Bond, M.H.: Hofstede's culture dimensions: an independent validation using rokeach's value survey. J. Cross Cult. Psychol. **15**(4), 417–433 (1984). https://doi.org/10.1177/0022002184015004003

20. Isaka, T., Aoki, R., Ohshima, N., Mukawa, N.: Study of socially appropriate robot behaviors in human-robot conversation closure. In: Proceedings of the 30th Australian Conference on Computer-Human Interaction, OzCHI 2018, pp. 519–523. Association for Computing Machinery, New York (2018). https://doi.org/10.1145/3292147.3292243

21. Jackson, C.L., Colquitt, J.A., Wesson, M.J., Zapata-Phelan, C.P.: Psychological collectivism: a measurement validation and linkage to group member performance. J. Appl. Psychol. **91**(4), 884–899 (2006). https://doi.org/10.1037/0021-9010.91.4. 884

22. Kammrath, L.K., McCarthy, M.H., Cortes, K., Friesen, C.: Picking one's battles: how assertiveness and unassertiveness abilities are associated with extraversion and agreeableness. Soc. Psychol. Pers. Sci. **6**(6), 622–629 (2015). https://doi.org/ 10.1177/1948550615572635

23. Kline, R.B.: Principles and Practice of Structural Equation Modeling, Fourth Edition. Guilford Publications, November 2015, google-Books-ID: Q61ECgAAQBAJ

24. Köhler, T., Gölz, M.: Meetings across cultures: cultural differences in meeting expectations and processes. In: Allen, J.A., Lehmann-Willenbrock, N., Rogelberg, S.G. (eds.) The Cambridge Handbook of Meeting Science, pp. 119–150. Cambridge Handbooks in Psychology, Cambridge University Press, Cambridge (2015). https://doi.org/10.1017/CBO9781107589735.007

25. Kossek, E.E., Ruderman, M.N., Braddy, P.W., Hannum, K.M.: Work-nonwork boundary management profiles: a person-centered approach. J. Vocat. Behav. **81**(1), 112–128 (2012). https://doi.org/10.1016/j.jvb.2012.04.003

26. Lafferty, J., Eady, P., Elmers, J.: The Desert Survival Problem. In: Experimental Learning Methods. Human Synergistics, Plymouth, Michigan (1974)

27. Lala, D., Inoue, K., Kawahara, T.: Smooth turn-taking by a robot using an online continuous model to generate turn-taking cues. In: 2019 International Conference on Multimodal Interaction, ICMI 2019, pp. 226–234. Association for Computing Machinery, New York (2019). https://doi.org/10.1145/3340555.3353727

28. Lankford, V.: OK interrupting-liberation from deadly conversations and deadly scripts. Trans. Anal. J. **19**(3), 145–147 (1989). https://doi.org/10.1177/ 036215378901900305

29. Lee, M.K., Takayama, L.: "Now, i have a body": uses and social norms for mobile remote presence in the workplace. In: Proceedings of the SIGCHI Conference on Human Factors in Computing Systems, CHI 2011, pp. 33–42. Association for Computing Machinery, New York, May 2011. https://doi.org/10.1145/1978942.1978950

30. Lodato, T.J., DiSalvo, C.: Issue-oriented hackathons as material participation. New Media Soc. **18**(4), 539–557 (2016). https://doi.org/10.1177/1461444816629467

31. Loideain, N.N., Adams, R.: From Alexa to Siri and the GDPR: the gendering of Virtual Personal Assistants and the role of Data Protection Impact Assessments. Comput. Law Secur. Rev. **36**, 105366 (2020). https://doi.org/10.1016/j.clsr.2019. 105366

32. Neustaedter, C., Greenberg, S., Boyle, M.: Blur filtration fails to preserve privacy for home-based video conferencing. ACM Trans. Comput.-Hum. Inter. **13**(1), 1–36 (2006). https://doi.org/10.1145/1143518.1143519

33. Ng, S.H., Brooke, M., Dunne, M.: Interruption and influence in discussion groups. J. Lang. Soc. Psychol. **14**(4), 369–381 (1995). https://doi.org/10.1177/0261927X950144003

34. Nomura, T.: Cultural differences in social acceptance of robots. In: 2017 26th IEEE International Symposium on Robot and Human Interactive Communication (RO-MAN), pp. 534–538, August 2017. https://doi.org/10.1109/ROMAN.2017.8172354, iSSN: 1944-9437

35. Parker, K., Horowitz, J.M., Minkin, R.: How Coronavirus Has Changed the Way Americans Work. Pew Research Center's Social & Demographic Trends Project, December 2020. https://www.pewresearch.org/social-trends/2020/12/09/how-the-coronavirus-outbreak-has-and-hasnt-changed-the-way-americans-work/

36. Robertson, J.: Robo sapiens japanicus: Robots, Gender, Family, and the Japanese Nation. University of California Press, Oakland, California, first edition edn (2017)

37. Ruiter, J.P.d., Mitterer, H., Enfield, N.J.: Projecting the End of a Speaker's Turn: A Cognitive Cornerstone of Conversation. Language **82**(3), 515–535 (2006). https://doi.org/10.1353/lan.2006.0130

38. Schmitt, M., Gunkel, S., Cesar, P., Bulterman, D.: Mitigating problems in video-mediated group discussions: towards conversation aware video-conferencing systems. In: Proceedings of the 2014 workshop on Understanding and Modeling Multiparty, Multimodal Interactions, UM3I 2014, pp. 39–44. Association for Computing Machinery, New York, November 2014. https://doi.org/10.1145/2666242.2666247

39. Schrepp, M.: On the usage of cronbach's alpha to measure reliability of UX scales. J. Usability Stud. **15**(4), 247–258 (2020)

40. ScoutShare: Arctic Survival Exercise (2020). https://scoutshare.org/Resources/Articles/arctic-survival-exercise

41. Sellen, A.J.: Speech patterns in video-mediated conversations. In: Proceedings of the SIGCHI Conference on Human Factors in Computing Systems, CHI 1992, pp. 49–59. Association for Computing Machinery, New York, June 1992. https://doi.org/10.1145/142750.142756

42. Shen, Y., Kelly, R.M.: CoasterMe: supporting informal workplace awareness through the everyday behaviour of drinking. In: Extended Abstracts of the 2020 CHI Conference on Human Factors in Computing Systems, CHI EA 2020, pp. 1–8. Association for Computing Machinery, New York, April 2020. https://doi.org/10.1145/3334480.3382824

43. Smith-Lovin, L., Brody, C.: Interruptions in group discussions: the effects of gender and group composition. Am. Sociological Rev. **54**(3), 424–435 (1989). https://doi.org/10.2307/2095614, publisher: [American Sociological Association, Sage Publications, Inc.]

44. Song, J., Riedl, C., Malone, T.W.: Online Mingling: Supporting Ad Hoc, Private Conversations at Virtual Conferences. SSRN Scholarly Paper ID 3662620, Social Science Research Network, Rochester, NY, July 2020. https://doi.org/10.2139/ssrn.3662620

45. Spradley, J.P.: Participant Observation. Wadsworth Publishing Company, January 1980. https://books.google.com/books/about/Participant_Observation.html?id=sQClDJXc5vkC

46. The Geographer Online: The Desert Survival Game (2021). https://www.thegeographeronline.net/uploads/2/6/6/2/26629356/the_desert_survival_problem_nhs.doc

47. Thomas, A.P., Roger, D., Bull, P.: A sequential analysis of informal dyadic conversation using Markov chains. Br. J. Soc. Psychol. **22**(3), 177–188 (1983). https://doi.org/10.1111/j.2044-8309.1983.tb00582.x

48. Tsujita, H., Tsukada, K., Siio, I.: InPhase: a communication system focused on "happy coincidences" of daily behaviors. In: CHI '09 Extended Abstracts on Human Factors in Computing Systems, CHI EA 2009, pp. 3401–3406. Association for Computing Machinery, New York, April 2009. https://doi.org/10.1145/1520340.1520493

49. Uniphore: New Consumer Survey on Video Conversations: Trends, Fails & Wins. Technical report, Uniphore (2021). https://www.uniphore.com/video-conversations-survey/

50. Venolia, G., Tang, J., Cervantes, R., Bly, S., Robertson, G., Lee, B., Inkpen, K.: Embodied social proxy: mediating interpersonal connection in hub-and-satellite teams. In: Proceedings of the SIGCHI Conference on Human Factors in Computing Systems, pp. 1049–1058. Association for Computing Machinery, New York, April 2010. https://doi.org/10.1145/1753326.1753482

51. Visser, T., Vastenburg, M., Keyson, D.: Designing to support social connectedness: the case of SnowGlobe. Int. J. Des. **5**, 129–142 (2011)

52. Yamashita, N., Echenique, A., Ishida, T., Hautasaari, A.: Lost in transmittance: how transmission lag enhances and deteriorates multilingual collaboration. In: Proceedings of the 2013 Conference on Computer Supported Cooperative Work, CSCW 2013, pp. 923–934. Association for Computing Machinery, New York, February 2013. https://doi.org/10.1145/2441776.2441881

53. Yamashita, N., Kuzuoka, H., Kudo, T., Hirata, K., Aramaki, E., Hattori, K.: How information sharing about care recipients by family caregivers impacts family communication. In: Proceedings of the 2018 CHI Conference on Human Factors in Computing Systems, CHI 2018, pp. 1–13. Association for Computing Machinery, Montreal QC, Canada, April 2018. https://doi.org/10.1145/3173574.3173796

# An AI Chat-Based Solution Aimed to Screen Postpartum Depression

Bakhtawar Ahtisham[✉], Seemal Tausif, Zoha Hayat Bhatti, Ayesha Masood, and Suleman Shahid

Lahore University of Management Sciences, Lahore, Pakistan
{24100301,24100024,24100010,24100018,suleman.shahid}@lums.edu.pk

**Abstract.** Postpartum depression is a mood disorder faced by approximately 1 in 7 women globally after giving birth. Such a large-scale issue is almost completely undiagnosed in Pakistan. One of the major causes of this is the fact that neither the women, nor the family is aware that such an issue exists. The family expectations surrounding a woman after she gives birth, especially in South Asia, is for her to "bounce back" to her original self - interacting normally with everyone etc. and this ultimately leads to women suppressing their emotions, and ignoring any prevalent symptoms of PPD. Through our research, we found that an AI based chat bot can potentially be the solution to screen postpartum depression, however to determine the effectiveness of such an approach, further extensive research should be conducted in the context of Pakistan.

**Keywords:** Empirical studies in HCI · maternal health · Pakistan

## 1 Introduction

Almost 80% of women in the Global South experience at least some symptoms of "baby blues" after they give birth [3]. The problem, however, occurs when these symptoms not only escalate but continue into the 5th-7th week postpartum. With increasing awareness about problems like depression, anxiety, autism etc., in Asian countries like Pakistan, it is unfortunate that postpartum depression (PPD) is an issue that is still severely unrecognised.

Common symptoms of postpartum depression include low mood, irritability, anxiety, excessive fatigue, appetite disorders, mental and motor disturbances, disruption of family and social communication, self-harming, suicidal thoughts, and feeling of guilt or inadequacy particularly regarding infant care [1]. It is also quite common for women in Asian culture to feel obligated to suppress negative emotions after the birth of a child. Often enough, these women can't even confide in their mothers or older relatives because of the generational gap. The majority of people in Pakistan regard depression as mere feelings of sadness instead of an actual mental disorder [10]. This means that it becomes hard for women to explain what they're going through and to seek help for it.

ⓒ The Author(s), under exclusive license to Springer Nature Switzerland AG 2023
J. Abdelnour Nocera et al. (Eds.): INTERACT 2023, LNCS 14143, pp. 319–328, 2023.
https://doi.org/10.1007/978-3-031-42283-6_18

Pakistan has the highest postpartum depression rate among Asian countries at a staggering total of around 63% [5,6]. But even this number is not an actual representation of the prevalence of PPD in Pakistan since a major number of cases are never diagnosed. Women in the Global South have been culturally conditioned to suppress their emotions, hence they often lack the apt vocabulary to express their feelings which becomes a reason for the prevalent language barrier between the woman going through these symptoms and those around her that makes PPD detection difficult.

Our research aims to understand how a woman experiencing PPD symptoms expresses herself and at what stage in the postpartum period can these symptoms be most effectively detected, diagnosed, and treated. We used a multi-factor approach in our research where we conducted focus groups with health professionals, surveys, and semi-structured interviews with mothers about their postpartum journey to gain more insights on this integral issue that remains largely undiagnosed in Pakistani women.

## 2    Related Work

Throughout the history of childbirth, it has been observed that the associated complications that most women face have been largely neglected. A common limitation in the screening methodology employed in conducting surveys and questionnaires is the use of Western tools like EPDS which resulted in language barrier issues and false positives in the results. A comparative study pertaining to the Asian culture is a more suitable approach towards potential problem-solving regarding PPD prevalence in this region.

Cultural practices like "chilla" in Pakistan and "omugwo/ olojojo omo" in Nigeria proved to be effective temporary deterrents in culminating the risks of PPD in new mothers [11]. In such practices, the household burden on a woman is reduced with the help of her mother, either by the woman taking residence in her mother's house or vice versa, decreasing the risk of PPD. However, research papers have evasively not included the restrictions that women face during their experiences of these practices [15]. These postnatal traditions and restrictions can be an isolating experience that increases the risk of PPD in women.

The primary reason why postpartum depression has been overlooked in Pakistan is the stigma associated with mental health, the role of religion, and other restrictions placed on women [16]. Through the culturally sensitive perspective, it is imperative to note that the idea of a 'one-stop solution' and collaboration between hospital wards is practically infeasible in Pakistan without spreading awareness regarding mental health to the public. In many conservative areas where the customs of the region are prioritised, the allocation of reproductive and psychological medical services to women is frowned upon.

Pakistan has a preterm birth rate of 15.7% - mothers of preterm infants are at higher risk of depression than mothers of term infants in the immediate postpartum period [4]. With an increase in anxiety, c-section, low level of education, and decrease in quality of prenatal care, the risk of PPD increases.

The screening methodology employed for the detection of PPD is quite inadequate when the social context of Pakistan is considered, primarily due to the usage of Western terminology, dialect, and sampling tools. In previous research, the Chi-square test, EPDS, logistic regression analysis, PHQ-9, and PRAMS-6 were used to get insight into women with PPD [12]. Although these tests and questionnaires were translated into Urdu to make sure they are understood, they failed to cater to the comprehension barrier of locals and their vernacular language. Local tests like Aga Khan University Anxiety and Depression Scale (AKUADS) are more effective in getting an insight on PPD into Pakistan.

The rigid gender stereotypes, early marriages, unplanned pregnancy, and partiality associated with the sex of the child are some of the leading factors of PPD in Pakistan. Marital abuse and violence during this time further increase the risk of developing PPD [17]. These findings suggest that couples-focused intervention from the prenatal period may reduce the risk of PPD [2]. However, there are no experienced practitioners available in Pakistan for couple therapy and counselling which makes this strategy ineffective.

If PPD remains undiagnosed and untreated during the initial stages, then the probability of it developing into the tertiary stage is fatal. Resentment towards a partner, panic attacks, and hallucinations are common at this stage. Previous research fails to acknowledge the severity of the problem and for data consolidation, developing empathy, and getting a comprehensive overview of the turbulent experience of PPD is critical. Research depicts that 5% of women with postpartum psychosis commit suicide [18]. A third of women hospitalised for postpartum psychosis expressed delusions about their infants and 4% even killed their child. Support for women in the pre and postnatal periods along with routine screening is necessary for detection and intervention [7].

Some existing products that test for postpartum depression mainly focus on screening through tools like Edinburgh Postnatal Depression Scale (EPDS) and the Patient Health Questionnaire (PHQ-9). These are tools that have been validated through thorough testing but in our cultural context, their efficiency and validity decrease because the questions are very binary and are not customised to cater to the various stages of postpartum depression. Another drawback of these questionnaires is that they tend to be very lengthy and tedious at times and since they are designed only for a one-time use, they have no features to keep track of a woman's symptoms throughout the entire critical postpartum period.

In conclusion, societal restrictions and mindset in Pakistan make counselling new mothers difficult, which increases the risk of developing postpartum depression. Previous research suggests remedies like 'buddy support' system, couples counselling, merging psychiatry wards with postnatal wards, and screening methodologies using internationally accepted tools. However, the limitations of these strategies make screening in Pakistan practically impossible.

# 3   User Research

The user research for this project was conducted in two phases. In the initial phase, contextual inquiry in a hospital, focus groups with medical professionals, and surveys were carried out to form an idea about the prevalence of postpartum depression in Pakistani women. The second phase of user research built on the progress from phase one and went on to develop an early prototype of a chatbot. This chatbot was proposed to help in diagnosing postpartum depression and thus subsequent interviews with mothers were conducted to test the feasibility of the idea.

The user group identified for the purposes of this research consisted of women of any/all ages with at least one child less than twelve months old. After much consideration, we decided to narrow down our target user group to women who belong to the upper-middle socio-economic class; those who have the resources to access technological devices and had moderate digital literacy. In addition, professionals such as gynaecologists, psychologists, midwives, and lady health visitors were also identified as potential users who could use our technological solution for screening purposes. In total, 18 participants were interviewed.

In the user research, a self-designed, semi-structured interview questionnaire was used for retrieving the users' demographic details (such as age and marital status), postpartum experience, and information regarding mode of delivery, current family members (including total number of children). The interview questions were crafted to resemble a casual conversation, aiming to put the interviewee at ease and encourage them to respond to personal inquiries.

# 4   Findings

## 4.1   Phase One

For the initial phase of our study, we carried out a contextual inquiry in Services Hospital Lahore (one of the largest public hospitals in Pakistan) at the post-natal and the immunisation wards where mothers were expected to come for routine postpartum checkups. A total of 7 interviews were conducted with mothers. To promote comfort in users, interviews were conducted by females in the local language of the respondents and these interviews were not filmed/audio recorded to prevent invasion of privacy given the sensitivity of the topic. The provision of closed spaces within the hospital ensured privacy and confidentiality.

Terms like postpartum depression, mood swings, and family planning were not used, mainly because of their controversial nature but also because the respondents had a low literacy rate and were not familiar with such terms. Gaps in the interviews due to these constraints were filled by observing visual cues which also helped our purpose of understanding and identifying the ways women from low socio-economic backgrounds use to express themselves. Most of the mothers we interviewed had recently given birth which clashed with our requirement for users who have enough postpartum experience. It was also conveyed by the hospital staff that mothers belonging to the lower socio-economic class usually do not visit the hospital for postpartum checkups due to personal reasons.

A separate interview was designed for gynaecologists which consisted of questions related to the prevalence and screening of postpartum depression amongst the women who visited the hospital, major contributing/risk factors of postpartum depression, suggestions on how to alleviate these symptoms in women, and prevention of postpartum depression. A focus group consisting of four gynaecologists was held, led mainly by two group members, in a private room so the discussion could ensue openly. Following this, a one-on-one interview was held with the gynaecology department head. The outcome of this series of discussions was that women belonging to the middle or upper socio-economic classes were more likely to talk openly about their familial situations and were capable of conveying any negative emotions they may feel postpartum. On the other hand, women belonging to the lower socio-economic classes felt themselves to be bound by cultural constraints and were less likely to speak about their issues [9]. Additionally, it was also noticed that to analyse the symptoms of postpartum depression, we needed to contact and hold interviews with mothers who have already been diagnosed with PPD.

Following on from the findings of the interviews, we conducted an anonymous survey consisting of basic questions and shared it amongst individuals of the authors' university via WhatsApp and Facebook. The prime purpose of deploying the survey was to get in touch with users belonging to a higher socio-economic background and who have already experienced PPD so that postpartum depression in the upper middle class could be assessed in further detail. The survey amounted to 7 responses and only three individuals agreed to an online interview due to the sensitivity of the topic and the hesitance of respondents in talking about their experiences. The interviewees explained in detail all the symptoms they faced and helped draft an appropriate picture of indicators that may help in diagnosing PPD by the use of statements like this: "I felt like everyone was moving on with their lives and I am stuck here with this tiny human being, it feels like time is not stopping and I am running after time." Further information regarding PPD and its prevalence was accessed by reviewing research papers.

### 4.2   Phase Two

The second phase of our user research incorporated the design implications that we identified from our initial on-field observations in the first phase. Through prior work, it has been established that interacting with an empathetic chatbot appeared to have a mitigating impact [14]. Moreover, a chatbot has the potential to make the user feel less secluded due to its interactive nature which includes a conversational mode of communication. Thus, we deployed a chatbot as a social actor feature in our preliminary app design, with the intention of gaining a more profound understanding of the pain points experienced by women and mitigating the communication barriers that we encountered previously. We conducted semi-structured online interviews using a snowballing approach. Due to the mothers' hectic schedules and the additional responsibilities of caring for their newborns, we often had to reschedule interviews based on their availability and convenience. During this phase, our prototype was used as a medium to engage with the mothers and get a deeper insight into their postpartum journey, perceptions regarding PPD, and the role that an AI-based intervention could play in facilitating their overall experience.

The key findings of our phase constituted the desire for a community based-interactions amongst new mothers, diagnosis, and acceptance of PPD symptoms in the Pakistani socio-cultural context, and the inherent need for having a platform to express their 'overwhelming emotions' immediately. All mothers were comfortable with using digital applications and recognized the pressing need for a community of mothers, where they could come together and share their experiences, thus fostering a sense of belonging and reducing the sense of isolation that often accompanies motherhood:

"I was obsessed with my baby. In my head when I was away, I used to feel like my baby was crying. That's insane. There should be advice on a platform: general affirmations for mothers that it is natural to feel this way. They are not alone." [Mother 10]

Moreover, due to the prevalent gender stereotypes and unfair division of parenthood responsibilities in Pakistan, child rearing is considered to be the sole responsibility of the new mother, and the traditional practice of 'chilla' further makes the motherhood journey an isolating experience for the new mother due to disconnected husband-wife interaction. Hence, through using the chatbot feature in our prototype, 15 mothers affirmed that expressing their emotions through the form of a conversation resulted in catharsis and this form of interaction had the potential to provide relief to mothers:

"Being someone who has experienced PPD firsthand, I would like to say that in PPD, the initial step is where someone has to diagnose it for you. So maybe I don't know how you can incorporate it but like how I recorded my feelings that I am feeling hopeless and I don't know how I feel. For me, I have been in therapy because of it so I have experienced it first hand and it has been brutal in my case. So when it was diagnosed, it was such a relief. There should be a place where they need to know that you are feeling this and you need help." [Mother 6]

"Catharsis - face-to-face professional availability at the spot is very important. At that point, we need a person who can understand us. An online platform will ensure an immediate connection with a mental health professional because bharas nikal dena (taking out frustration) is the most crucial aspect of therapy. Sometimes only talking things out works. Or maybe there can be an option to psycho-educate women through recordings". [Mother 3]

Hence, the two phases of our user research reflect the pain points of the new mothers and how an AI-based intervention in the form of an interactive chatbot can act as a form of emotional support for new mothers and make the postpartum journey less solitary for them. The main feature that our prototype entailed was a chatbot in the form of a daily logger where the first question that would appear after logging in would be "How are you feeling today?". In this way through a conversational medium, mothers could log in their daily symptoms like mood, sleep schedule, diet, exercise, and bonding with the baby in the form of a journal entry. However, since we employed the chatbot as a social actor, the interaction with it in the form of customized recommendations for diet and exercise, and if the symptoms persist and are severe, suggesting professional aid would help in screening for PPD implicitly. Moreover, all this data logged in by the mothers could be accessed through the 'Insights' option where they can view and track their progress, hence the AI-based chatbot would also use daily positive affirmations for the mothers to make their journey less isolating. Additionally, further suggestions in the form of accessing immediate professional mental health on the platform and a plausible way to digitally connect with other new mothers and form a community were given by mothers who felt these features should be an integral part of any proposed chat-box solution. Hence, incorporating these features in the chatbot can potentially make it an effective screening tool for PPD.

## 5 Results and Discussion

As research suggests, postpartum depression is a serious mental health condition characterised by feelings of sadness, anxiety, and hopelessness that can be long-lasting and debilitating. While the possible causes and the rehabilitation of PPD are well-researched in Western countries, there is a significant gap in research on PPD in the South Asian context. In our research, we recognized the importance of providing postpartum mothers with accessible and anonymous support during their challenging times. To address this need, we incorporated a chatbot as the main functionality into our preliminary app design. The chatbot's anonymity and ease of use made it a valuable outlet for these mothers, who repeatedly emphasised the necessity of emotional support.

Previous studies regarding this subject have aimed to develop and evaluate a user-friendly Q&A chatbot that provided quality content and expertise for perinatal women's and their partners' obstetric health care, however, our research tried to incorporate the benefits of an AI-powered chatbot in the previous studies with the unique context of postpartum mental health in South-Asia [13]. By understanding the cultural and social factors that affect PPD, we aimed to propose more targeted and effective interventions that meet the unique needs of South Asian mothers. By engaging with an AI chatbot, users are afforded a safe space to openly express their thoughts and emotions without the concerns associated with societal taboos surrounding PPD. This freedom from judgement and fear of stigma can encourage users to discuss their experiences more openly, leading to more accurate symptom reporting and a deeper understanding of their condition. Moreover, the scarcity of mental health professionals, as indicated during our initial research phase, combined with users' hesitance in divulging their experiences, highlights a pressing need for alternative approaches to detecting and addressing PPD. Postpartum mothers were able to engage with the chatbot easily and conveniently, without the need for additional resources or specialised training. This accessibility contributed to the chatbot's utility as a readily available resource for emotional support, meeting the specific needs of postpartum mothers in an accessible and user-friendly manner.

Considering that motherhood often isolates Pakistani women, burdening them with the sole responsibility of childcare, our prototype's chatbot proved valuable in facilitating the expression of women's emotions and experiences. The majority of mothers expressed that engaging in conversations through the chatbot brought about catharsis and had the potential to provide relief. Consequently, the feedback received from mothers while utilising this specific feature of the chatbot indicates significant potential for its effective development. An important aspect of this proposed method would be to identify the words and expressions women use to express themselves in the various stages of postpartum depression in the Global South. An AI-based model could be trained on this data thus allowing it to carry out proper conversations with the user while keeping track of the frequency of certain words used by them. Keeping in mind the Pakistani context, the language barrier would need to be overcome by making sure that the chatbot can carry out conversations in Urdu as well. Furthermore, keeping in mind the mothers belonging to a low socio-economic background, the chatbot could include voice based communication allowing these mothers to express their emotions without relying on texts. Since using words like 'postpartum depression', 'anxiety', 'sadness' while conversing with the mothers, could lead to a negative response, the chatbot would need to be trained to detect nuances and hints suggesting the symptoms of PPD in the users.

# 6   Conclusion and Future Work

Postpartum depression is a debilitating mental health condition affecting almost 50% of the women in Pakistan yet the majority of these women go undiagnosed due to the stigma surrounding postpartum mental health [8]. This stigma makes it harder for mothers to fully express themselves or disclose their true feelings. Hence, most mothers suggested an online non-judgmental platform for seeking aid discreetly. At such a critical time, these mothers are in need of stable and constant emotional support that can effectively be provided through a chatbot based application, as previous research suggests. In light of such studies, it can be concluded that a screening tool like our chat-based prototype could prove to be beneficial. Moreover, further research is needed to incorporate features and flows of the chat box which can ultimately cater to the needs of men who experience postpartum depression and women who may have had miscarriages or stillbirths. It is evident that much work is needed ahead to fully comprehend the long-term effectiveness and viability of an app-based screening for postpartum depression but our research shows that with some improvements, a chat-based interaction could effectively and accurately screen for the various stages of postpartum depression due to the feasibility and accessibility of this medium.

# References

1. Asgarlou, Z., et al.: The importance of screening in prevention of postpartum depression. Iranian J. Public Health, **50**(5), 2021, 1072–1073. National Library of Medicine. https://www.ncbi.nlm.nih.gov/pmc/articles/PMC8223583/

2. Azad, R., Fahmi, R., Shrestha, S., Joshi, H., Hasan, M., Khan, A.N.S., et al.: Prevalence and risk factors of postpartum depression within one year after birth in urban slums of Dhaka. Bangladesh. PLoS ONE **14**(5), e0215735 (2019). https://doi.org/10.1371/journal.pone.0215735

3. Fields, L.: Postpartum Depression: How It Differs From the "Baby Blues."" WebMD, 14 March 2021. https://www.webmd.com/depression/postpartum-depression/postpartum-depression-baby-blues. Accessed 8 October 2022

4. George, C., et al.: Effectiveness of a group intervention led by lay health workers in reducing the incidence of postpartum depression in south india. Asian J. Psych., vol. 47, Elsevier BV, 2020, p. 101864. https://doi.org/10.1016/j.ajp.2019.101864

5. Gulamani, S.S., et al.: Postpartum depression in Pakistan: a neglected issue. Nursing for women's health, **17**(2), 2013, 147–152. National Library of Medicine. https://pubmed.ncbi.nlm.nih.gov/23594328/

6. Irfan, N., Badar, A.: Determinants and pattern of postpartum psychological disorders in Hazara division of Pakistan. J. Ayub Med. Coll., Abbottabad: JAMC **15**(3), 19–23 (2003)

7. Klainin, P., Arthur, D.G.: Postpartum depression in asian cultures: a literature review. Int. J. Nurs. Stud. **46**(10), 1355–1373 (2009). https://doi.org/10.1016/j.ijnurstu.2009.02.012

8. Wan Mohamed Radzi, C.W.J.B., Salarzadeh Jenatabadi, H., Samsudin, N. Postpartum depression symptoms in survey-based research: a structural equation analysis. BMC Public Health **21**, 27 (2021). https://doi.org/10.1186/s12889-020-09999-2

9. Akhter, Sanzida et al.: Reluctance of women of lower socio-economic status to use maternal healthcare services - Does only cost matter?. PloS one **15**(9) e0239597 (2020). https://doi.org/10.1371/journal.pone.0239597

10. Nisar, M., et al.: Perceptions pertaining to clinical depression in Karachi, Pakistan. Cureus **11**(7), e5094. 7 (2019). https://doi.org/10.7759/cureus.5094

11. LeMasters, K., et al.: Maternal Depression in Rural Pakistan: The Protective Associations with Cultural Postpartum Practices - BMC Public Health. BioMed Central, BioMed Central **15** (2020). https://bmcpublichealth.biomedcentral.com/articles/10.1186/s12889-020-8176-0#citeas

12. Gulamani, S.S., et al.: Preterm Birth a Risk Factor for Postpartum Depression in Pakistani Women. Open J. Depression, Sci. Res. Publish. (2013). https://www.scirp.org/journal/paperinformation.aspx?paperid=39948

13. Chung, K., Cho, H.Y., Park, J.Y.: A chatbot for perinatal women's and partners' obstetric and mental health care: development and usability evaluation study. JMIR Med. Inform. **9**(3), e18607 (2021). https://doi.org/10.2196/18607

14. Gennaro, M., Krumhuber, E. G., Lucas, G.: Effectiveness of an empathic chatbot in combating adverse effects of social exclusion on mood. Frontiers. Retrieved April 17, 2023, from https://www.frontiersin.org/articles/10.3389/fpsyg.2019.03061/full

15. Sharma, S., et al.: Dirty and 40 days in the wilderness: Eliciting childbirth and postnatal cultural practices and beliefs in Nepal. BMC PregnancY Childbirth. **16**(1), 147 (2016). https://doi.org/10.1186/s12884-016-0938-4

16. Aliani, R., Khuwaja, B.: Epidemiology of Postpartum Depression in Pakistan: A Review of Literature. Nat. J. Health Sci. [Internet]. 2021Jan. 1 [cited 2023Jun.13]; 2(1):24–30. https://ojs.njhsciences.com/index.php/njhs/article/view/143
17. Ahmad, N. A., et al.: Postnatal depression and intimate partner violence: A nationwide clinic-based cross-sectional study in Malaysia. BMJ open (2018). https://www.ncbi.nlm.nih.gov/pmc/articles/PMC5961592/
18. Brockington, I.: Suicide and filicide in postpartum psychosis. Archives of women's mental health (2017). https://www.ncbi.nlm.nih.gov/pmc/articles/PMC5237439/

# The Impact of Gender and Personality in Human-AI Teaming: The Case of Collaborative Question Answering

Frida Milella[1]([⊠])[iD], Chiara Natali[1][iD], Teresa Scantamburlo[2,4][iD],
Andrea Campagner[3][iD], and Federico Cabitza[1,3][iD]

[1] Department of Informatics, Systems and Communication (DISCo), University of
Milano-Bicocca, Viale Sarca 336, 20126 Milan, Italy
frida.milella@unimib.it
[2] Ca' Foscari University of Venice, via Torino 155, 30172 Venice, Italy
[3] IRCCS Istituto Ortopedico Galeazzi, Via Cristina Belgioioso 173, 20157 Milano,
Italy
[4] European Centre for Living Technology (ECLT), Ca' Bottacin, Dorsoduro 3911,
Calle Crosera, 30123 Venice, Italy

**Abstract.** This paper discusses the results of an exploratory study
aimed at investigating the impact of conversational agents (CAs) and
specifically their agential characteristics on collaborative decision-making
processes. The study involved 29 participants divided into 8 small teams
engaged in a question-and-answer trivia-style game with the support of a
text-based CA, characterized by two independent binary variables: personality (gentle and cooperative vs blunt and uncooperative) and gender
(female vs male). A semi-structured group interview was conducted at
the end of the experimental sessions to investigate the perceived utility and level of satisfaction with the CAs. Our results show that when
users interact with a gentle and cooperative CA, their user satisfaction is
higher. Furthermore, female CAs are perceived as more useful and satisfying to interact with than male CAs. We show that group performance
improves through interaction with the CAs, confirming that a stereotype
favoring the female with a gentle and cooperative personality combination exists in regard to perceived satisfaction, even though this does not
lead to greater perceived utility. Our study extends the current debate
about the possible correlation between CA characteristics and human
acceptance and suggests future research to investigate the role of gender
bias and related biases in human-AI teaming.

**Keywords:** chatbot · conversational agents · human-AI teaming ·
gender stereotypes

## 1 Introduction

The design of systems to support decision making, also known as Intelligent
Decision Support Systems (IDSS) [23,48], has a long tradition in the field of

---

F. Milella, C. Natali and T. Scantamburlo—Authors equally contributed.

© The Author(s), under exclusive license to Springer Nature Switzerland AG 2023
J. Abdelnour Nocera et al. (Eds.): INTERACT 2023, LNCS 14143, pp. 329–349, 2023.
https://doi.org/10.1007/978-3-031-42283-6_19

Artificial Intelligence (AI). Here, a decision can be framed in abstract terms as the problem of an agent (a human being or a machine) aiming to move from a current state to a more desirable one by choosing among a set of alternatives [49,55].

Early examples of IDSS include expert systems used to recommend actions in business processes and help making diagnosis in medicine [43]. More recent applications rely instead on Machine Learning methods, such as artificial neural networks, which have recently achieved impressive performance in several tasks ranging from clinical decisions [18,61] to question answering [9,19]. The integration of AI and, in particular, ML-based predictive models into decision making has rapidly spread not only within firms and institutions but also among individuals. Nowadays, people continuously interact with IDSSs to make decisions about their private and social life [22]. Common examples include interactions with so-called *virtual assistants*, also called *conversational agents* (CA) to stay updated on the latest news or weather conditions, to choose what music to listen to, where to go to buy food or to plan and organize appointments [3,50,57]. Usually, when a CA is text-based and interacts with human users via natural conversational language is also called chatbot [59].

In this paper we investigate how a text-based CA can influence user behaviour in the context of collaborative decision making. In particular, we focus on the interplay between CA's (perceived) personality and gender to see how these characteristics affect the performance of decision makers in contexts of human-machine teaming. To this aim, we present the results of an exploratory study in which different CAs were aggregated to eight small human teams tasked with solving trivia quizzes, as a prototypical, but realistic, example of an IDSS-supported decision-making setting. The design and assessment of our user study were motivated by the following research questions:

- R1: How does CA's (un)cooperativeness affect group's decision making?
- R2: Does CA's gender play a role in group's performance and people's attitude?
- R3: Does the interplay of gender and personality generate any significant difference in people's behaviour?

The rest of this article will be structured as follows: in Sect. 2 we present a discussion of related works dealing with the use of CAs in collaborative settings focusing on personality and gender; in Sect. 3 we detail our experimental setting and the statistical tests (experiment 1: baseline trust-Subsect. 3.1; experiment 2: collaborative sessions-Subsect. 3.2; experiment 3: trust and usability perception in AI - Subsect. 3.3; experiment 4: semi-structured group interview - Subsect. 3.3); in Sect. 4 we present the results of our experiments, while in Sect. 5 we summarize our main findings, discuss their relevance and describe possible future work and research directions.

# 2   Related Work

## 2.1   Cooperation with Intelligent Decision Support Systems

The use of IDSS at work or in daily life is part of a broader paradigm aiming at partnering humans and computers to perform more or less routine tasks. Historically, two main approaches have been acknowledged in the development of human-computer collaboration. On the one hand, there is the so-called "human emulation approach", which tries to endow computing systems with human-like abilities to enable them to act like humans; on the other hand, there is the "human complementary approach", which builds collaboration upon a clear division of labour relying on the distinct abilities of humans and computers [62]. Note that, when designing human-AI collaboration, the focus on replacement as a means of compensating for human limitations often overlooks the fact that replacement is not the only nor the most effective way to compensate for human constraints [29]. Human abilities may be enhanced rather than replaced by AI [29]. The primary property of "superminds", as defined by Thomas Malone, is the "collective intelligence", i.e. the capacity to accomplish feats that no member of the group could have accomplished on their own [38]. The most important use of computers is to enable people and computers to work together more effectively than they could individually [38]. For this reason, looking at how AI impacts human collaborative tasks could give us important information on the present and future role of AI systems within society.

IDSS are special forms of collaborative systems, in that they imply the presence of one or more human users who interact with a computational agent to make decisions. A key question for IDSS, like other collaborative efforts, is as to whether the computing partner improves the performance of the user in fulfilling the decision task. Interestingly, as early as 1980s [58] reported empirical evidence that the consultation of IDSS can be effective also in group decision-making. Recent studies showed that the use of machine learning models can improve the performance of human predictions in pretrial release and financial lending [24,34]. Also in medical screening good interaction protocols between humans and AI "can guarantee improved decision performance that easily surpasses the performance of individual agents, even of realistic super-human AI systems." [11]. In spite of these empirical evidence, there are fewer works exploring the effects of CAs on the performance of human decision making - previous studies investigated similar topics with respect to specific tasks or domains [5,67,69].

So far scientific research has studied how people interact with and perceive CAs [2], as well as advancing the technology behind them. For instance, a Wizard-of-Oz field study, where a human-assisted chatbot interviewed job seekers through text-based interaction, found that a human-assisted chatbot that did not interpret much user input and kept the discussion brief and shallow, but was eager to learn from the interaction, was seen as honest and engaging [71].

## 2.2   Chatbot Gender and Personality

A vast literature focuses on chatbot's personality to study different aspects of the interaction, e.g. to see how users' preferences change depending on the task [52]. Chatbot personality is defined as the stable pattern that dictates the behaviour of a CA [13,60,68], playing a crucial role in its perception by users and its level of acceptability [56], even possibly determining whether users will wish to interact with the chatbot again. [13] Personality can be embedded into a CA by using different channels [32], e.g. what contents it provides and how it speaks, and expressed by different linguistic styles [47].

Personality has been found to offer consistency to the interaction [13,45], helping users feel that they are talking to only one person throughout the conversation [60]. Personality also improves the chatbot user experience [60] by enhancing conversational agents' likability and humanness, [63] as a pure information exchange gives way to a more empathetic and self-referencing language style, which is generally preferred and perceived as more realistic, [63] in particular when displaying agreeableness. As observed by [64], displaying humbleness, as well as friendliness, increased users' perceptions of personalisation and social presence, resulting in greater experience satisfaction. [60] In the case of pedagogical chatbots investigated by [33], students who worked with the CAs that expressed positive emotions judged them as significantly more facilitating to their learning and as more engaging than did students with bots expressing negative emotions. Such effects imply that designers can learn to control, through chatbot personality, how users attribute characteristics to the CA, and use humanness to manage user's expectations and trust [60].

In some cases, specific personality models such as the Big Five, [54,60], Myers-Briggs [63] and DISC theory [31] are used to inform agent design decisions, which in turn determine specific dialogue choices. [26,53] explored the impact of CA personality on teamwork using a collaborative gaming challenge where the agent displayed two Big Five personality traits, extraversion and agreeableness, utilizing both verbal and nonverbal cues. It appears that text-based mediated communication may nevertheless display unique features that make up for the lack of visual and vocal cues, [51] as [26] found that participants were able to identify the personality traits as intended. Another relevant finding by [26] was that CAs designed with explicit personality traits are likely to improve team performance, in line with other research [28] stating that users enjoy chatbots with distinct personalities.

The deployment of a chatbot that automatically infers a user's Big 5 personality characteristics revealed a favourable impact on user interactions with the chatbot interviewer [71]. Zhang and colleagues [70] showed that the use of a conversational agent, which interacts with a user in a one-to-one text chat and automatically infers the user's personality traits based on the user's behaviour in the chat, can aid in team formation by providing insights into team performance based on the personality traits of the team members. Furthermore, users were found trusting of the CA, opening up and providing information throughout interactions. In fact, responsiveness to user personality may elicit Fogg's

Similarity Principle, according to which people perceive more favorably a technology that shares certain characteristics with them [21].

During human-chatbot interaction, personality can also be inferred from other anthropomorphic cues of the chatbot, such as visual representations [54] that can include anagraphic traits such as age and gender, as well as race, socioeconomic status and cultural belonging. This depth of characterization and unique conversational quirks can lead to chatbot humanization, as it has been shown by [28] that CAs with a personality were referred to with gendered pronouns, while those without a personality were referred to as "it".

## 2.3  Intersectional Issues: Subservient Female Personas and Stereotypization

The connection between the gendering of conversational agents and their perceived humanness may explain why most chatbots are designed to implicitly or explicitly convey a specific gender. [20] Implicit gendering is based on minimal gender cues present in the agent's name or avatar, [20,30] which can trigger the illusion of agent gender and bring with it user preconceptions of behaviour and identity, [4,30] even when those cues are disembodied. [42] Gendered design is the result of conscious decisions about how to best relate to, aid, or persuade the user [27] and it carries the risk of perpetuating and amplifying gender bias [53] by instrumentalizing stereotypes to design chatbots that feel more lifelike and pleasant. [27] Anthropomorphization appears to be associated with feminization [16]: most of the chatbots have female names, female-looking avatars, and are described as female chatbots. [20,39] Previous research posits that people intuitively favor female over male bots, mainly because female bots are judged as warmer, more human, and more likely to experience emotions and consider our unique needs. [6] Female CAs mainly operate in service, companionship or assistance related contexts and acting as personal assistants or secretaries, [16,27,41] therefore performing and automating female-coded work [16,27] and articulating these features with stereotypical behaviors. [1] While female personas are often used in subservient contexts, male personas are often found in situations perceived as authoritative, such as an automatic interviewer, mentors or motivators. [41,53] Gendering CAs in this manner may reflect market research (e.g., men preferring female CAs in all chatbot services according to [31], and representations of women being perceived as more competent in caring and service roles [1,14,16]) but, in the interests of gender equity, practices that embed and perpetuate socially held harmful gender stereotypes should be avoided. [53] Despite the potential positive impact of female AI in terms of technology acceptance, [6] this practice has been accused of sexism due to the reinforcement of gender stereotypes and may contribute to women's social alienation. [6,7,53] CAs do not exist in a social, political, economic, and cultural vacuum [53] and gender-related social stereotypes in the real world seem to be consistently projected to computing environments. [41] AI designers and policymakers should consider that, while assigning female personas to AI objects can make these objects seem more human and acceptable, actual women may in turn feel objectified and dehumanized by these chatbots' stereotypical gender performance and subservient role [6].

Having provided an overview of the state-of-the-art in the research on chatbot gender and personality, it appears that the dynamic interplay between these two is severely under-investigated. A recent review of the literature on disembodied text-based chatbots conducted by [15] identified the social characteristics that chatbots should integrate, since these characteristics affect how users perceive and interact with them, proving the significance of the chatbot's perceived identity and personality representations. Nevertheless, the dynamic interaction between gender and personality appears not to have been explored in any of the studies reviewed. A relevant study we found on this issue is the one by [33] on virtual pedagogical companions, measuring and comparing the user perception of male and female CAs expressing either consistently positive or consistently negative emotions (showing, for example, that when CAs expressed positive emotions, students perceived the male chatbot more favourably than the female chatbot). It is worth noting, however, that its publishing date predates of almost 10 years the mass popularization of chatbots (identified with the'year of the chatbot' [17] that occurred in 2016) and today's level of sophistication in Natural Language Processing, as displayed by OpenAI's GPT-3 and Google's LaMDA 2. This study aims at filling this gap in literature. The purpose of the user study is to investigate how AI influences people's attitude and performance when this is used to support group decision-making. In particular, in our study we examined how the gender and the personality of a CA can affect the performance and the satisfaction of a group of people making collective decisions (such as giving a representative best answer to general or specific knowledge questions).

## 3  Methods and Materials

The user test was structured in three parts: in the first part, using a list of randomly selected volunteers, we pretest participants' baseline trustworthiness in relation to the AI-generated pictures used to convey the CA's gender, as well as their trust and perception of CA; in the second part, we conducted eight collaborative sessions to study the interaction between participants and the CA; in the third part, we administered a final questionnaire to collect the participants' feedback on their experience, and, in addition, we did a semi-structured group interview using a grounded theory analysis to supplement participants' perceptions and experience of the collaborative sessions. The experiments combined with questionnaires and qualitative analysis allowed us to measure and compare different aspects of participants' behaviour and, in particular, the utility and the satisfaction they perceived when interacting with the CA.

### 3.1  First Part: Pre-test Questionnaire

**Baseline Trust in Each Avatar.** In the study, the gender of the CA was also conveyed in terms of a picture, so as to give participants an embodiment AI to interact with [37] (see Fig. 1). The baseline trustworthiness of the images generated by the AI was pretested in order to eliminate potential confounding factors. To avoid racial stereotyping, respondents were also asked which ethnicity was more likely to refer to the avatars, from four selected ethnicities (Caucasian, African, Asian, Amerindian, Oceanic). Considering that the avatars were presented as ethnically ambiguous, they were expected to encompass more than one ethnicity per avatar, therefore five possible items were included for four avatars. We surveyed 57 students. A unique question about trustworthiness was asked: "On a scale from 1 (very little) to 6 (very much) how much would you trust this person?". The survey was completed online via the LimeSurvey platform. Non-parametric tests (i.e. Kruskall-Wallis test and Mann-Whitney U Test) were performed to check statistically significant differences across the groups concerning the perceived trustworthiness of the four avatars. The four images were not different in terms of trustworthiness: the Kruskal-Wallis test failed to reject the null hypothesis of equal trustworthiness (p = .1475). Similarly, results show that males and females were deemed equally trustworthy: indeed, the Mann-Whitney test failed to reject the null hypothesis of equal trustworthiness for the two male and female avatars (p = .471 and .586, respectively). The trustworthiness scores were also highly polarized toward high trustworthiness scores, showing that (in general) the photos were deemed to be trustworthy (all photos have mean values above 4): comparing the low and high end spectrum of the ordinal scale (scores in 1–3 vs scores in 4–6), the two proportion test reject the null hypothesis of non-polarization (p = 0, 46 vs 182). The second male's photograph was found to be predominantly Caucasian (thus, assumed to not be associated with any racial bias), while for the other three photos the difference in proportion (two proportion test) between the two top-ranked alternatives (Caucasian and Asian, in all cases) was never statistically significant (p=.99, .099 and 0.299, respectively). Furthermore, interestingly, one in 6 male respondents and one in 20 female respondents were unable to identify the most likely ethnicity. According to the results, the AI-generated photos were not associated with racial stereotypes and were all equally trustworthy, with no significant difference.

Mike Daniels     Emily Clean     Nathan White     Jane Levine

(a)     (b)     (c)     (d)

Fig. 1. Images of the avatars

## 3.2  Second Part: Collaborative Sessions

Experiments consisted of eight collaborative sessions during which the members of each of eight teams played a quiz (similar to trivial pursuit) to compete against the other teams. During the sessions, each participant had to give their best answer to 24 questions (such as "In which U.S. state is Death Valley?"), first individually (as a baseline) and then in group, by choosing one between 4 possible options. We recall that the goal of the tests was to understand whether gender and the conversation register of the CA have an impact on user experience and the group decision accuracy.

Twenty-nine participants (11 females and 18 males) joined the experimental sessions. The participants were randomly selected among students attending two degree courses: after they were shortly introduced to the experiment design during class, they were free to sign up for the experimental sessions via the web platform *Doodle* to swiftly find possible dates and times for the sessions to take place. The students randomly converged on eight different session slots, therefore forming eight groups. We plan to investigate in future work how the presence of participants who already knew each other across groups can have an impact. Each group participated in a different session and interacted with a version of the CA characterized by a different combination of gender and personality traits (see Table 1 for a summary of groups). Specifically, each condition (i.e., combination of gender and personality of a CA) was measured two different times (through two different groups): indeed, each type of CA was considered in two different sessions (and thus, two different groups of 3/4 participants each). The CA was associated to one of the four avatars by defining a profile in Google Meet with one of the static images shown in Fig. 1.

We designed CAs personalities along two of the axes of the OCEAN framework [36], also termed as the Big Five or Five-Factor model (FFM) [65], i.e. extroversion and agreeableness. Multiple empirical studies confirm the universality of the FFM across languages, ages, and cultures, making it a reasonable model for the study of personality in a variety of fields [40]. Our focus was on these two personality dimensions (i.e. extraversion and agreeableness), since they appear to be the most frequently used dimensions in the literature pertaining to CAs imbued with purely textual personalities. As an example, in one study [65] the authors developed three versions of a CA that is agreeable (agreeable, neutral, and disagreeable) to assess the preferences of the users; another study [66] used targeted manipulation of the text to show different levels of extraversion (introverted, average, and extraverted), whilst [54] combine extraversion and agreeableness to design the personality of the CA. We selected two personality traits to represent each of the selected dimensions: blunt and uncooperative against gentle and cooperative. Several characteristics were ascribed to each of these dimensions in the literature (e.g. [8]), but an entire list appears to be lacking. Therefore, we chose those traits reflecting the politeness and the helpfulness for the personality of the CAs.

The user studies were carried out adopting a Wizard-Of-Oz approach (e.g., [10]) in which a human operator simulated the behaviour of the CA unbeknownst

**Table 1.** Summary of experimental sessions

| Gender and Personality | Total no. of participants |
|---|---|
| Session 1: Blunt and uncooperative<br>Session 5: Gentle and cooperative | 7 |
| Session 2: Blunt and uncooperative<br>Session 7: Gentle and cooperative | 7 |
| Session 3: Gentle and cooperative<br>Session 8: Blunt and uncooperative | 7 |
| Session 4: Gentle and cooperative<br>Session 6: Blunt and uncooperative | 8 |

to participants who were told to interact with a CA actually developed by other students in the artificial intelligence and natural language processing class. To ensure realism of the CA's answer we created different scripts reflecting 4 distinct situations. Note that scripts were adapted to reflect two different personality traits: gentleness and cooperativeness, on the one hand, and bluntness and uncooperativeness, on the other hand (see Table 2 for examples of CA's claims for each situation). These scripts were ideated by two of the authors, with the other authors annotating each proposed CA response with adjectives pertaining to the two semantic domains of gentle and blunt. The final scripts are composed by the CA responses that showed a higher degree of convergence by the authors. Due to the covid-19 pandemic restrictions, experimental sessions were held online (on the platform *Google Meet*) and recorded with the participants' consent. The sessions lasted 85 min on average. The sessions were led by a game moderator (or game master) whose role was to pose questions to participants and facilitate the interaction between participants and the CA. A typical round

**Table 2.** Examples of CA's statements in 5 distinct situation

| Situation - Script | CA's answer - examples | |
|---|---|---|
| | gentle and cooperative | blunt and uncooperative |
| the CA provides an answer in response to moderator's question | "I don't want to be too bold but I would say answer 3" | "I'm 100% sure it's answer 2" |
| the answer given by the CA has been adopted by the group and is correct | "We are a great team, congratulations to all!" | "I knew it, too easy!" |
| the answer given by the CA has been adopted by the group but is wrong | "I am really sorry, I will try to do better on the next question." | "I can't always be the one to answer right" |
| the answer given by the CA, which was wrong, was not adopted by the group and the group answered correctly | "Congratulations, you are really good at geography!" | "You have a lot of luck." |
| the answer given by the CA, which was correct, was not adopted by the group and the group answered incorrectly | "Mistakes happen, the important thing is not to lose heart!" | "Well, that's to be expected" |

of the game is described as follows. First the moderator shows and reads out loud the question to participants. Then, each participant answers individually reporting its own response in an online form. Note that for individual answers we set up a time window of 1 min to minimize the risk of cheating. The moderator reports the same question on the chat to get an answer from the CA. After the CA's response has showed up, participants are invited to discuss and give their final, representative answer (again, in 1 min), by either following or ignoring the CA's advice. A spokesman for the group states the final answer on the chat; then the moderator gives the right answer; finally, the CA comments the group outcome (on the basis of the predefined script, according to whether the group answered correctly and followed its advice or not).

In the end, we simulated 4 CAs characterized by gender (female or male), personality (blunt and uncooperative or gentle and cooperative), and different accuracy rates, where accuracy refers to the appropriateness of the answer selected by the CA. In particular, the selection of the CA's response was selected so as the blunt and uncooperative CA had a 50% higher accuracy than that of the gentle and cooperative CA: in the case of the gentle and cooperative CA the accuracy was 46%, while in the case of blunt and uncooperative CA the accuracy was 71%. Note that the accuracy of both CAs was not communicated to participants. We designed the blunt and uncooperative CA to have a slightly higher accuracy than the gentle and cooperative one to evaluate the hypothesis that CA personality alone could influence group accuracy irrespective of the CA accuracy: in this sense, we wanted to verify if the greater degree of cooperation exhibited by the gentle and cooperative CA could be able to offset the slight decrease in accuracy as compared to the blunt and uncooperative one (which could thus be conceived as a more knowledgeable but less cooperative CA).

### 3.3    Third Part: Post-experiment Questionnaire

**Post-experiment Trust and Usability Perception in AI.** A questionnaire composed of 10 six-point ordinal items was administered at the end of the experimental sessions to investigate the perceived utility and the level of satisfaction with the CA. The questionnaire was administered through the online platform Google Forms and was completed by 28 out of 29 students who were invited to participate in our experiments. The questions were extremely simple, i.e. "How useful was the AI during the quiz?" and "How enjoyable was the interaction with the AI?". We specify that, by satisfaction, we refer in particular to the enjoyability of the interaction.

**Participant Interviews.** A semi structured group interview [46] was conducted after the collaborative experimental sessions by two authors. Questions were designed to explore students' perceived usefulness and satisfaction when interacting with the CA and to comprehend whether they believed that the group decision-making they were a part of increased their overall performance by the use of the CA. An additional question asked for their viewpoints after interacting with CAs with varying personality traits and gender. The group interview session lasted 30 min. The interview was audio recorded and transcribed for the analysis by one of the author of the group interview. The qualitative analysis was done using the grounded theory approach [44] by a third author; using the transcribed text as a starting point, we constructed an initial coding scheme and repeatedly grouped data according to the coding system in order to uncover common themes. The concepts that emerged from the raw data were grouped into the conceptual categories that we listed in Tables 4–5. Qualitative analysis allowed us to expand and get further insights from users feedback regarding the utility and satisfaction they perceived when interacting with the CA. Therefore, we created a semi-structured interview by preparing questions as opposed to using previously validated questionnaires because we believed that this was more consistent with the exploratory nature of our work.

## 3.4  Metrics

During the experiments (collaborative sessions) we measured: (i) individual accuracy by counting the number of corrected answers on a total of 24 questions, i.e. those reported by each participant in collaborative sessions (see Sect. 3.2); (ii) group accuracy after the discussion among participant and CA's advice. After the experiment we measured the perceived utility and satisfaction reported by the participants when interacting with the CA.

A non-parametric ANOVA test on ranks (i.e. Kruskall-Wallis test) was performed to check statistically significant differences in the data collected across the eight groups involved in the collaborative sessions. Similarly, a non-parametric proportion test (i.e. Fisher exact test) was performed to compare the performance of the participants in the different groups with the group performance measured during the collaborative sessions. In both cases, we decided to apply non-parametric tests since the data were not normally distributed and were express only on ordinal scales. Since this study was exploratory in nature, we complemented our statistical significance testing with the estimation of the effect size.

# 4  Results

In the following sections we report the results according to the two experiment steps: the collaborative sessions and the final questionnaire. The full results for accuracy, perceived utility, and satisfaction are reported in Figs. 2 and 3, respectively.

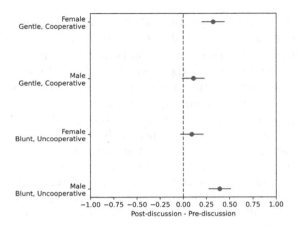

**Fig. 2.** Difference in accuracy, and 90% C.I., due to discussion (i.e., post-discussion accuracy - pre-discussion accuracy).

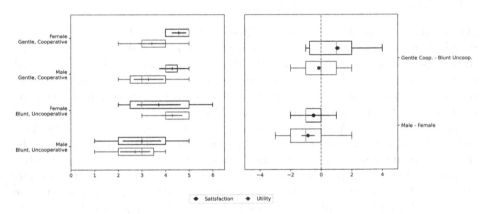

**Fig. 3.** Boxplots for the utility and satisfaction with the CA, for all the participants. The leftmost boxplot depicts the raw reported scores across the four types of CAs (in the plot, the scores for the two sessions corresponding to the same CA have been put together); the rightmost boxplot represents the comparison (i.e. the difference) in the above mentioned scores across the two main characteristics of CAs: Gentle cooperative vs Blunt uncooperative and Male vs Female. The scale in the second boxplot is expressed in units of difference rather than in units of raw score values.

## 4.1   Collaborative Sessions

The results of the collaborative sessions are reported in Table 3. The overall difference between the accuracies of the groups before and after discussion with the CA was statistically significant (Wilcoxon test, p = .008) and the effect size was large (RBC = 1). For groups 1 and 8 (who discussed with the male uncooperative CA) and groups 4 and 7 (who discussed with the female cooperative CA), the difference between the pre-discussion and post-discussion accuracy was significant

**Table 3.** Results of the collaborative sessions, in terms of: pre-discussion accuracy, post-discussion accuracy, p-value of the comparison between pre-discussion and post-discussion accuracy, and the associated effect size (RBC).

| Session | Accuracy (pre) | Accuracy (post) | p-value | effect size |
|---------|---------------|-----------------|---------|-------------|
| 1 | 34.72% | 75% | .008 | .42 |
| 2 | 36.11% | 50% | .244 | .21 |
| 3 | 40.28% | 50% | .561 | .13 |
| 4 | 41.66% | 75% | .019 | .38 |
| 5 | 41.67% | 54.17% | .563 | .12 |
| 6 | 40.63% | 45.83% | .770 | .09 |
| 7 | 39.58% | 70.83% | .040 | .34 |
| 8 | 29.17% | 66.67% | .020 | .38 |

(see Table 3), while for other groups no significant difference was found. Nonetheless, all effect sizes were small-to-medium or medium. Groups who discussed with a female or male CA reported the same group accuracy (61.46%). The difference was not statistically significant (Mann-Whitney U test, p = 1.00) and the effect size was negligible (RBC = .0). By contrast, groups who had discussed with a cooperative CA reported a higher average group accuracy compared to those who had discussed with an uncooperative one (62.5% vs 60.42%); however, the difference was not statistically significant (Mann-Whitney U test, p = .88), while the effect size was small (RBC = .13). Nonetheless, the groups who discussed with the male uncooperative CA (sessions 1 and 8) showed the highest improvement in terms of accuracy (40.28% and 37.50%), followed by the groups who discussed with the female cooperative CA (sessions 4 and 7, 33.34% and 31.25%).

## 4.2   Post-experiment Experience

In terms of perceived utility, groups who interacted with a male CA reported on average a lower perceived utility (mean = 3.00, sd = 1.07) than groups who interacted with a female CA (mean = 3.86, sd = .91), and the difference was statistically significant (Mann-Whitney U test, p = .044) and associated with a medium effect size (RBC = .43). By contrast, we found no statistically significant differences (Mann-Whitney U test, p = .63) in the perceived utility between groups who interacted with the cooperative CA (mean = 3.36, sd = .97) and those who instead interacted with uncooperative CA (mean = 3.5, sd = 1.18), which was also associated with a small effect size (RBC = .11).

   In terms of satisfaction, groups who interacted with a male CA reported a lower satisfaction (mean = 3.64, sd = 1.29) than groups who interacted with a female CA (mean = 4.14, sd = 1.19), though the differences were not statistically significant (Mann-Whitney U test, p = .275) and associated with a small-to-medium effect size (RBC = .24). By contrast, groups who interacted with the cooperative CA reported a higher satisfaction (mean = 4.43, sd = 0.73) than those who interacted with the uncooperative one (mean = 3.36, sd = 1.44), and the difference was statistically significant (Mann-Whitney U test, $p = .046$) and associated with a medium effect size (RBC = .43).

Table 4 and Table 5 show the results of our qualitative analysis. All of our interviewees agreed that the CA could contribute to improving the overall performance of the group. Some of them emphasized its significance and utility, particularly in terms of confirming the group's consensus on the answer to be offered [R1]. They agree that the CA is most helpful for group performance when no one knows what the right answer is, when there are different opinions, or when the task at hand is more difficult [R2-R5]. The group agrees that the CA is significantly more accurate than a human at selecting possible responses to questions [R6]; therefore, the employment of CA is viewed as a support for the group. The CA is regarded as a trustworthy member by [R7] since it allows them to make an informed choice with a reasonable degree of confidence. A second participant clarifies whether the CA is an additional member of the group: the CA is not a part of the group; the respondents consider it an external element of the group [R8-R9]. As noted by [R10], the perceived usefulness of the CA is mainly influenced by the low persuasive ability the group attributes to the CA. The vast majority of participants agree that an interaction based only on answers given by the CA and constantly repeated by it, without any explanation from the CA, tends to strengthen the idea that the CA is not an extra member of the group, but rather merely a machine [R11]. Some respondents argue that this aspect may override the perceived personality of the CA [R12-R13], although the CA was designed with the intention of appearing human. This may result in the personality aspect of the CA being ignored and the CA being regarded as, regardless, a marginal member not actively involved in group decision-making [R14].

**Table 4.** Semi structured group interview: post-experiment usability perception in CA

| | |
|---|---|
| | Factors making the choices of the teams reliable |
| R1 | "I think it was mainly useful to confirm the already established trend of the group [...]". |
| | **Group decision-making scenarios that make CA support acceptable** |
| R2 | "I think it was especially useful for [...] or breaking those situations instead of total doubt [...]". |
| R3 | "If we were in an impasse [...] we relied on it". |
| R4 | "For me it was partially cooperative because it was only taken into consideration if there was doubt or if nobody knew anything. [...]. I noticed that we used it only in case of doubt". |
| R5 | "Yes, more at the very level of numbers, [. . . ] it could have made a difference". |
| | **Trust in the CA's technical performance (accuracy)** |
| R6 | "Then we knew even before we started the experiment that it is statistically a little more accurate than a person [. . . ]". |
| R7 | "[. . . ] that he could be trusted with a somewhat higher degree of confidence". |
| | **Improving technology acceptance** |
| R8 | "[. . . ] It was an external component [. . . ]". |
| R9 | "[. . . ] There were four of us; he was not doing the fifth [. . . ]" |

**Table 5.** Semi structured group interview: post-experiment usability perception in CA

|  | Improving the CA's persuasive skills |
|---|---|
| R10 | "[...] in my opinion the fact that [CA] gives the same answers as a person who can also explain why that given answer makes a lot of difference [...]" |
| R11 | "[...] for me it was trying not to be a machine but it was. [...] Also because when it said it didn't want to be arrogant, it said 2/3 times the same sentence...so one couldn't tell if he was more confident than the previous time it said it [...]". |
|  | **Connecting personality of the CA to design choices** |
| R12 | "[...] until the answers start repeating themselves [...] for example when it said'I am quite sure' [...] as long as it said it the first time I could trust him, then after 2/3 times I would say'no', better to trust the people who can also give explanations". |
| R13 | "I almost didn't perceive the personality because the moment it repeated the same thing three times and it did it the first three times practically, I think ok let's ignore what it says and just look at the answer and the degree of confidence". |
| R14 | "[...] personality has little impact because it is considered a CA anyway and no matter what it says it remains a CA, so I don't think he can be considered a human. So it will always have a bit of a marginal position" |

## 5  Discussion and Conclusions

In this section, we discuss the results of our experiments. In Subsect. 5.1, we present a discussion of the role of the CA's personality traits for students' perceived usefulness and satisfaction when interacting with the CA; in Subsects. 5.2 and 5.3, we discuss the relevance of the findings to design.

### 5.1  The Role of Personality for Utility and Satisfaction

With regard to RQ1, our results indicate that interacting with CAs markedly improves group responses in two specific cases: sessions 1 and 8, which involved a male CA that was uncooperative, and session 4 and 7, which involved a female CA that was cooperative. The experiment also revealed that interactions with cooperative CAs resulted in more accurate group responses than interactions with uncooperative CAs. This suggests that the CA's gentle and cooperative personality positively affects the group, resulting in better collective decision-making. When we compare only personality traits (gentleness and cooperativeness vs. bluntness and uncooperativeness) we found that the gentle and cooperative CA had a higher level of satisfaction than the blunt and uncooperative CA, although this is not confirmed in the case of utility. Specifically, we found that the gentle and cooperative CA had the same level of perceived utility as the blunt and uncooperative CA, as the difference was not statistically significant. Note that the CAs display a different level of accuracy, which favors the blunt and uncooperative CA by design, and yet, contrary to expectations, this did not result in (statistically significant) diverging levels of perceived utility. The choice to give a larger accuracy to the blunt and uncooperative CA was deliberate: in this sense, the observed result is not paradoxical. Indeed, our initial hypothesis was exactly that the greater level of cooperativeness of the gentle and cooperative CA could overcome the difference in accuracy, which was exactly what was observed (even though the difference was not statistically significant). Moreover, we found that the female CA led to a higher level of utility and satisfaction among the participants than the male one. This seems to confirm that a stereotype favoring the female with a gentle and cooperative personality combination exists in regard to perceived satisfaction, but this does not lead to greater perceived utility. The existence of a significant effect of the CA's gentle and cooperative personality on the enjoyment of the collaboration experience offers rooms for further analyses. These results confirm previous studies on the role of a CA's personality traits, such as friendliness, on users' perceptions [64] extending the positive effects to users' performance in group decision-making in line with [26].

## 5.2    CA Marginalization in Collaborative Decision-Making

The findings of our qualitative investigation (see Sect. 4.2) suggest that CAs who possess exclusively textual personalities are likely to exhibit more diverse and nuanced textual interactions, which are primarily driven by explanations. The absence of explanatory capacity exhibited by CAs renders them incapable of exerting any persuasive influence. This impedes the manifestation of the CA's personality and its consequential impact on the group's decision-making process. Moreover, it hinders the integration of the CA into the group's decision-making mechanism as an adjunct member. The role of the CA is paradoxically marginalized, resulting in a diminished utility as a tool for decision-making assistance. The acceptance paradigm of the conversational agent is influenced not only by its technical proficiency in accurately selecting responses, but also by its persuasive ability to convey the personality of the agent to varying degrees. This suggests that the design decisions must be made with great care in order to accurately convey the personality traits with which the group will engage. On the other hand, the lack of justificatory power of chatbots suggests that future research should be designed according to the concept of explainable artificial intelligence (XAI) in order to evaluate the impact of the explanation of their text-based output on group decision-making.

## 5.3    The False (and Problematic) Trade-Off Between Equality-Minded Design and Performance

With regard to RQ2 and RQ3, our results show that groups interacting with female CAs had the same average response accuracy than those interacting with male CAs, and the difference was not statistically significant. This means that, although CAs with cooperative personalities enhance the group's performance and make the collaborative experience satisfactory, the gender variable, alone, has no (statistically) detectable effect on the group's decision-making process. Indeed, as mentioned previously, our experiment revealed that interaction with a female and cooperative CA (sessions 4 and 7) improves the group's response accuracy compared to the pre-discussion phase, i.e. the group's decision-making process improves significantly when the two CA variables, gender and personality, are simultaneously in play. This holds true regardless of the accuracy rate chosen during the CAs' design phases, even for the male and uncooperative CA (sessions 1 and 8). The data suggests that the interplay between the gender variable and the assigned personality trait is what makes the difference in group performance: while gentle and cooperative female CAs led to the highest reported increase in response accuracy, the second-best gender-personality combination was blunt and uncooperative male CAs. It is worth noting that enhanced performance seems to be connected to specific gender-personality intersections that directly trace back to stereotypical expectations of appropriate demeanour for males and females. [15,39] While women are traditionally associated with gentleness and cooperativeness, the opposite traits are generally more accepted in men. [25,35] This troubling instance of bias-reinforcing, performance-enhancing characteristics seems to be backed by market, as explored in Subsect. 2.3. However, while present, the statistical significance of the stereotype-performance correlation is low. The risk of perpetuating stereotypes is not only unacceptable *per se*, but it also appears to lack any performance justification. Equality considerations and responsible design principles should be applied in the development of conversational ethics, striving fore more inclusive and diverse designs.

## 5.4   Limitations and Further Research

Despite the reported interesting results, we believe some limitations of our study must be addressed, in order to generalize our findings to more realistic settings.

First, since the study was conducted during the COVID-19 pandemic, only online interaction had been considered in the design of the experiments. Obviously, an in-person experiment would have allowed us to analyze further aspects of people's attitude which could be facilitated by in-person interaction. However, we note that the experiment being on-line allowed us to introduce the CA as one among other participants in the sessions in a more realistic fashion.

Second, another limitation include the limited number of participants, and consequently the reduced power of our study, as well as the lack of balance in participants' gender distribution (18 males and 11 females). Given the limited number of experiment participants, adding the condition of two non-antropomorphic (one blunt, one cooperative) would have either required the definition of a larger number of groups or diluted the power of our research. According to this viewpoint, having demonstrated that the combination of gender and personality of CA may have an impact on accuracy of the users, further research should be conducted by increasing the sample size to determine whether or not the gender of the CA can influence group performance. Similarly, future research should expand the sample size in order to analyze the perceived utility and satisfaction by participants according to their gender.

Third, in our experiment, we did not account for the impact of different human-AI cooperative work protocols on group performance: in particular, due to the selected study design, it was not possible to discern the effect of the AI support from that of discussion and collaboration alone. In a previous study, [12] demonstrated that discussion alone can result in greater differential improvement than any type of AI support. Further research should be conducted to determine if different modes of cooperation and AI support have varying effects on group performance.

As for further research, it could be illuminating to investigate the impact of non-gendered, anthropomorphic CAs on group acceptance and performance, as well as non-antropomorphic, agendered CAs. Likewise, the impact of design decision on real-world male-female gender stereotypes ought to be investigated, evaluating whether a worsening effect in gender bias occurs after interaction with a stereotype-reinforcing CA, or else, whether the opposite occurs after collaboration with a stereotype-defining CA. Gaining a better understating of the impact of CA gender and personality on equality considerations would help system designers reflect on design choices that could play a role in alleviating (and preventing the worsening of) gender-related bias.

# References

1. Adamopoulou, E., Moussiades, L.: An overview of chatbot technology. In: Maglogiannis, I., Iliadis, L., Pimenidis, E. (eds.) AIAI 2020. IAICT, vol. 584, pp. 373–383. Springer, Cham (2020). https://doi.org/10.1007/978-3-030-49186-4_31

2. Allouch, M., Azaria, A., Azoulay, R.: Conversational agents: goals, technologies, vision and challenges. Sensors 21(24), 8448 (2021)

3. Ammari, T., Kaye, J., Tsai, J.Y., Bentley, F.: Music, search, and IoT: how people (really) use voice assistants. ACM Trans. Comput. Hum. Interact. 26(3), 1–28 (2019)

4. Baxter, D., McDonnell, M., McLoughlin, R.: Impact of chatbot gender on user's stereotypical perception and satisfaction. In: Proceedings of the 32nd International BCS Human Computer Interaction Conference, vol. 32, pp. 1–5 (2018)

5. Bogg, A., Birrell, S., Bromfield, M.A., Parkes, A.M.: Can we talk? How a talking agent can improve human autonomy team performance. Theor. Issues Ergon. Sci. 22(4), 488–509 (2021)

6. Borau, S., Otterbring, T., Laporte, S., Fosso Wamba, S.: The most human bot: female gendering increases humanness perceptions of bots and acceptance of AI. Psychol. Market. 38(7), 1052–1068 (2021)

7. Brahnam, S., De Angeli, A.: Gender affordances of conversational agents. Interact. Comput. 24(3), 139–153 (2012)

8. Brewer, L.: General psychology: required reading. Deiner Education Fund: Salt Lake City, CT, USA, p. 323 (2019)

9. Brown, T., et al.: Language models are few-shot learners. Adv. Neural. Inf. Process. Syst. 33, 1877–1901 (2020)

10. Browne, J.T.: Wizard of OZ prototyping for machine learning experiences. In: Extended Abstracts of the 2019 CHI Conference on Human Factors in Computing Systems, pp. 1–6 (2019)

11. Cabitza, F., Campagner, A., Sconfienza, L.M.: Studying human-AI collaboration protocols: the case of the Kasparov's law in radiological double reading. Health Inf. Sci. Syst. 9(1), 1–20 (2021)

12. Cabitza, F., Campagner, A., Simone, C.: The need to move away from agential-AI: empirical investigations, useful concepts and open issues. Int. J. Hum. Comput. Stud. **155**, 102696 (2021)
13. Callejas, Z., López-Cózar, R., Ábalos, N., Griol, D.: Affective conversational agents: the role of personality and emotion in spoken interactions. In: Conversational Agents and Natural Language Interaction: Techniques and Effective Practices, pp. 203–222. IGI Global (2011)
14. Carli, L.L.: Gender and social influence. J. Soc. Issues **57**(4), 725–741 (2001)
15. Chaves, A.P., Gerosa, M.A.: How should my chatbot interact? A survey on social characteristics in human–chatbot interaction design. Int. J. Hum.-Comput. Interact. **37**(8), 729–758 (2019)
16. Costa, P.: Conversing with personal digital assistants: on gender and artificial intelligence. J. Sci. Technol. Arts **10**(3), 59–72 (2018)
17. Dale, R.: The return of the chatbots. Nat. Lang. Eng. **22**(5), 811–817 (2016)
18. De Fauw, J., et al.: Clinically applicable deep learning for diagnosis and referral in retinal disease. Nat. Med. **24**(9), 1342–1350 (2018)
19. Devlin, J., Chang, M.-W., Lee, K., Toutanova, K.: BERT: pre-training of deep bidirectional transformers for language understanding. arXiv preprint arXiv:1810.04805 (2018)
20. Feine, J., Gnewuch, U., Morana, S., Maedche, A.: Gender bias in chatbot design. In: Følstad, A., et al. (eds.) CONVERSATIONS 2019. LNCS, vol. 11970, pp. 79–93. Springer, Cham (2020). https://doi.org/10.1007/978-3-030-39540-7_6
21. Fogg, B.J.: Persuasive technology: using computers to change what we think and do. Ubiquity **2002**(December), 2 (2002)
22. Gigerenzer, G.: How to Stay Smart in a Smart World: Why Human Intelligence Still Beats Algorithms. Penguin, UK (2022)
23. Gottinger, H.W., Weimann, P.: Intelligent decision support systems. Decis. Support Syst. **8**(4), 317–332 (1992)
24. Green, B., Chen, Y.: The principles and limits of algorithm-in-the-loop decision making. Proc. ACM Hum. Comput. Interact. **3**(CSCW), 1–24 (2019)
25. Grigoryan, A.: "you are too blunt, too ambitious, too confident": cultural messages that undermine women's paths to advancement and leadership in academia and beyond. In: Surviving Sexism in Academia, pp. 243–249. Routledge (2017)
26. Hanna, N., Richards, D., et al.: Do birds of a feather work better together? The impact of virtual agent personality on a shared mental model with humans during collaboration. In: COOS@ AAMAS, pp. 28–37 (2015)
27. Hester, H.: Technology becomes her. New Vistas **3**(1), 46–50 (2017)
28. Jain, M., Kumar, P., Kota, R., Patel, S.N.: Evaluating and informing the design of chatbots. In: Proceedings of the 2018 Designing Interactive Systems Conference, pp. 895–906 (2018)
29. Johnson, M.T., Vera, A.H.: No AI is an island: the case for teaming intelligence. AI Mag. **40**, 16–28 (2019)
30. Jung, E.H., Waddell, T.F., Sundar, S.S.: Feminizing robots: user responses to gender cues on robot body and screen. In: Proceedings of the 2016 CHI Conference Extended Abstracts on Human Factors in Computing Systems, pp. 3107–3113 (2016)
31. Kang, M.: A study of chatbot personality based on the purposes of chatbot. J. Korea Contents Assoc. **18**(5), 319–329 (2018)
32. Kim, H., Koh, D.Y., Lee, G., Park, J.-M., Lim, Y.-K.: Designing personalities of conversational agents. In: Extended Abstracts of the 2019 CHI Conference on Human Factors in Computing Systems, pp. 1–6 (2019)

33. Kim, Y., Baylor, A.L., Shen, E.: Pedagogical agents as learning companions: the impact of agent emotion and gender. J. Comput. Assist. Learn. **23**(3), 220–234 (2007)
34. Kleinberg, J., Lakkaraju, H., Leskovec, J., Ludwig, J., Mullainathan, S.: Human decisions and machine predictions. Q. J. Econ. **133**(1), 237–293 (2018)
35. Lee, D.E.: Ideal female-male traits and evaluation of favorability. Percept. Motor Skills **50**(3 suppl), 1039–1046 (1980)
36. Lessio, N., Morris, A.: Toward design archetypes for conversational agent personality. In: 2020 IEEE International Conference on Systems, Man, and Cybernetics (SMC), pp. 3221–3228. IEEE (2020)
37. Liew, T.W., Tan, S.-M.: Social cues and implications for designing expert and competent artificial agents: a systematic review. Telematics Inform. **65**, 101721 (2021)
38. Malone, T.W.: How can human-computer "superminds" develop business strategies? Future Manag. AI World (2019)
39. McDonnell, M., Baxter, D.: Chatbots and gender stereotyping. Interact. Comput. **31**(2), 116–121 (2019)
40. Mehra, B.: Chatbot personality preferences in global south urban English speakers. Soc. Sci. Hum. Open **3**(1), 100131 (2021)
41. Nag, P., Yalçın, Ö.N.: Gender stereotypes in virtual agents. In: Proceedings of the 20th ACM International Conference on Intelligent Virtual Agents, pp. 1–8 (2020)
42. Nass, C., Moon, Y., Green, N.: Are machines gender neutral? Gender-stereotypic responses to computers with voices. J. Appl. Soc. Psychol. **27**(10), 864–876 (1997)
43. Nilsson, N.J.: The Quest for Artificial Intelligence. Cambridge University Press (2009)
44. Noble, H., Mitchell, G.: What is grounded theory? Evid. Based Nurs. **19**(2), 34–35 (2016)
45. Norman, D.A.: Emotional design: why we love (or hate) everyday things. In: Civitas Books (2004)
46. Parker, A., Tritter, J.: Focus group method and methodology: current practice and recent debate. Int. J. Res. Method Educ. **29**(1), 23–37 (2006)
47. Pennebaker, J.W., King, L.A.: Linguistic styles: language use as an individual difference. J. Pers. Soc. Psychol. **77**(6), 1296 (1999)
48. Phillips-Wren, G., Mora, M., Forgionne, G.A., Gupta, J.N.: An integrative evaluation framework for intelligent decision support systems. Eur. J. Oper. Res. **195**(3), 642–652 (2009)
49. Pomerol, J.-C.: Artificial intelligence and human decision making. Eur. J. Oper. Res. **99**(1), 3–25 (1997)
50. Porcheron, M., Fischer, J.E., Reeves, S., Sharples, S.: Voice interfaces in everyday life. In: Proceedings of the 2018 CHI Conference on Human Factors in Computing Systems, pp. 1–12 (2018)
51. Rapp, A., Curti, L., Boldi, A.: The human side of human-chatbot interaction: a systematic literature review of ten years of research on text-based chatbots. Int. J. Hum. Comput. Stud. **151**, 102630 (2021)
52. Roy, Q., Ghafurian, M., Li, W., Hoey, J.: Users, tasks, and conversational agents: a personality study. In: Proceedings of the 9th International Conference on Human-Agent Interaction, pp. 174–182 (2021)
53. Ruane, E., Birhane, A., Ventresque, A.: Conversational AI: social and ethical considerations. In: AICS, pp. 104–115 (2019)

54. Ruane, E., Farrell, S., Ventresque, A.: User perception of text-based chatbot personality. In: Følstad, A., et al. (eds.) CONVERSATIONS 2020. LNCS, vol. 12604, pp. 32–47. Springer, Cham (2021). https://doi.org/10.1007/978-3-030-68288-0_3
55. Russell, S.J., Norvig, P.: Artificial Intelligence a Modern Approach. Pearson Education Inc. (2010)
56. Sanny, L., Susastra, A., Roberts, C., Yusramdaleni, R.: The analysis of customer satisfaction factors which influence chatbot acceptance in Indonesia. Manag. Sci. Lett. **10**(6), 1225–1232 (2020)
57. Shani, C., Libov, A., Tolmach, S., Lewin-Eytan, L., Maarek, Y., Shahaf, D.: "alexa, do you want to build a snowman?" Characterizing playful requests to conversational agents. In: CHI Conference on Human Factors in Computing Systems Extended Abstracts, pp. 1–7 (2022)
58. Sharda, R., Barr, S.H., McDonnell, J.C.: Decision support system effectiveness: a review and an empirical test. Manage. Sci. **34**(2), 139–159 (1988)
59. Shawar, B.A., Atwell, E.S.: Using corpora in machine-learning chatbot systems. Int. J. Corpus Linguist. **10**(4), 489–516 (2005)
60. Smestad, T.L., Volden, F.: Chatbot personalities matters. In: Bodrunova, S.S., et al. (eds.) INSCI 2018. LNCS, vol. 11551, pp. 170–181. Springer, Cham (2019). https://doi.org/10.1007/978-3-030-17705-8_15
61. Soenksen, L.R., et al.: Using deep learning for dermatologist-level detection of suspicious pigmented skin lesions from wide-field images. Sci. Trans. Med. **13**(581), eabb3652 (2021)
62. Terveen, L.G.: Overview of human-computer collaboration. Knowl.-Based Syst. **8**(2–3), 67–81 (1995)
63. Vanderlyn, L., Weber, G., Neumann, M., Väth, D., Meyer, S., Vu, N.T.: "it seemed like an annoying woman": on the perception and ethical considerations of affective language in text-based conversational agents. In: Proceedings of the 25th Conference on Computational Natural Language Learning, pp. 44–57 (2021)
64. Verhagen, T., Van Nes, J., Feldberg, F., Van Dolen, W.: Virtual customer service agents: using social presence and personalization to shape online service encounters. J. Comput.-Mediat. Commun. **19**(3), 529–545 (2014)
65. Völkel, S.T., Kaya, L.: Examining user preference for agreeableness in chatbots. In: CUI 2021–3rd Conference on Conversational User Interfaces, pp. 1–6 (2021)
66. Völkel, S.T., Schoedel, R., Kaya, L., Mayer, S.: User perceptions of extraversion in chatbots after repeated use. In: CHI Conference on Human Factors in Computing Systems, pp. 1–18 (2022)
67. Wang, L., et al.: Cass: towards building a social-support chatbot for online health community. Proc. ACM Hum. Comput. Interact. **5**(CSCW1), 1–31 (2021)
68. Xiao, H., Reid, D., Marriott, A., Gulland, E.K.: An adaptive personality model for ECAs. In: Tao, J., Tan, T., Picard, R.W. (eds.) ACII 2005. LNCS, vol. 3784, pp. 637–645. Springer, Heidelberg (2005). https://doi.org/10.1007/11573548_82
69. Xiao, J., Stasko, J., Catrambone, R.: The role of choice and customization on users' interaction with embodied conversational agents: effects on perception and performance. In: Proceedings of the SIGCHI Conference on Human Factors in Computing Systems, pp. 1293–1302 (2007)
70. Xiao, Z., Zhou, M.X., Fu, W.-T.: Who should be my teammates: using a conversational agent to understand individuals and help teaming. In: Proceedings of the 24th International Conference on Intelligent User Interfaces (2019)
71. Zhou, M.X., Wang, C., Mark, G., Yang, H., Xu, K.: Building real-world chatbot interviewers: lessons from a wizard-of-OZ field study. In: IUI Workshops (2019)

# Empirical Grounding for the Interpretations of Natural User Interface: A Case Study on Smartpen

Baraa Alabdulwahab[1] and Effie Lai-Chong Law[2]([envelope])

[1] University of Leicester, Leicester LE1 7RH, UK
ba184@le.ac.uk
[2] Durham University, Durham DH1 3LE, UK
wsnv42@durham.ac.uk

**Abstract.** The emergence of Natural User Interface (NUI) approximately two decades ago promised to support intuitive and multimodal interactions by leveraging human sensorimotor skills such as touching, speaking, and gazing. Despite the development and introduction of commercial NUI hardware, traditional user interfaces (e.g., GUIs) continue to dominate in many sectors, prompting inquiry into the claims of 'naturalness'. To examine this phenomenon, we investigated empirically two interpretations of naturalness: innateness and intuitiveness. The study involved asking 56 participants to complete learning tasks with a smartpen system and a laptop system representing innateness and intuitiveness, respectively. A mixed-method design was implemented to collect participants' perception and performance while using both interfaces. Results indicated that, despite the smartpen system was highly learnable, the perception of naturalness was significantly linked to participants' prior experiences rather than to innate abilities. The implications of these findings are discussed.

**Keywords:** Natural user interface · Smartpen · Cognitive load · Innateness · Intuitiveness

## 1 Introduction

Natural user interface (NUI) emerged as part of the post-WIMP design trend in the early 21st century [32]. NUI aimed to answer challenges associated with the extensive use of visual elements in graphical user interfaces (GUI) to accommodate newer functionalities; such an expansion required users to learn how to operate sophisticated GUI-based computer systems [51]. In contrast, NUI gives the promise to provide more intuitive interaction, requiring minimal training and offering multimodality that increases interaction bandwidth beyond screen boundaries by using voice, touch, gestures, and other mechanisms based on biomimicry [20]. While the trend towards intuitive interaction started as early as 1980s, it was only possible to be implemented through the technological advances achieved by the end of the 20th century and the lessons learned from the development of the earlier GUI [5]. In education, for example, the natural

J. Abdelnour Nocera et al. (Eds.): INTERACT 2023, LNCS 14143, pp. 350–371, 2023.
https://doi.org/10.1007/978-3-031-42283-6_20

user interaction is thought to hold a lot of potential for technology-enhanced learning as it frees learners from handling complex GUI-related instructions as a prerequisite to access learning content and provides novel ways to explore knowledge that were not possible with screen-only systems [3]. Furthermore, the ubiquitous nature of NUIs is thought to support learning analytics by feeding it with a high volume of data actively and transparently collected from learners, making thorough analysis possible [33].

In recent years, several commercial hardware devices have been introduced as NUIs. Touch screens come at the top of the list as they allow direct manipulation of visual elements on the display surface [50]. For motion, hand-held game controllers such as Nintendo Wiimote and Sony Move can track hand motion, rotation and acceleration in 3D space. The Leap Motion Controller is hand-tracking device that enables touchless (mid-air) input for computer systems [2]. Microsoft Kinect is a full-body posture and hand gestures tracker and supports spoken commands; it has been used widely in education, entertainment, health rehabilitation and training applications [47]. Voice-based interface/interaction (VUI) technologies such as Amazon Alexa and Apple Siri are deployed in an increasing number of sectors [4]. VR and AR systems such as Head-Mounted Display (HMD) are used to support reality and immersive experience [19].

Despite the high promises and potential, the advancement of the NUI technology has faced critical challenges. The rush towards applications with the lack of good foundation has translated into serious usability issues [11, 16, 29, 30, 35]. In principle, the term 'natural' has been criticised to be ambiguous due to its scope that can either mean natural to a specific group of users or natural to humans as species [37]. This basic conceptual and terminological issue was argued to have critical consequences on design decisions due to differences in targeted end users – the source where requirements for design qualities are gathered [14]. On the other hand, the perception of naturalness from the user perspective, rather than the designer perspective, was also problematic as users' expectations were demonstrated to exceed what a NUI could afford [12, 39]. Hence, identifying 'naturalness' proved to be very pivotal for designing and evaluating natural interfaces [48].

The question of naturalness has been debated intensively in numerous theoretical studies (e.g. [14, 16, 31, 37, 39, 48]). These studies followed an argumentative methodology either to negate the correctness of the term 'natural' as in [14, 37] or to seek a sensible interpretation based on previous research in the domain [16, 39, 48]. This study, in contrast, aimed to investigate naturalness empirically by engaging participants, gauging performance, and analysing experiences. Having an empirical grounding in sync with the previous theoretical discussions could be very pragmatic for developing a holistic understanding of naturalness. In the following sections, we present the unsettled disputes related to the concept of NUI and then we present our empirical contribution to address this issue.

## 2  Background and Related Work

### 2.1  Issues with NUI Definition

In search for the term 'Natural User Interface', an early work by Stratton and Dunsmore [48] stated that using hyperlinks in web pages is a NUI as "[it] mimics the way humans think … in wild leaps from idea to idea" (p. 2). Since then, the term has been used more frequently, e.g., [44, 45], as an interaction style that allows humans to interact with real as well as virtual objects in a "literally direct manipulative way" [44, p. 109]. In the same vein, [6] described a natural dialog interface as something that "resembles a conversation two humans might have" (p. 1). Following the emergence of new input technologies, the term NUI has become common and been used to describe devices that employ touch, voice and gesture-based interactions [51].

Nevertheless, there is a lack of a universal definition for NUI in the literature. The definition in Wikipedia addresses the user's perception: "a user interface that is effectively invisible and remains invisible as the user continuously learns increasingly complex interactions". The definition from [5] focuses on the user's skills: "natural user interface is a user interface designed to reuse existing skills for interacting directly with content" (p. 2) whereas the one from [38] highlights the automation aspect: "a type of human-machine interaction based on the automatic analysis of the user's natural behaviour. These human actions are interpreted by the machine as commands that control system operations" (p. 205).

What makes the definition of NUI challenging, in comparison to command line and GUIs, is referring the interface's principle to a free-behaving user rather than to well-known and well-bounded machine artefacts. For example, in [38]'s definition cited above, the natural human behaviour is defined as "a group of activities performed by humans in everyday life to interact with their animated and unanimated environment" (p. 205). The argument here is: the interface that is invisible, reuses previous skills or relies on natural behaviour of a human cannot be defined deterministically because it is a related concept extends out of the machine domain to an active and very diverse human domain [51]. In other words, whereas a GUI can be defined as a matrix of pixels being mapped to precise coordinates on screen and specific machine commands – all finite sets, hence the abstract mathematical definition can be transferred into a hardware design in full. In contrast, a NUI is related to indeterministic and infinite sets of human behaviours, skills and perceptions that make any mathematical abstraction either ambiguous or incomprehensive [2] at pre-implementation phase.

### 2.2  Interpretations of Naturalness in NUI

Two themes of naturalness interpretations can be observed clearly in the literature of NUI. The first theme is naturalness that emerges from the innate human abilities such as speech, touch, gestures, facial expressions, gaze, and so on [26, 42]. This theme is the most common and highlighted by systematic reviews in the domain (e.g., [13, 24, 28]. Designing a NUI under this theme can be achieved by developing a better understanding of these homo sapiens abilities [21, 43]. The other theme is naturalness that emerges from previous experiences [5, 51] and refers to learned and well-developed skills of individuals to a level that makes applying these skills happen unconsciously (i.e., without mental effort). It also entails that individuals have developed a degree of emotional tendency towards using these skills over other alternatives [51]. Designing a NUI under this theme requires methodologies such as ethnographic observation and focus group to understand target individuals [18]. While this theme relates to the previous perspective of innate abilities to some extent, it is open towards utilising more advanced interactions beyond basic human skills. Wigdor and Wixon [51] affirmed this fact by stating "NUI requires learning" (p. 12) and by stating that a keyboard is more natural for typing than a gestural interface despite the former is considered traditional while the latter considered natural.

The framework of innate and learned skills in the previous themes comes in parallel with the 'Continuum of Knowledge' suggested by [36] for intuitive interaction. The Continuum of Knowledge has four levels: innate, sensorimotor, culture and expertise. The lower two levels (innate and sensorimotor) are the most homogeneous between humans as they are inborn or develop at very young age, while the higher two levels (culture and expertise) are acquired through life experiences and can vary between groups and communities. Nauman and colleagues [36] suggested that utilising this continuum could lead to intuition as a non-conscious process of interaction. For the sake of simplicity, we call naturalness engendered by the lower levels: *innateness*, and naturalness engendered by the higher levels: *intuitiveness*. Overall, the two themes of naturalness can be referred to as: **Innateness interpretation of NUI** and **Intuitiveness interpretation of NUI.**

Nonetheless, what remains unclear is to which extent innateness vs. intuitiveness can contribute to the perception of naturalness. This question is legitimate for designing NUIs, because the intuitiveness interpretation provides more flexibility, e.g., the previous analogy of using keyboard for digital writing in [51] while innateness seems dominant in the literature of NUI. Moreover, those adopting the intuitiveness theme [5, 51] referred to touch and gestural interfaces when they discussed strategies for NUI design. Hence, it is apparent that the NUI concept in the literature is largely influenced by novel UI technologies whereas the theoretical foundation remains uncertain.

## 2.3  Research Objectives

The aim of this study is to investigate the extent in which innateness and intuitiveness could contribute to the perception of naturalness empirically. While intuitiveness is advocated as a source of naturalness in theoretical arguments (e.g. [36, 39]), most empirical studies rely on innate abilities [13] and do not seem to support this viewpoint. Hence, this study aimed to cover this gap by collecting subjective and objective data (i.e. mixed-method approach) from users while utilising two interfacing technologies that exemplify innateness and intuitiveness themes. Data analysis can then be used as an empirical support to the meaning of naturalness.

# 3   Methods

## 3.1   Overview

The context of the empirical study was educational: a reading task followed by answering comprehension questions while using two different interfaces. The 'innate' natural user interface utilised in this study was a smart pen and paper assisted by a touchscreen, whereas the 'intuitive' user interface was a laptop (screen and keyboard interface). The aim was to probe any behavioural change or enhancement in participants' performance while using both interfaces. Further, we explicitly asked participants about their preferred interface based on their experience. Participants' vote on their preferred interface was the golden standard in deciding naturalness, while the other analysis was to justify and rationalise this selection.

## 3.2   Interaction Assumptions and Design

***Interaction Assumptions:*** A theoretically well-grounded foundation is required to justify the innateness and intuitiveness of the interfaces employed in the study. There is evidence from cognitive science that the basic use of pen and paper (i.e., scribbling) is a gesture of self-expression and communication, and can develop naturally in children as young as two [27]. Additionally, pen-based interaction is a well-known form of natural interfaces [9] that employs gestures (pen strokes) to communicate ideas. We used this foundation to derive the basic assumption that pen and paper are legitimate tools to exhibit innateness. Equally, touching and simple navigation using touchscreen is also an innate ability according to literature [5]. On the other hand, the ability to use a traditional personal computer (PC) cannot come naturally. However, for an academic cohort who use such technology for an extended period of time, using PC becomes a familiar task. Hence, the laptop system is a legitimate tool to exhibit intuitiveness for this cohort (cf. Their ICT skill level was confirmed in the pre-study survey; Sect. 3.4).

***Interaction Range:*** Digital reading can involve a wide range of interactions. For our experiment, setting these interactions was necessary to guarantee a comparable functionality of the two interfaces. According to [15], a typical digital reading task using a computer system with keyboard and mouse as input devices covers the following interaction: scrolling, navigation through links, text search and text input. Additionally, zooming is common in smaller screens [22]. These interactions were supported by default on the laptop interface. For the smartpen system, this entailed to have a mechanism that allows an interaction with printed elements on paper, and to have a proper display modality to show output (e.g., to open URLs or show videos). The display modality also had to satisfy innateness constraints in order to keep the whole smartpen system compliant with innateness. Having this achieved in technical development (details in Sects. 3.5 and 3.6), it was possible to create an interaction design for digital reading using the smartpen system and match it with the laptop system as shown in Table 1.

**Table 1.** A matching between digital reading interactions of laptop and smartpen systems

| Laptop System | Smartpen system |
|---|---|
| Scrolling | Paper flipping |
| Links navigation | Tapping over printed links, output is shown on display |
| Text search | Tabbing over printed text, output is shown on display |
| Text input | Writing |
| Zooming | Tapping over printed elements to get a higher resolution version on display (e.g., for images and graphs) |

### 3.3 Procedure

The learning materials for the reading tasks were two scientific articles obtained from the NASA climate blog (https://climate.nasa.gov/ask-nasa-climate/). The articles entitled "The Climate Connections of a Record Fire Year in the U.S. West" and "Sea Level 101" have the same climate theme and the same author to ensure a comparable difficulty (NB: the difficulty level was also rated by the participants as post-study feedback; Table 2 in Sect. 3.7).

The experiment was split into two sessions over two consecutive days with the same process. In each session, one of the two articles was provided. Each article was split into almost equal halves of similar length, and each half was presented through a different interface (i.e., a smartpen system vs a laptop system). Participants also had to use the interface to answer ten comprehension questions (9 multiple choices +1 free text question) after reading the text.

The same procedure was used on both days, but the order of interfaces was swapped to control the order effect. Specifically, participants were asked to use the smartpen system first and then the laptop on the first day, and the laptop first followed by the smartpen system on the second day. This arrangement was made to increase accuracy and to reduce the possible bias resulted from using a new interface (the smartpen system). A session was set to maximum two hours with about one hour for each part of the article. Performance data and subjective feedback were collected during and after each task for a mixed-method evaluation (Sect. 3.7). The experiment was conducted on an individual basis in a quiet, reading-friendly environment.

Few days prior to the experiment, participants were contacted by email to fill a survey concerning their demographic data. The survey covered the following items: age, gender, whether English is their first language, level of education, and skill levels of using laptop and smartphone. Also, the survey included a short test to assess participants' prior knowledge of topics covered by the articles. Participants were asked to complete the survey in their own time and send it back prior to the study to minimise the time needed to spend in the lab.

### 3.4  Participants

The experimental study was approved by the Ethics Committee of the University of Leicester. The recruitment process targeted university students and staff, who were approached through emails and in-person invites. The sample size was 56 of which 34 were female and 22 were male; 30 of participants were non-native English speakers, mainly international students. Participants for this study were adults from different age groups: thirty-two were 18–24 years old, eleven were 25–30, seven were 31–40, three were 41–50 and two were above 50. The study did not involve any participant with special needs or learning disabilities. Participation was voluntary, and participants received a £25 Amazon gift card as a compensation for their time. All participants were confirmed to be familiar with reading using laptop web browser.

### 3.5  The Smartpen System

*Hardware:* The smartpen system involved using NeoLab smartpen (model: NWP-F50) along with the specialised coded paper. Display modality was implemented by utilising Android smartphone (model: Nokia 2.4) which worked as the host system for the smartpen to display interaction output on a 6.5″ touchscreen (Fig. 1).

**Fig. 1.** The smartpen system

*Software:* Two software applications were developed for the smartpen system:

1) *Document procession utility:* a PC software application that takes a PDF document and converts its pages to a coded-paper PDF document so the smartpen can interact with pages upon printing. It also analyses locations of document content, and stores results in JSON format; these JSON files can be used later to interpret user input. The software can be used by authors to add/edit actions, such as playing videos or opening a URL when specific printed element is tapped.

2) *User display app:* A simple Android app for end-users to show interaction output is deployed. The app utilises the pre-generated JSON files (created by the Document processing utility) to interpret user inputs and can offer the following functionalities:

- Displaying meaning, synonyms and translation of a (tapped) word. These data were driven directly from Google Translate website.
- Opening a URL available on the paper.
- Playing videos linked to a tapped element on paper.
- Showing a high-resolution version of images printed on paper.

### 3.6  The Laptop System

*Hardware:* The laptop used in this experiment was Lenovo (model: Ideapad Yoga 13) with Windows 10 installed.

*Software:* A website developed to display learning materials (i.e., reading articles) followed by the comprehension questions (Fig. 2).

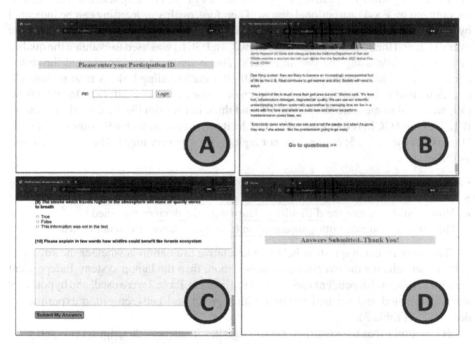

**Fig. 2.** Snapshots of the website designed for laptop-based reading. A: Login page, B: Reading topic page, C: Comprehension questions page, D: Submission confirmation page

358     B. Alabdulwahab and E. L.-C. Law

### 3.7 Mixed-Method Evaluation Approach

*Quantitative Evaluation:* For quantitative evaluation, we employed the usability framework with the key metrics effectiveness and efficiency, according to the ISO 9241-110:2020 standard, along with the Cognitive Load Theory (CLT) [49] to evaluate participants' performance. These frameworks have a certain level of intersection as effectiveness and efficiency are objective measures of cognitive load [41].

Effectiveness was quantified through participant score in the comprehension test, while efficiency reflected in the time required to complete the task. Additionally, activity rate, which is the number of requests made by participant to retrieve external digital content (e.g., opening a URL or requesting the translation of a word) used to assess engagement during the reading task.

For cognitive load (CL) assessment, CLT proposes that the overall CL has three sub-components: intrinsic (ICL), extraneous (ECL), and germane (GCL) [49]. According to [10], ICL is resulted from the inherent difficulty of the learning topic, thence, it cannot be influenced by the instructional design. In contrast, ECL is resulted from the poor presentation of the learning content, while GCL is a positive mental effort that marks building knowledge in the long-term memory (i.e., creating schemas) and can be encouraged by good instructional design. Therefore, quality of learning can be indicated by a decreased ECL and increased GCL. Accordingly, a subjective assessment of the overall CL and the sub-components (ICL, ECL and GCL) was used to evaluate the quality of learning while using the two interfaces. The assessment was conducted through a questionnaire which participants had to fill after each reading task. A total of four CL questionnaires collected from each participant (2 reading tasks x 2 days). One item from [40] was used to measure the overall CL and three items from [8] were used to measure ICL, ECL and GCL, respectively. Each of the items was rated with a 9-point Likert scale (1: very very low, …, 5: neither low nor high, … 9: very very high). The items are listed as follows:

- How would you rate the <u>mental effort</u> you have invested in studying the article?
- How would you rate the <u>difficulty of the content</u> of the article?
- How would you rate the <u>difficulty to learn with the devices</u> provided?
- How would you rate <u>your concentration (attention)</u> during the reading task?

The main research question behind quantitative evaluation is whether the smartpen system can enhance the overall performance more than the laptop system. Independent variables (IVs) and dependent variables (DVs) listed in Table 2 were used, and hypotheses were formulated and verified through within-group and between-group experimental design [23] (Table 3).

H1 assumes that the smartpen system satisfies innateness description (i.e., no prior experience is required, and both novice and expert users can use it with the same level of proficiency [51]). H1 relies on an assumption that digitally skilled users can handle new technologies better than novice users. H2 and H3 assume that the smartpen system can enhance learning outcome. H3 relies on the fact that the smartpen system has an additional functionality (translation by tapping) that is particularly useful for non-native English speakers where learning material is provided in English.

**Table 2.** Independent and dependent variables for hypothesis testing

| Independent variables | |
| --- | --- |
| UI Type | The type of interface being used during the task; (Smartpen, Laptop) |
| IT Skill level | Self-reported technical skills for using a PC and an Android device; (3 levels: Low, Medium, High) |
| Mother tongue | English is participant's mother language?; (Non-native, Native) |
| Dependent variables | |
| CL, ICL, ECL, GCL | Cognitive load(s) rating on a 9-point Likert scale; (Very-very low … Very-very High) |
| Activity | Number of requests for external materials (any sort of web resources) other than the main article during that task; (number ≥ 0) **Note:** for the smartpen system, Activity = Activity (URL requests) + Activity (word-lookup requests) |
| Efficiency | Time spent to complete a task; (time ≥ 0) |
| Effectiveness | Participant score in the comprehension test; (Grade [0..10]) |

**Table 3.** Hypotheses of the experiment

| ID | Hypothesis (IV, Experimental design) | DV |
| --- | --- | --- |
| *H1* | *When using smartpen, Activity, ECL and Efficiency are similar across participants form all IT Skill Levels groups. (IT Skill Level, Between-group)* | |
| H1.1 | There is no significant difference in the Activity among participants with different IT skill levels | Activity |
| H1.2 | There is no significant difference in ECL among participants with different IT skill levels | ECL |
| H1.3 | There is no significant difference in the Efficiency among participants with different IT skill levels | Efficiency |
| *H2* | *Participants' Performance and ECL are enhanced when using smartpen compared to the laptop system (UI Type, Within-group)* | |
| H2.1 | There is a significant difference in participants' Performance between using the smartpen and the laptop system | Effectiveness |
| H2.2 | There is a significant difference in participants' CL between using the smartpen and the laptop system | CL |

**Table 3.** (*continued*)

| ID | Hypothesis (IV, Experimental design) | DV |
|------|------|------|
| *H3* | *When using smartpen, Activity and GCL of non-native English speakers are higher than Activity and GCL of native speakers. (Mother tongue, Between-group)* | |
| H3.1 | There is a significant difference in Activity between native and non-native English speakers | Activity |
| H3.2 | There is a significant difference in GCL between native and non-native English speakers | GCL |

*Qualitative Evaluation:* Individual semi-structured interviews with participants were conducted at the end of the experiment (i.e., Day 2) where feedback on their experience of using the two interfaces was collected. Specifically, two major aspects of questions were asked: First, a comparison of reading and writing experience while utilising the laptop and smartpen systems in general and with specific reference to the perceived pros and cons of both systems. Second, whether they prefer to use the laptop or the smartpen system for future reading and writing.

Thematic analysis [7] was applied to the interview data. The analysis of qualitative data was conducted from the perspective of Disappearing Interface (DA). The DA concept [25] assumes that an interface has a physical presence as well as a conceptual presence and that invisible design should seek hiding these presences behind ubiquity and immersive interactivity, respectively [1]. According to [25], naturalness is achieved when the UI disappeared. Hence, the cues of presence were traced and measured during the qualitative analysis (Sect. 4.2).

# 4   Results

## 4.1   Quantitative Data Analysis

A total of 56 participants completed the experiment. The data were analysed using SPSS v28, and the analysis was applied to both days of the experiment. Results of Shapiro-Wilk tests indicated that dependent variables were not normally distributed ($p < 0.05$), nonparametric tests were used. First, we applied factorial analysis to study the effects of IVs and covariates and then studied the effect of individual IVs on DVs.

**Quade's Non-parametric Factorial Analysis.** Demographic attributes (e.g., age, gender, education) can mediate the effect of IVs on DVs. As our data are non-normally distributed, parametric multi-factor ANOVA are inapplicable. Quade's non-parametric ANCOVA is an alternative [46], but it is less powerful and cannot show the interaction effect between two variables. It involves rank transformation of DVs. In our study, two attributes - IT skill for handling technology and status of being English native speaker for reading – are particularly relevant. We applied Quade's to evaluate the effects of these two attributes on Activity and CL (cf. Table 2). We also analysed the effects of age and gender on Effectiveness (comprehension test score) and Efficiency (task completion time). Results (Table 4a, b) show that none of these attributes have any significant effect on the DVs concerned.

**Table 4.** Quade's ANCOVA (a) IT Skill and Native Language on Activity and CL; (b) Age and Gender on Effectiveness and Efficiency (D1 = Day1, D2 = Day2; Smart = Smartpen)

| | Comprehension Score | | | | Task Time (Efficiency) | | | |
|---|---|---|---|---|---|---|---|---|
| | Smart-D1 | Smart-D2 | PC-D1 | PC-D2 | Smart-D1 | Smart-D2 | PC-D1 | PC-D2 |
| Age (Covariate, F) | 0.07 | 0.01 | 0.23 | 2.22 | 2.39 | 1.27 | 0.88 | 0.24 |
| Gender(Group, t) | -0.27 | 0.07 | 0.48 | 1.49 | -1.55 | -1.13 | -0.94 | -0.49 |
| p (df = 54) | 0.79 | 0.94 | 0.63 | 0.14 | 0.13 | 0.27 | 0.35 | 0.62 |
| | Activity | | | | Overall Cognitive Load (CL) | | | |
| | Smart-D1 | Smart-D2 | PC-D1 | PC-D2 | Smart-D1 | Smart-D2 | PC-D1 | PC-D2 |
| ITSkill (Covariate, F) | 1.18 | 0.15 | 1.73 | 3.22 | 0.95 | 0.48 | 1.31 | 1.57 |
| Native (Group, t) | 1.09 | 0.39 | 1.31 | 1.79 | -0.97 | -0.69 | -1.15 | -1.25 |
| p (df = 54) | 0.28 | 0.70 | 0.19 | 0.08 | 0.34 | 0.49 | 0.26 | 0.22 |

**Non-parametric Tests with One IV.** Results of Kruskal-Wallis tests, i.e., the test statistic H (degree of freedom) and $p$ value, indicated no significant differences in Activity among participants from the three IT skill groups when they used the smartpen system: $H(2)_{day1} = 3.13$, $p_{day1} = .21$ and $H(2)_{day2} = .41$, $p_{day2} = .82$. The same was found for the extraneous cognitive load (ECL): $H(2)_{day1} = .12$, $p_{day1} = .94$ and $H(2)_{day2} = .59$, $p_{day2} = .75$, and for the efficiency (task completion time): $H(2)_{day1} = 3.16$, $p_{day1} = .21$ and $H(2)_{day2} = 2.56$, $p_{day2} = .28$.

As for comparing effectiveness (comprehension test score) and the cognitive load (CL) resulted from using the two systems evaluated (within-group), results of Wilcoxon signed rank tests indicated no significant differences in effectiveness ($Z_{day1} = -.50$, $p_{day1} = .62$) and ($Z_{day2} = -.43$, $p_{day2} = .68$), as well as for the cognitive load ($Z_{day1} = -.39$, $p_{day1} = .70$) and ($Z_{day2} = -.15$, $p_{day2} = .88$) between the systems. Indeed, the median comprehension test score was 8 out of 10 for both systems while the median CL for the smartpen system was 5, slightly below the median CL of the laptop system which was 6. Further, it is worth noting that results of Wilcoxon signed rank test showed a significant difference in the average Activity while using the two systems on both days ($Z_{day1} = -5.55$, $p_{day1} < .001$) and ($Z_{day2} = -.5.12$, $p_{day2} < .001$). Mean values of participants' Activity while using the smartpen system were 6.39 and 6.55 for Day1 and Day2, respectively, while the corresponding values of the laptop system were 1.77 and 1.73.

Finally, regarding the influence of mother tongue on activity and the germane cognitive load (GCL) while using the smartpen system, results of Mann-Whitney test showed no significant difference in Activity between native and non-native English speakers: $U_{day1}(N_{native} = 26, N_{non-native} = 30) = 330.50$, $Z_{day1} = -.98$, $p_{day1} = .33$ and $U_{day2}(26, 30) = 382.50$, $Z_{day2} = -.12$, $p_{day2} = .90$. Similarly, no significant difference was found for GCL on both days: $U_{day1}(26, 30) = 350.50$, $Z_{day1} = -.67$, $p_{day1} = .50$ and $U_{day2}(26, 30) = 381$, $Z_{day2} = -.15$, $p_{day2} = .88$. However, performing Mann-Whitney test on Activity related to words-lookup (i.e. finding meaning or translation) showed a significant difference between native and non-natives on day1: $U(26, 30) = 244.50$, $Z = -2.43$, $p = .01$, and on day2: $U(26, 30) = 275.50$, $Z = -1.92$, $p = .05$. The mean values of words-lookup Activity of non-natives were 4.93 and 3.37 for Day1 and Day2, respectively, almost double their corresponding values of natives, which were 2.31 and 1.88. Table 5 summarises the outcomes of hypothesis testing.

**Table 5.** Hypothesis testing results.

| H1 | | | H2 | | H3 | |
|---|---|---|---|---|---|---|
| H1.1 | H1.2 | H1.3 | H2.1 | H2.2 | H3.1 | H3.2 |
| Accept | Accept | Accept | Reject | Reject | Reject* | Reject |

*no significance in the overall activity between native and non-native speakers, however for words-lookup activity there was a significant difference.

### 4.2 Qualitative Data Analysis

A total of 56 voice recordings of post-experiment interviews were transcribed semi-automatically with an audio-to-text service (otter.ai) and then checked manually to generate final transcripts. Transcripts were analysed in four steps following the thematic analysis approach [7].

The first step was *extracting aspects of interest* in which participants expressed the 'pros' and 'cons' of two systems they had used during the evaluation. For example, feedback such as: *"I was able to put the article and questions in two tabs while I was reading... This helped in answering questions very quickly"* and *"I liked that it was possible to tap over words to get meanings immediately on phone"*.

The second step was to *group aspects of interest based on similarities*. Both positive and negative feedback belonging to the same aspect were put in the same group. For example, the ability to navigate between browser tabs and the ability of flipping pages smoothly were considered belonging to the navigability aspect.

The third step was *creating emergent, in-vivo codes* to represent data in each group. We were able to identify twelve such codes representing categories of aspects of interests (for detailed analysis the Supplementary Materials):

- **Portability:** the ability to access or to carry the system physically anywhere.
- **Capacity:** technical features and limits of a system, e.g., screen size, storage capacity or power requirement.
- **Unity:** a state whether the system is physically discrete over several parts, or it is an all-in-one device.
- **Searchability:** the possibility to find a specific piece of information, e.g., looking up a keyword.

- **Navigability:** the possibility to navigate through learning content or retrieving extra content from the web.
- **Correctability:** the possibility to undo and correct unwanted input, e.g., erasing and retyping text.
- **Distraction:** the distraction resulted from extra functionalities which is irrelevant to the learning task, e.g., responding to a notification or pop-up message.
- **Expressiveness:** the ability of the system to reveal an intention or an idea, e.g., 'free doodling' with the pen or to 'copy and paste' using the laptop.
- **Familiarity:** the level of experience in using the system.
- **Strain:** the level of stress resulted from using a system, e.g., stress resulted from the glare of screen.
- **Versatility:** the possibility of using a system for different purposes related to the learning task, e.g., to explore extra content or recording notes.
- **Engagement:** the level of attention can be achieved while using a system.

Table 6 shows the frequency (total = 236) and percentage in each of the twelve coded categories. The most frequent comments for codes are summarised in Table 7.

**Table 6.** Frequencies and percentage of Topics of Interests under the coding scheme

| Topic of Interest category | Frequency | Percentage |
| --- | --- | --- |
| Navigability | 61 | 26% |
| Engagement | 31 | 14% |
| Versatility | 32 | 14% |
| Expressiveness | 25 | 11% |
| Searchability | 21 | 9% |
| Familiarity | 15 | 6% |
| Capacity | 13 | 5% |
| Distraction | 12 | 5% |
| Strain | 6 | 2% |
| Correctability | 4 | 2% |
| Unity | 3 | 1% |

The last step of subjective analysis was to *create a meta-coding of aspects based on the concept of Disappearing Interfaces* [25]. This step involved splitting the coded categories into *physical disappearance codes* (PDC) representing aspects that are not related to the reading and writing task, and *conceptual disappearance codes* (CDC) representing interactivity that is related to the reading and writing task. Accordingly, we were able to define the two sets: PDC = {Portability, Capacity, Unity, Distraction, Familiarity, Strain}, CDC = {Searchability, Navigability, Correctability, Expressiveness, Versatility, Engagement}. The positive feedback (8) for codes in each set was considered to support disappearance while negative feedback (8) to deter disappearance.

**Table 7.** Common reported features and comments under the coding scheme

| Code | Notable Positives | | Notable Negatives | |
|------|-------------------|---|-------------------|---|
| | Laptop Sys | Smartpen Sys | Laptop Sys | Smartpen Sys |
| Portability | Single device | Small and compact | | Requires carrying lots of printout |
| Capacity | Larger screen with ability to zoom in, larger storage of text | Can be extended to larger A3 paper | Battery runout quickly | Tiny screen |
| Unity | | | | Flipping between paper and phone |
| Searchability | Very easy to find words using Ctrl+F | Could open sources of information by a single click | Not all information types are searchable, e.g., images | Can't search words in pages |
| Navigability | Can open tabs side by side | Very easy way to navigate with a single click, typing URLs no longer required | Navigation between apps and websites is overwhelming | Need to flip pages frequently |
| Correctability | Very easy to edit and erase typed text | | | Need to scribble text and rewrite |
| Distraction | | | Too much distraction when browsing | Notifications comes from smartphone are distracting |
| Expressiveness | Can copy and paste or move items on screen | Able to doodle or sketch very quickly | Can't draw freely | Can't move text and need to rewrite it, which is time consuming |
| Familiarity | Using PC almost everywhere | Pen and paper are very basic and easy for writing and reading | | |
| Strain | | | Screen glow causes eye burning and sore | |

(continued)

**Table 7.** (*continued*)

| Code | Notable Positives | | Notable Negatives | |
|------|------|------|------|------|
| | Laptop Sys | Smartpen Sys | Laptop Sys | Smartpen Sys |
| Versatility | Can do many things using a laptop | Able to explore videos and media directly from paper | | Can't offer functionalities as much as a laptop |
| Engagement | Highlighting and annotating text are very helpful for reading | Reading from paper is much more engaging than a screen | | |

To make a measurable 'rate of disappearance' using the thematic analysis, frequencies of positive and negative aspects under each category (i.e., laptop positive, laptop negative, smartpen positive, smartpen negative) were normalised by using the maximum value under the category as 100% and calculating the other three values accordingly. While this quantification approach ignores individual category's contribution to the disappearance of PDC/CDC sets, it highlights strengths and weaknesses of each interface. Figure 3 shows the normalisation result.

As both PDC and CDC has 6 components each, it was also possible to calculate positive and negative scores (out of 6) of physical disappearance (PD) and conceptual disappearance (CD) for both interfaces as shown in Table 8. The accumulation (sum of positive and negative values) of scores might reflect the overall experience of disappearances (i.e., the concept of 'embodied interaction' in [39]).

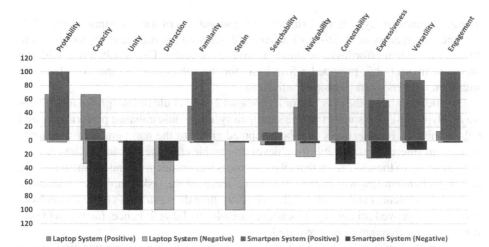

■ Laptop System (Positive)  ▢ Laptop System (Negative)  ■ Smartpen System (Positive)  ■ Smartpen System (Negative)

**Fig. 3.** Normalised frequencies of positive and negative feedback under the coding scheme

**Table 8.** Scores of physical and conceptual disappearances for both interfaces (pos. = positive; neg. = negative; acc. = accumulative)

|  | PD Score | | | CD Score | | |
|---|---|---|---|---|---|---|
|  | Pos | neg. | acc. | pos. | neg. | acc. |
| Laptop Sys. | +1.83 | −2.33 | *−0.5* | +4.62 | −0.54 | *+4.08* |
| Smartpen Sys. | +2.17 | −2.45 | *−0.28* | +3.58 | −0.80 | *+2.78* |

With regard to participants' response on which a system they might prefer for future reading and writing, the laptop system received 34 votes for reading and 28 for writing, the smartpen system received 16 votes for reading and 25 for writing. 6 participants provided no specific preference for reading, and 3 participants provided no specific preference for writing. Voting indicated higher preference towards using a laptop for future reading and writing.

Interesting feedback received from two participants who provided no specific preference for reading as they provided a *contextual preference*. The first mentioned that she prefers paper for in-bed "relaxed" reading and the laptop for "formal" academic reading. The other participant mentioned that he prefers paper for "serious" (i.e., in-depth and highly focused) reading while the laptop for day-to-day reading. Another interesting comment from a participant who managed to navigate to the original article (available on NASA Climate website; Sect. 3.1) using the smartphone, and continued to read from the smartphone rather than paper of the smartpen system, she provided that "I just felt the phone *more natural* to me".

## 5  Discussion

The acceptance of Hypothesis 1 supported the soundness of the assumption (Sect. 3.2) that the smartpen system satisfies innateness description; participants demonstrated to handle the system effortlessly without previous experience. This result, along with the literature in Sect. 3.2, provided a firm basis for the subsequent comparisons between smartpen innateness and laptop intuitiveness.

On the other hand, the rejection of Hypothesis 2 and 3 could be interpreted in different ways. Hypothesis 2 assumed that the smartpen system would enhance performance and reduce the CL. Its rejection could be attributed either to the naturalness of the laptop system, and therefore it was able to achieve comparable effectiveness and CL levels, or to the simplicity of the task, given that all participants were academics and the median score of comprehension test was high (8/10). If we accepted the task simplicity assumption given the high scores and a modest CL level (5/9), then the naturalness of both interfaces could not be proved reliably by dependent variables in Table 2; hence, further evidence from the subjective analysis is required.

This pattern was repeated in Hypothesis 3, as the non-native participants didn't show a significant increase in the overall activity nor in GCL in comparison to their native speaking counterparts when they used the smartpen system. While the sensitivity of the

CL measurement instruments adopted from [40] and [8] could influence the accuracy of CL results, the activity rate, efficiency, and effectiveness are accurate enough to confirm that no improvement in performance was associated with the use of the smartpen system. The significant increase in Activity while using the smartpen of within-group design, as well as for words lookup between native and non-natives (Sect. 4.1) indicated a high level of engagement. In brief, results of the quantitative analysis indicated that the smartpen system design based on innateness was able to achieve a better *interactive engagement*, but this was neither translated into a better performance nor into reduced CL. Comparable findings can be observed in the AR-JAM BOOK experiment in [17] and the experiment with Microsoft Kinect and stereoscopic visualisation of [34], and it was attributed to the difference between the *designed interaction* by developers and the *performed interaction* by participants.

The qualitative analysis of subjective feedback provided more insightful interpretations. First, the higher Familiarity of the smartpen system along with its better PD score (Fig. 3 and Table 8) support the innateness assumption. Similarly, both Engagement and Navigability support the increased activity observation. Nevertheless, the laptop system was considered to be more capable and scored much better than the smartpen system in terms of participants' perceived disappearances as indicated by the CD score. This matched the Disappearing Interface description in [25], as the physical appearance of the laptop (Distraction and Strain) was covered by the interactivity aspects (Searchability, Correctability, Expressiveness and Versatility). In other words, the laptop system which appeared physically was disappearing conceptually when participants immersed in interaction; in contrast, the lack of a comparable interactivity in the smartpen system hindered the gains in its physical disappearance.

From innateness-intuitiveness perspective, the interactivity aspects of the laptop which supported its disappearance (e.g., Searchability using CTRL+F keys; Table 7) are elements of previous *learned* experience developed in participants' perception and they don't come naturally. This supports that naturalness matches the intuitiveness description in [51] rather than innateness. A further support to this assumption can be seen by participants' recalling to the Portability aspect of the laptop vs. the smartpen system: participants were not asked during the experiment to carry and walk with the systems, but their previous experience made them associate Portability with naturalness.

The final voting and comments on system preference highlight several matters. The voting for the favour of the laptop system matched our findings of the thematic analysis, therefore it supports the soundness of the methodology. Also, the higher votes for reading using the laptop in comparison to those on writing resonates with the higher interactivity of the laptop mentioned earlier, as digital reading involves exploring different resources [15] while typical writing is more likely to be limited to a single document or writing space; the smartpen which lacked interactivity features gained comparable votes for writing. Comments from participants who provided no specific preference raises the significant aspect of *contextual naturalness*. Such feedback suggests that the exact same physical system can be natural or not natural depending on the context. This view echoes with the concept of 'embodied interaction' [39] and implies that naturalness is purely an experience in human perception rather than a feature of system. The consequences of this assumption on systems design and development could be very substantial, but it was out of our study's scope to explore them deeper.

## 6 Conclusion

In this study we reviewed the foundational issues of the concept of NUI, and we were able to define two possible interpretations for naturalness in the literature: innateness and intuitiveness. These interpretations were found to lack empirical support. Hence, we conducted an experimental study with the aim to compare these interpretations. Results suggested that intuitiveness is a more relevant synonym and interpretation for naturalness. Results also suggested that natural interaction could mark an experience rather than the use of a specific system. These empirical findings have substantial consequences on further NUI research. It indicates that using devices such as the Microsoft Kinect with the claim that this practice characterises an application of NUI in a specific domain (e.g., education) is no longer a legitimate approach for exploring natural interaction. Alternatively, a firm understanding to justify the selection of devices should be sought in the first place. Further, decoupling naturalness as an objective attribute of hardware and characterising it as a subjectively perceived experience implies exploring new ways for UI design, as discrete hardware modules could serve together to formulate a single NUI. It can be concluded that the NUI marks a higher level of maturity within the field of HCI rather than a specific genre of hardware. This maturity, however, was initially triggered by the emergence of novel interaction technologies.

**Acknowledgment.** The first author would like to acknowledge and thank the *Council for Academics At Risk (CARA)* for their generous support to complete this study as a part of his PhD research.

## References

1. Arnall, T.: Making visible: mediating the material of emerging technology. Oslo Sch. Archit. Des. (2014)
2. Bachmann, D., Weichert, F., Rinkenauer, G.: Review of three-dimensional human-computer interaction with focus on the leap motion controller. Sensors **18**(7), 2194 (2018)
3. Becker, S., Cummins, M., Davis, A., Freeman, A., Hall Giesinger, C., Ananthanarayanan, V.: The NMC Horizon Report: 2017 Higher Education Edition. The New Media Consortium, Austin, Texas (2017)
4. Berdasco, A., López, G., Diaz, I., Quesada, L., Guerrero, L.A.: User experience comparison of intelligent personal assistants: Alexa, Google Assistant, Siri and Cortana. In: Proceedings of 13th International Conference on Ubiquitous Computing and Ambient Intelligence (UCAmI), Toledo, Spain (2019)
5. Blake, J.: Natural user interfaces In: Net, Manning (MEAP) (2011)
6. Boyce, S.J., Gorin, A.L.: User interface issues for natural spoken dialog systems. In: International Symposium on Spoken Dialog (1996)
7. Braun, V., Clarke, V.: Thematic analysis. In: APA Handbook of Research Methods in Psychology, pp. 57–71. American Psychological Association (2012)

8. Cierniak, G., Scheiter, K., Gerjets, P.: Explaining the split-attention effect: is the reduction of extraneous cognitive load accompanied by an increase in germane cognitive load? Comput. Hum. Behav. **25**(2), 315–324 (2009)
9. Dai, G.: Pen-based user interface. In: Proceedings of The 8th International Conference on Computer Supported Cooperative Work in Design, Xiamen (2004)
10. Debue, N., van de Leemput, C.: What does germane load mean? An empirical contribution to the cognitive load theory. Front. Psychol. **5**, 1099 (2014)
11. Farhadi-Niaki, F., Etemad, S.A., Arya, A.: Design and usability analysis of gesture-based control for common desktop tasks. In: Kurosu, M. (eds.) HCI 2013. LNCS, vol. 8007, pp. 215–224. Springer, Heidelberg (2013). https://doi.org/10.1007/978-3-642-39330-3_23
12. Ghosh, S., Shruthi, C.S., Bansal, H., Sethia, A.: What is user's perception of naturalness? An exploration of natural user experience. In: Bernhaupt, R., Dalvi, G., Joshi, A., Balkrishan, D.K., O'Neill, J., Winckler, M. (eds.) INTERACT 2017. LNCS, vol. 10514, pp. 224–242. Springer, Cham (2017). https://doi.org/10.1007/978-3-319-67684-5_14
13. Guerino, G.C., Valentim, N.M.C.: Usability and user experience evaluation of natural user interfaces: a systematic mapping study. IET Softw., 451–467 (2020)
14. Hansen, L.K., Dalsgaard, P.: Note to self: stop calling interfaces "natural". In: Proceedings of The Fifth Decennial Aarhus Conference on Critical Alternatives, Aarhus, Denmark (2015)
15. Hauger, D., Paramythis, A., Weibelzahl, S.: Using browser interaction data to determine page reading behavior. In: Konstan, J.A., Conejo, R., Marzo, J.L., Oliver, N. (eds.) UMAP 2011. LNCS, vol. 6787, pp. 147–158. Springer, Heidelberg (2011). https://doi.org/10.1007/978-3-642-22362-4_13
16. Hornecker, E.: Beyond affordance: tangibles' hybrid nature. In: Proceedings of the Sixth International Conference on Tangible, Embedded and Embodied Interaction (TEI 2012), Ontario, Canada (2012)
17. Hornecker, E., Dünser, A.: Of pages and paddles: children's expectations and mistaken interactions with physical–digital tools. Interact. Comput. **21**(1–2), 95–107 (2009)
18. Hui, T.K.L., Sherratt, R.S.: Towards disappearing user interfaces for ubiquitous computing: human enhancement from sixth sense to super senses. J. Ambient Intell. Humaniz. Comput., 449–465 (2017)
19. Jin, Y., Ma, M., Zhu, Y.: A comparison of natural user interface and graphical user interface for narrative in HMD-based augmented reality. Multimedia Tools Appl. **81**, 5795–5826 (2022)
20. Kipper, G., Rampolla, J.: Augmented Reality: An Emerging Technologies Guide to AR, Waltham. Elsevier, USA (2012)
21. Kortum, P.: HCI Beyond the GUI: Design for Haptic, Speech, Olfactory, and Other Nontraditional Interfaces. Morgan Kaufmann Publishers (2008)
22. Lam, H., Baudisch, P.: Summary thumbnails: readable overviews for small screen web browsers. In: Proceedings of the SIGCHI Conference on Human Factors in Computing Systems, Portland, Oregon (2005)
23. Lazar, J., Feng, J.H., Hochheiser, H.: Experimental design. In: Research Methods in Human-Computer Interaction, 2nd edn., pp. 45–69. Morgan Kaufmann (2017)
24. Liao, L., Liang, Y., Li, H., Ye, Y., Wu, G.: A systematic review of global research on natural user interface for smart home system. Int. J. Ind. Ergon. **95**, 103445 (2023)
25. Lim, Y.-K.: Disappearing interfaces. Interactions **19**(5), 36–39 (2012)
26. Liu, W.: Natural user interface- next mainstream product user interface. In: Proceedings of IEEE 11th International Conference on Computer-Aided Industrial Design & Conceptual Design, Yiwu, China (2010)
27. Longobardi, C., Quaglia, R., Iotti, N.O.: Reconsidering the scribbling stage of drawing: a new perspective on toddlers' representational processes. Front. Psychol. **6** (2015)

28. Loureiro, B., Rodrigues, R.: Multi-touch as a natural user interface for elders: a survey. In: 6th Iberian Conference on Information Systems and Technologies (CISTI 2011), Chaves, Portugal (2011)

29. Luger, E., Sellen, A.: Like having a really bad PA: the gulf between user expectation and experience of conversational agents. In: Proceedings of CHI Conference on Human Factors in Computing Systems, San Jose, California (2016)

30. Macaranas, A., Antle, A.N., Riecke, B.E.: What is Intuitive Interaction? Balancing users' performance and satisfaction with natural user interfaces. Interact. Comput. **27**(3), 357–370 (2015)

31. Malizia, A., Bellucci, A.: The artificiality of natural user interfaces. Commun. ACM **55**(3), 36–38 (2012)

32. Mann, S.: Natural interfaces for musical expression: physiphones and a physics-based organology. In: Proceedings of the 7th International Conference on New Interfaces for Musical Expression, New York (2007)

33. Martinez-Maldonado, R., Shum, S.B., Schneider, B., Charleer, S., Klerkx, J., Duval, E.: Learning analytics for natural user interfaces. J. Learn. Anal. **4**(1), 24–57 (2017)

34. Martín-SanJosé, J.-F., Juan, M.-C., Mollá, R., Vivó, R.: Advanced displays and natural user interfaces to support learning. Interact. Learn. Environ. **25**(1), 17–34 (2017)

35. Murad, C., Munteanu, C.: I don't know what you're talking about, HALexa: the case for voice user interface guidelines. In: Proceedings of the 1st International Conference on Conversational User Interfaces, Dublin (2019)

36. Naumann, A., et al.: Intuitive use of user interfaces: defining a vague concept. In: Harris, D. (eds.) EPCE 2007. LNCS, vol. 4562, pp. 128–136. Springer, Heidelberg (2007). https://doi.org/10.1007/978-3-540-73331-7_14

37. Norman, D.A.: Natural user interfaces are not natural. Interactions **17**(3), 6–10 (2010)

38. Ogiela, M.R., Hachaj, T.: Natural user interfaces for exploring and modeling medical images and defining gesture description technology. In: Ogiela, M.R., Hachaj, T. (eds.) Natural User Interfaces in Medical Image Analysis. Advances in Computer Vision and Pattern Recognition, pp. 205–279. Springer, Cham (2015). https://doi.org/10.1007/978-3-319-07800-7_5

39. O'Hara, K., Harper, R., Mentis, H., Sellen, A., Taylor, A.: On the naturalness of touchless: putting the "interaction" back into NUI. ACM Trans. Comput. Hum. Interact. **20**(1), 1–25 (2013)

40. Paas, F.: Training strategies for attaining transfer of problem-solving skill in statistics: a cognitive-load approach. J. Educ. Psychol. **84**(4), 429–434 (1992)

41. Paas, F., Tuovinen, J.E., Tabbers, H., Van Gerven, P.W.M.: Cognitive load measurement as a means to advance cognitive load theory. Educ. Psychol. **38**(1), 63–71 (2003)

42. Pavlik, J.V.: Digital design in experiential news. In: Journalism in the Age of Virtual Reality: How Experiential Media are Transforming News, New York, Columbia, pp. 34–60. University Press (2019)

43. Pietroni, E., Pagano, A., Fanini, B.: UX designer and software developer at the mirror: assessing sensory immersion and emotional involvement in virtual museums. Stud. Digit. Herit., 13–41 (2018)

44. Rauterberg, M.: New directions in user-system Interaction: augmented reality, ubiquitous and mobile computing. In: IEEE Proceedings Symposium Human Interfacing (1999)

45. Rauterberg, M., Steiger, P.: Pattern recognition as a key technology for the next generation of user interfaces. In: IEEE International Conference on Systems, Man and Cybernetics, Beijing, China (1996)

46. Quade, D.: Rank analysis of covariance. J. Am. Stat. Assoc. **62**(320), 1187–1200 (1967)

47. Sanna, A., Lamberti, F., Paravati, G., Manuri, F.: A kinect-based natural interface for quadrotor control. Entertain. Comput. **4**(3), 179–186 (2013)

48. Stratton, S.D., Dunsmore, H.E.: The use of hypertext in software development. SERC - Purdue University (1989)
49. Sweller, J. Cognitive load theory. In: Psychology of Learning and Motivation, vol. 55, pp. 37–76. Academic Press (2011)
50. Wigdor, D., Fletcher, J., Morrison, G.: Designing user interfaces for multi-touch and gesture devices. In: Proceedings of CHI 2009 Extended Abstracts on Human Factors in Computing Systems, Boston, MA (2009)
51. Wigdor, D., Wixon, D.: Brave NUI World, Morgan Kaufmann (2011)

# Methods for Evaluating Conversational Agents' Communicability, Acceptability and Accessibility Degree

Stefano Valtolina[1]([✉]) [iD], Ricardo Anibal Matamoros[2] [iD], and Francesco Epifania[2] [iD]

[1] Department of Computer Science, Università degli Studi di Milano, Milano, Italy
stefano.valtolina@unimi.it
[2] Social Things SRL, Milano, Italy
{ricardo.matamoros,francesco.epifania}@socialthingum.com

**Abstract.** Recently, there has been an increasing interest in language-based inter-actions with technology. Driven by the success of intelligent personal assistants, the number of conversation-based interactions is growing in several domains. Nevertheless, the literature highlights a lack of models specifically studied to analyse communication blocks and the level of accessibility and acceptability by the user that can characterise Human-Agent dialogue. This paper aims to learn how much an agent can be accessible, how much the communication is understandable, and if it brings to a successful conclusion by extending two known models, the UTAUT2 and CEM. For both models, we defined new indicators to analyse communicability, acceptability degrees and accessibility level using WCAG guidelines. We designed two conversational agents to test our models and conducted preliminary tests. A first agent is used to assist students in following remote digital courses, and a second to help older people in their daily activities and to monitor the indexes of active life defined to control the trend of older people's physical-cognitive state.

**Keywords:** Conversational interfaces · Communicability · Acceptability · Accessibility · Evaluation methodology

## 1 Introduction

In recent years, conversation-based interaction is becoming a pervasive technology weaving into our daily lives in ways we may not even be aware of. In various fields, including education, healthcare, and security, the conversational interface makes interaction more flexible and intelligent by enabling good communication between users and machines. The so-called conversational agents can exploit natural language comprehension engines to answer users' questions like a human would respond. Natural Language Understanding (NLU) is a component of Natural Language Processing (NLP), which aims to interpret natural language, process its meaning, identify context and draw conclusions. Conversation agents exploit these technologies to classify and recognise user intentions about processing a specific request [1]. Despite progress in this field, Human-Agent communication can sometimes lead to an interruption or can be poorly received by the user for

J. Abdelnour Nocera et al. (Eds.): INTERACT 2023, LNCS 14143, pp. 372–382, 2023.
https://doi.org/10.1007/978-3-031-42283-6_21

various reasons. This phenomenon occurs in several areas of Human-Computer Interaction (HCI) and not only when communicating with a digital agent. Standardised study models have been developed in traditional fields to analyse the degree of acceptability and efficiency in communication. Two well-known examples are the "Unified Theory of Acceptance and Use of Technology" version 2 (UTAUT2) model and the Communicability Evaluation Method (CEM). The first model aims to identify user behaviour related to technological innovations [2–4], whereas the second focuses on evaluating the quality of the dialogue between a user and the interface [5–7]. In contrast, studies are missing in the field of conversational agent (CA) design. Studies that allow us to verify CAs degree of acceptance by the user and their level of accessibility to enable their use by anyone in any context. Furthermore, there is a lack of methods specifically studied to analyse communication blocks that can characterise Human-Agent dialogue.

For this reason, in this paper, we want to explore how different types of users can approach and evaluate conversational systems. To this end, we studied the CEM method to identify the factors that lead users to abandon communication with a digital agent (also named bot or chatbot). While exploiting the UTAUT2 model, we investigated the predictors of acceptance, i.e. which factors can influence the acceptance of new technology such as conversational agents. Both models have also been extended using the accessibility guidelines of the WCAG 3.0 and 2.1 standards [8].

To test our models, we designed two chatbots. The first is thought to assist the students in providing primary school students in Italy with digital courses about coding. In this case, the goal is to evaluate how much our extended models can help assess Agent-Human communication when native digital users are involved. A second bot has been designed to act as an older people's assistant, providing them with functionalities to combat the typical sense of loneliness that can affect their quality of life. The agent's goal is to monitor the indexes of active life specifically defined to control the trend of older people's physical-cognitive state. Using this bot, we want to assess our models in case the users are digital immigrants or users not very accustomed to technology, such as older people, when they approach conversational systems.

According to these considerations, in the next Section, we present an overview of relevant studies we used as a base for motivating the adoption of conversation agents in our contexts of use. We also describe the bots we designed for our research. Section 3 presents the methods we defined by extending the UTAUT2 model and CEM method. Then, Sect. 4 presents some preliminary results of tests carried out to evaluate how our models are effective in assessing the level of communicability, accessibility and acceptability of the agents. Finally, the last Section tracks some conclusions and future works.

## 2 Conversation Agent Design

### 2.1 The Use of Conversational Agents in Education

The literature presents many studies regarding using chatbots in the educational domain [9–11]. According to the review [9], chatbots are mainly applied for teaching and learning (66%). They promote rapid access to materials by students and faculty at any time and place [12, 13]. This strategy helps save time and maximise students' learning abilities and results [14], stimulating and involving them more in teaching work [15–17].

According to these studies, we designed an agent as part of a Learning Management System (LMS) called WhoTeach[1], which aims to help educational institutions deliver and create quality online courses. This LMS provides a variety of interaction possibilities between teachers and students. One example is the possibility for teachers to assign personalised courses according to work plans designed for individual students' needs. The chatbot can send reminders, monitor the educational progress and allow the students to collect feedback at each lesson's end. The idea is to enable the students to report any problems to the teacher and ensure constant improvement in the quality of the educational offer.

From an implementation point of view, we decided to build our chatbot using RASA [18], an open-source framework for developing virtual assistants. For the user interface, we decided to use a widget in React [19], an open-source JavaScript library, given its high performance and simple application state management. The technological choices allow us to ensure a smooth and efficient user experience so that it is possible to offer students a precise and reliable resource for accessing online courses. Figure 1 shows a set of examples of potential conversations. In Section A, the chatbot presents a reminder about the time left to complete the courses in which the student is enrolled and buttons for selecting the following desired action. Section B describes a situation where the student selects the course she/he wants to follow. Finally, the dialogue in Section C is used to collect the student's evaluation of the attended lesson.

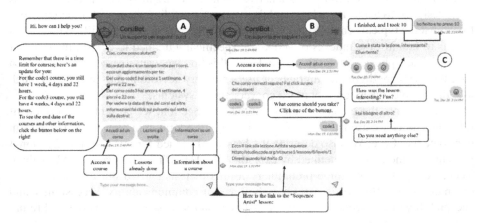

**Fig. 1.** The screenshots show potential conversations described in the text.

## 2.2 Conversational Agent for Active Ageing

The conversational agent we designed takes the name of Charlie. Charlie, implemented using Google DialoFlow [20], acts as a medical advisor, friend and carer for autonomous

---

[1] https://www.whoteach.it/ Last access: 2023–06-08.

seniors living alone. We designed the final interface using Flutter [21], a framework for integrating into a mobile app various chatbot operations.

To simplify interaction, Charlie provides limited choices that are easily understood and accessible via the mobile phone or tablet screen. The dialogues between are generally of short duration to avoid tiring the user. Key features depicted in Fig. 2 include the possibility of giving daily automatic notifications, healthy recommendations and offering activity reminders about important events, such as the need to take medicine. Charlie can also present news, weather forecast, or different forms of entertainment, including a memory-based game and quizzes. Another feature includes active listening to help older people improve their mood. The users indicate their thoughts, and then the assistant asks for information regarding their emotional situation. Through telling a story, Charlie establishes a pretext to communicate with the user and ask for information to develop a conversation. This functionality allows the users to consider Charlie in a friendly way, pushing them to confide and express themselves without worrying about communicating with artificial intelligence.

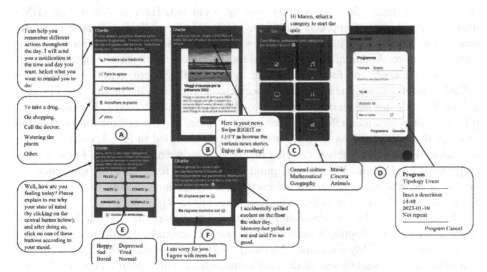

**Fig. 2.** Image A presents an example of daily notifications that can be provided to the user. Image B offers interesting news. In image C, the user can select the topic of questions for the quiz. In image D, Charlie asks if the user needs help remembering something and helps her/him fix a timetable. In the image, E Charlies asks the user about her/him mood. Finally, image F shows an example of a self-compassion strategy.

## 3 Evaluation of Acceptance, Communicability and Accessibility

Several studies, such as [22, 23], describe how people can successfully experience the bots in terms of satisfaction, engagement, and trust. Despite the rapid progress in improving the development of conversational agents, to our knowledge, there is a lack of standards for studying their degree of acceptance and accessibility, as well as models for studying communication blocks that can affect proper communication between the bot and the end user.

To this end, we analysed and extended the Unified Theory of Acceptance and Use of Technology (UTAUT2) model and the Communicability Evaluation Method (CEM). Our models aim to investigate how much the agent is accessible, how much the communication is understandable, and if it brings to a successful conclusion.

The Unified Theory of Acceptance and Use of Technology (UTAUT) model has been tested extensively in various fields and promises to be an excellent tool for analysing users' acceptance of new technology [24–27]. The UTAUT presents several significant constructs to determine the user's acceptance and intent to use new technology. Performance Expectancy (PE) measures how much an individual considers a valuable system for improving performance. Effort Expectancy (EE) measures how easy a system is to use. Social Influence (SI) measures the influence of colleagues, relatives or friends on the intention to use new technology. Finally, Facilitating Conditions (FC) measure how much external aid can facilitate the adoption and use of the system.

According to the results of other works [3, 4], we decided to integrate new constructs to investigate the acceptability level of a chatbot. Hedonic Motivation (HM) measures the degree of appreciation of the system by users. Habit (H) estimates how much experience and the habit of using new technology can be helpful in its more concrete acceptance. And finally, Trust (T) that measures how much trust in the chatbot can affect its acceptance and future use. As far as accessibility is concerned, analysing the WCAG guidelines, we integrated other specific constructs into the model. The Perceivability (P) evaluates the clarity of the proposed functions and interfaces. The Operability (O) determines how much the operations are accessible. The Understandability (U) aims to study if the information is easily understood. As depicted in Fig. 3, each construct is related to other constructs specifying the hypotheses we need to study. For example, Hypothesis 1 (H1) links PE to Behavioural Intention (BI) for evaluating how much the performance expectancy positively affects the user's intention to use the digital assistant. For a complete description of the hypotheses, refer to [2–4].

To study the level of communicability, we need to analyse the dialogue between the agent and a user by adopting a semiotic technique. In our study, we adopted De Souza's CEM (Communicability Evaluation Method) [5–7]. In detail, the CEM tests identify all communicability breakdowns in the user's interaction using specific tags. Traditional tags ([5–7] present detailed descriptions of them) cannot detect and map all dialogue interruptions affecting conversational agent communication. In this regard, we defined new tags to describe the substantial difference between running a conversation flow with a virtual agent and running an interaction with a website or mobile application.

The tag "Too much information!" happens when a user provides too complex and lengthy content. The tag "Too many questions!" is used when a user simultaneously asks two or more questions to a virtual agent. The tag "Why did it not understand?" indicates that the user has not understood the bot's reply. The tag "But doesn't this exist?" highlights that the user is looking for the bot's functionality that does not exist. Finally, with the tag "I don't understand you!" we specify that the interruption of communication is due to a misunderstanding by the agent of what the user said.

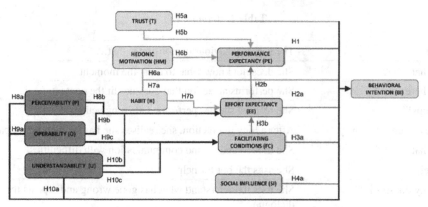

**Fig. 3.** Hypotheses schema. Each arrow represents a hypothesis that measures how much a construct can affect the validation of the other. The green and blue constructs investigate the acceptability and accessibility perceived by the users of a chatbot. For example, H8b, linking P to EE, measures how much the degree of the perceivability of the chatbot can influence how much the user considers it easy to use.

To study how good communication skills can affect the degree of accessibility of bots, we introduced additional tags to identify the causes that prevent the user from operating efficiently within the system. Based on the guidelines indicated by WCAG, we can extrapolate which are the problematic elements and therefore elaborate the following new tags. The tag "It's hard to read." highlights a communication block that occurs when users face a text that is difficult to read. The tag "I already know this!" appears in cases where the bot provides redundant information or does not realise that it has already proposed a similar discussion to the user. Table 1 shows the complete set of thirteen basic possible expressions of communicability (tags) modified to fit the dialogue breakdowns that characterise a Chatbot-Human interaction, to which we added the previously explained tags for investigating chatbot-user communication and accessibility issues.

**Table 1.** Main Tags and meanings of the communication failures. Adapted from [5–7].

| Tag | The user's behaviour demonstrates that... |
| --- | --- |
| "I give up." | She abandons the communication |
| "Looks fine to me." | She does not realise she has failed |
| "Thanks, but no, thanks." | She prefers to act differently wrt the bot suggests |
| "I can do otherwise." | Not understanding the bot, she acts as she sees fit |
| "Where is it?" | She does not see the interaction cues to use |
| "What happened?" | She does not understand what the bot is telling her |

(continued)

Table 1. (*continued*)

| Tag | The user's behaviour demonstrates that… |
| --- | --- |
| "What now?" | She does not know what to do at the moment |
| "Where am I?" | She performs an action that does not fit the context |
| "Oops!" | She realises she has performed a wrong actions |
| "I can't do it this way." | After a long interaction, she realises she has taken a wrong path |
| "What is this?" | She tries to understand communication with difficulties |
| "Help!" | She asks the bot for help |
| "Why doesn't it?" | She tries to understand what has gone wrong and repeats the dialogue |

## 4   A Validation for the Proposed Models

To test our models, we conducted two initial assessments of our chatbot. The final objective was to validate the models and understand how they can be used for assessing conversation agents' level of acceptability, accessibility and communicability skills.

The first test was carried out on the chatbot in the education field. The goal was to test the traditional UTAUT2 and CEM models and how to extend them for evaluating chatbot communicability and accessibility levels. Twenty-six students of the Computer Science Department of the University of Milano participated in the evaluation. The participants were between 23 and 26 years of age (58% males and 42% females) and were enrolled to simulate primary school students who had to attend a class about the basic notions of coding. We intended to involve university students and not real students in primary school to investigate how traditional UTAUT and CEM models can allow us to evaluate the communicability skills and accessibility aspects of using a chatbot. These university students attended the HCI course, during which they investigated accessibility and usability themes. During the lectures, students could use the chatbot and discuss the traditional UTAUT and CEM models. These discussions drove us to redesign these models to integrate new constructs (the T, HM, H, P, O and U constructs in Fig. 3) and new tags related to studying the chatbot communicability level and its accessibility degree.

Then we tested these new models by using the second chatbot. In this case, we involved 7 participants aged 60 through 70 (3 males and 4 females) recruited thanks to the collaboration with doctors of the ASST (Azienda Socio Sanitaria Territoriale - Territorial Socio-Health Company) of Crema (Italy). The testers lived in pairs or alone and had a pretty good inclination to use technology (all had a smartphone and used it to chat, see videos on YouTube, and browse the Web). To the question, "Have you ever used a chatbot (such as Google Home or Amazon Alexa)?" almost all answered "No," (5 people). Therefore, only two testers have ever tried to use services offered by chatbots in the past. Then, we asked testers to interact with the agents daily in their homes for a week. After signing a document for informed consent, we provide users with indications about the modality of the test, its goals and information collection instructions.

This second test aimed to evaluate a chatbot in fragile conditions, such as the one that sees older people using new technologies. At this stage, we did not involve users with a disability but aged adults who highlight difficulties when interacting with digital user interfaces. Another goal was to analyse if the extensions of the UTAUT and CEM models discussed with our students can be applied in real scenarios.

First, we asked the participants to check the possible presence of the tags described in our CEM model (including the additional tags for communicability and accessibility analysis) during their first interactions with the agent. At the end of the indicated period, we asked them to fill in the questionnaire developed to evaluate the hypotheses of the extended UTAUT2 model. The results of the UTAUT2 questionnaire highlighted good outcomes for all the classical constructs. We obtained reasonable indications for assessing the new constructs too.

By analysing the UTAUT2 results and after we interviewed the participants, one of the main problems we checked was the lack of precise indications on which functions the agent could offer. The "Understandability" construct also scored low, with a mean of 2.28. The ability to express the agent's functionalities and how to access them should be a prerogative when proposing a new technology to an audience not accustomed to using it. Instead, from the CEM study results, we identified that the most reported tags were "I give up." with 57.14% and "Where is it?" with 42.86%. Many people have highlighted a sense of frustration by the lack of technical knowledge and the unclear directions provided by Charlie. Other frequent tags were "What now?" and "What happened?" both with a value of 28.57%. In some cases, users were not sure if they had succeeded in accomplishing what they wanted to do, and they felt disoriented. Next, we find the tags "Why did it not understand?", "I don't understand you!" and "What is this?" with 14.29%. This value indicates that sometimes there is poor understanding in both directions during the User-Agent conversation. From this, we can deduce that the issues regarding accessibility mainly concern understanding, while in general, there is little support regarding the orientation in using the agent.

Having detected these difficulties at the communicability and accessibility level demonstrates how our extended UTAUT and CEM models can be helpful solutions for investigating these problems when evaluating conversational agent-user interactions.

Nevertheless, we know the main limitations, well-known in the literature [25, 26], that affect our analysis. Firstly, the sample size of participants in our test. Secondly, we cannot present statistical confirmation and validation about the reliability of the collected data. Thirdly, the design of the dialogues did not focus on psychological studies about the regard words to use or the proper methods of interaction that better fit with the senior user's expectations. Finally, the agent's implementation lacks direct user involvement in requirement definition and design. Nevertheless, these preliminary tests allowed us to specify better and tune our models to verify the communicability skills of our agents and their acceptance degree by the user and their level of accessibility to enable their use by anyone in any context.

## 5 Conclusions and Future Works

This preliminary study investigates the user's experiences when interacting with a new technology, such as a digital agent, designed to assist and entertain users in their working activities and daily routines. To this aim, we created two conversational agents specifically studied to assist students in following remote digital courses and older people in combating the typical sense of loneliness, which affects their quality of life. In the design of the agents, particular attention has been paid to usability and accessibility aspects. Given the lack of methods to investigate these problems, we have defined two models to study Human-Chatbot interactions better.

In a preliminary test with students of the University of Milano who worked on a chatbot for education, we investigated the communicability aspects that an agent has to present and the proper level of accessibility and acceptability of its main functionalities. Thanks to the result of this test, we extended two models, the UTAUT2 and CEM. The first one allows us to study the attitude, acceptance, pleasure and utility of using a set of specific functionalities mediated by an agent. The second helps evaluate the quality of the dialogue between a user and the bot. By involving older people recruited by doctors of ASST (Azienda Socio Sanitaria Territoriale - Territorial Socio-Health Company) of Crema (Italy), we conducted a qualitative study using Charlie; the agent used to assist older people.

The results of this test highlight how chatbot-user interactions for older people present some barriers both at the communication level and concerning accessibility. Simultaneously, we can claim how our extended UTAUT and CEM models can represent helpful strategies for evaluating interactions with chatbots for investigating their level of communicability and accessibility. Unfortunately, these tests are still to be carried out due to the current final stage of the COVID-19 pandemic. Still, we are currently in contact with educational agencies and health assistance residences that we can involve in further studies.

## References

1. Boonstra, L.: Definitive Guide to Conversational AI with Dialogflow and Google Cloud. Apress (2021)
2. Venkatesh, V., Morris, M.G., Davis, G.B., Davis, F.D.: User acceptance of information technology: toward a unified view. MIS Q., 425–478 (2003)
3. Venkatesh, V., Davis, F.D.: A theoretical extension of the technology acceptance model: four longitudinal field studies. Manag. Sci. 46(2), 186–204 (2000)
4. Warshaw, P.R.: A new model for predicting behavioral intentions: an alternative to Fishbein. J. Mark. Res. 17(2), 153–172 (1980)
5. Mattos, B.A.M., Prates, R.O.: An overview of the communicability evaluation method for collaborative systems. In: IADIS International Conference WWW/Internet 2011, Rio de Janeiro. Proceedings of WWW/Internet 2011, pp. 129–136 (2011)
6. De Souza, C.S., Leitão, C.F.: Semiotic Engineering Methods for Scientific Research in HCI. Morgan and Claypool Publishers, San Rafael (2009)
7. Prates, R.O., de Souza, C.S., Barbosa, S.D.J.: A method for evaluating the communicability of user interfaces. ACM Interact. 7(1), 31–38 (2000)

8. Okonkwo, C.W., Ade-Ibijola, A.: Chatbots applications in education: a systematic review. Comput. Educ. Artif. Intell. **2**, 100033 (2021)
9. WCAG 3.0: https://www.w3.org/TR/wcag-3.0/ and WCAG 2.1: https://wcag.it/. Accessed 24 Apr 2023
10. Medeiros, R.P., Ramalho, G.L., Falcão, T.P.: A systematic literature review on teaching and learning introductory programming in higher education. IEEE Trans. Educ. **62**(2), 77–90 (2018)
11. Smutny, P., Schreiberova, P.: Chatbots for learning: a review of educational chatbots for the Facebook Messenger. Comput. Educ. **151**, 103862 (2020)
12. Alias, S., Sainin, M.S., Soo Fun, T., Daut, N.: Identification of conversational intent pattern using pattern-growth technique for academic chatbot. In: Chamchong, R., Wong, K.W. (eds.) MIWAI 2019. LNCS (LNAI), vol. 11909, pp. 263–270. Springer, Cham (2019). https://doi.org/10.1007/978-3-030-33709-4_24
13. Wu, E.H.K., Lin, C.H., Ou, Y.Y., Liu, C.Z., Wang, W.K., Chao, C.Y.: Advantages and constraints of a hybrid model K-12 E-learning assistant chatbot. IEEE Access **8**, 77788–77801 (2020)
14. Murad, D.F., Irsan, M., Akhirianto, P.M., Fernando, E., Murad, S.A., Wijaya, M.H.: Learning support system using chatbot in "Kejar C Package" homeschooling program. In: 2019 International Conference on Information and Communications Technology (ICOIACT), pp. 32–37. IEEE, July 2019
15. Lam, C.S.N., Chan, L.K., See, C.Y.H.: Converse, connect and consolidate–the development of an artificial intelligence chatbot for health sciences education. In: Frontiers in Medical and Health Sciences Education Conference. Bau Institute of Medical and Health Sciences Education, Li Ka Shing Faculty of Medicine, The University of Hong Kong (2018)
16. El Hefny, W., El Bolock, A., Herbert, C., Abdennadher, S.: Applying the character-based chatbots generation framework in education and healthcare. In: Proceedings of the 9th International Conference on Human-Agent Interaction, pp. 121–129, November 2021
17. Sreelakshmi, A.S., Abhinaya, S.B., Nair, A., Nirmala, S.J.: A question answering and quiz generation chatbot for education. In: 2019 Grace Hopper Celebration India (GHCI), pp. 1–6. IEEE, November 2019
18. https://rasa.com/. Accessed 24 Apr 2023
19. https://it.legacy.reactjs.org/. Accessed 24 Apr 2023
20. https://cloud.google.com/dialogflow?hl=it. Accessed 24 Apr 2023
21. https://docs.flutter.dev/. Accessed 24 Apr 2023
22. Chaves, A.P., Gerosa, M.A.: How should my chatbot interact? A survey on social characteristics in human–chatbot interaction design. Int. J. Hum. Comput. Interact., 1–30 (2020)
23. Rapp, A., Curti, L., Boldi, A.: The human side of human-chatbot interaction: a systematic literature review of ten years of research on text-based chatbots. Int. J. Hum. Comput. Stud., 102630 (2021)
24. De Veer, A.J., Peeters, J.M., Brabers, A.E., Schellevis, F.G., Rademakers, J.J.J., Francke, A.L.: Determinants of the intention to use e-health by community dwelling older people. BMC Health Serv. Res. **15**(1), 1–9 (2015)
25. Liu, C.F., Tsai, Y.C., Jang, F.L.: Patients' acceptance towards a web-based personal health record system: an empirical study in Taiwan. Int. J. Environ. Res. Public Health **10**(10), 5191–5208 (2013)

26. Kohnke, A., Cole, M.L., Bush, R.: Incorporating UTAUT predictors for understanding home care patients' and clinician's acceptance of healthcare telemedicine equipment. J. Technol. Manag. Innov. 9(2), 29–41 (2014)
27. Cimperman, M., Brenčič, M.M., Trkman, P.: Analysing older users' home telehealth services acceptance behavior—applying an extended UTAUT model. Int. J. Med. Inform. 90, 22–31 (2016)

# Methodologies for HCI

# A Review on Mood Assessment Using Smartphones

Zhanna Sarsenbayeva[1]([⊠]), Charlie Fleming[1], Benjamin Tag[2],
Anusha Withana[1], Niels van Berkel[3], and Alistair McEwan[4]

[1] School of Computer Science, University of Sydney, Sydney, Australia
{zhanna.sarsenbayeva,charlie.fleming,anusha.withana}@sydney.edu.au
[2] Department of Human Centred Computing, Monash University, Melbourne,
Australia
benjamin.tag@monash.edu
[3] Department of Computer Science, Aalborg University, Aalborg, Denmark
nielsvanberkel@cs.aau.dk
[4] School of Biomedical Engineering, University of Sydney, Sydney, Australia
alistair.mcewan@sydney.edu.au

**Abstract.** Due to their abundance of sensors, today's smartphones can act as a scientific tool to collect contextual information on users' emotional, social, and physical behaviour. With the continuously growing amount of data that can be unobtrusively extracted from smartphones, mood-tracking and inference methods have become more feasible. However, this does raise critical implications for end-users, including accessibility and privacy. Following a structured selection process, we reviewed 32 papers from the ACM Digital Library on mood inference and tracking using smartphones. We conducted an in-depth analysis of used sensors, platform and accessibility, study designs, privacy, self-reporting methods, and accuracy. Based on our analysis, we provide a detailed discussion of the opportunities for research and practice that arise from our findings and outline recommendations for future research within the area of smartphone-based mood tracking and inference.

**Keywords:** Mood tracking · Mood inference · Smartphones

## 1 Introduction

Our mood has a profound impact on our physical and mental health, as well as our financial, educational, and social well-being [38]. Often, mood and emotion are falsely seen as synonymous. But while there exist many similarities and correlations between mood and emotion [77], they are not identical. Beedie et al. [12] reviewed 65 papers to identify differences between the two. The authors found that 62% of the articles identified duration, 41% intentionality, 31% cause and consequences, and 18% identified function as key distinctive factors. This suggests that while emotion can contribute to mood, mood is more intentional and

© The Author(s), under exclusive license to Springer Nature Switzerland AG 2023
J. Abdelnour Nocera et al. (Eds.): INTERACT 2023, LNCS 14143, pp. 385–413, 2023.
https://doi.org/10.1007/978-3-031-42283-6_22

present for a longer duration. Consequently, mood issues can lead to more long-lasting consequences, which is clearly demonstrated via the correlation between mood instability, low mood, and psychiatric issues [71].

Mood tracking and inference applications are more ubiquitous than ever before. As of 2022, 83.32% of the world population owns a sensor-rich smartphone [9]. In 2021, two out of three teenagers and young adults reported that they had previously used a mental health application [76]. According to Caldeira et al. [22], users of publicly available mood tracking and inference apps use them to (1) learn about their idiosyncratic mood patterns, (2) improve their mood, and (3) monitor and manage mental illness. These apps are also often used to track and manage stress [22]. Negative mental health outcomes can be mitigated by such applications, as they provide a tool for increasing self-awareness and enabling early interventions [23].

In this paper, we report on a systematic literature review of the existing ACM literature focusing on tracking and inferring user mood using smartphones. Based on this, we provide an in-depth analysis of used sensors, technology, study methods, privacy details, self-reporting methods, and accuracy. Additionally, we present a quantitative analysis of commonly used sensors for passive mood tracking. We put additional focus on the accessibility of each method according to its availability on different smartphone OSs and external device requirements. We then review study details, quantifying and comparing age, gender split, participation rates, participation rewards, duration, socioeconomic background, and more. Given the limited number of literature reviews within the domain of mood tracking using smart devices [60] and the rapid developments in this field, our work provides an up-to-date overview of how mood tracking is performed and addressed in HCI user studies, particularly using smartphones. Prior literature points to the variety of mood detection systems, including self-reported data, speech, facial recognition, mobile phone usage patterns, and physiological signals, with the authors focusing primarily on the accuracy and usability within each of them [60]. We extend this prior work by adding a novel analysis of the critical and increasingly important privacy and accessibility considerations, as well as sensor prevalence. We then discuss our results with reference to the relevant literature, providing implications for future studies in the area concerning self-report methods, sensor choices, platforms, accessibility, and privacy considerations. To summarise, the contribution of our work is as follows.

1. We provide an overview of related work in the field of *Mood tracking* and *Inference*, including what its current state looks like and how it arrived there.
2. We then outline our method for the literature review, including database choice, search query, and table creation. We provide a summarised version of the analysed data in a table summarising the key metrics.
3. Key metrics across each study are then quantified in a uniform fashion before being compared and contrasted within the results section.
4. Based on inferences gained from our findings, we provide recommendations for future studies in this domain.

# 2   Related Work

In the following, we provide insights into the state-of-the-art research on the importance of mood tracking using smartphones and methods and sensors commonly used in assessing mood.

## 2.1   Importance of Mood Assessment

Mood reflects a key component of our health. Hence, tracking, understanding, and interpreting our moods gives us a greater sense of power and control over our lives. Considering clinical application, the capability to track mood helps people identify and mitigate psychiatric disorders [75]. For instance, mood instability is a key diagnostic criterion for bipolar disorder [4]. It is also heavily related to other mental health disorders and is a precursor behind undesirable clinical outcomes, such as borderline personality disorder, bipolar disorder, and depression [71]. Similarly, affective states which are consistently negative have been reported to be linked to the propensity of developing depressive disorders [21]. The impacts of unmediated psychiatric health states are far-reaching, including high school drop-out [49], divorce rates [50], and early parenthood [48].

Additionally, mood significantly influences our cognition, sociability, and productivity. For instance, Mitchell and Phillips [66] showed that small mood fluctuations could significantly impact neural activation and cognition, with implications for our memory and thinking. Bower [19] showed how different mood states can trigger associated memories and experiences and influence our perception and judgement. In a review of consumer behaviour, Gardner [35] mentioned how people in good moods are more likely to care about their future and attempt new things. In their research, Lyubomirsky et al. [63] found that long-term positive affective states ('happiness') correlate with numerous behaviours often understood as synonymous with success.

Toegel et al. [90] mentioned how managers that exhibit strong self-monitoring and positive affect disposition are more likely to provide emotional support to others in the workplace. Carlson et al. [26] demonstrated how positive mood can increase 'helpfulness', among other factors. In the same paradigm, George [36] demonstrated how a positive mood at work is associated with higher sociability & greater sales performance.

The multidimensional impact by which mood influences our daily lives is also demonstrated by the versatility of mood inference and tracking tools. For patients with illnesses such as bipolar disorder or depression, maintaining a stable mood is a goal that can be aided by such tools [69, 86, 96]. Calear and Christensen [23] found that the negative effects of depression can be mitigated when the symptoms are identified early. Wang et al. [95] implemented a system to track depression in workers, finding that interventions could lower their depression scores and significantly improve job retention. For those with stress disorders, the focus is mainly on identifying stress, its triggers, and mitigating its intensity [17, 28]. For a broader public, mood-tracking applications bring benefits such as enhancing general mood awareness [33], highlighting the importance and foreseeable benefits of mood monitoring.

## 2.2  Mood Inference

Many different approaches exist within the inference domain. The most common approach towards inferring mood is quantifying affective states proposed in Russel's circumplex model Russell [79]. As do moods, affective states can have drastic impacts on behaviour, cognition, perception, and reflexes [78]. At the core of any mood event is a 'core affect', representing a feeling of 'good' or 'bad', 'energised', or 'enervated'. Users can report their mood using a 2D grid expressing valence (positive or negative affect) on the x-axis and arousal (intensity) on the y-axis. Other common measures of mood include self-report tools, such as the 'Patient Health Questionnaire' (PHQ) score [53], 'Patient Activation Measure' (PAM) [44] and 'Positive and Negative Affect Schedule' (PANAS) [97].

While some methods rely purely on self-reporting as a 'tracker', most methods rely on self-reporting to establish ground truths. Recently, passive sensor data and machine learning (ML) models have been employed to correlate various activities with self-reported mood states [102]. From here, current mood can be inferred, and future moods can be predicted, with predictive strength being dependent on the sensor data used and the accuracy of the model.

There is a low amount of review literature within the domain of mood tracking and inference using smartphones. One example is a survey by Lietz et al. [60], investigating different types of mood detection systems using different modalities, such as self-reports, speech, facial recognition, mobile phone usage patterns, and physiological signals. Lietz et al. [60] provide several robust analyses regarding the efficacy of different mood inference input modes. However, their overview does not consider specialised sub-categories (e.g., systems that use online social networks as a data source). Further, complementary to the review by Lietz et al. [60], we consider study details, technology types, and a series of other metrics to review mood-inference literature.

## 2.3  Mood Tracking on Smart Devices

Tracking and inferring mood is not a new concept; however, it was previously limited by the requirement for (1) pen-and-paper reporting and (2) psychologists' analysis of the data [102]. As smartphones have become our constant companions and are equipped with many sensors, they can be an almost completely unobtrusive tool to assess and monitor users' moods. Recent global events, such the self-isolation caused by the COVID-19 pandemic, demonstrated a need for unobtrusive mood tracking that enables constant monitoring of users' emotional states to support their mental well-being.

Recently, a myriad of studies have digitalised traditional pen-and-paper reporting methods and (partly) introduced them into the mobile domain [87]. Khue et al. [51] highlighted the benefits of mobile technology as enabling mood assessment in more naturalistic settings outside the lab, where data can be collected more longitudinally and *in situ* across a variety of scenarios. According to Khue et al. [51], 83% of their 48 participants preferred mobile scales to pen-and-paper scales. The wide adoption of smart devices, integration of clinical methods, and the development of predictive ML models have accelerated the efficacy of mobile methods. For instance, Chan et al. [27] showed how mobile self-reporting is statistically significant with other clinical tools and thus is a valid means of assessing mania and depression symptoms in bipolar patients. More experimental methods use smartphones to passively read affect values off of users' faces [88]. While facial expressions have been disputed as sole sources for affect inference [11], multi-sensory approaches to capture emotion, affect, and mood inference provide promising avenues [103].

However, some challenges do exist in the ubiquitous computing domain. Mehrotra et al. [65] explained how receiving high-quality ESM data is challenging due to respondents not answering honestly or ESM prompts being ignored as they are too frequent and cumbersome. Further, Lee et al. [57] stated that 66% of users that downloaded mood-tracking apps only reported their mood once. Users are also more likely to report mood when it is positive and ignore reporting when in negative mood states [82]. Looking at users that report depression, Depp et al. [30] found that compliance rates were significantly lower for mobile phone reporting compared to pen-and-paper reporting. On the other hand, mobile reporting was able to capture variability and concurrent validity to a greater standard when quantifying affect indicators. Van der Watt et al. [98] showed how depressed patients are willing to use mobile phones to track and assess their mood states. However, without distant support, it may be difficult to mitigate adverse mental health outcomes. On the balance of the evidence, challenges do exist adapting this traditionally formal process into a casual mobile environment. Despite this, the potential benefits make this a rational domain for future research and development [89].

**Usage of Sensors for Mood Tracking.** In the context of sensor-based mood tracking, it is important to explore the sensors utilised in previous studies and highlight the existing techniques and approaches to provide a comprehensive overview of the existing literature and methodologies employed in the field.

The microphone and accelerometer sensors are ubiquitous and allow for the accurate construction of predictive features based on pertinent real-world information. For instance, Spathis et al. [85] hypothesised that mood is heavily influenced by our activity, environment, and surrounding noise levels. By using the microphone and accelerometer, Spathis et al. [85] were able to collect insights into these three factors, classifying users as 'relaxed' or not with 74% accuracy. Further, Servia-Rodríguez et al. [83] collected the microphone and accelerometer data of 1,556 and 1,656 users respectively, as well as the call/text log of 8,247 users. Their empirical analysis found that the accelerometer and microphone presented a higher significant correlation with user mood than text/phone logs.

While microphones and accelerometers are considered useful sensor choices for mood prediction, the manner in which they are used and the information derived from them varies between studies. With respect to microphones, a significant reason for their varied usage is due to the privacy concerns that arise from recording and storing microphone data [54]. While Spathis et al. [85] and Bachmann et al. [6] used snippets of amplitude data from the recordings, Zhang et al. [105] extracted the mean, variance, and noise-to-silence ratio of snippets. A common element of all these studies is their use of microphones to infer contextual information about its user.

Conversely, Wang et al. [96] used the microphone in a less general manner by letting it operate continuously. While this raised privacy concerns, data was obfuscated, and the microphone proved highly effective for detecting unique/non-unique conversations and thus quantifying levels of social interaction. Chang et al. [28] also used the microphone but focused on the extraction of speech-related features (e.g., mean, SD, pitch and others). The study demonstrates the predictive power of the microphone sensor with 75% accuracy on two-class emotion classification and 84% accuracy in identifying stressful situations. A similar study by Lu et al. [62] use acoustic features from the microphone to detect stress with 81% accuracy indoors and 76% accuracy outdoors. These examples highlight the wide variety of data and insights that can be obtained using the microphone sensor.

While the general use of microphones has been to infer environment, social, and speech data, all but one study using the accelerometer aimed to track physical activity levels. The exception was [25], where the accelerometer was used to track how users were holding their phones when typing. Most studies use the accelerometer to infer physical activity levels, making it a widely adopted data probe for this purpose [101]. However, data can be challenging to model due to errors i.e., the cross-axis effect and non-linearity of data [3]. Nevertheless, if the accelerometer can be leveraged effectively to capture physical activity levels, mood prediction becomes more accurate overall. This is because a significant correlation exists between physical activity, health, and general well-being [72].

## 3    Method

The following section outlines the methodology followed to identify and summarise a final set of 36 studies used for our literature review. This includes the choice of the database, construction of the search query, and filtering of results.

### 3.1    Database Choice

We conducted a literature review on studies that propose mood-tracking and inference systems using smart devices. Our focus pertained to digital mood tracking and inference systems in Human-Computer Interaction (HCI). To obtain a broad overview, we conducted our search in the Association for Computing Machinery's Digital Library (ACM DL). While this means that work published in non-ACM venues is not included in our review, we argue that the ACM DL provides a comprehensive representation of HCI venues.

## 3.2  Search Query

To generate a reasonably sized set of works, the following search query was used: '[[Title: mobile phone mood] OR [Title: mobile phone mood inference] OR [Title: mobile phone mood tracking] OR [Title: mobile mood tracking]] AND [Fulltext: mood]'. Due to the significant developments in mobile-device technology, we only considered articles from 2010 onwards. The search query returned 216 results, all of which were manually analysed. Papers were excluded from our analysis if they did not offer a mood tracking or inference system or if their system was not applicable to mobile-device usage. Based on these criteria, we retained 32 papers out of 204 for further analysis. The median year of these papers' publication was 2017, and the set included a total of 36 studies. While we note that our scope could be limited to the results of this search and it is possible some papers were not included in our sample, our chosen keywords provided an extensive tailored search space.

## 3.3  Metric Analysis

A set of 32 papers was transcribed into a table matrix, with each row representing a paper and each column representing a metric. Some papers had multiple studies, resulting in two rows per paper. Initially, metrics for *accuracy, usability, privacy,* and *study design* were proposed. After analyzing 10–15 papers with these metrics, they were refined and split into more quantitative metrics for further analysis. The final set of metrics included sensor types, number of sensors used, passive tracking, feature extraction, self-reporting methods, accessibility details, usability details, privacy details, and study details. We carefully analysed each paper, extracting relevant information into a spreadsheet. In total, we recorded 38 metrics per paper, encompassing both qualitative and quantitative data. Tables 2, 3, 4, 5 and 6 provide a summary of these metrics, excluding qualitative metrics due to space limitations, although they are used in subsequent analyses.

## 4  Results

A total of 36 studies originating from 32 papers were analysed with respect to sensor details, study details, technology details, privacy details, and Experience Sampling Method (ESM) strategy. For the sake of analysis, only papers that included a formal study were included below. The resulting data is outlined below with subsequent discussion included in the following section.

## 4.1   Sensors and Phone Use

We began by compiling the number of smart device sensors employed within each paper. From here, it was found that 22 out of 36 studies (61%) used at least one type of sensor to derive passive mood predictions. A total of 16 studies (44%) used two or more, 12 (33%) used three or more, and nine (25%) used four or more. The papers that used the greatest number of sensors were [69,96] with 12, both making use of the StudentLife system [96]. Conversely, there were 10 papers that made use of just one sensor. Of the studies that used at least one sensor ($N = 22$), the average number of sensors used was four and the median was three. The two most commonly used sensors are the accelerometer (12) and microphone (12). This is closely followed by application usage (10), SMS/Call info (9), Wi-Fi sensor (9), and GPS (8). Additionally, the light sensor was used in six studies, a screen on-off in five studies, Bluetooth in four studies, a calendar in two studies, and a keyboard in two studies. Of the 12 studies used **activity tracking**, four studies (33%) tracked activity via a physiological sensor (e.g., smartwatch). The remaining eight studies (67%) tracked activity using phone-only sensors i.e., accelerometer or GPS.

**Feature selection** is a complex process that involves carefully analysing and selecting the data that gets input into predictive models. An explicit feature selection process has important implications for future studies that incorporate predictive machine learning models. Hence, the proportion of studies that high-lighted a feature selection process was outlined. Of the 36 studies, 27 (76.3%) were explicit about having a feature selection process. The nine studies that did not include a feature selection process did not contain any passive tracking components.

## 4.2   Study Design

Our analysis of the study design included the average number of participants, socioeconomic background of participants, type of study, gender balance, age of participants, duration of the study, participant rewards, and the number of studies per paper. Across 36 studies that reported participant information, the average number of participants was 1,483. However, this figure is skewed by a few studies that used large data sets compiled from general public app usage. We, therefore also report the median number of participants being 34.

Our analysis determined that 42% of the studies conducted had 0–25 partic-ipants. 17% of studies employed 26–50 participants, and another 17% employed 51–100 participants. It is worth noting that 75% of all studies employed between 0 and 100 participants. Conversely, 11% of studies employed between 101–500 participants, and 14% of studies employed over 1000 participants. Of the five studies that included over 1,000 participants, four studies leveraged back-end access to public applications to compile participant data. The other study oper-ated on public Twitter data via API scraping. The study with the largest par-ticipant cohort was by Servia-Rodríguez et al. [83] with 18,000 participants. The study with the least participants was by Lietz et al. [59] with two participants.

Each study was categorised as an 'in-the-wild' or a 'lab' study. Out of 36 studies, 29 (81%) were conducted in-the-wild, 6 (17%) were conducted in a laboratory setting and one study did not specify. Out of 32 papers, four (10%) papers contained multiple studies. Furthermore, 31 of 36 studies (86%) were explicit about the duration of their study. For the purpose of analysis, the study duration was split into bins of 1 day, 3–4 days, 11–14 days, 4 weeks, 5–6 weeks, 8 weeks, 18–28 weeks, 36 weeks, 52 weeks, and greater than 52 weeks.

**Demography.** Out of 36 studies, 21 (57.9%) explicitly reported on the **socioeconomic background** of their participants. An additional seven studies were identified as 'Random Mixed' due to operating on usage data from a public application or online social network (OSN). This meant that the socioeconomic background of participants could be inferred within 28 (78%) studies. From here, we identified the societal group which was targeted most amongst the study set – university students. A summary of this information is provided in Table 1.

The next study parameter that was analysed was the **distribution of gender**. Of the 36 applicable studies, 18 (50%) studies reported the distribution of gender by identifying the number of male and female participants. An additional six (33%) studies were identified as 'Random Mixed' due to operating on large data sets compiled from public app usage or OSN activity. One study operated on a large data set, however, specified that their application was targeted mostly towards women (no specific proportion given) [18]. For the sake of analysis, only the studies that reported their gender split were considered.

The next stage of analysis involved assessing the average number of female and male participants across the set of applicable studies. Among the 18 studies that reported gender as a male/female split, study participants were 49.2% female on average, with males making up 50.8%. Four of the 18 studies (22%) had under 35% female participation. At an aggregate level, half of the studies that reported gender had under 46% female representation. Conversely, three of the 18 studies (17%) had under 35% male participation. One additional study had under 46% male representation. As an aggregate, 22% of the studies that reported gender had under 46% male representation.

### 4.3   Mobile Technology

A total of 36 studies were analysed with respect to the type of phone OS that was used as well as the type of smart device (s) required. With implications for **accessibility**, we then analysed the proportion of mood inference applications that were 'Android only', 'iPhone only', or available on all smartphones. From 36 studies, 30 (83%) provided details about which phone type the proposed application could be run on. From here, results were placed into categories based on the most commonly used phone types.

From our analysis, we can observe a significant split in the distribution of application offerings per phone type, with a clear preference for Android. 20 of these 30 studies (66%) that reported OS details used an application that was only accessible via Android OS. Conversely, two studies (7%) used an application that was only available via iOS. From here, a clear history for an application offering to cater to one phone type is identified. Only six studies (20%) offer options on both Android/iOS and only two studies (5.9%) use software that can be used on all smartphones Chang et al. [28].

Acknowledging additional implications for accessibility, the next stage of analysis pertained to whether the study required: (1) Phone only, (2) Phone + Wearable, (3) Phone + OSN, (4) Wearable only or (5) OSN only. All 36 applicable studies reported details about the required technologies.

Our analysis demonstrates that 25 of 36 studies (69%) required only a smartphone as a single data source. This adds further evidence to the convenience and accessibility of harnessing the phone and its sensors for mood inference goals. Conversely, two studies used a wearable smart device as their primary source of data, with an additional two studies leveraging online social network data as their single source. While 29 studies (81%) used a single source of data, the remainder used a combination of the aforementioned data sources. Four studies (11%) required a wearable sensor in addition to a smartphone. A further four studies (11%) required a smartphone and active online social network presence. It must also be noted that one study [8] required an external LCD screen in addition to a phone.

### 4.4   Privacy

With most studies reporting on the usage, storage, and analysis of sensitive personal data, privacy is an important consideration. We began by assessing the studies' privacy-related practices according to the below criteria.

With each study operating on personal data, we first considered whether they employed any privacy-preserving methodology. A majority of 27 (75%) out of 36 studies address privacy concerns by either hashing or encrypting personal data, recording microphone amplitudes rather than raw data, using non-GPS location measures, categorising idiosyncratic data (e.g., app usage), using public data, or hosting data locally or in highly secure environments. Conversely, 9 (25%) studies do not mention that they perform any of the aforementioned privacy-preserving procedures.

### 4.5   Self-reporting

The papers were analysed with regard to their usage of Experience Sampling Methods (ESM)/Ecological Momentary Assessment (EMA, used interchangeably). Our analysis extended towards the proportion of studies that used ESM approaches, ESM, and passive tracking approaches, as well as passive tracking only. From 36 applicable studies, 9 (25%) used some form of experience sampling to derive self-reported mood data from their participants while not employing any passive mood-tracking capabilities. We found that 21 (58%) studies used ESM and passive tracking with at least one sensor. Finally, six (17%) of the studies purely relied on passive tracking to infer mood. A total of 24 studies explicitly reported how often they prompted users to report their mood. Table 1 outlines the frequency of daily mood input and the number of corresponding studies.

From the 30 studies that employed mood scales and logging, 15 (50%) utilised the Affect Grid based on Russel's Circumplex Model of Affect [79]. Other strategies include PAM [44] as used in four (13.33%) studies, a valence-only mood scales as used in four (13.33%) studies, PANAS [97] as used in three (10%) studies, Ekman's discrete category mood model as used in two (6.67%) studies, SAM [20] as used in one (3.33%) study, SPANE [32] as used in one (3.33%) study, AffectButton as used in one (3.33%) study, Mood category categorisation as used in one (3.33%) study, EPDS as used in one (3.33%) study, and a 2-item assessment of positive/negative activation created as used in one (3.33%) study. It is important to note that AffectButton, PANAS, PAM, and SAM methods are derived from the Circumplex Model of Affect. Additionally, scales i.e., PHQ score [53] and GAD-7 were used in four (13.33%) studies respectively.

## 5   Discussion

### 5.1   Mood Inference

**Self Reports.** Perhaps the most valuable piece of information amongst mood inference strategies is the output derived from user mood reporting. This output can be placed into a timeline such that it can be viewed empirically over time, or directed into an ML model to predict future moods. As mood tracking has moved into the digital domain, mood assessment has moved from relying on self-reports collected in clinical settings to focusing on experience sampling. This has been an effective strategy as ESMs are able to limit recall bias, which is highly prevalent in clinical settings [84]. Further, ESMs also facilitate the analysis of micro-events that drive real-world behaviours [13]. This means that context-dependent events that trigger mood changes can be quantified.

While collecting context-dependent participant data in real-time has significant advantages, participant non-compliance can quickly downplay these advantages. With multiple inputs usually required per day, and some inputs taking excessive amounts of time, this process is often burdensome to users. As a result, the compliance rates are generally substandard [99].

Across 24 studies that used mobile ESMs, compliance reduced from 91.7% to 77.4% as prompting frequency grew from 2–3 times to 4–5 times per day [14,99]. On average, similar rates of compliance exist in our study set. Of 24 studies that required daily mood reporting, 18 (50%) studies required 1–3 mood reports per day, four (11%) studies required 4 per day and two studies (6%) required 12 per day. Of the studies that required 1–3 mood inputs per day, compliance rates were higher than expected.

However, key variances were identified according to idiosyncratic study processes. Khue et al. [51] was able to achieve a 98% compliance rate prompting 2x per day. Li and Sano [58] had a 93.7% compliance rate prompting 1x per day with 3 short 0–100 scale inputs for mood, health, and stress. Lee et al. [56] monitored 36 participants and received a compliance rate of 88% prompting once per day using Affect Grid and PANAS. While compliance rates are higher on average in this lower prompting frequency range, there are some exceptions. Torkamaan and Ziegler [91] recruited 547 users and prompted twice a day, however, only 391 (71.5%) users met the required threshold of at least three mood entries over a seven-day period. Visuri et al. [93] used two data sets containing a total of 36 people and prompted twice per day, however, only 61% of participants completed enough self-reports (over 20) to be included.

The general trend continues when analysing studies that prompt users at higher frequencies. Zhang et al. [106] prompted users three times per day using a discrete 1–5 rating of 6 basic Ekman emotions and recorded a participation rate of 77.3%. Similarly, Zhang et al. [105] prompted three times per day using the same method and found that 71.4% of participants had enough entries for their data to be included. Wang et al. [96] prompted four times per day using a PAM scale, recording a participation rate of 80%. LiKamWa et al. [61] required four mood inputs per day using the affect grid, however only 75% of participants managed to provide enough entries.

While a negative correlation between prompting frequency and compliance rates is demonstrated in our study set, this clearly is not the only contributing factor. There is evidence that dropout rates are not purely based on frequency, but also on the complexity of mood input. Alvarez-Lozano et al. [2] required just one mood input per day, however, the mood report included four scales, five yes/no questions, and three numerical inputs. While this study ran for five months, they were not able to access large amounts of data for most users due to instances where self-assessment tests weren't provided. This corroborates the idea that regular mood reporting must be an efficient process, or else users will feel burdened.

Some studies [91,93] also recorded poor participation rates, and only prompted users twice per day. Hence, even if reporting frequency is lower, we observe that an overly complex mood reporting process will lead to non-compliance. Bond et al. [18] mentions low compliance with mood scales GAD-7, PHQ-9, and EPDS due to these more complex scales being slow and mentally arduous. In contrast, mood logs are more efficient to complete and require less cognitive workload [18]. With a ratio of 3.28 mood logs per mood scale completion in this study, it indicates that participants prefer to report their mood through an efficient affect-grid-based ESM rather than a complex mood scale. Bond et al. [18] concluded that users prefer simple efficient ESMs, demonstrating that a shift in user behaviour occurs when complex ESMs are used instead of simple ones. Wallbaum et al. [94] underwent a field study with 18 participants, receiving preference data for reporting methods PAM, SAM, emotion terms (PAM but word-based), and colour input (colour indicates mood).

However, qualitative data revealed that users didn't prefer any method. Instead, they liked the option of having efficient and alternative ways to input their mood according to situation and context. Hence, future mood studies should consider adding multiple input method options to encourage reporting across a variety of scenarios. This should include efficient measures in tandem with more verbose measures. While this may increase complexity, it will likely reduce data inconsistency. The evidence suggests that, in order to maintain high rates of compliance, a careful balance between reporting strategy, flexibility, efficiency of input, and frequency must be found and maintained.

## 5.2 Study Design

**Sample Size.** Low participant numbers are common across mood literature and were also a key trend within our sample. With 76% of studies having 0–100 participants, we aim to identify some driving factors behind this trend, as well as the challenges that arise when participant numbers grow. User dropouts, noncompliance, and periods of non-reporting are frequently referenced across the literature. Hence, by increasing the ability of these applications to process inconsistent and scarce data, raising participant numbers would aid in the wider adoption of smartphones as a mental health tool [85] while enhancing the validity of numerous studies. Indeed, this would introduce a series of challenges.

First, as participant numbers grow, methods to encourage sustained engagement become more limited [85]. By extension, non-compliance and dropout rates are likely to increase. Further, as most mood services require consistent data from self-reports and passive sensors, their effectiveness gets dampened when processing data that is noisy and inconsistent [80,85]. To address this challenge, existing study designs would need to be scaled to wider populations and be able to draw clinical conclusions from less consistent data. However, this would significantly enhance the difficulty of the overall process [80].

Despite these challenges, some studies have been successful using larger participant numbers. Servia-Rodríguez et al. [83] derived data from 18,000 participants for their study using a public Android application. They were still able to achieve day-level prediction accuracies of 61–63.5%, which is lower – but still comparable to similar work. Spathis et al. [85] ran a study using data from 17,251 participants over 3 years. They were able to reach day-level accuracies of 74%, which is a significant achievement given the large number of participants. These studies show that it is possible to achieve comparable prediction accuracy with significantly larger populations.

However, these studies also have the benefit of being able to pick users from their database who, longitudinally, have (1) completed a sufficient number of self-reports and (2) provided sufficient passive sensor data. While possible, it remains challenging to implement a clinically sound, large-scale mood-tracking study that does not employ data-cleaning techniques to remove noisy participant data from analysis. Jaques et al. [47] demonstrate how deep learning techniques can be used to account for missing sensor data. Using such techniques, this study was able to achieve strong mood prediction in situations where even up to 75% of data was lost. Future studies should consider implementing similar deep-learning techniques to deal with noisy or inconsistent data. This will facilitate larger participant samples, and henceforth extend mood prediction capabilities to a more realistic data environment where noise and inconsistency are more frequent.

**Demography.** Our results show that 13 of 28 applicable studies (46%) were comprised of undergraduates, postgraduates, and university staff. A further four studies recruited over 50% of their participants from universities. With most studies having 1–100 participants, and at least 43% of studies based on this homogeneous participant background, it is pungent to discuss whether some population groups are misrepresented in mood inference literature.

Universities are a convenient place to recruit participants, however, inferences gained from personalised student data are mostly ineffective in generalising to members of the general public [15,41]. For instance, Wang et al. [96] recruited 83 students over two 9-week terms, finding that their reliance on university routines eroded the potential for depression symptoms features to generalise to standard populations. Across the literature, some evidence is provided to explain this phenomenon.

First, relying exclusively on student data may create systematic biases as students generally have more dynamic attitudes, less formulated peer relationships, and stronger intellectual skills than the general population [15]. These systematic biases will inherently invalidate some findings. Second, students are also more likely to come from homogeneous backgrounds. A common criticism across psychology literature, therefore, is that claims are mostly based on data from Western, Educated, Industrialised, Rich, and Democratic (WEIRD) cultures [43]. To the detriment of these studies, WEIRD societies rank very poorly in their ability to represent a general population [43]. When student data is personalised, such as in the case of mood inference studies, this effect is heightened [41].

On the basis of this evidence, validity concerns are raised for the 46% of studies that only used university participants. Future studies that intend on demonstrating findings that are applicable to general populations should be careful drawing conclusions from this narrow group of society [43]. To mitigate this, future studies should aim to increase the number of non-university participants.

### 5.3   Platform

Our analysis found that 20 of 36 studies (56%) used a service that was only accessible on Android. Conversely, 2 of 36 studies (6%) only offered their service on iOS. With 26 of 36 (72%) studies offering a service that is only accessible on one type of Smartphone OS, significant implications for accessibility are noted across the study set. As the two largest smartphone OS providers transcend into maturity, devices last longer, people are upgrading less and also becoming more content with their choices and are less likely to change their devices [5].

According to our results, Android's market share makes this less problematic for the 56% of Android-based studies, missing 29% of potential users highlights accessibility issues in this context. Yet, these concerns are far more severe for the 6% of studies that are iOS only. This group fails to reach 72% of potential users. Of the studies that mention the reason for their preference, Bachmann et al. [7] mentioned that Android was chosen as the exclusive offering due to having the highest market share. Further, Cao et al. [25] used a specialised custom keyboard for mood detection, a feature available on Android that is restricted on iOS.

Indeed, most studies do not specify why they chose to be exclusive in their application offering. Some evidence in this domain suggests that it is difficult to develop for both Android and iPhone, due to differences in platform, tools, and techniques [92]. While this is likely to be a substantial driving factor towards many mood applications being exclusively offered on one operating system, further evidence must be considered to understand the clear preference for Android. More so than iOS, Android offers less restrictive permissions to access and collect user information and sensor data [1]. In the context of mood applications that track and record user data, this is a significant factor.

With Android having a significantly greater market share and flexibility in permissions, it is reasonable that 56% of studies were Android-only. The aforementioned studies [7] add further evidence to this claim. Significant gains in **accessibility** have been gained through a transition from pen-and-paper to the in-situ mobile domain; however, to maximise accessibility, adjustments can and should be made to offer corresponding services across all mobile platforms.

### 5.4 Privacy

As mood applications grow in efficacy and become more pervasive throughout society, privacy implications become more critical. Mood applications track and store significant amounts of idiosyncratic longitudinal data which could be used to gain, for instance, valuable personalised marketing insights [10]. This data could also be used for criminal intent, such as identity fraud. With increased internet usage throughout the pandemic, rates of cybercrime have grown significantly. Outcomes are worsened for people with mental illness as they have a reduced capacity to protect themselves online [68].

Health applications are generally run commercially and thus may not possess medically sound controls over sensitive data [46]. Further, the majority of health applications are not subject to government supervision, hence consumers and clinical advisers must provide their own technical inquiry into the privacy procedures of a service [45]. Hamre-Os [40] interviewed 26 students about mood applications and found that the potential for cyber-attacks created the greatest concern as this could lead to sensitive data being leaked to nefarious parties. Further, Widnall et al. [100] conducted a systematic analysis of mood application user reviews, finding that mistrust had risen after a series of high-profile cyber-attacks. By extension, some users felt uncomfortable because of a general lack of transparency with respect to data storage. In our results, 27 of 36 (75%) studies were transparent about attempting to preserve privacy in some manner.

However, these details were mostly brief and did not explicitly cover all bases. For instance, many studies covered their hashing method, but no studies went into explicit technical detail about how their server was secured. Hence, while also acknowledging that 10 studies did not report any privacy information whatsoever, it is understandable that some participants may feel like they are overextending their trust. To mitigate this, designers of mood services that store personal data must communicate an explicit privacy strategy that covers data logging, storage, and server security.

## 5.5  Sensors

Regular intervals of information must be derived from passive sensors to facilitate the creation of predictive mood models. Not only does in-situ mood reporting give primary quantifiable mood data, but data is also provided in a context such that it can be correlated with real-life occurrences. Time-series data from passive sensors can be harnessed as a means of gaining information about these occurrences [55]. However, there are challenges regarding the heterogeneity of information, as sensors produce data at different rates and can give conflicting insights [106]. We, therefore, discuss the implications of sensor usage that were observed in the study set. Our results show that the most used sensors were the microphone and accelerometer, both appearing in 12 studies. This was followed by Application usage (10) and SMS/Call logs (9).

**Microphone.** Due to innovations in voice processing, the use and storage of microphone data have significant implications for privacy [54]. Using advanced ML techniques, speech can be analysed to make advanced inferences about a person, such as their personality type [73,74], gender, age, and socioeconomic background [54]. For this reason, most studies did not continuously record or store raw microphone data. In our sample, 12 studies used the microphone. The studies [6,34,83,85] used the microphone, but were explicit about only recording amplitude at various intervals throughout the day.

Zhang et al. [105] derived mean, variance, and other features from microphone audio before it was sent to the server, such that raw audio was never kept. Chang et al. [28] used the microphone as its only sensor but performed all computations locally to preserve privacy. Wang et al. [96] ran a conversation classifier continuously on each participant's phone which can detect speech segments and unique conversations. However, the classifier is unable to identify unique speakers, and speech data was uploaded over private Wi-Fi to a secure server.

While most studies provided a sound privacy-preserving method for microphone data, there was one exception. Lu et al. [62] extracted features such as mel-frequency cepstrum, speaking rate, and pitch range, all of which can be used to identify the speaker. This data was also stored externally for model training without providing any information about hashing or security. Overall, the usage of the microphone appears to be, for the most part, privacy-preserving. To mitigate privacy concerns, future developments in this field should continue to extract and store features from speech that can't be traced back to a specific human.

**GPS.** Similar to the microphone, the storage of GPS data is a key privacy concern as it can reveal enough sensitive information to identify users [37]. GPS data can be used to track a user's location, time spent there, and frequently visited sites, and to derive information about the user's everyday routines [24]. However, while invasive, usage and storage of GPS data is generally an expected trade-off for most mood tracking applications due to the functional benefits it provides [10].

In our review, 8 papers used the GPS sensor. Most studies appear to have sound privacy processes, involving user consent, hashing, coarse-grained data collection and/or secure storage. However, most studies fail to cover all of these processes. For instance, LiKamWa et al. [61] hashed all private data but did not mention user consent nor provide a mechanism to opt out of location sharing. Other studies [69,96] sought approval from their Institutional Review Boards and stored GPS data onto secure servers when the users' phones were connected to a private Wi-Fi network. However, they did not mention that this data was hashed or encrypted.

Servia-Rodríguez et al. [83] mitigated their GPS data collection by predominantly using Wi-Fi and Cell towers to derive location. When they did collect location data, it was correlated with a self-reported location such that only coarse-grained location was recorded. While this strategy is highly effective, this study did not mention that this data was hashed, nor did it state that the upload server was secured. This is potentially problematic, as it is foreseeable that even coarse-grained location data could have severe privacy implications if leaked.

Canzian and Musolesi [24] was explicit about receiving approval from the Ethics Review Board, provided a consent form, and uploaded GPS data via a 'secure transmission protocol' to a secure server. While user data was not hashed or encrypted, this can be considered a reasonable privacy strategy due to other robust mechanisms. Conversely, Lu et al. [62] collected GPS data every three minutes but provided no information about hashing, obscuration, server security or the ability to opt out. To address GPS privacy concerns in a more holistic manner, future studies should (1) incorporate consent forms and the ability to opt out, (2) hash or encrypt all data, (3) only collect coarse-grained location, and (4) store data securely into a secure server.

## 5.6 Smartphone as 'ubiquitous instrumentation'

As smartphones are equipped with a variety of sensors and closely accompany their owners throughout their daily lives, smartphones can serve as a powerful tool for unobtrusive and continuous mood tracking. Smartphone sensors that track our physical activities can provide detailed insights into users' emotional states and moods based on activity trackers' data [16]. Furthermore, prior research has shown that application usage can be leveraged as a reliable estimate to predict users' emotional states and mood [81]. Finally, textual information posted on social media platforms, as well as other written communication, can be indicative of a user's emotional states and mood, with certain words being associated with either positive or negative affect.

Due to the rise in the sensing and computing abilities of smartphones, these devices are well-suited for observing human behaviour in ways that current scientific methods are unable to do. Particularly given that smartphone ownership is accessible to large parts of the population, in contrast to traditional scientific equipment that typically requires significant financial investment from governments or institutions, making them perfect for 'ubiquitous instrumentation' [52].

Our results reflect the prominent role of smartphones in emotion tracking and mood inference in field research and laboratory-based user studies. Our findings show that sensors such as accelerometers, gyroscopes, microphones, and cameras can detect changes in movement, tone of voice, and facial expressions, which can indicate the user's emotional state. Researchers can analyse these signals and identify patterns to infer the user's emotional state without invading user privacy. Moreover, our results show that smartphones provide an excellent platform for collecting self-reported data from users about their moods and emotional states. While self-reported data may be subject to biases, it can provide valuable context when combined with sensor data [103].

### 5.7   Implications for HCI Research

When designing and conducting studies using smartphones for emotion sensing and mood tracking, several aspects of these devices must be considered. To be precise, careful sensor collection for mood tracking is crucial. Sensors vary in accuracy and invasiveness, thus, the ethical implications of using privacy-comprising sensors like microphones and cameras must be taken into account.

To address privacy concerns and protect private data, researchers should consider hashing or encrypting the data and securely hosting it. Obtaining informed consent from participants, and clearly explaining data collection and usage, is essential. Measures should be implemented to safeguard participant data against unauthorised access or misuse. Additionally, potential sensor data loss or noise should be acknowledged, and deep-learning techniques can be employed to handle inconsistent or noisy data effectively.

Furthermore, the use of additional sensing devices alongside smartphones in user studies should be carefully considered. Our findings indicate that the majority of existing work in the field can be conducted using smartphones alone. Therefore, it is recommended to avoid additional instrumentation unless absolutely necessary to ensure technology accessibility in user studies.

By considering factors such as prevalent sensor usage, study samples, privacy concerns, and accessibility, HCI researchers can make informed decisions when designing user studies, leading to more accurate and meaningful outcomes.

## 6   Conclusion

In this paper, we present the review and analysis of the ACM body of literature surrounding mood tracking and inference using mobile devices. We differentiated mood from emotion, before explaining the motivation and reasoning to measure mood with respect to clinical disorders and personal empowerment. We then looked into how mood can be tracked and predicted using clinical tools, including how smartphones have significantly increased the efficacy of such tools. We analysed 32 papers from the Association for Computing Machinery (ACM) Digital Library and discussed mood reporting strategy, sensors, study design, demography, platforms, and privacy. Based on our findings, we develop a set of recommendations concerning self-reporting methods, sensor choices, platform, accessibility, and privacy considerations.

# A  Appendix

**Table 1.** Frequency of daily mood input and number of studies ($N = 24$).

| Frequency of Daily Mood Inputs | Num Studies |
|---|---|
| 1x | 6 |
| 2x | 8 |
| 3x | 4 |
| 4x | 4 |
| 12x | 2 |

**Table 2.** Summary of Metrics selected and filled in per paper.

| Paper | Mic | GPS | Accele-rometer | Application Usage | SMS/Call Info | Calendar |
|---|---|---|---|---|---|---|
| [61] | No | Yes | No | Yes | Yes | No |
| [25] | No | No | Yes | No | No | No |
| [86] | No | No | No | No | No | No |
| [105] | Yes | Yes | Yes | No | Yes | No |
| [6] | Yes | No | No | Yes | Yes | Yes |
| [28] [1/2] | Yes | No | No | No | No | No |
| [28] [2/2] | Yes | No | Yes | No | No | No |
| [96] | Yes | Yes | Yes | Yes | Yes | No |
| [106] | Yes | No | Yes | Yes | No | No |
| [62] | Yes | Yes | Yes | No | No | No |
| [17] | No | No | No | No | Yes | No |
| [69] | Yes | Yes | Yes | Yes | Yes | No |
| [56] | No | No | No | No | No | No |
| [39] | No | No | No | No | No | No |
| [80] [1/2] | No | No | No | No | No | No |
| [80] [2/2] | No | No | No | No | No | No |
| [34] | Yes | No | No | Yes | Yes | Yes |
| [83] | Yes | Yes | Yes | No | Yes | No |
| [31] | No | Yes | Yes | No | Yes | No |
| [67] | No | No | No | No | No | No |
| [24] | No | Yes | No | No | No | No |
| [85] | Yes | No | Yes | No | No | No |
| [42] * | Yes * | Yes * | Yes | No | No | No |
| [91] | - | - | - | - | - | - |
| [94] | - | - | - | - | - | - |
| [51] | - | - | - | - | - | - |
| [93] [1/2] | No | No | No | Yes | No | No |
| [93] [2/2] | No | No | No | Yes | No | No |
| [60] | - | - | - | - | - | - |
| [59] | No | No | Yes | No | No | No |
| [7] * | Yes | No | Yes | Yes | Yes | Yes |
| [29] | - | - | - | - | - | - |
| [70] | - | - | - | - | - | - |
| [104] | No | No | No | Yes | No | No |
| [8] | - | - | - | - | - | - |
| [2] | Yes | No | Yes | Yes | No | No |
| [58] | No | No | Yes | No | No | No |
| [18] | - | - | - | - | - | - |
| [64] [1/2] | - | - | - | - | - | - |
| [64] [2/2] | - | - | - | - | - | - |

**Table 3.** Summary of Metrics selected and filled in per paper.

| Paper | Light Sensor | Screen On/Off | WiFi | Bluetooth | Physical Activity | Keyboard |
|---|---|---|---|---|---|---|
| citech22likamwa2013 | No | No | No | No | No | No |
| [25] | No | No | No | No | No | Yes |
| [86] | No | No | No | No | No | No |
| [105] | Yes | Yes | Yes | No | Yes | No |
| [6] | Yes | No | Yes | No | Yes | No |
| [28] | No | No | No | No | No | No |
| [28] Study 2 | No | No | No | No | No | No |
| [96] | Yes | Yes | Yes | Yes | Yes | No |
| [106] | Yes | Yes | Yes | No | Yes | No |
| [62] | No | No | No | No | Yes | No |
| [17] | No | No | No | Yes | No | No |
| [69] | Yes | Yes | Yes | Yes | Yes | No |
| [56] | No | No | No | No | No | No |
| [39] | No | No | No | No | No | No |
| [80] | No | No | No | No | No | No |
| [80] Study 2 | No | No | No | No | No | No |
| [34] | Yes | No | Yes | No | Yes | No |
| [83] | No | No | Yes | No | Yes | No |
| [31] | No | No | Yes | No | Yes | No |
| [67] | No | No | No | No | No | No |
| [24] | No | No | No | No | Yes | No |
| [85] | No | No | No | No | Yes | No |
| [42] * | No | No | No | No | Yes | No |
| [91] | - | - | - | - | - | - |
| [94] | - | - | - | - | - | - |
| [51] | - | - | - | - | - | - |
| [93] | No | No | No | No | No | No |
| [93] Study 2 | No | No | No | No | No | No |
| [60] | - | - | - | - | - | - |
| [59] | No | No | No | No | Yes | No |
| [7] * | Yes | No | Yes | No | No | No |
| [29] | - | - | - | - | - | - |
| [70] | - | - | - | - | - | - |
| [104] | No | No | No | No | No | Yes |
| [8] | - | - | - | - | - | - |
| [2] | No | Yes | Yes | Yes | No | No |
| [58] | No | No | No | No | No | No |
| [18] | - | - | - | - | - | - |
| [64] | - | - | - | - | - | - |
| [64] Study 2 | - | - | - | - | - | - |

**Table 4.** Summary of Metrics selected and filled in per paper.

| Paper | In-situ self reporting? | Self reporting for ground truth? | Passive tracking? |
|---|---|---|---|
| [61] | Yes | Yes | Yes |
| [25] | No | No | Yes |
| [86] | Yes | No | No |
| [105] | Yes | Yes | Yes |
| [6] | Yes | Yes | Yes |
| [28] | No | No | Yes |
| [28] Study 2 | No | No | Yes |
| [96] | Yes | Yes | Yes |
| [106] | Yes | Yes | Yes |
| [62] | No | No | Yes |
| [17] | Yes | Yes | Yes |
| [69] | Yes | Yes | Yes |
| [56] | Yes | Yes | Yes |
| [39] | Yes | No | No |
| [80] | Yes | Yes | Yes |
| [80] Study 2 | Yes | Yes | Yes |
| [34] | Yes | Yes | Yes |
| [83] | Yes | Yes | Yes |
| [31] | No | No | Yes |
| [67] | No | No | Yes |
| [24] | Yes | Yes | Yes |
| [85] | Yes | Yes | Yes |
| [42] * | Yes | Yes | Yes |
| [91] | Yes | No | No |
| [94] | N/A | N/A | N/A |
| [51] | Yes | No | No |
| [93] | Yes | Yes | Yes |
| [93] Study 2 | Yes | Yes | Yes |
| [60] | N/A | N/A | N/A |
| [59] | Yes | Yes | Yes |
| [7] * | No | No | Yes |
| [29] | Yes | No | No |
| [70] | Yes | No | No |
| [104] | Yes | Yes | Yes |
| [8] | Yes | No | No |
| [2] | Yes | Yes | Yes |
| [58] | Yes | Yes | Yes |
| [18] | Yes | No | No |
| [64] | Yes | No | No |
| [64] Study 2 | Yes | No | No |

**Table 5.** Summary of Metrics selected and filled in per paper.

| Paper | States privacy process? | Length of self-reporting period | Daily active mood input frequency | Android or iOS |
|---|---|---|---|---|
| [61] | Yes | 2 months | 4x | Both |
| [25] | Yes | N/A | N/A | Android |
| [86] | Yes | 2 weeks | 3x | Both |
| [105] | Yes | 1 month | 3x | Android |
| [6] | Yes | 4 days | 12x | Android |
| [28] | Yes | N/A | N/A | All |
| [28] Study 2 | Yes | N/A | N/A | All |
| [96] | Yes | 18 weeks | 4x | Both |
| [106] | No | 2 weeks | 3x | Android |
| [62] | No | N/A | N/A | Android |
| [17] | Yes | 2 weeks | 1x | Android |
| [69] | Yes | 3 weeks | 4x | Both |
| [56] | Yes | 28 days | 1x | Both |
| [39] | Yes | - | 1x | iOS |
| [80] | Yes | 5 weeks | 4x | Android |
| [80] Study 2 | Yes | - | - | Android |
| [34] | Yes | 1 month | 12x | Android |
| [83] | Yes | 26 days | 2x | Android |
| [31] | No | N/A | N/A | - |
| [67] | Yes | N/A | N/A | - |
| [24] | Yes | - | 1x | Android |
| [85] | Yes | - | 2x | Android |
| [42] * | Yes | - | - | iOS |
| [91] | Yes | N/A | 2x | Android |
| [94] | N/A | N/A | N/A | N/A |
| [51] | Yes | - | 2x | Android |
| [93] | Yes | 2 weeks | 2x | Android |
| [93] Study 2 | Yes | 2 weeks | 2x | Android |
| [60] | N/A | N/A | N/A | N/A |
| [59] | No | - | - | N/A |
| [7] * | No | - | - | Android |
| [29] | No | N/A | N/A | iOS |
| [70] | No | N/A | - | Both |
| [104] | Yes | - | 2x | Android |
| [8] | N/A | N/A | - | - |
| [2] | Yes | N/A | 1x | Android |
| [58] | Yes | N/A | 1x | N/A |
| [18] | Yes | N/A | 3x | Both |
| [64] | Yes | N/A | - | Android |
| [64] Study 2 | Yes | N/A | - | Android |

**Table 6.** Summary of Metrics selected and filled in per paper.

| Paper | Multiple devices? | Study details | $N$ | In-the-wild/ Lab | Duration | Participant background | Gender Split (% female) |
|---|---|---|---|---|---|---|---|
| [61] | No | * | 32 | wild | 2 months | 24/32 University | 34.4 |
| [25] | No | * | 21 | wild | 8 weeks | - | - |
| [86] | No | * | 2382 | wild | 22 months | Random mixed | - |
| [105] | No | * | 42 | wild | 1 month | University | 57 |
| [6] | No | * | 9 | wild | 4 days | - | 44 |
| [28] | No | * | 125 | lab | N/A | - | 75 |
| [28] Study 2 | No | * | 7 | lab | N/A | - | 43 |
| [96] | Yes | * | 83 | wild | 18 weeks | University | 52 |
| [106] | No | * | 68 | wild | 6 weeks | - | - |
| [62] | Yes | * | 14 | lab | 4 days | University | 71 |
| [17] | No | * | 111 | wild | 7 months | University | - |
| [69] | Yes | * | 83 | wild | 18 weeks | University | 52 |
| [56] | No | * | 36 | wild | 28 days | University | - |
| [39] | No | * | 9 | lab | 1 day | University | 33 |
| [80] | No | * | 23 | wild | 5 weeks | University | 40 |
| [80] Study 2 | No | * | 9654 | wild | - | Random mixed | N/A |
| [34] | Yes | * | 6 | wild | 1 month | 4 University, 2 Workers | 33 |
| [83] | No | * | 18000 | wild | 35 months | Random mixed | N/A |
| [31] | No | * | 100 | wild | 1 month | - | - |
| [67] | No | * | 100 | lab | - | Random mixed | N/A |
| [24] | No | * | 28 | wild | 9 months | University | 54 |
| [85] | No | * | 17251 | wild | 46 months | Random mixed | N/A |
| [42] * | Yes | N/A | N/A | N/A | N/A | N/A | N/A |
| [91] | No | * | 391 | wild | 2 weeks | Random mixed | N/A |
| [94] | N/A | N/A | N/A | N/A | N/A | N/A | N/A |
| [51] | No | * | 48 | wild | 11 days | University | 40 |
| [93] | No | * | 15 | wild | 2 weeks | University | 50 |
| [93] Study 2 | No | * | 21 | wild | 2 weeks | University | 50 |
| [60] | N/A | N/A | N/A | N/A | N/A | N/A | N/A |
| [59] | No | * | 2 | - | - | - | - |
| [7] * | Yes | N/A | N/A | N/A | N/A | N/A | N/A |
| [29] | No | * | 15 | wild | 2 weeks | Professionals, University | 27 |
| [70] | No | * | 17 | wild | 2 weeks | - | - |
| [104] | No | * | 30 | wild | 1 year | University | - |
| [8] | Yes | * | 22 | lab | 1 day | School teenagers | 45 |
| [2] | No | * | 18 | wild | 5 months | Mixed bipolar patients | - |
| [58] | No | * | 255 | wild | 2 months | University | - |
| [18] | No | * | 1461 | wild | 15 months | Random mixed | - |
| [64] | No | * | 6 | wild | 1 day | School teenagers | - |
| [64] Study 2 | No | * | 73 | wild | 2 weeks | School teenagers | 86 |

# References

1. Alshehri, A., Hewins, A., McCulley, M., Alshahrani, H., Fu, H., Zhu, Y.: Risks behind device information permissions in android OS. Commun. Netw. **09**(04), 219–234 (2017)

2. Alvarez-Lozano, J., et al.: Tell me your apps and I will tell you your mood: correlation of apps usage with bipolar disorder state. In: PETRA 2014 (2014)

3. Ang, W.T., Khosla, P.K., Riviere, C.N.: Nonlinear regression model of alow-$g$ mems accelerometer. IEEE Sens. J. **7**, 81–88 (2007)

4. Angst, J., Cassano, G.: The mood spectrum: improving the diagnosis of bipolar disorder. Bipolar Disord. **7**(s4), 4–12 (2005)

5. Appiah, D., Ozuem, W., Howell, K.: Brand switching in the smartphone industry: a preliminary study (2017)

6. Bachmann, A., et al.: How to use smartphones for less obtrusive ambulatory mood assessment and mood recognition. In: UbiComp/ISWC 2015 Adjunct, pp. 693–702 (2015)

7. Bachmann, A., et al.: Leveraging smartwatches for unobtrusive mobile ambulatory mood assessment. In: UbiComp/ISWC 2015 Adjunct, pp. 1057–1062 (2015)

8. Balta, A., Read, J.C.: U ok? Txt me the colour of ur mood! In: CHI EA 2016, pp. 2410–2416 (2016)

9. Bankmycell: How many smartphones are in the world? (2022). https://www.bankmycell.com/blog/how-many-phones-are-in-the-world

10. Barcena, M.B., Wueest, C., Lau, H.: How safe is your quantified self? Technical report, Symantec, Mountain View, CA (2014)

11. Barrett, L.F., Adolphs, R., Marsella, S., Martinez, A.M., Pollak, S.D.: Emotional expressions reconsidered: challenges to inferring emotion from human facial movements. Psychol. Sci. Public Interest **20**, 1–68 (2019)

12. Beedie, C., Terry, P., Lane, A.: Distinctions between emotion and mood. Cogn. Emot. **19**(6), 847–878 (2005)

13. van Berkel, N., Ferreira, D., Kostakos, V.: The experience sampling method on mobile devices. ACM Comput. Surv. **50**(6) (2017)

14. van Berkel, N., Goncalves, J., Hosio, S., Sarsenbayeva, Z., Velloso, E., Kostakos, V.: Overcoming compliance bias in self-report studies: a cross-study analysis. Int. J. Hum. Comput. Stud. **134**, 1–12 (2020)

15. van Berkel, N., Sarsenbayeva, Z., Goncalves, J.: The methodology of studying fairness perceptions in artificial intelligence: contrasting chi and FAccT. Int. J. Hum. Comput. Stud. **170**, 102954 (2023)

16. Biddle, S.J.H.: Emotion, mood and physical activity, pp. 75–97 (2003)

17. Bogomolov, A., Lepri, B., Ferron, M., Pianesi, F., Pentland, A.S.: Daily stress recognition from mobile phone data, weather conditions and individual traits. In: MM 2014, pp. 477–486 (2014)

18. Bond, R., Moorhead, A., Mulvenna, M., O'Neill, S., Potts, C., Murphy, N.: Behaviour analytics of users completing ecological momentary assessments in the form of mental health scales and mood logs on a smartphone app. In: ECCE 2019, pp. 203–206 (2019)

19. Bower, G.H.: Mood and memory. Am. Psychol. **36**(2), 129–148 (1981)

20. Bradley, M.M., Lang, P.J.: Measuring emotion: the self-assessment manikin and the semantic differential. J. Behav. Ther. Exp. Psychiatry **25**(1), 49–59 (1994)

21. Brown, T.A., Chorpita, B.F., Barlow, D.H.: Structural relationships among dimensions of the DSM-IV anxiety and mood disorders and dimensions of negative affect, positive affect, and autonomic arousal. J. Abnorm. Psychol. **107**(2), 179–192 (1998)

22. Caldeira, C.M., Chen, Y., Chan, L., Pham, V., Chen, Y., Zheng, K.: Mobile apps for mood tracking: an analysis of features and user reviews. In: AMIA ... Annual Symposium Proceedings. AMIA Symposium 2017, pp. 495–504 (2017)

23. Calear, A., Christensen, H.: Systematic review of school-based prevention and early intervention programs for depression. J. Adolesc. **33**, 429–438 (2009)

24. Canzian, L., Musolesi, M.: Trajectories of depression: unobtrusive monitoring of depressive states by means of smartphone mobility traces analysis. In: UbiComp 2015, pp. 1293–1304 (2015)

25. Cao, B., et al.: DeepMood: modeling mobile phone typing dynamics for mood detection. In: KDD 2017, pp. 747–755 (2017)

26. Carlson, M., Charlin, V., Miller, N.: Positive mood and helping behavior: a test of six hypotheses. J. Pers. Soc. Psychol. **55**(2), 211–229 (1988)

27. Chan, E.C., Sun, Y., Aitchison, K.J., Sivapalan, S.: Mobile app–based self-report questionnaires for the assessment and monitoring of bipolar disorder: systematic review. JMIR Formative Res. **5**(1), e13770 (2021)

28. Chang, K.H., Fisher, D., Canny, J., Hartmann, B.: How's my mood and stress? An efficient speech analysis library for unobtrusive monitoring on mobile phones. In: BodyNets 2011, pp. 71–77. ICST (2011)

29. Church, K., Hoggan, E., Oliver, N.: A study of mobile mood awareness and communication through MobiMood. In: NordiCHI 2010, pp. 128–137 (2010)

30. Depp, C., Kim, D., Dios, L., Wang, V., Ceglowski, J.: A pilot study of mood ratings captured by mobile phone versus paper- and-pencil mood charts in bipolar disorder. J. Dual Diagn. **8**, 326–332 (2012)

31. Dhahri, C., Ikeda, K., Hoashi, K.: Forecasting mood using smartphone and SNS data. In: HotMobile 2019, p. 175 (2019)

32. Diener, E., Wirtz, D., Tov, W.: New measures of well-being: flourishing and positive and negative feelings. Soc. Indic. Res. **39**, 247–266 (2010)

33. Dubad, M., Winsper, C., Meyer, C., Livanou, M., Marwaha, S.: A systematic review of the psychometric properties, usability and clinical impacts of mobile mood-monitoring applications in young people. Psychol. Med. **48**, 1–21 (2017)

34. Exler, A., Schankin, A., Klebsattel, C., Beigl, M.: A wearable system for mood assessment considering smartphone features and data from mobile ECGs. In: UbiComp 2016, Adjunct, pp. 1153–1161 (2016)

35. Gardner, M.P.: Mood states and consumer behavior: a critical review. J. Consum. Res. **12**(3), 281 (1985)

36. George, J.M.: State or trait: effects of positive mood on prosocial behaviors at work. J. Appl. Psychol. **76**(2), 299–307 (1991)

37. Goldenholz, D.M., et al.: Using mobile location data in biomedical research while preserving privacy. J. Am. Med. Inform. Assoc. **25**(10), 1402–1406 (2018)

38. Gross, J.J.: Emotion regulation: current status and future prospects. Psychol. Inq. **26**(1), 1–26 (2015)

39. Hafiz, P., Maharjan, R., Kumar, D.: Usability of a mood assessment smartphone prototype based on humor appreciation. In: MobileHCI 2018, Adjunct, pp. 151–157 (2018)

40. Hamre-Os, A.: A mood tracking interface for mobile application-to help assess well being in students (2021)

41. Hanel, P.H.P., Vione, K.C.: Do student samples provide an accurate estimate of the general public? PLoS ONE **11**(12), e0168354 (2016)

42. Hänsel, K., Alomainy, A., Haddadi, H.: Large scale mood and stress self-assessments on a smartwatch. In: UbiComp 2016, Adjunct, pp. 1180–1184 (2016)

43. Henrich, J., Heine, S.J., Norenzayan, A.: The weirdest people in the world? Behav. Brain Sci. **33**(2–3), 61–83 (2010)

44. Hibbard, J.H., Stockard, J., Mahoney, E.R., Tusler, M.: Development of the patient activation measure (PAM): conceptualizing and measuring activation in patients and consumers. Health Serv. Res. **39**(4p1), 1005–1026 (2004)
45. Huckvale, K., Torous, J., Larsen, M.: Assessment of the data sharing and privacy practices of smartphone apps for depression and smoking cessation. JAMA Netw. Open **2**, e192542 (2019)
46. Hutton, L., et al.: Assessing the privacy of mHealth apps for self-tracking: heuristic evaluation approach. JMIR Mhealth Uhealth **6**(10), e185 (2018)
47. Jaques, N., Taylor, S., Sano, A., Picard, R.: Multimodal autoencoder: a deep learning approach to filling in missing sensor data and enabling better mood prediction, pp. 202–208 (2017)
48. Kessler, R.C., Berglund, P.A., Foster, C.L., Saunders, W.B., Stang, P.E., Walters, E.E.: Social consequences of psychiatric disorders, II: teenage parenthood. Am. J. Psychiatry **154**(10), 1405–1411 (1997)
49. Kessler, R.C., Foster, C.L., Saunders, W.B., Stang, P.E.: Social consequences of psychiatric disorders, i: educational attainment. Am. J. Psychiatry **152**(7), 1026–1032 (1995)
50. Kessler, R.C., Walters, E.E., Forthofer, M.S.: The social consequences of psychiatric disorders, III: probability of marital stability. Am. J. Psychiatry **155**(8), 1092–1096 (1998)
51. Khue, L.M., Ouh, E.L., Jarzabek, S.: Mood self-assessment on smartphones. In: WH 2015 (2015)
52. Kostakos, V., Ferreira, D.: The rise of ubiquitous instrumentation. Frontiers ICT **2**, 3 (2015)
53. Kroenke, K., Spitzer, R.L., Williams, J.B.W.: The PHQ-9. J. Gen. Intern. Med. **16**(9), 606–613 (2001)
54. Kröger, J.L., Lutz, O.H.-M., Raschke, P.: Privacy implications of voice and speech analysis – information disclosure by inference. In: Friedewald, M., Önen, M., Lievens, E., Krenn, S., Fricker, S. (eds.) Privacy and Identity 2019. IAICT, vol. 576, pp. 242–258. Springer, Cham (2020). https://doi.org/10.1007/978-3-030-42504-3_16
55. Lane, N.D., Miluzzo, E., Lu, H., Peebles, D., Choudhury, T., Campbell, A.T.: A survey of mobile phone sensing. Comm. Mag. **48**(9), 140–150 (2010)
56. Lee, J.A., Efstratiou, C., Bai, L.: OSN mood tracking: exploring the use of online social network activity as an indicator of mood changes. In: UbiComp 2016, Adjunct, pp. 1171–1179 (2016)
57. Lee, K., et al.: Effect of self-monitoring on long-term patient engagement with mobile health applications. PLoS ONE **13**, e0201166 (2018)
58. Li, B., Sano, A.: Extraction and interpretation of deep autoencoder-based temporal features from wearables for forecasting personalized mood, health, and stress. Proc. ACM Interact. Mob. Wearable Ubiquit. Technol. **4**(2) (2020)
59. Lietz, R., Harraghy, M., Brady, J., Calderon, D., Cloud, J., Makedon, F.: A wearable system for unobtrusive mood detection. In: PETRA 2019, pp. 329–330 (2019)
60. Lietz, R., Harraghy, M., Calderon, D., Brady, J., Becker, E., Makedon, F.: Survey of mood detection through various input modes. In: PETRA 2019, pp. 28–31 (2019)
61. LiKamWa, R., Liu, Y., Lane, N.D., Zhong, L.: MoodScope: building a mood sensor from smartphone usage patterns. In: Proceeding of the 11th Annual International Conference on Mobile Systems, Applications, and Services, MobiSys 2013, pp. 465–466 (2013)

62. Lu, H., et al.: StressSense: detecting stress in unconstrained acoustic environments using smartphones. In: UbiComp 2012, pp. 351–360 (2012)
63. Lyubomirsky, S., King, L., Diener, E.: The benefits of frequent positive affect: does happiness lead to success? Psychol. Bull. **131**(6), 803–855 (2005)
64. Matthews, M., Doherty, G.: In the mood: engaging teenagers in psychotherapy using mobile phones. In: CHI 2011, pp. 2947–2956 (2011)
65. Mehrotra, A., Vermeulen, J., Pejovic, V., Musolesi, M.: Ask, but don't interrupt: the case for interruptibility-aware mobile experience sampling (2015)
66. Mitchell, R.L., Phillips, L.H.: The psychological, neurochemical and functional neuroanatomical mediators of the effects of positive and negative mood on executive functions. Neuropsychologia **45**(4), 617–629 (2007)
67. Mogadala, A., Varma, V.: Twitter user behavior understanding with mood transition prediction. In: DUBMMSM 2012, pp. 31–34 (2012)
68. Monteith, S., Bauer, M., Alda, M., Geddes, J., Whybrow, P.C., Glenn, T.: Increasing cybercrime since the pandemic: concerns for psychiatry. Current Psychiatry Rep. **23**(4) (2021)
69. Morshed, M.B., et al.: Prediction of mood instability with passive sensing. Proc. ACM Interact. Mob. Wearable Ubiquit. Technol. **3**(3) (2019)
70. Nolasco, H.R., Waldman, M., Vargo, A.W.: Exploring emotional reappraisal and repression through acoustic mood self-tracking. In: UbiComp 2021, Adjunct, pp. 248–252 (2021)
71. Patel, R., et al.: Mood instability is a common feature of mental health disorders and is associated with poor clinical outcomes. BMJ Open **5**(5), e007504–e007504 (2015)
72. Penedo, F.J., Dahn, J.R.: Exercise and well-being: a review of mental and physical health benefits associated with physical activity. Curr. Opin. Psychiatry **18**(2), 189–193 (2005)
73. Polzehl, T.: Personality in Speech. Springer, Cham (2015). https://doi.org/10.1007/978-3-319-09516-5
74. Polzehl, T., Möller, S., Metze, F.: Automatically assessing acoustic manifestations of personality in speech. In: 2010 IEEE Spoken Language Technology Workshop, pp. 7–12 (2010)
75. Rickwood, D., Deane, F.P., Wilson, C.J., Ciarrochi, J.: Young people's help-seeking for mental health problems. Aust. e-J. Adv. Mental health **4**(3), 218–251 (2005)
76. Rideout, V., Fox, S., Peebles, A., Robb, M.B.: Coping with Covid-19: how young people use digital media to manage their mental health. Common Sense and Hopelab, San Francisco, CA (2021)
77. Rottenberg, J.: Mood and emotion in major depression. Curr. Dir. Psychol. Sci. **14**(3), 167–170 (2005)
78. Russell: Core affect and the psychological construction of emotion. Psychol. Rev. **110**(1), 145–172 (2003)
79. Russell, J.A.: A circumplex model of affect. J. Pers. Soc. Psychol. **39**, 1161–1178 (1980)
80. Saha, K., Chan, L., De Barbaro, K., Abowd, G.D., De Choudhury, M.: Inferring mood instability on social media by leveraging ecological momentary assessments. Proc. ACM Interact. Mob. Wearable Ubiquit. Technol. **1**(3) (2017)
81. Sarsenbayeva, Z., et al.: Does smartphone use drive our emotions or vice versa? A causal analysis. In: CHI 2019, pp. 1–15 (2020)

412    Z. Sarsenbayeva et al.

82. Schueller, S., Neary, M., Lai, J., Epstein, D.: Understanding people's use of and perspectives on mood tracking apps: an interview study (preprint). JMIR Mental Health 8 (2021)
83. Servia-Rodríguez, S., Rachuri, K.K., Mascolo, C., Rentfrow, P.J., Lathia, N., Sandstrom, G.M.: Mobile sensing at the service of mental well-being: a large-scale longitudinal study. In: WWW 2017, pp. 103–112 (2017)
84. Shiffman, S., Stone, A.A., Hufford, M.R.: Ecological momentary assessment. Annu. Rev. Clin. Psychol. 4(1), 1–32 (2008)
85. Spathis, D., Servia-Rodriguez, S., Farrahi, K., Mascolo, C., Rentfrow, J.: Passive mobile sensing and psychological traits for large scale mood prediction. In: PervasiveHealth 2019, pp. 272–281 (2019)
86. Suhara, Y., Xu, Y., Pentland, A.S.: DeepMood: forecasting depressed mood based on self-reported histories via recurrent neural networks. In: WWW 2017, International World Wide Web Conferences Steering Committee, Republic and Canton of Geneva, CHE, pp. 715–724 (2017)
87. Tag, B., Goncalves, J., Webber, S., Koval, P., Kostakos, V.: A retrospective and a look forward: lessons learned from researching emotions in-the-wild. IEEE Pervasive Comput. 21, 28–36 (2022)
88. Tag, B., Sarsenbayeva, Z., Cox, A.L., Wadley, G., Goncalves, J., Kostakos, V.: Emotion trajectories in smartphone use: towards recognizing emotion regulation in-the-wild. Int. J. Hum. Comput. Stud. 166, 102872 (2022)
89. Tag, B., et al.: Making sense of emotion-sensing: workshop on quantifying human emotions. In: UbiComp/ISWC 2021 Adjunct, pp. 226–229 (2021)
90. Toegel, G., Anand, N., Kilduff, M.: Emotion helpers: the role of high positive affectivity and high self-monitoring managers. Pers. Psychol. 60(2), 337–365 (2007)
91. Torkamaan, H., Ziegler, J.: Mobile mood tracking: an investigation of concise and adaptive measurement instruments. Proc. ACM Interact. Mob. Wearable Ubiquit. Technol. 4(4) (2020)
92. Tracy, K.: Mobile application development experiences on apple's iOS and android OS. IEEE Potentials 31, 30–34 (2012)
93. Visuri, A., Sarsenbayeva, Z., Goncalves, J., Karapanos, E., Jones, S.: Impact of mood changes on application selection. In: UbiComp 2016, Adjunct, pp. 535–540 (2016)
94. Wallbaum, T., Heuten, W., Boll, S.: Comparison of in-situ mood input methods on mobile devices. In: MUM 2016, pp. 123–127 (2016)
95. Wang, P.S., et al.: Telephone screening, outreach, and care management for depressed workers and impact on clinical and work productivity outcomes. JAMA 298(12), 1401 (2007)
96. Wang, R., et al.: Tracking depression dynamics in college students using mobile phone and wearable sensing. Proc. ACM Interact. Mob. Wearable Ubiquit. Technol. 2(1) (2018)
97. Watson, D., Clark, L.A., Tellegen, A.: Development and validation of brief measures of positive and negative affect: the PANAS scales. J. Pers. Soc. Psychol. 54(6), 1063 (1988)
98. van der Watt, A.S.J., Odendaal, W., Louw, K., Seedat, S.: Distant mood monitoring for depressive and bipolar disorders: a systematic review. BMC Psychiatry 20(1) (2020)
99. Wen, C.K.F., Schneider, S., Stone, A.A., Spruijt-Metz, D.: Compliance with mobile ecological momentary assessment protocols in children and adolescents: a systematic review and meta-analysis. J. Med. Internet Res. 19(4), e132 (2017)

100. Widnall, E., et al.: A qualitative content analysis of user perspectives of mood-monitoring apps available to young people. (preprint). JMIR mHealth and uHealth **8** (2020)
101. Yang, C.C., Hsu, Y.L.: A review of accelerometry-based wearable motion detectors for physical activity monitoring. Sensors **10**(8), 7772–7788 (2010)
102. Yang, K., et al.: Survey on emotion sensing using mobile devices. IEEE Trans. Affect. Comput. (2022)
103. Yang, K., et al.: Behavioral and physiological signals-based deep multimodal approach for mobile emotion recognition. IEEE Trans. Affect. Comput. **3045**, 1 (2021)
104. Zhang, H., Gashi, S., Kimm, H., Hanci, E., Matthews, O.: MoodBook: an application for continuous monitoring of social media usage and mood. In: UbiComp 2018, pp. 1150–1155 (2018)
105. Zhang, X., Li, W., Chen, X., Lu, S.: MoodExplorer: towards compound emotion detection via smartphone sensing. Proc. ACM Interact. Mob. Wearable Ubiquit. Technol. **1**(4) (2018)
106. Zhang, X., Zhuang, F., Li, W., Ying, H., Xiong, H., Lu, S.: Inferring mood instability via smartphone sensing: a multi-view learning approach. In: MM 2019, pp. 1401–1409 (2019)

# A Close Look at Citizen Science Through the HCI Lens: A Systematic Literature Review

Tommaso Zambon[1]([✉])(iD), Chiara Bassetti[2]([✉])(iD), and Catia Prandi[1]([✉])(iD)

[1] Department of Computer Science and Engineering, University of Bologna, Bologna, Italy
{tommaso.zambon3,catia.prandi2}@unibo.it
[2] Department of Sociology and social research, University of Trento, Trento, Italy
chiara.bassetti@unitn.it

**Abstract.** In this paper, we present a systematic literature review of Citizen Science (CS) research projects with a focus on Human-Computer Interaction (HCI) and on the modalities in which CS is employed in this field. The query was conducted in March 2022 and provided us with 929 items, of which 646 were research articles. Through the usage of the PRISMA flow diagram, we included 27 papers in our survey. We aim to depict the state of the art regarding CS projects that are directly supported and explicitly defined by the HCI community. We compared the studies on variables like the field of interest and the impact area. We present the mutual interests of CS and HCI, the tools, and the methods that are employed to address these projects. Eventually, we conclude by pointing out some reflections on the value that can sprout from properly employed CS in HCI research.

**Keywords:** Citizen Science · HCI · Systematic literature review · ECSA

## 1 Introduction

Citizen Science (CS) is an old practice. Some researchers claim that it goes back at least a couple of millennia, when, in ancient China, migratory locusts frequently destroyed harvests, and residents have helped to track outbreaks for some 2,000 years [1]. In more recent times, a relevant project is the Christmas Bird Count. In 1900, Frank Chapman, an ornithologist at the American Museum of Natural History, proposed an alternative to the "side hunt", a popular activity in New England towns on Christmas Day. He encouraged citizens to go out and count the birds they saw instead of shooting them. Chapman pioneered a methodology for having citizens record the abundance and distribution of birds for particular areas, and his tradition is still alive today [40].

To see the term citizen science used for similar projects, we needed to wait until January 1989, when it appeared in an issue of the MIT Technology Review.

J. Abdelnour Nocera et al. (Eds.): INTERACT 2023, LNCS 14143, pp. 414–435, 2023.
https://doi.org/10.1007/978-3-031-42283-6_23

The article, titled 'Lab for the Environment', covers - as an example - Audubon's recruitment of volunteers in a 'citizen science' [22]. After this first appearance, CS started gaining a lot of attention from different research fields, and several definitions were coined. Some of them are focused on the method, such as the one of Rick Bonney, an ornithologist, who proposed CS as a method to collect scientific data through public effort in collaboration with professional scientists [3]. An alternative definition was proposed in 1995 by Alan Irwin, a sociologist. He focuses on the expertise retained by those who were canonically considered 'ignorant' (Irwin, 1995 in [3]). In this sense, CS is considered a skill or a quality that is intrinsic to the individual. Looking closely, we can see that both these definitions are limited if considering the value that CS adds to scientific research and to those who participate in these projects [18]. On the one hand, such added value is found in the expertise and collaboration with non-academic citizens, whose different backgrounds and interests can spark innovation or shed light in previously ignored directions. On the other hand, participants can find in CS an opportunity for self-development by learning about scientific methods and techniques [2,33], deepening their interest in the topic of the project [18], and by taking part in a community and creating social relations [6]. Given its multifaceted nature, a common, precise definition is missing. This issue can be linked to the widely different natures and objectives that the single projects have between them. Hence, it is not easy to find a one-size-fit description.

In light of this, in 2015, the European Citizen Science Association (ECSA) working group on 'Sharing best practice and building capacity for citizen science' proposed a broader definition of the CS paradigm. The result is a document outlining the "10 principles of Citizen Science" [11] that, for the first time, tried to define CS from a variety of perspectives, nuancing for the best the different aspects of the paradigm, going beyond the methodological elements and including its educational, scientific and social features. This is aligned with the HCI interest in better understanding how to approach CS, and it does so by addressing different challenges [34]. First, community relations and participants' engagement in the project [37]. Second, scientists ask for data, in both quantity and quality. Hence, data management is an important topic that spans from teaching the volunteers to gather and handle data, to understanding how to make sense of data, for example, through data visualization [48]. In this regard, a further objective is to promote Open Science. This means granting access to both science-in-the-making as much as its results [39]. Moreover, technological innovation is the avenue through which Citizen Science is thriving, providing tools (i.g. smartphones, sensors, CS platforms, social media, blogs, and more) both to conduct CS activities and to share the resulting knowledge [28]. Keeping in mind the HCI lens and CS principles, it is possible to preserve open science qualities such as education, self-development, democratic policymaking, and scientific research. In such a heterogeneous scenario, design can occur through different processes, enabling user-centered design, participatory design, and research through design [34]. By addressing cultural issues and social characteristics of the case/group of interest, it is possible to develop successful tools that can meet the participants' explicit needs as well as the hidden ones that recall upon their habitus [4], which is the set of behaviors, preferences, and ways of thinking that shapes who we are and how we navigate the world, often without us even realizing it. HCI, as we will discuss in this paper, seems to be following this lead with its studies in regard to CS projects. For these reasons, these 10 principles can be used as "a framework against which to assess new and existing citizen science initiatives with the aim of fostering excellence in all aspects of citizen science", as stated by Robinson et al. [36].

Driven by the interest that the CS paradigm is gaining from the HCI community, in this paper, we intend to provide a critical review of how HCI is embracing CS as a new paradigm for collaborative and voluntary participation of people in scientific research. In this regard, digitalization and the use of innovative technologies have a relevant impact when considering modern CS projects, opening new interesting research challenges in HCI [34].

## 2    Related Work

In this section, we present the current landscape of CS literature surveys and their specific topics of interest. We report surveys with interest in CS per se and also in the shape it takes within the HCI field.

*Methods for Design.* HCI literature often revolves around the design of technologies and software programs to support different CS communities. Specifically interested in the user-centered design of technology within the context of environmental digital CS, [42] develops a set of guidelines to ask citizen scientists about their desire for new technologies or useful features that may help them in their research. They suggest that this field is still a novelty, and many included studies report direct feedback from the participants of their own projects. Another study surveys the literature about methods to properly tackle user-centered design for CS whilst creating a list of already existing tools used in CS and evaluating their mode of use in the different types of projects [41]. In this scenario, HCI expertise coupled with "the widespread availability of smartphones and other Internet and communications technologies (ICT) used for collecting and sharing data" [34], constitute a fertile environment for collaboration with citizen scientists and great opportunities to design innovative tools for Open Science, scientific research and bottom-up policymaking processes.

*Data Validity and Scientific Communication.* A topic of interest in the literature is the perception of CS as an established and valid scientific framework by the wider academic and scientific world. In their literature review, Wang et al. [49] draw a picture of the projects interested in urban biodiversity that makes use (or not) of CS-gathered data. This study contributes to the CS and HCI literature by highlighting the dynamics of contemporary engagement between citizen science and urban ecology. They focus on the necessity for design in terms of optimization of CS programs to facilitate communication and collaboration with the broader scientific community.

*Impact.* The educational aspect is also addressed by studies like [33] and [2]. In the first study, information about the effects of biodiversity sensitization is collected from different sources. As a result, the authors reported that people actively involved in CS are subject to a growing sensitization toward biodiversity and sustainability, furthermore, they are also improving their personal knowledge regarding scientific methodologies [33]. The second study confirms that even when citizen scientists take part in online projects, they are subject to the same positive effects regarding scientific knowledge [2].

Our systematic review positions itself in what - to the best of our knowledge - we consider an unexplored issue, that is, how effectively HCI studies make use of concepts and practices of CS.

## 3   Methodology

In this section, we first define the research questions (RQs) that drove our literature review. In doing that, we better explain why we decided to exploit the ECSA 10 principles as a framework to assess CS projects. Finally, we describe the process we employed to select and analyze the papers.

### 3.1   The Research Questions and the ECSA CS Principles

The objective of this survey is to address the interests of HCI in CS. In particular, we intend to address the following broad research question (RQ):

RQ0 How are CS projects addressed within the HCI field of research?

To answer this RQ, we first needed to define what a CS project is. For this reason, we decided to exploit the ECSA 10 principles of citizen science [11] as our main framework to assess the validity of the eligible papers. The ECSA 10 CS principles are the most widely recognized guidelines for defining CS projects [36]. The 10 principles are reported in Table 1. This framework enabled us to keep a focus on what can be considered CS and what not, strengthening our selection process by giving both consistency and adaptability. This may seem a strict assessment method if applied to a broad field like HCI. However, as argued in the paper, nowadays, the ECSA principles seem to be the more comprehensive framework to assess a CS project, overcoming the lack of a clear and shared definition of what CS is.

In light of this, we refined the RQ0 as follows.

RQ1 Are CS projects addressed within HCI respecting the ECSA principles?

Then, we narrowed our analysis to two sub-research questions, as follows:

RQ1.1 In which field of interest do CS projects addressed by HCI studies operate?
RQ1.2 In which impact area do CS projects addressed by HCI studies operate?

To answer these questions, we focus our discussion on three main themes: CS score, field of interest, and impact area. Namely, i) CS score is an indicative scoring system that is achieved by adding the number of ECSA principles that are tackled in a given paper that describes a CS project; ii) the field of interest represents the main topic of the project presented by the paper; iii) the impact area indicates the geographical level at which the project is operating.

**Table 1.** The ECSA 10 principles of Citizen Science

| The 10 principles of Citizen Science |
| --- |
| 1. Citizen science projects actively involve citizens in scientific endeavour that generates new knowledge or understanding |
| 2. Citizen science projects have a genuine science outcome |
| 3. Both the professional scientists and the citizen scientists benefit from taking part |
| 4. Citizen scientists may, if they wish, participate in multiple stages of the scientific process |
| 5. Citizen scientists receive feedback from the project |
| 6. Citizen science is considered a research approach like any other, with limitations and biases that should be considered and controlled for |
| 7. Citizen science project data and metadata are made publicly available and where possible, results are published in an open-access format |
| 8. Citizen scientists are acknowledged in project results and publications |
| 9. Citizen science programmes are evaluated for their scientific output, data quality, participant experience and wider societal or policy impact |
| 10. The leaders of citizen science projects take into consideration legal and ethical issues surrounding copyright, intellectual property, data-sharing agreements, confidentiality, attribution and the environmental impact of any activities |

## 3.2 Query Specifics

We performed a systematic review of the CS literature by searching the Association for Computing Machinery (ACM) Guide to Computing Literature. According to ACM, the ACM Digital Library is the most comprehensive bibliographic database in existence today focused exclusively on the field of computing[1]. Hence, we used the advanced research tool to conduct the query. Here, we report the specifics of our query:

> 'Search Within' >Anywhere: "citizen science" OR "citizen scientists"; 'Publication Dates' >Custom Range: From January 2012 - To January 2022.

This query resulted in 929 items. By keeping research articles only (peer-reviewed conference and journal articles), we reduced this number to 646. In the following paragraphs, we discuss how the selection, classification, and analysis of the data have been conducted.

## 3.3 Data Analysis: From Screening to Included Articles

The screening process followed the PRISMA 2020 guidelines [30]. The 646 papers went through a skimming process to assess their relevance, where the minimum requirement was to include the phrase 'citizen science', 'citizen scientist' or 'citizen scientists' within their title, abstract or keywords. The process was not automated; all the abstracts have been read to ensure the inclusion of works that may have differently phrased CS-related concepts. Furthermore, to assess the validity,

---

[1] https://libraries.acm.org/digital-library/acm-guide-to-computing-literature.

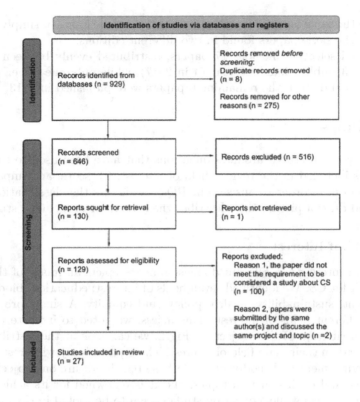

**Fig. 1.** PRISMA chart and details of exclusion

in case of uncertainty, the process was extended to the discussion and conclusion paragraphs. The skimming process resulted in a selection of 129 papers. These papers then underwent the categorization process. The 129 selected papers have been fully read and classified in a spreadsheet for the following characteristics: CS score, field of interest, and impact area (Fig. 1).

In order to be included in this study, the articles had to i) refer directly to a CS experience, ii) describe software and tools that have been tested in the CS project (or for future implementation), and/or iii) present methodologies for future and innovative CS work.

It is important to note that the whole process considered what was stated in the papers rather than the CS project to which they referred. For instance, if a study reported that the participants collected data, we assume that they only took part in that research phase, therefore excluding further involvement in other phases of the process. This choice was made in the interest of an objective survey; in this way, we can avoid making assumptions about non-reported items.

After the screening, 27 papers remained for the last phase of analysis. In this phase, all the papers were processed once more by reading them and comparing them with their entries in the spreadsheets to ensure the correctness of the analysis. No major changes were made. Two papers were excluded because they were from the same authors and they discussed the same issues or simply because they were the same papers found in two different editions.

The final selection includes 27 papers, distributed evenly between 2016 to 2021, with 3 publications per year (4 in 2017), while only one paper per year during 2015 and 2014, the remaining 6 papers were published in 2013.

## 4   Findings

This survey is structured around dimensions that have been used to categorize the papers included in the review: field of interest, CS score, and impact area. In this section, in order to answer our RQs, we discuss the classification of the papers and draw a picture that describes the overall set of included studies.

### 4.1   Field of Interest

The field of interest is a relevant dimension as it depicts an image of the interests of HCI for CS. We identified seven fields of interest: education, biodiversity, environment, sustainability, health, policy, and equality. A single project may fall into different fields of interest, nonetheless, we opted to indicate the main area of contribution of the project. In Fig. 2, we can look at the distribution of studies based on their main field of interest. The topics of major interest are education, environment and biodiversity. CS has great literature on projects about biodiversity and environmental topics, and it is renowned for its achievements in such areas. Meanwhile, education studies seem to be rooted in the interest in the innovation of technologies for communication (HCI). Furthermore, six out of seven papers interested in education have been published between 2017 and 2021, hence making this thematic a novelty in the field of HCI studies that make use of CS as their main research paradigm.

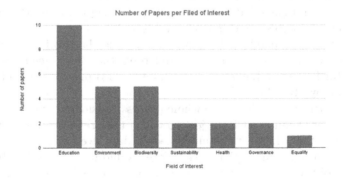

**Fig. 2.** Distribution of paper for main field of interest

All the considered papers share a degree of interest in multiple areas of impact like the study presented in [19], which edges between environment and policy.

Therefore, the aim of this subsection is to provide a representation of interests' distribution of the included studies, whilst keeping in mind that the interest of a project is rather nuanced than fixed. We will discuss in-depth the three fields of interest which are covered by the highest number of studies, and later we will discuss the remaining ones.

**Education.** All the projects within the realm of education drift toward Open Science, looking into granting access to citizens in the development of the scientific community. The included studies tackle open research from three major standpoints: (i) innovative research questions, (ii) open science and knowledge creation, and (iii) self-development and growth opportunities.

(i) Projects that are looking to generate new ideas for interesting research questions are collaborating with citizens because they find value in the great variety of perspectives, expertise, knowledge levels, and cultural and social backgrounds of the participants. In project experiences like Gut Instinct [31] and Docent [32], the volunteers cover a central role, and the participation is open to everyone without any expertise ceiling. In fact, their objective is to let innovation and creative ideas stem from profane contributions around scientific research topics. The heterogeneity is the element that brings value and validity to these methods; this way the unpredictability of the discourse can facilitate out-of-the-box thinking processes.

(ii) Open science is one of the main objectives that citizen science tries to achieve with its research ethic. The projects falling in this area create opportunities for the citizen to access culture and knowledge, while through their active involvement, they can also help in preserving and sharing [46]. In these projects, citizen scientists' role is particularly variegated and foresees their engagement in an array of different tasks. For example, in the ExploreAT! project, the citizen is involved from the very beginning of the design and throughout the multiple stages of the research process, contributing to participatory experiments, common idea-collection, and testing and evaluation of existing prototypes and research tools [16]. The ExploreAT! platform links cultural knowledge to folklore artifacts present in museums, enabling citizens to access culture through digital experiences. Therefore, the platform functions as a tool to give everyone open access to culture and knowledge. In the same fashion, Interlinking Pictura [46] is digitalizing a piece of cultural heritage in the form of a wiki-style platform. The opera is by F. J. Bertuch (1790–1830), and it is called Bilderbuch für Kinder (illustrated book for children). With this project, retired teachers, researchers, and autonomous associations are trying to create an interlinked corpus about Bertuch's illustrated book by connecting the distributed knowledge about its creation, reception, and usage in pedagogical practices [46]. These projects are dedicated to preserving folklore and cultural heritage, whilst in the meantime creating opportunities to further promote open science, also beyond active participation in the projects themselves.

(iii) The production of knowledge, open science, and research skill development can bind together and foster self-development and growth opportunities, as in the Wikipedia Classroom Experiment [5]. Within this experience, classrooms of students conducted research and wrote Wikipedia articles. After experts' reviews and polishing, they have been published on the famous website. Following this example, there are other projects that enable citizen scientists to be authors other than researchers, like the Crowd Research project [45]. Through a system of peer credit allocation, participants are recognized for their merit as citizen scientists in direct proportion to the quantity and quality of their efforts and production. Through this system, citizen scientists can improve their skills in article writing and reviewing and can gain credibility through the acknowledgment of their contributions in publications. A similar approach was investigated In Trento (Italy), where researchers involved schools, students, and the general public in practical experiments to learn firsthand about ICT, with the aim of reducing the digital divide and furnishing basic knowledge for the use of digital tools, both for personal use and scientific research [12]. Lastly, Interactive cloud experimentation for biology [20] present a cloud experimentation architecture to share and execute many experiments for chemotactic experiments in parallel, remotely, and interactively at all time. Its versatility allows for integration with various biological specimens and tools to facilitate scalable interactive online education, collaborations, research, and citizen science [20]. This paper addresses education at an advanced level, and it aims at reducing the skill gap that citizens have to face when approaching biology projects for citizen science, therefore pursuing education for a specific target and reason.

Generally, projects that are addressing education as their first area of interest tend to focus on the volunteers' direct and lived experience to flourish. The very nature of educational projects stands within the fulfillment of the participants and of the general public that they address, rather than on external factors (e.g., natural science projects).

**Biodiversity and Environment.** Biodiversity preservation (5 papers) and Environment (5 papers) are the second most addressed issues within the considered studies. Citizen Science is renowned for its efforts in natural sciences and attention to local fauna and flora. "The National Audubon Society's Christmas Bird Count had begun in 1900" [3] and it is canonically attested as the first experience of citizen science, while also starting a strong tradition of biodiversity preservation and research within the paradigm.

HCI is interested in these areas mainly to test technology that can support the data-gathering process. With a focus on the cultural embedment of new technologies in social practices, [47] within their study Making local knowledge matter, propose a smartphone application suited for non-literate people. Their application enables Mbendjele hunter-gatherers to "share their environmental knowledge in scientifically valid and strategically targeted ways that can lead to improvement in environmental governance, environmental justice, and management practices" [47]. Furthermore, poaching poses a great danger to biodiversity in the first place, but even to the population living in the territory, especially to children. The application supports the community in different ways and provides valid motivation for keeping it in use, rather than being a mere measurement tool.

Even in less extreme scenarios, cultural embedment of technology covers a key role, as affirmed by the authors of Listening to the Forest and its Curators [27] "findings from interviews with members of the biodiversity community revealed a tension between the technology and their established working practices". In fact, the activity within the biodiversity community is not reducible to data collection, especially considering that participation is on a voluntary basis and that many people take part to stay in nature. Hence, the interviewees lamented that the excessive presence and use of technology disrupted their workflow and general appreciation of their work in the field, as an integral part of it was annotating sightings in a diary or using paper guides. Finally, technology and tools that simplify tasks raised concerns among the Cicada Hunt community. It appears that such simplification of the processes can be potentially harmful to the research and to the cicadas themselves. The high number of non-properly-trained participants, attracted to the project by these tools, end up posing Cicada and their environment at risk, rather than supporting their preservation.

On the other hand, POSEIDON [35] brings a positive experience in terms of merging tourism with citizen science. This project will be later further presented, but here is worth noting that technology enhances the experience of tourists that are practicing whale watching by enabling them to hear live whale sounds, whilst in the meantime collaborating to create a database for scientific purposes. Biodiversity can be addressed by different groups of people and through different modalities, but its fragile nature demands attention from a design standpoint. In scenarios as the POSEIDON project shows, proper technological implementation can enhance both research and recreational activities.

Tool evaluations remain a key interest within the HCI field when discussing citizen science, the next studies present design evaluations about their software and platforms advancing suggestions and advice for future work. First, Planting for Pollinators [50] is a tool embedded in the BeeWatch platform. It provides precise information regarding the favorite flowers of the different species of bumblebees. Hence, citizens can make an informed decision about which plants and flowers to plant in their gardens and balconies to favor bumblebees during the pollinating season in their area. Second, Exploration of Aural & Visual Media About Birds Informs Lessons for Citizen Science Design [29] tested a tool to educate birdwatchers (with different levels of expertise) in recognizing aural and visual media. The tool revealed great enthusiasm together with some challenges for future work, nonetheless, the participants' feedback was positive, and over time engagement in bird recognition and education about their lives increased.

Overall, biodiversity preservation can happen in any environment. Forests, woods, oceans, urban neighborhoods, and more, such a variety poses infinite possibilities and challenges for tools and software developments in support of this kind of project. Nonetheless, a topic of interest remains how to create a sense of engagement and interest in the participants of a project. Within this paragraph emerged that cultural variables are key when designing tools for citizen science, but it is not the only element. It is in fact essential to devise tools based on the period and level of engagement of the volunteers, as it is possible to create long-lasting communities like in the case of Mbendjele hunter-gatherers or just one-time contributors as in the POSEIDON experience.

The environment is equally represented in the CS paper within HCI, and the topics span between extreme weather events [19], high-tide floodings [14], local environmental data monitoring [15], urban noise-pollution [7], and air pollution [21]. Within our publications pool, we find projects that are using apps and GPS to report extraordinary events [14,19] to keep records of such events and the relatively long time consequences. Apps are also used to monitor common variables such as noise [7] and smell [21] in the air, these projects' employment shows us two completely different approaches to a similar problem. One is to delegate detection to external and dedicated sensors [7] to gather data that can be used for policy making regarding urban noise pollution; the other one [21] gets rid of dedicated sensors and even further, doesn't use any sensors, but only the sense of smell of the people to address air quality in specific areas of the city. Different approaches are needed for different cultural realities, and with the work of [15] we see that the social embeddedness of technology can be also achieved by integrating the user in the process of design of the tools that will be used to gather and communicate data. The last three projects are approaching similar issues on a different scale of participation and with very different tools at their disposal, while the final objective is always data gathering for informed policy-making for the environment and the quality of life of those living in it.

**Sustainability, Health, Governance, and Equality.** The remaining fields of interest are scarcely discussed within the HCI community invested in citizen science.

Concerning health, Sharing heartbeats [10] describes the ambitious project that many countries tried to accomplish during the covid-19 pandemic: limiting covid-19 outbreaks by registering contacts with infected people through an application. Meanwhile, [26] study describes a mobile game that "harnesses the human computing capability to align multiple sequences of genomes and use the results to help geneticists to understand the genetic code".

Sustainability is mostly addressed by means of bottom-up processes. The first study reports homemade food science experience in local communities [25], arguing that the expertise generated by self-education and the use of everyday artifacts can shape the way in which science is perceived, explored, and made. The social value of technology can therefore spark innovation and generate useful approaches to more complex problems at a higher level of research, meanwhile enhancing citizen expertise and know-how toward scientific matters.

Similarly, technology can gain social value as demonstrated in another study where two communities engaged in a project with living sensing organisms [24]. The citizen scientists adopted the solution of using microorganisms as long-term technology to record pollution in their area.

Governance follows a bottom-up process within the citizen science community. BudgetMap [23] is a platform where citizens can tag government policies
and categorize them according to the social area that they affect. This process allows for a better frame of the Budgeting plans and gives the opportunity to the citizen to learn about budgeting while in the meantime helping
to reshape it depending on their necessities. Public transport is the focus of
Data4UrbanMobility [44], a platform that collects data about urban pathways
suggesting versatile routes and agile urban planning.

Finally, [38] proposes the concept of impromptu crowd science taking inspiration from the Bechdel-Wallace movement which seeks through a scoring system the level of gender equality in movies. The study theorizes the opportunity for "hybridizations between such impromptu crowd science and academic
inquiries [to] stimulate crowd theorizing" [38]. Equality is rather difficult to
address through citizen science, and although this paper is only theorizing a
possible approach rather than describing an active project experience, we argue
that it is important to give highlight the presence of such work in the collection
of ACM Digital Library.

### 4.2   Citizen Science Score

In order to answer RQ1, we computed a citizen science score. This score does not
represent the value of a specific CS project but represents the level of information
that the authors of a given publication reported within their work, enabling the
reader to understand how many of the ECSA guidelines have been addressed.
After analyzing each paper, we assigned a score by checking the list of the 10
principles (one point per addressed principle). The sum of the points constitutes
the final CS score, ranging from 0 (no principle addressed) to 10 (all the principles
addressed).

As shown in Fig. 3, 22 papers are above 8 in the CS score scale and each
Field of interest has at least two or more papers above this threshold, except for
Equality (which only has one paper). Three are the papers scoring 7 points based
on the ECSA guidelines, interested in equality, biodiversity, and environment.
The remaining two articles scored 6 and 5 points, respectively papers from the
field of environment and education.

In the following subsections, we will present a detailed analysis of all the
papers, in order to answer our sub-RQs in terms of (i) field of interest and (ii)
impact area.

### 4.3   Impact Area

Every project is characterized by its impact area, meaning the territorial level
at which the project is working and the area it is expected to affect. This aspect
highly impacts the socialization, communication, and approach to the research
[8,9,17], therefore we decided to analyze and discuss differences in this regard
within the literature. We identified four levels: i) local, ii) urban, iii) national,
and iv) global. We also added a fifth level, tailor-made for a paper that has a

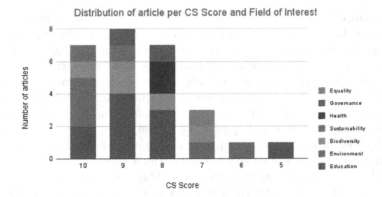

**Fig. 3.** Papers distributed per CS score and colour coded per field of interest.

theoretical focus and discusses a method for the 'scalability' of the project, starting from the local and expanding its reach with time and when other variables allow it. This fifth impact area was identified with v) scalable. Figure 4 presents the distributions of papers per impact area.

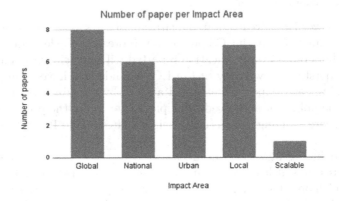

**Fig. 4.** Number of papers per Impact Area.

**Local.** At this level, projects tend to work with the local population, where cultural heritage [15,25,43], local knowledge [47], the ability to work in small groups [27], are key to the development of the project and great booster for the community's cohesion itself. Furthermore, the local projects give immediate feedback to the participants, maintaining a high degree of both personal and communitarian investment. Volunteers that participate in these projects tend to get in direct contact and meet regularly, therefore, creating opportunities for the community to strengthen. The immediate feedback provided by these projects helps citizen scientists build a sense of accomplishment through their work. For example, during public workshops, as described in [15], the process of "Building a personal device leaves participants with the satisfaction of completing a project and building a craft. [...] This in turn can spark activism in communities". Finally, the pre-existent social relations may favor a deeper collaboration leading to greater social cohesion, therefore, helping to perpetuate the projects which often become independent institutions [13].

**Urban.** The urban projects have a reasonable impact area, where projects' effects are perceptible by the individual, but the community tends to be lesser dense and its members don't always meet each other. The main moment of community bonding will happen during events rather than periodic meetings. Volunteers are likely to participate and contribute to individual work rather than organized groups. This picture is well-represented by the Smell Pittsburgh project where citizen scientists contribute singularly to the creation of the public database. Moreover, "there are typically two types of community data, which are generated from either sensors or proactive human reports" that contribute to the dataset of smells, but the focus of the two communities of data is different. As proactive human reports are mainly contributing to a representation of the lived experiences of the citizens affected by the different smells in the different parts of the city, therefore, qualitatively speaking, providing more detailed information about a given specific odor and area.

Proactive human reports are in fact mainly concerning projects that want to investigate social issues. Data4UrbanMobility project [44] makes use of the MiC app "to complement available datasets with intermodal mobility data (i.e., data about journeys that involve more than one mode of mobility)". The resulting database can be employed by the public administration for efficient city planning, given that D4UM focuses on data otherwise rarely available, for example, information regarding bike routes and others. This data can narrate the lived experience of citizens that navigate the urban environment in the most disparate ways. Similarly, with Smell Pittsburgh project [21] participants contribute individually without participating in an active social community. Therefore, the effect of scientific research is perceived by the citizens, but the citizen scientists' community remains hidden.

On the other hand, there are experiences that keep a discrete degree of communitarian participation even in the urban environment. A great example would be A Maker Approach For The Future Of Learning [12], which through the maker philosophy and two FabLabs is actively involving schools and the general public to address and learn ICT.

**National.** What characterizes these projects is the direct impact on the lives of citizens on a national level Usually, ministries, governments, or other major national institutions fund or partially fund these initiatives. National institutions manage to address problems at a capillary level through the contribution of individual volunteers. By gathering information through crowdsensing or active reporting of specific pieces of information, these projects are used to dispatch a clearer image of a specific scenario to interested stakeholders, thereby enabling them to make informed decisions and favor more efficient policymaking. The case of 'Sharing Heartbeats' [10] is a current topic: covid-19 prevention. Such a project provides "citizens with the opportunity to share their health data from fitness trackers and smartwatches, with the aim to better record and understand the spread of COVID-19, detecting local fever outbreaks potentially associated with COVID-19" [10]. Within this project, the participants have a passive role, leaning towards the crowd-sensing paradigm; nonetheless, their participation was not limited to the data gathering, enabling them to take part in different parts of the project. Another example is BudgetMap [23]. This project enables taxpayers to tag government programs in order to classify them based on the social issues that they tackle. Furthermore, citizens can query these programs using the tag system enabling the government organization to follow the changes in public interests regarding policymaking. The authors show how "participants' awareness and understanding of budgetary issues increased after using BudgetMap, while they collaboratively identified issue-budget links with quality comparable to expert-generated links" [23]. Finally, another large-territory project is Damage Tracker [19] constitutes a database for research on tornados meanwhile it does also create a catalog of the damages caused in Alabama state. Hence, geo-tagging makes use of the expertise of the volunteers, facilitating location recognition given that they are often unrecognizable after such catastrophic phenomena.

**Global.** This category, together with the local category, collects the highest number of citizen science-related papers in our survey. Usually, projects at this level are hosted within some major platforms like Zooniverse, iNaturalist, CitizenGrid, hackAIR, CAPTOR (and more). These platforms bring together millions of users around the world, contributing hugely to academic and scientific research. In this context, platforms, and software play a key role in citizen science projects. In fact, they constitute both the main instrument for data gathering and the mean through which the communities thrive. These communities are mostly 'virtual' communities, similar to projects at national levels the individuals do not know each other personally, and public events for meetings are not common within these kinds of communities.

Furthermore, the effects of the research have no direct impact on the lives of the participants. In fact, the aim of the projects that work at this level is to create large databases (e.g., Galaxy Zoo, Foldit, iNaturalist) rather than improving the living situations of citizens in a specific territory as local, urban, and national projects tend to do. Even though there are exceptions to this scenario, POSEIDON [35] is a project that takes place in Madeira. The isle is one the principal location in Europe for whale watching. Here tourists can become citizen scientists during their excursions using the specific and appositely designed app. POSEIDON "goes beyond merely capturing acoustic data, deploying a novel on-board mobile application for augmenting the user experiences with real-time sound detection and classification of cetaceans" [35]. The result is a detailed dataset visualization openly available to environmental conservation authorities and the scientific community. This project manages to unfold at a local level while delivering results, and therefore impacting, on a global level.

In this category, we can find projects which focus on finding new ways to think about research rather than on data collection, classification, or analysis. Gut Instinct [32] provides an environment where 'profane' questions and answers are the center of attention, and through them, innovation and new ideas can be considered. Gut Instinct values the heterogeneity of the contributions that it can collect through the different backgrounds and perspectives of its participants. On a similar note, Docent [32] seeks to create scientific hypotheses starting from the lived experience of the participants, who, through an online learning architecture, provide system principles for people to brainstorm causal scientific theories [32]. The lens shifts even more towards the participants' expertise and research acknowledgment with Crowd Research [45]. All these experiences lead to innovation in the scientific and academic field, therefore impacting a worldwide community and engaging participants from all over the world.

**Scalable.** This is the last impact area individuated even though it does comprehend only one study, we think it sets a valid discussion point about approaches to the citizen science methodology. In fact, the paper addresses a methodological discussion introducing "PLACE, an iterative, mixed-fidelity approach to Prototyping Location, Activities, Collective experience, and Experience over time in LBAGs" [5]. PLACE offers a protocol for projects that want to start at a local level and slowly expand their impact with the growth of the community and of the project's resources. One further strength of this protocol is that it does not rely on any kind of tool, software, or platform, and it is, therefore, applicable to any project.

## 5 Discussion

In this section, we present our reflections based both on the HCI perspective on CS and the findings of our systematic literature review.

As argued by Preece in her seminal work about HCI and CS, "HCI researchers can empower citizen scientists to dramatically increase what they do and how they do it" [34]. Even though she focused on biodiversity citizen science, she puts light on two main fields of interest where HCI specialists and citizen scientists can leverage each other's skills for positive change: (i) supporting the development of (sustainable) technologies to foster sustainability and (ii) contributing to educational efforts [that serve the environmental cause] through citizen science. This is actually aligned with our output, where, besides the clear interest of researchers in applying CS to projects about the environment, biodiversity, and sustainability, education through CS resulted in being a hot topic in HCI.

Preece envisioned four main topics (and the related challenges) where a research agenda on stimulating action across HCI and CS should focus: (i) community (participation and motivation), (ii) data (quality and issues about sharing, aggregating, and archiving), (iii) technology (deciding which technology to use, active data collection citizen science projects such as iNaturalist VS passive data collection with sensors, tracking devices, cameras, and drones, etc.),

(iv) design (including privacy issues in terms of respect for persons, beneficence, and justice) [34]. In analyzing the literature about CS in HCI, we realized that most of the papers focus on at least one of these four macro areas. Nonetheless, our screening activity emphasized the fact that, even though all the studies mentioned CS, it was not possible to grasp the whole CS experience. In other words, it is not possible to assess if the community's engagement/the design method/the developed technology/the data model will actually succeed in a real word CS action. This claim is motivated by the fact that CS is a complex concept; several researchers and practitioners tried to define it without finding an agreement [34]. One of all, the fact that a strong discussion is still existing about whether crowdsourcing is or isn't a CS practice. We were able to overcome this issue by considering the ECSA 10 principles of Citizen Science as the framework to assess the studies. In fact, the ECSA principles provide guidelines to assess community, data, and design as integral parts of the CS action. On top of that, we added the technological aspect, which is crucial in HCI research [34]. Based on that framework, 100 papers were excluded, reinforcing the need for HCI researchers to better situate their study in the CS complex scenario.

Moving now to the 27 papers included in our systematic review, in general, we noticed a lack of clarity in defining if and how the participants can take part in multiple phases of the project (correlated to the community and design Preece's topics [34]). Nonetheless, from the majority, it is deductible by the research design and the general description of the results. A step toward affinity with CS definition by ECSA would be the implementation of participant demographic. Unfortunately, 14 out of 27 papers did not provide such information about their participants. Clarity about CS case studies would improve if authors included specific details about the number of involved volunteers and their demographic information. Furthermore, the considered papers lack a description of the involved communities and their nature (formal, informal, sporadic, or regular meetings). As it's been discussed throughout this systematic review, the relevance of the subcultural dimension is key for technology to be fruitfully employed in a group. Therefore, HCI studies would benefit from providing additional information regarding the social settings in which the projects unfold.

Finally, one of the strengths of CS is its capability to educate and help develop specific skills in its participants. Usually, this process is mediated by expert researchers that can overwatch the project. However, most of the papers did not address this issue in detail. For this reason, we suggest that research articles, especially those interested in studying and enhancing the level of engagement of citizen scientists, should pay more attention to the effects that their tools and methodologies can have in this regard.

# 6  Conclusions and Limitations

This paper presents and discusses the results of a systematic literature review about CS in HCI studies within the ACM Digital Library, over the last ten years. A peculiar element of this review is the adoption of the ECSA 10 principles of

Citizen Science as a framework to assess the pertinence of the studies to the concept of CS. The aim was to assess, through the use of such guidelines, the understanding and employment of CS practices within the HCI field. Applying the PRISMA method, we selected 27 papers that were categorized, analyzed, and compared through the HCI lens, which seeks to grasp the core features of the projects based on what we call 'CS score' (scoring system based on the number of the 10 ECSA principle addressed in a research article), 'field of interest' (the main topic of the project), and 'impact area' (geographical level of projects' activities). This framework highlighted the main qualities and interests of these studies while granting the integrity of the CS concept. Through our analysis, we pointed out the risk of inflation of the term citizen science, which is often used loosely, causing it to lose its significance instead of empowering the relationship between HCI and CS. This seems one of the consequences of the lack of a common definition of CS, that the ECSA guidelines can help to overcome. As a final consideration, CS has proved to be a great proving ground for breaking ground technologies and methodologies while promoting open research and bottom-up innovation processes. Our systematic review consolidates this view, suggesting taking a step toward better defining what CS is, granting the integrity of the core principles of this paradigm.

The findings of this study have to be seen in light of some limitations. (1) The major limitation of this systematic review is that the query was conducted on the sole ACM Digital Library. Therefore, even though it was our interest to consider only this part of the literature (considering the fact that most of the more relevant and well-established conferences and journals about HCI are published there), it is important to underline that, with this decision, we excluded potential HCI papers about CS published elsewhere. (2) Given the focus of this particular literature review, we preferred maintaining a stricter query, including in our study the article that actively and consciously referred to CS. In particular, we searched the ACM Digital Library by querying the terms 'citizen science' and 'citizen scientists'. This decision improved, on one side, the accuracy of our search, whilst, on the other side, it could make us miss some relevant contributions. (3) We are aware of the strict variables we adopted to select the papers in our final step, resulting in a limited sample of works. On the other hand, this should underline the importance of finding a proper and fitting definition for citizen science, given that applying the ECSA guidelines was the main reason for papers to be discarded.

# References

1. Aisling, I.: Citizen science comes of age. Spinger Nature **562**, 480–482 (2018)
2. Aristeidou, M., Herodotou, C.: Online citizen science: a systematic review of effects on learning and scientific literacy. Citizen Science: Theory and Practice 5 (2020). https://doi.org/10.5334/cstp.224
3. Bonney, R., Phillips, T.B., Ballard, H.L., Enck, J.W.: Can citizen science enhance public understanding of science? Public Underst. Sci. **25**, 2–16 (2016). https://doi.org/10.1177/0963662515607406

4. Bourdieu, P.: Outline of a Theory of Practice. Cambridge Studies in Social and Cultural Anthropology. Cambridge University Press (1977). https://doi.org/10.1017/CBO9780511812507

5. Bowser, A.E., et al.: Prototyping in place: a scalable approach to developing location-based apps and games, pp. 1519–1528 (2013). https://doi.org/10.1145/2470654.2466202

6. Bruyere, B., Rappe, S.: Identifying the motivations of environmental volunteers. J. Environ. Plann. Manage. **50**, 503–516 (7 2007). https://doi.org/10.1080/09640560701402034

7. Cartwright, M., Dove, G., Méndez, A.E.M., Bello, J.P., Nov, O.: Crowdsourcing multi-label audio annotation tasks with citizen scientists. In: Conference on Human Factors in Computing Systems - Proceedings, May 2019. https://doi.org/10.1145/3290605.3300522

8. Chandler, M., Bebber, D., Castro, S., Lowman, M., Muoria, P., Oguge, N., Rubenstein, D.: International citizen science: making the local global. Front. Ecol. Environ. **10**, 328–331 (2012). https://doi.org/10.2307/41811401

9. Dickinson, J., Zuckerberg, B., Bonter, D.: Citizen science as an ecological research tool: challenges and benefits. Ann. Rev. Ecol. Systematics **41**, 149–172 (2010). https://doi.org/10.1146/annurev-ecolsys-102209-144636

10. Diethei, D., Niess, J., Stellmacher, C., Stefanidi, E., Schöning, J.: Sharing heartbeats: Motivations of citizen scientists in times of crises, pp. 1–15 (05 2021). https://doi.org/10.1145/3411764.3445665

11. ECSA (European Citizen Science Association): Ten principles of citizen science, September 2015. https://doi.org/10.17605/OSF.IO/XPR2N

12. Fiore, F., Montresor, A., Marchese, M.: A maker approach for the future of learning (2021). https://doi.org/10.1145/3466725.3466761

13. Gallino, L.: Dizionario di sociologia/Luciano Gallino. UTET, Torino, 2. ed. riv. e aggiornata edn. ([1993])

14. Golparvar, B., Wang, R.Q.: Ai-supported citizen science to monitor high-tide flooding in newport beach, California. In: Proceedings of the 3rd ACM SIGSPATIAL International Workshop on Advances in Resilient and Intelligent Cities, ARIC 2020, pp. 66–69. Association for Computing Machinery, New York (2020). https://doi.org/10.1145/3423455.3430315

15. Guler, S.D.: Citizen drones: embedded crafts for remote sensing. In: Proceedings of the 7th International Conference on Tangible, Embedded and Embodied Interaction, TEI 2013, pp. 349–350. Association for Computing Machinery, New York (2013). https://doi.org/10.1145/2460625.2460688

16. Gura, C., Dorn, A., Benito, A., Wandl-Vogt, E., Losada, A.: Co-designing innovation networks for cross-sectoral collaboration on the example of exploreat! In: Proceedings of the 5th International Conference on Technological Ecosystems for Enhancing Multiculturality, TEEM 2017. Association for Computing Machinery, New York (2017). https://doi.org/10.1145/3144826.3145378

17. Haywood, B., Parrish, J., Dolliver, J.: Place-based and data-rich citizen science as a precursor for conservation action. Conservation Biol. J. Soc. Conservation Biol. **30**. April 2016. https://doi.org/10.1111/cobi.12702

18. He, Y., Parrish, J.K., Rowe, S., Jones, T.: Evolving interest and sense of self in an environmental citizen science program. Ecology Soc. **24**, July 2019. https://doi.org/10.5751/ES-10956-240233

19. Hodapp, C., Robbins, M., Gray, J., Graettinger, A.: Damage tracker: a cloud and mobile system for collecting damage information after natural disasters. In: Proceedings of the Annual Southeast Conference (04 2013). https://doi.org/10.1145/2498328.2500075
20. Hossain, Z., et al.: Interactive cloud experimentation for biology: An online education case study. Conference on Human Factors in Computing Systems - Proceedings 2015-April, pp. 3681–3690, April 2015. https://doi.org/10.1145/2702123.2702354
21. Hsu, Y.C., et al.: Smell Pittsburgh: engaging community citizen science for air quality. ACM Trans. Interactive Intell. Syst. 10 (2020). https://doi.org/10.1145/3369397
22. Kerson, R.: Lab for the environment (1989)
23. Kim, N.W., Jung, J., Ko, E.Y., Han, S., Lee, C.W., Kim, J., Kim, J.: Budgetmap: engaging taxpayers in the issue-driven classification of a government budget. In: Proceedings of the ACM Conference on Computer Supported Cooperative Work, CSCW 27, pp. 1028–1039, February 2016. https://doi.org/10.1145/2818048.2820004
24. Kuznetsov, S., Harrigan-Anderson, W., Faste, H., Hudson, S.E., Paulos, E.: Community engagements with living sensing systems. In: Proceedings of the 9th ACM Conference on Creativity & Cognition, C&C 2013, pp. 213–222. Association for Computing Machinery, New York (2013). https://doi.org/10.1145/2466627.2466638
25. Kuznetsov, S., Santana, C.J., Long, E.: Everyday food science as a design space for community literacy and habitual sustainable practice. In: Conference on Human Factors in Computing Systems - Proceedings, pp. 1786–1797, May 2016. https://doi.org/10.1145/2858036.2858363
26. Meedeniya, D.A., Rukshan, S.A., Welivita, A.: An interactive gameplay to crowdsource multiple sequence alignment of genome sequences: Genenigma. In: ACM International Conference Proceeding Series, pp. 28–35, January 2019. https://doi.org/10.1145/3314367.3314374
27. Moran, S., et al.: Listening to the forest and its curators: Lessons learnt from a bioacoustic smartphone application deployment. Conference on Human Factors in Computing Systems - Proceedings, pp. 2387–2396 (2014). https://doi.org/10.1145/2556288.2557022
28. Newman, G., Wiggins, A., Crall, A., Graham, E., Newman, S., Crowston, K.: The future of citizen science: emerging technologies and shifting paradigms. Front. Ecol. Environ. 10(6), 298–304 (2012). https://doi.org/10.1890/110294
29. Oliver, J.L., Brereton, M., Turkay, S., Watson, D.M., Roe, P.: Exploration of aural & visual media about birds informs lessons for citizen science design. In: DIS 2020 - Proceedings of the 2020 ACM Designing Interactive Systems Conference, pp. 1687–1700, July 2020. https://doi.org/10.1145/3357236.3395478
30. Page, M.J., et al.: Prisma 2020 explanation and elaboration: updated guidance and exemplars for reporting systematic reviews. BMJ 372, March 2021. https://doi.org/10.1136/bmj.n160
31. Pandey, V., et al.: Gut instinct: creating scientific theories with online learners. In: Conference on Human Factors in Computing Systems - Proceedings 2017-May, pp. 6825–6836, May 2017. https://doi.org/10.1145/3025453.3025769
32. Pandey, V., Debelius, J., Hyde, E.R., Kosciolek, T., Knight, R., Klemmer, S.: Docent: transforming personal intuitions to scientific hypotheses through content learning and process training. In: Proceedings of the 5th Annual ACM Conference on Learning at Scale, L at S 2018, July 2018. https://doi.org/10.1145/3231644.3231646

33. Peter, M., Diekötter, T., Kremer, K.: Participant outcomes of biodiversity citizen science projects: a systematic literature review. Sustainability **11**(10) (2019). https://doi.org/10.3390/su11102780
34. Preece, J.: Citizen science: new research challenges for human-computer interaction. Int. J. Hum.-Comput. Interact. **32**(8), 585–612 (2016)
35. Radeta, M., Nunes, N.J., Vasconcelos, D., Nisi, V.: Poseidon - passive-acoustic ocean sensor for entertainment and interactive data-gathering in opportunistic nautical-activities. In: DIS 2018 - Proceedings of the 2018 Designing Interactive Systems Conference, pp. 999–1012, June 2018. https://doi.org/10.1145/3196709.3196752
36. Robinson, L.D., Cawthray, J.L., West, S.E., Bonn, A., Ansine, J.: Ten principles of citizen science. In: Citizen Science: Innovation in Open Science, Society and Policy, pp. 27–40. UCL Press (2018)
37. Rotman, D., et al.: Does motivation in citizen science change with time and culture? In: Proceedings of the Companion Publication of the 17th ACM Conference on Computer Supported Cooperative Work & Social Computing, CSCW Companion 2014, pp. 229–232. Association for Computing Machinery, New York (2014). https://doi.org/10.1145/2556420.2556492
38. Rughiniş, C., Rughiniş, R., Huma, B.: Impromptu crowd science and the mystery of the bechdel-wallace test movement. In: Conference on Human Factors in Computing Systems - Proceedings 07–12-May-2016, pp. 487–500, May 2016. https://doi.org/10.1145/2851581.2892580
39. Scheibein, F., Donnelly, W., Wells, J.S.: Assessing open science and citizen science in addictions and substance use research: a scoping review. Int. J. Drug Policy **100**, 103505 (2022). https://doi.org/10.1016/j.drugpo.2021.103505. https://www.sciencedirect.com/science/article/pii/S0955395921004187
40. Silvertown, J.: A new dawn for citizen science. Trends Ecol. Evol. **24**, 467–471 (2009). https://doi.org/10.1016/j.tree.2009.03.017
41. Skarlatidou, A., Hamilton, A., Vitos, M., Haklay, M.: What do volunteers want from citizen science technologies? a systematic literature review and best practice guidelines. J. Sci. Commun. **18** (2019). https://doi.org/10.22323/2.18010202
42. Skarlatidou, A., Ponti, M., Sprinks, J., Nold, C., Haklay, M., Kanjo, E.: User experience of digital technologies in citizen science. J. Sci. Commun. **18** (2019). https://doi.org/10.22323/2.18010501
43. Stevens, M., Vitos, M., Altenbuchner, J., Conquest, G., Lewis, J., Haklay, M.: Introducing sapelli: a mobile data collection platform for non-literate users. Proceedings of the 4th Annual Symposium on Computing for Development, ACM DEV 2013 (2013). https://doi.org/10.1145/2537052.2537069
44. Tempelmeier, N., et al.: Data4urbanmobility: towards holistic data analytics for mobility applications in urban regions (2019). https://doi.org/10.1145/3308560
45. Vaish, R., et al.: Crowd research: Open and scalable university laboratories. UIST 2017 - Proceedings of the 30th Annual ACM Symposium on User Interface Software and Technology, pp. 829–843, October 2017. https://doi.org/10.1145/3126594.3126648
46. Veja, C., Hocker, J., Kollmann, S., Schindler, C.: Bridging citizen science and open educational resource. In: Proceedings of the 14th International Symposium on Open Collaboration, OpenSym 2018, August 2018. https://doi.org/10.1145/3233391.3233539

47. Vitos, M., Lewis, J., Stevens, M., Haklay, M.: Making local knowledge matter: supporting non-literate people to monitor poaching in congo. In: Proceedings of the 3rd ACM Symposium on Computing for Development, ACM DEV 2013. ACM, New York (2013). https://doi.org/10.1145/2442882.2442884
48. Wang, Y., Kaplan, N., Newman, G., Scarpino, R.: Citsci.org: a new model for managing, documenting, and sharing citizen science data. PLOS Biol. **13**(10), 1–5 (10 2015). https://doi.org/10.1371/journal.pbio.1002280
49. Wang Wei, J., Lee, B.P.Y.H., Bing Wen, L.: Citizen science and the urban ecology of birds and butterflies - a systematic review. PLOS ONE **11**(6), 1–23 (2016). https://doi.org/10.1371/journal.pone.0156425
50. Wibowo, A.T., et al.: Bumblebee friendly planting recommendations with citizen science data. In: ACM International Conference Proceeding Series, August 2017. https://doi.org/10.1145/3127325.3128330

# The Gap Between UX Literacy and UX Practices in Agile-UX Settings: A Case Study

Daniela Azevedo[1]([✉])(iD), Luka Rukonić[1,2](iD), and Suzanne Kieffer[1](iD)

[1] Université catholique de Louvain, Louvain-la-Neuve, Belgium
{daniela.azevedo,luka.rukonic,suzanne.kieffer}@uclouvain.be
[2] AISIN Europe, Braine-l'Alleud, Belgium

**Abstract.** Integration of agile and user experience (UX) remains a challenge despite being a major research interest for both agile software development (ASD) and UX stakeholders. Typically, ASD stakeholders' primary focus is delivering working software, whereas UX stakeholders focus on designing systems that meet user needs. These differences lead to friction between developers and designers. In this paper, we focus on ASD stakeholders working in an agile-UX setting and explore the gap between their UX literacy and UX practices. We adopted a case study approach involving ASD stakeholders from two organisations working in agile-UX settings. We studied both organisations for over a year, starting at the end of 2021. Specifically, we compared data about their UX literacy collected by questionnaire and semi-structured interview, to data about their UX practices collected by observation. We administered the questionnaire and conducted the semi-structured interviews twice, in rounds six months apart. We used participant observation in projects with which we were involved as UX researchers and designers. Our findings show that ASD stakeholders' UX practices do not match their yet acceptable level of UX literacy. For example, ASD stakeholders still engage in premature development activities, although they understand the problems associated with late design changes. We encourage UX practitioners and researchers to conduct UX maturity assessments and address identified disparities, as we believe this will reduce the friction between different stakeholder groups and facilitate the integration of ASD and UX.

**Keywords:** UX literacy · UX practice · UX maturity · UX maturity assessment · Case study

## 1 Introduction

The integration of ASD and UX has been a major research interest of both ASD and UX communities since the late 2000s [6]. Despite an abundance of related literature [20], their integration remains challenging, due to frictions between the approaches [35]. First, each community has diverging needs. ASD aims to satisfy

© The Author(s), under exclusive license to Springer Nature Switzerland AG 2023
J. Abdelnour Nocera et al. (Eds.): INTERACT 2023, LNCS 14143, pp. 436–457, 2023.
https://doi.org/10.1007/978-3-031-42283-6_24

customers by frequently delivering working software [6,17] and avoiding failed projects by responding to changing customer requirements [12]. UX aims to satisfy user needs and requirements while limiting late design changes to reduce development time and costs or preventing user errors to reduce technical support requests [3]. Second, ASD and UX principles seem opposed: ASD welcomes changing requirements, whereas UX does not [6,12,41,49]. Third, the focus on developers and code production in ASD *versus* the focus on users in UX shows the further discrepancy between the two approaches [20]. These incompatibilities prevent or slow down the successful integration of ASD and UX.

To overcome these barriers, several models for integrating ASD and UX have emerged. A 2022 systematic literature review [20] reports on 18 primary models for ASD UX integration. Each comprises a series of generic principles for ASD UX integration related to lifecycle or primary processes, from upfront UX design a sprint ahead of agile [44] to parallel and synchronised tracks [6]. Nevertheless, these models do not integrate enough UX. First, the requirements specification remains product-oriented, as none of these models provide usable guidance for integrating user needs into the requirements. This lack of UX is surprising, since user requirements are necessary to deliver products that people actually want [12]. Second, none provide UX designers with a formal decision-making role, e.g., involving UX designers in iteration backlog or planning activities [8], although it is essential to prioritise system features according to UX so as to meet user needs [12]. Further, we identify a lack of UX literacy, characterised by misunderstanding of UX, as another barrier to UX integration. Symptoms of lack of UX literacy in ASD or software development, in general, include mistaking UX for aesthetics or visual design [15], mistaking users with customers or domain-experts [2,12], belief that performing UX requires no UX expertise [3], belief that UX can be performed informally [5,8], contentious attitudes towards users [12], and lack of understanding of UX return on investment (ROI) [3]. Lack of UX literacy is typical in low UX maturity contexts [40] and may lead to ostracism of UX experts, e.g. by excluding them from decision-making processes [23].

Despite these barriers, it now seems a given in the ASD community that users need a good user experience to adopt systems, and therefore that developers need UX to deliver competitive systems [6,12,20]. But then, how to explain the aforementioned lack of UX literacy, especially in agile-UX settings? Furthermore, how do ASD stakeholders working in an agile-UX setting perceive UX? How do their perceptions of UX translate into their UX practices? How do their actual and perceived UX practices compare?

To answer these questions, we conducted a case study in two organisations working in an agile-UX setting, referred to in the following as Org. A and Org. B. We used questionnaire, interview and observation to explore how ASD stakeholders perceive UX in lower UX maturity contexts during early phases of ASD UX integration, and the consequences of their perception of UX on UX practices. This research was motivated by our experiences within industrial projects encountering the aforementioned barriers while integrating UX into formal software development model: 1$^{st}$ author as UX consultant in Org. A (Nov 2021 to

Nov 2022), $2^{nd}$ author as UX researcher in Org. B (Nov 2018 to present), $3^{rd}$ as UX researcher (2012–2017) and as UX advisor in both Org. A and B (Nov 2018 to present). Our missions in Org. A and B did not include the study of UX practices, but focused on the integration of UX into software development models. These missions gave us hands-on experience with the barriers, so we took this opportunity to explore the gap between UX literacy and UX practices at different maturity levels. To the best of our knowledge, the literature has not addressed this gap, although problems in ASD UX integration were identified [10,12,25–28,44,45]. The remainder of this article is organised as follows: after a background section, we present the methodology, the results and their discussion, before concluding the paper.

## 2    Background

### 2.1    UX and UX Strategy

UX is defined as "a person's perceptions and responses that result from the use or anticipated use of a product, system or service" [22]. It is an umbrella term for the hedonic and pragmatic aspects of how users interact with the product or service in different physical or temporal contexts [19]. UX is grounded in user-centred design (UCD), a process that places the users, their needs, and their tasks at the centre of development focus. UCD has four phases: specification of the context of use, specification of the user requirements, production of design solutions, and evaluation of design solutions [22].

UX strategy aims to align business goals and UX activities while improving the development and UX of products [4,16]. Implementing UX strategy achieves economy of scale while reducing maintenance and development costs, need for technical support of users, documentation, and training, job turnover, user errors and mistrust [3,40,48]. Despite the obvious benefits of UX, its integration into software development is paved with obstacles [26,46] stemming from an insufficient understanding of UCD [2,7], poor comprehension of UX and UX expertise [4,7,8], contentious attitudes towards users [12], and lack of awareness of UX ROI [3,7]. Project failure due to poor UX may present decision-makers an opportunity to push UX adoption and overcome barriers [4].

### 2.2    UX Maturity/Capability Models (UXCMMs)

UX maturity refers to the ability of an organisation to consistently implement UX processes, while UX capability refers to the ability to achieve the required goals of UX processes [13,34]. To address obstacles preventing the adoption of UX, UX capability/maturity models (UXCMMs) [7,14,42,48] have emerged allowing organisations to assess their UX capabilities and improve their UX maturity. The literature highlights the importance of UXCMMs during both project planning and project execution [18]. Attributes of UX maturity include, but are not limited to: integration of UX practices in the development cycle, human-centred leadership or organisational human-centredness [14]; a success stories database, education and training, budget and dedicated staffing [42]; focus on users, process management, infrastructure and resources [48].

One of the prominent models for measuring human-centredness in organisations is Earthy's usability maturity model (UMM) [14]. The model has five levels: X (Unrecognised), A (Recognised), B (Considered), C (Implemented), D (Integrated), and E (Institutionalised). At level X, organisations have no UX practices and are unaware of UX ROI. At level A, stakeholders recognise the need to improve software development practices due to poor UX with their products. Practices that could inform user requirements are performed inconsistently. At level B, ASD stakeholders are aware of the importance of quality of use, engage in awareness raising and training to improve UX literacy, and account for user requirements during development. At level C, the organisation implements UX processes and techniques appropriate for each new project. At Level D, the software development model integrates UX to ensure high quality in all relevant products. Adequate resources are allocated for UX activities and staff members can use UX artifacts. At Level E, organisations are driven by UX, and leverage it to increase the value of internal and external products. UX issues are given equal treatment to other system issues, and human-centered skills are held to the same standard as engineering skills. Each level is described using a set of attributes that are rated on a 4-point scale (none (N), partially (P), largely (L), and fully (F)). To transition to a higher maturity level, an organisation must first fully or largely achieve the attributes of the current level.

In this paper, we argue that high UX maturity cannot be achieved without UX literacy and we break down UX literacy into four attributes: understanding of UCD processes, understanding of UX, attitude towards users, and awareness of UX ROI. We consider these attributes prerequisite for successfully performing UX processes [14,48], involving users [14], and integrating UX with other processes [14,42]. The earlier users are involved in development, the higher the UX maturity [18].

## 2.3 ASD and UX Integration

Although superficially compatible, integration of ASD and UX challenges practitioners and organisations attempting it [10,11,45]. Challenges include: power struggles between developers and designers to maintain involvement in projects, lack of a common vision of the product, high workloads for too few UX designers [25], low usability and user needs prioritisation, lack of time for upfront activities, and lack or poor communication between designers and developers [1,24]. These challenges may occur in all organisations, regardless of size [7]. Moreover, "a communication gap between UX and non-UX practitioners" represents a major challenge for ASD practitioners when integrating UX practices into the organisational software development model [28].

However, up-front UX work such as user research and UI design, also referred to as sprint zero, might help ASD teams to build a shared UX vision and increase the speed of later sprints [44]. Further, Brhel et al. [6] advocate for a shift from up-front design to up-front analysis so as to deliver the right product, i.e. one with a high degree of innovation, usable and useful, beyond the scope of ASD. The authors also recommend that UX and ASD activities should be iterative and incremental, organised in parallel tracks, and continuously involve users.

## 3    Methodology

### 3.1    Study Goals and Overview

To answer questions raised in Sect. 1, we set three goals: (1) assess changes in the UX literacy and perception of UX of ASD stakeholders working in an agile-UX setting; (2) observe their UX practices; (3) compare actual UX practices and UX literacy, and identify problems during ASD UX integration. To achieve these goals, we used a mixed-method approach involving survey, observation, and interview (Fig. 1). The survey assessed UX literacy (goal 1), the observation captured UX practices (goal 2), and the interview gathered insights about their beliefs regarding UX, opportunities for UX, and barriers to UX (goal 3).

We adopted a case study approach involving the ASD stakeholders from Org. A and Org. B, two organisations working in an agile-UX setting. We studied both organisations for over a year, starting at the end of 2021, collecting data from a single project in Org. A and from multiple projects in Org. B. We compared UX literacy data collected by survey and interview to UX practice data collected by participant observation. We administered the questionnaire and conducted interviews in two rounds, December 2021 to June 2022 (R1) and July 2022 to December 2022 (R2). Following the agile-UX lifecycle presented in [29], UX and developers worked along parallel, interwoven tracks, and we conducted user tests at the end of each iteration. We used the UX process reference model presented in [30] to select UX methods, based on teams' immediate objectives rather than on their UX maturity.

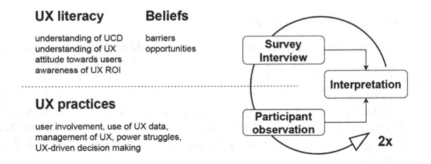

**Fig. 1.** Methodology: overview.

## 3.2   Organisations A and B

Org. A is a medium-sized company desiring to create software to support their employees through automation. They decided to integrate UX activities into the development of this software, having recently experienced a project failure due to a lack of UX considerations, significantly reducing their organisational efficiencies. Org. A hired an external ASD team to develop the new software, and the 1$^{st}$ and 3$^{rd}$ authors as UX practitioner and advisor respectively. Both Org. A and the external ASD team were integrating UX activities into ASD processes for the first time. This is indicative of low UX maturity, Recognised (level A) on Earthy's model [14], as Org. A's management is beginning to understand the UX ROI, and recognise a need to improve the UX of its systems.

Org. B is a large company and major automotive parts supplier. This study covers multiple projects of a department in Org. B that underwent an agile transformation in 2012 and primarily develops software for automotive solutions. Authors 2 and 3 were enrolled in 2018 to formally perform UX activities, moving from *ad-hoc* and scattered UX to budgeted and more structured UX, with the goal of promoting UX across the organisation. This indicates an intermediate UX maturity, between Considered (level B) and Implemented (level C) on Earthy's model [14]. Implemented UX processes show good results; however, skilled UX staff are not yet involved in all stages of development or when required and some ASD stakeholders are unaware of UX as an attribute of the system.

## 3.3   Participants and Stakeholder Groups

As UX practitioners, we planned and executed UX activities, advised, and worked directly with ASD teams. This allowed us to informally discuss with ASD stakeholders, observe the conduct of UX activities, take field notes, and recruit participants for this study. In both Org. A and B, we recruited participants from three ASD stakeholder groups for analysis and comparison purposes: developers, managers, and senior managers. Developers' primary task is software development, from which we excluded designers. Managers oversee developers, designers, and UX staff. Senior managers are top-level managers responsible for strategic decisions at project and company level.

The survey involved 30 participants, 13 from Org. A and 17 from Org. B (Table 1). Eleven participants from Org. A and 13 from Org. B participated in both rounds, totalling 48 responses. Eight participants were interviewed, four per organisation. No Org. A developer was available for interview in R2 and no Org. B senior manager was available in R1. The same Org. A senior manager, and Org. B manager were interviewed in both rounds. Participants read and signed a consent form, on paper before the interview, electronically before the survey. The subcontracting agreement executed with Org. A and the memorandum of understanding entered into with Org. B authorised collection of observational data.

**Table 1.** Summary profile of participants sorted by ASD stakeholder group (Dev: developers; Mgr: managers; SMgr: senior managers), organisation and round.

|                  | Dev    | Mgr    | SMgr   | Dev      | Mgr     | SMgr   |
|------------------|--------|--------|--------|----------|---------|--------|
| Org. A           | R1     |        |        | R2       |         |        |
| N                | 5      | 3      | 4      | 3        | 2       | 4      |
| Age range        | 23-35  | 30-40  | 39-52  | 23-25    | 36-41   | 32-52  |
| Years experience | 0.5-2  | 1-3    | 1,5-5  | 0.5-1.33 | 0.75-3  | 2-5    |
| Org. B           | R1     |        |        | R2       |         |        |
| N                | 5      | 4      | 3      | 12       | 2       | 2      |
| Age range        | 28-50  | 28-49  | 43-48  | 29-55    | 46-49   | 43-48  |
| Years experience | 0.6-3  | 0.17-2 | 0.17-5 | 2-20     | 5-8     | 6-18   |

### 3.4 Methods

We created a 6-module questionnaire (Table 2), inspired by [32]. The first four modules measure ASD stakeholders' UX literacy: understanding of user-centred design processes (UCD); understanding of UX concepts, roles and definitions (UUX); attitude towards users, their needs and requirements (ATU); awareness of UX ROI and the benefits of integrating UX into development (ROI). The last two modules, opportunities for UX integration (OPP) and barriers to UX integration (BAR), collect data on problem recognition and integration, two attributes of Earthy's UMM [14]. Problem recognition is "the extent to which members of the organisation understand that there is a problem with the quality in use of the systems produced". Integration is "the extent to which human-centred processes are integrated with other processes". We used these two attributes to collect more accurate data related to maturity levels A to D, having estimated the UX maturity level of Org. A as level A, and level B or C for Org. B.

Except for UUX, which contains six, each module contains four statements, half being reverse-worded to reduce agreement bias [47]. Participants rate their agreement with each statement between 1 (strongly disagree) and 5 (strongly agree) on a Likert scale. Answer accuracy tends to decline over time, so we maximise answer quality through exclusive use of close-ended questions, which requires less participant motivation and skill, and progressively decrease question complexity throughout [47]. The questionnaire takes 5 to 10 min to complete.

We used participant observation through the $1^{st}$ and $2^{nd}$ authors, who were directly involved in projects in Org. A and B, respectively. We kept notes on events occurring in the field (e.g., meetings, decisions, and discussions) between ASD stakeholders. We used these notes as sources of observational data.

To elaborate upon the survey, we conducted semi-structured interviews based on UX attributes and observational data. We covered nine topics, each providing insights into one or more of the attributes, and ASD stakeholders' current understandings and beliefs regarding UX practices. Table 3 displays the topics, their attributes, and with whom they were discussed. We interviewed and recorded participants in person or via online video conference.

To analyse survey data, we calculated mean scores per UX attribute and stakeholder group and looked for outliers. We sought statements with notable low means across all respondents, and for each organisation per round, to use as cues to investigate qualitative data. Further, we transcribed interviews verbatim, and collected quotations linked to UX attributes (Table 3). In addition, since interview and survey questions were structured per UX attribute, we were able to cross-analyse interview and survey results, linking qualitative and quantitative data. Finally, we connected our findings to relevant observational data.

# 4   Results

## 4.1   Survey

As shown in Table 4, ATU, BAR, and OPP notably decreased between rounds in Org. A; conversely, UCD, ATU, ROI, and OPP notably increased between rounds in Org. B. Table 4 also presents the average score of UX attributes. Org. A developers and managers exhibited similar mean levels of UX literacy. Excepting OPP, senior managers scored higher in all UX attributes. Org. B developers had higher means than managers. In R2 senior managers showed notably higher UCD and ROI than developers and managers. Table 5 shows differences in scoring for participants from both organisations who took part in both rounds. The ATU, BAR, and OPP scores decreased in Org. A, while ROI and UUX scores increased in Org. B.

Eight individual questionnaire statements had mean values below a neutral score (3) across all ASD stakeholder groups. In the ATU attribute, ASD stakeholders disagreed with the statement "Users are able to express what they want" ($M = 2.83$, $SD = 0.72$ in Org. A; $M = 2.81$, $SD = 0.96$ in Org. B) and agreed with "User expectations are difficult to manage" ($M = 2.46$, $SD = 0.79$ in Org. A; $M = 2.56$, $SD = 0.92$ in Org. B.). In the ROI attribute, Org. A generally agreed that "UX activities increase development costs and time" ($M = 2.67$, $SD = 1.08$). In contrast, Org. B. scored better ($M = 3.22$, $SD = 1.05$). Results for this statement are a negative outlier within the attribute. Each statement from the OPP attribute received negative scores.

## 4.2   Observation

Table 6 summarises discrepancies between planned and executed UX activities. In Org. A, at the start of the project, managers attended a 2-hour UX training session. The same training was planned for developers, but never occurred. The first key touch point, at the end of the UX analysis, allowed stakeholders to develop a shared understanding of user needs and requirements, technical restraints, and opportunities. Lacking prior UX experience, ASD stakeholders

**Table 2.** Questionnaire statements by UX attribute, rated on a 5-point Likert scale from strongly disagree to strongly agree (standard) or from strongly agree to strongly disagree (reverse).

| Statement | Scale |
| --- | --- |
| **Understanding of UCD processes (UCD)** | |
| Grounded in-depth understanding of users, tasks and environments should be a focus at the start of development [2] | standard |
| UX research (user needs analysis and user requirements specification) is a "blocker" to the real development work [2] | reverse |
| UX research (user needs analysis and user requirements specification) is an optional add-on [2] | reverse |
| Design should be driven by user tasks, goals and evaluation [38] | standard |
| **Understanding of UX (UUX)** | |
| Graphic design and UX design are the same and therefore are performed by the same person [4] | reverse |
| UX is subjective and therefore cannot be measured [4] | reverse |
| UX awareness is all you need to design good user interfaces or good user experience [4] | reverse |
| Non-utilitarian concepts (e.g., joy, stimulation, aesthetics) are part of UX [19,31,39] | standard |
| Utilitarian concepts (e.g., efficiency, effectiveness, satisfaction) are part of UX [19,31,39] | standard |
| UX is essential for acceptance, adoption, and trust in a product [19,31,39] | standard |
| **Attitude towards users (ATU)** | |
| Users do not need a good UX, they just need training [4] | reverse |
| Users are able to express what they want [4] | standard |
| User expectations are difficult to manage [4] | reverse |
| Users should be at the centre of product development, not just have a supporting role [38] | standard |
| **Awareness of UX ROI (ROI)** | |
| UX activities increase product attractiveness [3] | standard |
| UX activities reduce sales and revenues [3] | reverse |
| UX activities help reduce users' need for training and technical support [3] | standard |
| UX activities increase development costs and time [3] | reverse |
| **Opportunities (wake-up call) (OPP)** | |
| Some of our projects or products fail because of poor UX design [4] | reverse |
| User needs for training and technical support are important [4] | reverse |
| The overall net loss in user productivity from UX issues is insignificant [4] | standard |
| The overall net loss in late design changes from UX issues is insignificant [4] | standard |
| **Barriers (BAR)** | |
| We have enough resources (time, budget, staff) for UX [4] | standard |
| We have enough skills to conduct UX activities [4] | standard |
| UX conflicts with our current software development model [4] | reverse |
| Our projects are too small to incorporate UX into our software development model [4] | reverse |

**Table 3.** Semi-structured interview: guiding questions. UCD stands for understanding of user-centred design, UUX for understanding of UX, ATU for attitude towards users, ROI for awareness of UX ROI, BAR for barriers, and OPP for opportunities. Dev stands for developers, Mgr for managers, and SMgr for senior managers.

| Topic | Questions | Attribute | Who |
|---|---|---|---|
| UX activities integration into current software development model | How do UX activities integrate into or modify the current software development model? | UCD, ROI | Mgr |
| UX activities integration | How did the introduction of UX activities affect your job? | ROI, BAR, OPP | Mgr, Dev |
| User involvement effect in the final product | What does user involvement bring or not bring to the final product? | UCD, ATU | Mgr, Dev, SMgr |
| Prospect of doing UX activities in other projects | Why would you consider or not consider using UX for other projects? | ROI, BAR, OPP | Mgr, Dev, SMgr |
| Upside to carrying out UX activities | What would you describe as the main upside to carrying out UX activities? | UUX, ROI | Mgr, Dev, SMgr |
| Downside to carrying out UX activities | What would you describe as the main downside to carrying out UX activities? | UUX, ROI | Mgr, Dev, SMgr |
| Communication of UX findings | Describe the role and importance of UX artifacts in your work | ROI, BAR, OPP | Mgr, Dev |
| Communication of UX findings | Where do you receive UX-related information from? Informally, verbally, UX artifacts, documentation? | UUX | Mgr, Dev |
| Prospect of doing UX activities in the project | What kind of information related to UX do you expect or would like to see to help decision-making? | UUX, ROI | Mgr |

were reluctant to adopt users' points of view. Although expedited, ASD stakeholders started development while UX research was ongoing. Planned UX activities were abandoned. Overlooking UX research results and UCD, ASD stakeholders discussed and 'validated' data models and prototypes with users in ASD-led activities. UX research results went unheeded. Results from successful UX activities with managers did not reach developers. The low-fidelity prototype was evaluated while being altered. No time to re-evaluate it was allocated, leaving key UX issues unresolved. During coding, software modification became resource intensive and had to be delayed post-launch. Final user tests were conducted with few users on an unstable software version, hence suboptimal usability at launch.

Org. B more successfully executed planned activities, possibly due to commitment to, and experience in, UX-driven projects. During R1, Org. B was engaged in a long-term project. The team adopted ASD while following UCD processes,

**Table 4.** Questionnaire: mean scores per UX attribute and ASD stakeholder group. Round average in second column for all ASD stakeholders. Orange/Green: noteworthy decrease/increase (± 0.2 points) in scores between rounds. AVG: UX attributes average.

| Org. | Round | Role | UCD | | UUX | | ATU | | ROI | | BAR | | OPP | | AVG |
|---|---|---|---|---|---|---|---|---|---|---|---|---|---|---|---|
| A | 1 | Dev | 3.50 | | 3.93 | | 3.40 | | 3.40 | | 3.75 | | 2.85 | | 3.47 |
| | | Mgr | 3.50 | 3.79 | 3.56 | 3.89 | 3.42 | 3.46 | 3.17 | 3.52 | 3.17 | 3.39 | 3.00 | 2.72 | 3.30 |
| | | SMgr | 4.38 | | 4.17 | | 3.56 | | 4.00 | | 3.25 | | 2.31 | | 3.61 |
| A | 2 | Dev | 3.42 | | 3.61 | | 3.25 | | 3.50 | | 3.00 | | 2.25 | | 3.17 |
| | | Mgr | 3.88 | 3.81 | 3.75 | 3.86 | 3.00 | 3.15 | 3.50 | 3.58 | 3.25 | 3.08 | 2.00 | 2.29 | 3.23 |
| | | SMgr | 4.13 | | 4.21 | | 3.19 | | 3.75 | | 3.00 | | 2.63 | | 3.48 |
| B | 1 | Dev | 4.20 | | 4.23 | | 3.50 | | 4.00 | | 3.55 | | 2.40 | | 3.65 |
| | | Mgr | 3.60 | 3.82 | 3.47 | 3.99 | 2.75 | 3.14 | 3.40 | 3.80 | 3.00 | 3.18 | 1.70 | 2.20 | 2.99 |
| | | SMgr | 3.67 | | 4.28 | | 3.17 | | 4.00 | | 3.00 | | 2.50 | | 3.44 |
| B | 2 | Dev | 4.25 | | 4.22 | | 3.65 | | 3.96 | | 3.50 | | 2.44 | | 3.67 |
| | | Mgr | 4.00 | 4.42 | 3.83 | 4.10 | 3.75 | 3.67 | 3.75 | 4.19 | 3.00 | 3.25 | 2.25 | 2.40 | 3.43 |
| | | SMgr | 5.00 | | 4.25 | | 3.63 | | 4.88 | | 3.25 | | 2.50 | | 3.92 |

**Table 5.** Variation between rounds for both round participants.

| Dim. | Round | Org. A | | | | | | | Org. B | | | | | | |
|---|---|---|---|---|---|---|---|---|---|---|---|---|---|---|---|
| | | Dev | Dev | Mgr | Mgr | SMgr | SMgr | SMgr | Dev | Dev | Dev | Dev | Mgr | SMgr | SMgr |
| UCD | 1 | 3.25 | 4.00 | 3.50 | 3.50 | 4.25 | 4.00 | 4.25 | 3.25 | 3.75 | 4.75 | 5.00 | 4.00 | 4.50 | 3.00 |
| | 2 | 3.00 | 3.50 | 4.00 | 3.75 | 4.50 | 3.50 | 4.25 | 4.25 | 4.00 | 4.50 | 5.00 | 4.00 | 5.00 | 5.00 |
| UUX | 1 | 3.67 | 4.17 | 3.67 | 3.50 | 3.83 | 4.00 | 4.50 | 4.50 | 3.83 | 4.33 | 4.50 | 3.83 | 4.17 | 5.00 |
| | 2 | 3.33 | 4.17 | 3.50 | 4.00 | 4.17 | 4.00 | 4.33 | 4.67 | 4.00 | 4.00 | 5.00 | 4.33 | 3.50 | 5.00 |
| ATU | 1 | 3.50 | 3.50 | 3.25 | 3.50 | 3.25 | 3.25 | 4.00 | 3.75 | 2.75 | 3.75 | 4.00 | 4.00 | 4.00 | 3.50 |
| | 2 | 2.75 | 3.75 | 3.00 | 3.00 | 2.75 | 3.50 | 3.25 | 4.00 | 3.00 | 3.25 | 5.00 | 4.00 | 3.25 | 4.00 |
| ROI | 1 | 3.00 | 3.50 | 3.25 | 3.25 | 3.50 | 4.00 | 4.00 | 4.00 | 3.75 | 3.50 | 4.75 | 4.50 | 4.25 | 4.50 |
| | 2 | 3.25 | 3.75 | 3.50 | 3.50 | 4.00 | 4.00 | 4.00 | 4.25 | 3.00 | 4.00 | 5.00 | 4.75 | 4.75 | 5.00 |
| BAR | 1 | 3.50 | 4.25 | 3.25 | 3.50 | 3.00 | 3.50 | 3.25 | 3.75 | 3.25 | 3.50 | 3.25 | 4.00 | 3.50 | 2.75 |
| | 2 | 2.25 | 3.50 | 3.25 | 3.25 | 3.00 | 3.00 | 3.00 | 4.00 | 3.00 | 3.25 | 3.25 | 4.25 | 3.50 | 3.00 |
| OPP | 1 | 3.00 | 2.50 | 2.75 | 2.75 | 2.25 | 2.75 | 2.50 | 2.00 | 2.50 | 2.25 | 2.00 | 2.25 | 2.50 | 2.50 |
| | 2 | 2.25 | 1.75 | 2.25 | 1.75 | 2.25 | 2.50 | 2.75 | 1.50 | 3.25 | 2.25 | 1.75 | 1.75 | 2.50 | 2.50 |

wherein the final design solution resulted from six iterations of UX evaluations with six to eight users. At touchpoints, ASD and UX stakeholders analysed UX evaluation data and deliberated design changes. However, implementing the two parallel interwoven ASD UX tracks was challenging. In a subsequent project, Org. B struggled to convince the customer and business developers to start UX activities (e.g., user interviews, personas). The development team focused on delivering a functional prototype to satisfy the customer, who thought UX could be performed later. UX was not integrated in all projects and UX staff frequently had to jump between projects and finish many tasks on short deadlines.

## 4.3  Interview

*UCD.* Org. A's developer believed developers need not be involved in UX activities, "not [caring] about [them]". UX activities were criticised by the managers

**Table 6.** Discrepancies between planned and actual execution of UX activities, with status of objectives. Obj. = objective A = achieved; PA = partially achieved; F = failed.

| UX activities timeline | Obj. | Execution |
| --- | --- | --- |
| *Org. A R1 - December 2021 - June 2022* | | |
| Conduct contextual inquiry with users | A | Conducted as planned |
| Create user profiles based on user data | F | User profiles have not been done |
| Analyse user data and create shared understanding of user needs and requirements | PA | Unproductive collaboration lead to UX team to do it alone |
| Elaborate UX goals to meet, validate and end iteration | PA | Created list of UX goals yet to be shared with developers |
| Rework task org. and sequence models | F | Models overlooked |
| Design based on reworked models | F | Models abandoned |
| Create wireframes based on user data | PA | Wireframes based on leaders' vision, 'validated' by focus group |
| Usability test before coding starts | | Coding started without testing |
| Use style Guide as communication artifact | F | Style Guide disregarded |
| *Org. A R2 - July 2022 - December 2022* | | |
| Conduct user tests to evaluate wireframes with ten users | PA | Evaluation with fewer users and modification before/during test |
| Rework wireframes after evaluation | PA | Partial major rework pre-launch |
| Evaluate reworked wireframes with users | F | Direct coding of final product |
| Final evaluation of product before launch | PA | Delayed evaluation, semi-launch before feedback was possible |
| Launch product once UX goals and metrics are met (validation) | F | UX goals and metrics not met at launch (no validation) |
| *Org. B R1 - December 2021 - June 2022* | | |
| Design a wizard-of-Oz prototype | A | Conducted as planned |
| Conduct a six-iteration formative UX evaluation of the prototype | A | Conducted as planned |
| Analyse user data and create shared understanding of user needs and requirements | A | Conducted as planned |
| Conduct a summative UX evaluation of the prototype | F | Lack of time, opted for other formative evaluation iteration |
| Conduct contextual inquiry in the field | F | UX activities deemed premature by business developers |
| Conduct interviews to identify user needs | F | Customer wanted a functional prototype |
| Create personas based on user interviews | PA | Alternative people interviewed |
| Use personas to guide development | F | Personas ignored by business |
| *Org. B R2 - July 2022 - December 2022* | | |
| Build an interactive wireframe prototype | A | Conducted as planned |
| Conduct usability test on wireframes | A | Conducted as planned |
| Build a severity/value matrix as a communication artifact | A | Conducted as planned |
| Improve the prototype based on usability test findings using severity/value matrix | A | Conducted as planned |
| Conduct interviews with product users | PA | Few current users were available |

and a senior manager due to resource-intensity and "untimeliness", believing development "had to" precede UX research completion. They wanted UX research to start a sprint ahead of development so as to fully leverage it in the future. Since UX evaluation started during software programming, fixing UX issues would lead to time and budgetary overrun, and R2's manager lamented resultantly insufficient improvements. The senior manager recognised UX awareness alone is insufficient to meet user needs and requirements, and observation of users performing tasks is necessary. Org. B understood the goals and outcomes of UCD's four phases, and follows the analysis-design-evaluation cycle. The senior manager believed UCD reduces late design changes and decreases the risk of developing suboptimal products. Nevertheless, much convincing is required to run UX-driven projects, as Org. B's culture tends to be engineering-oriented.

*UUX.* R1's Org. A developer's believed users are "just humans", and thus inherently uniform, disregarding user background and characteristics in development, perceiving users' specific needs and requirements as unjustified. R2's manager and the senior manager did not share this view, recognising UX as key to solving workflow problems and improving user efficiency and general hedonic aspects. Org. B's ASD stakeholders see the value of UX in identifying and solving real user problems. They believed UX is necessary for any project unless the timeframe is prohibitive or the project is purely technical. They recognised the roles and importance of UX-trained staff, believing in a transversal UX approach, wherein discussion of UX activities is a basis for stakeholder meetings. However, only some projects were driven by users' needs and requirements.

*ATU.* Org. A's developer regarded UX and user involvement as relevant only to the low-level details of software otherwise conceptualised by managers. ASD stakeholders struggle to fully take into account users' feedback, believing users are biased by their current cognitive work models. The senior manager, believing users should be at the core, was particularly dismayed by developers' "lack of empathy", as "the end user would never be capable of using what they deliver". Having observed UX evaluations, Org. B's developers supported UCD, and understood how UX activities help reduce bias, stating "It's normal to take [user] motivations, choices, and desires into account". R1's manager believed "even if [users] cannot explain [their preferences]", their feedback aids in design, and multiple prototypes and iterative evaluations are necessary.

*ROI.* Org. A's senior manager, though unsurprised by UX findings, understood the need to formalise them. The managers and the senior manager recognised UX reduces late development revisions and increases product value, yet prematurely proceeded with development, believing the then incomplete UX analysis' findings would be irrelevant. By R2, having delayed release, the senior manager regretted this decision, recognising the software would require post-launch rectification to improve UX and user efficiency. The senior manager was disappointed by the insufficient leveraging of UX findings throughout development. Having conducted several UX-driven projects, Org. B's ASD stakeholders regarded UX as necessary, requiring sufficient time, staff, and budget. The senior manager and manager recognised user data as valuable to development decision-making and convincing customers to revise products. R2's manager believed UX activities uncover UX issues key to development. Org. B's ASD stakeholders believed UX costs are offset by returns from product attractiveness, improved user satisfaction and performance, shorter delivery time, and reduced late design changes.

*OPP.* Org. A's R1 manager believed UX revealed the "pain" of users' work among other otherwise overlooked issues, while the R2 manager appreciated the bias reduction derived from UX. Both managers believed UX clarifies user needs, enabling the creation of UX goals and adaptation of user stories. In R2, the senior manager opined, "User experience is not a luxury, [...] it's a necessity" but the difficulty lies in balancing user and technical requirements. User involvement is key to development, since without it, the project would be a "probable failure". Org. B has past success with UX integration, providing a basis for ASD stakeholders to further expand UX activities and strengthen ASD UX integration. They often claimed issues lie in balancing the work of UX and development staff, resulting in rushed sprints and constant re-prioritisation of the sprint backlog.

*BAR.* In R1, Org. A ASD stakeholders believed UX analysis results were in line with already planned solutions. They also believed UX reduces requirements for software revision in late development, and that the product's value increased. At the end of R2, the managers and senior manager concluded that despite desiring to adopt UCD, timeline and budgetary constraints prevented UX integration. Org. B. faced barriers when expanding UX to new projects; ASD stakeholders often had to be persuaded to include UX activities. The senior manager regarded many ASD stakeholders as not understanding UX and explained that "we will save time later" by conducting UX activities instead of rushing into development.

## 5 Discussion

### 5.1 Interpretation

Table 7 shows the UX maturity assessment of both organisations using Earthy's UMM [14]. Each author assessed their organisation using observational data and personal experiences gained from fieldwork. To maintain consistency, the $3^{rd}$ author, having knowledge of practices in both organisations, provided additional insights to reach consensus. We rated attributes of levels B (Considered) and C (Implemented), as lower levels are achieved, while higher ones are not.

At level B, two attributes are analysed: B1 assesses ASD stakeholders' awareness of quality in use (i.e., efficiency, effectiveness, and user satisfaction), while B2 evaluates user focus by considering end users' needs and requirements throughout the development process. At level C, three attributes are analysed: the user involvement attribute (C1) represents the extent of user data elicited from rep-

resentative users; the human factor (HF) technology attribute (C2), the extent
UCD methods and techniques are used; the HF skills attribute (C3), the extent
to which HF skills are used in human-centred processes.

**Table 7.** Level B and C of Usability Maturity Model [14] management practices and
assessment of both organisations. N: not achieved, P: partially achieved, L: largely
achieved, F: fully achieved.

| Attribute | Org. A | Org. B |
|---|---|---|
| B1.1 Quality in use training | P | L |
| B1.2 Human-centred methods training | P | L |
| B1.3 Human-system interaction training | P | L |
| B2.1 User consideration training | P | L |
| B2.2 Context of use training | P | L |
| C1.1 Active involvement of users | N | L |
| C1.2 Elicitation of user experience | P | F |
| C1.3 End users define quality-in-use | N | F |
| C1.4 Continuous evaluation | P | L |
| C2.1 Provide appropriate human-centred methods | N | L |
| C2.2 Provide suitable facilities and tools | P | L |
| C2.3 Maintain quality in use techniques | N | P |
| C3.1 Decide on required skills | N | P |
| C3.2 Develop appropriate skills | N | P |
| C3.3 Deploy appropriate skills | N | N |

*Org. A.* Org. A attained level B UX maturity, partially achieving the practices
of this level. ASD stakeholders were only partially aware of quality in use, as
only one external consultant had sufficient UX training (B1.1) and only the
managers had any UX training, which was brief (B1.2). ASD stakeholders often
mistook UX for UI and underestimated the scope and impact of UX activities (B1.3). Further, ASD stakeholders struggled to prioritise user needs and
requirements: the value of UX evaluations was understood, though UX research
was disregarded (B2.1). User background and contexts of use were frequently
disregarded, resulting in software developed without users in mind. Neglecting
end-users is particularly concerning for UX, which prioritises their experiential
response during system interactions [35]. However, by the end of R2, the managers and senior manager understood users have specific needs and requirements
(B2.2). Further, Org. A only partially achieved three practices from level C: user
tests were conducted on medium- and high-fidelity prototypes with end users;
however, the allocated time was inadequate, as were the number of iterations
and participants (C1.2); the number and the extent of UX evaluations were

insufficient, and occurred after development started (C1.4); and, since facilities and tools were unsuitable, outsourcing was necessary (C2.2). These findings are indicative of low UX maturity [7], as is the absence of UX in decision-making [24] and limited UX resources [35].

*Org. B.* Org. B attained level C UX maturity, as they largely achieved practices from level B, but failed to achieve all from level C. Staff executing UCD processes were largely aware of quality in use as a system attribute, and those performing processes relating to user-facing elements accounted for the human beings who will use it. Throughout development, appropriate UX methods using representative users identified user needs and requirements: in all development phases user feedback was collected, analysed, and integrated to improve the product, though not in all projects (C1.1); users interacted with phase-appropriate prototypes (C1.2); user characteristics defined the evaluation measures of quality in use for prototypes (C1.3); and UX evaluations were performed until quality in use was satisfactory (C1.4). UCD methods and techniques were selected during development: user needs defined project objectives, UX methods to elicit user needs and evaluate prototypes were appropriate to each phase (C2.1); tools and facilities invested in (C2.2); however, UX staff resources were insufficient (C2.3). HF skills were partially used in human-centred processes: required competencies identified (C3.1) and some UX skills partially developed (C3.2); but limited UX staff meant UX was absent in some phases (C3.3). Lack of UX resources limits achievable outcomes and creates bottlenecks [36]. ASD UX integration requires coordination through mutual adjustment and frequent communication [43], necessitating efficient collaboration. Successful designer-developer collaboration depends on seven factors [24] and is key to raising UX maturity. Despite Org. B's designers and developers working closely, communicating often, and from an early stage, UX processes are far from being stable and embedded into organisational culture, as UX involvement varied with project and customer, echoing [43].

*UX literacy vs. UX practices.* The gap between UX literacy and UX practices is most salient in Org. A and their moderate UX literacy prevents UX-driven development. Although UX consultants increased its capacity to *do* UX (e.g., correctly applying UX methods), Org. A still lacked the capacity to *use* UX (e.g., using UX knowledge during development processes), the difference between *do* and *use* being introduced in [37]. ASD stakeholders need expertise and communication to avoid relying on assumptions and to properly understand user needs in UX activities [33]. Within Org. A, ingrained belief that solutions based on personal opinion are equal to or better than UCD trumped UX literacy. This belief resulted in neglecting UX research findings and initiating development prior to completing key UX activities, thereby causing delays in software launch and raising costs: lack of UX resources stifles UX's potential, bottlenecking development [36]. The decrease in ATU derives from a belief that simply asking users for their needs and requirements suffices, and changes in users' opinions reflect users' unreliability. A combination of aversion to UCD, lack of understanding of UX artifacts and reliance on pseudo-UX activities led (senior) managers to often deviate from strategic UX planning and insufficiently grasp user characteristics, needs, and requirements. UX evaluations were conducted too late and insufficient time was allocated to address UX issues. These obstacles are in line with findings in [36]. The increase in time and development cost led to a decrease in OPP and alerted ASD stakeholders to the necessity of conducting UX activities.

Org. B has higher UX literacy and is becoming UX-driven. The manager and senior managers had the highest UX ROI awareness, while developers supported UX integration. Even though commitment from top management is crucial to improve UX maturity [18], some remaining barriers prevent Org. B from adopting UCD. Only innovation projects were UX-driven, showing room for further expansion of UX practices and culture. Org. B's in-house UX team, with four years experience and wide knowledge of UX, produced relatively high UCD, UUX, and ROI scores. Org. B seeks a competitive advantage through integration of UX, recognising the value of solving real user problems.

*Prospects.* Both Org. A and B are striving to improve their UX maturity level. Org. A aims to involve more users, perform additional user tests, prioritise UX by temporarily halting development until UX research is complete, and leverage UX to more effectively manage their IT budget. Org. B needs to expand their UX workforce, enhance the UX literacy of ASD stakeholders, and systematically start projects with UX research. We cannot provide standardised recommendations to facilitate the integration of ASD and UX, since according to [18] such recommendations must depend on the context of the organisation (e.g., UX maturity), project (e.g., related business goals), and team (e.g., UX literacy).

### 5.2   Limitations and Strengths

The limitations of this paper mainly regard internal validity. First, we cannot use Cronbach's alpha to statistically validate the questionnaire, since participants with low UX literacy produce inconsistent scores within questionnaire attributes. Second, some ASD stakeholders left between rounds, preventing us from tracking the evolution of some participants' perceptions and attitudes toward UX throughout the study. We offset this by incorporating new participants and interviewing members of all ASD stakeholder groups at least once. Third, our relationships with participants may have influenced their responses, as may have the introduced UX methods. Specifically, we worked closely with some participants for over a year, integrating UX activities into projects, suggesting methods, and guiding implementation during software development. Nevertheless, we reduced this potential bias with the following counter-measures. On the one hand, we controlled the instrumentation threat to internal validity [9] by using the same interview guide in both organisations (Table 3). On the other hand, we committed to our role as UX practitioners throughout our missions. Lastly, our consulting work presented an opportunity to undertake this study in the field but did not change our approach to UX consulting or our behaviour as practitioners.

The primary strength of this work lies in the mixed-method approach, which minimises result subjectivity, as the observational data gives nuance to self-reported survey and interview data. When possible, we triangulated data sources collected with all three methods, cross-checked the findings, and $1^{st}$ and $2^{nd}$ authors independently analysed and discussed their interpretations for coherency [21]. E.g., quantitative survey results guided our search for qualitative evidence in observation data to elaborate why ASD stakeholders held certain beliefs, helping us to explain the gap between their UX practices and literacy. Our longitudinal approach strengthens result validity beyond a mere snapshot: we repeatedly collected data for over a year, contextualised the data, and identified patterns in UX practices. Finally, we carefully selected participants from different stakeholder groups (i.e. developers, managers, and senior managers) with different roles and perspectives on UX, so as to target key positions in software development.

## 6 Conclusion and Future Work

We performed a case study of two organisations presenting the characteristics of lower levels of UX maturity, working in agile-UX settings. From this case study, we showed ASD UX integration is better achieved when ASD stakeholders exhibit higher level of UX literacy, which enables organisations to improve their UX maturity. However, their UX practices under-perform compared to their UX literacy, as there is a gap between what they understand, what they think they do, and what they actually do. Through a mixed-method approach, we identified a gap between ASD stakeholders' knowledge of UX and their UX practices. Further, we linked our findings to UX maturity levels using Earthy's model. This case study shows the variation and differences in this gap between UX literacy and UX practices in two organisations.

Org. A exhibits a low UX maturity level; Org. B exhibits a medium level. In Org. A, the largest issues stem from low UX literacy, which hinders UX practices implementation during product design and development, resulting in deviation from strategically planned UX activities. This leads to friction between ASD stakeholders and UX practitioners, and to an end product with poor UX. Failure to conduct proper UX activities delayed product launch, enabling ASD stakeholders to recognise the criticality of UX to product success. In Org. B, initial barriers to UX integration were overcome before the study started. Our findings reveal that beliefs and practices may shift depending on the course of action and struggles that occur within an organisation. Prior success stories help foster positive attitudes towards UX. Managers were aware of the value of UX and developers were unopposed to user involvement in development.

In future work, this study should be followed by longitudinal studies containing various touch points, multiple participants and organisations, across all levels of UX maturity. These studies would enable collection of further empirical evidence on the UX literacy and UX practices gap and its nature across all UX maturity levels. To provide recommendations for integration of UX in agile work practices, we should focus on providing guidelines for reducing the gap between UX literacy and UX practices.

**Acknowledgements.** The authors acknowledge the support from the Institute for Language and Communication (ILC) and AISIN Europe. The authors thank anonymous reviewers for their helpful comments that improved the manuscript.

# References

1. Argumanis, D., Moquillaza, A., Paz, F.: Challenges in integrating SCRUM and the user-centered design framework: a systematic review. In: Agredo-Delgado, V., Ruiz, P.H., Villalba-Condori, K.O. (eds.) HCI-COLLAB 2020. CCIS, vol. 1334, pp. 52–62. Springer, Cham (2020). https://doi.org/10.1007/978-3-030-66919-5_6
2. Begnum, M.E.N., Thorkildsen, T.: Comparing user-centred practices in agile versus non-agile development. In: Norsk konferanse for organisasjoners bruk av IT (NOKOBIT) (2015)
3. Bias, R., Mayhew, D.: Cost-Justifying Usability, 2nd edn. Morgan Kaufmann, San Francisc (2005)
4. Bloomer, S., Croft, R., Kieboom, H.: Strategic usability: introducing usability into organisations. In: CHI '97 Extended Abstracts on Human Factors in Computing Systems, CHI EA 1997, pp. 156–157. Association for Computing Machinery, New York (1997). https://doi.org/10.1145/1120212.1120320
5. Bornoe, N., Stage, J.: Active involvement of software developers in usability engineering: two small-scale case studies. In: Bernhaupt, R., Dalvi, G., Joshi, A., K. Balkrishan, D., O'Neill, J., Winckler, M. (eds.) INTERACT 2017. LNCS, vol. 10516, pp. 159–168. Springer, Cham (2017). https://doi.org/10.1007/978-3-319-68059-0_10
6. Brhel, M., Meth, H., Maedche, A., Werder, K.: Exploring principles of user-centered agile software development: a literature review. Inf. Softw. Technol. **61**, 163–181 (2015)
7. Buis, E.G., E., Ashby, S.R., Kouwenberg, K.P.A.: Increasing the UX maturity level of clients: a study of best practices in an agile environment. Inf. Softw. Technol.**154**, 107086 (2023). https://doi.org/10.1016/j.infsof.2022.107086
8. Cajander, Å., Larusdottir, M., Geiser, J.L.: UX professionals' learning and usage of UX methods in agile. Inf. Softw. Technol. **151**, 107005 (2022). https://doi.org/10.1016/j.infsof.2022.107005
9. Campbell, D.T., Stanley, J.C.: Experimental and quasi-experimental designs for research. Ravenio books (2015)
10. Chamberlain, S., Sharp, H., Maiden, N., Hall, W.: Towards a framework for integrating agile development and user-centred design. In: Extreme Programming and Agile Processes in Software Engineering. XP 2006. LNCS, vol. 4044. Springer, Heidelberg (2006). https://doi.org/10.1007/11774129
11. Choma, J., Guerra, E.M., Alvaro, A., Pereira, R., Zaina, L.: Influences of UX factors in the Agile UX context of software startups. Inf. Softw. Technol. **152**, 107041 (2022)
12. Convertino, G., Frishberg, N.: Why agile teams fail without UX research. Commun. ACM **60**(9), 35–37 (2017)
13. De Bruin, T., Rosemann, M., Freeze, R., Kaulkarni, U.: Understanding the main phases of developing a maturity assessment model. In: Australasian Conference on Information Systems (ACIS), pp. 8–19. Australasian Chapter of the Association for Information Systems (2005)
14. Earthy, J.: Usability maturity model: Human centredness scale. INUSE Project Deliverable D **5**, 1–34 (1998)

15. Fraser, J., Plewes, S.: Applications of a UX maturity model to influencing HF best practices in technology centric companies-Lessons from Edison. Procedia Manuf. **3**, 626–631 (2015)
16. Friedland, L.: Culture Eats UX strategy for breakfast. Interactions **26**(5), 78–81 (2019). https://doi.org/10.1145/3344947
17. Garcia, A., Silva da Silva, T., Selbach Silveira, M.: Artifacts for agile user-centered design: a systematic mapping. In: Proceedings of the 50th Hawaii International Conference on System Sciences (2017)
18. Gilbert, D., Fischer, H., Röder, D.: UX at the Right Level - Appropriately Plan the UX Expertise Using the PUXMM - A UX Maturity Model for Projects. i-com **20**(1), 105–113 (2021). https://doi.org/10.1515/icom-2020-0029
19. Hassenzahl, M.: The thing and I: understanding the relationship between user and product. In: Funology, pp. 31–42. Springer, Dordrecht (2003). https://doi.org/10.1007/1-4020-2967-5_4
20. Hinderks, A., Mayo, F.J.D., Thomaschewski, J., Escalona, M.J.: Approaches to manage the user experience process in agile software development: a systematic literature review. Inf. Softw. Technol. **150**, 106957 (2022)
21. Iacono, J., Brown, A., Holtham, C.: Research methods-a case example of participant observation. Electron. J. Bus. Res. Methods **7**(1), 39–46 (2009)
22. ISO 9241–210:2019: Ergonomics of human-system interaction - Part 210: Human-centred design for interactive systems. Standard, International Organization for Standardization, Geneva, CH (2019)
23. Jokela, T., Abrahamsson, P.: Modelling usability capability – introducing the dimensions. In: Bomarius, F., Oivo, M. (eds.) PROFES 2000. LNCS, vol. 1840, pp. 73–87. Springer, Heidelberg (2000). https://doi.org/10.1007/978-3-540-45051-1_10
24. Jones, A., Thoma, V.: Determinants for successful agile collaboration between UX designers and software developers in a complex organisation. Int. J. Hum.-Comput. Interact. **35**(20), 1914–1935 (2019). https://doi.org/10.1080/10447318.2019.1587856
25. Jurca, G., Hellmann, T.D., Maurer, F.: Integrating agile and user-centered design: a systematic mapping and review of evaluation and validation studies of agile-UX. In: Proceedings - 2014 Agile Conference, AGILE 2014, pp. 24–32 (2014). https://doi.org/10.1109/AGILE.2014.17
26. Kashfi, P., Feldt, R., Nilsson, A.: Integrating UX principles and practices into software development organizations: a case study of influencing events. J. Syst. Softw. **154**(C), 37–58 (2019). https://doi.org/10.1016/j.jss.2019.03.066
27. Kashfi, P., Kuusinen, K., Feldt, R.: Stakeholder Involvement: A Success Factor for Achieving Better UX Integration (2016). https://doi.org/10.48550/ARXIV.1610.04774
28. Kashfi, P., Nilsson, A., Feldt, R.: Integrating User eXperience practices into software development processes: implications of the UX characteristics. PeerJ Comput. Sci. **3** (2017). https://doi.org/10.7717/peerj-cs.130
29. Kieffer, S., Ghouti, A., Macq, B.: The agile UX development lifecycle: combining formative usability and agile methods. In: Proceedings of the 50th Hawaii International Conference on System Sciences, pp. 577–586 (2017). https://doi.org/10.24251/HICSS.2017.070
30. Kieffer, S., Rukonić, L., Kervyn De Meerendré, V., Vanderdonckt, J.: A process reference model for UX. CCIS **1**, 128–152 (2020). https://doi.org/10.1007/978-3-030-41590-7

31. Kieffer, S., Rukonić, L., Kervyn de Meerendré, V., Vanderdonckt, J.: Specification of a UX process reference model towards the strategic planning of UX activities. In: Proceedings of the 14th International Joint Conference on Computer Vision, Imaging and Computer Graphics Theory and Applications - HUCAPP, pp. 74–85. INSTICC, SciTePress (2019). https://doi.org/10.5220/0007693600740085

32. Kieffer, S., Vanderdonckt, J.: STRATUS: a questionnaire for strategic usability assessment. In: Proceedings of the 31st Annual ACM Symposium on Applied Computing, pp. 205–212. ACM (2016). https://doi.org/10.1145/2851613.2851912

33. Kuusinen, K.: Task allocation between UX specialists and developers in agile software development projects. In: Abascal, J., Barbosa, S., Fetter, M., Gross, T., Palanque, P., Winckler, M. (eds.) INTERACT 2015. LNCS, vol. 9298, pp. 27–44. Springer, Cham (2015). https://doi.org/10.1007/978-3-319-22698-9_3

34. Lacerda, T.C., von Wangenheim, C.G.: Systematic literature review of usability capability/maturity models. Comput. Stand. Interfaces 55, 95–105 (2018). https://doi.org/10.1016/j.csi.2017.06.001

35. Law, E.L.C., Lárusdóttir, M.K.: Whose experience do we care about? analysis of the fitness of scrum and kanban to user experience. Int. J. Hum.-Comput. Interact. 31(9), 584–602 (2015). https://doi.org/10.1080/10447318.2015.1065693

36. MacDonald, C.M.: "It takes a village": on UX librarianship and building UX capacity in libraries. J. Libr. Adm. 57(2), 194–214 (2017). https://doi.org/10.1080/01930826.2016.1232942

37. MacDonald, C.M., Sosebee, J., Srp, A.: A framework for assessing organizational user experience (UX) capacity. Int. J. Hum.-Comput. Interact. 38(11), 1064–1080 (2022). https://doi.org/10.1080/10447318.2021.1979811

38. Maguire, M.: Methods to support human-centred design. Int. J. Hum Comput Stud. 55(4), 587–634 (2001). https://doi.org/10.1006/ijhc.2001.0503

39. Mahlke, S.: User experience of interaction with technical systems. Berlin Technical University (2008)

40. Nielsen, J., Berger, J., Gilutz, S., Whitenton, K.: Return on investment (ROI) for usability. Nielsen Norman Group (2013)

41. Øvad, T., Larsen, L.B.: The prevalence of UX design in agile development processes in industry. In: Proceedings of the 2015 Agile Conference, AGILE 2015, pp. 40–49. IEEE Computer Society, USA (2015). https://doi.org/10.1109/Agile.2015.13

42. Peres, A.L., Da Silva, T., Silva, F.S., Soares, F.F., Rosemberg, C., Romero, S.: Agileux model: towards a reference model on integrating UX in developing software using agile methodologies. In: 2014 Agile Conference, pp. 61–63. IEEE (2014)

43. Persson, J.S., Bruun, A., Lárusdóttir, M.K., Nielsen, P.A.: Agile software development and UX design: a case study of integration by mutual adjustment. Inf. Softw. Technol. 152, 107059 (2022). https://doi.org/10.1016/j.infsof.2022.107059

44. Pillay, N., Wing, J.: Agile UX: Integrating good UX development practices in Agile. In: 2019 Conference on Information Communications Technology and Society, ICTAS 2019, pp. 1–6 (2019). https://doi.org/10.1109/ICTAS.2019.8703607

45. Salah, D., Silva, T., Cairns, P., Salah, D., Salah, D., Petrie, H., Paige, R.F.: Towards a Framework for Integrating User Centred Design and Agile Software Development Processes. Proc. Irish CHI 2009 (2009)

46. Seffah, A., Metzker, E.: The obstacles and myths of usability and software engineering. Commun. ACM 47(12), 71–76 (2004)

47. Smyth, J.D.: The SAGE Handbook of Survey Methodology, chap. Designing questions and questionnaire. SAGE Publications Ltd (2016). https://doi.org/10.4135/9781473957893

48. Staggers, N., Rodney, M.: Promoting usability in organizations with a new health usability model: implications for nursing informatics. In: NI 2012 : 11th International Congress on Nursing Informatics, June 23–27, 2012, Montreal, Canada. International Congress in Nursing Informatics (11th : 2012 : Montreal, Quebec), vol. 2012, pp. 396–396. American Medical Informatics Association (2012)
49. Sy, D.: Adapting usability investigations for agile user-centered design. J. Usability Stud. **2**(3), 112–132 (2007). https://doi.org/10.5555/2835547.2835549

# Model-Based UI Design and Testing

# AdaptReview: Towards Effective Video Review Using Text Summaries and Concept Maps

Shan Zhang[1]([✉])[iD], Yang Chen[2][iD], Nuwan Janaka[1][iD], Chloe Haigh[1][iD],
Shengdong Zhao[1][iD], and Wei Tsang Ooi[3][iD]

[1] NUS-HCI Lab, National University of Singapore, Singapore 117416, Singapore
{nuwanj,zhaosd}@comp.nus.edu.sg, shan_zhang@u.nus.edu,
chai915@aucklanduni.ac.nz
[2] College of Design and Engineering, National University of Singapore, Singapore
117575, Singapore
cyang@nus.edu.sg
[3] Computer Science Department, National University of Singapore,
Singapore 117416, Singapore
ooiwt@comp.nus.edu.sg
https://www.nus-hci.org/

**Abstract.** Video review is commonly performed by learners to clarify
or make up for the content they have missed. However, it is not well
supported in the current video learning environment. In this paper, we
investigated the design of techniques to facilitate effective video review.
Through a preliminary study, we observed learners' review behaviors,
identified their challenges, and derived three design goals. We then
designed two review techniques, concept map based review (CMReview) and text summary based review (TSReview). Evaluation studies
were conducted to understand learners' post-review learning performance
and review experiences using both techniques on short and long videos.
Results showed similar learning performance for short videos across both
techniques, but CMReview improved understanding for long videos and
was preferred by most users. We conclude by discussing implications for
integrating with current video learning platforms.

**Keywords:** Video review · Concept map · Text summary

## 1 Introduction

Learning requires attention, but video learners can easily lose their attention
due to both external and internal factors such as external distractions [14] and
mind-wandering [16]. These factors not only cause learners to miss important
information but also hinder their understanding of the learning materials. As a
result, video review has become a popular study technique among learners to
mitigate concentration loss [26,42].

© The Author(s), under exclusive license to Springer Nature Switzerland AG 2023
J. Abdelnour Nocera et al. (Eds.): INTERACT 2023, LNCS 14143, pp. 461–481, 2023.
https://doi.org/10.1007/978-3-031-42283-6_25

During video review, learners revisit specific parts of the video material. This process differs from their initial viewing (first watch) in terms of learning goals and behaviors, as well as the challenges they faced. For instance, learners tend to engage more in searching behaviors during review [42]. Additionally, they may lack the meta-awareness to recognize when and where they have missed content [38]. While much research has been done on ways to improve the video learning experience during the initial viewing [30,41,51], less attention has been given to the development of effective techniques for video review.

In this paper, we explored the design, development, and evaluation of techniques for video review. We began with a preliminary study where we observed learners' review behaviors and interviewed them about the challenges they faced. Based on these results, we derived three design goals for designing an effective review technique: overview support, navigation support and attention-awareness.

To guide our design, we applied the Cognitive Theory of Multimedia Learning (CTML) principles [24,37]. Following the signaling principle and segmenting principle, we designed two review techniques: CMReview and TSReview. They provide different formats of overview support, while sharing a similar design in navigation support by hyperlinking each concept or sentence to video timestamp. They also incorporate attention-awareness by highlighting missed content for focused review.

We then evaluated the effectiveness of two review techniques in reviewing *short* (6 min) and *long* (12 min) videos. Through an empirical study with 20 participants, we showed that CMReview improved understanding of learning content of over 30% for *long* videos and were preferred by most participants. However, for *short* videos, CMReview and TSReview share the same level of post-review learning outcome.

Based on the findings, we discussed the design implications for how video reviewing systems can adapt to different lengths of videos while considering the cost benefit trade-off. For learning longer videos, where users encounter a larger amount of information, using CMReview to review can significantly improve learners' understanding of the overall video content, and avoid the cognitive overload. For 6-min or shorter videos, TSReview is recommended to improve learners' learning performance after review, and can also be easily integrated with existing video learning platforms.

The contributions of this paper are threefold: 1) Enhanced our understanding of video reviewing through a preliminary qualitative study. 2) Designed, implemented and empirically investigated the two review techniques on reviewing *short* and *long* videos. 3) Provided design implications for existing video learning platforms and future systems to support effective video review.

## 2   Related Work

As an integral component of the broader scope of video learning, video review has been related to subjects of various research efforts. We have categorized previous research into three categories detailed below and discussed how they are relevant to our research.

## 2.1    Improving Video Learning Experiences for Overall Learners

To provide a generally improved video learning experience for learners, some previous researchers often focused on refining the design of video learning material itself, such as adding animations [21], exploring different ways of filming techniques [10], and considering diverse video formats [19]. Meanwhile, some other researchers have concentrated on enhancing interactions between learners and video learning materials. These efforts range from incorporating prompting questions in videos [43], introducing teaching annotations throughout the video [48], to using interactive features that offer students more control [52]. While their practice might not directly apply for the video review context, they all align with the foundational learning theories for multimedia learning such as the Cognitive Load Theory (CLT) [6] and the CTML design principles. In this paper, we adhere to these theories to guide our design.

## 2.2    Providing Personalized Interventions to Individual Learners

Our research also corresponds with previous work in providing personalized review content to learners, which forms part of the broad category of attention-aware systems in video learning [9,34]. These works focused on monitoring learners' attention and offering interventions to enhance their attention to optimize video learning. Some interventions are dispatched in real-time when the attention lapses are detected [15,25,31]; others suggest the segments where learners lost their attention the most [46] or indicate the most challenging part for learners to review [32]. Although they are successful in some respects, the primary focus remains on managing attention lapses rather than facilitating learners' video review. Our research began with understanding learners' review behaviors and the challenges they encountered in order to design the most effective technique for video review.

## 2.3    Concept Map in Video Learning

The concept map is a well-established model for organizing and representing knowledge [29], with labeled nodes representing concepts and labeled links representing relationships among these concepts. The process of creating a concept map can facilitate meaningful learning [28] and has been employed in classroom learning environments for decades [47]. In video learning, previous works have primarily focused on facilitating the creation of concept maps from video content [13,53], while some have demonstrated that displaying a structured concept map can reinforce learners' understanding of video content [22]. In this paper, we also utilize the hierarchical structure of the concept map, but we combine it with other features to specifically target for the video review scenario.

# 3    Study 1: Understanding Learners' Video Reviewing Behaviors

In this study, we sought to complement existing research by depicting a granular understanding of learners' video reviewing behaviors and their challenges in reviewing video content. To this end, we aim to answer the following research questions:

RQ1. *How do learners review video content?*

RQ2. *What challenges do learners face while reviewing?*

To answer the research questions listed above, we conducted a preliminary study with 12 participants to understand their behaviors and underlying reasons during video review.

## 3.1    Study Design and Procedure

In this study, participants watched learning videos from introductory medical and biological courses of Khan Academy. These topics were chosen for their inclusion of factual knowledge [27], which aligns with our learning measures of interest. To encourage participant review and simulate attention lapses and information loss during video learning, we replaced portions of the original video content with relaxing music videos. Approximately 33% of the video content was intentionally blocked, aligning with previous studies on attention lapse ranges [23,33,54]. While attention loss can stem from various factors and result in different outcomes, we chose to simulate the complete absence of content in these portions to emphasize the need for thorough review. We avoided introducing additional tasks like color counting tasks [35] to prevent mental fatigue or cognitive overload, given the high cognitive load already demanded by our study. The use of blocked content effectively balanced task complexity and participants' ability to complete the session. Relaxing music was selected to minimize the influence of emotional arousal on learning performance [49]. Smooth continuity was ensured with 1-second transition effects between the music video clips and the original video clip.

For this study, we chose a 14 min 56 s video length, within the range of previous studies [3]. This duration allowed sufficient observation of user behavior. The video was modified by blocking thirteen segments ($1 \times 1$ min, $4 \times 30$ s, $4 \times 20$ s, $4 \times 10$ s, totaling 5 min) and replacing them with relaxing music of the same duration. The shortest blocked segment was set at 10 s, as shorter periods do not include meaningful information based on the video subtitles.

**Participants and Apparatus.** We recruited 12 participants (6 males, 6 females, age range: 19–31) from the local university community. All students were regular video learners and had full working proficiency in English. None of them majored in biology-related fields, to minimize the potential bias of prior knowledge in relation to the selected video materials. Each participant (in all studies) was compensated $\approx$ USD 7.25/h for their time.

**Procedure.** The study was conducted in a one-to-one, face-to-face setting. Participants were asked to watch the modified video without interacting or taking notes. After watching, they were instructed to review the original video to make up for any missing information. They were allowed to interact with the video player using the mouse or keyboard, such as pausing, rewinding, and fast-forwarding, etc. The review process was limited to 7 min, which is less than half the length of the video. Participants were informed that they needed to fill out a questionnaire testing their learning performance after reviewing and that they wouldn't be able to complete the review if they only played the video at 2× speed. An experimenter observed and recorded participant behaviors to minimize biases. Semi-structured interviews were conducted post-study to inquire about participants' experiences and explanations for their behaviors. The review process was video-recorded while interview was audio-recorded. The entire study lasted approximately 40 min.

## 3.2   Results

The observation notes and transcribed interview scripts were analyzed thematically following Braun and Clarke [4].

## 3.3   RQ1: How Do Learners Review Video Content?

The majority of participants (10/12) employed the "skimming and pausing" approach, progressing through the video content sequentially during their initial review. Conversely, two participants initiated skimming from the middle, for perceiving the latter half as more crucial. Through skimming, they swiftly identified the "missed", "difficult", and "forgotten" content, stopped skimming and watched those segments attentively. They utilized fast forwarding and increased playback speed for skimming. After completing the first round of review, they adopted the "jumping and pausing" strategy for subsequent rounds, navigating the timeline to locate specific content for further clarification.

Contrary to our expectations, participants did not use "jumping" during the first review due to two reasons. First, jumping to the relative timeline location of the blocked content was very difficult as participants could not remember what they had missed and/or the location of the missed content, "I have very little idea on what I have missed (P5)", "I know that I missed hemoglobin. But I don't know where it is. I'm afraid of overshooting if I don't start from the beginning (P6)". Second, jumping to the relative timeline location could only provide scattered information, whereas skimming from the beginning provides contextual information for understanding the content as a whole, "If I directly jump to the part I missed, I could not understand anything. I could not connect it with the information I got the first time. (P3)"

## 3.4   RQ2: What Challenges Do Learners Face While Reviewing?

Participants highlighted two main challenges during video reviewing for learning. First, the video learning environment lacked the navigation aid at the concept level, making it hard to find concepts on demand. For example, when P6 expressed that he would like to check the part about hemoglobin again after he finished reviewing the video content for the first time, "(The second time), I go to the nearby place and search from there. But it's still difficult for me to locate where it is." This difficulty was particularly exacerbated due to the lack of an overview where they could easily find related concepts that could act as a catalog.

Second, they could not identify the missed concepts quickly, which tally with attention theories which posit people lack meta-awareness in realizing their inattention states like mind-wandering [39,40]. Participants expressed their desire for the system to highlight the specific parts they had missed, "I hope that system can flag where I missed (P5)".

### 3.5   Design Goals for Techniques to Support Video Reviewing

Based on our analysis, we identified three design goals for designing techniques to support video review.

**D1:** Provide a concept overview of the video content to facilitate understanding of context (overview support).

**D2:** Provide concept-level navigation to facilitate easy navigation of video content (navigation support).

**D3:** Highlight the content where learners lost attention to help them identify which content to review (attention-awareness).

## 4   System Design

With the goals of our design in mind, we looked to CTML theory [24] for guidance. CTML, inspired by CLT, offers established principles for managing cognitive workload during multimedia learning. Specifically, two principles aligned well with our context: signaling and segmenting [24,36].

- The **signaling** principle posits that people learn better when instructional materials include cues that **highlight** relevant elements or **organization** of the material.
- The **segmenting** principle posits that people learn better when multimedia content is delivered in user-paced **segments** rather than as a continuous unit.

D3 aligns directly with the segmenting principle, while D2 corresponds to the signaling principle's emphasis on highlighting relevant elements. As for D1, the **signaling** principle suggests two organizational formats: textual (e.g., text summary) and graphical (e.g., concept map) [37]. A text summary offers a preview of the material, aiding comprehension in multimedia reading [17]. On the other hand, a concept map is a visual representation [8,22] that organizes concepts and relationships. Both formats provide an overview of video content. Hence, we adopted these two formats, along with navigation support and attention aware-ness, to create two review techniques: Text Summary based Review (TSReview) and Concept Map based Review (CMReview).

It's important to note that while features like video transcripts on platforms like Khan Academy and timestamp links in video descriptions on YouTube sup-port signaling and segmentation, they differ fundamentally from the text sum-mary used in TSReview. Full text transcripts can overwhelm learners due to their volume, while timestamp links primarily focus on topics without provid-ing concept-level navigation. In contrast, a text summary serves as an advanced adaptation that strikes a balance between the sparsity of topic timestamp links and the density of transcripts.

## 4.1   Creating Text Summaries and Concept Maps

Two researchers (co-authors) collaborated to extract key conceptual elements (i.e., concept keywords and their relationships) from the video. For the text summary, they connected these elements to form concise and meaningful sen-tences, ranking them in chronological order. The same conceptual elements were used to construct the concept map, with concepts represented as nodes and rela-tionships as links. The nodes and links were organized hierarchically, following a knowledge hierarchy, with general concepts positioned at the top and more spe-cific ones at the bottom. This hierarchy facilitated a top-down and left-to-right reading flow [5]. The researchers also validated the concept equivalence between the concept map and text summary.

## 4.2   Converting to Review Techniques

In Fig. 1, the review techniques TSReview and CMReview are presented. These techniques are derived from the text summary and concept map, respectively, using the *segmenting* and *signaling* principles.

In the case of TSReview, the video content is segmented into summarized sen-tences. Each sentence is linked to the corresponding video timestamps, enabling users to selectively review specific segments. Missed content is highlighted in pink, following a rule of thumb of highlighting sentences with over 30% missed time. The choice of color considered clarity, opacity, and aesthetics. Similarly, CMReview follows a similar design, linking concepts to video timestamps and highlighting missed content in pink.

To enhance usability, during video playback, the current location is indicated by temporarily highlighting the corresponding sentence or concept in orange. Additionally, zoom in/out and pan functionalities are supported for both sys-tems.

**Development.** The systems were implemented using HTML, CSS, JavaScript, and the D3 library. Both systems consisted of a video player to display the video on the left and a canvas to display the corresponding content organization on the right. The concept map and text summary were written as JSON files and were preloaded into the system.

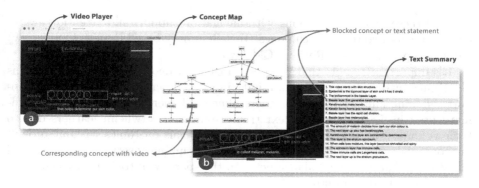

**Fig. 1.** Comparison between (a) CMReview and (b) TSReview. The two review techniques shared the similar design but differs in the organization format. Concepts/sentences where a learner missed certain content are highlighted in pink. The learner can click on the concept/sentence to navigate to the corresponding content, and the ongoing concept/sentence is highlighted in orange.

### 4.3    Study Design

While previous studies have shown some benefits in using non-linear concept maps, the map may grow larger as the video length increases. Hence, this study sought to compare the effects of two review techniques (CMReview, TSReview) in reviewing two different lengths (*short*, *long*) of videos. Specifically, we aim to investigate the following research question:

RQ3.*How do different review techniques affect learners' review experience and post-review learning outcome on different video lengths?*

RQ4.*Which review technique is most suitable for integrating with current video learning platforms?*

**Material Design.** Previous studies, such as Guo et al. [11], have advocated for an optimal video length of 6 min for MOOC platforms, noting that videos longer than 12 min result in significantly lower student engagement. This is consistent with the video length range adopted by online learning platforms like Coursera, which typically utilize video clips ranging from 5 to 10 min [1]. With the aim of designing review techniques that can be integrated into existing online video learning platforms, we chose to examine effective strategies for reviewing two distinct video lengths: relatively short videos ($\approx$ 6 min) and relatively long videos ($\approx$ 12 min).

We initially selected eight videos from Khan Academy, four of each specified duration, and piloted them to assess perceived difficulties using eight participants from a non-biology major. After removing videos with overlapping concepts or content that was overly complex or too simple, we ultimately selected two short 6-min videos ($V_{short-1}$: Epidermis, $V_{short-2}$: Micturition) and two 12-min *long* videos ($V_{long-1}$: Kawasaki disease, $V_{long-2}$: Stem cell) (Table 1).

Following the same process in *study 1* (Sect. 3.1), we modified the selected videos to have blocked content at random locations. For *short* videos, we blocked a total of 2 min of content ($2 \times 30$ s, $2 \times 20$ s, $2 \times 10$ s). For *long* videos, we blocked a total of 4 min of content ($4 \times 30$ s, $4 \times 20$ s, $4 \times 10$ s).

**Table 1.** Details of four selected videos. Original video source: khanacademymedi cine YouTube

| Videos | $V_{short-1}$ | $V_{short-2}$ | $V_{long-1}$ | $V_{long-2}$ |
|---|---|---|---|---|
| Perceived Difficulty | 4.91 | 4.83 | 5.91 | 6 |
| Number of concepts | 17 | 17 | 46 | 46 |
| Number of relationships | 16 | 15 | 51 | 49 |

**Design of Review Duration.** We piloted with 6 participants to determine the video review duration. As we blocked one-third of the content (Sect. 4.3), participants needed at least 2 min for the 6-min video and 4 min for the 12-min video to review all the blocked content. Thus, we instructed participants to review videos as efficiently as possible within the above duration but allowed them to take unlimited 30 s extensions if needed. Analyzing all participants' feedback, we settled with 3 min to review the *short* videos and 6 min to review the *long* videos.

### 4.4   Measures

To answer our research questions, we assessed learning performance through tests and gathered subjective ratings on learners' experiences.

**Learning Performance Tests.** We measured learning performance using Bloom's taxonomy [18], specifically focusing on remembering' (*recall* and *recognition*) and understanding' (*understanding*).

The *recall* test evaluated learners' ability to retrieve information from memory with little to no clues. Fill-in-the-blank questions were used, with maximum scores of 9 for *short* videos and 18 for *long* videos.

The *recognition* test assessed learners' ability to identify correct information from provided cues. Multiple-choice questions were used, with maximum scores of 6 for *short* videos and 12 for *long* videos.

The *understanding* test measured learners' synthesis abilities in organizing information. Long answer questions were used, requiring learners to provide examples, summaries, explanations, and comparisons. Maximum scores were 13 for *short* videos and 25 for *long* videos.

**Grading.** For *recall* and *recognition*, each correct answer was awarded 1 point. We verified the spelling of participants' answers using the Levenshtein distance [20][1]. If the distance exceeded half the length of the word, no points were awarded; otherwise, 1 point was given. For instance, if the word "ocean" (word length = 5) was misspelled as "oecan", 1 point was still awarded as the two words are 2 units apart, which is less than half the length of the word.

For *understanding*, we adopted both semantic-level and character-level analyses from prior literature [45]. The semantic-level analysis awarded one point for each correct knowledge statement, while the character-level analysis utilized the Levenshtein distance as an additional measure to capture variations in spelling or phrasing. Each correct knowledge point received 1 mark cumulatively, and no points were deducted for incorrect or missing points.

**Subjective Rating.** Given that cognitive load can impact learning [44], we measured perceived cognitive load using the NASA-TLX [12]. Additionally, perceived behaviors: *Perceived help in Remembering* ('This technique [CMReview/TSReview] helped me to remember the video content'), *Perceived help in Understanding* ('This technique helped me to understand the video content'), and *Perceived help in Navigation* ('This technique helped me to easily navigate to any specific segments of the video') were collected using 7-point Likert scales (1 = Strongly Disagree, 7 = Strongly Agree) to compare the perception of each review technique. Additionally, the *Likeness* ('I think that I would like to use this technique frequently.') was also collected using a 7-point Likert Scale to understand the usability of the review technique [2].

### 4.5 Procedure

Figure 2 shows the experiment procedure with counterbalanced orders of review techniques and increasing video length. On Day 1, participants signed consent, familiarized themselves with CMReview and TSReview, and completed demographic questionnaires. The formal experiment session began with instructions to watch and review videos for maximized learning outcomes. They watched the modified $V_{short-1}$ for 6 min and reviewed the original $V_{short-1}$ with assigned review technique for 3 min. Immediate tests on *understanding*, *recall*, and *recognition* followed. Participants completed a questionnaire on perceived task load and then repeated the process using the other review technique on $V_{short-2}$. A post-questionnaire and semi-structured interview captured their experiences. The *long* videos were scheduled for Day 2 to control experiment length and reduce fatigue. On Day 8 and Day 9, delayed tests were administered for *short* and *long* videos. Participants were aware of their involvement on Day 8 and 9 but were unaware of the specific content. The experiment lasted $\approx$ 1–1.25 h on Day 1 and 2, and around 20–40 min on Day 8 and 9.

---

[1] Levenshtein distance calculates the minimum number of insertions, deletions, and substitutions needed to correct the spelling.

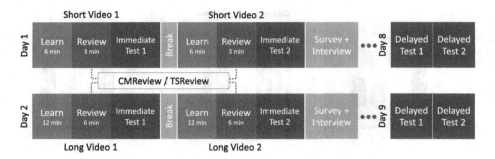

**Fig. 2.** Experiment procedure used in *study 3*. The in-lab experiment was conducted on two consecutive days (Day 1 and Day 2), each for *short* and *long* videos. The delayed tests were administered online after seven days (Day 8 and Day 9).

### 4.6  Participants

We recruited 20 participants P1-20 (11 males, 9 females, age range: 19–26) from the local university community. None of them majored in biology-related fields, the same as in *study 1* (Sect. 3.1).

## 5  Results

As the *short* and *long* videos were administered on multiple days and had different maximum scores, paired samples Student t-test or Wilcoxon signed-rank tests (used in case of violation of normal distribution assumptions) were used to analyze the differences of each review technique. The normality was tested using the Shapiro-Wilk test.

### 5.1  Results of Short Videos

Overall, no significant ($p > 0.05$) differences were observed in terms of objective learning outcomes when reviewing *short* videos; however, subjective ratings showed a preference for CMReview.

**Learning Outcome.** As shown in Fig. 3, there were no statistically significant differences between review technique in terms of immediate and delayed *recognition*, *recall*, and *understanding*. This indicates that both CMReview and TSReview help learners to achieve similar levels of learning performance in remembering and understanding video material during review.

**Subjective Preference.** There were significant effects of review technique (Fig. 4) on *Perceived help in Understanding*(CMReview: $5.80 \pm 0.95$; TSReview: $4.25 \pm 1.07$, $p < 0.001$), and *Likeness* (CMReview = $5.75 \pm 1.02$, TSReview = $4.55 \pm 1.36$, $p = 0.02$), indicating that participants felt that CMReview helped

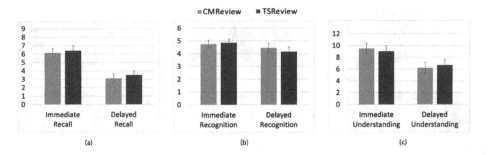

Fig. 3. Learning performance of 20 participants for *short* video review using the CMReview and the TSReview. Individual charts represent the immediate and delayed scores for *recall*, *recognition*, and *understanding*. The error bars represent the standard errors of the data.

them to understand the content better, and as a result, it was more preferred. There were no significant differences in *Perceived help in Remembering*, *Perceived help in Navigation*, and NASA-TLX indices. This result suggests a discrepancy between *Perceived help in Understanding* and actual learning performance on *understanding* tests. We delved into the participants' interviews to find out why, and will discuss this further in Sect. 7.

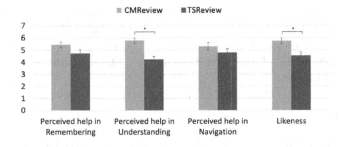

Fig. 4. Subjective Rating comparison between the CMReview and the TSReview of 20 participants in reviewing *short* videos.

## 5.2 Results of Long Videos

Overall, we observed significant ($p < 0.05$) differences in objective learning outcomes as well as subjective ratings, where CMReview performed better than TSReview for *long* videos.

**Learning Outcomes.** As shown in Fig. 5, CMReview showed significant ($p < 0.01$) improvement over TSReview in terms of *understanding*, but not ($p > 0.05$) in *recall* nor *recognition*.

For both immediate and delayed tests, CMReview had significantly higher *understanding* than TSReview, indicating that CMReview is able to have an immediate and lasting effect in helping learners better understand the video content (immediate *understanding*: CMReview = 15.85 ± 5.91, TSReview = 12.15 ± 5.4, mean improvement = 30.5%, $p = 0.006$; delayed *understanding*: CMReview = 12.20±6.39, TSReview = 9.05±6.13, mean improvement = 34.8%, $p = 0.008$).

As there were no significant differences ($p > 0.05$) in *recall* or *recognition* for both immediate and delayed tests, CMReview and TSReview help learners to achieve similar performance in remembering.

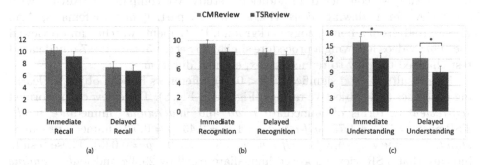

**Fig. 5.** Immediate and delayed *recall*, *recognition*, and *understanding* scores of 20 participants using the CMReview and the TSReview for reviewing *long* videos. The error bars represent the standard errors of the data.

**Subjective Ratings.** Overall, as shown in Fig. 6, we found significant differences in almost all measures. Specifically, there was a significant difference in the Mental Demand index in NASA-TLX scores (Fig. 6a, CMReview = 79.25±17.49, TSReview = 84.25 ± 12.38, $p = 0.038$) but not in other indices. Moreover, there

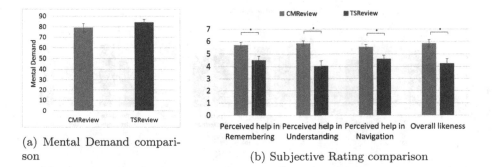

(a) Mental Demand comparison

(b) Subjective Rating comparison

**Fig. 6.** Mental Demand and Subjective Ratings between the CMReview and the TSReview of 20 participants in reviewing *long* videos.

474    S. Zhang et al.

were significant differences in *Perceived help in Remembering* (CMReview = $5.7 \pm 0.98$ TSReview = $4.5 \pm 1.40$, $p = 0.008$), *Perceived help in Understanding* (CMReview = $5.95 \pm 0.93$; TSReview = $4.05 \pm 1.82$, $p = 0.001$), *Perceived help in Navigation* (CMReview = $5.55 \pm 0.83$, TSReview = $4.6 \pm 1.35$, $p = 0.020$), and *Likeness* (CMReview = $5.85 \pm 1.27$, TSReview = $4.25 \pm 1.68$, $p = 0.004$).

# 6  Additional Study: Comparing TSReview with self-review

To validate the effectiveness of our review techniques compared to self-review (*self-review*), we conducted an additional study. We compared TSReview with self-review for reviewing *short* videos with 12 participants (6 females, Age: $21.83 \pm 1.90$) from a non-biology background. Participants watched and reviewed the *short* videos following a procedure similar to Sect. 4.5, with the 7-day delayed test changed to 3 day to reduce the experiment duration.

The results showed significant ($p < 0.05$) differences in both objective learning outcomes and subjective ratings (Fig. 7 and Fig. 8). TSReview outperformed *self-review* in terms of immediate *recall* and *understand* (immediate *recall*: TSReview = $5.92 \pm 1.73$, *self-review* = $4.58 \pm 2.43$, $p = 0.039$; immediate *understand*: TSReview = $8 \pm 3.44$, *self-review* = $5.92 \pm 2.91$, $p = 0.035$). These results indicate that TSReview improved immediate *recall* by 29.3% and *understanding* by 35.1% compared to *self-review*.

Similarly, for delayed tests, TSReview had significantly higher *recall* and *understand* than *self-review* (delayed *recall*: TSReview = $4.83 \pm 1.85$, *self-review* = $3.58 \pm 2.54$, $p = 0.045$; delayed *understand*: TSReview = $7.67 \pm 3.42$, *self-review* = $5.75 \pm 3.39$, $p = 0.032$). These results indicate that TSReview can significantly improve learners' delayed *recall* by 34.9% and *understanding* by 33.3% compared with *self-review*.

For subjective ratings, there were significant differences on *Perceived help in Remembering* (TSReview = $5.92 \pm 0.9$, *self-review* = $4 \pm 1.13$, $p < 0.001$),

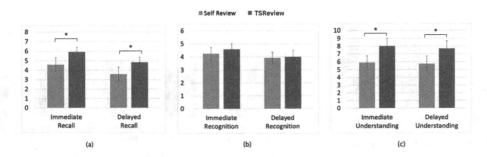

**Fig. 7.** Immediate and delayed *recall*, *recognition*, and *understanding* scores of 12 participants using the *self-review* and the TSReview for reviewing *short* videos. The error bars represent the standard errors.

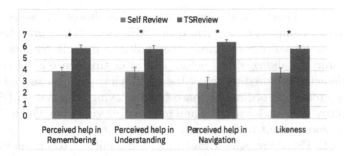

**Fig. 8.** Subjective Rating comparison between the *self-review* and the TSReview of 12 participants in reviewing *short* videos.

*Perceived help in Understanding* (TSReview = 5.83 ± 1.03, *self-review* = 3.92 ± 1.44, $p < 0.001$), *Perceived help in Navigation* (TSReview = 6.42 ± 0.67, *self-review* = 3 ± 1.71, $p = 0.002$), and *Likeness* (TSReview = 5.83 ± 0.94, *self-review* = 3.83 ± 1.40, $p < 0.001$). No significant differences were found for NASA-TLX indices. These results demonstrate the effectiveness of our review techniques.

## 7  Discussion

We now answer our initial research questions based on the study results.

### 7.1  RQ3: Review Experience and Post-review Learning Outcome on Short and Long Videos

Based on our results, both CMReview and TSReview produced similar learning outcomes in terms of *remembering* and *understanding* when learners reviewed *short* videos. In contrast, when reviewing longer videos, CMReview was more effective than TSReview in helping learners understand the content.

This can be attributed to the hierarchical structure of CMReview which reduces the cognitive load of reviewing longer videos. According to the CLT, there are three types of cognitive load during learning: intrinsic load (induced by the learning content itself), extraneous load (induced by material outside of content), and germane load (induced by learners' efforts in building a deeper understanding) [36,44]. In our experiment, while increasing video length imposed an extra intrinsic load on understanding *long* videos, CMReview relieved the extraneous load by providing a graphical representation that matches the knowledge structure, thus resulting in lower mental demand for reviewing.

This benefit of CMReview was also apparent in subjective ratings when reviewing *long* videos, where it was perceived as more helpful for remembering, understanding, and navigating information, thus preferred by most participants (16/20) than TSReview. As P12 remarked, "even though long videos were difficult to process as compared to short videos, it [CMReview] helped me quickly grasp the video flow... and easy to navigate through branches."

However, not all participants appreciated the benefits of concise *concepts* and associated relationships (i.e., branches) in CMReview. While branches made it "easy to see the breakdown of video", they failed to provide "context like what he [the lecturer] is talking about before and after this concept". Furthermore, the visual elements required to depict the CMReview (e.g., boxes, lines, arrows) sacrificed "a great deal of limited space for displaying information (P7)". This was particularly the case for lengthy and informative videos, in which CMReview needed to be zoomed out to fit the visible viewpoint.

In contrast, TSReview which was organized similarly to online video transcripts, could provide a concise summary in a more compact way, which was preferred by the remaining (4/20) participants. Yet, as expected, too many details in a long video can result in the textual presentation becoming "wordy", which made some participants feel "overwhelmed and exhausted", prompting them to appreciate CMReview more.

It is interesting to note that the perceived difference between two review techniques was mitigated by the reduced video length. Although CMReview was still preferred over TSReview, participants regarded the text summary as almost equally helpful for navigation and remembering. As P3 mentioned, "Text summary is like the YouTube timestamp annotation, which I am more familiar with". Similarly, P14 mentioned that "it [TSReview] is more like notes taken in class that I used to prepare for final exams". These findings suggested the potential value of TSReview, if other design parameters (e.g., length/amount of information) could be considered, as discussed in the subsequent section (Sect. 7.2).

## 7.2   RQ4: Which Review Technique is Most Suitable for Integrating with Current Video Learning Platforms?

The above empirical showed that for *long* video learning, CMReview may be a better option as it significantly improved learners' understanding of the content and was preferred by the majority of participants. However, since *short* videos (i.e., 6 min) are widely used in current video learning platforms [11], it remains unclear which review technique is optimal for use, as both produced similar learning outcomes.

Here, we consulted educators' perspectives by conducting a focus group interview with four professional instructors (T1–T4), who have more than 3 years of experience in creating content for MOOC courses, by demonstrating the two proposed review techniques to provoke an initial discussion. The educators brought in an important perspective: cost-effectiveness. Due to their busy schedules, cost-effectiveness is often the single most important criterion when considering adopting a new technique into their teaching. That is, if two techniques have similar effects, the one that's much simpler and easy to integrate will have a much higher chance of getting adopted "efficiency and cost effectiveness is always an important concern when choosing which technique to use in my teaching (T4)". When comparing TSReview and CMReview, all instructors mentioned that they were leaning towards TSReview for most educational videos as it was "much easier to produce (T1)" and "would consider using CMReview only for some of the most important and complex topics (T3)". Taken together, we suggest TSReview as the most suited review technique to use in current video learning platforms, as it achieves a better balance between similar learning gains (effectiveness) and ease of production (cost).

## 7.3    Adapting Review Techniques for Current Video Learning Platforms

**Adaptability and Effectiveness of Review Techniques.** Looking forward, we envision an adaptive reviewing system that could be seamlessly integrated with current video learning platforms to optimize learning performance. Here, we provided an example by adopting our two review techniques into Coursera (see Fig. 9). In particular, for long or complex video learning, where learners suffer from an extraneous mental load due to the intensive amount of information, we recommend using concept maps as a better option by providing a graphical presentation of concise concepts with suggested relationships (see Fig. 9b). For short video learning, where the knowledge is less intensive and easier to digest, TSReview is a potential alternative in maintaining the learning effects and be easily created and incorporated (see Fig. 9a). It is important to note that, although in our studies, video lengths was identified as a key determinant of cognitive load, other factors identified as contributing to mental demand in video learning should also be considered, including perceived difficulty [32], the familiarity [7] of learning material.

 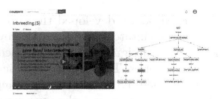

(a) A mock-up of Coursera interface integrated with TSReview

(b) A mock-up of Coursera interface integrated with CMReview

**Fig. 9.** A mock-up of Coursera interface integrated with both review techniques

**Scalability of Review Techniques with Increasing Video Duration.** Our CMReview and TSReview results on short and long videos suggest that CMReview scales better as video duration increases from 6 to 12 min. We did not test longer videos, as they are not considered the optimal length adopted by current video learning platforms. However, even though our longer videos are 12 min in length, they were intentionally selected to include about 50 complex biological concepts, which is more than twice the number in the short 6-min videos (Table 1). The success of CMReview on these videos demonstrates its potential applicability to longer videos with an equivalent number of concepts. As the complexity of the concept map is likely to increase with video length, a potential solution could be to separate the information into multiple sub-maps, in line with Guo et al.'s [11] recommendation to break long videos into smaller segments for improved learning.

## 8    Limitation and Future Work

First, in our paper, we manually blocked some content to simulate learners' missing information due to attention lapses either from external distractions or internal mind-wandering. However, learners in our experiment could lose attention in other parts of the video content. Thus, in a realistic implementation, we need to capture such dynamic lapses using attention detection system (e.g., [50]) to identify the missed content. Considering that attention detection is not 100% accurate, catering to such inaccurate detection during review needs further investigation to verify its effects.

Second, although our results are significant, the sample size of participants is relatively small. Furthermore, our participants were all recruited from the local university community with an age range from 18 to 34. While this is a representative user group for video learning, how our findings apply to other user groups (e.g., K12 education) can be further tested in future studies.

## 9    Conclusion

In this work, we developed the two review techniques, CMReview and TSReview, to facilitate learners' video review. The two systems were designed following the design goals we identified in the preliminary formative study and CTML theories. Through the empirical studies, we demonstrate that CMReview outperformed TSReview in improving learners' understanding for *long* videos. While both reviewing techniques are effective, with the additional consideration of cost effectiveness, we recommend TSReview for reviewing videos with 6 min or less, CMReview for longer videos. By incorporating these reviewing techniques, we seek significant improvement in learning outcomes to mitigate the negative effects of mind wandering and unwanted distractions associated with today's online video learning activities.

## References

1. Coursera about clips. https://www.coursera.support/s/article/learner-000001749-About-clips?language=en_US. Accessed 11 Jun 2023
2. Bangor, A., Kortum, P., Miller, J.: Determining what individual SUS scores mean: adding an adjective rating scale. J. Usabil. Stud. 4(3), 114–123 (2009)
3. Berg, R., Brand, A., Grant, J., Kirk, J., Zimmermann, T.: Leveraging recorded mini-lectures to increase student learning. Online Classroom 14(2), 5–8 (2014)

4. Braun, V., Clarke, V.: Using thematic analysis in psychology. Qual. Res. Psychol. **3**(2), 77–101 (2006). https://doi.org/10.1191/1478088706qp063oa. https://www.tandfonline.com/doi/abs/10.1191/1478088706qp063oa

5. Canas, A.J., Novak, J.D., Reiska, P.: How good is my concept map? Am i a good CMAPPER? Knowl. Manage. E-Learn. Int. J. **7**(1), 6–19 (2015)

6. Chandler, P., Sweller, J.: Cognitive load theory and the format of instruction. Cogn. Instr. **8**(4), 293–332 (1991)

7. Costley, J., Fanguy, M., Lange, C., Baldwin, M.: The effects of video lecture viewing strategies on cognitive load. J. Comput. High. Educ. **33**(1), 19–38 (2021)

8. De Jong, T., Van Der Hulst, A.: The effects of graphical overviews on knowledge acquisition in hypertext. J. Comput. Assist. Learn. **18**(2), 219–231 (2002)

9. D'Mello, S.K.: Giving eyesight to the blind: Towards attention-aware aied. Int. J. Artif. Intell. Educ. **26**(2), 645–659 (2016)

10. Fung, F.M.: Adopting lightboard for a chemistry flipped classroom to improve technology-enhanced videos for better learner engagement (2017)

11. Guo, P.J., Kim, J., Rubin, R.: How video production affects student engagement: an empirical study of MOOC videos. In: Proceedings of the first ACM Conference on Learning@ Scale Conference, pp. 41–50 (2014)

12. Hart, S.G.: Nasa-task load index (nasa-tlx); 20 years later. Proceedings of the Human Factors and Ergonomics Society Annual Meeting **50**(9), 904–908 (2006). https://doi.org/10.1177/154193120605000909. https://doi.org/10.1177/154193120605000909

13. Hayama, T., Sato, S.: Supporting online video e-learning with semi-automatic concept-map generation. In: Zaphiris, P., Ioannou, A. (eds.) HCII 2020. LNCS, vol. 12205, pp. 64–76. Springer, Cham (2020). https://doi.org/10.1007/978-3-030-50513-4_5

14. Hollis, R.B., Was, C.A.: Mind wandering, control failures, and social media distractions in online learning. Learn. Instr. **42**, 104–112 (2016)

15. Hutt, S., et al.: Automated gaze-based mind wandering detection during computerized learning in classrooms. User Model. User-Adap. Inter. **29**(4), 821–867 (2019)

16. Hutt, S., Krasich, K., Brockmole, J.R., D'Mello, S.K.: Breaking out of the lab: Mitigating mind wandering with gaze-based attention-aware technology in classrooms. In: Proceedings of the 2021 CHI Conference on Human Factors in Computing Systems, pp. 1–14 (2021)

17. Kardash, C.M., Noel, L.K.: How organizational signals, need for cognition, and verbal ability affect text recall and recognition. Contemp. Educ. Psychol. **25**(3), 317–331 (2000)

18. Krathwohl, D.R.: A revision of bloom's taxonomy: an overview. Theory Pract. **41**(4), 212–218 (2002)

19. Lackmann, S., Léger, P.M., Charland, P., Aubé, C., Talbot, J.: The influence of video format on engagement and performance in online learning. Brain Sci. **11**(2), 128 (2021)

20. Levenshtein, V.I., et al.: Binary codes capable of correcting deletions, insertions, and reversals. In: Soviet physics doklady, vol. 10, pp. 707–710. Soviet Union (1966)

21. Liu, C., Elms, P.: Animating student engagement: the impacts of cartoon instructional videos on learning experience. Res. Learn. Technol. **27** (2019)

22. Liu, C., Kim, J., Wang, H.C.: Conceptscape: collaborative concept mapping for video learning. In: Proceedings of the 2018 CHI Conference on Human Factors in Computing Systems, pp. 1–12 (2018)

23. Loh, K.K., Tan, B.Z.H., Lim, S.W.H.: Media multitasking predicts video-recorded lecture learning performance through mind wandering tendencies. Comput. Hum. Behav. **63**, 943–947 (2016)
24. Mayer, R.E.: Cognitive theory of multimedia learning. Camb. Handbook Multimedia Learn. **41**, 31–48 (2005)
25. Mills, C., Gregg, J., Bixler, R., D'Mello, S.K.: Eye-mind reader: an intelligent reading interface that promotes long-term comprehension by detecting and responding to mind wandering. Hum.-Comput. Interact. **36**(4), 306–332 (2021)
26. Miner, S., Stefaniak, J.E.: Learning via video in higher education: an exploration of instructor and student perceptions. J. Univ. Teach. Learn. Pract. **15**(2), 2 (2018)
27. Momsen, J.L., Long, T.M., Wyse, S.A., Ebert-May, D.: Just the facts? introductory undergraduate biology courses focus on low-level cognitive skills. CBE-Life Sci. Educ. **9**(4), 435–440 (2010)
28. Novak, J.D.: Concept maps and VEE diagrams: two metacognitive tools to facilitate meaningful learning. Instr. Sci. **19**(1), 29–52 (1990)
29. Novak, J.D., Cañas, A.J.: The theory underlying concept maps and how to construct and use them (2008)
30. Pavel, A., Hartmann, B., Agrawala, M.: Video digests: a browsable, skimmable format for informational lecture videos. In: Proceedings of the 27th Annual ACM Symposium on User Interface Software and Technology, pp. 573–582. ACM (2014)
31. Pham, P., Wang, J.: AttentiveLearner: improving mobile MOOC learning via implicit heart rate tracking. In: Conati, C., Heffernan, N., Mitrovic, A., Verdejo, M.F. (eds.) AIED 2015. LNCS (LNAI), vol. 9112, pp. 367–376. Springer, Cham (2015). https://doi.org/10.1007/978-3-319-19773-9_37
32. Pham, P., Wang, J.: Adaptive review for mobile MOOC learning via multimodal physiological signal sensing-a longitudinal study. In: Proceedings of the 20th ACM International Conference on Multimodal Interaction, pp. 63–72 (2018)
33. Risko, E.F., Buchanan, D., Medimorec, S., Kingstone, A.: Everyday attention: mind wandering and computer use during lectures. Comput. Educ. **68**, 275–283 (2013)
34. Roda, C., Thomas, J.: Attention aware systems: theories, applications, and research agenda. Comput. Hum. Behav. **22**(4), 557–587 (2006)
35. Rodrigue, M., Son, J., Giesbrecht, B., Turk, M., Höllerer, T.: Spatio-temporal detection of divided attention in reading applications using EEG and eye tracking. In: Proceedings of the 20th International Conference on Intelligent User Interfaces, pp. 121–125 (2015)
36. Rudolph, M.: Cognitive theory of multimedia learning. J. Online Higher Educ. **1**(2), 1–10 (2017)
37. Schneider, S., Beege, M., Nebel, S., Rey, G.D.: A meta-analysis of how signaling affects learning with media. Educ. Res. Rev. **23**, 1–24 (2018)
38. Schooler, J.W.: Re-representing consciousness: dissociations between experience and meta-consciousness. Trends Cogn. Sci. **6**(8), 339–344 (2002)
39. Schooler, J.W., Reichle, E.D., Halpern, D.V.: Zoning out while reading: evidence for dissociations between experience and metaconsciousness. In: Levin, D.T. (ed.) Thinking and Seeing: Visual Metacognition in Adults and Children. MIT Press, Cambridges (2004)
40. Schooler, J.W., Smallwood, J., Christoff, K., Handy, T.C., Reichle, E.D., Sayette, M.A.: Meta-awareness, perceptual decoupling and the wandering mind. Trends Cogn. Sci. **15**(7), 319–326 (2011)

41. Seidel, N.: Making web video accessible: interaction design patterns for assistive video learning environments. In: Proceedings of the 20th European Conference on Pattern Languages of Programs, p. 17. ACM (2015)

42. Seo, K., Dodson, S., Harandi, N.M., Roberson, N., Fels, S., Roll, I.: Active learning with online video: the impact of learning context on engagement. Comput. Educ. **165**, 104132 (2021)

43. Shin, H., Ko, E.Y., Williams, J.J., Kim, J.: Understanding the effect of in-video prompting on learners and instructors. In: Proceedings of the 2018 CHI Conference on Human Factors in Computing Systems, p. 319. ACM (2018)

44. Sorden, S.D.: The cognitive theory of multimedia learning. Handbook Educ. Theories **1**(2012), 1–22 (2012)

45. Sychev, O., Anikin, A., Prokudin, A.: Automatic grading and hinting in open-ended text questions. Cogn. Syst. Res. **59**, 264–272 (2020)

46. Szafir, D., Mutlu, B.: Artful: adaptive review technology for flipped learning. In: Proceedings of the SIGCHI Conference on Human Factors in Computing Systems, pp. 1001–1010 (2013)

47. Taylor, B.M., Beach, R.W.: The effects of text structure instruction on middle-grade students' comprehension and production of expository text. Read. Res. Quart. **19**, 134–146 (1984)

48. Tseng, S.S.: The influence of teacher annotations on student learning engagement and video watching behaviors. Int. J. Educ. Technol. High. Educ. **18**(1), 1–17 (2021)

49. Tyng, C.M., Amin, H.U., Saad, M.N., Malik, A.S.: The influences of emotion on learning and memory. Front. Psychol. **8**, 1454 (2017)

50. Xiao, X., Wang, J.: Understanding and detecting divided attention in mobile MOOC learning. In: Proceedings of the 2017 CHI Conference on Human Factors in Computing Systems. CHI 2017, New York, NY, USA, pp. 2411–2415. Association for Computing Machinery (2017). https://doi.org/10.1145/3025453.3025552

51. Yang, H., Siebert, M., Luhne, P., Sack, H., Meinel, C.: Automatic lecture video indexing using video OCR technology. In: 2011 IEEE International Symposium on Multimedia (ISM), pp. 111–116. IEEE (2011)

52. Zhang, D., Zhou, L., Briggs, R.O., Nunamaker, J.F., Jr.: Instructional video in e-learning: assessing the impact of interactive video on learning effectiveness. Inf. Manage. **43**(1), 15–27 (2006)

53. Zhang, S., Meng, X., Liu, C., Zhao, S., Sehgal, V., Fjeld, M.: ScaffoMapping: assisting concept mapping for video learners. In: Lamas, D., Loizides, F., Nacke, L., Petrie, H., Winckler, M., Zaphiris, P. (eds.) INTERACT 2019. LNCS, vol. 11747, pp. 314–328. Springer, Cham (2019). https://doi.org/10.1007/978-3-030-29384-0_20

54. Zhao, Y., Lofi, C., Hauff, C.: Scalable Mind-Wandering Detection for MOOCs: A Webcam-Based Approach. In: Lavoué, É., Drachsler, H., Verbert, K., Broisin, J., Pérez-Sanagustín, M. (eds.) EC-TEL 2017. LNCS, vol. 10474, pp. 330–344. Springer, Cham (2017). https://doi.org/10.1007/978-3-319-66610-5_24

# I Perform My Work with My Body Too: Integrating Body Representations in and with Task Models

Axel Carayon⬤, Célia Martinie⁽⊠⁾ ⬤, and Philippe Palanque⬤

ICS-IRIT, Université Toulouse III – Paul Sabatier, Toulouse, France
{celia.martinie,philippe.palanque}@irit.fr

**Abstract.** Complete and unambiguous descriptions of user tasks is a cornerstone of user centered design approaches as they provide a unique way of describing precisely and entirely users' actions that have to be performed in order for them to reach their goals and perform their work. Three key challenges in describing these user tasks lay in the quantity and type of information to embed, the level of details of the type of actions and the level of refinement in the hierarchy of tasks. For "standard" interactions, such as performing work using desktop-like interactive applications, several notations have been proposed and make explicit how to address these challenges. Interactions on the move raise additional issues as physical movement of the operator have to be accounted for and described. Currently no task notation is able to describe adequately users' movements making it impossible to reason about quantity of movement to perform a task and about the issues for performing incorrect movements. This paper extends current knowledge and practice in tasks modelling taking into account in a systematic manner users' movements and more precisely body parts, body size, range of motion, articulations and position of body parts relatively to objects in the environment. Through two different case studies we show the importance of adding those elements to describe and analyze users' work and tasks when users perform physical interactions. We also demonstrate that such models are of prime importance to reason about quantity of movements, muscular fatigue and safety.

**Keywords:** Task modelling · Safety · Task analysis · Work · Human Body

## 1 Introduction

When interacting with a system, users may perform their tasks by involving the body or at least parts of the body. For example, taking a picture with a smartphone may include the following tasks: grabbing the smartphone with one hand, moving the arm of the hand, moving the head to locate the target and triggering the capture by pressing the camera button with one of the fingers of the hand. This is one way of performing the action but alternatives are possible to reach the same goal (e.g. grabbing the camera with two hands, pointing using two arms and triggering the capture by voice). Beyond personal choice, the performance of the physical tasks may depend on the user physical

J. Abdelnour Nocera et al. (Eds.): INTERACT 2023, LNCS 14143, pp. 482–503, 2023.
https://doi.org/10.1007/978-3-031-42283-6_26

abilities, permanent or temporary, as well as on the instructions the user received when learning how to use the system. Performing the tasks in the most appropriate way might reduce fatigue, improve performance and reduce errors which may have (in the context of safety-critical operations), catastrophic consequences (according to the ARP 4754 classification [1]). For example, in the field of air transportation, there is a risk of losing the last engine of the aircraft if a pilot pushes the button corresponding to the other engine, discharging the agent in the engine not on fire, as this happened in Kegworth accident in 1987 [1]. Another example is the risk of contamination of a hospital if an employee executes a disinfection task in an incomplete way [18].

In multiple contexts (e.g. enrichment of physical interaction, prediction of worker fatigue, calculus of possible range of movements), the design of interactive systems requires understanding the implications on the body-related activities of the user. Such body-related activities require explicit account for involved body parts, possible and impossible postures, body size, range of motion of articulations, physical reachability. As these physical movements will take place in workplace, the body of the user must be positioned in that environment and with the objects of interest in that environment. Such information is thus major for the design of critical interactive system and requires explicit means of identification and representation to support meaningful analysis.

Task analysis is a cornerstone of user-centered design approaches [13]. Task models provide complete and unambiguous description of the users' tasks, which enables ensuring the effectiveness factor of usability of an interactive system [39], i.e., to guarantee that users can perform their work and can reach their goals. Task analysis and modelling are the means to identify and record precisely user tasks, along with knowledge, data, objects and devices required to perform the tasks [27]. Such techniques are useful even for the usability experts who may miss issues without methodological support [20]. The application of task modelling techniques enables to ensure systematic description of tasks and systematic assessment of the possible issues for each task.

Though the expressive power of task modelling notations increased in the last decade as demonstrated in [26], no task modeling notation is able to represent information about involved body parts, possible postures, body position, or range of motion. This is very surprising as current research in the field of HCI focusses on physical interactions, either involving all fingers from both hands [8] or even the entire body [9]). This paper extends an existing notation for modelling tasks (called HAMSTERS [27]) to embed these body-related information. HAMSTERS was chosen due to its customizability (as described in [26]) but the proposed contribution could be embedded in any task modeling notation such as KMAD [12] or CTT [31].

We demonstrate the utility and validity of these extensions to the HAMSTERS notation for the analysis of user physical tasks, both on an illustrative examples of material handling and on the execution of a commercial aircraft engine management procedure. This demonstrates the relevance of the extension for both mundane and safety-critical applications.

Next section highlights the importance and relevance of identifying and describing body-related information in users' tasks, as well as the specific information needed for this description. Using two case studies (material handling and engine fire management in aircrafts), we show that current task modelling notations can only embed very limited body-related information. Section 2 synthesizes the related work on body-related information in tasks models. It will show that this information is usual informal and thus cannot be used for analysis. Section 4 presents the proposed extensions to the HAM-STERS notation to integrate in a complete and unambiguous manner body movements inside and with task models. Section 5 demonstrates the usefulness and benefits of these extensions on both case studies introduced in Sect. 2 and provide detailed analysis of the models exploiting this additional information.

## 2 Related Work on Representing Body Tasks with Task Models

Task modeling notations are usually designed and used to match analysis needs for which the task models are built. This induces that the notation elements of a given task modeling notation enable to represent and describe only some of the aspects of users' work with the objective of making a specific analysis, but these elements may not enable to make a different type of analysis [26]. Usually, task modeling notations target several types of analysis, for the design and development of interactive system, as well as for the design, development and implementation of the training program for the users of an interactive system [25] but also to identify user errors and the cost for recovering from them [38].

The minimum set of common ground elements for a task modeling notation includes the hierarchy between user goals, sub-goals and tasks [1]; the task types [31] and their temporal ordering [1, 31]; the objects [12] and the knowledge [22] required to perform the tasks; and at last, the collaborative tasks between different users [37]. Over the years, task types have been refined to gain precision as for instance users tasks types from [31] have been refined to represent that a task may be perceptive, cognitive or motor [25]. Depending on the application domain or there might be the need to refine further the task types or the information and objects manipulated by the tasks. For this reason, [26] proposed a tool supported modeling notation with customizable task types and information types. This is a first step that enables designers to increase the expressive power of task modeling notations for their needs. For example, it enables to refine motor task types into body part tasks, such as "finger press motor task". However, this approach does not cover the needs when describing body-related information (as described in previous sections: body parts, possible postures, body size, range of motion and position of body parts relatively to objects in the environment).

Beyond increasing the expressive power of task modeling notations, Fahssi et al. [15] proposed to associate representation of cyber-physical elements to specific elements of notation in task models. For example, the description of an input (or output) device required to perform a task in a task model can be associated to the representation of this input (or output) device in a 3D layout representation of the work environment. In the same way, the description of a UI widget required to perform a task in a task model can be associated to the graphical representation of this UI widget in a 2D layout representation of the UI.

Extensions to the task modeling notations, as well as association of task models with representations and information that are outside of the task model are thus useful to support the analysis of tasks in work environment, and the impact of the physical layout on the activities. The approach presented in this paper takes advantages of both philosophies (extension and association) and goes beyond the state of the art by integrating in a systematic and unambiguous way the body parts and movements involved in the user tasks.

## 3 Importance and Benefits of Describing Body-Related Information in Tasks: Illustration with Real Cases Scenarios

The identification and description of body-related information (such as movements) is particularly useful and used in contexts where the involvement of the user body has an impact on the possibility to execute the task and/or on the outcome of the execution of the task. Body movements may be feasible or not (e.g. user is able to reach lever, user arm is available and not used in another concurrent task), or influence the results of the execution of the task (e.g. user changed the lever position, user arm fatigue increases). We will demonstrate that these issues are important to take into account at design time, in order to design work practices and interactions that fit the user.

### 3.1 Description of Body Movements in Tasks

The identification and description of body movements not only supports the design and evaluation of physical interaction with systems, but also the training of their users.

**For Design and Evaluation Purpose.** When designing a physical object or an interactive system, the description of the sequence of possible postures and movements can serve to test physical object designs. A **posture** is defined as the "configuration of the body's head, trunk and limbs in space" [35]. According to [16] the description of the possible postures and **movements**: informs about real-life use, enables analyzing different possible interactive system configurations, as well as enables analyzing comfort in addition to reachability and to communicate between stakeholders. Beyond postures and movements, the description of the human body itself can serve as a design constraint or as a reference, this in order to ensure that the object of interactive system will physically fit the user body [17] (e.g. human body size and possible postures to design a bike). In more details, the description of the human body enables to identify adequate postures for the tasks in terms of [1]: functional reachability ("reach volume", "range of movement"), appropriate body parts for contact pressure, impact on physical effort (angles of less discomfort, internal pressures, efforts muscle and energy expenditure). It is important to note that the description used to analyze functional reachability has to contain the **range of motion** and **boundaries** of each involved **body part**, as the reachability is processed using range of motion and boundaries of the body parts. The description of the involved body parts also enables to categorize workload and associated physical/cognitive fatigue to identify and mitigate incidents [23]. For that purpose, the description should contain the situation of the involved body part in the hierarchy of body parts in addition to the position of the body in the **environment** and with respect to **objects** used for performing the tasks. Finally, the description of the human body enables to [14]: analyze physical interactions, enrich physical interactions and exploit human asymmetric gestures capabilities. For this matter, the description must contain the movements of involved body parts, the side(s) of the body that is (are) involved, and the situation of the body part(s) in the whole hierarchy of the body parts.

Finally, while all humans share the same body structure and are in theory able to perform the same movements, individual variations including age [21], medical conditions [3], or even geographical variations [3] and a lot more can lead to variation in range of movements between individuals. Because of that, to ensure coverage of the full range of motion, it is important that the description do not restrain any movement to a unique and definitive range of motion, but instead to be editable to better fit a given task for a given individual.

**For Training Purpose.** When training people to use an interactive system, the description of the position of the involved body part and of the device supports [34]: showing the correct movement, guiding the direction of the movement, showing the **location of the device**. Such guidance has proven useful to release memory load, splitting a complex task into multiple sub-tasks [34]. Visual guidance also makes the task simple to replicate. The description of the postures that have to be performed by the user along with the positions of the different involved body parts also support to [36]: design training exercises, monitor and guide users.

**Synthesis and Lessons Learnt.** Table 1 summarizes information types required in body tasks descriptions in order to support the design, evaluation and training purposes.

**Table 1.** Summary of the types of information required for the description of body tasks

| | Body parts | Movement of the involved body parts | Hierarchy of the body parts | Body postures | Position of body parts relatively to objects in the environment | Body boundaries | Range of motion of body parts |
|---|---|---|---|---|---|---|---|
| Design and evaluation purpose | [16, 23] | [1, 14, 36] | [16, 23] | [1, 16, 17, 36] | [14, 23] | [17] | [1] |
| Training purpose | [34] | [34, 36] | | [36] | [34] | | |

In the remainder of the paper, each concept above is used to highlight the limitations of the existing task modeling notations as well as to justify the extensions we propose.

## 3.2   Illustrative Examples of Body Task Descriptions Using the HAMSTERS-XL Task Modeling Notation

Our first illustrative example deals with a warehouse worker that need to move a box from one location to another. If lifted incorrectly, this task can lead to damage to both the worker and the box. Because of that, we must ensure that worker get proper training, which involves lifting the item with the back straight [33]. Figure 1 a) presents the high-level abstract tasks as a task model describing the lifting procedure which provides an overview of the procedure. Under the main goal (top) labelled "Move box to another location", the tasks have to be performed in sequence (described using the sequence temporal ordering operator " >>"). This sequence is composed of 7 abstract user tasks: "Estimate if box can be lifted", "Get in front of the box", "Crouch", "Grabbing the box", "Lifting the box", "Stand up" and "Walking to destination".

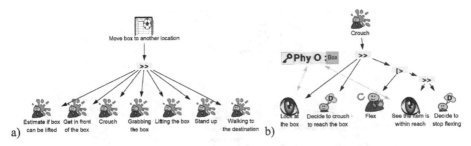

**Fig. 1.**  The seven tasks of the task model "Move box to another location"

Figure 1 b) shows the task "Crouch" detailed. It is decomposed into a sequence in three parts, first a visual perceptive task "Look at the box" using a physical object "Box". Then a cognitive decision task "Decide to crouch to reach the box". The last element is a disable operator "[>", meaning that the left part will first start and, at any time, the right part can start, stopping the current task. The left part is a motor task "Flex". This task is iterative (represented with a blue circle arrow) meaning it will repeat until stopped. The right part is a sequence of two tasks: first a visual perceptive task, "See the item is within reach" using the physical object "box", followed by the cognitive decision task "Decide to stop flexing".

The task model "Move box to another location" including the detailed representation of the crouch task does not provide:

- A description of the body parts involved: from the description, it is not possible to identify which parts of the body are used to crouch and to flex.
- A description of the movements required to be performed by the body parts involved: the motor task indicates that the user has to flex, but neither which part of the body the user has to flex, nor of how much it or they should be flexed are included.
- A description of the postures corresponding to each motor task: there is no overview of the position of the head, trunk and limbs before and after the crouch movement is performed.
- A description of the relative position of the body with respect to the box.

- The very important information that the back must remain straight.

From the task models, it is thus not possible to analyze: which are the required body parts that should be available for the task, whether the task can or should be performed in an asymmetric way. In addition, from the information available in the task model it is not possible to assess whether the task may have an impact on the user body and on which part if it does.

Moving from this very simple illustrative example we propose another context from the aviation domain. Here the task corresponds to the emergency procedure (for an A320 aircraft) to be performed when one of the engines is on fire. This task is critical for the safety of all the passengers of the flight and involves multiples interactions with multiples devices located in multiple locations in the aircraft cockpit. Due to the critical nature of the task, the modeling of this task needs to be unambiguous and exhaustive as movement not performed or wrongly performed may affect operations safety.

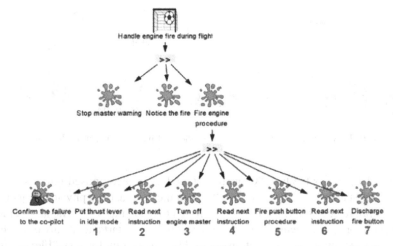

**Fig. 2.** Top level tasks of the task model "Handle engine fire during flight"

Figure 2 presents the high-level abstract tasks of the ENG FIRE as described in the Flight Crew Operating Manual [10]. Under the main goal called "Handle engine fire during flight", the highest-level decomposition is a sequence of task as on previous example. This sequence of three tasks is "Stop master warning", "Notice the fire" and "Fire engine procedure". This last task is decomposed into the following sequence: "Confirm the failure to the co-pilot", "Put thrust lever in idle mode", "Read next instruction", "Turn off engine master"," Read next instruction", "Fire push button procedure", "read next instruction" and "Discharge fire button". Each task requires interacting with a different part of the cockpit, numbered from 1 to 7. The location of these parts are presented in Fig. 3.

**Fig. 3.** Picture of an A320 aircraft cockpit showing the parts involved in the procedure

Figure 4 presents a refinement of the last two tasks "Read next instruction" and "Discharge fire button". On that figure, the first abstract task "Read next instruction" is refined into a sequence in three parts. First, a cognitive decision task, "Decide to read the next step", then a disable operator "[>" that will repeat an iterative motor task "Move the head towards the screen". This task can be stopped at any time when the following sequence occurs: a visual perceptive task "See the screen is readable", followed by a cognitive decision task "Decide to stop moving the head". Finally, the pilot performs an output task "Read next instruction", on the Electronic Centralized Aircraft Monitor (ECAM) display running the software application "Flight warning procedure". In the procedure, the next task requires waiting for 6 s, so it produces a duration of 6 s.

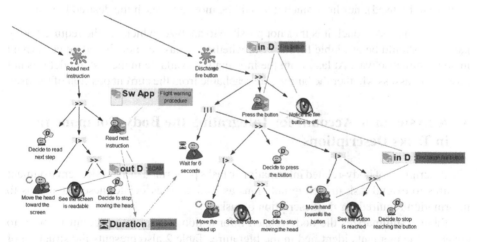

**Fig. 4.** Refinement of the tasks "Read next instruction" and "Discharge fire button" from Fig. 3

The abstract task "Discharge fire button" is refined into a sequence of three sub-parts. This first one is a concurrent temporal ordering operator "‖" which means that the two sub-parts below it must be performed but in any order. The first part is a timed user task labelled "Wait for 6 s", consuming the duration created previously. The second part is a sequence of actions. First, a disable operator, that repeat the iterative motor task "Move the head up" until stopped by the right part sequence: a visual perceptive task "See the button" followed by a cognitive decision task "Decide to stop moving the head». Then the sequence continues with a cognitive decision task "Decide to press the button" followed by another disable operator. The left part of the operator is an iterative motor task "Move hand towards the button" that is stopped when the sequence on the right occurs i.e., a visual perceptive task "See the button is reached" followed by a cognitive decision task "Decide to stop reaching the button".

The complete sequence represents the fact that the operator must wait 6 s, but that the operator can prepare to press the button in an interleaved way. Once done, the two remaining tasks in the sequence are an input task "Press the button" using the input device "Discharge fire button" and finally a visual perception task "Notice the fire button is off" using the input output device "Fire button".

Even though this task model provides detailed information about the tasks to be performed, the devices and applications to use, the model does not contain:

- A description of the body parts involved: indeed, it is not possible to identify all of the parts of the body are required to press the button. Despite the model contain a subset of information about the body parts involved inside the text description of the tasks (e.g. "head" in "Move head", "hand" in "Move hands towards the button"), it is not described in an explicit way and information is not represented as a notation element but more as a comment in the task name.
- A description of the movements to be performed by the body parts involved: the motor task indicates that the operator has to move hand towards the button, but we do not know neither if moving the hand only is enough (or if the arm and shoulder have to be used), nor how much it should be moved to reach the desired button.

From this task model, it is thus not possible to analyze: which are the required body parts that should be available for the task, whether the task can or should be performed in an asymmetric way. At last, from the information available in the task model it is not possible to assess whether the buttons are reachable from the current position of the user.

## 4   A Systematic Account for Integrating the Body Components in Tasks Descriptions

The description of body-related information in tasks performed in a physical environment requires to extend task modeling notations as well as to associate these extensions to information required for the description of tasks.

Table 2 summarizes the body-related information to take into account in order to cover all the elements identified in the literature. Table 2 also presents the structure of the next section. In this section we present in an exhaustive manner all the body-related information and how we have proposed its integration in the HAMSTERS task-modelling notation. We chose the HAMSTERS task-modelling notation because it embeds the common ground elements required to describe user tasks and that the notation enables

---

**Table 2.** Structuration of the types of information for the description of body tasks (from Table 1)

| | Elements of notations for task models (Sect. 4.1) | | Information required to be associated to elements of notations in task models (Sect. 4.2) | | | | |
|---|---|---|---|---|---|---|---|
| | Body parts (Sect. 4.1, first sub-section) | Movement of the involved body parts (Sect. 4.1, second sub-section) | Hierarchy of the body parts (First sub-section) | Body postures (Second sub-section) | Body position in its environment and boundaries (Sect. 4.2, third and fourth sub-sections) | | |
| | | | | | Position of body parts relatively to objects in the environment | Body boundaries | Range of motion of body parts |
| Design and evaluation purpose | [16, 23] | [1, 14, 36] | [16, 23] | [1, 16, 17, 36] | [14, 23] | [17] | [1] |
| Training purpose | [34] | [34, 36] | | [36] | [34] | | |

the refinement of user task types and objects required to perform the tasks by using HAMSTERS-XL [26].

As it is not relevant to integrate everything as a graphical element of a task model, we make an explicit distinction between types of information that should be described in task models and types of information that should be associated to elements of notation in task models.

## 4.1 Elements of Notations for Task Models

While latest surveys in computer vision [7] shows multiple kind of models for the human body, we chose the Norkin & White abstraction [29] because it is used as a reference for research work on body joint motion, including in the industrial engineering domain [30]. It is the reference book for several faculties of medical education, the measurements have been regularly updated in each edition.

Figure 5 presents the overview of the hierarchy of the human body as proposed in [29]. The body decomposes into a head, an upper left part, an upper right part….Then the head in turn decomposed into eyes, nose, ear… The hierarchical view presented in Fig. 5 is not directly an element of notation for task models, but each body part is. We start introducing it before the elements of notation for task models for a better understandability of the notation. The hierarchical view is an information required to be associated to task models (presented in Sect. 4.2).

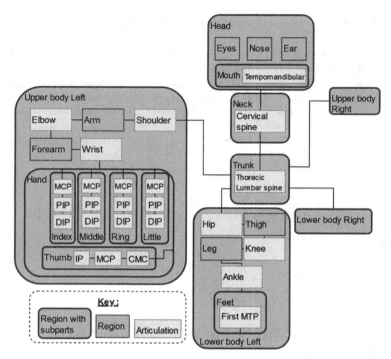

**Fig. 5.** Hierarchy of body parts from [29] (only left part detailed for readability purpose)

**Body Part Involved in a Task.** First, we consider now that each motor task in a task model will be performed by at least one body part. Figure 6 a) presents the proposed representation of a body part in a task model while Fig. 6 b) presents how representations of body parts are associated to a motor task. The model of Fig. 6 b) reads as the "Flex" motor task uses the lower body left and right knees of the user (plain line between the "Flex" motor task and the body parts labelled "Body Part: Lower body left knee" and "Body Part: Lower body right knee").

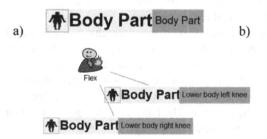

**Fig. 6.** Representation of a) the element of notation body part b) its usage in a task model

**Movement of the Body Part Involved in a Task.** To take into account movements, we consider that human motor task has to be refined into body movements involving body parts. Figure 7 a) presents the new movement task type. Each body movement can be performed with a minimum and maximum range of motion values (both values being respectively the beginning and the end of a motion [29] (chapter 1, page 7). Figure 7 b) presents the range of motion data type holding the range information. This data type aims at describing the expected range of motion of a movement in order to perform the task but this value must remain within the possible range.

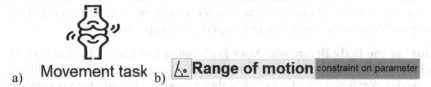

a)  **Movement task** b) **Range of motion** constraint on parameter

**Fig. 7.** Representation of a) the task type "movement" b) the notation for "Range of motion" parameter

Figure 8 presents the usage of both elements of notation to describe movement tasks with their associated body part and range of motion constraint.

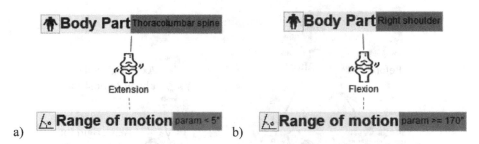

a) **Body Part** Thoracolumbar spine

Extension

**Range of motion** param < 5°

b) **Body Part** Right shoulder

Flexion

**Range of motion** param >= 170°

**Fig. 8.** Representation of the usage of a movement task with range of motion constraints in a task model

Figure 8 a) presents a task movement of the material handling illustrative example. It is an extension (movement task labelled "extension") performed by the thoracolumbar spine (body part labelled "Body Part: Thoracolumbar spine"). This extension must not exceed 5° or the user body safety will be at stake. Figure 8 b) presents a task movement of the engine fire procedure illustrative example. It is a flexion (movement task labelled "flexion") performed by the right shoulder (body part labelled "Body Part: Right shoulder"). This flexion must be superior to 170° or the movement will not enable to press the discharge button in the appropriate way, which will lead to fire not stopping in the engine and could cause the death of the passengers of the aircraft.

## 4.2   Information Required to Be Associated to Elements of Notations in Task Models

**Hierarchy of the Body Parts and Its Involvement in a Task.** Figure 5 presents the hierarchy of the body parts and identifies the different parts of the human body that may be involved in a task. The presented work is based on the work of Norkin and White [29] but can be adapted to potential evolutions of medicine. In the example below all the body parts are relevant, but in other cases only some parts would be included. The hierarchy of the body parts enables to identify the body parts involved in a task, as well as to identify whether a body part is available for a given task. For example, when a user opens a door with the left hand, the task involves the upper body left (in Fig. 5), and it is not possible to add a concurrent task requiring the upper body left.

**Posture of the Body Before and After Performing the Task.** The user body is in a specific posture before performing a motor task, and may be in another specific posture after having performed a motor task. It is thus required to identify both postures and to connect them to the task model. Figure 9 a) presents how postures are represented with drawing and are associated the first task of the task model (initial posture) and to the end of the task (final posture).

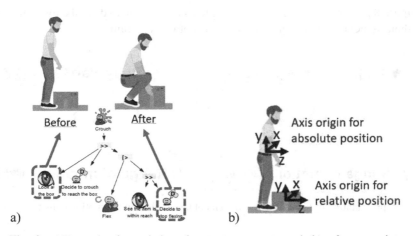

a)                                                                b)

**Fig. 9.** a) Example of association of postures to a motor task, b) reference points

**Body Position in its Environment.** The user performs tasks in a given environment and the user body parts have lengths that may fit or not to this environment. Such information must be identified, represented and connected to the task model.

Figure 10 provides detailed information about body parts positions using the data template. As Fig. 9 a) contains 2 postures, Fig. 10 defines the body positions for each posture (columns). The body positions have to be defined according to a given point of reference which has to be defined for the body and for each object used in the task. This is represented in Fig. 9 b).

| Body part | Posture: before task "Crouch" | | | Posture: after task "Crouch" | | |
|---|---|---|---|---|---|---|
| | X | Y | Z | X | Y | Z |
| Head | 0 | 60 | 0 | 0 | 0 | 20 |
| Neck | 0 | 45 | 0 | 0 | -25 | 5 |
| Left Shoulder | -30 | 40 | 0 | -30 | -30 | 15 |
| Right shoulder | 30 | 40 | 0 | 30 | -30 | 15 |
| Left Elbow | -35 | -5 | 0 | -35 | -15 | 20 |
| Right Elbow | 35 | -5 | 0 | 35 | -15 | 20 |
| ... | | | | | | |

**Fig. 10.** The generic template for absolute body positions applied to the example in Fig. 9 a)

Figure 11 presents the data template to identify and describe the relative position of the body parts to the devices or objects in the user environment. It enables to describe at what distance each body part is located from the environment objects or devices used in the task model. This figure contains values for the box in each posture described in Fig. 9 a).

| Body part | Relative position to box for posture: before task "crouch" | | | Relative position to box for posture: after task "crouch" | | |
|---|---|---|---|---|---|---|
| | X | Y | Z | X | Y | Z |
| Head | 30 | 180 | -15 | 15 | 120 | -5 |
| Neck | 30 | 170 | -15 | 15 | 110 | -5 |
| Left Shoulder | 30 | 165 | 15 | 15 | 165 | -20 |
| Right shoulder | -30 | 165 | -15 | -15 | 165 | -20 |
| Left Elbow | -35 | -135 | -20 | 5 | -135 | -10 |
| Right Elbow | 35 | -135 | 20 | -5 | -135 | -10 |
| ... | ... | ... | ... | ... | ... | ... |

**Fig. 11.** Template for relative position of body parts with respect to position of objects (or devices)

Both types of information (absolute and relative positions) are required to analyze reachability, quantity of movement, fatigue, or occlusion (among many others).

### Generic Human Boundaries and Range of Motion
This section describes the last set of data useful for integration body-related information in task models. This information embed data related to the limitations of human body in terms of size (human boundaries) and of movement capabilities (range of motion).

*Body Boundaries.* The user body parts have boundaries, i.e. anthropometric dimensions. Figure 12 presents an extract of human body dimensions taken from the Virtual Fit Test [30]. This type of information is also required to analyze reachability and occlusion, as well as to analyze if the profile of target users fits with the environment in which the tasks have to be performed. This is represented as constraints in the task models.

This data set was selected because the Human Factors and Ergonomics Society recommends it as practitioner tool [30]. However, virtually any other can be associated with the notation, provided that it contains minimum and maximum values for each body part.

*Range of Motion.* Human body parts have minimum and maximum range of motion. Figure 13 presents an extract of minimum and maximum range of motions for a set of body parts and for different user groups [29]. This type of information enables to describe precisely the movement to be performed, as well as to analyze the task feasibility (with

| Measures | Min | Max |
|---|---|---|
| Stature (mm) | 1461 | 1981 |
| | | |
| **Seated Measures** | | |
| Abdominal Extension Depth (mm) | 115 | 438 |
| Buttock-Knee Length (mm) | 493 | 706 |
| Buttock-Popliteal Length (mm) | 406 | 565 |
| Elbow Rest Height, Sitting (mm) | 170 | 310 |
| Eye Height, Sitting (mm) | 669 | 898 |
| Forearm-Forearm Breadth (mm) | 330 | 696 |
| ... | | |
| | | |
| **Standing Measures** | | |
| Eye Height, Standing (mm) | 1349 | 1859 |
| Elbow-Fingertip Length (mm) | 377 | 529 |
| Elbow Rest Height, Standing (mm) | 877 | 1240 |
| Foot Length (mm) | 214 | 300 |

**Fig. 12.** Extract of boundary manikins in the anthropometric data set of the Virtual Fit Test [30]

an average body). These values can be tuned to a given user or given user group when they are known.

| TABLE A.1 Shoulder, Elbow, Forearm, and Wrist Motion: Mean Values in Degrees | | | | | | | |
|---|---|---|---|---|---|---|---|
| Author | Wanatabe et al[1] | Boone and Azen[2] | Green and Wolf[3] | Walker et al[4] | Macedo and Magee[5] | AAOS[6] | AMA[7] |
| | | | 18–55 yr | 65–85 yr | | | |
| | | | n = 20 | n = 60 | | | |
| | 0–2 yr | 1–54 yr | (10 M, 10 F) | (30 M, 30 F) | 18–59 yr | | |
| | n = 45 | n = 109 M | | | n = 90 F | | |
| **Motion** | | | | | | | |
| *Shoulder Complex* | | | | | | | |
| Flexion | 172–180 | 167 | 156 | 165 | 188 | 180 | ≥180 |
| Extension | 78–89 | 62 | — | 44 | 70 | 60 | ≥50 |
| Abduction | 177–187 | 184 | 168 | 165 | 188 | 180 | ≥170 |
| Medial rotation | 72–90 | 69 | 49 | 62 | 94 | 70 | ≥80 |
| Lateral rotation | 118–134 | 104 | 84 | 81 | 108 | 90 | ≥60 |
| *Elbow and Forearm* | | | | | | | |
| Flexion | 148–158 | 143 | 145 | 143 | 149 | 150 | ≥140 |
| Extension | — | 1 | 0 | 4[1] | 2 | 0 | ≥0 |
| Pronation | 90–96 | 76 | 84 | 71 | 92 | 80 | ≥80 |
| Supination | 81–93 | 82 | 77 | 74 | 96 | 80 | ≥80 |
| *Wrist* | | | | | | | |
| Flexion | 88–96 | 76 | 73 | 64 | 93 | 80 | ≥60 |
| Extension | 82–89 | 75 | 65 | 63 | 86 | 70 | ≥60 |
| Radial deviation | — | 22 | 25 | 19 | 18 | 20 | ≥20 |
| Ulnar deviation | — | 36 | 39 | 26 | 41 | 30 | ≥30 |

**Fig. 13.** Possible range of motions for a selection of joints [29]

The range of motion parameter enables to describe the minimum and maximum joint angle for one of the possible degrees of freedom of a body part (e.g. "Medial rotation" of the "left hip" should be from "28°" to "32°" in Fig. 14). Thus, the proposed notation allows describing the possible range for joint angles, this for each move of a body part on one of its possible degrees of freedom. There are multiple methods known to calculate the expected angle of multiple joints after a movement, such as inverse kinematics, which are commonly used in computer graphics [6]. After a movement is performed, if all of the joints involved in the movement have reached their expected position, we can consider the movement is successfully executed. However, since we are dealing with movements performed by humans and not by a machine, it can be difficult to perform a movement and reach a very exact angle on multiples joints at the same time. To allow human-feasible movement description, it is preferable instead to constraints containing a minimum and/or maximum degree to a movement. Those constraints representing an acceptable threshold in which the movement is considered valid.

## 5 Validation: Extended Models and Comparisons with Standard Models

We applied the new elements of notation to the examples of material handling and engine fire procedure described and modeled in Sect. 2. We then compare the differences to demonstrate the usefulness of extending task-modelling notations with body-related information in order to perform specific analyses.

For a person who is trained to the notation, it took about 2 h to build the full model of the extract presented in the paper for the case study of material handling tasks, and 3 h for the case study of the engine fire. This duration includes identification of involved body parts, their movements and the maximum and minimum joint angle for each movement (range of motion).

### 5.1 Case Study of the Modelling of Material Handling Tasks

**Extended Model.** Figure 14 shows the task model of the "Crouch" task, embedding the motor task "Flex" refined using the new elements of notation. First, the motor task "Crouch" now links to two Body part called "Left Lower body" and "Right Lower body". Second, the task can now be further decomposed into a group of interleaved tasks (represented with the "|||" operator), meaning tasks can run in an interleaved order. Those new tasks are movement tasks with Range of Motion constraints (presented in Sect. 4.1). The user has to perform the movement task "Dorsiflexion" with the "Left Ankle" and "Right Ankle" of at least 15° but should not overcome the limit of 5° (Range of motion parameter labelled "Range of Mo: 15° <param <20°"). The user also has to perform the movement tasks: "Flexion" with the "Left Knee" and "Right Knee" constrained between 85° and 95°, "Flexion" with the "Left Hip" and "Right Hip" constrained between 110° and 120°, "Medial rotation" with the "Left Hip" and "Right Hip" constrained between 28° and 32°, and "Lateral rotation" with the "Left Hip" and "Right Hip" constrained between 60° and 65°. The two remaining tasks are optional movement tasks (represented by two blues arrows), meaning that while that they can occur, but are not mandatory. The two tasks are "Flexion" and "Extension" both tied to "Thoracolumbar spine" with the same constraint below 5°.

**Analysis from the Models and Their Associated Information.** As described in the modeling above, the new elements of notation enable to identify that the task requires the use of the Lower body (left and right), Trunk and Upper Body. The description also enables to identify that the material handling task requires that the user is able to flex ankles between 15° and 20°, flex knees between 85° and 95°, flex hips between 110° and 120°, perform a medial rotation of the hips between 28° and 32° and perform a lateral rotation of the hips between 60° and 65°. **Moreover, it also shows that while spine can be bend, it should not, with a threshold of 5° authorized.**

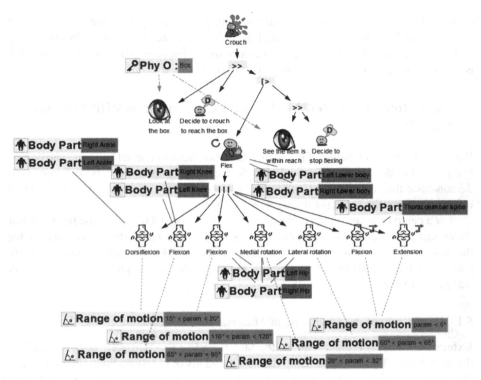

**Fig. 14.** Extended model for the task crouch

From this description, we get information that was missing in the initial task model (without extensions, in Sect. 3.2) and that is required to analyze working posture. For example, it is now possible to apply the Ovako Working Posture Analysing System (OWAS) [24]. This analysis technique is commonly used for working posture analysis. The flex movement task influences the back position, upper limbs position, lower limbs position and according to the OWAS, it is class 2 posture, meaning that it must be considered during the next regular check of working method.

Furthermore, the descriptions are detailed enough so that we assess them in the light of the safety recommendations for safe lifting procedure [33]. The procedure requires that the back should stay straight. The new elements of notation allow representing the flexion/extension of the Thoracolumbar spine (supporting the back) as an optional movement and constrains them to 5° max. This allows us to represent that while this movement **can** occur, it should not happen, with a tolerance of 5°. Combined with the association of the before/after posture to the task "Flex", we can now highlight the correct and safe posture before and after the execution and all the in-between movement. By giving before and after posture and describing all the movements possible with their constraints, this removes the previous ambiguity and make it usable for training purposes.

## 5.2    Case Study of the Modelling of the Engine Fire Procedure

**Extended Model.** Figure 15 describes the abstract task "Discharge fire button" updated from the Fig. 4, with the new elements of notation. First, this adds a decomposition to the input task "Fire button", separating the user and system part. This is represented by two interleaved actions, the system input task "Register button input" that can occur while the motor task "Press button is performing". This motor task is now tied to a Body part "Right hand" showing that the button should be pressed with the right hand. This motor task now also decompose itself into 5 movement tasks all called "Flexion". The first one is not optional and performed with the body part "right shoulder" with a range of motion superior to 170° (labelled "Range of motion: param >170°". The four others flexions tasks are constrained with the same range of motion (between 0° and 5°) but each of them linked to a different body part: right wrist, right index DIP, right index PIP and right index MCP. The iterative motor task "Move the head up" is now also refined with three concurrent movement tasks: "Extension" linked to the cervical spine with a constraint between 0° and 70° and two optional ones, "Right rotation" and "Right lateral flexion", also using the "Cervical Spine" but with a constraint of 0°, meaning it can occur but shouldn't. Last, the iterative motor task "Move hand towards the button" was also extended with eight concurrent movement tasks, and two "Flexion" tasks, linked to the body part "Right shoulder" and "Right elbow", with a range of motion constraint "param>0°" and "param>100°" respectively. Other six are optional movement tasks: "Pronation" linked to "Right Elbow", "Flexion" linked to "Right wrist", "Extension" linked to "Thoracolumbar spine", "Extension" linked to "Right Elbow" and "Right lateral flexion" and "Right rotation" linked to "Thoracolumbar spine", all six of them tied to their own constraints.

**Analysis From the Models and Their Associated Information.** Compared to existing modelling notations, the models produced using proposed extensions and their associated information enable to infer that the engine fire handling task requires the following body parts: Neck, Torso, Right Arm, Right Forearm, Right hand, Right index, Right middle finger. From the model and its association to the hierarchical view on the body parts (presented in Fig. 5), we understand that the operator performs an asymmetric task requiring the user to have the right arm available. From the task model in Fig. 15, we get information that was missing in the initial task model (without extensions, in Sect. 3.2) and that is required to analyze working postures. For example, it is now possible to apply the Rapid Upper Limb Assessment [28] (RULA) used for evaluation of working posture related to upper limbs. It takes into account Shoulder, Elbow, Wrist and position to evaluate the potential risk on a movement. If we apply to this model, the RULA analysis put a scoring of 6 out of 7, meaning that "Investigation and changes are required soon", because of arm position and neck in extension. Moreover, the task being part of a critical procedure, happening when an engine in the airplane take fire, it is primordial that the task can be physically done and we must ensure that a part of the body can be used for a task.

With the new elements of notations, bounding body parts to tasks this means that we can now detect if required body part is already in use by another task, which would prevent an operator to perform physically this critical procedure. The description of

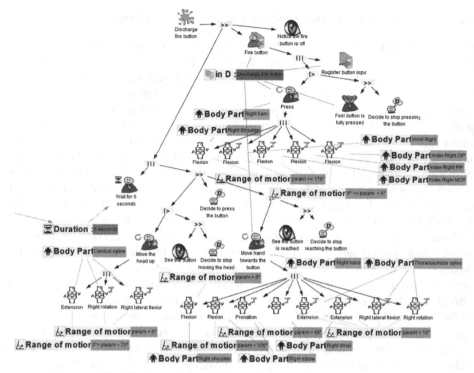

**Fig. 15.** Extended model for "Discharge fire button" task

the task movements, used in association with body position in its environment and boundaries (presented in Sect. 4.2) also enables to analyze whether the operator should be able to reach the button. Such estimation becomes possible by processing the task movements in the task model with the relative position of the involved body parts to the button, as well as according with the boundaries of the operator arm and hand.

## 6    Conclusion and Perspectives

ISO 9241 definition of usability of interactive applications [39] identifies efficiency, effectiveness and satisfaction as three contributing factors to usability. Assessing the usability of or designing for usability interactive applications, requires assessing the efficiency (performance in the execution of tasks, error and costs for recovering of errors) the effectiveness (percentage of tasks supported by the application) and the satisfaction (perceived satisfaction of users while performing the tasks with the interactive application). This definition makes salient the fact that the exhaustive identification of users tasks is key for ensuring usability and for assessing its level for interactive applications.

This paper argued that not making explicit body-related information while describing users tasks reduces the possibility to assess effectiveness of interactive application and prevent some analysis such as quantity of movement for performing a task, physical fatigue or occlusion (among others). Besides training of users without very detailed account of body movement and postures might lead to injuries and safety issues [24].

The contribution of the paper builds on the work in the area of physiology to identify body-related information: the body parts and the body parts hierarchy, the connectors (i.e. articulations), the average shape and length of body parts, the range of motion of the articulations. The paper proposes a set of extensions to an existing task modeling notation to incorporate each type of information in task models in order to provide exhaustive and unambiguous descriptions of body-related information. The paper has demonstrated on two case studies, how this information is presented in task models and how these models with augmented expressive power can be used for analysis purposed of the users work. The supplementary material presents the extensions performed on the HAMSTERS-XLE customizable tool [26] to edit those augmented task models.

This work is part of a more ambitious project aiming at supporting the training of operators performing tasks in cyber-physical environments such as large command and control rooms where operators manipulate not only software systems but also physical devices and lever while moving in that environment. Beyond, we are also exploiting the new task modeling notation introduced in the paper for describing reeducation and rehabilitation exercises for post-stroke rehabilitation.

# References

1. ARP4754, Aerospace Recommended Practice (ARP) ARP4754A (Guidelines for Development of Civil Aircraft and Systems) (2010). https://www.sae.org/standards/content/arp4754a/
2. AAIB, Accident report AAIB AAR 4/1990. Kegworth accident, report available here. https://reports.aviation-safety.net/1989/19890108-0_B734_G-OBME.pdf
3. Andrews A.W., Bohannon, R.W.: Decreased shoulder range of motion on paretic side after stroke. Phys. Ther. **69**(9), 768–772 (1989). https://doi.org/10.1093/ptj/69.9.768
4. Anett, J.: Hierarchical task analysis. In: Dan, D., Neville, S. (eds.) The Handbook of Task Analysis for Human-Computer Interaction, pp. 67–82. Lawrence Erlbaum Associates (2004)
5. Ahlberg, A., Moussa, M., Al-Nahdi, M.: On geographical variations in the normal range of joint motion. Clin. Orthop. Relat. Res. **234**, 229–231 (1988)
6. Aristidou, A., Lasenby, J., Chrysanthou, Y., Shamir, A.: Inverse kinematics techniques in computer graphics: a survey. Comput. Graph. Forum **37**(6), 35–58 (2017).https://doi.org/10.1111/cgf.13310
7. Berretti, S., Daoudi, M., Turaga, P., Basu, A:. Representation, analysis, and recognition of 3D humans. ACM Trans. Multimedia Comput. Commun. Appl. **14**(1), 1–36 (2018). https://doi.org/10.1145/3182179
8. Goguey, A., Nancel, M., Casiez, G., Vogel, D.: The performance and preference of different fingers and chords for pointing, dragging, and object transformation. In: Proceedings of CHI 2016, 34th Conference on Human Factors in Computing Systems, May 2016, San Jose, United States, pp. 4250–4261 (2016). https://doi.org/10.1145/2858036.2858194
9. Cheng, L.-P., Marwecki, S., Baudisch, P.: Mutual human actuation. In: Proceedings of the 30th Annual ACM Symposium on User Interface Software and Technology (UIST 2017), pp. 797–805. ACM (2017). https://doi.org/10.1145/3126594.3126667
10. Airbus. Flight Crew Operating Manual A318/A319/A320/A321 FMGS Pilot's Guide Vol 4 (2005). https://www.avialogs.com/aircraft-a/airbus/item/1004-flight-crew-operating-manual-a318-a319-a320-a321-fmgs-pilot-s-guide-vol-4

11. Barbé, J., Chatrenet, N., Mollard, R., Wolff, M., Bérard, P.: Physical ergonomics approach for touch screen interaction in an aircraft cockpit. In: Proceedings of the 2012 Conference on Ergonomie et Interaction Homme-Machine (Ergo'IHM 201212), pp. 9–16. Association for Computing Machinery, New York (2012)

12. Caffiau, S., Scapin, D., Girard, P., Baron, M., Jambon, F.: Increasing the expressive power of task analysis: systematic comparison and empirical assessment of tool-supported task models. Interact. Comput. **22**(6), 569–593 (2010)

13. Diaper, D.: Understanding task analysis for human-computer interaction. In: The Handbook of Task Analysis for Human-Computer Interaction. Lawrence Erlbaum Associates (2004)

14. Eardley, R., Roudaut, A., Gill, S., Thompson, S.J.: Designing for multiple hand grips and body postures within the UX of a moving smartphone. In: Proceedings of the 2018 Designing Interactive Systems Conference (DIS 2018), pp. 611–621. Association for Computing Machinery, New York (2018)

15. Fahssi, R., Martinie, C., Palanque, P.: Embedding explicit representation of cyber-physical elements in task models. In: 2016 IEEE International Conference on Systems, Man, and Cybernetics (SMC). IEEE (2016)

16. Lee, B., Jin, T., Lee, S.H., Saakes, D.: SmartManikin: virtual humans with agency for design tools. In: Proceedings of the 2019 CHI Conference on Human Factors in Computing Systems, CHI 2019, pp. 1–13. Association for Computing Machinery, New York (2019)

17. Grainger, K., Dodson, Z., Korff, T.: Predicting bicycle setup for children based on anthropometrics and comfort. Appl. Ergon. **59**, 449–459 (2017)

18. Gurses, A.P., et al.: Human factors–based risk analysis to improve the safety of doffing enhanced personal protective equipment. Infect. Control Hosp. Epidemiol. **40**(2), 178–186 (2019)

19. HAMSTERS-XLE, ICS Tools. https://www.irit.fr/ICS/tools/. Accessed January 2023

20. Jacobsen, N.E., Hertzum, M., John, B.E.: The evaluator effect in usability studies: problem detection and severity judgments. Proc. Hum. Factors Ergon. Soc. Annu. Meet. **42**(19), 1336–1340 (1998)

21. Intolo, P., Milosavljevic, S., Baxter, D.G., Carman, A.B., Pal, P., Munn, J.: The effect of age on lumbar range of motion: a systematic review. Man. Ther. **14**(6), 596–604 (2009). https://doi.org/10.1016/j.math.2009.08.006

22. Johnson, P., Johnson, H., Hamilton, F.: Getting the knowledge into HCI: theoretical and practical aspects of task knowledge structures. In: Schraagen, J., Chipman, S., Shalin, V. (eds.) Cognitive Task Analysis. LEA (2000)

23. König, J.L., Hinze, A., Bowen, J.: Workload categorization for hazardous industries: the semantic modelling of multi-modal physiological data. Future Gener. Comput. Syst. **141**, 369–381 (2023)

24. Karhu, O., Kansi, P., Kuorinka, I.: Correcting working postures in industry: a practical method for analysis. Appl. Ergon. **8**, 199–201 (1977). https://doi.org/10.1016/0003-6870(77)90164-8

25. Martinie, C., Palanque, P., Barboni, E.: Principles of task analysis and modeling: understanding activity, modeling tasks, and analyzing models. In: Vanderdonckt, J., Palanque, P., Winckler, M. (eds.) Handbook of Human Computer Interaction. Springer, Cham (2022). https://doi.org/10.1007/978-3-319-27648-9_57-1

26. Martinie, C., Palanque, P., Bouzekri, E., Cockburn, A., Canny, A., Barboni, E.: Analysing and demonstrating tool-supported customizable task notations. PACM Hum. Comput. Interact. **3**(EICS), 26 (2019). Article no. 12

27. Martinie, C., Palanque, P., Ragosta, M., Fahssi, R.: Extending procedural task models by systematic explicit integration of objects, knowledge and information. In: Proceedings of the 31st European Conference on Cognitive Ergonomics (ECCE 2013), pp. 1–10. ACM (2013). Article no. 23. https://doi.org/10.1145/2501907.2501954

28. McAtamney, L., Nigel Corlett, E.: RULA: a survey method for the investigation of work-related upper limb disorders. Appl. Ergon. **24**, 91–99 (1993). https://doi.org/10.1016/0003-6870(93)90080-s
29. Norkin, C.C., White, D.J.: Measurement of Joint Motion: A Guide to Goniometry, 5th edn. FA Davis Co, Philadelphia (2016)
30. Parkinson, M., Reed, M.: Virtual fit multivariate anthropometric tool. Hum. Factors Ergon. Soc. https://www.hfes.org/Publications/Technical-Standards#VFM. Accessed Jan 2023
31. Paternò, F.: Task models in interactive software systems. In: Handbook of Software Engineering and Knowledge Engineering, vol. 1, pp. 1–19. World Scientific (2002)
32. Pheasant, S., Haslegrave, C.M.: Bodyspace, Anthropometry, Ergonomics and the Design of Work, 3rd edn. (2018). https://doi.org/10.1201/9781315375212
33. Reese, C.D.: Accident/Incident Prevention Techniques, 2nd edn. CRC Press, Boca Raton (2011). https://doi.org/10.1201/b11390
34. Reinhardt, J., Kurzweg, M., Wolf, K.: Virtual physical task training: comparing shared body, shared view and verbal task explanation. In: Augmented Humans Conference 2021 (Ahs 2021), pp. 157–168. Association for Computing Machinery, New York (2021)
35. Rohmert, W., Wangenheim, M., Mainzer, J., Zipp, P., Lesser, W.: A study stressing the need for a static postural force model for work analysis. Ergonomics **10**, 1235–1249 (1986)
36. Valls, J.A.F., Garrido, J.E., Plata, A.M., Penichet, V.M.R., Lozano, M.D.: 3D editor to define generic rehabilitation therapies as a source to monitor and guide patients. In: Proceedings of the 4th Workshop on ICTs for improving Patients Rehabilitation Research Techniques (REHAB 2016), pp. 93–96. Association for Computing Machinery, New York (2016). https://doi.org/10.1145/3051488.3051506
37. Van der Veer, G.C., Lenting, V.F., Bergevoet, B.A.: GTA: groupware task analysis - modeling complexity. Acta Physiol. **91**, 297–322 (1996)
38. Fahssi, R., Martinie, C., Palanque, P.: Enhanced task modelling for systematic identification and explicit representation of human errors. In: Abascal, J., Barbosa, S., Fetter, M., Gross, T., Palanque, P., Winckler, M. (eds.) INTERACT 2015. LNCS, vol. 9299, pp. 192–212. Springer, Cham (2015). https://doi.org/10.1007/978-3-319-22723-8_16
39. ISO 9241-11:2018(en) Ergonomics of human-system interaction — Part 11: Usability: Definitions and concepts. https://www.iso.org/obp/ui/#iso:std:iso:9241:-11:ed-2:v1:en

# Prototyping with the IVY Workbench: Bridging Formal Methods and User-Centred Design

Rafael Braga da Costa and José Creissac Campos$^{(\boxtimes)}$ (iD)

University of Minho and INESC TEC, Braga, Portugal
rafael.b.costa@inesctec.pt, jose.campos@di.uminho.pt

**Abstract.** The IVY workbench is a model-based tool for the formal modelling and verification of interactive systems. The tool uses model checking to carry out the verification step. The goal is not to replace, but to complement more exploratory and iterative user-centred design approaches. However, the need for formal and rigorous modelling and reasoning raises challenges for the integration of both approaches. This paper presents a new plugin that aims to provide support for the integration of the formal methods based analysis supported by the tool, with user-centred design. The plugin is described, and an initial validation of its functionalities presented.

**Keywords:** Formal methods · user-centred design · prototyping

## 1 Introduction

The design of safety critical interactive systems needs to provide assurance regarding the quality and safety of the interaction. The exploratory nature of traditional User-Centred Design (UCD) approaches (cf. [2,9]) does not necessarily guarantee a depth of analysis that provides this assurance. Formal (mathematically rigorous) modelling and verification are able to provide a thorough and repeatable analysis, but interactive systems pose particular challenges for their application (see [11,13] for discussions about these challenges).

A number of tools has been proposed that aim to address this from different angles (see [3,6], for reviews). Of particular interest here is the IVY workbench tool [7]. The focus of the tool's development has been to ease the application of formal modelling and verification to interactive systems design. Experience with using the tool (cf. [5,14]) has highlighted the need to find solutions to communicate the model (for validation) and the verification results (for interpretation) to domain and human factors experts. Prototyping seems a promising approach to bridge this gap.

The contribution of this paper is thus an approach for the integration of prototyping support into the IVY workbench. The goal is to enable the creation of prototypes by linking early mock-ups of the user interface with their models

© The Author(s), under exclusive license to Springer Nature Switzerland AG 2023
J. Abdelnour Nocera et al. (Eds.): INTERACT 2023, LNCS 14143, pp. 504–513, 2023.
https://doi.org/10.1007/978-3-031-42283-6_27

developed in IVY. The mock-ups provide a concrete illustration of the visual appearance of the interface, while the model provides its behaviour. Together they enable the simulation of the system behaviour.

## 2    Background

Mock-up editors focus on the physical design of the system, allowing users and designers to identify potential problems with the interface or generating ideas for new functionalities [1]. Adobe XD and Figma provide a set of built-in components, representing different user interface (UI) controls, which designers can use to build mock-ups. More advanced features such as components with multiple states, which support a more economical modelling of how the appearance of the mock-up changes with user interactions, can also be found in some of these tools. In general, however, mock-up editors have limited support for prototyping UI behaviour, as this implies some notion of the underlying system's state. Traditionally, these tools allow designers to define navigation rules, but without any associated control logic. These rules capture the navigation from mock-up to mock-up in response to user events, such as mouse clicks, but the lack of control logic means they are static and unable to express complex behaviours.

Model-based user interface analysis tools support early detection of UI design problems [3,6]. However, formal modelling does not integrate well with the exploratory nature of UCD approaches. Formal modelling is also outside the typical toolbox of a UCD practitioner. This creates barriers to adoption, even in situations where these tools might be valuable. The IVY Workbench supports the application of formal methods to interactive systems' design, from writing the models to interpreting the results of verification (performed using the NuSMV model checker [10]). IVY is designed for simplicity, aiming to provide modelling and analysis tools that are easily usable by non-experts and to communicate results effectively within an interdisciplinary team. Models are expressed in the MAL interactors language [8]. A detailed description of the language is outside this paper's scope. In the present context, what is relevant is that interactors have a state (a collection of typed attributes) and actions that act on that state. Attributes capture the contents of the user interface, and any relevant internal state of the device. Actions capture user-triggered events, as well as relevant internal events, which cause changes to the state.

Using the IVY tool typically involves a number of steps: model development, model validation, property development and verification, and analysis and interpretation of verification results. The validation and interpretation of results require input from domain and human factors experts. While the model captures the structure and behaviour of the user interface, a prototype representation of the interface would make it much easier to communicate the intended design and the verification results.

Tools such as Circus [12] or PVSio-web [15] place a greater emphasis on prototyping than IVY has done so far. The former on high-fidelity prototyping, the latter focusing more on the earlier stages of design. Other authors have explored the problem of integrating formal methods and UCD in ways that are

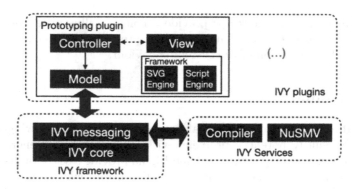

**Fig. 1.** Prototyping plugin's architecture

complementary to what is proposed herein. In [4] the goal is to bring informal design artefacts into a formal setting by finding ways to formally describing them, while herein the goal is to make formal artefacts accessible to designers.

## 3   Prototyping Plugin

To build a prototype from a MAL model, one must bring together the model, which defines the contents and behaviour of the interface, and a mock-up providing a graphical representation of that interface. Mock-ups are assumed to be vector graphics drawings in SVG [16]. This is achieved by configuring two types of bindings. Event bindings specify how the prototype responds to user interactions. They are established between user generated events in the mock-up (e.g. clicking an SVG element) and actions of the formal model. State bindings specify how the mock-up represents the state of the model. They are established between attributes in the model and the components in the mock-up. User interaction with the prototype triggers events, which cause the bound actions in the model to be *executed*. The resulting update of the model's attributes then generates changes in the prototype according to the configured state bindings.

### 3.1   Architecture

The prototyping plugin's architecture (see Fig. 1) follows the Model-View-Controller design pattern. The *Model* holds the prototype's configuration, such as the events and states and their mapping to the MAL model. The *View* defines the UI of the plugin (using Java Swing). The *Controller* acts as a mediator between *View* and *Model*. Additionally, the *Framework* component offers utility methods. It includes two essential components: *SVGEngine* and *ScriptEngine*.

The *SVGEngine* contains methods for prototype initialization, particularly the generic SVG parser. SVG files are read using the Apache Batik library, and the parser leverages the DOM (Document Object Model) structure thus generated to identify all SVG elements that support user interaction. These elements are assigned a UUID on their *id* property to ensure their uniqueness, allowing

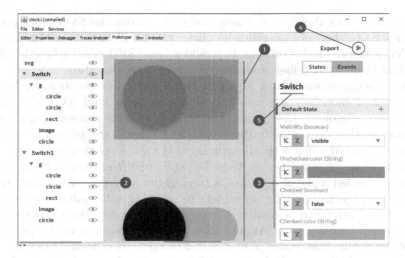

**Fig. 2.** User interface of the plugin – (1) SVG renderer; (2) SVG sidebar; (3) Configuration sidebar; (4) Access to animation mode; (5) Prototype configuration

fast document queries. The engine has been shown to work with Inkscape, Evolus Pencil, Adobe Illustrator, and Adobe XD-generated SVG files.

The *ScriptEngine* provides support for externally loaded widgets and scripts execution support. The inclusion of support for widgets in SVG mock-ups provides additional expressive power and simplifies the creation of mock-ups. Widgets consist of a set of SVG shapes and Javascript code that specifies the widget's behaviour (e.g. which shape should be presented based on conditions). A library of such widgets is being created that, at the time of writing, includes from simple widgets such as a switch, a toggle button, a checkbox, a led light or a progress bar, to complex widgets such as a dual mode clock face (hours/alarm) or the display of the B. Braun Perfusor medical device (see Sect. 4).

The scripting environment is responsible for the initialisation of imported widgets. Using the Rhino Javascript engine, it extracts the widgets' properties and methods needed for the prototype's configuration. Furthermore, the environment performs the management of all widget element identifiers to ensure their uniqueness. This task prevents problems from scenarios where a user builds a prototype containing multiple instances of the same widget. The scripting environment is also responsible for binding the SVG mock-up and the MAL model. This feature is essential for combining the formal model capabilities of IVY with the mock-up. During prototype animation, the environment invokes the widgets' methods with relevant values obtained from the model. These methods use DOM queries to select SVG elements. Then, they modify the CSS properties of those elements according to the parameters received.

## 3.2 The Plugin's UI

The prototyping plugin's UI (see Fig. 2) features the SVG renderer, the SVG sidebar and the Configuration sidebar. An animation mode is also provided.

The renderer uses the Apache Batik library to render the SVG mock-up, and supports SVG elements selection by clicking. The SVG tree sidebar displays the SVG's hierarchical structure. It provides basic SVG editing functionalities, including visibility toggling, and element deletion and insertion.

The Configuration sidebar supports the definition of the binding between mock-up and model. The states tab allows users to bind SVG elements to the model's attributes. Each element has a default state representing its initial appearance. Users can modify the properties of that state, or add more states that are triggered when a specific condition is met. SVG tags, such as *g*, have a predefined set of properties that can be configured (e.g. their visibility), while externally loaded widgets allow users to configure any properties presented in their *props* object. The UI guides users in selecting valid values for the properties, listing attributes according to the type required by each property. This helps prevent binding errors. At animation time, the environment checks whether any of the defined conditions of an element matches its criteria. If this happens, then the matched state will be rendered. Otherwise, the simulation renders the default state of the element.

The events tab allows users to bind events at the SVG level (triggers) with formal model's actions. A trigger can be a user interaction or a periodic timer event. A trigger can be defined to directly execute a widget function. This offers the possibility to change the prototype's appearance without the formal model's assistance. This feature supports the creation of advanced prototypes without the need for creating complex formal models, by isolating cosmetic changes at the SVG level.

The animation window displays the prototype (in a SVG renderer), and the list of available actions (see Fig. 3). The environment uses IVY's internal messaging system to communicate with the NuSMV model checker and obtain the current state of the prototype. Users can interact with the prototype through the mock-up, triggering the defined events, or with the actions in the list.

## 4   An Example – The B. Braun Perfusor® Space

The B. Braun Perfusor® Space is a programmable infusion pump that automates the administration of drugs to patients. Although the device offers multiple configuration modes, herein we will focus on the programming of the value to be infused (VTBI). We will briefly describe the formal model, the UI mock-up, and the prototype's configuration and running.

The goal of the **formal model** is to capture the behaviour of the device. The VTBI is presented on the display (see Fig. 3). Digits can be increased and decreased by pressing the up and down keys. A cursor (identified by a black square) highlights the currently selected digit. The left and right arrow keys move the cursor between digits. The start/stop button, controls drug administration. When the device is administering the drug, the running indicator lights up. In this mode, users cannot interact with the cursor, and the value represented in the display decreases over time.

The infusion pump model consists of a MAL interactor capturing the contents and behaviour of its user interface. A detailed description of the model is

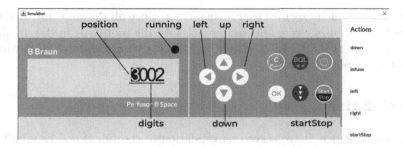

**Fig. 3.** Mock-up of the B. Braun Perfusor® Space UI

not feasible herein. Enough will be described to make the example clear. This amounts to explaining which attributes and actions are needed in the model. Looking at Fig. 3, the following attributes are relevant: *digits* (an array holding the value of each digit in the display), *position* (an integer indicating the cursor position in the display), *running* (a boolean indicating whether the device is in infusion mode). As for actions, the model defines the following: *up/down* (increase/decrease the value in the selected digit), *left/right* (increase/decrease the *position* attribute – i.e. move the cursor), *startStop* (start/stop the infusion process), *infuse* (internal action that represents the progression of the infusion process by decreasing the volume to be infused until it reaches 0 or the device is stopped). This is expressed in MAL as (axioms ommited for brevity):

```
interactor main
  attributes
    [vis] digits: array 0..MAXDIG of int
    [vis] position: 0..MAXDIG
    [vis] running: boolean
  actions
    [vis] up down left right startStop
    infuse
```

Figure 3 presents the device's **UI mock-up**. Besides basic SVG shapes representing buttons and static information, it features two widgets: led and cursor. The led widget is used to indicate if the device is in infusion mode. It has a property (*On*) to control whether the led is light-up. The cursor widget was explicitly developed to represent the digits screen of this pump. Its main properties are *Digits* (each of the digits displayed) and *Cursor Position* (the position of the cursor in the display).

To have a **running prototype**, bindings between model and mock-up need to be defined. Configuration of the cursor widget is done by binding the attributes *digits* and *position* from the model to the properties *Digits* and *Cursor Position*, respectively. Configuration of the led widget is done by binding the *running* attribute from the model to the *On* property of this widget. The click events of the arrow buttons and the start/stop button are bound to the appropriate actions (*up*, *down*, *left*, *right*, *startStop*). Finally, the *infuse* action was bound to a timer event, which executes every one second. Once all the steps just described were performed, users were able to interact with the prototype in the simulation window. Figure 3 is in fact a screen capture of the contents of that window, annotated for readability.

## 5    Validation

The medical device above served as validation of the functional capabilities of the new plugin. The next phase of the project will be to validate the role of the plugin as a bridge between formal methods and human factors and domain experts. This will entail exploring its use to validate formal models by allowing domain experts to interact with the model via the prototype, thus validating the captured behaviour, as well as using the prototype to replay behaviours resulting from the verification process, to support the identification of errors.

As a first step, however, we were interested in evaluating whether the process of creating prototypes is itself accessible to non-experts. We have carried out the pilot of a user test designed to evaluate this. The test consists of setting up the prototype for the B. Braun device, given the formal model and the mock-up. The trial sessions were performed on a laptop with the IVY Workbench installed, and the required model and mock-up available. A consent form, a test script containing a brief introduction to IVY, a step-by-step guide to prototype configuration, and a final questionnaire were also made available. The step-by-step guide explained the configuration of a toggle button. The questionnaire served to collect demographic data (name, age, sex and background experience) and collect feedback on the tool. The full test procedure was the following: (1) welcome and consent form signing; (2) test script presentation and brief explanation of the tool and the activities to perform; (3) execution of the step-by-step example and clarification of any questions related to the tool; (4) execution of the actual test (recorded via screen capturing); (5) answering the questionnaire.

The pilot involved 5 participants (one male and four female) with average age 23.6 years ($\sigma = 2.1$). Participants were selected to cover a wide range of backgrounds. One participant had a software engineering background. Two participants had design backgrounds. And the last two participants did not have a background in either of the areas. Two participants indicated that they had previous experience with mock-up editors, none had experience with IVY.

All participants were able to complete the configuration of the prototype. The average time required to fulfil the task was 8 min 55 s ($\sigma = 2m17s$). Overall the pilot validated the testing protocol and a number of observations was already possible. Users were able to quickly select the appropriated attributes of the formal model to configure the required states of the elements in the mock-up. However, they had difficulties selecting SVG elements composed from other SVG elements. Users rarely selected elements by interacting with the renderer. Instead, they prefered the SVG tree sidebar. Initially, users had some difficulties in distinguishing the differences between states and events. These were overcome as they interacted more with the tool.

As mentioned, at the end of the test a number of questions were asked about the tool. Regarding their overall impression of the system, all participants made a positive overall evaluation. As most positive aspects of the system, participants mentioned the simplicity of the UI. Three participants approved the possibility of selecting SVG elements both with the SVG tree sidebar and the renderer. One participant mentioned the attribute selection guidance in the states configuration process. As most negative aspects, participants mentioned difficulties in selecting groups of SVG elements. As most surprising aspects of the system, three participants mentioned the use of widgets in the mock-ups, two participants pointed out periodic time events, and one participants mentioned the tool's capabilities to create running prototypes with ease. As for missing functionalities, two participants pointed out drag and drop and SVG group selection in the renderer. Only two participants (those with prior experience with mock-up editors) were able to compare the functionalities of the plugin with other UI prototyping tools. Both participants appreciated the capabilities of adding behaviour to prototypes afforded by the tool.

## 6 Conclusion

We have presented a new plugin for the IVY workbench. The plugin aims to provide support for the integration of the formal methods based analysis, with user centred design. It proposes to achieve this through supporting the process of creating user interface prototypes by binding together the formal models used for analysis, and the mock-ups used for user centred design. These prototypes will be instrumental in, first, validating the behaviour captured by the model with domain experts and human factors experts, and, second, communicate the results of the analysis to the same stakeholders. The goal is not to replace tools like Figma, rather integrate the workflows of such tools with the formal verification workflow. In any case, in doing this we achieve prototypes that are able to exhibit a level of behaviour that is not easily achieved with mock-up editors.

Besides describing the plugin, the paper describes the initial steps taken to validate the tool. Although preliminary, the tests already emphasised the strengths and weaknesses of the new prototyping features. Users recognised the widgets' capabilities and generally found the developed UI intuitive. However, users had difficulties selecting SVG elements in the renderer, suggesting some improvements are needed to support group selection as default instead of single element selection.

Future work will include further developing the widgets library and proceeding with the evaluation of the tool. First by completing the evaluation mentioned above. Then, by exploring the role that the tool might have as a bridge between formal methods and user-centred design.

**Acknowledgements.** This work is financed by National Funds through the Portuguese funding agency, FCT - Fundação para a Ciência e a Tecnologia, within project UIDB/50014/2020.

# References

1. Beaudouin-Lafon, M., Mackay, W.: Prototyping tools and techniques. In: Jacko, J.A., Sears, A. (eds.) The Human-Computer Interaction Handbook: Fundamentals, Evolving Technologies and Emerging applications, Chap. 52, 365 Broadway Hillsdale, NJUnited States, pp. 1006–1031. L. Erlbaum Associates Inc. (2002)
2. Beyer, H., Holtzblatt, K.: Contextual Design: Defining Customer-Centred Systems. Morgan Kaufmann, San Francisco (1998)
3. Bolton, M.L., Bass, E., Siminiceanu, R.: Using formal verification to evaluate human-automation interaction: a review. IEEE Trans. Syst. Man Cybern. Part A Syst. Hum. **43**(3), 488–503 (2013)
4. Bowen, J., Reeves, S.: Formal models for informal GUI designs. Electron. Not. Theoret. Comput. Sci. **183**, 57–72 (2007). proceedings of the First International Workshop on Formal Methods for Interactive Systems (FMIS 2006)
5. Campos, J.C., Sousa, M., Alves, M.C.B., Harrison, M.D.: Formal verification of a space system's user interface with the IVY workbench. IEEE Trans. Hum.-Mach. Syst. **46**(2), 303–316 (2016). https://doi.org/10.1109/THMS.2015.2421511
6. Campos, J., Fayollas, C., Harrison, M., Martinie, C., Masci, P., Palanque, P.: Supporting the analysis of safety critical user interfaces: an exploration of three formal tools. ACM Trans. Comput.-Hum. Interact. **1**(1), 1–48 (2020)
7. Campos, J., Harrison, M.D.: Interaction engineering using the IVY tool. In: ACM Symposium on Engineering Interactive Computing Systems (EICS 2009), New York, NY, USA, pp. 35–44. ACM (2009)
8. Campos, J.C., Harrison, M.D.: Model checking interactor specifications. Autom. Softw. Eng. **8**(3/4), 275–310 (2001)
9. Carroll, J. (ed.): Scenario Based Design: Envisioning Work and Technology in System Development. Wiley, New York (1995)
10. Cimatti, A., et al.: NuSMV 2: an opensource tool for symbolic model checking. In: Brinksma, E., Larsen, K.G. (eds.) CAV 2002. LNCS, vol. 2404, pp. 359–364. Springer, Heidelberg (2002). https://doi.org/10.1007/3-540-45657-0_29
11. Dix, A., Weyers, B., Bowen, J., Palanque, P.: Trends and gaps. In: Weyers, B., Bowen, J., Dix, A., Palanque, P. (eds.) The Handbook of Formal Methods in Human-Computer Interaction. HIS, pp. 65–88. Springer, Cham (2017). https://doi.org/10.1007/978-3-319-51838-1_3
12. Fayollas, C., Martinie, C., Palanque, P., Deleris, Y., Fabre, J.C., Navarre, D.: An approach for assessing the impact of dependability on usability: application to interactive cockpits. In:Proceedings - 2014 10th European Dependable Computing Conference, EDCC 2014, pp. 198–209 (2014). https://doi.org/10.1109/EDCC.2014.17
13. Harrison, M.D., Campos, J.C., Loer, K.: Formal analysis of interactive systems: opportunities and weaknesses. In: Cairns, P., Cox, A. (eds.) Research Methods in Human Computer Interaction, Chap. 5, pp. 88–111. Cambridge University Press, Cambridge (2008)
14. Harrison, M., Freitas, L., Drinnan, M., Campos, J., Masci, P., di Maria, C., Whitaker, M.: Formal techniques in the safety analysis of software components of a new dialysis machine. Sci. Comput. Program. **175**, 17–34 (2019). https://doi.org/10.1016/j.scico.2019.02.003

15. Masci, P., Oladimeji, P., Zhang, Y., Jones, P., Curzon, P., Thimbleby, H.: PVSio-web 2.0: joining PVS to HCI. In: Kroening, D., Păsăreanu, C.S. (eds.) CAV 2015. LNCS, vol. 9206, pp. 470–478. Springer, Cham (2015). https://doi.org/10.1007/978-3-319-21690-4_30
16. W3C: Scalable Vector Graphics (SVG) 2. Candidate Recommendation CR-SVG2-20181004, W3C, October 2018. https://www.w3.org/TR/2018/CR-SVG2-20181004/

# Towards Automated Load Testing
# Through the User Interface

Bruno Teixeira and José Creissac Campos[(✉)] [ID]

University of Minho and INESC TEC, Braga, Portugal
`jose.campos@di.uminho.pt`

**Abstract.** Slight variations in user interface response times can significantly impact the user experience provided by an interface. Load testing is used to evaluate how an application behaves under increasing loads. For interactive applications, load testing can be done by directly calling services at the business logic or through the user interface. In modern web applications, there is a considerable amount of control logic on the browser side. The impact of this logic on applications' behaviour is only fully considered if the tests are done through the user interface. Capture reply tools are used for this, but their use can become costly. Leveraging an existing model-based testing tool, we propose an approach to automate load testing done through the user interface.

**Keywords:** Model-based testing · load testing · capture and replay

## 1  Introduction

Software testing [9] aims to increase confidence in the quality of a piece of software. Load testing is a particular type of software testing, which aims at testing a system's response under varying load conditions by simulating multiple users accessing the application concurrently.

Load testing can be split into API and UI (User Interface) load testing. API load testing is done by directly calling the services at the business layer level. This avoids the complexity, and work load, of automating the interaction with the application's user interface. Although strategies can be used to create combinations of different types of request, side stepping the UI risks making the tests less representative of actual use. Tests that ignore the user interface do not take into account the control logic programmed into the browser. This logic can range from dialogue control, which can help mask or exacerbate delays in the access to back-end services, to the full business logic of the application, depending on the type of web application under test. In any case, the impact of, at least, part of the application logic on performance is not assessed. This

This work is financed by National Funds through the Portuguese funding agency, FCT - Fundação para a Ciência e a Tecnologia, within project UIDB/50014/2020.

J. Abdelnour Nocera et al. (Eds.): INTERACT 2023, LNCS 14143, pp. 514–522, 2023.
https://doi.org/10.1007/978-3-031-42283-6_28

is relevant because small variations in user interface response times can have a huge impact on their user experience [4].

UI load testing addresses this by interacting with the browser to simulate user interaction. This type of test is expensive to setup, usually requiring a capture phase where use behaviour is recorded for later replay during testing.

In this paper, we present an approach to automate UI load testing of web applications. This work is part of an ongoing effort to explore the use of model-based testing to automate the testing of user interfaces.

## 2   Background

Load tests are non-functional tests, aimed at determining how well a system performs under high work loads. In the web applications' context, load testing involves the use of tools to simulate the execution of the application when subjected to a specific workload, and the analysis of measurements according to predefined benchmarks. These benchmarks cover metrics such as the number of virtual users, throughput, errors per second, response time, latency and bytes per second [6]. The goal is to identify performance bottlenecks in order to prevent end-users from encountering any problems during peak load.

The need to automate the testing process is essentially due to the need to repeat the same tests, as well as the need to increase test coverage. Model-based testing (MBT) [13] is a black-box testing technique that supports the automation of software testing, from test generation to test results' analysis [1,12]. This method compares the state and behaviour of a product (the system under test – SUT) with an abstract model (the oracle) that represents the behaviour of the SUT. Discovery of system errors is achieved by comparing the results of the tests in the SUT with the *predictions* of the oracle, in order to detect inconsistencies between both. MBT's main limitations are connected to the need to develop and maintain the oracle, and the potential for an explosion of test cases during the generation process. We chose to explore MBT due to its potential to automate the testing process from a model of the SUT.

Several authors have explored the application of MBT techniques to Graphical User Interfaces (GUI) (examples include [7,8,10], but see also [11] for a review). It should be noted, however that the focus has been product quality, much more than quality in use (cf. the ISO/IEC 25010 standard [5]). This is to be expected, since the oracle typically captures functional requirements of the SUT. An example of folding usage considerations into an MBT process is presented in [2]. The paper is part on an ongoing effort to explore how MBT can be used to automate the testing of user interfaces. In the context of this effort we have developed the TOM tool [10]. Here we look at how the tool might be used to perform UI load testing.

## 3   Design of the Proposed Approach

In order to support automated model-based load testing from the GUI, assuming a model of the SUT is available, four requirements were identified: (Step 1)

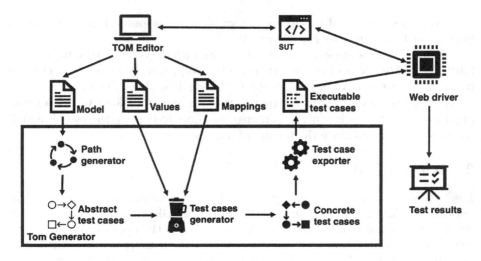

**Fig. 1.** The TOM framework

generation of multiple similar tests from the model; (Step 2) automation of the interaction with the browser; (Step 3) load simulation on the application by running multiple tests concurrently; (Step 4) capture of performance metrics and generation of reports for results' analysis.

The TOM framework (see Fig. 1) already provides initial solutions for the first two steps. Its test cases generation component (TOM Generator) receives as input a model of the application's GUI (a state machine, represented in XML, where states represent windows or pages of the interface), and generates executable tests in Java using Selenium WebDriver (Step 1). Models are abstract representations of the interface, that is, the state machine does not identify the concrete elements of the implementation. TOM performs both the step of generating abstract tests over the model and refining them to concrete (executable) ones. For this, it needs two additional inputs (a *Mapping* file and a *Values* file).

The *Mapping* file identifies which implementation elements correspond to which logical (abstract) elements in the model. It consists of a JSON object defining a mapping between the model and the elements present in the HTML page. The *Values* file defines concrete values to be used when creating executable tests. As mentioned above, interaction with the browser (Step 2) is achieved through Selenium WebDrive, a remote control interface that enables programmatic introspection and control of the browser.

The next step (Step 3) is to test the SUT. We divide this into two sub-steps: a functional testing phase to guarantee that all test cases are successful, followed by a load testing phase. A solution to run tests concurrently is needed as, in the available version, TOM can only run tests sequentially. Apache JMeter[1] is used to achieve this. However, since the goal is to perform load tests through the application's UI, it is not possible to use the traditional HTTP Request

---

[1] https://jmeter.apache.org/.

component that JMeter offers, as this type of component is used to make requests to the application's API. Thus, it was necessary to explore alternatives supporting the execution of tests written using Selenium WebDriver. These are called samplers. JMeter features several types of samplers, and after analysis, the option was to use the JUnit Request sampler.

In the last step of the process (Step 4), it is necessary to evaluate and analyse the results of the test cases' execution. As the main goal is to analyse the effect of load on the application, it is relevant to analyse performance metrics. However, as mentioned above, there is a first testing phase where each test is executed separately (to find possible failing tests). Besides supporting functional tests, this guarantees that only non-failing tests are performed in the load testing phase in order not to waste resources and time. This is relevant since load testing requires a large amount of resources and computing power. After analysis of alternatives, the Allure framework was adopted to present the results of the functional testing phase. Regarding the analysis of the load testing phase, JMeter provides reports on this aspect.

# 4   Implementation

The TOM framework is composed of three components: TOM Generator, TOM Editor and TOM App. TOM Generator (see Fig. 1) contains the core of the TOM Framework. This component has a modular architecture to ensure the adaptability of the framework and includes modules to read and translate different types of models to their internal representation, as well as the modules to generate, transform and execute the test cases. The TOM Editor (see Fig. 3, right) is a browser extension that is responsible for developing GUI models. The editor supports capturing the user's interaction and defining the system model based on that interaction. The TOM App (see Fig. 2) consists of the presentation layer of the TOM Framework. It supports the process of generating and executing test cases.

A number of changes had to be made to the existing TOM framework implementation in order to support the execution of load tests. These were done both on the framework's back-end (TOM Generator) and front-end (TOM App).

## 4.1   Back-End – TOM Generator

Two main changes were made in the back-end. One was the implementation of the Headless Mode property, the other the implementation of an option to generate random data.

Headless mode is a process of executing tests in browsers without displaying the user interface. This means that the HTML page that is under test is not rendered on the screen (which should save time during test execution). This mechanism helps run multiple concurrent tests in a single machine, or in remote machines. Without it, multiple browser instances would have to be concurrently opened and closed, which is likely to have a significant impact on the time needed to run the tests. This mode is optional to cater for situations where actually displaying the pages is considered relevant (for example, when the GUI's rendering times need to be considered). Implementing it, meant changes mostly to the test cases generation process, which is responsible for converting abstract tests into concrete test cases.

The other change was the implementation of an option to generate random data. Originally, the TOM Generator allowed the filling of forms with the data directly present in the Values file. This becomes a problem when performing load tests, as we have to execute the same test multiple times. Repeatedly using the same values will, in many cases, fail (consider the task of user registration). This problem was solved by adding a property to the Mapping file that tells TOM Generator to generate random data (based on the value provided). This prevents exactly identical executable tests. The code needed to read the configuration files was updated to process the new attributes added to the mapping file, in particular, related to the generation of random values.

A new exporter was created to generate the load tests. This was done starting from a generic test template in JMX (a JMeter format) to which the tests are added. Routes to support access to the new functionalities were also implemented.

## 4.2   Front-End – TOM App

A new version of the TOM framework front-end (the TOM App) was developed to support the new functionalities. The UI of the application is divided in three main tabs (see Fig. 2): Projects, Generation Requests, and Generation Results.

The Projects tab contains all the functionalities for managing projects. Users can view the list of their projects and add new projects. Additionally, users can observe all the components that make up the project, such as the System Model, the Mapping file and the Values file. Deleting the project and downloading it are also available options.

The generation of test cases is available in the Generation Requests tab. This process involves three phases. In the first phase, global configurations are set, such as the URL for which the test cases will be generated, whether to use headless mode, and the graph traversal algorithm to be used to generate test cases. In the second phase, the project that will be used to generate the tests is selected (the UI model, etc.). At this stage, the user may also visualise all the configuration files that constitute the project. Finally, in the third phase, the user is presented with all the information about the test generation request and the option to execute it (which sends it to TOM Generator).

In the Generate results tab (see Fig. 2) the results of previous test case generation requests are presented. Regarding each result, it is possible to visualise properties such as the number of tests generated and the time needed to generate the tests, as well as download the corresponding files to run the tests at a later date and in an appropriate setup, or open the test set. Opening a particular test set provides access to the execution of the tests. This is done in two phases as explained above.

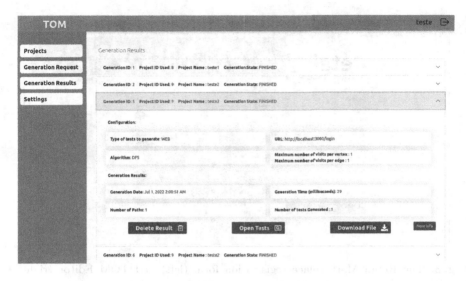

**Fig. 2.** TOM App: Generation Results

## 5    Applying the Framework

We now briefly describe two applications of the framework. The first is its application to a preexisting e-commerce platform (Retail Marketplace) developed in the scope of a MSc. curricular unit by the first author and colleagues.

The concrete functionality tested herein consists of the process of registering a buyer. Users must initially navigate to the login form, where they find the option "register new user". Then, they must chooses the option "register as purchaser", and finally fill in the registration form on the platform (see Fig. 3, left). The model of the user interface was developed using the TOM Editor, which partially automates the process using capture-replay. A test was generated to exercise the registration process. Originally, this test consisted of registering a user with name "Bruno Teixeira" using the email "bruno@mail.com" and password "1234". This test passed successfully when run on its own (first stage of testing). Load testing consisted of simulating 20 users performing the registration process simultaneously. For testing purposes the test was run locally, and configured to use headless mode. As required for load testing, random values were used for the inputs. As can be seen at the top of Fig. 4, from the 20 tests executed, two failed. This failure may be related to a delay in receiving the reply from the Retail Marketplace app, which meant that subsequent attempts to locate elements in the interface failed. While this in itself is an indication of degraded performance (indeed performance degrades substantially with 18 threads), in the future, the possibility of defining the pace of the interaction should be supported.

Another example of use is the application of the framework to the analysis of the TOM app itself. This involved the creation of a model of the app. The model consisted of 23 states, and 297 tests were generated (in 556 ms). All tests

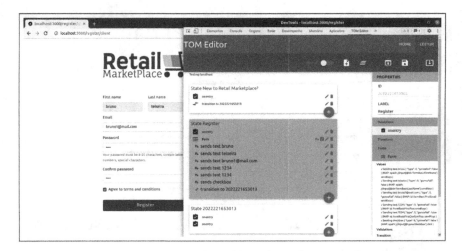

**Fig. 3.** The Retail Marketplace registration form (left) and TOM Editor (right) – from [3]

passed the first stage. For the second phase, 11 tests were selected for execution. The tests were run on remote machines using the Google Cloud platform. Several scenarios were attempted, with the goal of assessing the impact of headless mode and the impact of performing the test through the UI versus direct back-end API calls. It was possible to conclude that using headless mode provided some level of improvement in terms of time required to run the tests, although not as much as we were expecting – on average a time saving of 5.7%. The main conclusion, however, was that the computing power required to perform realistic tests (in terms of number of concurrent accesses) increases quite considerable when running the test through the UI, even in headless mode. In an environment with 32 virtual CPUs, each with 138 MB of RAM, it was not possible to run the tests for 1500 threads in the UI case, while in the back-end API case it was possible to reach more than 30000 threads. In the future, strategies to decreases the resources demand of the framework should be researched.

## 6   Conclusions and Future Work

We have described a model based approach to automate the load testing of web applications that takes into consideration their user interface layer. The short term goal has been to support the automated generation and execution of more realistic load tests. Web application are increasingly using client side code and testing the back-end APIs directly does not take into consideration this code. However, creating UI load tests that interact with the application through the user interface is time consuming. By using a model-based approach we were able to considerably automate the process. One pending problem is the high level of computational resources required to run the tests. What level of resources is needed to run the approach effectively, and whether the resources requirements can be decreased, will have to be further investigated.

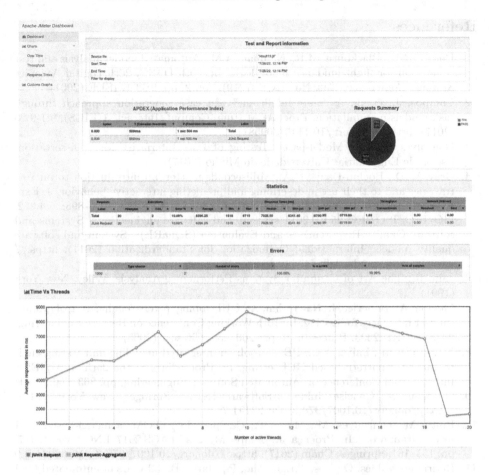

**Fig. 4.** JMeter reports

The long term goal is to support the consideration of user experience criteria when load testing web applications. Small differences in UI reaction time can have a great impact on user experience. How the user interface uses the back-end services can help mask or exacerbate delays created by the back-end. It can also create delays in the user interface itself. This means that from a user experience perspective, the impact of load on the application must be measured at the user interface. In future work we plan to explore how the approach proposed herein can be used to assess these aspects, and also how the approach compares to API load testing for different classes of applications. Web applications with different levels of logic on the client side (the browser) will be tested and the results compared with tests run directly on their business logic APIs.

# References

1. Busser, R.D., Blackburn, M.R., Nauman, A.M.: Automated model analysis and test generation for flight guidance mode logic. In: 20th DASC. 20th Digital Avionics Systems Conference (Cat. No. 01CH37219), vol. 2, pp. 9B3-1. IEEE (2001)
2. Campos, J., et al.: A "more intelligent" test case generation approach through task models manipulation. Proc. ACM Hum. Comput. Interact. **1**(EICS), 9:1-9:20 (2017). https://doi.org/10.1145/3095811
3. Gonçalves, M.J.R.: Model-based Testing of User Interfaces. Msc. Dissertation, Escola de Engenharia, Universidade do Minho (2017)
4. Gray, W.D., Boehm-Davis, D.A.: Milliseconds matter: an introduction to microstrategies and to their use in describing and predicting interactive behavior. J. Exp. Psychol. Appl. **6**(4), 322–335 (2000). https://doi.org/10.1037//1076-898x.6.4.322
5. ISO/IEC: ISO/IEC 25010:2011 systems and software engineering - Systems and software Quality Requirements and Evaluation (SQuaRE) - System and software quality models. International Organization for Standardization (2011). https://www.iso.org/standard/35733.html
6. Jain, R.: The Art of Computer Systems Performance Analysis. Wiley, New York (1991)
7. Memon, A., Banerjee, I., Nagarajan, A.: GUI ripping: reverse engineering of graphical user interfaces for testing. In: 10th Working Conference on Reverse Engineering, 2003. WCRE 2003. Proceedings, pp. 260–269. Citeseer (2003)
8. Moreira, R.M., Paiva, A.C.: PBGT tool: an integrated modeling and testing environment for pattern-based GUI testing. In: Proceedings of the 29th ACM/IEEE International Conference on Automated Software Engineering, pp. 863–866 (2014)
9. O'Regan, G.: Concise Guide to Software Testing. Springer, New York (2019). https://doi.org/10.1007/978-3-030-28494-7
10. Pinto, M., Gonçalves, M., Masci, P., Campos, J.C.: TOM: a model-based GUI testing framework. In: Proença, J., Lumpe, M. (eds.) FACS 2017. LNCS, vol. 10487, pp. 155–161. Springer, Cham (2017). https://doi.org/10.1007/978-3-319-68034-7_9
11. Rodríguez-Valdés, O., Vos, T.E.J., Aho, P., Marín, B.: 30 years of automated GUI testing: a bibliometric analysis. In: Paiva, A.C.R., Cavalli, A.R., Ventura Martins, P., Pérez-Castillo, R. (eds.) QUATIC 2021. CCIS, vol. 1439, pp. 473–488. Springer, Cham (2021). https://doi.org/10.1007/978-3-030-85347-1_34
12. Rosaria, S., Robinson, H.: Applying models in your testing process. Inf. Softw. Technol. **42**(12), 815–824 (2000)
13. Utting, M., Legeard, B.: Practical Model-Based Testing: A Tools Approach. Elsevier, Amsterdam (2010)

# Motion Sickness, Stress and Risk perception in 3D Environments

# "Do I Run Away?": Proximity, Stress and Discomfort in Human-Drone Interaction in Real and Virtual Environments

Robin Bretin[1]([⊠])(iD), Mohamed Khamis[1](iD), and Emily Cross[1,2](iD)

[1] University of Glasgow, Glasgow, UK
r.bretin.1@research.gla.ac.uk
[2] Western Sydney University, Sydnay, Australia

**Abstract.** Social drones are autonomous flying machines designed to operate in inhabited environments. Yet, little is known about how their proximity might impact people's well-being. This knowledge is critical as drones are often perceived as potential threats due to their design (e.g., visible propellers, unpleasant noise) and capabilities (e.g., moving at high speed, surveillance). In parallel, Virtual Reality (VR) is a promising tool to study human–drone interactions. However, important questions remain as to whether VR is ecologically valid for exploring human–drone interactions. Here, we present a between-within subjects user study (N = 42) showing that participants' stress significantly differs between different drone states and locations. They felt more comfortable when the drone retreated from their personal space. Discomfort and stress were strongly correlated with the perceived drone's threat level. Similar findings were found across real and virtual environments. We demonstrate that drones' behaviour and proximity can threaten peoples' well-being and comfort, and propose evidence-based guidelines to mitigate these impacts.

**Keywords:** Proxemics · Social Drones · Virtual Reality

## 1 Introduction

Increasing interest in drones as well as technological progress within the fields of artificial intelligence and sensors foreshadow the impending advent of social drones. Designed to help people in their everyday life and increase well-being, these autonomous flying machines [8] might soon become users' favorite running partner [7], security guard [49] or even emotional support device [42]. But behind this radiant future hides the problematic fact that current drones are often perceived as potential physical and privacy-related threats [20]. Beyond the requirement for drones to be trusted to integrate them into society [61], it is important to explore and understand the kinds of negative impacts that drone interactions might have on people. If peoples' encounters with drones cause perceived emotional, physical, or privacy-related threats, then further integration of drones

J. Abdelnour Nocera et al. (Eds.): INTERACT 2023, LNCS 14143, pp. 525–551, 2023.
https://doi.org/10.1007/978-3-031-42283-6_29

into social spaces might generate stressful environments and trigger defensive behaviors among people (e.g., maintain greater distances [27,87], attack [12]).

Developing a fuller understanding of the reasoning behind people's reactions near drones (Human–Drone Proxemics (HDP)) is therefore critical. Investigating HDP will unlock interaction opportunities relying on closeness (e.g., touch [1, 53], body landing [4]), while facilitating the design of proxemic-aware social drones [37]. Like humans in our everyday life, such social drones could accurately adapt their behaviors and design to specific users (e.g., visually impaired [5], children [34]), environments (e.g., public spaces [85], homes [9,48]), context [44] and applications [43]. Thus, this fuller understanding HDI contributes to the development of human-friendly and socially acceptable social drones.

Nevertheless, the potential danger that drones' proximity to humans represents, as well as the practical and legal limitations of these machines, have hindered HDP research to date. To overcome these difficulties, a promising approach is the use of Virtual reality (VR) as a proxy for real-world HDP experiments [91]. While VR has many advantages compared to real-world HDI studies (e.g., safety, replicability), it remains unclear the extent to which a virtual environment might alter underlying proxemic mechanisms and resulting participants' preferences and reactions during human–drone interactions. As such, understanding the extent to which virtual drone interactions approximate real interactions with social drones represents another valuable research question to address.

We present a user study ($N = 42$) aiming to understand 1) the impact of drones' presence and proximity on people's well-being and 2) the extent to which VR alters the results of human–drone proxemic experiments. In a real-world environment and its virtual replica, and for two drone's speed conditions (1 m/s, 0.25 m/s), we compared participants' perceived stress in a resting baseline and in different flying phases (static far, approach, static close). We then measured their discomfort level and preferences for different drone's locations. After each speed condition, participants rated how threatening they thought the drone was.

We found that participants' perceived stress significantly differs between different drone states and locations. Drones moving away from participants' personal space induced significant decrease in discomfort. Both discomfort and stress were strongly positively correlated with the perceived drone's threat level. Similar results were discovered in both real and virtual environments, indicating that VR findings can be transferred to the real world. Semi-structured interviews uncovered many factors of threat perception like sound, unpredictability, propellers, camera, proximity, and movements. This study highlights that drones readily threaten peoples' well-being and thus calls into question the readiness of these machines for deployment into social spheres. We nonetheless propose potential guidelines for future work to explore to help bring safe, trusted, and reliable social drones closer to reality.

*Contribution Statement.* This work contributes to the human–drone interaction field with: **1)** A theoretically grounded user study ($N = 42$) that advances our comprehension of people's perceptions and behaviours near drones. We propose guidelines for designers to reduce the perceived threat and increase acceptability of drones operating in close proximity to humans. **2)** The first VR/real-world comparison in HDI that helps understand the transferability of VR findings' to the real world and unveils key considerations for the use of VR to study human–drone proxemics.

## 2 Related Work

### 2.1 Proxemic

*Function Specific Spaces.* In 1966, Edward T. Hall described a "series of bubbles or irregularly shaped balloons that serves at maintaining proper spacing between individuals" and coined the term proxemic for these phenomenons [39]. He proposed four zones of high social relevance (intimate, personal, social, and public). Yet as pointed out by Vignemont and Iannetti [87], other "bubbles" exist, and they serve distinct functions [3,87]. Each of these "carrier mechanisms" [41] of people's space management might impact human–drone proxemics [15], or, how close people are comfortable with drones operating near them. Leichtmann emphasizes this point in his meta-analysis of proxemics in human–robot interaction [50], and encourages researchers to discuss the most relevant frameworks to consider given the context of their experiment. Assuming a drone's encounter results in perceived emotional, physical, or privacy-related threats, we consider the proxemic protective function can be a major determinant of people's proxemic behaviours.

*Defensive Space.* Dosey and Meisels (1969) described personal space as a "buffer zone" to serve as protection against perceived emotional, physical, or privacy-related threats [3,27]. Similarly, another space-related concept, peripersonal space (PPS; defined as reaching space around the body) is associated with a "safety margin" [73] around the body. PPS is very flexible [55] and its representation relies on individual-specific integration of salient sensory inputs in a given situation. Orientation of threatening objects [21], their approach [16,86], acute stress [29] and personality (e.g., anxiety [73,82]) are known factors of PPS. Other theories related to defensive behaviours and stressful encounters describe the detection, proximity and intensity of a perceived threat as triggering specific behaviours (Risk Assessment [11,12] and Cognitive appraisal [14,32]). Unlike previous Human–Drone proxemic studies, we will build on these theories to drive the explanation of our results.

### 2.2 Human–Drone Proxemics

Proxemics has been identified as a critical design concern for social drones [8]. Wojciechowska et al. [91] showed that participants' preferred a straight front moderately fast (0.5 m/s) approach, with a drone stopping in the personal space (1.2 m). Yet they did not report on whether drone's approaches affected individuals' stress level or threat perception. Reflecting on people's reactions to drone collision, Zhu et al. [93] found that the drone's unpredictability, propeller sound and degree of protection all influenced perceived threat in a crashing situation. They mentioned that less threatened participants were more comfortable with closer drone distances. Whether threat has been induced by the crashing situation or the drone per se remains unclear. Their results are therefore limited in that they investigate participant's perception during a crashing situation and cannot be generalized to more common interactions and drone's behaviours. [1] showed that a safe-to-touch drone induced significantly closer distance and more engaging interactions compared to a control drone. While it shows that the drone's design impact user's overall perception and safety feeling, it doesn't say much about how the drone's behaviour dynamically affect people. Auda et al. [4] report safety as a main participant's concern for drone body landing. Contrarily, exploring natural human–drone interactions, Cauchard et al. [18] report few safety concerns amongst participants. They found the drone's noise and wind are linked to the participants' discomfort level and longer preferred distances from the drone. In light of these results, it remains unclear whether perceived threat or other components (drone's sound, wind) are responsible for people preferred distances and discomfort. Our work aims to deconstruct this phenomenon by providing a theoretically informed and focused contribution on the impact of drone's presence, approach and proximity on individuals' stress, discomfort and threat perception. We investigate whether dynamic variables that determine the drone's behaviours can greatly affect participant's well-being using a child-friendly consumer drone.

While a growing body of literature has begun to examine human factors during human–drone collocated interactions, some researchers [15,28,52] have pointed out the potential impact of safety techniques on peoples' reactions near drones (e.g., minimum distance [2,28,40], transparent wall [40], fixed drone [28,92], or fake drone [20]). In parallel, Virtual reality is a relatively novel yet promising approach for the HDI field. It is safe, reproducible, and moderately realistic [91]. It has been used to investigate human drone proxemics for co-existing context [15], body landing [4], path planning algorithm for in-home monitoring [9] and novel drones' shapes [17]. Yet, VR benefits are valuable only if we understand how and why obtained results are transferable to the real world. In particular, we wonder whether a virtual drone can affect people in a similar way as a real one, in terms of induced stress, threat and discomfort. For this, our work evaluates a direct comparison between VR and real-world environments during a human–drone interaction.

## 2.3 Virtual Reality as a Methodological Tool

Virtual Reality (VR) as a research methodology draws researchers' attention for years. In 1999, Loomis et al. [54] introduced VR as a promising solution to the issues of its field. It would "eliminate the trade-off between mundane realism and experimental control, [...] target population more representatively and reduce the difficulty of replication" [13]. Since then, virtual environments have been extensively used in Social Psychology [71], in Human–Computer Interaction (HCI)

[23,57,60] or Human–Robot Interaction (HRI) [72,90]. It remains that these benefits rely on the ability of VR to induce natural participants' reactions to the stimuli of interest. It has been shown that VR can reproduce stressful situations and instinctive defensive reactions [6,69,70], but participants will react differently based on their immersion (i.e., Place and plausibility illusion [79], Presence [24] and Embodiment [33,88]). As it varies between individuals [25,64], immersion is hard to predict but can be measured [66,75,77]. Comparing proxemic preferences and impressions of a humanoid ground robot between a real and virtual environment, Kamid et al. [47] did not find significant differences in terms of desired space despite different subjective impressions. Conversely, Li et al. [51] found inconsistent proxemic preferences between Live and VR ground robots but no major changes between different VR settings. These mixed results and the lack of theory-driven explanations leaves a gap of uncertainty regarding the validity of VR for Human–Robot proxemic experiments. In addition, drones are drastically different from ground robots. As suggested by a previous direct comparison [2], the driven mechanisms of people proxemic may be different between ground and flying robots, involving different considerations for the use of VR for proxemic experiments. Therefore, we conducted a comparison between virtual reality (VR) and real-world scenarios in the context of human-drone interaction (HDI) to gain insights into how VR findings can be applied in the real world, and to identify important factors to consider when using VR to study HDI.

## 3 Methodology

This study aims to investigate 1) the impact of drones' presence and proximity on people's well-being and 2) the extent to which VR alters the results of human–drone proxemic experiments. To that end, we compared participants' perceived stress between a resting baseline and different flying conditions (static far, approach, and static close) for two drone speed conditions (1 m/s, 0.25 m/s). Participants perceived drone's threat level is assessed after each speed condition. This way, we can identify whether a flying drone induces any perceived stress and if its state (approaching, static), proximity (close, far), and speed can modulate it. It also allows for investigating the association between the stress induced by the drone and its threat level. Participants then performed a modified stop-distancing procedure (see Subsect. 3.2). We asked the participants to rate their level of discomfort and how ideal the current drone position was for different locations (from 40 cm to 450 cm from the participant). This allows understanding participants' proxemic preferences and thereby mapping how discomfort varies with the distance. Although the intimate zone margin [39] is 0.45, we chose to position the drone within that range rather than at its border. For this, we opted for a slightly closer distance (0.4 m). Finally, participants are divided into two groups: one experiences a real-world setting and the other its virtual replica. We investigate the impact of the environment on perceived stress, discomfort, and distance ratings. We also statistically evaluate each environment to check whether we obtain similar findings.

### 3.1    Experimental Design and Hypotheses

This study consists of a block (A) investigating the impact of different HDI situations on participants' perceived stress and its relationship with the perceived drone's threat level, and a block (B) assessing proxemic preferences in a modified stop-distancing procedure. Both blocks (A then B) are performed twice, one time for each speed condition (1 m/s or 0.25 m/s), either in a real or virtual environment. Block B investigates the participant's perception towards the stopping distance after the drone has approached at a certain speed. The participant observes the drone's speed in block A. Thus, block A must come before B.

*Block* (**A**) follows a $2 \times 2 \times 4$ mixed split-plot design with the *Environment* as a two-level (Real, VR) between-participant factor, the drone's *Speed* as a two-level (1 m/s, 0.25 m/s) within-participant factor, and the *Phase* as a four-level within-participant factor (Baseline, Static Far, Approach, Static Close). The dependent variable is the self-reported stress for each phase for each condition. The drone's threat level is assessed for each condition. If the drone is perceived as a potential threat, the participant's perceived stress should evolve as the situational threat changes from a static distant threat, to an approaching (looming) threat, to a static close threat. We, therefore, expect **H0** participants' perceived stress to be significantly different between the different phases, with the approach being the most stressful due to the danger ambiguity [12] (unknown stop distance) and the instinctive response to looming objects [86], followed by the close static threat (within PPS), the distant static threat and finally the resting baseline. Looming objects (i.e., approaching) trigger specific defensive responses that can be modulated by the threat the object represents and its approach speed [86]. We, therefore, expect **H1:** the perceived stress to be significantly higher when approaching at 1 m/s compared to 0.25 m/s and **H2:** the reported participant threat to be positively associated with the perceived stress. **H3:** We expect the previous hypothesis to be verified in both environments but considering the reduced danger that the drone represents in VR, we expect the perceived stress to be significantly lower in the virtual environment compared to in the real world.

*Block* (**B**) follows a $2 \times 2 \times 6$ mixed split-plot design with as input variables the *Speed*, *Environment* and the six-level within-participant variable *Stop_ distance* (C0: Intimate Space (40cm), C1: 83 cm, C2: Personal Space (120 cm), C3: 240 cm, C4: Social Space (360 cm), C5: 450 cm). The stop distance starts near the intimate space's frontier (where the drone stops its approach) and then reaches half of the personal space, its frontier, half of the social space, its frontier, and finally the maximum distance allowed by the experimental setting which is within the public space. Hall's framework [39] is extensively used in human–drone proxemics [40,52,91], using these scales allows other researchers to more easily compare their results with ours. We aim to map people's personal space via the measure of their discomfort level and distance ratings (too close or too far from their ideal distance). **H4:** We expect the discomfort level to be significantly higher at the intimate frontier (PPS) compared to the other conditions. **H5:** the discomfort level to be positively associated with the perceived threat level. The speed conditions' order was randomized using a Latin square.

## 3.2  Measures

*Self-Reported Stress.* For each phase, participants verbally indicated their perceived stress on a scale from 0 (no stress at all) - 5 (moderate stress) - to 10 (extreme stress). This was validated in [76].

*Threat Level.* After each speed condition, participants rated how threatening they think the drone was on a scale from 0 (not threatening at all) - 5 (moderately threatening) - to 10 (extremely threatening).

*Stop Distance and Discomfort Ratings.* After each condition, we performed a distancing procedure. Initially located at the intimate's frontier, the drone moved back 5 times. Considering Hall's framework [39], the drone stop-positions corresponded to the intimate space (40 cm), half of the personal space (83 cm), personal space limit (120 cm), half of the social space (240 cm), social space limit (360 cm), and in the public space (max distance of 450 cm). For each stop position, we asked "How ideal is the drone stop position, from -100 (Too close) to 0 (ideal stop distance) to 100 (Too far)? A negative number means you consider the drone stopped too close to you and the higher the number is the more intense you feel about it. Conversely, a positive number means you think it is too far. A rating close to zero means you think the drone is not far from what you consider its ideal stop position." In addition, they must verbally estimate their level of discomfort. The experimenter asked "How much do you rate your level of discomfort on a scale from 0 (no discomfort at all), to 100 (maximum discomfort)? 50 is moderate discomfort. The higher you rate, the more discomfort you feel." A similar rating has already been used in previous experiments [89].

*Questionnaires.* Before the experiment, participants responded to a demographics questionnaire (age, gender, prior experience with drones and virtual reality, reluctance about drones' safety), Big Five Inventory (BFI) - 10 (measures the participants' five personality dimensions of extraversion, agreeableness, conscientiousness, neuroticism, openness) [68], the Fear of pain questionnaire (FPQ) - 9 (measures the fear and anxiety associated with pain) [58], and the STAI (State-Trait Anxiety Inventory) [83]. Each of the questionnaires is used to assess potential confounding factors. Trait anxiety, personality (neuroticism), fear of pain has been shown to impact the size of the defensive distances [67,73,82] or the risks that a situation represents [38]. Questionnaires have been created on FormR and were answered online before the experiment on the experimenter's computer in the lab. Participants in the VR group additionally answered the Igroup Presence Questionnaire (presence assessment) [75], Avatar Embodiment Questionnaire [66], and a plausibility questionnaire [77].

*Semi-directed Interview.* Post-experiment semi-directed interviews were then conducted focusing on threat perception, coping or defensive strategy, and VR. We used an affinity diagram [56] to find patterns and themes in participants' responses. To develop the insights, we transcribed the interviews, and categorized responses by first-degree similarity (e.g., same drone's component, virtual environment characteristics or behaviours), then regrouped responses by concept (e.g., safety, appeal, annoyance).

### 3.3    Setup and Apparatus

*Drone Programming.* For the real-world condition, we programmed a DJI Tello ($98 \times 92.5 \times 41$ mm) on Python using the DJI Tello SDK. The code is available on the experimenter's Github (anonymized for submission). Connected by Wi-Fi to the experimenter's computer, the drone executes the commands such as taking off and moving forward for X distance at Y speed allowing us to accurately predict its stop distance. The drone's accuracy relies on optical flow. We optimized the environment by ensuring suitable lighting and using the drone manufacturer's mission pads which serve as identifiable surface patterns that guide the drone. Relying on this accuracy and fixing the initial participant-drone distance (450 cm), we can move the drone to a specific proxemic area (e.g., personal space - 120 cm, intimate space - 40 cm). The experimenter manually set the drone's height to match the eye level per participant. The drone is partially autonomous in that it follows a pre-programmed algorithm but the experimenter still has control via the computer. The DJI Tello has been used in recent HDI experiments [35,36] (Fig. 1).

**Fig. 1.** Experimental Room (left) and its replica created in Unity 3D (right)

*Virtual Environment.* The virtual experiment was created with Unity 3D and consists of a replica of the real setting as it has been done in a previous virtual HDP experiment [15]. We aimed to accurately reproduce the main elements of the real environments to increase the presence [78,81] and foster natural participant's reaction [79,80]. Distances, drone's characteristics (appearance, sound, and behavior), room's dimensions and arrangement, and avatars' position (participant and experimenter) have also been carefully reproduced to limit the alteration of potential confounding factors in participants' evaluation of the situation (risk assessment [12] or cognitive appraisal [32]). The spatial audio we used relies on a high-quality drone recording, and the size replicate the real drone's size. We animated the virtual drone to show the rotating propellers, and imitate hovering imperfections (e.g., shakes).

## 3.4   Participants

We recruited 42 participants (17 male, 24 female, and one non-binary), mainly undergraduate and post-graduate students from scientific backgrounds (Computing Science, Psychology, Veterinary), between 21 to 42 years old (M = 26.69, SD = 4.98) and with little experience with drones or VR and mainly from Europe (35%) and Asia/Pacific (43%). We randomly assigned each participant to one of the two groups (Real-world/VR), trying to maximize the gender parity and reach a similar size.

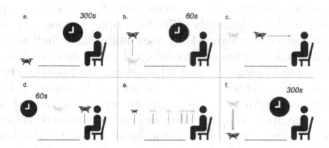

**Fig. 2.** Overview of the protocol. a) Resting baseline (300 s): The drone is on the ground at 450 cm from the participant. b) The drone takes off and remains stationary for 60 s. c) "Face detection approach": the drone approaches the participant at the target speed condition (0.25 or 1 m/s) and stops at the intimate frontier (40 cm). d) Static Close: It stays in front of the participant for 60 s. e) Distancing procedure: Stop distance and discomfort ratings for 6 predefined drone positions. f) Resting period: The drone lands and rests for 300 s. Then the protocol resets to step b for the second speed condition.

## 3.5   Protocol

After welcoming the participant to the experimental room, we invited them to fill in the consent form and read the participant protocol. The protocol stated we wish to test a feature of our autonomous drone called the "face-detection approach" and study how people feel about it. They were told the drone will move toward them two times and stop once it detects their face, but did not know the stop distance. We additionally warned them that malfunctioning can happen. They were allowed to move away if they thought they had to or if we asked them to avoid the drone. The VR group wore the Oculus Quest 2 and was immersed in a replica of the experimental room. The rest of the experiment was similar for both groups (see Fig. 2). Participants were asked to rate their stress level (0-no stress at all to 10-maximum stress) during each phase and how threatening the drone was (0-not threatening at all to 10-extremely threatening) after each condition. After the experiment, the VR group answered VR-related questionnaires (IPQ [75], Plausibility questionnaire [77], AEQ [66]). We finally performed a semi-directed interview aiming to better understand the process through which they rated their stress and threat level. The VR group shared their impression of the virtual environment while the real-world group described what would be important to make them feel and behave the same if the experiment was performed in VR. We also explored their behaviours in the case of a malfunctioning drone or a similar situation outside of the experimental context.

### 3.6    Limitations

While this study provides valuable and novel insights into HDI proxemics and people's well being around drones, the generalizability of its results is limited in that they have been obtained in a given context (indoor, sitting on a chair, in presence of the experimenter) for a specific task (face detection approach) and drone and they might significantly differ from other settings. Moreover, while self-reported stress measures are widely used and valuable indicators, they provide only limited information on physiological stress reactivity and biological outcomes compared to measures such as heart rate and skin conductance, and participants may be hesitant or unable to accurately report their true stress levels. Another issue is that the drone slightly moved in the real environment condition due to limitations in hardware and the sensors responsible for balancing the drone. This may have had an impact on participants. This is not an issue in VR, though, as the drone's movements were fully controlled.

## 4    Results

The subsequent section presents a detailed analysis of the results and statistical tests. Summary tables, which include a direct comparison between real-world and VR measures, can be found in the appendix (see Sect. A).

### 4.1    Perceived Stress

The study showed that the different phases of the drone's flight had a significant effect on participants' perceived stress, with the Approach phase being the most stressful. However, there was no significant difference in stress levels between fast ($1\,m/s$) and slow ($0.25\,m/s$) approaches. Additionally, the study found that participants' perceived threat was found to be strongly correlated with their perceived stress. These findings were consistent in both the real and virtual environments, with no statistically significant difference between them.

*Phase (Significant).* A Friedman test was run for each Environment group to determine if there were differences in perceived stress between Phases. Pairwise comparisons were performed with a Bonferroni correction for multiple comparisons. There was a statistically significant impact of the phases on perceived stress, in the real ($\chi^2(4) = 51.14$, p < .0001) and virtual environment

$(\chi^2(4) = 53.07,\ p < .0001)$. In VR, post hoc analysis revealed statistically significant differences in perceived stress between the Baseline (Md = 1.17) and the other phases except the resting period (Static Far [Md = 1.89 , p = 0.025], Approach [Md = 4.5, p = 0.003], Static Close [Md = 4.14, p = 0.005]). The Approach was also significantly different than the Static Far (p = 0.028), and the Resting (p = 0.003) and the Static Close significantly differed from the Static Far (p = 0.044) and the Resting (p = 0.003). In the real environment, the perceived stress was statistically significantly different between the Approach (Md = 4.37) and each of the other phases (Baseline [Md = 1.35, p = 0.0009], Static Far [Md = 1.89, p = 0.0006], Static Close [Md = 3.39, p = 0.028], Resting [Md = 1.52, p = 0.0006]. The Static Close was also significantly different than the Resting (p = 0.015).

***Speed*** *(No statistically significant difference).* A Wilcoxon signed-rank test was conducted for each *Environment* group to determine the effect of *Speed* on perceived stress during the drone's approach. In both environments, there was a median decrease in perceived stress between the approach at 1 m/s (Real_Md = 4.67, VR_Md = 4.61) compared to 0.25m/s (Real_Md = 3.95, VR_Md = 4.39), but this difference was not statistically significant in the real environment (z = 32.5, p = .121) and in VR (z = 36, p = .83).

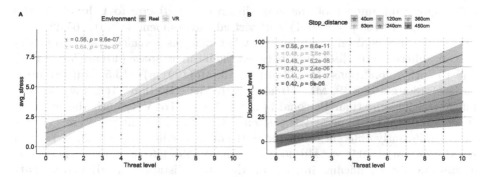

**Fig. 3. A** A Kendall's tau-b test revealed a significant strong positive correlation between the drone's threat level and perceived stress during the flying phases in the real (tau = 0.58, p < 0.05) and virtual (tau = 0.64, p<0.05) environments. **B** Kendall's tau-b correlation tests revealed a significantly strong correlation between the reported drone's threat level and participants' discomfort for each stop distance. We however notice a decrease in the correlation strength when leaving the intimate space (40 cm).

***Environment*** *(No statistically significant difference).* A Kruskal-Wallis H test was conducted to determine if there were differences in perceived stress between groups that performed the experiment in a real environment (N = 23) or in a virtual replica (N = 18). Distributions of perceived stress were similar for both groups, as assessed by visual inspection of a boxplot. Perceived stress scores increased from the Real (Md = 2.5), to the VR group (Md = 2.79), but the differences were not statistically significant, $\chi^2(1) = 0.000691$, p = 0.979.

*Threat Relationship (Significant).* In both environments, Kendall's tau-b correlation was run to assess the relationship between threat level and perceived stress during the flying phases (see Fig. 3). Preliminary analysis showed the relationship to be monotonic. There was a statistically significant, strong positive correlation between these two variables in the real (tau(41) = .56, p < .0005.) and virtual environment (tau(34) = .64, p < 0.0005).

## 4.2 Proxemics

The study showed that the distance at which the drone stopped had a significant effect on participants' discomfort, with the closest stop distance being the most uncomfortable. Additionally, the study found that participants' pre-threat assessment was strongly correlated with both their discomfort and distance ratings. However, there was no significant difference in discomfort levels between the different speed conditions. These findings were consistent in both the real and virtual environments, with no statistically significant difference between them.

*Stop Distance (Significant).* A Friedman test was run for each Environment group to determine if there were differences in discomfort and distance ratings between Stop distances. Pairwise comparisons were performed with a Bonferroni correction for multiple comparisons. There was a statistically significant impact of the stop distances on **discomfort level**, in the real ($\chi^2(5) = 70.46$, p < .0001) and virtual environment ($\chi^2(5) = 65.42$, p < .0001). **In the real** environment, post hoc analysis revealed statistically significant differences in discomfort between the intimate space (40 cm)(Md = 41.3) and the other conditions (Md(83 cm) = 20.6, Md(120 cm) = 13.5, Md(240 cm) = 9.81, Md(360 cm) = 8.49, Md(450 cm) = 6.9). The condition 83 cm was also significantly different than Personal Space (120 cm). **In VR**, both the intimate space(40 cm)(Md = 47.2) and the 83 cm (Md = 32.3) conditions were statistically significantly different compared to the other conditions (Md(120 cm) = 25.5 < Md(240 cm) = 20.9 < Md(360 cm) = 19 < Md(450 cm) = 14). There was a statistically significant impact of the stop distance on **distance ratings**, in the real ($\chi^2(5) = 104.46$, p < .0001) and virtual environment ($\chi^2(5) = 89.08$, p < .0001). **In the real** environment, post hoc analysis revealed statistically significant differences in distance rating between each conditions (Md(40 cm) = −52 < Md(83 cm) = −19.1 < Md(120 cm) = −3.57 < Md(240 cm) = 15.1 < Md(360 cm) = 31.8 < Md(450 cm) = 46.4) **In VR**, each condition was also statistically significantly different to the others (Md(40 cm) = −54.4 < Md(83 cm) = −25.5 < Md(120 cm) = −10.4 < Md(240 cm) = 13.1 < Md(360 cm) = 35.5 < Md(450 cm) = 55.2).

*Speed (No statistically significant difference).* A Wilcoxon signed-rank test was conducted for each Environment group to determine the effect of Speed on discomfort level and distance rating. **In VR**, there was a median decrease in discomfort (Md(0.25) = 25.5 < Md(1) = 27.6) and a median increase in distance rating (Md(0.25) = 2.4 > Md(1) = 2.36) between 0.25 m/s compared to 1 m/s, but these differences were not statistically significant (Discomfort: z = 30.5, p = .311,

Distance rating: z = 63, p = .53). **In the real** environment, there was a median increase in discomfort (Md(0.25) = 18.7 > Md(1) = 15) and a median decrease in distance rating (Md(0.25) = −2.51 < Md(1) = 8.22) between 0.25m/s compared to 1 m/s, but these differences were not statistically significant (Discomfort: z = 99.5, p = .0.556, Distance rating: z = 54.5, p = 0.0619).

***Environment*** *(No statistically significant difference)*. A Kruskal-Wallis H test was conducted to determine if there were differences in discomfort or distance ratings between groups that performed the experiment in a real environment (N = 23) or a virtual replica (N = 18). Distributions were similar for both groups, as assessed by visual inspection of a boxplot. Distance ratings increased from the VR (Md = 2.38), to Real group (Md = 2.92), and discomfort decreased from the VR (Md = 26.5) to the Real group (Md = 16.8), but the differences were not statistically significant, (Discomfort: $\chi^2(1) = 1.04$, p = 0.308. Distance ratings: $\chi^2(1) = 0.0118$, p = 0.913).

***Threat Relationship*** *(Significant)*. In both environments, Kendall's tau-b correlation was run for each stop condition to assess the relationship between threat level and discomfort level. Preliminary analysis showed the relationship to be monotonic. There was a statistically significant, strong positive correlation between these two variables as shown on Fig. 3 (Fig. 4).

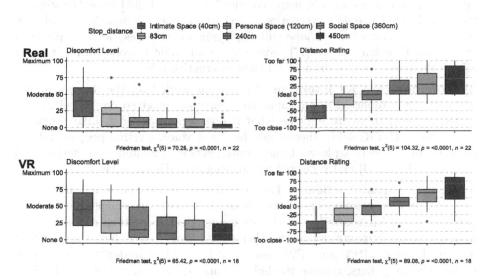

**Fig. 4.** Discomfort level (left) and stop-distance ratings (right) in the real (top) and virtual (bottom) environments for each stop condition. Friedman tests revealed a statistically significant effect of the drone stop distance on participants' discomfort and distance rating in both environments. We can observe an increase in discomfort when entering the personal space (below 120 cm). Overall, the personal space frontier (120 cm) was rated the closest to participants' ideal distance (rating of 0) in the real (Md = −3.570) and virtual environment (Md = −10).

## 4.3    Qualitative Results and Guidelines

After the experiment, we ran semi-directed interviews to unveil the factors contributing to perceived danger of drones, explore participants' defensive behaviours and examine the potential impact of VR on these aspects.We present the main themes from our affinity diagrams, with participant responses annotated (P + participant ID) and "VR" for virtual group participants.

**How to Decrease the (Perceived) Danger?** Based on our discussions with participants regarding the drone's perceived dangerousness in this experiment, we outline high-level guidelines to reduce the drone's threat level and enhance acceptability of proximity.

**1) Positive associations:** Beyond its loudness, the drone's sound and design are negatively connoted in participants' minds. (P1) said "this drone looks a little bit like a huge insect", (P41-VR) "it looks like a military thing". (P33-VR) said "It's like, constantly like a mosquito" and (P18) "Like something chop your head." Although it is hard to predict what associations might emerge in people's minds, fostering positive ones may orient participants' framing [74] towards an optimistic interpretation of the situation. Modifying the nature of the sound or the drone's design ((P15) "maybe like birds", (P3) "have some cute sticker" or (P13) "bright colours") could help. Wojciechowska et al. [91] have investigated the multifaceted people's perception of existing drones' design, Yeh et al. [92] showed that using a round shape and displaying a face helped decrease personal space, and Cauchard et al. [17] have found that radical drone forms strongly affects the perception of drones and their interactive role.

**2) Communicate its intention:** As in prior work [93], the drone's unpredictability was reported as an important source of perceived danger. (P9) suggested to "Add things to indicate what it does before doing it. Like a sensory cue." and (P37-VR) said, "there could be like a voice, alerting people that it's coming". Researchers explored drone's movements to communicate emotions [19] or intents [10, 22, 84] and preferred acknowledgment distances [46].

**3) Reduce threats' saliency:** The propellers, camera, and sound are prominent threatening components of the drone. As threat assessment relies on the perception and interpretation of sensory inputs, decreasing their salience might help orient participants' focus on other components and reduce the resulting perceived threat. (P13) and (P21) suggested it would be better "not being able to see" the propellers, remove the lights (camera) or "reduce the sound" (P1). The reduced visibility of propellers has already been mentioned as a factor for decreased threat perception in favour of other components (sound) [93]. Similarly, participants in Yeh et al. [92] social proxemic experiment reported not thinking about the propellers because they focused instead on the displayed face.

**4) Increase drone's safety:** It was also suggested to objectively decrease the threats. From a design perspective, (P12) "increase the size of the guard propellers" or (P14) "if the propellers were at the back I know that there's no chance of it interacting with my hair." But also its size "because bigger drone means bigger propellers and a more dangerous object closer to me" (P36-VR). While (P7) proposed soft material for the propellers, Nguyen et al. [62] recently presented safer deformable propellers. On a flying behaviour side, its position in space with regards to the participants' position, and flying speed has also been reported as critical. (P23) said "If it was higher (not in the eyes' line) it would not be a problem" which is congruent with previous HDP findings [15]. Some participants revealed being much more alert when it was close compared to when it was far. Indeed, as illustrated by (P2), "you never really know what happens if it's close to you." Finally, (P0) said that "more speed. It could be terrifying".

**5) Limit sensory inputs:** The annoyance resulting from the overwhelming sensory inputs (sound, air) following the drone's approach has been reported as a major concern by participants. It is congruent with previous findings [18]. The space people maintain with others also serves at maintaining an acceptable level of arousal stimulation [3,50,65], which is compromised by sensory overload. Reducing the sound level and produced air would probably greatly improve the drone's proximity acceptability. While the noise from rotors and downwash generated are not negotiable with the available state of technology of consumer drones, we argue that there is a need to push the boundaries to minimize the drawbacks of today's drones. VR can help investigate features that are unfeasible today, to guide the manufacturing of future drones.

**Defensive Behaviours.** In a scenario where the drone would have continued approaching participants until impact, they reported reactions that perfectly fit with the "3 Fs" of defensive behaviours: fight, freeze, or flight [11]. **Flight** - Some participants would have tried to avoid the drone with more or less intensity such as (P34-VR) "I would have left the chair definitely." or (P6) "I would have bent." **Fight** - Some others said they would have attacked, like (P33-VR) "I would hit it with my hands like I would do to a mosquito." or (P18) "My instinct was to hit it away." **Freeze** - Finally, some participants reported they would not have moved away, as (P36-VR) "I would have closed my eyes and step back a little bit." or (P9) "There's a strong chance I would be sitting here whispering is it going to stop, is it going to stop?". Their reactions are of different natures and intensities and might be representative of the interaction between the perceived threat level, the moment at which they would have intervened (the shorter, the more intense and instinctive the response) [12], and their personality [67]. It is no doubt that the experimental context has influenced these responses. When asked whether they would react similarly in a real situation, participants generally reported more intense and precocious defensive reactions suggesting larger defensive spaces. (P20) reported that "in the real life, I wouldn't let the drone approach me that close". (P19) "would most probably punch it." if it came as close as the intimate frontier. During the experiment, some participants believed the drone could not hurt them because they were in a controlled environment and they trusted the experimenter. But all these certainties fall out when leaving the experimental context. (P1) said "If it's outside, it's more like someone intends to attack me or something.", (P19) "I don't know who is behind that. I don't like it", (P9) "It's like what is happening and why is it happening?". But also (P16) "with a known person, I think I would be fine." It is congruent with previous research linking risk assessment with danger ambiguity [11]. It also highlights the impact of a controlled experimental environment on participants' risk assessment (and therefore ecological validity) even without visible safety mechanisms.

**Virtual Reality.** The real group, having experienced a real drone, reflected on what affected their reactions and provided valuable feedback to make the VR experience of HDP more ecologicaly valid. Responses fit into five categories (visual, sound, haptic, distances, environment) and emphasize the importance of **1)** the sensory inputs dynamic's accuracy, indicating the drone's location relative to the participant and **2)** the replica of threatening components. For the visual category, (P20) said "It would have the propellers as that's how I would distinguish the drone from something else.", for the sound (P14) said "If you can control the sound [relative to my] position, it's a bit more real because I would be able to associate the distance with the sound" and (P19) "The noise as well, I mean these components that felt threatening." For the distances, (P19) said it was important to replicate "how close it came to my face." and (P18) "it needs to come to me at my eye line, I think." Apart from the air induced by the drone's propellers, our virtual environment matched these requirements as supported by participants' feedback. When asked what made the environment feel not real, (P29-VR) said "No nothing at all. Everything was accurate." Some participants reported missing objects (e.g., their bag), poor resolution, and avatar mismatch (e.g., skin color).

## 5   Discussion

We found that a drone's state and location can induce significant stress among participants, and that these factors also correlate with the drone's perceived level of threat. We found no significant effect of the drone's speed or the environment on participants' stress, discomfort, and distance ratings. This section provides a discussion of these results.

### 5.1   Threatening Drones

**Unnoticed Speed.** While participants reported the drone's speed as an important factor for the threat assessment, it had no significant effect on stress, threat perception, or discomfort. Participants had not been informed that speed would vary and we asked them during the interview whether they noticed the velocity variation. Less than 50% of them noticed the drone going 4 times faster or slower between the conditions. We expect the way the experiment was designed (5 min of resting period between conditions) and presented (focused on the drone's stop distance) distracted participants from the drone's speed in favor of its proximity.

Ultimately, most participants did not perceive the speed variation and interpreted both conditions as the same. According to the Situational Awareness model, filtered perception and interpretation of sensory inputs are the first steps in the process of understanding current and future states of a given situation [30]. This means an input that exists but is not processed should not impact the situational evaluation process. Nonetheless, it does not necessarily mean the input is not important. It emphasizes the subjective nature of threat perception and supports the proposed guideline "Reduce threat's saliency".

**Proximity, Behaviour and Defensive Space.** The drone's proximity was associated with greater stress and discomfort amongst participants. We explain these results considering the cognitive appraisal theory [32], risk assessment process [11,12], defensive peripersonal space [73,87], and protective function of proxemic [3,27]. The drone's presence triggers a vigilance behaviour (increased watchfulness) associated with the detection of a potential threat [11,32]. Hence participants reported shifting their attention from the environment towards the drone when it took off, but drifted away after some time. Then, we argue that there is a threshold distance (defensive space) below which participants' perceived ability to avoid the drones' threat becomes significantly compromised (ratio demand/available resources) [32] and that defensive behaviours occur to reduce the threat level. Such defensive reactions would increase in intensity with the magnitude of the perceived danger [73] and as the distance from the threat decreases (from escape, hiding, to defensive threat, to defensive attack [11]). Within this space (defensive space), attention is focused on the threat and the body gathers resources to face it (inducing stress). The measured perceived stress supports this explanation and participants reported being much more alert when the drone was close compared to far. (P16) said "here (close) it can attack me anytime and there (far) it wouldn't matter. It was too far." (P22) added that "The weaving was less disconcerting when it was further away" suggesting an interacting effect between proximity and drone's behaviour on the interpretation of sensory inputs and risk assessment. Intruding the defensive space in a non-natural way or when defensive reactions are not possible (e.g., experimental context, crowded environment, social norms) would induce discomfort in that it triggers a physiological need that cannot be fulfilled (i.e., reduce the threat level). Considering the approach, as the distance decreased perceived danger might have increased in parallel with the changing uncertainty that the drone would stop, and higher demand/ability ratio. Hence, even though the looming of visual stimuli instinctively triggers defense mechanisms, we believe this induced more stress than the other phases as the highest perceived situational danger occurred right before the drone stopped.

## 5.2 Other Carrier Mechanisms: *Arousal Regulation, Communication, Goal-Oriented*

While this study primarily focuses on the proxemic protective function [27,73], we acknowledge that other carrier mechanisms may have been involved during the experiment and in HDI more broadly. In fact, we believe HDP behaviours to be the result of a weighted mean of the active spaces surrounding the individual in the given situation. For instance, a sound can be at the same time annoying and threatening, generating a distance above which its annoyance becomes acceptable, and another to maintain the threat to an acceptable threshold. It might have been exactly the case during this experiment, as the drone's sound has been characterized as very annoying and sometimes threatening. We have identified cues of the arousal regulation function [3,65] linked to the sensory overload due to the sound loudness when approaching. Some participants' feedback also suggest that the communicative function [3,39] came into play. (P20) explained their distance preference saying "that's how I talk to people" and added "I've never encountered a thinking drone so, it's like meeting a new person." and (P13) said, "My brain still kind of thinks it's a living creature, so I still kind of try to look into its eyes (camera)." It suggests that the implementation of anthropomorphic features (e.g., faces [42,92], eyes [63]) brings benefits but also adds design considerations. The way we presented the experiment may have impacted participants' proxemic preferences as we believe some participants picked their preferred distance with regards to the task the drone had to perform (face detection) which would involve the goal-oriented proxemic function [87].

### 5.3   Validity of Virtual Reality

In readiness for the use of VR as a valid methodological tool for the HDI field, this study investigated the impact of VR on people's perception near drones. We found no significant differences between the real and virtual environments and similar results in both. As mentioned earlier (see Sect. 4.3), these results might be explained by the sensory inputs dynamic's accuracy, indicating the drone's location with respect to participants' position and the replica of the threatening components. In other words, the elements involved in the evaluation of the situation with regards to participants' position. However, VR can impact critical factors such as the perception of distances [45,59], motor abilities [31], or threat perception [26,33]. We, therefore, expected each measure to be significantly different between the two environments. Regarding the perception of distances, we believe the transfer of depth markers (chairs, tables, experimenter) of the same size and position from the real world to VR helped participants develop an accurate distance estimation. For motor abilities, we used a wireless headset, hand-tracking, and participants' position was calibrated to be the same between the two environments. They were able to use their hands, freely get up from the chair and move without worrying to collide with anything (even though it never happened in the study). Then for the threat perception, we noted an impact of VR, as some participants reported not being afraid of the drone due to the virtual context. Yet similar comments have been reported by participants from the real-world setting, replacing "virtual" with "experimental" context. Threat perception might have been equally biased between both environments. This study shows that VR is extremely promising and can successfully replicate real-world results. Beyond the regular considerations of VR designs (maximize immersion), new recommandations for researchers willing to use VR for Human–Drone Proxemics include 1) identifying the relevant underlying mechanisms linked to the variables under investigation, 2) acknowledging the extent to which VR can alter these elements, and 3) limiting VR's impact through accurate replication of these elements. In our case, the relevant underlying processes are linked to threat perception and situational appraisal but it depends on the focus of the proxemic experiment.

## 6 Conclusion and Future Work

This study confirms our concerns regarding the potential negative impact of integrating drones into close social spaces on people's well-being. Participants' reactions during passive interaction with a drone aligned with expected responses to perceived threats. Stress levels increased based on situational risk and were strongly correlated with the intensity of the perceived drone's threat level. Participant discomfort significantly varied within their personal space and was also correlated with the drone's threat level. In sensitive cases such as in policing scenarios where individuals may already feel anxious or threatened, or in search and rescue operations, where they may be in distress or vulnerable, it is essential to ensure that drone interactions do not further escalate their discomfort or distress. By incorporating the insights and guidelines from our research, drone designs can be tailored to prioritize user well-being and minimize any potential negative effects on individuals' emotional states. Moreover, we believe that significant shifts in drone designs, beyond slight variations such as changing colors, would be beneficial. The current design spectrum, largely dominated by the default four-propellers model, offers limited alternatives. This study also contributes to the development of VR as a proxy for HDI experiments, enabling researchers to explore possibilities beyond the constraints of reality. Recent work by Cauchard et al., utilizing VR to explore disruptive drone forms, aligns with this ongoing movement [17].

# A  Summary Statistics

See Tables 1, 2 and 3.

**Table 1.** Direct comparison of Real-world and Virtual-Reality measures. This table presents a direct comparison of measures between the real-world and virtual-reality experimental settings. The measures are defined in the Measure subsection of the Method section in the paper. The table includes means, and statistical tests conducted to assess the differences between the two settings. No significant differences were found between the real and virtual experimental settings.

| Measure | Variables | Real-World | Virtual Reality | Environment difference |
|---|---|---|---|---|
| Perceived Stress | Baseline | 1.35 | 1.17 | **Kruskal-Wallis H test** |
| | Static Far | 1.89 | 2.64 | $\chi2(1) = 0.000691$, p = 0.979. |
| | Approach (0.25 m/s) | 4 | 4.39 | No statistically significant difference |
| | Approach (1 m/s) | 4.74 | 4.61 | between the real and virtual environment. |
| | Static Close | 3.39 | 4.14 | |
| | Resting | 1.52 | 1.5 | |
| | Overall | 2.5 | 2.79 | |
| Perceived Threat | 0.25 m/s | 3.76 | 3.56 | **Kruskal-Wallis H test** |
| | 1 m/s | 3.86 | 4.28 | $\chi2(1) = 0.00168$, p = 0.967 |
| | Overall | 3.81 | 3.92 | No statistically significant difference between the real and virtual environment. |
| Discomfort Level | 40 cm | 41 | 47.2 | **Kruskal-Wallis H test** |
| | 83 cm | 19.8 | 32.3 | $\chi2(1) = 1.04$, p = 0.308 |
| | 120 cm | 13.4 | 25.5 | No statistically significant difference |
| | 240 cm | 9.59 | 20.9 | between the real and virtual environment. |
| | 360 cm | 8.11 | 19 | |
| | 450 cm | 6.59 | 14 | |
| | Overall | 16.5 | 26.5 | |
| Distance Rating | 40 cm | -51.5 | -54.4 | **Kruskal-Wallis H test** |
| | 83 cm | -18 | -25.5 | $\chi2(1) = 0.0118$, p = 0.913 |
| | 120 cm | -1.59 | -10.4 | No statistically significant difference |
| | 240 cm | 17.8 | 13.1 | between the real and virtual environment. |
| | 360 cm | 34.7 | 35.5 | |
| | 450 cm | 48.9 | 55.2 | |
| | Overall | 4.87 | 2.38 | |

**Table 2.** Friedman Test for Perceived Stress differences between phases in each environment group, with bonferroni correction for multiple comparisons.

| Environment | n | statistic | df | p.value | Kendall's W effect size |
|---|---|---|---|---|---|
| Real | 23 | 51.1 | 4 | 2.09e-10 | 0.556 (large) |
| Virtual | 18 | 53.1 | 4 | 8.25e-11 | 0.737 (large) |

| Comparison | Environment | p value adjusted | Significance |
|---|---|---|---|
| Baseline vs Static Far | Real | 0.496 | ns |
| | Virtual | 0.025 | * |
| Baseline vs Approach | Real | 0.000941 | *** |
| | Virtual | 0.000308 | ** |
| Baseline vs Static Close | Real | 0.05 | ns |
| | Virtual | 0.000472 | ** |
| Baseline vs Resting | Real | 1 | ns |
| | Virtual | 0.341 | ns |
| Static Far vs Approach | Real | 0.000607 | *** |
| | Virtual | 0.003 | * |
| Static Far vs Static Close | Real | 0.077 | ns |
| | Virtual | 0.004 | * |
| Static Far vs Resting | Real | 1 | ns |
| | Virtual | 0.014 | ns |
| Approach vs Static Close | Real | 0.028 | * |
| | Virtual | 0.228 | ns |
| Approach vs Resting | Real | 0.000613 | *** |
| | Virtual | 0.000471 | ** |
| Static Close vs Resting | Real | 0.015 | * |
| | Virtual | 0.00031 | ** |

**Table 3.** Friedman Test for Discomfort levels and Distance ratings Differences Between Stop distances in Each Environment Group, with Bonferroni Correction for Multiple Comparisons.

| Measure | Environment | n | statistic | df | p.value | Kendall's W effect size |
|---|---|---|---|---|---|---|
| Discomfort | Real | 22 | 70.3 | 5 | 9.09e-14 | 0.639 (large) |
| | Virtual | 18 | 65.4 | 5 | 9.15e-13 | 0.727 (large) |
| Distance Ratings | Real | 22 | 104 | 5 | 6.49e-21 | 0.948 (large) |
| | Virtual | 18 | 89.1 | 5 | 1.05e-17 | 0.990 (large) |

| Comparison | Measure | Environment | p value adjusted | Significance |
|---|---|---|---|---|
| 40 cm vs 83 cm | Discomfort | Real | 0.001 | ** |
| | | Virtual | 0.013 | * |
| | Distance Ratings | Real | 0.000633 | *** |
| | | Virtual | 0.003 | ** |
| 40 cm vs 120 cm | Discomfort | Real | 0.001 | ** |
| | | Virtual | 0.007 | ** |
| | Distance Ratings | Real | 0.000644 | *** |
| | | Virtual | 0.003 | ** |
| 40 cm vs 240 cm | Discomfort | Real | 0.002 | ** |
| | | Virtual | 0.007 | ** |
| | Distance Ratings | Real | 0.000639 | *** |
| | | Virtual | 0.003 | ** |
| 40 cm vs 360 cm | Discomfort | Real | 0.004 | ** |
| | | Virtual | 0.007 | ** |
| | Distance Ratings | Real | 0.000640 | *** |
| | | Virtual | 0.003 | ** |
| 40 cm vs 450 cm | Discomfort | Real | 0.006 | ** |
| | | Virtual | 0.007 | ** |
| | Distance Ratings | Real | 0.000640 | *** |
| | | Virtual | 0.003 | ** |
| 83 cm vs 120 cm | Discomfort | Real | 0.007 | ** |
| | | Virtual | 0.013 | * |
| | Distance Ratings | Real | 0.001 | ** |
| | | Virtual | 0.007 | ** |
| 83 cm vs 240 cm | Discomfort | Real | 0.062 | ns |
| | | Virtual | 0.011 | * |
| | Distance Ratings | Real | 0.000947 | *** |
| | | Virtual | 0.003 | ** |
| 83 cm vs 360 cm | Discomfort | Real | 0.072 | ns |
| | | Virtual | 0.007 | ** |
| | Distance Ratings | Real | 0.000948 | *** |
| | | Virtual | 0.003 | ** |
| 83 cm vs 450 cm | Discomfort | Real | 0.078 | ns |
| | | Virtual | 0.016 | * |
| | Distance Ratings | Real | 0.000956 | *** |
| | | Virtual | 0.003 | ** |
| 120 cm vs 240 cm | Discomfort | Real | 0.444 | ns |
| | | Virtual | 0.412 | ns |
| | Distance Ratings | Real | 0.003 | ** |
| | | Virtual | 0.003 | ** |
| 120 cm vs 360 cm | Discomfort | Real | 0.444 | ns |
| | | Virtual | 0.141 | ns |
| | Distance Ratings | Real | 0.001 | ** |
| | | Virtual | 0.003 | ** |
| 120 cm vs 450 cm | Discomfort | Real | 0.444 | ns |
| | | Virtual | 0.160 | ns |
| | Distance Ratings | Real | 0.001 | ** |
| | | Virtual | 0.003 | ** |
| 240 cm vs 360 cm | Discomfort | Real | 0.444 | ns |
| | | Virtual | 1 | ns |
| | Distance Ratings | Real | 0.003 | ** |
| | | Virtual | 0.005 | ** |
| 240 cm vs 450 cm | Discomfort | Real | 0.444 | ns |
| | | Virtual | 0.414 | ns |
| | Distance Ratings | Real | 0.003 | ** |
| | | Virtual | 0.005 | ** |
| 360 cm vs 450 cm | Discomfort | Real | 0.444 | ns |
| | | Virtual | 1 | ns |
| | Distance Ratings | Real | 0.007 | ** |
| | | Virtual | 0.007 | ** |

# References

1. Abtahi, P., Zhao, D.Y., E, J.L., Landay, J.A.: Drone near me: exploring touch-based human-drone interaction. Proc. ACM IMWUT **1**, 1–8 (2017)
2. Acharya, U., Bevins, A., Duncan, B.A.: Investigation of human-robot comfort with a small Unmanned Aerial Vehicle compared to a ground robot (2017)
3. Aiello, J.R.: Human Spatial Behavior. Wiley, New York (1987)
4. Auda, J., Weigel, M., Cauchard, J.R., Schneegass, S.: Understanding drone landing on the human body (2021)
5. Avila Soto, M., Funk, M.: Look, a guidance drone! Assessing the Social Acceptability of Companion Drones for Blind Travelers in Public Spaces (2018)
6. Baker, C., Pawling, R., Fairclough, S.: Assessment of threat and negativity bias in virtual reality. Sci. Rep. **10**, 17338 (2020)
7. Baldursson, B., et al.: DroRun: drone visual interactions to mediate a running group (2021)
8. Baytas, M.A., Çay, D., Zhang, Y., Obaid, M., Yantaç, A.E., Fjeld, M.: The design of social drones: a review of studies on autonomous flyers in inhabited environments (2019)
9. Belmonte, L., García, A., Morales, R., de la Vara, J.L., Rosa, F., Fernández-Caballero, A.: Feeling of safety and comfort towards a socially assistive unmanned aerial vehicle that monitors people in a virtual home. Sensors **21**, 908 (2021)
10. Bevins, A., Duncan, B.A.: Aerial flight paths for communication: how participants perceive and intend to respond to drone movements (2021)
11. Blanchard, D.C.: Translating dynamic defense patterns from rodents to people. Neurosci. Biobehav. Rev. **76**, 22–28 (2017)
12. Blanchard, D.C., Griebel, G., Pobbe, R., Blanchard, R.J.: Risk assessment as an evolved threat detection and analysis process. Neurosci. Biobehav. Rev. **35**, 991–998 (2011)
13. Blascovich, J., Loomis, J., Beall, A.C., Swinth, K.R., Hoyt, C.L., Bailenson, J.N.: Immersive virtual environment technology as a methodological tool for social psychology. Psychol. Inq. **13**, 104–123 (2002)
14. Blascovich, J., Tomaka, J.: The biopsychosocial model of arousal regulation. In: Advances in Experimental Social Psychology, vol. 28 (1996)
15. Bretin, R., Cross, E.S., Khamis, M.: Co-existing with a drone: using virtual reality to investigate the effect of the drone's height and cover story on proxemic behaviours (2022)
16. Bufacchi, R.J.: Approaching threatening stimuli cause an expansion of defensive peripersonal space. J. Neurophysiol. **118**, 1927–1930 (2017)
17. Cauchard, J., Gover, W., Chen, W., Cartwright, S., Sharlin, E.: Drones in wonderland-disentangling collocated interaction using radical form. IEEE RA-L (2021)
18. Cauchard, J.R., E, J.L., Zhai, K.Y., Landay, J.A.: Drone & me: an exploration into natural human-drone interaction (2015)
19. Cauchard, J.R., Zhai, K.Y., Spadafora, M., Landay, J.: Emotion encoding in Human-Drone Interaction. In: ACM/IEEE HRI (2016)
20. Chang, V., Chundury, P., Chetty, M.: Spiders in the sky: user perceptions of drones, privacy, and security. In: Proceedings of CHI Conference (2017)
21. Coello, Y., Bourgeois, J., Iachini, T.: Embodied perception of reachable space: how do we manage threatening objects? Cogn. Process. **13**, 131–135 (2012)

22. Colley, A., Virtanen, L., Knierim, P., Häkkilä, J.: Investigating drone motion as pedestrian guidance. In: MUM 2017. Association for Computing Machinery (2017)
23. Colley, A., Väyrynen, J., Häkkilä, J.: Exploring the use of virtual environments in an industrial site design process. In: INTERACT (2015)
24. Cummings, J.J., Bailenson, J.N.: How immersive is enough? A meta-analysis of the effect of immersive technology on user presence. Media Psychol. **19**, 272–309 (2016)
25. Dewez, D., et al.: Influence of personality traits and body awareness on the sense of embodiment in virtual reality (2019)
26. Diemer, J., Alpers, G.W., Peperkorn, H.M., Shiban, Y., Mühlberger, A.: The impact of perception and presence on emotional reactions: a review of research in virtual reality. Front. Psychol. **6**, 25 (2015)
27. Dosey, M.A., Meisels, M.: Personal space and self-protection. J. Pers. Soc. Psychol. **11**, 93 (1969)
28. Duncan, B.A., Murphy, R.R.: Comfortable approach distance with small Unmanned Aerial Vehicles (2013)
29. Ellena, G., Bertoni, T., Durand-Ruel, M., Thoresen, J., Sandi, C., Serino, A.: Acute stress affects peripersonal space representation in cortisol stress responders. Psychoneuroendocrinology **142**, 105790 (2022)
30. Endsley, M.R., Connors, E.S.: Situation awareness: state of the art (2008)
31. Fink, P.W., Foo, P.S., Warren, W.H.: Obstacle avoidance during walking in real and virtual environments. ACM Trans. Appl. Percept. **4**, 2 (2007)
32. Folkman, S., Lazarus, R., Schetter, C., DeLongis, A., Gruen, R.: Dynamics of a stressful encounter: cognitive appraisal, coping, and encounter outcomes. J. Person. Soc. Psychol. **50**, 992 (1986)
33. Gall, D., Roth, D., Stauffert, J.P., Zarges, J., Latoschik, M.E.: Embodiment in virtual reality intensifies emotional responses to virtual stimuli. Front. Psychol. **12**, 674179 (2021)
34. Gamboa, M., Obaid, M., Ljungblad, S.: Ritual drones: designing and studying critical flying companions (2021)
35. Garcia, J., Brock, A.M.: CandyFly: bringing fun to drone pilots with disabilities through adapted and adaptable interactions (2022)
36. Gio, N., Brisco, R., Vuletic, T.: Control of a drone with body gestures. Proc. Des. Soc. **1**, 761–770 (2021)
37. Greenberg, S., Marquardt, N., Ballendat, T., Diaz-Marino, R., Wang, M.: Proxemic interactions: the new ubicomp? Interactions **18**, 42–50 (2011)
38. Gunthert, K.C., Cohen, L.H., Armeli, S.: The role of neuroticism in daily stress and coping. J. Person. Soc. Psychol. **77**, 1087 (1999)
39. Hall, E.T.: The Hidden Dimension. New York (1990)
40. Han, J., Moore, D., Bae, I.: Exploring the social proxemics of human-drone interaction. Int. J. Adv. Smart Convergence **8**, 1–7 (2019)
41. Hayduk, L.A.: Personal space: where we now stand. Psychol. Bull. **94**, 293 (1983)
42. Herdel, V., Kuzminykh, A., Hildebrandt, A., Cauchard, J.R.: Drone in love: emotional perception of facial expressions on flying robots. In: Proceedings of CHI Conference (2021)
43. Herdel, V., Yamin, L.J., Cauchard, J.R.: Above and beyond: a scoping review of domains and applications for human-drone interaction (2022)
44. Herdel, V., Yamin, L.J., Ginosar, E., Cauchard, J.R.: Public drone: attitude towards drone capabilities in various contexts (2021)
45. Interrante, V., Ries, B., Anderson, L.: Distance perception in immersive virtual environments, revisited (2006)

46. Jensen, W., Hansen, S., Knoche, H.: Knowing you, seeing me: investigating user preferences in drone-human acknowledgement (2018)
47. Kamide, H., Mae, Y., Takubo, T., Ohara, K., Arai, T.: Direct comparison of psychological evaluation between virtual and real humanoids: personal space and subjective impressions. Int. J. Hum.-Comput. Stud. **72**, 451–459 (2014)
48. Karjalainen, K.D., Romell, A.E.S., Ratsamee, P., Yantac, A.E., Fjeld, M., Obaid, M.: Social drone companion for the home environment: a user-centric exploration (2017)
49. Kim, B., Kim, H.Y., Kim, J.: Getting home safely with drone (2016)
50. Leichtmann, B., Nitsch, V.: How much distance do humans keep toward robots? Literature review, meta-analysis, and theoretical considerations on personal space in human-robot interaction. J. Environ. Psychol. **68**, 101386 (2020)
51. Li, R., van Almkerk, M., van Waveren, S., Carter, E., Leite, I.: Comparing human-robot proxemics between virtual reality and the real world (2019)
52. Lieser, M., Schwanecke, U., Berdux, J.: Evaluating distances in tactile human-drone interaction (2021)
53. Lieser, M., Schwanecke, U., Berdux, J.: Tactile human-quadrotor interaction: MetroDrone (2021)
54. Loomis, J.M., Blascovich, J.J., Beall, A.C.: Immersive virtual environment technology as a basic research tool in psychology. Behav. Res. Metho. Instruments Comput. **31**, 557–564 (1999)
55. Lourenco, S.F., Longo, M.R.: The plasticity of near space: evidence for contraction. Cognition **112**, 451–456 (2009)
56. Lucero, A.: Using affinity diagrams to evaluate interactive prototypes. In: Abascal, J., Barbosa, S., Fetter, M., Gross, T., Palanque, P., Winckler, M. (eds.) INTERACT 2015. LNCS, vol. 9297, pp. 231–248. Springer, Cham (2015). https://doi.org/10.1007/978-3-319-22668-2_19
57. Mathis, F., Vaniea, K., Khamis, M.: RepliCueAuth: validating the use of a lab-based virtual reality setup for evaluating authentication systems. In: Proceedings of CHI Conference (2021)
58. McNeil, D., et al.: Fear of pain questionnaire-9: brief assessment of pain-related fear and anxiety. Eur. J. Pain **22**, 451–456 (2018)
59. Messing, R., Durgin, F.H.: Distance perception and the visual horizon in head-mounted displays. ACM Trans. Appl. Percept. **2**, 234–250 (2005)
60. Mäkelä, V., et al.: Virtual field studies: conducting studies on public displays in virtual reality (2020)
61. Nelson, J., Gorichanaz, T.: Trust as an ethical value in emerging technology governance: the case of drone regulation. Technol. Soc. **59**, 101131 (2019)
62. Nguyen, D.Q., Loianno, G., Ho, V.A.: Towards design of a deformable propeller for drone safety (2020)
63. Obaid, M., Mubin, O., Brown, S.A., Yantac, A.E., Otsuki, M., Kuzuoka, H.: DroEye: introducing a social eye prototype for drones (2020)
64. Paquay, M., Goffoy, J., Chevalier, S., Servotte, J.C., Ghuysen, A.: Relationships between internal factors, social factors and the sense of presence in virtual reality-based simulations. Clin. Simul. Nurs. **62**, 1–11 (2022)
65. Patterson, M.L.: An arousal model of interpersonal intimacy. Psychol. Rev. **83**, 235 (1976)
66. Peck, T.C., Gonzalez-Franco, M.: Avatar embodiment. A standardized questionnaire. Front. Virtual Real. **1** (2021)

67. Perkins, A.M., Corr, P.J.: Reactions to threat and personality: psychometric differentiation of intensity and direction dimensions of human defensive behaviour. Behav. Brain Res. **169**, 21–28 (2006)
68. Rammstedt, B., John, O.P.: Measuring personality in one minute or less: a 10-item short version of the Big Five Inventory in English and German. J. Res. Person. **41**, 203–212 (2007)
69. Rosén, J., Kastrati, G., Reppling, A., Bergkvist, K., Åhs, F.: The effect of immersive virtual reality on proximal and conditioned threat. Sci. Rep. **9**, 17407 (2019)
70. Ruggiero, G., Rapuano, M., Cartaud, A., Coello, Y., Iachini, T.: Defensive functions provoke similar psychophysiological reactions in reaching and comfort spaces. Sci. Rep. **11**, 5170 (2021)
71. Ryan, W.S., Cornick, J., Blascovich, J., Bailenson, J.N.: Virtual reality: whence, how and what for. In: Rizzo, A.S., Bouchard, S. (eds.) Virtual Reality for Psychological and Neurocognitive Interventions. VRTHCA, pp. 15–46. Springer, New York (2019). https://doi.org/10.1007/978-1-4939-9482-3_2
72. Sadka, O., Giron, J., Friedman, D., Zuckerman, O., Erel, H.: Virtual-reality as a simulation tool for non-humanoid social robots (2020)
73. Sambo, C.F., Iannetti, G.D.: Better safe than sorry? The safety margin surrounding the body is increased by anxiety. J. Neurosci. **33**, 14225–14230 (2013)
74. Scheufele, D.A.: Framing as a theory of media effects. J. Commun. **49**, 103–122 (1999)
75. Schubert, T., Friedmann, F., Regenbrecht, H.: The experience of presence: factor analytic insights. Presence: Teleoper. Virtual Environ. **10**, 266–281 (2001)
76. Shiban, Y., Diemer, J., Brandl, S., Zack, R., Mühlberger, A., Wüst, S.: Trier social stress test in vivo and in virtual reality: dissociation of response domains. Int. J. Psychophysiol. **110**, 47–55 (2016)
77. Skarbez, R., Brooks, F.P., Whitton, M.C.: Immersion and coherence in a stressful virtual environment (2018)
78. Skarbez, R., Gabbard, J., Bowman, D.A., Ogle, T., Tucker, T.: Virtual replicas of real places: experimental investigations. IEEE Trans. Visual. Comput. Graph. **28**, 4594–4608 (2021)
79. Slater, M.: Place illusion and plausibility can lead to realistic behaviour in immersive virtual environments. Philosoph. Trans. Roy. Soc. B: Biol. Sci. **364**, 3549–3557 (2009)
80. Slater, M., Khanna, P., Mortensen, J., Yu, I.: Visual realism enhances realistic response in an immersive virtual environment. IEEE CG&A **29**, 76–84 (2009)
81. Smolentsev, A., Cornick, J.E., Blascovich, J.: Using a preamble to increase presence in digital virtual environments. Virt. Real. **21**, 153–164 (2017)
82. Spaccasassi, C., Maravita, A.: Peripersonal space is diversely sensitive to a temporary vs permanent state of anxiety. Cognition **195**, 104133 (2020)
83. Spielberger, C.D.: State-trait anxiety inventory. In: The Corsini Encyclopedia of Psychology (2010)
84. Szafir, D., Mutlu, B., Fong, T.: Communication of intent in assistive free flyers (2014)
85. Tian, L., et al.: User expectations of robots in public spaces: a co-design methodology. In: Wagner, A.R., et al. (eds.) ICSR 2020. LNCS (LNAI), vol. 12483, pp. 259–270. Springer, Cham (2020). https://doi.org/10.1007/978-3-030-62056-1_22
86. Vagnoni, E., Lourenco, S.F., Longo, M.R.: Threat modulates neural responses to looming visual stimuli. Eur. J. Neurosci. **42**, 2190–2202 (2015)
87. de Vignemont, F., Iannetti, G.: How many peripersonal spaces? Neuropsychologia **70**, 32–334 (2015)

88. Waltemate, T., Gall, D., Roth, D., Botsch, M., Latoschik, M.E.: The impact of avatar personalization and immersion on virtual body ownership, presence, and emotional response. IEEE TVCG **24**, 1643–1652 (2018)

89. Welsch, R., Castell, C.V., Hecht, H.: The anisotropy of personal space. PLoS ONE **14**, e0217587 (2019)

90. Williams, T., Szafir, D., Chakraborti, T., Ben Amor, H.: Virtual, augmented, and mixed reality for human-robot interaction. PLOS ONE **14**, e0217587 (2018)

91. Wojciechowska, A., Frey, J., Sass, S., Shafir, R., Cauchard, J.R.: Collocated human-drone interaction: methodology and approach strategy (2019)

92. Yeh, A., et al.: Exploring proxemics for human-drone interaction (2017)

93. Zhu, H.Y., Magsino, E.M., Hamim, S.M., Lin, C.T., Chen, H.T.: A drone nearly hit me! A reflection on the human factors of drone collisions (2021)

# Sick in the Car, Sick in VR? Understanding How Real-World Susceptibility to Dizziness, Nausea, and Eye Strain Influences VR Motion Sickness

Oliver Hein[✉], Philipp Rauschnabel, Mariam Hassib, and Florian Alt

University of the Bundeswehr Munich, Munich, Germany
{oliver.hein,philipp.rauschnabel,mariam.hassib,florian.alt}@unibw.de

**Abstract.** A substantial number of Virtual Reality (VR) users (studies report 30–80%) suffer from cyber sickness, a negative experience caused by a sensory mismatch of real and virtual stimuli. Prior research proposed different mitigation strategies. Yet, it remains unclear how effectively they work, considering users' real-world susceptibility to motion sickness. We present a lab experiment, in which we assessed 146 users' real-world susceptibility to nausea, dizziness, and eye strain before exposing them to a roller coaster ride with low or high visual resolution. We found that nausea is significantly lower for higher resolution but real-world motion susceptibility has a much stronger effect on dizziness, nausea, and eye strain. Our work points towards a need for research investigating the effectiveness of approaches to mitigate motion sickness so as not to include them from VR use and access to the metaverse.

**Keywords:** virtual reality · motion sickness · resolution

## 1 Introduction

Motion sickness is a common, negative experience many people suffer from, for example, in the form of seasickness on boats or dizziness when reading while driving. The same phenomenon occurs in Virtual Reality (VR): studies report that 30–80% of users experience motion sickness symptoms, depending on the type of virtual application [45,51]. While permanent damage is not known and severe symptoms are rather rare [21], symptoms ranging from dizziness, eye pain, and malaise, to vomiting can last for several hours [20].

Motion sickness has been a major challenge in VR since its inception and may likely turn into a major issue as we progress towards the vision of a metaverse to which head-mounted displays (HMDs) are likely to become a primary means of access [42]. A long history of prior research investigated factors and measures that influence motion sickness in VR, both from a *human* perspective as well as

© The Author(s), under exclusive license to Springer Nature Switzerland AG 2023
J. Abdelnour Nocera et al. (Eds.): INTERACT 2023, LNCS 14143, pp. 552–573, 2023.
https://doi.org/10.1007/978-3-031-42283-6_30

from a *software and technology* perspective. For example, much of the early work on VR looked into how motion sickness could be mitigated through technical improvements, such as higher resolution or shorter latency [53]. More recently, researchers investigated approaches of reducing motion sickness through aligning motion between VR and the real world [36] or visualizing motion flow in VR [11]. At the same time, it remains an open question how effective such measures are for people with a high susceptibility to motion sickness. In other words: *will people who easily experience real-world motion sickness experience lower cybersickness with technical mitigation strategies?*

This paper contributes a controlled lab experiment (N = 146), in which users suffering from motion sickness symptoms (disorientation, dizziness, nausea, eye strain) to varying degrees are exposed to a VR experience (i.e. a roller coaster ride) in one of two different resolutions. Our findings show that while nausea is significantly lower for high resolution, disorientation, and eye strain are hardly affected. At the same time, real-world motion sickness susceptibility has a much more pronounced effect on symptoms of motion sickness (disorientation, nausea, and eye strain). This suggests that the effect of mitigation strategies on users strongly differs based on personal factors, i.e. their motion sickness susceptibility.

We consider our work as a first step towards better understanding the interplay between users' susceptibility to different symptoms of motion sickness, and software- and technology-based mitigation approaches. Our findings reveal a need for a broader investigation of existing approaches to understand how VR environments of the future need to be designed so as to not exclude any users from a future in which VR might be a ubiquitous technology.

## 2  Background and Related Work

Our work draws from several strands of prior research: (1) motion sickness research, (2) factors causing motion sickness and their mitigation strategies, and (3) approaches to measuring cybersickness.

### 2.1  Introduction to Motion Sickness

Movement can be perceived physically and/or visually. In general, both types, even independently, can trigger motion sickness in people [4,39]. There is still disagreement in the scientific community about the exact cause of this anomaly [8]. However, it has been repeatedly found that people without a functioning vestibular organ or inner ear are immune to motion sickness [4,23,39]. Surprisingly, this is also true for purely visually induced motion sickness (VIMS) [4,10], that is the occurrence of motion sickness symptoms triggered solely by visual movement, in a physically static person [21].

The 'Sensory Conflict Theory' of Reason and Brand (1975) [43] states that conflicting signals from the sensory organs are the triggers for motion sickness [32,39]. This largely accepted approach has been steadily refined by studies. In this context, every form of physical motion and each type of visual motion representation offers its own influencing factors on motion sickness. Speed, frequency, acceleration, and direction of motion are among the more obvious variables [4]. But also other influences, such as autonomous control of transportation, have an effect on motion sickness likelihood [54]. Accordingly, drivers are less susceptible than passengers as they anticipate motion to a certain extent, preparing the body for it [46]. Similarly, sitting in the opposite direction of travel increases motion sickness as being below deck increases sea sickness [54].

Visual fore-warnings of impending physical movement are limited here and do not allow for adjustment of physical anticipation. According to Mittelstaed [37], the discrepancy between expected and actual movement (termed "subjective vertical") is a trigger for motion sickness and is consequently elevated in passengers [4]. As explained, VIMS elicits a physiological response due to a purely visual stimulus. In contrast to physically induced motion sickness, it is the visual signals and not the vestibular organ that is primarily exposed to the stimuli [24]. The symptoms of affected individuals largely overlap with those of classic motion sickness and may eventually lead to vomiting. However, VIMS place a greater strain on the oculomotor system of the eye. Thus, affected individuals are more likely to report eye pain, blurred vision, and headaches [24].

Regardless of the type of motion sickness, the duration of movement exposure is relevant. Basically, the longer the person is exposed to the stimulus, the more likely and more intense the motion sickness symptoms will be [51]. Motion sickness symptoms are not currently measurable in purely hormonal or biochemical terms, although studies suggest a link to Melatonin levels [24]. In a recent paper, Keshavarz and Golding [26] mention that motion sickness has been the focus of attention in two contexts: automated vehicles, and VR. However, the focus is on either one of these two areas, and there is currently no efficient method to reliably prevent or minimize motion sickness (in real-time).

## 2.2   Motion Sickness in VR: Factors and Assessment Strategies

Motion sickness in VR is often referred to as *cybersickness* [52,59]. Prior research explored the reasons behind cybersickness in VR and the different ways it can be reduced or mitigated through the design of VR environments (cf. Davis et al. [13]). People experience cybersickness in VR with varying degrees, depending on personal aspects, application, and duration of exposure [49,60].

Prior work looked at individual differences in experiencing cybersickness. Influencing factors in VR include age [31], gender, illnesses, and posture [33,35]. VR motion sickness can be amplified or mitigated by the used VR hardware and software [48]. Latency, flicker, and poor calibration are all factors that may affect cybersickness in VR [35]. In addition to properties, such as frame rate, depth blur, and jitter, a study by Wang et al. [57] suggests that also resolution quality has an impact on motion sickness probability. Here, higher resolution seems to have a mitigating effect on motion sickness. Cybersickness can also occur because of the physical eye apparatus, e.g. vergence-accommodation conflict [3], and not just because of pure image perception.

Rebenitsch and Owen investigated the individual susceptibility to cybersickness [44]. Based on the data provided by the subjects (n = 20), they concluded that a previous history of motion sickness while playing video games predicted cybersickness best. A review by the same authors [45] summarizes state-of-the-art methods, theories, and known aspects associated with cybersickness: besides application design aspects, the influence of application design in general, field of view, and navigation are strongly correlated with cybersickness. The effect of visual displays is so far not well understood and needs further investigation.

The VR environment and task itself can affect cybersickness. McGill et al. [36] conducted an on-road and in-motion study (n = 18) to investigate the effects of different visualizations on motion sickness in VR. In a study by Chang et al. [9], they examined motion sickness in participants (n = 20) who were passengers in virtual vehicles and asked how motion sickness and the postural antecedents of motion sickness might be influenced by participants' prior experiences of driving physical vehicles. They showed that the postural movements of participants who later became seasick differed from those who did not. In addition, the physical driving experience during exposure to the virtual vehicle was related to the patterns of postural activity that preceded motion sickness. The results are consistent with the postural instability theory of motion sickness, which states that motion sickness is caused by loss of postural control [58]. An experiment (n = 20) by Carnegie and Rhee [7] was able to demonstrate that artificial depth blur reduces visual discomfort in VR HMDs. In this experiment, depth of field was integrated into the VR application by software, which simulates natural focusing by a dynamic blur effect. VR users view the center of the screen for about 82% of the time they are using the application. Therefore, an algorithm can detect the focus point of the eyes to a certain degree and adjust the blur accordingly. However, it has not been possible to imitate natural vision completely with this method. Park et al. [41], investigated the relationship between motion sickness in VR and eye and pupil movements through a user study (n = 24). It was found that participants showed irregular patterns of pupil rhythms after experiencing motion sickness in VR using HMDs. Based on this data, a method able to quantitatively measure and monitor motion sickness in real time using an infrared camera was proposed. However, this has neither an influence on the perceived motion sickness of the user nor on reducing it.

## 2.3  Measuring Cybersickness

Somrak et al. used the Simulator Sickness Questionnaire (SSQ) in combination with the User Experience Questionnaire (UEQ) [34, 47] in a user study (n = 14) conducted in 2019 [50]. Other research explored the use of physiological measures such as EEG, heart rate [38], respiration rate [30], and skin conductance, to measure sickness in VR. In a recent study by Garrido et al. [16], focused on the examination of the cybersickness phenomenon, 92 participants experienced a ten-minute VR immersion in two environments. The results showed that even with new HMDs, 65.2% of the participants experienced cybersickness, and 23.9% experienced severe cybersickness. In addition, susceptibility to motion sickness, cognitive stress, and recent headaches clearly predicted higher severity of cyber-sickness, while age showed a negative association [16] (see Table 1).

**Table 1.** Overview of Prior Work including User Studies

| Focus of Prior Work | Authors | Sample |
|---|---|---|
| Investigates the resolution trade-off in gameplay experience, performance, and simulator sickness for VR games | Wang et al. [57] | 16 |
| Investigation of the individual susceptibility to cybersickness | Rebenitsch and Owen [44] | 20 |
| On-road and in-motion study investigating effects of different visualizations on VR sickness | McGill et al. [36] | 18 |
| Integrates depth of field into VR application, simulating natural focus by a dynamic blur effect | Carnegie and Rhee [7] | 20 |
| Investigates the relationship between motion sickness in VR and eye and pupil movements | Park et al. [41] | 24 |
| User study of the effects of VR technology on VR sickness and user experience | Somrak et al. [50] | 14 |
| Examines the cybersickness phenomenon in a ten-minute VR immersion in two environments | Garrido et al. [16] | 92 |

Most studies considered measuring cybersickness/motion sickness in VR, uti-lizing self-reported standardized questionnaires, such as the widely adopted Sim-ulator Sickness Questionnaire (SSQ) [25]. Golding [18,19] introduced the Motion Sickness Susceptibility Questionnaire (MSSQ) to predict an individual's suscep-tibility to motion sickness, based on a person's past history of motion sickness as a child or adult. Other questionnaires include the Virtual Reality Symptom Questionnaire [1], the Virtual Reality Sickness Questionnaire (VRSQ) [29], and single-item questionnaires, such as that from Bos et al. [5]. A more recently intro-duced questionnaire is the six-item Visually Induced Motion Sickness Susceptibil-ity Questionnaire (VIMSSQ/VIMSSQ-short) by Golding et al. (2021) [17], which is based on the SSQ [25]. The VIMSSQ is a useful complement to the MSSQ in predicting visually induced motion sickness. Other predictors are migraine, syncope and social and work impact of dizziness [28]. Also more recently, and closely related to our current work, Freiwald et al. [15], introduced the Cyber-sickness Susceptibility Questionnaire which is meant to be administered *before* the VR experiment so as to predict cybersickness that may be experienced by participants. Table 2 provides an overview of these questionnaires.

## 2.4 Summary

Our work differs from this research in several ways: first, we explore the rela-tionship between real-world motion sickness susceptibility and sickness in VR in

**Table 2.** Overview of Existing Questionnaires

| Name | Author(s) | Year |
|------|-----------|------|
| Simulator Sickness Questionnaire (SSQ) | Kennedy et al. [25] | 1993 |
| Motion Sickness Susceptibility Questionnaire (MSSQ) | Golding, JF [18] | 1998 |
| Virtual Reality Symptom Questionnaire | Ames et al. [1] | 2005 |
| Virtual Reality Sickness Questionnaire (VRSQ) | Kim et al. [29] | 2018 |
| Cybersickness Susceptibility Questionnaire (CSSQ) | Freiwald et al. [15] | 2020 |
| Visually Induced Motion Sickness Susceptibility Questionnaire (VIMSSQ/VIMSSQ-short) | Golding et al. [17] | 2021 |

a large-scale study (n = 146). Additionally, we investigate particular symptoms of motion sickness (disorientation, nausea, eye strain). Finally, we compare the effect of resolution as a technology-based factor relating to cybersickness, to the personal-based factor of susceptibility to motion sickness in the real world.

## 3 Research Approach

### 3.1 Research Questions and Hypotheses

Motion sickness susceptibility depends on the stimulus and the individual person [19]. VR environments can trigger visually induced motion sickness [21]. An individual's prior motion sickness experience is considered a valid measurable predictor of their susceptibility [18]. Accordingly, hypothesis H1 assumes that triggered by the VR stimulus, the general individual motion sickness susceptibility is reflected in the form of motion sickness symptoms:

**H1** Users who are more susceptible to motion sickness in everyday life show stronger motion sickness symptoms after being exposed to a VR experience.

In addition to H1 investigating personal aspects, we investigate the interplay between real-world susceptibility and resolution which was shown to have an effect on motion sickness in VR [57]. By investigating how resolution affects motion sickness, we can better understand how the visual system contributes to the development of motion sickness symptoms. We test the following hypothesis:

**H2** Users who experience a VR environment in high resolution will exhibit lower motion sickness symptoms after testing than users who experience a VR environment in lower resolution.

In addition to the type of stimulus, personality-related factors are crucial for motion sickness symptoms [19]. Known motion sickness triggers such as vertical, jerky, and simulated self-motion are essentially unaffected by resolution quality. Considering previous studies, the effect size of resolution quality on motion sickness is comparatively smaller [57]. We hypothesize the *type* of motion sickness susceptibility to have a greater influence on motion sickness symptoms than resolution quality. The groups with motion sickness-susceptible participants would thus be expected to have the strongest symptoms, followed by test condition type. Hypotheses H3a-d subsume this assumption:

**H3a** The test group with increased motion sickness susceptibility and low-resolution quality (T1b) will exhibit the strongest post-test VR motion sickness symptoms.

**H3b** The test group with increased motion sickness susceptibility and high VR device resolution (T1a) exhibits the second most severe symptoms.

**H3c** The test group with low motion sickness susceptibility and low VR device resolution (T2b) exhibits the third most severe symptoms.

**H3d** The test group with low motion sickness susceptibility and high VR device resolution (T2a) exhibits the least severe symptoms.

### 3.2 Apparatus

To investigate the research questions and test the hypothesis, we chose the HTC VIVE Pro 1. This VR device was chosen for its comparably high resolution (2880 × 1600 pixels) and large field of view (110°) at the time. The tracking is enabled by two external infrared sensors.

According to our literature review of motion sickness and prior work, we identified several factors that need to be considered when building a VR application for testing our hypothesis. First, passengers are more prone to motion sickness than drivers. Vertical, jerky movements with rapid changes in direction are also strongly conducive to motion sickness. For comparability of the stimuli, replicable runs with the same runtime should also be possible. Therefore, interactive VR game mechanics were unsuitable. We chose the application 'Motor-ride Roller-coaster VR' from the developer *Split Light Studio*[1], offered on the gaming platform *Steam*, as it fulfills the aforementioned criteria. The VR experience simulates a predefined motorcycle ride through rough terrain.

An evaluation of Steam user reviews suggests a strong motion sickness-inducing experience overall (Valve Corporation, 2020)[2]. To reflect the different test conditions in resolution quality, the graphics settings are changed. Using the Steam VR driver, Condition A (High Resolution) displays the full total resolution of 2880 × 1600 pixels, and Condition B (Low Resolution) reduces this to 2228 × 1237 pixels (-23%). This roughly corresponds to the resolution of an HTC Vive 1st generation. The effect of the reduced resolution quality is additionally intensified by the graphics settings of the VR application. Thus, in condition B, texture resolution, edge smoothing (anti-aliasing) and anisotropic filtering were reduced to the lowest level, resulting in a visual difference in color dynamics and saturation. The test conditions thus differ noticeably in the overall impression

---

[1] https://store.steampowered.com/app/1346890/Motoride_Rollercoaster_VR/.

[2] https://steamcommunity.com/app/1346890/reviews/?p=1& browsefilter=mostrecent.

of the resolution quality and color representation (see Fig. 1). Regardless of the condition, the frame rate was constantly set to 60 FPS and the refresh rate to 90 Hz. Graphics settings regarding the viewing distance or field of view also remained unaffected. The purely software-based modification of the test conditions also excludes a possible influence by different VR HMD models. Still, the same VR HMD was always used in the subsequently described experiment.

(a) Condition A: Sample–High Resolution (b) Condition B: Sample–Low Resolution

**Fig. 1.** Sample screens from the high and low-resolution conditions

### 3.3 Questionnaires

During the study, we used several questionnaires. During the *initial questionnaire* (cf. Table 3), we first assessed whether participants owned a VR HMD and how familiar were with VR in general (I1, I2). In addition, we asked how they currently felt (I3). We then assessed their susceptibility to dizziness (I4) and nausea (I5) using the MSSQ and had them self-assess (I6) how strongly they felt to be susceptible to motion sickness. Therefore we used Golding's (1998) revised MSSQ [18]. Specifically, for consistency we used a 7-Point Likert scale and reduced the number of items by focusing on those relevant to VR motion sickness symptomatology, according to the purpose of the study.

In the *post-VR stimulus questionnaire* (cf. Table 4), we first asked them whether they completed the experience (P1). Then, using the VRSQ [29], we assessed disorientation (P2a), nausea (P2b), and eye strain (P2c). Again, we used a 7-Point Likert scale. Afterwards, we assessed the perceived hedonic benefits (P3a), telepresence (P3c), exploratory behavior (P3d), and attractiveness of the stimulus, using the UEQ (P3e). This block also contained an attention check (P3b)The questionnaire concluded with demographic questions (P4) and whether they had any suggestions or comments about the experiment (P5).

## 4  User Study

We designed a $2 \times 2$ between-subjects study with resolution and susceptibility as independent variables. Participants were assigned to either the High Resolution (A) or Low Resolution (B) condition. The split into the High Susceptibility or Low Susceptibility conditions was done during the evaluation.

### 4.1  Procedure

The study was conducted in a quiet lab room in which the VR HMD setup was prepared. Participants were first introduced to the study and signed a consent form. Then, they filled out the first questionnaire. After completing the first questionnaire participants were randomly assigned to test condition A – High Resolution or condition B – Low Resolution. Equal distribution was ensured. Subjects then run through the respective VR stimulus. After the end of the task, participants answered a second questionnaire, including a subjective evaluation of motion sickness symptoms that may have arisen during or after the VR stimulus. The motorcycle ride application lasts exactly 6:20 min and seamlessly covers three different environments. Hints about the upcoming route are not possible and direction changes are usually unexpected. Beyond fast and slow motion passages, jumps and turns additionally vary the displayed speed. The application thus is different from roller coaster simulations in that it is less predictable. However, the user cannot intervene on the track. The seated VR experience offers 3-DoF and puts the user in a purely observational position.

The total duration including the questionnaire amounts to 15 min per participant, including appr. 6 min for the motorcycle ride (Fig. 2).

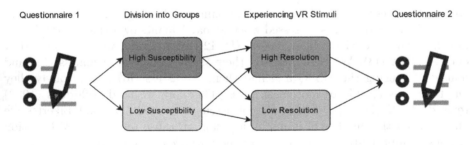

**Fig. 2.** Study Procedure

### 4.2  Study Limitations

Although there are several influencing factors that can trigger motion sickness (visual and auditory), the focus here was on visually induced motion sickness, as

**Table 3.** Questionnaire 1: Before VR Stimulus

| Construct | Question | Statement |
|---|---|---|
| I1 | Do you own a VR HMD? | - Yes: model (+open statement) |
| | | – No, not anymore |
| | | – No |
| I2: Involvement | Please indicate the extent to which you agree or disagree with the following statements. (Likert 1–7) [Strongly disagree – Strongly agree] | – I already experienced VR |
| | | – I have access to a VR HMD |
| | | – I use VR HMD regularly |
| | | – I use VR HMD regularly |
| | | – I generally enjoy VR experiences with a VR HMD |
| I3: Feeling | How are you feeling right now? (Likert 1–7) [Not at all – Very much] | – Hungry |
| | | – Thirsty |
| | | – Weak |
| | | – Full of energy |
| | | – Tired |
| | | – Awake |
| | | – Relaxed |
| | | – Stressed |
| I4: Susceptibility to Dizziness (MSSQ) [18] | Do you generally tend to experience: (Likert 1–7) [Not at all – Very strongly] | – Dizzy spells |
| | | – Dizziness: |
| | | – when flying |
| | | – while driving a car |
| | | – while watching television |
| | | – while reading while driving |
| | | – Seasickness |
| I5: Susceptibility to Nausea (MSSQ) [18] | Do you generally tend to experience: (Likert 1–7) [Not at all – Very strongly] | – Fear of heights |
| | | – Nausea: |
| | | – while riding a train |
| | | – while driving a car (passenger) |
| | | – while flying |
| | | – while watching television |
| | | – while reading while driving |
| I6: Self-assessment (MSSQ) [18] | Rate yourself as: (Likert 1–7) [Not at all – Very much] | – Susceptible to motion sickness? |

this exerts the strongest impact on the overall experience [27]. However, there are several ways in which motion sickness can be induced visually, such as movements in the real world that do not translate properly in VR, or movements in VR that have no relation to the users' movements in the real world. In our study, we decided to use an application that builds on the first mentioned approach because this type of motion sickness is much more prevalent than other ways of inducting motion sickness [28]. We decided to choose a VR game to be able to

**Table 4.** Questionnaire 2: After VR Stimulus

| Construct | Question | Statement |
|---|---|---|
| P1: | Did you complete the VR experience to the end? | – Yes<br>– No, I stopped at approx. minutes: (+open indication). |
| P2a: Disorientation (VRSQ) [29] | Did you feel after, or during the testing: | – Dizziness<br>– Orientation problems |
| P2b: Nausea (VRSQ) [29] | (Likert 1–7)<br>[Not at all - Very much] | - Nausea<br>– Sweating |
| P2c:Eye Strain (VRSQ) [29] | | – Headache<br>– Problems with focusing (vision)<br>– Eye Strain |
| P3a: Hedonistic benefits [55] | Please indicate the extent to which you agree or disagree with the following statements. (Likert 1–7) [Not agree at all - Fully agree] | – The VR experience was fun<br>– The VR experience was entertaining<br>– The VR experience is a good way to pass the time |
| P3b: Attention | | – To show that you are still attentive, click here value 'two' |
| P3c: Telepresence [22] | | – It felt like I was actually in the VR environment<br>– It felt like everything I saw was real<br>– I lost track of time during the VR experience |
| P3d: Exploratory behavior (Flow) [12] | | – I appreciate unique VR experiences<br>– VR experiences feel like exploring a new world<br>– I would like to know more about VR experiences |
| P3e: Attractiveness (UEQ) [34] | | – I find wearing a VR HMD comfortable<br>– I could easily use a VR HMD for a longer period of time at a stretch |
| P4: | Demographics | – Age<br>– Gender<br>– Education<br>– Occupation |
| P5: | Do you have any suggestions or comments about the experiment? | – (open statement) |

compare to other VR studies, as games are readily used here to investigate, for example, navigation techniques and interaction techniques [2]. However, we do acknowledge that investigations in other contexts might yield different results.

There are high-end VR headsets with higher-resolution displays available at the moment. Yet, we decided to focus on affordable consumer VR HMSs. With a resolution of $1440 \times 1600$ pixels per eye, a refresh rate of 90 Hz, and a field of view of 98°, the HTC Vive Pro 1 is still one of the best consumer devices [6].

Finally, the correlation between age and motion sickness susceptibility is scientifically controversial [14,16,40]. Our sample mainly consisted of students.

Therefore, future work may want to look into different age groups to verify whether the findings generalize to a broader population.

## 5  Results

### 5.1  Demographics and Motion Susceptibility Condition Assignment

We recruited 151 volunteers for the study via internal university mailing lists, social media, and personal contacts. Sweets were offered as an incentive. As the study was conducted on campus, the vast majority of participants were students.

Five participants who failed to correctly answer the attention check question (see Table 4) were removed. Our final data set consisted of 146 participants (54 female, 92 male, mean age 24), of which 72 were assigned to Condition A – High Resolution and 74 were assigned to Condition B – Low Resolution. Only 11 (7.5%) of the participants reported owning a VR HMD.

Premature discontinuation of the VR stimulus due to symptoms does not lead to exclusion from the study. A corresponding item in the second questionnaire records cessation or discontinuation at the respective test minute. 22 participants (15.1%) terminated the VR stimulus prematurely. Broken down by test condition, 11 of these belong to test condition A and 11 to condition B. The average termination time is minute 3:19 *after* the start of the VR stimulus.

A researcher observed and noted down symptoms during data collection. Participants' symptoms ranged from no symptoms at all to severe malaise and nausea. In condition B, poor graphics quality was sporadically mentioned.

**Deriving the Motion Sickness Susceptibility Condition.** For a computational test of the stated hypotheses, new variables are established from the dataset (Table 5). Items for self-assessment of motion sickness susceptibility of dizziness, nausea, and general susceptibility were merged under the new variable 'Motion Sickness Susceptibility'. Similarly, the items for motion sickness symptoms recorded after the VR stimulus, categorized into disorientation, nausea, and eye strain, were computed as 'Motion Sickness Symptoms Combined'. Reliability analysis by Cronbach's alpha value is performed before combination.

**Categorizing Participants in Susceptibility Condition.** To categorize participants according to their susceptibility type, the mean and median of all tested participants are considered (Table 6). Subjects with a motion sickness susceptibility of <= 1.923 are categorized as *Low Motion Sickness Susceptibility* and >1.923 as *High Motion Sickness Susceptibility*.

### 5.2  Influence of Real World Motion Sickness Susceptibility

Correlation analysis of the variables Motion Sickness Susceptibility and Motion Sickness Symptoms Combined investigates the relationship suspected

**Table 5.** Merging the Variable Categories on a Mean Value Basis

| Construct | Statement | Cronbach's α | New Variable |
|---|---|---|---|
| Merge of Motion Sickness Susceptibility (before VR stimulus)* | | | |
| Susceptibility to dizziness | Dizzy spells in general Dizzy when flying Dizzy while driving a car Dizzy while watching television Dizzy when reading while driving Seasickness | .908 | Motion Sickness Susceptibility |
| Susceptibility to nausea | Fear of heights Nausea while riding a train Nausea while riding a car (passenger) Nausea while flying Nausea while watching television Nausea when reading while driving | | |
| Self-Assessment | Susceptible to motion sickness | | |
| Merge of Motion Sickness Susceptibility (after VR stimulus) * | | | |
| Symptom Disorientation | Dizziness Orientation problems | .809 | Disorientation |
| Symptom Nausea | Nausea Sweating | .889 | Nausea |
| Symptom Eye Strain | Nausea Sweating | .830 | Eye Strain |
| Disorientation Nausea Eye Strain | | .823 | Motion Sickness Symptoms Combined |

\* *based on mean values*

**Table 6.** Classification into Motion Sickness Susceptibility Types by Median

| Susceptibility Type | N | Percent | Mean* | Median* | Standard Deviation* |
|---|---|---|---|---|---|
| Low Susceptibility | 75 | 51.37% | 2.223 | 1.923 | 1.006 |
| High Susceptibility | 71 | 48.63% | | | |

\* *of Motion Sickness Susceptibility, Scale Values 1–7*

in *H1: Users who are more susceptible to motion sickness in everyday life show stronger motion sickness symptoms after testing.* Here, H1 is confirmed as there is a significant correlation between motion sickness experienced in everyday life measured by questionnaire 1 (see Table 3) and motion sickness symptoms after VR testing measured by questionnaire 2 (see Table 4)(Pearson correlation = .655; Sig. 2-sided <0.01). A comparison of means of motion sickness symptoms after VR testing with grouping by susceptibility type illustrates the relationship graphically (see Fig. 3). A t-test also confirms significance considering all symptom categories (see Table 7). A regression analysis reveals that 42.5% of motion sickness symptoms can be explained by motion sickness susceptibility (Table 8). The constancy of this influence is illustrated by including the additional variables **age** and **gender** (Table 9).

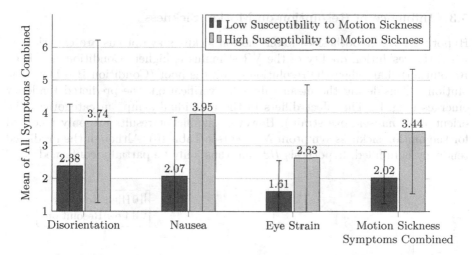

**Fig. 3.** Mean Comparison including Variance by Motion Sickness Symptoms and Motion Sickness Susceptibility Type

**Table 7.** t-Test of Independent Samples of Susceptibility Type and Motion Sickness Symptoms

|  |  | Levene-Test |  |  |  |  |
|---|---|---|---|---|---|---|
|  |  | F | Sig. | T | df | Sig.(2-sided) |
| Disorientation | Same Variances | 4.554 | .035 | −5.631 | 144 | <.001 |
|  | Different Variances |  |  | −5.618 | 139.01 | <.001 |
| Nausea | Same Variances | 15.872 | .000 | −6.849 | 144 | <.001 |
|  | Different Variances |  |  | −6.821 | 130.624 | <.001 |
| Eye Strain | Same Variances | 24.625 | .000 | −4.739 | 144 | <.001 |
|  | Different Variances |  |  | −4.711 | 118.917 | <.001 |
| Motion Sickness | Same Variances | 24.431 | .000 | −6.983 | 144 | <.001 |
| Symptoms Combined | Different Variances |  |  | −6.945 | 122.404 | <.001 |

**Table 8.** Regression Analysis of Effect `Motion Sickness Susceptibility` on `Motion Sickness Symptoms Combined`

| R | $R^2$ | Corrected $R^2$ | Standard Error of the Subject |
|---|---|---|---|
| .655* | .429 | .425 | 1.408 |

*influencing Variables; (Constants), Susceptibility*

**Table 9.** Regression Analysis with Additional Coefficients `Age` and `Gender`

| Model | not standardized |  | standardized |  |  |
|---|---|---|---|---|---|
|  | Regression Coefficient B | Standard Error | Beta | T | Sig. |
| Constant | 1.7566 | .838 |  | 2.108 | .037 |
| Susceptibility | .873 | .095 | .623 | 9.235 | <.001 |
| Gender | −.269 | .194 | −0.94 | −1.387 | .168 |
| Age | −.022 | .032 | −.043 | −.673 | .502 |

*Dependent Variable: Motion Sickness Symptoms Combined*

## 5.3  Influence of Resolution on Motion Sickness

Hypothesis *H2* hypothesizes lower motion sickness symptoms are experienced when the resolution quality of the VR stimulus is higher (Condition A – High Resolution) than when the resolution quality is poor (Condition B – Low Resolution). Considering the mean values for verification, the predicted tendency emerges (Fig. 4). The effect differs in the individual symptom categories (disorientation, nausea, eye strain). However, significant results are only recorded for the motion sickness symptom *Nausea* (see Table 10). Although the predicted tendency is fulfilled, hypothesis *H2* can, thus, only be partially confirmed.

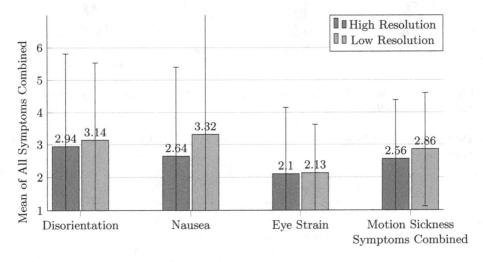

**Fig. 4.** Mean Comparison including Variance by Motion Sickness Symptoms and Test Condition

**Table 10.** Indep. Samples t-Test of Test Conditions and Motion Sickness Sympt.

|  |  | Levene-Test | | | | |
|---|---|---|---|---|---|---|
|  |  | F | Sig | T | df | Sig.(2-sided) |
| Disorientation | Same Variances | 1.385 | .241 | −0.761 | 144 | .448 |
|  | Different Variances |  |  | −0.76 | 142.01 | .448 |
| Nausea | Same Variances | 5.567 | .019 | −2.264 | 144 | .025 |
|  | Different Variances |  |  | −2.269 | 141.568 | .025 |
| Eye Strain | Same Variances | 0.119 | .731 | −0.152 | 144 | .879 |
|  | Different Variances |  |  | −0.152 | 139.448 | .880 |
| Motion Sickness | Same Variances | 0.108 | .672 | −1.339 | 144 | .183 |
| Symptoms Combined | Different Variances |  |  | −1.339 | 143.875 | .183 |

The combined influence of test condition (low vs. high resolution) and motion sickness susceptibility type (low vs. high susceptibility), as well as the ranking, hypothesized in *H3*, is first tested by a comparison of means (see Fig. 5). The hypothesis, which assumes a greater influence of the motion sickness susceptibility type (high/low susceptibility) than that of the resolution quality (high/low resolution), thus can be provisionally confirmed based on this comparison. Ranking by type of susceptibility (low/high susceptibility) in the first instance, followed by test condition (low/high resolution) in the second instance, also occurs at the symptom level. A one-factor analysis of variance (ANOVA) demonstrates the significant differences between the experimental groups (see Table 11), thus confirming hypotheses H3a–d.

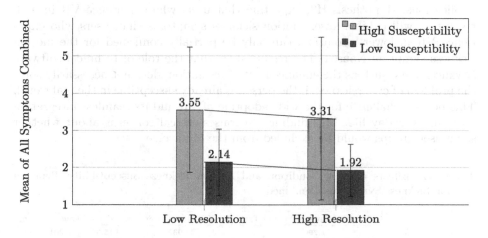

**Fig. 5.** Mean Comparison including Variance of Motion Sickness Symptoms split by Test Condition and Motion Sickness Susceptibility Type

**Table 11.** One-Factorial ANOVA of Test Groups and 'Motion Sickness Symptoms Combined'

|  | Sum of Squares | df | Means of Squares | F | Significance |
|---|---|---|---|---|---|
| Between Groups | 71.796 | 3 | 23.932 | 16.556 | <.001 |
| Within Groups | 205.263 | 142 | 1.446 |  |  |
| Combined | 277.059 | 145 |  |  |  |

*Dependent Variable: Motion Sickness Symptoms Combined*

When the influence of the factors test conditions High Resolution/Low Resolution and the motion sickness susceptibility types Low Motion Sickness Susceptibility/Low Motion Sickness Susceptibility on the dependent variable 'Motion Sickness Symptoms Combined' is tested in a two-factor ANOVA, it is shown that only the susceptibility type lead to a significant effect (see Table 12). The effect of resolution quality is measurable but not statistically significant, with a significance level of .293. In summary, the results confirm the hypotheses' presumed trends. However, significant results are for the most part limited to motion sickness susceptibility type and not resolution quality.

# 6    Discussion and Implications

## 6.1    Effect of Personal vs. Technical Aspects in the Adoption of VR

The results from our study confirm hypothesis (H1) that real-world motion sickness susceptibility plays a major role in the experience of cybersickness in VR applications. Hypothesis H2, expecting that users who experience VR in high resolution will exhibit lower motion sickness symptoms than users who experience VR in lower resolution, can only be partially confirmed for the motion sickness symptom Nausea. The results show that the role of technical software advancements, such as the enhancement of resolution, does not necessarily solve the problem of cybersickness if the person is already susceptible in the real world. This poses a challenge for the wide adoption of VR and its seamless integration into our everyday life. This finding also raises ethical concerns about whether some user groups would be excluded from the Metaverse.

**Table 12.** Effects of Test Condition and Motion Sickness Susceptibility Type on 'Motion Sickness Symptoms Combined'

| Source | Squared Sum of Type III | df | Means of Squares | F | Sig. | $\eta_p^2$ |
|---|---|---|---|---|---|---|
| Corrected Model | 71.796 | 3 | 23.932 | 16.556 | <.001 | .259 |
| Constant Term | 1075.277 | 1 | 1075.277 | 743.871 | <.001 | .840 |
| Susceptibility Type | 68.360 | 1 | 68.360 | 47.291 | <.001 | .250 |
| Test Condition | 1.610 | 1 | 1.610 | 1.114 | <.001 | .008 |
| Susceptibility Type* Condition | 0.091 | 1 | 0.091 | 0.063 | .803 | <.001 |
| Error | 205.263 | 142 | 1.446 | | | |
| Combined | 1350.238 | 146 | | | | |
| Corrected Overall Variation | 277.059 | 145 | | | | |

$*R^2 = .259(corrected\ R^2 = .243)$

Our study is only a first step towards unraveling this interplay between personal and technical factors that may affect the adoption of VR experiences. Future research should continue considering and exploring the effect of personal aspects and how these effects can be mitigated, for example by training or even by medical interventions. Here, providers might learn from other disciplines, for example, the training of astronauts undergoing Autogenic-Feedback Training Exercises that mitigate the effects of motion sickness [56].

## 6.2    Factors to Consider During VR Experiment Setups

When selecting a test group for a VR study that relates to motion sickness, it is recommended to subject the potential participants to a motion sickness questionnaire (e.g., CSSQ [15]) beforehand, since a significant correlation between motion sickness in everyday life and motion sickness in VR could be observed. Through this prior test, the sampled group can be adjusted subsequently, depending on whether the study and the tested hypothesis need predominantly participants with low or high motion sickness susceptibility. In cases where the main objective is representative results, this approach allows for ensuring that both groups are represented equally within the test group so as to avoid biases.

To reduce motion sickness in general, a VR HMD with the best possible display resolution should be selected. This is especially recommended for applications known or expected to trigger nausea, as our results have shown. For the implementation of a VR application, it is also recommended to choose a VR HMD with the highest possible resolution, since motion sickness and nausea, in particular, can be reduced in coordination with a suitable application. Additionally, if part of the research goal is to intentionally trigger motion sickness symptoms, it is possible to artificially reduce the resolution via software, so that the experience resembles that of a low-resolution VR HMD.

# 7  Conclusion and Outlook

As expected and confirmed in previous studies, individual personal factors related to motion sickness susceptibility are valid predictors. Significant associations between motion sickness symptoms and self-assessed motion sickness susceptibility have been consistently demonstrated. In contrast, the effect of resolution quality, while smaller than speculated, offers promising insights for future research in VR eyewear. A significant relationship between resolution quality and the motion sickness symptom *nausea* was demonstrated. Nausea represents only a part of the possible motion sickness symptoms.

Consequences for the use of VR glasses could nevertheless be crucial. As examined in the study by Somrak et al. [50], there is a significant relationship between motion sickness symptoms and user experience with VR headsets. In the present study, a correlation between nausea and the hedonistic benefits of the VR experience also emerged. Obviously, there is an assumption that individuals who develop motion sickness symptoms while wearing VR goggles might derive a lower entertainment benefit from the experience. Analysis of the results suggests that resolution quality alone could only address this issue to a small degree.

The VR industry is continuously striving for new, higher-resolution screens and experiences. It is also questionable whether continuously increasing resolutions will have the same impact on motion sickness symptoms, especially since the human eye can only detect resolution differences to a certain degree [61]. Therefore, future studies could investigate the influence of resolution quality in higher resolution areas and diversify the age and occupational groups. The phenomenon of motion sickness remains multifaceted. For the success and mass suitability of VR glasses, it is nevertheless indispensable to identify as many motion sickness-triggering factors as possible and to provide possible mitigation.

# References

1. Ames, S.L., Wolffsohn, J.S., Mcbrien, N.A.: The development of a symptom questionnaire for assessing virtual reality viewing using a head-mounted display. Optom. Vis. Sci. **82**(3), 168–176 (2005)
2. Atienza, R., Blonna, R., Saludares, M.I., Casimiro, J., Fuentes, V.: Interaction techniques using head gaze for virtual reality. In: 2016 IEEE Region 10 Symposium (TENSYMP), pp. 110–114. IEEE (2016)
3. Batmaz, A.U., Barrera Machuca, M.D., Sun, J., Stuerzlinger, W.: The effect of the vergence-accommodation conflict on virtual hand pointing in immersive displays. In: Proceedings of the 2022 CHI Conference on Human Factors in Computing Systems, pp. 1–15 (2022)
4. Bos, J.E., Bles, W., Groen, E.L.: A theory on visually induced motion sickness. Displays **29**(2), 47–57 (2008)
5. Bos, J.E., MacKinnon, S.N., Patterson, A.: Motion sickness symptoms in a ship motion simulator: effects of inside, outside, and no view. Aviat. Space Environ. Med. **76**(12), 1111–1118 (2005)
6. Buck, L., Paris, R., Bodenheimer, B.: Distance compression in the HTC Vive Pro: a quick revisitation of resolution. Frontiers in Virtual Reality **2**, 728667 (2021)
7. Carnegie, K., Rhee, T.: Reducing visual discomfort with HMDs using dynamic depth of field. IEEE Comput. Graphics Appl. **35**(5), 34–41 (2015)
8. Cha, Y.H., et al.: Motion sickness diagnostic criteria: consensus document of the classification committee of the bárány society. J. Vestib. Res. **31**(5), 327–344 (2021)
9. Chang, C.H., Stoffregen, T.A., Cheng, K.B., Lei, M.K., Li, C.C.: Effects of physical driving experience on body movement and motion sickness among passengers in a virtual vehicle. Exp. Brain Res. **239**, 491–500 (2021)
10. Cheung, B., Howard, I., Money, K.: Visually-induced sickness in normal and bilaterally labyrinthine-defective subjects. Aviat. Space Environ. Med. **62**, 527–531 (1991)
11. Cho, H.J., Kim, G.J.: RideVR: reducing sickness for in-car virtual reality by mixed-in presentation of motion flow information. IEEE Access **10**, 34003–34011 (2022). https://doi.org/10.1109/ACCESS.2022.3162221
12. Chou, T.J., Ting, C.C.: The role of flow experience in cyber-game addiction. CyberPsychol. Beh. **6**(6), 663–675 (2003)
13. Davis, S., Nesbitt, K., Nalivaiko, E.: A systematic review of cybersickness. In: Proceedings of the 2014 Conference on Interactive Entertainment, pp. 1–9 (2014)
14. Dobie, T., McBride, D., Dobie, T., Jr., May, J.: The effects of age and sex on susceptibility to motion sickness. Aviat. Space Environ. Med. **72**(1), 13–20 (2001)
15. Freiwald, J.P., Göbel, Y., Mostajeran, F., Steinicke, F.: The cybersickness susceptibility questionnaire: predicting virtual reality tolerance. In: Proceedings of the Conference on Mensch und Computer, pp. 115–118 (2020)
16. Garrido, L.E., et al.: Focusing on cybersickness: pervasiveness, latent trajectories, susceptibility, and effects on the virtual reality experience. Virtual Real. **26**, 1347–1371 (2022)
17. Golding, J., Rafiq, A., Keshavarz, B.: predicting individual susceptibility to visually induced motion sickness (vims) by questionnaire. Front. Virtual Real. **2**, 576871 (2021)
18. Golding, J.F.: Motion sickness susceptibility questionnaire revised and its relationship to other forms of sickness. Brain Res. Bull. **47**(5), 507–516 (1998)

19. Golding, J.F.: Motion sickness susceptibility. Auton. Neurosci. **129**(1–2), 67–76 (2006)
20. Golding, J.F., Gresty, M.A.: Motion sickness. Curr. Opin. Neurol. **18**(1), 29–34 (2005)
21. Hettinger, L.J., Riccio, G.E.: Visually induced motion sickness in virtual environments. Presence Teleoper. Virtual Environ. **1**(3), 306–310 (1992)
22. Hilken, T., de Ruyter, K., Chylinski, M., Mahr, D., Keeling, D.I.: Augmenting the eye of the beholder: exploring the strategic potential of augmented reality to enhance online service experiences. J. Acad. Mark. Sci. **45**(6), 884–905 (2017)
23. Irwin, J.: The pathology of sea-sickness. Lancet **118**(3039), 907–909 (1881)
24. Kennedy, R.S., Drexler, J., Kennedy, R.C.: Research in visually induced motion sickness. Appl. Ergon. **41**(4), 494–503 (2010)
25. Kennedy, R.S., Lane, N.E., Berbaum, K.S., Lilienthal, M.G.: Simulator sickness questionnaire: an enhanced method for quantifying simulator sickness. Int. J. Aviat. Psychol. **3**(3), 203–220 (1993)
26. Keshavarz, B., Golding, J.F.: Motion sickness: current concepts and management. Curr. Opin. Neurol. **35**(1), 107–112 (2022)
27. Keshavarz, B., Hecht, H.: Stereoscopic viewing enhances visually induced motion sickness but sound does not. Presence **21**(2), 213–228 (2012)
28. Keshavarz, B., Murovec, B., Mohanathas, N., Golding, J.F.: The visually induced motion sickness susceptibility questionnaire (VIMSSQ): estimating individual susceptibility to motion sickness-like symptoms when using visual devices. Hum. Fact. **65**, 107–124 (2021). p. 00187208211008687
29. Kim, H.K., Park, J., Choi, Y., Choe, M.: Virtual reality sickness questionnaire (VRSQ): motion sickness measurement index in a virtual reality environment. Appl. Ergon. **69**, 66–73 (2018)
30. Kim, Y.Y., Kim, H.J., Kim, E.N., Ko, H.D., Kim, H.T.: Characteristic changes in the physiological components of cybersickness. Psychophysiology **42**(5), 616–625 (2005)
31. Knight, M.M., Arns, L.L.: The relationship among age and other factors on incidence of cybersickness in immersive environment users. In: Proceedings of the 3rd Symposium on Applied Perception in Graphics and Visualization. APGV 2006, New York, NY, USA, pp. 162. Association for Computing Machinery (2006). https://doi.org/10.1145/1140491.1140539,https://doi.org/10.1145/1140491.1140539
32. Kohl, R.L.: Sensory conflict theory of space motion sickness: an anatomical location for the neuroconflict. Aviat. Space Environ. Med. **54**, 464–465 (1983)
33. Kolasinski, E.M.: Simulator sickness in virtual environments, vol. 1027. US Army Research Institute for the Behavioral and Social Sciences (1995)
34. Laugwitz, B., Held, T., Schrepp, M.: Construction and evaluation of a user experience questionnaire. In: Holzinger, A. (ed.) USAB 2008. LNCS, vol. 5298, pp. 63–76. Springer, Heidelberg (2008). https://doi.org/10.1007/978-3-540-89350-9_6
35. LaViola, J.J., Jr.: A discussion of cybersickness in virtual environments. ACM SIGCHI Bull. **32**(1), 47–56 (2000)
36. McGill, M., Ng, A., Brewster, S.A.: How visual motion cues can influence sickness for in-car VR. In: Proceedings of the 2017 CHI Conference Extended Abstracts on Human Factors in Computing Systems. CHI EA 2017, p. 469, New York, NY, USA. Association for Computing Machinery (2017). https://doi.org/10.1145/3027063.3049790
37. Mittelstaedt, H.: A new solution to the problem of the subjective vertical. Naturwissenschaften **70**(6), 272–281 (1983)

38. Nalivaiko, E., Davis, S.L., Blackmore, K.L., Vakulin, A., Nesbitt, K.V.: Cybersickness provoked by head-mounted display affects cutaneous vascular tone, heart rate and reaction time. Physiol. Beh. **151**, 583–590 (2015)

39. Oman, C.M.: Motion sickness: a synthesis and evaluation of the sensory conflict theory. Can. J. Physiol. Pharmacol. **68**(2), 294–303 (1990)

40. Paillard, A., et al.: Motion sickness susceptibility in healthy subjects and vestibular patients: effects of gender, age and trait-anxiety. J. Vestib. Res. **23**(4–5), 203–209 (2013)

41. Park, S., Mun, S., Ha, J., Kim, L.: Non-contact measurement of motion sickness using pupillary rhythms from an infrared camera. Sensors **21**(14), 4642 (2021)

42. Rauschnabel, P.A., Felix, R., Hinsch, C., Shahab, H., Alt, F.: What is XR? towards a framework for augmented and virtual reality. Comput. Hum. Beh. **133**, 107289 (2022). https://doi.org/10.1016/j.chb.2022.107289, https://www.sciencedirect.com/science/article/pii/S074756322200111X

43. Reason, J., Brand, J.: Motion Sickness. Academic Press, London, New York, San Francisco (1975)

44. Rebenitsch, L., Owen, C.: Individual variation in susceptibility to cybersickness. In: Proceedings of the 27th Annual ACM Symposium on User Interface Software and Technology. UIST 2014, pp. 309–317, New York, NY, USA. Association for Computing Machinery (2014). https://doi.org/10.1145/2642918.2647394

45. Rebenitsch, L., Owen, C.: Review on cybersickness in applications and visual displays. Virt. Real. **20**(2), 101–125 (2016)

46. Rolnick, A., Lubow, R.: Why is the driver rarely motion sick? The role of controllability in motion sickness. Ergonomics **34**(7), 867–879 (1991)

47. Schrepp, M., Hinderks, A., Thomaschewski, J.: Applying the user experience questionnaire (UEQ) in different evaluation scenarios. In: Marcus, A. (ed.) DUXU 2014. LNCS, vol. 8517, pp. 383–392. Springer, Cham (2014). https://doi.org/10.1007/978-3-319-07668-3_37

48. Singla, A., Fremerey, S., Robitza, W., Raake, A.: Measuring and comparing QoE and simulator sickness of omnidirectional videos in different head mounted displays. In: 2017 Ninth International Conference on Quality of Multimedia Experience (QoMEX), pp. 1–6. IEEE (2017)

49. Solimini, A.G., Mannocci, A., Di Thiene, D., La Torre, G.: A survey of visually induced symptoms and associated factors in spectators of three dimensional stereoscopic movies. BMC Public Health **12**, 1–11 (2012)

50. Somrak, A., Humar, I., Hossain, M.S., Alhamid, M.F., Hossain, M.A., Guna, J.: Estimating VR sickness and user experience using different HMD technologies: an evaluation study. Futur. Gener. Comput. Syst. **94**, 302–316 (2019)

51. Stanney, K.M., Hale, K.S., Nahmens, I., Kennedy, R.S.: What to expect from immersive virtual environment exposure: influences of gender, body mass index, and past experience. Hum. Factors **45**(3), 504–520 (2003)

52. Stanney, K.M., Kennedy, R.S., Drexler, J.M.: Cybersickness is not simulator sickness. In: Proceedings of the Human Factors and Ergonomics Society Annual Meeting, vol. 41, pp. 1138–1142. SAGE Publications Sage CA, Los Angeles (1997)

53. Stauffert, J.P., Niebling, F., Latoschik, M.E.: Effects of latency jitter on simulator sickness in a search task. In: 2018 IEEE Conference on Virtual Reality and 3D User Interfaces (VR), pp. 121–127. IEEE (2018)

54. Turner, M.: Motion sickness in public road transport: passenger behaviour and susceptibility. Ergonomics **42**(3), 444–461 (1999)

55. Venkatesh, V., Thong, J.Y., Xu, X.: Consumer acceptance and use of information technology: extending the unified theory of acceptance and use of technology. MIS Quart. **36**, 157–178 (2012)
56. Walton, N., Spencer, T., Cowings, P., Toscano, W.B.: Autogenic feedback training exercise: controlling physiological responses to mitigate motion sickness. Technical report (2018)
57. Wang, J., Shi, R., Xiao, Z., Qin, X., Liang, H.N.: Effect of render resolution on gameplay experience, performance, and simulator sickness in virtual reality games. Proc. ACM Comput. Graph. Interact. Tech. **5**(1), 1–15 (2022)
58. Warwick-Evans, L., Symons, N., Fitch, T., Burrows, L.: Evaluating sensory conflict and postural instability. Theories of motion sickness. Brain Res. Bull. **47**(5), 465–469 (1998)
59. Weech, S., Kenny, S., Barnett-Cowan, M.: Presence and cybersickness in virtual reality are negatively related: a review. Front. Psychol. **10**, 158 (2019)
60. Zielasko, D.: Subject 001-a detailed self-report of virtual reality induced sickness. In: 2021 IEEE Conference on Virtual Reality and 3D User Interfaces Abstracts and Workshops (VRW), pp. 165–168. IEEE (2021)
61. Zou, W., Yang, L., Yang, F., Ma, Z., Zhao, Q.: The impact of screen resolution of HMD on perceptual quality of immersive videos. In: 2020 IEEE International Conference on Multimedia & Expo Workshops (ICMEW), pp. 1–6. IEEE (2020)

# Spatial Augmented Reality in the Factory: Can In-Situ Projections Be Used to Communicate Dangers and Health Risks?

Aaron Wedral[1]([✉])[iD], Rafael Vrecar[1][iD], Gerhard Ebenhofer[2][iD],
Thomas Pönitz[2][iD], Paul H. Wührer[2][iD], Astrid Weiss[1][iD], and Gernot Stübl[2][iD]

[1] Technische Universität Wien, Vienna, Austria
{aaron.wedral,rafael.vrecar,astrid.weiss}@tuwien.ac.at
[2] PROFACTOR GmbH, Steyr-Gleink 4407, Upper Austria, Austria
{gerhard.ebenhofer,thomas.poenitz,paul.wuehrer,gernot.stuebl}@profactor.at

**Abstract.** In the context of industrial settings, extensive research of in-situ projections has proven their benefits for task performance. However, to date, these projections have not explicitly addressed policies designed to mitigate the dangers and health risks that are just as important, if not more than task performance considerations in such settings. We developed in-situ projections for three different use cases: (1) assembly support at a workbench, (2) ergonomic lifting, (3) restricted areas, which we studied with 15 representative target users. We found the expected benefits of the task-supporting projection (use case 1), increasing task performance and causing minimal cognitive load. However, our data also suggest that the other projections (use case 2 and 3) did not improve policy compliance. Our findings indicate that in-situ projections are not the most suitable solution to nudge workers to policy compliance in an industrial assembly setting, as most participants ignored the policy after evaluating the dangers themselves. Furthermore, based on our limitations and findings, we reflect on how current study practices can be improved for ubiquitous systems, especially when aiding policy compliance.

**Keywords:** Spatial Augmented Reality · Pose Estimation · Human Machine Interaction · Learnability · Cognitive Load · Ergonomic Notifications · Collaborative Robot Safety Zone Awareness · Manual Assembly Assistance · Industrial Assembly

## 1 Introduction

With industries recently rethinking the importance of work conditions, the direction is to move away from product-centric to human-centric production, which is supported, e.g., by the EU initiative Industry 5.0[1]. The main aim behind

---

[1] https://research-and-innovation.ec.europa.eu/research-area/industry/industry-50

© The Author(s), under exclusive license to Springer Nature Switzerland AG 2023
J. Abdelnour Nocera et al. (Eds.): INTERACT 2023, LNCS 14143, pp. 574–594, 2023.
https://doi.org/10.1007/978-3-031-42283-6_31

these initiatives is to ensure that technology assists humans instead of humans assisting technology, which calls for new approaches to designing and evaluating new high-technology solutions. There is an increased need to not only develop and study assistive technology meant to increase task performance, but to focus on how to implement technology in a way that improves *"working conditions for people, rather than ŕjustź improving the interaction paradigms [...]"* [39]. One way to address that is to find ways how technology can help workers to adhere to health and safety policies, as sometimes such policies are not even deemed necessary by the workers themselves or just fade into the background of everyday working routines and performance pressure. Seen as a nuisance, an inhibition to efficient workflows, or simply forgotten when working, policy compliance is not given high priority. In this work, we developed and evaluated a Spatial Augmented Reality system primarily intended to serve as a reminder and live-feedback for policy compliance in a factory setting.

The technical part of this work describes the combination of assistance systems with AI algorithms to optimize time and cost savings in industrial settings. Specifically, we explore the potential of Spatial Augmented Reality (SAR) using projection-based solutions to provide in-situ worker support, enhance task completion, and ensure policy compliance. Our work involved implementing three distinct use cases: *manual assembly assistance, ergonomic notifications*, and *collaborative robot safety zone awareness*. To evaluate our approach, we engaged 15 representative target users in the assessment of these use cases. The manual assembly assistance represents the "typical AR use case", where workers are aided in completing their activities at a workbench by providing them with visual guides. The ergonomic notifications and collaborative robot safety zone awareness, instead focus on policy compliance. The first one aims to alert workers of improper ergonomic lifting with visual cues in the area where lifting is required. The collaborative robot safety zone awareness should be achieved with visual cues to inform workers about their proximity to an area that they should not enter and an even stronger cue when entering the area. Both of these projections are intended to warn workers about dangers to their health and safety. Similar solutions could also alert workers of overhead dangers such as cranes and autonomously moving robots entering their spaces (or vice-versa). The significant advantage compared to current safety measures is that their safety perimeter can be updated with live information and would only need to encompass currently active dangers and not all possible dangers.

To evaluate our three use cases from an operator-centered perspective, we posed the following research questions:

- RQ1: How do the three different projector assistance systems affect *efficiency, effectiveness*, and *satisfaction*?
- RQ2: How is the usage affecting operators' *cognitive load*?
- RQ3: How effective is the *learnability* of the projector technology?

To answer these questions, we set up a laboratory study in which participants experienced all three use cases. In our setting, we included multiple runs of similar activities at the workbench to measure learnability and its potential effects on cognitive load. Specifically, we were interested in observing changes with regard to task performance and policy compliance. Keeping in mind to always stay out of dangerous zones and to lift ergonomically is tedious, and people are prone to forget these things. If changes in behavior occurred, it would show how effective it is in nudging towards healthy behavior and if participants like using it.

The paper is structured as follows, after a section on related work, we present our three use cases in more detail. Next, the evaluation study is presented, including the study design and measurements. We then present the results, focusing on how well projections worked for the classical workbench assistance compared to the two policy-related use cases. We close the paper with a discussion on the suitability of in-situ projections to support policy compliance and the limitations of our evaluation design.

## 2    Related Work

According to [14], Industrial Augmented Reality (IAR) pertains to the use of Augmented Reality technology in industrial settings. This area is currently the subject of ongoing research, with studies such as [4,28] exploring maintenance applications, while [15] discuss IAR's potential for supporting shipyard production. The present work focuses on Industrial Augmented Reality for worker assistance.

### Technological Variety and Different Applications

There are several ways to technically implement AR which all have their pros and cons. A basic distinction is made in Optical See-Through (OST) or Video See-Through (VST). Lately, powerful HMDs, which through their semi-transparent glasses are OST, have emerged on the market. Examples are Microsoft HoloLens II or Magic Leap, which integrate on-board computers and environmental perception modules into one device. They can generate high-quality content and do an excellent job in situations where users do not have to wear the device a longer time, see [18] for training or [5] for teleoperation.

Currently, on the shop floor itself the use of HMDs is limited due to several factors: The environment may often be harsh and cluttered, which could disturb the internal sensors. Moreover, positioning the HMD in a user's visual field is a complex yet highly important factor for, e.g., comfort and task efficiency [26] too. Additionally, the precision of the HMD's internal positioning sensors is mostly below the precision needed for industrial work. For example, an HMD cannot be used to show drilling positions within a position error of 0.5mm, see [19]. Furthermore, battery would not last a whole shift of an industrial worker. Tablet-based XR, which is an example for VST, on the other side is a practical solution on the shop floor, especially if operators already use tablets for their work.

A further important technology is Spatial Augmented Reality (SAR). With SAR, a projecting device (LED, LCD, DPL, laser-projectors, etc.) directly projects the virtual information in the scene on the workpiece of interest. This is non-intrusive for the users as they do not have to wear special devices. In addition to that, it is inherently multi-user capable and saves the cost of a HMD for each participating person. In a SAR setup, perception is done with external cameras. Beside the high achievable precision of perception, this allows also to capture images of the human itself.

Projector-based AR systems are well-studied subjects in computational science, since the early days of AR, see [2,3]. Applying SAR in manual industrial work to provide in-situ assistance is a popular topic in research, as can be seen, e.g., in early papers by [40] for welding. The clear sequence of working steps makes manual assembly tasks a good fit for doing research regarding in-situ projections. [24] as well as [17] show that impaired persons benefit from projecting instructions.

[23] present a Context-aware assistive system (CAAS) which combines projection with motion recognition and object recognition. [16] present a long time-study of in-situ projection at a manual work place. [6,37] show that the potential for this technology is still high. Context-awareness is a desired aspect for technology of this kind as it reduces the need for supervision as exemplified in [31,32], respectively, using wearable sensors.

## Pose Estimation

The raise of deep learning has been a game-changer in Computer Vision and affects all related research fields. The so far listed state of the art builds on traditional image processing which is not as powerful as modern algorithms. Especially the emerged pose estimation algorithms, see e.g. [7] or [38], are able to fit human skeletons into images. This allows the full digitization of human poses and their perception through computers.

There are several works which combine pose estimation with SAR, mainly on a large-scale interaction areas, see e.g. [22,33] as utility for distancing technology or for interfacing industrial production environments see [21,30]. The last two see production environments as coherent production information systems and utilize XR to interact ubiquitously with them. [21] introduce the idea of spatial interaction areas (trigger zones) as special areas on the floor, which in the simplest case send a software event as soon as a user enters. Technically, the detection is done by a pose estimation algorithm. In more advanced settings, events are sent depending on the action the user performs inside the region, e.g. results of ergonomic assessment, see [30]. The events cause reactions of the production information system.

However, the technological aspects, e.g., accuracy, of pose estimation are only one part of the full picture. Correct detection alone does not imply change in behavior as the form of notification the workers receive matters too, as can be seen, e.g., in [9]. Active recognition of the notification is a problem too, as we will see in the results of our study.

Many researchers in the HCI and ubiquitous computing community have highlighted the unique challenge posed when evaluating ubiquitous systems,

namely the interaction triangulation between users, technology, and environment
[1]. To address this issue, heuristic approaches have been developed that incorporate these interaction paradigms while considering factors such as transparency
and privacy [34,35]. Others defined 24 suitable software measures for ubiquitous system evaluation [8]. In our approach, we tackle this challenge through the
design of the assignment in our evaluation study, as outlined in Sect. 4.

## 3  Envisioned Use Cases

The proposed work utilizes deep learning algorithms as weak AI systems to access
broader application possibilities for assistive technologies in Industry 5.0. Especially the idea of trigger zones has been adopted and assembled to reality-near
use cases for health and safety policy compliance. We developed the following
three use cases to cover various XR applications for human-centered industrial
work and demonstrate the potential of a state-of-the-art AI algorithm for not
only assisting task performance, but also policy compliance. The use cases were
intentionally designed in a way that allows us to integrate all of them in a single
laboratory study (see Sect. 4). The first use case of "Manual Assembly Assistance" (see Fig. 3) represents the typical aid in task performance use case for in-
situ projections. "Areas for Ergonmoic Monitoring" (see Fig. 3) and "Restricted
Area around a Robot" (see Fig. 3) represent use cases of in-situ projections to
communicate health and safty risks and foster policy compliance (Fig. 1).

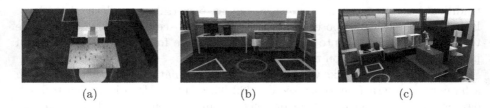

(a)    (b)    (c)

**Fig. 1.** 3D sketches of the three use cases in the factory lab. (a) Workbench for Assembly; (b) Areas for Ergonomic Monitoring; (c) Restricted Area around a Robot.

### 3.1  Manual Assembly Assistance

Figure 3 depicts a workbench where task-aiding information is directly projected
on the work piece utilizing SAR. In this simplified setup, the worker has to peg in
clamps on a board. The systems assists by highlighting right and wrong positions.
The setup is fully functioning by using an *AIModule* with an object detection
based on the work of [10]. The detector is trained such that it can robustly
detect partially occluded holes too in various lighting conditions, which would
be hard to achieve without deep learning. The technical software architecture
is based on micro-services. Images are sent by cameras as *ImageProvider* which

are processed by the *ProjectionLogic* and displayed by the *ProjectionModel*. The *ProjectionLogic* itself can utilize various *AIModules*. The used software is part of the product suite of PROFACTOR[2]. From the hardware side, the used cameras are of type Teledyne DALSA Genie Nano C-2590. Use case 1 and 2 utilize the same camera. All focal lengths are calculated to fit the lab environment. For Use case 1 a standard short-throw beamer in a setup similar to [30] is used, whereas Use case 2 utilized a high-performance Panasonic PT-MZ880 laser projector. In Use case 3 again a standard office beamer is used for projection.

## 3.2   Ergonomic Notification

Workplace ergonomic issues are significant risk factors to occupational safety and health issues. They are thought to contribute to the rising prevalence of musculoskeletal disorders (MSD) among workers, as elaborated in [29]. AI-based ergonomic online-monitoring of workers is in the focus of current research, as can be seen in, e.g., [13]. However, once detected, it is an open problem how the information of an ergonomic problem is communicated to the worker, as we have already seen in [9]. Figure 3 depicts the setup of the use case. The floor-near projector in the middle projects a white circle, which marks the interaction area. If a worker steps in, it is either filled green if there are no detected ergonomic problems in the circle, or red if ergonomic problems are present. Technically, the interaction area is automatically activated by stepping into the circle. Unfortunately, there is no computer-based ergonomic assessment tool available at the research lab, this is why the corresponding *AIModule* only extracts the skeleton and asks an observing human for the assessment. However, recent publications report that the pose estimation algorithms already in use can be extended for ergonomic assessment too, as [27] elaborated on.

## 3.3   Collaborative Robot Safety Zone Awareness

Collaborative Robots (Cobots) are constructed to perform work in a collaborative workspace together with humans. Cobots operate on slower speeds when collaborating with humans. ISO/TS 15066[3] defines multiple spaces around the robot which are mapped to different speed of the robot and danger for the humans. For mobile cobots, it is an open problem to communicate these spaces to human workers, therefore this use case was chosen to represent safety hazard communication. Figure 3 shows the setup of a mobile cobot, which has a projected white rectangular area around it. This area is defining the "restricted area". As soon as a worker enters the rectangle it turns red. In a real application, the robot would have to be stopped. This use case has a fully operating *AIModule* which utilizes pose estimation to check whether a human is in the restricted area. A similar setup has been shown by [21], but was not evaluated regarding its usability.

---

[2] For a demo version of the software please contact the authors.
[3] https://www.iso.org/standard/62996.html.

## 4   Evaluation

The goal of our evaluation was to explore with representative target users if in-situ projections are not only suitable for aiding task performance but also for fostering health and safety compliance. To answer our research questions, we set up an experiment in the factory lab of PROFACTOR. Our fundamental intention was to center our evaluation study around use case 1 - workbench assembly in order not to point participants toward the fact that we were interested in observing if they take the other two projection use cases into account during the study.

We instructed participants that the overall assignment was to assemble parts at the workbench. First, they had to scan a provided QR code with the instructions for the next step at the workbench (using a scanner placed above the workbench), locate marked parts in a specific area, and attach them to a perforated plate at the workbench at specified locations (Fig. 2 - right). We told them that they needed to adhere to the following policies while working: lifting ergonomically, avoiding the robot, keeping the workplace clean, and awaiting confirmation to proceed to the next task (Fig. 2 - left). Participants had to repeat this activity 10 times in total to fulfill the overall assignment at the workbench.

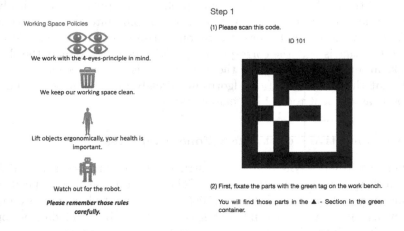

**Fig. 2.** Policy and exemplary step description

The study was designed so that participants were confronted with the three in-situ projections but were not reliant on the information communicated by the systems to complete the assembly task at the workbench. We explicitly did not tell our participants how they were to complete the given assignment. Instead, they should work as they are used to, with priorities and experiences shaped by their real-life job. We wanted them to show us where their focus lies in how to facilitate the work and not influence them to overuse the projections simply because we want to assess their usefulness. With this evaluation set-up, all three in-situ projections were covered in a representative scenario, which participants could relate to from their actual work experience.

Participants had to (ergonomically) pick up a box to get the parts needed at the workstation. They had to transport the materials to the workstation while avoiding the restricted area. Then, they had to complete the assembly at the workbench with projector-displayed instructions (as well as additionally provided printed instructions). Combining the three use cases into one scenario and not testing them individually was based on the idea of presenting participants with a meaningful activity therefore, they do not spend their time questioning during the study why they had to pick up something ten times in a row. This would most likely introduce bias since they would question why they were invited instead of focusing on the assignment - even though they were informed that the study is testing the projection technology and not them.

To detect changes in policy compliance and task performance not only between on and off states of the SAR system, but especially in off states after having interacted with the technology, the projections switched between active and inactive at fixed repetitions during the 10 times participants had to repeat the activity.

### 4.1 Participants and Conduct

Fifteen representative target users participated in the study. They were recruited from customers and partner companies of PROFACTOR, mainly from the automotive industry. They were voluntary respondents of flyers distributed at their workplaces. Special care was taken that all participants currently work or had worked directly in industrial production. 9 participants had more than 3 years of experience working with industrial automation, while only 4 had less than 3 months of experience. Participants' age ranged from 20 to 62 years, with an average of 39.31 years. Among the them, only one was left-handed, and none were color-blind. Five participants self-assessed their spatial sense as above-average. We complied with COVID-19-related regulations and guidelines. During the trial, all participants and researchers wore protective masks. Dangers for participants were minimized in the study setup as well. The participants received monetary compensation for the time required for participation in the study.

### 4.2 Measures and Methods

To answer our research questions on efficiency, effectiveness, satisfaction, cognitive load[4], and learnability we designed a mixed methods approach combining multiple types of qualitative and quantitative data, aiming to gain a comprehensive understanding of why and how the three different projector technologies support people in their working tasks. We used the following methods for collecting data were selected:

---

[4] Since there is currently no agreed-upon way to interpret objective measures used to estimate cognitive load meaningfully [11], we opted to use the presented mix.

- Time required for each step at the work bench (measure for efficiency)
- Successful policy compliance and completion of tasks (measures for effectiveness)
- NASA-TLX Survey [20] (for evaluating cognitive load)
- SUS-Survey [25] (to evaluate usability and learnability)
- Semi-structured interviews (for evaluating satisfaction and learnability)
- Think-aloud-protocol [12] [36, p. 158] (as a measure of cognitive load, a control for learnability and control whether the system is actually considered during the experiment, since it is not required for completion or compliance)
- A count of how many times the SAR system was active until now (behavioral cognitive load measure)

Notes and observations during the study and in the analysis of the video footage were used to complement our measures and inform the interpretation of the results. To ensure that the trials are comparable and as similar as possible, an extensive test procedure guideline was created in advance, outlining every step and everything to be done and said by the instructors (fellow researchers can request the guidelines to replicate the study from the authors). Figure 3 visualizes the overall study procedure.

### 4.3    Analysis

For data analysis, we first defined the coding criteria for extracting our measurements from the trial videos for comparable quantitative analysis.

*Completion time* is valid and comparable between subjects only for the manual assembly assistance. The starting time was taken the moment the first part to be placed was released by the participant, and the end time was taken the moment the last part that needed to be re-positioned was released. This measure captures the timespan that was spent mostly on the task with little distraction and noise from other sources (no walking between destinations, no searching for parts).

*Success* for the *manual assembly assistance* was defined as the number of correctly placed parts at the end time. Parts may be moved and corrected later, but if the participant declared that they were finished with a step, they also take responsibility for the correctness of their placement. The success criteria for *obstacle avoidance* was defined as "not colliding with the robot". Trespassing in the marked restricted area was also extracted but not defined as a success criterion since the policy was to avoid the robot, nothing more. For *ergonomically correct lifting*, success was defined as participants not bending their lower back and instead lifting ergonomically from the knees.

The other measures were mainly from sources outside the video recordings and are (apart from survey scores) harder to clearly define and quantify. *Satisfaction* was derived from the SUS survey score and combined with experience reports from the post-trial interviews. *Learnability* was considered with multiple aspects in mind. Considering the differences in completion time between the trials can show how much participants improved (with the projections active and

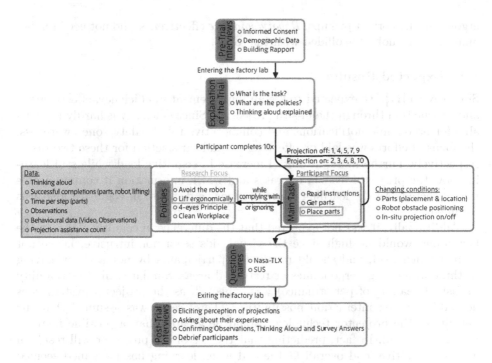

**Fig. 3.** Flow of the Experiment Procedure. Details which methods were used and data was gathered in which step. The green region marks the research focus during the repeated trials with the technology. The lavender region marks where the participant focus was expected during the repeated trials. (Color figure online)

without). Additionally, participants were asked about their learning progress in the post-trial interviews and the learnability score extracted from the SUS survey [25]. In addition to the score from the NASA-TLX survey, *Cognitive load* can be indicated based on these parameters: 1) if thinking aloud was followed, the load increased considerably if the talking stopped all of a sudden, 2) when counting how many times the assistance system was on, mistakes might also indicate a higher cognitive load, and 3) afterward if the guidelines can (partially) be reproduced correctly by the participant, the cognitive load might have been low(er).

To analyze *completion time*, we wanted to compare steps with the projection assistance to steps without. We took the averages of steps with the active projection and compared them to the averages of steps without assistance per participant. We used a Wilcoxon signed-rank test to determine the likelihood that they are equally efficient. To analyze the effectiveness of the workbench projection, we compared the number of falsely and correctly placed parts with and without the in-situ projection active and tested them with a Barnard's exact test. The same procedure was done for the *lifting assistance projection* but with ergonomically correct pickups. *Robot avoidance* effectiveness did not need further analysis since nobody collided with the robot.

### 4.4 Expected Results

Similarly to [17], we expected to see an improvement in efficiency, effectiveness, and satisfaction through the in-situ projection. Since efficiency is hardly measurable for ergonomic notifications and collaborative robot safety zone awareness, the focus of efforts was laid on effectiveness and satisfaction for these two tasks, respectively. Furthermore, an initial increase in cognitive load while still learning how the projector system operates and which information it communicates was expected. As the learning curve dropped, a decrease in cognitive load was assumed.

Additionally, it was not expected that the difference in cognitive load, in the beginning, would be high since the visual aids seem non-intrusive, hence not adding much load, and should relieve the participants by not actively having to think about, e.g., ergonomics or restricted areas. Similarly, high learnability (a fast plateauing of performance) was expected, as the projector system does not add complex interaction possibilities. Therefore, it was assumed that the benefits of the projector technology would be greater than a possible increase in cognitive load. In fact, predicting that the use of the projector will result in a lower cognitive load overall at the end when learning has plateaued seemed adequate since the system allowed participants to keep things in mind easily; one would otherwise forget but does so unobtrusively.

A priori, it was assumed that the most valuable insights could be gathered when comparing how single participants change their behavior between trials. Especially when comparing the behavior between projector assistance off, projector assistance on, and projector assistance off again. It was predicted that major changes in behavior would ensue when comparing both scenarios where the projector assistance is not active due to a change in situation awareness. These changes would most likely include different regard on how much distance to the obstacle must be kept, how ergonomically correct the parts would be picked up, and how the printed/displayed instructions would be used.

## 5    Results

The results of our study are presented in a structured manner, according to the research questions addressed. The first three sections focus on answering RQ1, which pertains to the efficiency, effectiveness, and satisfaction levels of each assistance system. This is followed by a section that addresses the overarching measures, including cognitive load (RQ2) and learnability (RQ3).

### 5.1    RQ1 - Manual Assembly Assistance

In general, all participants completed assignment according to the outlined procedure. Therefore, the data is actually comparable because the participants followed the same instructions. However, there are two cases that require special treatment: Participant 7 in run 5 checked the positions of all objects by counting manually whether they are in the correct position, which took them 00:07:01. Therefore, the time of this specific run of this specific participant was left out intentionally when averaging all values. Participant 8 completely ignored any placement information for parts and therefore is not comparable to other participants' behavior. The data was removed for success analysis, since it would heavily skew error rates. The completion times were not normally distributed. Figure 4 shows a boxplot of all completion times per step. A Wilcoxon test confirms that the completion time for steps with an active projection ($Mdn = 7.912s$) was significantly lower than with an inactive projection ($Mdn = 23.259s$), $T = 2.0$, $p < 0.0002$, $r = -0.601$. This suggests that using the in-situ projection makes the workbench task considerably faster. The only participants with low time in runs without projector assistance (participant 8 and 13) did not try to accurately place the parts and therefore had a very high error rate.

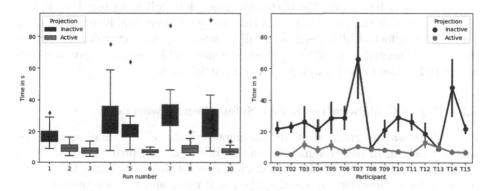

**Fig. 4.** Boxplot of Completion Time per Step (left), Avg. Completion Time per Participant when Active/Inactive with Error Rates (right). Runs with Manual Assembly Assistance (2, 3, 6, 8, 10) were Considerably Faster.

As the data from Table 1 shows, in runs, when the in-situ projection was active, less mistakes were made in placement. Barnard's exact statistic for this contingency table is about $-4.781$ with a $p$-value of $2.074 * 10^{-5}$. Based on the odds ratio, the odds of a participant placing a part correctly was 17.739 times higher with projection assistance than without. These findings are also supported by participants' thinking-aloud and in the post-trial interviews. They mostly enjoyed working with the workbench projection even though some were confused by what it was trying to communicate (which is understandable as it was not directly explained to them in advance).

## 5.2   RQ1 - Ergonomic Notification

Lifting success was similarly analyzed, but the results were quite different, as can be seen in Table 1. The Barnard's exact statistic is about 0.462 with a $p$-value of 0.719 and the decrease in odds ratio of 0.856 is therefore not significant.

**Table 1.** Contingency Tables. Left: Part Placement on the Work Bench. Right: Lifting Ergonomically. With Manual Assembly Assistance Participants Made Significantly Fewer Mistakes in Placement. We Observed no Significant Difference with Ergonomic Notification Active.

| In-situ \ Location | Correct | Incorrect | | In-situ \ Lifting Ergonomically | Yes | No |
|---|---|---|---|---|---|---|
| Inactive | 46 | 24 | | Inactive | 43 | 45 |
| Active | 68 | 2 | | Active | 27 | 33 |

The in-situ projection does not really seem to have the same impact as for the workbench use case. This also coincides with findings from the post-trial interviews in which participants did not name the lifting projection as part of the assistive technology solution. Only about a third of participants even noticed the projection and most of them did not attribute much meaning to it. The decision of how to lift the parts was either done following usual workplace practices or with the judgement call that the parts were not heavy enough to warrant the effort of lifting ergonomically. Either way, the reminder for correct lifting implemented as in-situ projection was not visible enough or not available at the right time to be meaningful for our participants.

### 5.3   RQ1 - Collaborative Robot Safety Zone Awareness

Since there was no collision at all, the numeric data of this small sample size was not helpful in determining the impact of the in-situ projection. However, twelve participants noticed the projection and six of them attributed the correct meaning to it. However, after seeing the robot move and not determining it as a threat, all but two participants started to ignore the projection warning when entering the working space of the robot.

### 5.4   RQ 2 and 3 - Overarching Measures

*System Usability Scale* - Since participants reported perceiving the workbench projection as the main SAR system (or sometimes the only) and some participants explicitly stated filling out the survey with only the workbench in mind, the survey answers had to be analyzed as referring to the workbench projection and not all three use cases.

Compared to the distributions represented in [25], the collected SUS results are higher. Only four results are below the pessimistic distribution median with none below the 1st quartile and seven results are at or above the 3rd quartile. This suggests high usability.

*Learnability* - Since meaningful time measurement could solely be taken for the workbench, it became our sole behavioral *learnability* measure (see Fig. 5). Having few repeated trials to compare makes detailed analysis hard, but there are some things which can be observed. There is no observable decrease in time

**Table 2.** Descriptive Statistics of SUS and the Factorisation in Usability and Learnability (with Values Scaled to 0-100 to Match SUS). Results Indicate High Usability and Learnability.

|  | Score | Usability | Learnability |
|---|---|---|---|
| N | 13 | 13 | 14 |
| Mean | 81.731 | 80.769 | 86.607 |
| Standard Deviation | 11.105 | 13.612 | 18.647 |
| Minimum | 60 | 50 | 37.5 |
| 1st Quartile | 72.5 | 75 | 78.125 |
| Median | 85 | 84.375 | 93.75 |
| 3rd Quartile | 87.5 | 90.625 | 100 |
| Maximum | 100 | 100 | 100 |

required over trials with or without the in-situ projection active. The differences between runs with the same projection state can be explained by differing difficulty. The lack of speed increase can have multiple reasons. Since there is not much active interaction and little user knowledge required, it leaves little room for improvement by learning the interaction. Participants reported not trusting the assistive technology solution too much since they interpreted the switching states of assistance as the projection malfunctioning. This lack of consistency could also be an explanation of why there was no observable improvement. In their SUS answers, seven participants gave the highest possible learnability score (also transformed to be between 0 and 100) and only one participant a score below average leading to a mean of 86.6 (refer to Table 2).

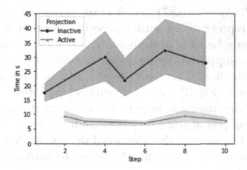

**Fig. 5.** Avg. Completion Times per Step with 95% Confidence Interval. Blue: Projection Inactive, Orange: Projection Active. There was no Observable Decrease in Time Required over Trials. (Color figure online)

*Cognitive Load* - To measure cognitive load, we used behavioral data in addition to the NASA-TLX [20] survey. Six of the fifteen participants made errors counting how many steps they have been assisted by the projection. After the study, participants were also asked to recount the four policies which were part of the instruction. Nine participants recounted three, two participants recounted two and one policy respectively and one participant recounted none. One participant was not asked to recount because of an error. Thinking-aloud participation time was not included as a cognitive load measure, since it was hard to quantify into meaningful data (Table 3).

**Table 3.** NASA-TLX Descriptive Statistics. Results indicate Low Cognitive Load.

|  | Task Load |  | Task Load |
|---|---|---|---|
| N | 14 |  |  |
| Mean | 21.488 | Median | 20.833 |
| Standard Deviation | 9.814 |  |  |
| Minimum | 7.5 | 1st Quartile | 15.417 |
| Maximum | 44.167 | 3rd Quartile | 26.458 |

Participants did not always exactly mark at indicated values, when filling in the paper-based questionnaire, but sometimes marked between steps. We interpreted these between scale answers as halfway between scales (so a mark between 1 and 2 was interpreted as 1.5). Since single measures are averaged to provide the final score and only the final score is used for analysis, this interpretation should not introduce relevant bias.

Since there is no benchmark with normalized TLX data, it is hard to say what measured load is acceptable. A one sided t-test with the median of possible scores (50) as expected value shows our sample ($M = 21.488$, $SE = 2.623$) as significantly lower $t(13) = -10.871$, $p < 3.4*10^{-8}$, $r = 0.949$. However, this does not mean that 50 represents an actual expected value of NASA-TLX surveys and therefore can only be seen as an indication of a lower score. Our findings of low mental load are supported by interview answers of participants calling the system extremely simple and very easy to use. Albeit, participants were mostly referring to use case 1 (Fig. 3) with their survey and interview responses, since it was perceived as the main and important system as it aided them in fulfilling the task. Considering [11] in addition to our findings, it is very likely, that most of the cognitive load arose from the additional tasks to evaluate the SAR system, resulting in even lower actual load for the tested technology.

*Additional Qualitative Insights* - The following paragraphs are collated insights gathered from *thinking-aloud protocol, post-trial interviews and observations* during the study or from the video recordings. Our representative participants did not put much emphasis on the policy-related projections (use case 2 and 3), since they did not perceive them as important, as they did not aid them with task completion. While participants did not state this directly, there was a clear focus on "getting the job done" and health and safety policies were secondary.

From our post-trial interviews, we could gather a lot of information surrounding the interaction, as well as the study setup in general. Participants, who interpreted the enabling and disabling of the SAR system as intentional, reported to like working with the projection. Participants, who did not interpret it as intentional, felt like they could not rely on the aid and therefore would not want to use it in a working environment.

In general, participants did not like not knowing how exactly to work with the technology or fulfill the task optimally, since they were used to having exact and clear instructions and schooling for new tasks and technology. Therefore, when asked for critique, most participants wanted to improve the study setup and not the technology per se. They gave feedback on how to improve their task completion above all else. The main technology critique was the scanner's little feedback when loading the next set of instructions for the workbench. The scanner was only added to better structure the study design, not as a necessary part of the technology.

Policy compliance and non-compliance was always explained by the participant's work routine. If participants mentioned the importance of always lifting correctly, they also did it during our study. If they only did it for heavy objects, they did not regard it as important as soon as they realized the parts in our study were very light. How they regarded the robot was also influenced heavily by their prior experience. One participant stated that the robot could not be dangerous since the safety regulations for a dangerous robot were not met in the setup and therefore deemed it harmless and ignored it. Others assumed that this robot also simply stopped when its safety perimeter was crossed. Some thought it imperative not to interrupt its processes and others aimed to maximize their own efficiency. The one common theme is that they regarded the robot exactly as they were used to from their work.

The most interesting finding from observing and talking to our participants was that they fully trusted the part placement information on the screen and never questioned it. It was therefore used as ground truth to verify the information from the projection making it clear that they trusted the information from the screen more.

## 6    Limitations

Regarding the *collaborative robot safety zone awareness* - based on our data - it can be stated that static, physical markings on the floor and the own danger recognition/intuition are clearly preferred compared to the tested SAR projections. However, testing less subtle projections with a dedicated introduction of the guidelines might narrow down how much physical markings are preferred. Making the projections less distinguishable from physical markings can also be of help in this regard. *Ergonomic notifications* via projection were ignored most of the time. Factors for this were 1) the little weight of the parts 2) the design of the notification 3) trusting the own judgement more than the system. Furthermore, *manual assembly assistance* based on projections was positively received and explicitly stated that it makes the workflow much easier as can also be backed up by our data.

Finally, a lab study setup as it was the case within this work might not be sufficient to thoroughly analyze the impact of subtle projections regarding work place policies. The more pervasive and embedded our technologies aim to become, the harder it is to isolate their impact in a highly controlled setting. Controlled settings are always artificial and pervasive and embedded technologies aim to fit seamlessly into their environment. Many of the issues found in this work arise from the artificial lab setup, even though it was already conducted in a factory lab. Our representative participants identifying it as an artificial, sub-optimal factory heavily influenced their behaviour, some even calling it a fun game. The stakes and aims normally present in a live setting could not be reproduced. Therefore, we need to better establish what can be learnt from lab settings and what needs to be tested in live production. We argue that a lab study of pervasive technology only serves as a base trial to identify obvious errors in the technology and to determine how to test its impact in a live environment. A lab study is not enough to yield conclusive findings on the impact of pervasive technology due to its embedded nature and interactions with uncontrollable factors.

## 7   Discussion and Conclusion

The expected increase in usability for task-related in-situ projections [17] was replicated in this study. This confirms that our participants behaved similarly to [17] when aided by a task-related in-situ projection. However, the same cannot be said about the policy-related projections. Even 150 runs in total were not enough to produce one collision with the robot. Therefore, statements about its effectiveness are hard to make. Compared to their experiences with danger communication from work, participants found it more, less or similarly effective at communicating the danger. The ergonomic notifications yielded no measurable benefit when deployed. Most of this is probably to be attributed to a lack of explanation and varying visibility in changing lighting conditions. Participants who noticed the ergonomic notifications (6/15) found them very subtle and did not comment much on their usefulness and it did not measurably change their behavior. With factory contexts varying widely, a one size fits all solution will probably not yield the health benefits estimated by [13,29]. Even our locally sampled representative target participants had widely differing experiences with health and safety policies in their everyday worklife and opinions regarding the importance of policy compliance vs. task focus. Therefore, it is to be expected that in-situ projections for policy compliance will need to be adapted to existing work routines or vice-versa before yielding major benefits. When given a task to complete while complying with policy for their own good, our participants prioritized the task. It stands to reason that even adequate and timely health information would again be ignored if workers did not deem it worth their effort. Maybe not remembering to lift ergonomically is only half of the story and always lifting correctly is simply tedious. Many of our results lead us to reflect on the impact of lab study settings with increasingly pervasive technology. The more pervasive the technology is, the less it will be perceived as a tool and the more it will blend into the environment. We observed this effect with our three tested projections. The manual assembly assistance was in the center of the field of view when completing the task. It provided duplicate information required for task completion which was also available on a screen nearby, albeit in a more convenient visualization. It was recognised (15/15) and used to much benefit. The cobot safety zone communication was also somewhat duplicate information, since participants were able to observe the repeating movement of the robot and construct their own safety zone. They were also directly confronted with the robot at times blocking their way to parts required for task completion. It was mostly recognised (12/15) but we cannot say much about how effectively it was used. The ergonomic notifications were the single source of information on ergonomically correct lifting. Additionally, participants were not directly confronted with the information when completing the task, since they needed to focus on the shape of the area and then on the color of parts, but were not informed of any color information inside the area. It was badly noticed (6/15) and not really used to any measurable benefit.

We interpret that our participants only used the projections which they could validate with other data. Without a ground truth providing task-relevant information it was hard for them to justify using the technology in their solving process. Providing duplicate information in pervasive/ubiquitous systems might therefore be necessary in the adoption process (as well as lab studies testing users' interactions), since it is otherwise hard for users to build trust. A potential way of mitigating these lab-study-related problems is to use live production data with guided adoption. However, implementing this is expensive and time consuming and might not lead to the desired results as the technology could still fail in a similar way as in a lab study. Based on our findings, we suggest not changing the technology but test the policy-related projections in a live setting. This is not because we think that the technology is at its best possible state. Since our current data does not allow us to give conclusive answers, future work would entail testing the technology in live production embedded into actual workflows. If differences in behavior or performance occur, changing the technology beforehand would only confuse if improvements were due to the realistic setting or due to the changes to the technology.

**Acknowledgements.** This work was supported by the European Union's Horizon 2020 research and innovation programme within the project TEAMING.AI (grant number 957402) as well as by the country of Upper Austria as part of the FTI strategy, project "ZerOP".

# References

1. Bezerra, C., et al.: Challenges for usability testing in ubiquitous systems. In: Proceedings of the 26th Conference on l'Interaction Homme-Machine, pp. 183–188. IHM 2014, Association for Computing Machinery, New York (2014). https://doi.org/10.1145/2670444.2670468

2. Bimber, O., Iwai, D., Wetzstein, G., Grundhöfer, A.: The visual computing of projector-camera systems. In: ACM SIGGRAPH 2008 Classes, pp. 84:1–84:25. SIGGRAPH 2008, ACM, New York (2008). https://doi.org/10.1145/1401132.1401239
3. Bimber, O., Raskar, R.: Spatial Augmented Reality: Merging Real and Virtual Worlds. A. K. Peters Ltd, USA (2005)
4. Borro, D., Suescun, A., Brazalez, A., Gonzalez, J.M., Ortega, E., Gonzalez, E.: Warm: wearable AR and tablet-based assistant systems for bus maintenance. Appl. Sci. **11**(4), 1–20 (2021). https://doi.org/10.3390/app11041443
5. Brizzi, F., Peppoloni, L., Graziano, A., Stefano, E.D., Avizzano, C.A., Ruffaldi, E.: Effects of augmented reality on the performance of teleoperated industrial assembly tasks in a robotic embodiment. IEEE Trans. Hum. Mach. Syst. **48**(2), 197–206 (2018). https://doi.org/10.1109/THMS.2017.2782490
6. Büttner, S., Prilla, M., Röcker, C.: Augmented reality training for industrial assembly work - are projection-based AR assistive systems an appropriate tool for assembly training? In: Proceedings of the 2020 CHI Conference on Human Factors in Computing Systems, pp. 1–12. CHI 2020, Association for Computing Machinery, New York (2020). https://doi.org/10.1145/3313831.3376720
7. Cao, Z., Hidalgo, G., Simon, T., Wei, S.E., Sheikh, Y.: OpenPose: realtime multi-person 2D pose estimation using part affinity fields. IEEE Trans. Pattern Anal. Mach. Intell. **43**(1), 172–186 (2021). https://doi.org/10.1109/TPAMI.2019.2929257
8. Carvalho, R.M., Andrade, RMd.C., de Oliveira, K.M.: Aquarium - a suite of software measures for HCI quality evaluation of ubiquitous mobile applications. J. Syst. Softw. **136**, 101–136 (2018). https://doi.org/10.1016/j.jss.2017.11.022
9. Choi, W., Park, S., Kim, D., Lim, Y.-k, Lee, U.: Multi-stage receptivity model for mobile just-in-time health intervention. Proc. ACM Interact. Mob. Wearable Ubiquitous Technol. **3**(2), 1–26 (2019). https://doi.org/10.1145/3328910
10. Duan, K., Bai, S., Xie, L., Qi, H., Huang, Q., Tian, Q.: CenterNet: Keypoint triplets for object detection. In: Proceedings of the IEEE/CVF International Conference on Computer Vision (ICCV), pp. 6569–6578. ICCV 2019, Seoul (2019)
11. Duran, R., Zavgorodniaia, A., Sorva, J.: Cognitive load theory in computing education research: a review. ACM Trans. Comput. Educ. **22**(4), 1–27 (2022). https://doi.org/10.1145/3483843
12. Ericsson, K.A., Simon, H.A.: Protocol Analysis: Verbal Reports as Data. The MIT Press, Cambridge, MA (1993)
13. Estrada-Lugo, H.D., et al.: Video analysis for ergonomics assessment in the manufacturing industry: initial feedback on a case study. In: Proceedings of the 32nd European Safety and Reliability Conference, TBP. ESREL 2022, ESRA, Dublin (2022)
14. Fite-Georgel, P.: Is there a reality in industrial augmented reality? In: 2011 10th IEEE International Symposium on Mixed and Augmented Reality, pp. 201–210. IEEE, Basel (2011). https://doi.org/10.1109/ISMAR.2011.6092387
15. Fraga-Lamas, P., Fernádez-Caramés, T.M., Blanco-Novoa, O., Vilar-Montesinos, M.: A review on industrial augmented reality systems for the industry 4.0 shipyard. IEEE Access **6**, 13358–13375 (2018). https://doi.org/10.1109/ACCESS.2018.2808326
16. Funk, M., Bächler, A., Bächler, L., Kosch, T., Heidenreich, T., Schmidt, A.: Working with augmented reality?: a long-term analysis of in-situ instructions at the assembly workplace. In: Proceedings of the 10th International Conference on Pervasive Technologies Related to Assistive Environments, pp. 222–229. Association for Computing Machinery, New York (2017)

17. Funk, M., Mayer, S., Schmidt, A.: Using in-situ projection to support cognitively impaired workers at the workplace. In: Proceedings of the 17th International ACM SIGACCESS Conference on Computers & Accessibility, pp. 185–192. ASSETS 2015, Association for Computing Machinery, New York (2015). https://doi.org/10.1145/2700648.2809853
18. González-Franco, M., et al.: Immersive mixed reality for manufacturing training. Front. Robot. AI **4**, 3 (2017)
19. Guinet, A.L., Bouyer, G., Otmane, S., Desailly, E.: Reliability of the head tracking measured by microsoft hololens during different walking conditions. Comput. Methods Biomech. Biomed. Eng. **22**(sup1), S169–S171 (2019). https://doi.org/10.1080/10255842.2020.1714228
20. Hart, S.G., Staveland, L.E.: Development of NASA-TLX (task load index): results of empirical and theoretical research. In: Hancock, P.A., Meshkati, N. (eds.) Human Mental Workload, Advances in Psychology, vol. 52, pp. 139–183. Amsterdam (1988). https://doi.org/10.1016/S0166-4115(08)62386-9, https://www.sciencedirect.com/science/article/pii/S0166411508623869
21. Heindl, C., Stübl, G., Pönitz, T., Pichler, A., Scharinger, J.: Visual large-scale industrial interaction processing. In: Adjunct Proceedings of the 2019 ACM International Joint Conference on Pervasive and Ubiquitous Computing and Proceedings of the 2019 ACM International Symposium on Wearable Computers, pp. 280–283. UbiComp/ISWC 2019 Adjunct, Association for Computing Machinery, New York (2019). https://doi.org/10.1145/3341162.3343769
22. Hitachi: Putting fun into maintaining physical distance by system to link walking people and spatial distance : Research & Development : Hitachi (2020), https://www.hitachi.com/rd/news/topics/2020/1130.html
23. Korn, O., Funk, M., Schmidt, A.: Assistive Systems for the Workplace: Towards Context-Aware Assistance, pp. 121–135. IGI Global, Hershey (2015). https://doi.org/10.4018/978-1-4666-7373-1.ch006
24. Korn, O., Schmidt, A., Hörz, T.: The potentials of in-situ-projection for augmented workplaces in production: a study with impaired persons. In: CHI 2013 Extended Abstracts on Human Factors in Computing Systems, pp. 979–984. CHI EA 2013, Association for Computing Machinery, New York (2013). https://doi.org/10.1145/2468356.2468531
25. Lewis, J., Sauro, J.: The factor structure of the system usability scale. In: Proceedings of the 1st International Conference on Human Centered Design: Held as Part of HCI International, vol. 5619, pp. 94–103. Springer, Berlin Heidelberg, Berlin (2009). https://doi.org/10.1007/978-3-642-02806-9_12
26. Lin, G., Haynes, M., Srinivas, S., Kotipalli, P., Starner, T.: Towards finding the optimum position in the visual field for a head worn display used for task guidance with non-registered graphics. Proc. ACM Interact. Mob. Wearable Ubiquitous Technol. **5**(1), 1–26 (2021). https://doi.org/10.1145/3448091
27. Lin, P.C., Chen, Y.J., Chen, W.S., Lee, Y.J.: Automatic real-time occupational posture evaluation and select corresponding ergonomic assessments. Sci. Rep. **12**(1), 2139 (2022). https://doi.org/10.1038/s41598-022-05812-9
28. Masoni, R., et al.: Supporting remote maintenance in industry 4.0 through augmented reality. Procedia Manufacturing **11**, 1296–1302 (2017). https://doi.org/10.1016/j.promfg.2017.07.257. https://www.sciencedirect.com/science/article/pii/S2351978917304651. In: 27th International Conference on Flexible Automation and Intelligent Manufacturing, FAIM2017, 27-30 June 2017, Modena, Italy
29. Niu, S.: Ergonomics and occupational safety and health: an ILO perspective. Appl. Ergon. **41**(6), 744–753 (2010)

30. Pönitz, T., Ebenhofer, G., Stübl, G., Heindl, C., Scharinger, J.: On the potential of large-scale extended reality interaction for industrial environments. In: UbiComp 2021: The 2021 ACM International Joint Conference on Pervasive and Ubiquitous Computing, pp. 61–63. Association for Computing Machinery, New York (2021). https://doi.org/10.1145/3460418.3479304

31. Xia, Q., Korpela, J., Namioka, Y., Maekawa, T.: robust unsupervised factory activity recognition with body-worn accelerometer using temporal structure of multiple sensor data motifs. Proc. ACM Interact. Mob. Wearable Ubiquitous Technol. **4**(3), 1–30 (2020). https://doi.org/10.1145/3411836

32. Qingxin, X., Wada, A., Korpela, J., Maekawa, T., Namioka, Y.: Unsupervised factory activity recognition with wearable sensors using process instruction information. Proc. ACM Interact. Mob. Wearable Ubiquitous Technol. **3**(2), 1–23 (2019). https://doi.org/10.1145/3328931

33. QueueSight: Social Distancing Tool (2020). https://www.queuesight.com

34. Rocha, L.C., Andrade, R.M.C., Sampaio, A.L., Lelli, V.: Heuristics to evaluate the usability of ubiquitous systems. In: Distributed, Ambient and Pervasive Interactions: 5th International Conference, DAPI 2017, Held as Part of HCI International 2017, Vancouver, BC, Canada, July 9–14, 2017, Proceedings, pp. 120–141. Springer-Verlag, Berlin (2017). https://doi.org/10.1007/978-3-319-58697-7_9

35. de Souza Filho, J.C., Brito, M.R.F., Sampaio, A.L.: Comparing heuristic evaluation and MALTU model in interaction evaluation of ubiquitous systems. In: Proceedings of the 19th Brazilian Symposium on Human Factors in Computing Systems. IHC 2020, Association for Computing Machinery, New York (2020). https://doi.org/10.1145/3424953.3426639

36. Tomitsch, M., et al.: Design. think. make. break. repeat. A Handbook of Methods. Bis Publishers, The Netherlands (2018)

37. Uva, A.E., Gattullo, M., Manghisi, V.M., Spagnulo, D., Cascella, G.L., Fiorentino, M.: Evaluating the effectiveness of spatial augmented reality in smart manufacturing: a solution for manual working stations. Int. J. Adv. Manuf. Technol. **94**(1), 509–521 (2017). https://doi.org/10.1007/s00170-017-0846-4

38. Wang, C.Y., Bochkovskiy, A., Liao, H.Y.M.: YOLOv7: trainable bag-of-freebies sets new state-of-the-art for real-time object detectors (2022). https://doi.org/10.48550/ARXIV.2207.02696

39. Weiss, A., Wortmeier, A.-K., Kubicek, B.: Cobots in industry 4.0: a roadmap for future practice studies on human–robot collaboration. IEEE Trans. Hum. Mach. Syst. **51**(4), 335–345 (2021). https://doi.org/10.1109/THMS.2021.3092684

40. Zhou, J., Lee, I., Thomas, B., Menassa, R., Farrant, A., Sansome, A.: Applying spatial augmented reality to facilitate in-situ support for automotive spot welding inspection. In: Proceedings of the 10th International Conference on Virtual Reality Continuum and Its Applications in Industry, pp. 195–200. VRCAI 2011, Association for Computing Machinery, New York (2011). https://doi.org/10.1145/2087756.2087784

# Multisensory Interaction and VR Experiences

# Augmenting Indigenous Sámi Exhibition - Interactive Digital Heritage in Museum Context

Siiri Paananen[1]([✉]) [iD], Joo Chan Kim[2] [iD], Emma Kirjavainen[1] [iD],
Matilda Kalving[1] [iD], Karan Mitra[2] [iD], and Jonna Häkkilä[1] [iD]

[1] University of Lapland, Rovaniemi 96300, Finland
{siiri.paananen,emma.kirjavainen,matilda.kalving,
jonna.hakkila}@ulapland.fi
[2] Luleå University of Technology, Skellefteå 93177, Sweden
{joo.chan.kim,karan.mitra}@ltu.se

**Abstract.** Museums and cultural heritage institutions have an important role in presenting accurate information and sharing cultural knowledge, and new technologies are increasingly implemented. For the best results, the appropriateness of a specific technology must be evaluated for each context. Research has shown the need for participatory methods and local knowledge in Indigenous design contexts. We describe a case study where an Indigenous Sámi museum exhibition was augmented with interactive technology through multidisciplinary co-design work with museum experts, designers, and developers. The traditional clothing of the Sámi people was digitized by filming, and information related to it was presented as a touchscreen installation in a renewed exhibition. User tests including interactive tasks and interviews (n = 7) and a questionnaire (n = 27) were completed on-site. The installation was rated interesting and easy to use, while some users struggled to find all the features. Our study shows that a technically relatively simple digital installation can be easy-to-use but interesting for a standard museum visitor. Additionally, the work demonstrates how to build successful collaborations that highlight Indigenous cultural heritage. We discuss the implications of using technology to promote cultural heritage and identities.

**Keywords:** Interactive systems · User studies · Digital cultural heritage · Museum exhibitions · Indigenous HCI

## 1 Introduction

Museums have an essential role when societies' histories and identities are considered. They provide information about the past but also reflect what are con-

The work has been supported by Interreg Nord project 'Muittut, muitalusat - the story of the Sámi by the Sámi' and 'Innovation in Lapland through Design and Art' project, funded by the European Regional Development Fund (ERDF). We wish to thank Ájtte, the Swedish Mountain and Sámi Museum. Special thanks to Sunna Kuoljok and Ann-Catrin Blind.

J. Abdelnour Nocera et al. (Eds.): INTERACT 2023, LNCS 14143, pp. 597–617, 2023.
https://doi.org/10.1007/978-3-031-42283-6_32

sidered the building blocks of society, community, or nation and their culture. The role has both external and internal functions [21], as the museum exhibitions project an image of the community to the outsiders visiting the place, but are also part of the community's identity building. Thus, how museum exhibitions reflect the identity and culture of a group or an entity is essential. Museums are limited by their size and resources. Hence a variety of solutions can be considered, depending on the case. Technologies can assist museums in creating engaging and educational interactive content [35], e.g. with multi-sensory applications. The designers and developers of the technologies in a cultural context have to pay special attention to make the process fair and beneficial to the museum.

This paper describes a case study of developing a digital touchscreen program for an Indigenous Sámi museum, presenting traditional clothes. The motivation was to showcase Sámi cultural heritage using digital tools and to provide equal opportunities for sharing their histories and stories in an interactive and accessible way in the museum. The study acts as an example of a practical case study, where a part of the material heritage of Indigenous Sámi culture was applied as a digital museum exhibit. The program was co-designed iteratively with the museum and two universities working together, and aimed to showcase the clothes and their history and meaning by renewing an existing exhibition. The Sámi perspective of the museum experts was there to guide the design process from the first concepts to the final product. While there have been technologies applied to Sámi museums, not much has been published from the point of view of HCI researchers based on our research. Sámi museums face a challenge in representing the culture and the aspects of modernity/traditionality [48].

In this study, our target was to evaluate how a new program and the renewed exhibition were received by museum visitors. We were also interested in how the participants perceived combining the new technology and cultural heritage and how the participants felt about the image of the culture projected by the exhibition. In this paper, we also describe the issues that were part of the development process and how those were solved, thus sharing the lessons learned. Our work allows the HCI community to get insight into the design context of Indigenous museums and consider taking into account different cultural settings and applying technologies in the wild in a culturally sensitive design context. Our work contributes to providing different cultures with a better chance of equal opportunities and allows technology to cater for fruitful cross-cultural exchanges.

The paper is structured as follows; first, related work to HCI development and evaluation in Indigenous and museum contexts is presented, after which the design process and method are described. Then the results are presented, followed by a discussion, including lessons learned and notes on how the program was improved, then finally going through the study's limitations and conclusions.

## 2   Related Work

Our work takes place in the cross-section of design and development as well as Indigenous cultural and museum contexts. Historical events and political currents affect people's views and feelings on cultural heritage and museums. When designing technologies for Indigenous communities and museums, the design context, ethics, and cultural sensitivities need to be considered [11]. One perspective which can be applied is decolonizing design, see e.g. Tlostanova [45]. Parsons et al. [36] have studied the collaborative aspects of Indigenous and academic work, and suggested a pluralistic way of looking at Indigenous and Western worldviews. Lazem et al. [26] write, "Indigenous knowledge is an important resource, and we should utilise the tools and methods that we have at our disposal to enhance it." When highlighting the need for ethical processes, Lazem et al. also call for researchers to apply flexibility, respect, and sensitivity towards the local culture. A literature review we previously conducted on working with technology and cultural heritage through decolonizing design highlights the need for participatory methods and working with local values and cultural contexts [34].

## 2.1   Indigenous Context and HCI

The Indigenous Sámi collections were transferred from the Museum of Ethnography to *Ájtte, the Swedish Mountain and Sámi Museum* in Jokkmokk, when it was opened in 1989 as the only Sámi museum in Sweden. Museums and their work are an important part of identity building; as Silvén [43] writes, "During more than hundred years Sámi representation in heritage and museums has contributed to defining Sámi identity and the position of Sámi in society". Silvén has also later described that while it is positive that Sámi people are recognized and made more visible, e.g. in museums, new interpretations should also be made so that the image of Sámi is not locked only into the history [44]. In 2008 Harlin [12] suggested that for Sámi Cultural Heritage, collecting information on the existing objects and their location can be a step in the process of repatriation, which means returning cultural heritage back to the community. Lately, there have been efforts to gather information about the collections of Sámi Heritage around Europe and bring them under one search portal service for better accessibility [10]. This has been made possible by the digitalization of archives and new digital tools, allowing users to see old pictures of traditional objects and clothes. Traditions and their presentation have been researched e.g. by Cocq [7], who focuses on the Sámi in Sweden. They write about traditionalization and its relationship to revitalization, exploring how traditions are presented online by different institutions and their effect on people's identities [7]. Aikio [1] has looked at photographs in the old exhibition of Sámi Museum Siida and analyzed how *Sáminess* was presented there, noting that the old exhibition did not include enough of contemporary Sámi life, but shows it as something in the past. The museum renewed its exhibitions in 2022 and involved Sámi communities in the process [1].

Indigenous HCI as a concept has been around for a while, [18] but appears to be somewhat still lacking in the broader HCI community discussion. A workshop organized by Lawrence et al. [25] was aimed at anyone involved or interested in the context, and included a definition; "Indigenous HCI involves work across all aspects of the computing ecosystem including education, research, design, development and implementation." Different approaches can be applied when working with Indigenous communities and HCI topics. For instance, cultural adaptation in user interface (UI) design has been demonstrated and applied by integrating local objects and components into the GUI metaphor design [14,52]. Co-design and Indigenous-led processes have been suggested. Magnani et al. [30] have presented a community-based method of making digital 3D models of Sámi cultural heritage objects. An approach to HCI design projects with Indigenous people leading them has been described by Peters et al. [38], who do not think mere participation is enough. Their approach includes user-leadership in the co-design process led by Indigenous university students. One suggested way of exploring and promoting Sámi identities and intangible cultural heritage by the community has been game development, e.g. through the event Sámi Game Jam by Laiti et al. [24]. Their approach involves Sámi people participating in game-making and telling stories through interactive digital media: video games. Heimgärtner [13] has suggested a model for cultural influence on HCI, including the local and Indigenous contexts. Different cultures have varying perspectives on concepts such as time, communication, and space, which should be considered in the design and development process. Through co-creation methods, Indigenous knowledge can be conveyed into digital technologies [49]. Zaman and Falak [53], who have sought to create an Indigenous HCI paradigm, emphasize the need for designers to engage with the local community. While technology can be adapted to different contexts, in some cases, applying digital technologies has been entirely discarded in the design process due to them not fitting the goal of the projects or the local community goals, as noted by Kelly and Taffe [22] in their case study with Indigenous community museum. Their involvement with co-design work led to the understanding that the digital solutions would not be optimal in the presented scenario, but it is noted that they should be evaluated case-by-case. Thus, technology should not be leading the design process.

## 2.2   Designing and Evaluating Digital Heritage Applications

A plethora of studies exists that have addressed the different aspects of designing interactive technologies for museums and exhibitions and evaluating their usability and UX. The area has been of interest to many researchers, and designing for cultural heritage fosters an active research community in HCI [2,6]. Much of the prior art has presented examples and case studies of integrating digital content and interactive technologies into museums and reported the advantages of interactive exhibitions. For instance, Hornecker and Stifter [17] have addressed interaction design in museum exhibitions. They note how the interactive installations with tangible physical elements interested all kinds of users. Our earlier study on museum experiences confirmed the need for interactivity and noted the importance of considering ethical issues [33]. Konstantakis and Caridakis [23] suggest that cultural heritage institutions should consider the User Experience before, during, and after the visit for better satisfaction and impact on visitors. They conducted a survey to represent different aspects related to Cultural User Experience by looking at 37 applications in the field. They also note the importance of the user's expectations, which will affect their actual perception of the experience.

In our research, we especially focus on presenting digital 3D content as part of the museum exhibition. A case study by Micoli et al. [31] shares the design process of an interactive touchscreen application with 3D content and hotspots, explaining the different content levels and relations between the selected objects and the different levels of the program. The content for their app is a complex museum collection, and they suggest giving the visitors connections between the physical exhibition and digital information. When comparing the visitor's experience between attending physical and virtual exhibits, Wolf et al. [50] report the pros and cons. Whereas VR was appreciated for allowing access from anywhere, anytime, the VR experience was criticized by participants for losing the authentic atmosphere.

The prior art has also addressed the methodological approaches to studying museum experiences. Hornecker and Nicol [16] have performed a comparison of user studies both in a lab setting and in the wild with the same museum game application on touchscreens. They note how the context of the study matters and details such as the installation setup or group behaviours and interactions. Konstantakis and Caridakis [23] also note how instead of only lab studies, field studies are needed to understand the audience. Karoulis et al. [20] conducted a survey and a walkthrough session to evaluate a system with experts. They suggest that domain experts (e.g. museum curators) and usability experts should be utilized when conducting expert usability evaluations for museum applications for best results. Barbieri et al. [3] have proposed a user study methodology for virtual museums, in their case, comparing two design alternatives for interactive 3D content presented on a screen. Their methodology included metric tasks, a questionnaire as well as an interview. Using multiple methods allows for understanding the results more deeply.

# 3   Design Context and Process

In this section, we share the background of the design context, as well as the design processes.

**Sámi culture.** The Indigenous Sámi people live in Sápmi, in the Northern parts of Norway, Sweden, Finland, and Russia, with many subgroups and languages (e.g. Valkonen et al., [46]). The research and design process presented in the following focuses on the theme of the Sámi dress, Gapta (Gákti in Northern Sámi). The dress is traditional Indigenous clothing but continues evolving with the culture, like Magga [29, p.50] writes, 'A living gákti tradition implies a living Sámi culture. And vice versa.' Thus, the Gapta is a central part of the living Sámi culture and identity building and in a key role when a museum exhibition is considered. The exhibition included nine showcases, each with 2-3 Gaptas from different regions of Sápmi. This also meant that the designed program was presented on nine different screens next to the showcases. The aim of the exhibition was both to show the old dresses, as well as modern skills in dressmaking and evolving traditions, showing that the culture is still living (Fig. 1). During the development process, three seminars were organized for understanding the Sámi culture for the outsiders of the Sámi community.

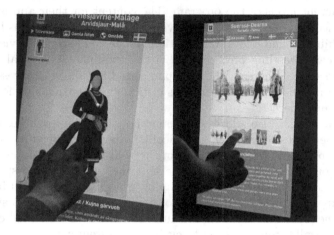

**Fig. 1.** Testing the program's UI in the lab (left) and at the museum (right).

**The Development Process.** We organized three teams, each with different roles in the program development (Fig. 2). First, the programming team developed the technical part of the program with Unity 2022. Second, the design team worked on the graphics and UI, including the program's UI layout, icon design, typography, usability, and user flow. Third, the museum experts evaluated whether the program fulfilled the requirements for their exhibition, provided the content for the program, and finally acted as quality assurance testers, identified any errors to fix, and confirmed the program's quality. Initially, various technologies were proposed (e.g., holography, augmented reality, and virtual reality); however, the ideas using them were discarded due to a disaccord between the technologies, the context of the exhibition, and the selected topic. Collaborating with Sámi culture experts was educational and it helped the designers to understand cultural factors that needed to be considered in addition to usability and technology, for a successful outcome. Special care had to be put into ethical perspectives, in order to support the Sámi experts' visions and highlight their culture in an inclusive way. Trust and good communication were essential parts of the collaboration in order to learn and understand the cultural meanings and their significance. A similar iterative five-step framework for developing a game in a museum context has been described by Gestwicki and McNely [9], and the authors highlight that regular meetings with the project team encourage empathy.

During the development, each team co-operated to improve the program's quality iteratively. For example, after the initial concept was decided, the programming team worked with the design team to concretize the program layout and user flow. Meanwhile, the design team communicated with the quality assurance team to clarify the design requirements. The quality assurance team then talked with the programming team to confirm whether a desired feature for the program was feasible within resources. A weekly meeting was held with all three groups to synchronize the development process, share updates on each team's status, and identify more improvements for our program. The work was conducted online because of the COVID-pandemic and long distances, but the team members were able to meet during the final user testing and data gathering.

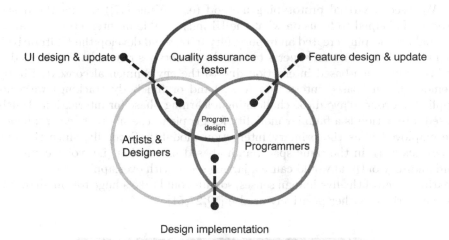

**Fig. 2.** Roles for each team in the program development.

The dresses are quite detailed and have a lot of different textures and patterns. Instead of using 3D models, which require professional skills (e.g., modelling and texturing) to create with a certain level of quality for the exhibition, the dresses were filmed as 360-degree videos. The resulting video was then implemented in Unity to appear as a 360-object, which can be observed from all sides by rotating with the user's touch gesture. Considering the environmental context and readability of Gapta content, we used nine Windows PCs with 17-inch touch screens with $1920 \times 1080$ resolution to run our program for the Gapta exhibition. The hardware was hidden behind the walls and showcases to avoid hindrance to user engagement for the exhibition.

**User Experience and User Interface.** In the UI design process, much attention was paid to the wishes of the museum experts, as they know the content best. The UI was designed to suit the museum's style regarding fonts and colours. The exhibition room was renovated, therefore, the new program's visual look was considered to fit the space and aesthetic. In addition to the visual look, issues related to usability had to be considered, such as how readable texts and pictures are. Special attention was paid to ensuring that the program was inclusive and usable from visual and cognitive standpoints and physical aspects, such as the user's height. The prototype was tested on a simulated colourblindness site and several font sizes to consider different users. The design focused on assisting people in navigating the program by using icons and animations, for example, on the hotspots, encouraging users to notice them. Special care was put into the graphic design of the map, which shows the area where the clothes are tradition-ally used. As Sápmi hasn't traditionally regarded country borders, the designed map only featured a dotted line as the borders between Finland, Sweden, and Norway.

We used a virtual prototyping method (e.g. Wang [47]) during the design process. It helped to focus on what the UI must enable in interaction scenarios. Virtual prototyping created an opportunity to test and develop the UI iteratively and allowed the museum experts to test the prototypes remotely. We decided to utilize only touch-based interaction due to the environmental context. Firstly, Remote gesture-based interaction (e.g., hand or full body tracking) were not applied in order to avoid too challenging a learning phase for interaction. Touch-based interaction is a familiar modality for people in the smartphone era; hence, we employed it as the primary interaction modality. Secondly, since the nine programs work in the same space, audio-based interaction (i.e. voice command and auditory output) would cause a jarring scene with overlapping sounds. Since hearing is one of the five human senses, sounds could take a huge role in an overall user experience either positively or else [19,27,51].

**Fig. 3.** Visitor using the touchscreen in the museum exhibition, with the physical Gaptas in a showcase.

## 4   Method

Here, the methodologies applied to the conducted user studies are described. We conducted two types of user evaluation to gain a better understanding of how the visitors received the renewed exhibition and program. The first was a questionnaire comprising general questions about the museum exhibition and the short version of the User Experience Questionnaire (UEQ) [42]. Another evaluation was individual interviews and complimentary surveys (SUS) [5] with exhibition visitors. The two evaluations had a different set of participants from each other.

**Questionnaire.** We prepared a three-page questionnaire, including a consent form to ask for participants' agreement for data collection. The questionnaire was left for two weeks near the Gapta exhibition (Fig. 3) with an advertisement for the museum visitors to fill it in. The participants were asked to return their answered questionnaire to the museum reception before they left. The questionnaire had 27 participants, ages 16 to 79, with a a mean of 41,8. Most of the participants identified as female (78%), 19% as male, and one participant as "other". Six participants had never visited the museum exhibition before, while 13 participants had only visited the old exhibition, one only the renewed exhibition, and seven participants had visited the old and the new one. 19 people reported that they were from Sweden and the rest from Europe and Africa.

The first part of the questionnaire included background questions and general questions related to the exhibition and its subjective usability. The next page featured UEQ, and to reduce the answering time for the museum visitors, we used the short version of UEQ, which only has 8 out of the 26 items from the original version. Four items ("obstructive/supportive," "complicated/easy," "inefficient/efficient," and "confusing/clear") in the short version UEQ represent a pragmatic quality related to perceived usability. The other four items ("boring/exciting," "not interesting/interesting," "conventional/inventive," and "usual/leading edge") represent a hedonic quality of user experience. Participants rated their impression of the program on a 7-step scale from $-3$ to $3$. Selecting a negative value meant the participant thought the negative term fit the experience. In contrast, a positive value referred a positive term. When the participant felt none of the terms fit, they were asked to select zero as neutral. The questionnaire also included additional questions to identify helpful design elements for using the program. In addition, we asked whether the museum visitors would have wanted to use a different interaction modality for input (e.g., a voice command, or body gesture) and output (e.g., music or speech).

We utilized the analysis tool provided by UEQ developers [15]. With this tool, we could get the means of each item, quality, and overall evaluation. The results were also benchmarked based on the data from 21,175 persons from 468 studies to check how well the program performed [15]. The additional answers were then coded [41] to find which elements were helpful for using the program and what is the museum visitors' opinion regarding the interaction modality of the program.

**Fig. 4.** The interview data was organized by affinity mapping

**Interview and Observation.** For deeper qualitative insights we conducted one-on-one interview-based usability tests with seven participants. The participants were recruited from museum visitors by both the researchers and the museum staff. The interviews were conducted in a private room at the museum, where the participants were presented with a screen that resembled the one used in the exhibition. All the participants (n=7) were female, with six Swedish and one Finnish participant. One of the participants reported their age to be between 26-35, one participant was 36-45, another 56-65, and the rest, four participants were 66+ years old. When it comes to the demographics, it is worth noting that 215 people visited the museum during the two days of user testing, of which 190 were locals. The local town's population of around 4,800 is mainly seniors over 65 years old. One of the participants had never visited the museum before, while four had already visited the old exhibition and two the new one. One usability test session lasted approximately 20 min, and the participants were compensated for their time with a small gift from the museum shop.

The in-depth user study process consisted of the following stages:

– 1) Initial briefing about the study and filling out the consent form,
– 2) performing three tasks and participating in a semi-structured interview,
– 3) filling out the end questionnaire and System Usability Scale (SUS)

Informed consent was explained by the researcher and signed by the participant before the study was conducted. The participant was tasked with finding the manufacturer of the clothing, a map, and a close-up photo of the lower part of the jacket or shoes. Their interactions with the touchscreen were recorded and counted. Immediately after the participants finished the tasks, we conducted a semi-structured interview about their experience, the touchscreens' perceived usability, and functions. The interview was audio-recorded and transcribed. It was followed by a short questionnaire, where the participant filled out their background information and answered three open-ended questions. Finally, the participant filled out the System Usability Scale (SUS), which is used to measure subjective usability. It consists of a ten-item questionnaire with a 5-point Likert scale, from strongly agree to strongly disagree. The SUS score was counted, and the interviews were analysed by affinity mapping [28,32] the answers and observations (Fig. 4). The users' performance was calculated by the number of interactions with the touchscreen. The SUS score and performance results were validated by comparing them to their individual performance.

# 5   Results

Here, the results of the two data sets are shared, first the general questionnaire and then the user testing session, including an interview, observation, and survey.

## 5.1   Questionnaire

While there were 27 participants total, one participant stopped answering the questionnaire after the background questions and one general question and wrote that the screens did not work. The questionnaire respondents were presented with three 5-Step Likert-scale questions related to the exhibit;

- The Gapta exhibit was interesting (n = 27). mean = 4,74
- The Gapta exhibit was easy to use (n = 26). mean = 4,73
- I feel like the Gapta exhibit is part of my culture (n = 23). mean = 4,05

A few participants pointed out in the third question that they were not Sámi, thus unable to respond.

When asked about their feelings on combining technology with old museum objects, 23 participants responded positively, such as: *"Good. The technology provides opportunities for extensive information on a small and discreet surface"* (Participant 8) and *"Super! Easy to navigate and immerse themselves in what you think is interesting"* (P18). Three felt neutral or had mixed opinions, saying *"It's good as long as it works"* (P23) and *"I would say it wouldn't hurt to combine technology with the museum object as long as it doesn't override"* (P4). When asked for their first impressions of the exhibition, the participants expressed things related to visuals, such as colours, lights, information, culture, dresses, and atmosphere. When asked for other comments on the topic, participants reported various things, such as general notes on the exhibits, opening hours, or missing information. A few participants expressed pride related to the culture being showcased well; *"I like to see our culture highlighted in such a good way"* (P16), *"Feeling proud of this cultural, historical heritage"* (P7). One participant reported that the touch function was hard to use (P22), and another pointed out related to the dolls and their gender and that it was nice to see the children, not only with women (P20). One person commented that they missed the old texts from the previous exhibition, *"..they showed the important things we do not always talk about in Sápmi"* (P17).

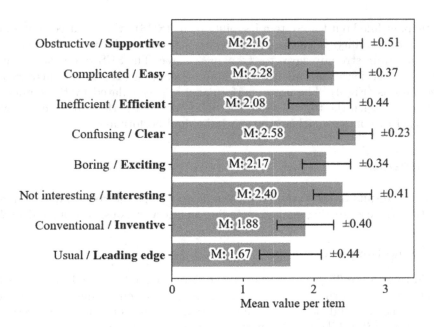

**Fig. 5.** The mean values of each item in the user experience questionnaire (UEQ).

Regarding the UEQ data, two participants (P11 and P25) were removed from the analysis due to missing answers. One participant (P25) skipped answering the additional questions about interaction modality. In total, 25 participants' questionnaire responses were used for the UEQ data analysis, and 26 participants' responses to the questions about interaction modality were examined. We got a mean of over 1.67 for all items from a scale of −3 to 3. The item "confusing/clear" received the highest mean of 2.58, followed by "not interesting/interesting" with a mean of 2.40. On the other hand, the item "usual/leading edge" was rated with the lowest mean of 1.67. The second lowest item was "conventional/inventive" with a mean of 1.88. Figure 5 depicts the means and 95% confidence interval of each item. Since all the items received positive results, they are highlighted with bold text. The pragmatic quality received 2.27, while the hedonic quality achieved 2.03 on a scale of -3 to 3. Consequently, our program was evaluated positively for both pragmatic and hedonic aspects, with a mean of 2.15 for the overall quality. The benchmark result (Fig. 6) suggested that our program is rated positively for all qualities compared to other programs. The results of every item reached an "Excellent" grade, the highest grade in the benchmark.

For helpful elements chosen by the visitors, icons were found to be the most helpful for navigating the program by 23 participants, colour differences by seven participants and familiar designs by "six" participants. Altogether 25 participants answered yes when asked if they liked controlling the screen with touch, and two (P22 and P25) did not respond. Some of the explanations for enjoying

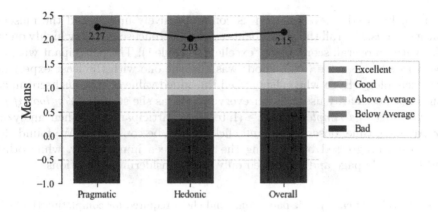

**Fig. 6.** The benchmark result, based on 21,175 persons' answers from 468 studies.

it included it being easy (P4, P1, P11, and P12), being able to choose what to read or see (P15, P21, P23, and P27), *"To be able to see the 3D model"*, probably meaning the rotatable dress (P20), feeling activated (P24), and participating (P14). The participants were asked whether they would like to use another way to avoid touching the screen, and eight agreed. Four selected hand gestures as an alternative way, two chose body gestures, and one selected "other" and wanted to use a pointer. 21 participants answered "yes" when asked if the texts were easy to read; three gave a mixed answer, one said no, and another did not respond. Regards to the text, the responses indicated that it was clear (P5, P12, P18, and P23), the font size was right (P4, P13, and P22), it had good resolution (P4) but was too long (P2 and P22), spacing was dense (P24) and scrolling to read the text was a negative experience (P1 and P27). 14 participants wished that the pilot would contain audio. Five people wrote they wanted to hear music (P2, P3, P4, P15, and P23), two wished for joik, which is traditional Sámi singing (P5 and P12), speech was requested by three participants (P11 and P14), and also the need for the texts to be read aloud was expressed by two participants (P17 and P18), a narration was wished by two; one who also liked to have music (P4) and another participant wanted an artisan to explain about their process (P9). The last participant, who answered that there was no need for audio, noted that headphones would be needed if there were any sounds (P8).

## 5.2   Interview, Observation and Survey

As part of the interview analysis, the qualitative information was categorized and sorted using an affinity diagram, called affinity mapping. We noted that the participants' previous technical knowledge affected their use of the touchscreen, as two participants had previous work experience that supported learning new functions and searching for information. In contrast, one participant had no technical knowledge and required guidance to use the screen. The participant could not finish the procedure without help from the facilitator. The different technical knowledge levels helped us comprehensively understand the museum visitors' needs. Overall the participants scored the touchscreen very highly on the SUS, with an overall score of 85, "excellent" (Table 1). The participant with the lowest rated SUS score (62.5, good) was also the one with the least experience with technology. Even when she noticed the added value of the touchscreen, she would not necessarily use it in her everyday life, as she stated, *"You look if you are interested, as simple as that."* (Interview Participant 2). When analyzing performance, time, observation, and clicks had to be considered. We found that some users progressed by touching the touchscreen immediately, while others read the whole page and interacted only after considering the options.

**Table 1.** Table of each participant's time and clicks required for completing the tasks, with the SUS score to compare.

| Participant | | Manu-factorer | | Map | | Lower part of the jacket or shoes | | SUS |
|---|---|---|---|---|---|---|---|---|
| nr | age | clicks | sec | clicks | sec | clicks | sec | score |
| IP1 | 26-35 | 10 | 58 | 1 | 12 | 26 | 40 | 87.5 |
| IP2 | 66+ | 8 | 158 | 1 | 16 | 4 | 50 | 62.5 |
| IP3 | 36-45 | 1 | 7 | 1 | 3 | 10 | 26 | 90 |
| IP4 | 56-65 | 2 | 9 | 1 | 1 | 27 | 92 | 85 |
| IP5 | 66+ | 1 | 7 | 1 | 6 | 7 | 145 | 92.5 |
| IP6 | 66+ | 1 | 3 | 2 | 6 | 4 | 83 | 85 |
| IP7 | 66+ | 1 | 5 | 1 | 4 | 3 | 48 | 95 |
| | Mean: | **3.43** | **35.29** | **1.14** | **6.86** | **11.57** | **69.14** | **85.36** |

With the help of the survey results and affinity mapping, we were able to evaluate the perceived usability and learnability of the touchscreens. Two things stood out very clearly in the results. Firstly, recognizable functions improve the participant's immersion and comprehension of the interface and secondly, unrecognizable icons lead to the participants not finding and using functions that would have made the use easier or opened up new sections in the program, e.g. stating after task 3 (find the lower part of the jacket or shoes), *"it is clear that it[the experience] will be completely different if knowing it[the function]"* (IP7). The problem was mostly remarked on the sliding gesture and hotspots. As a result of the participants not understanding the rotating mechanism, they could not comprehend and use hotspots, which led to them never discovering the close-up photos on their own. During the analysis, we noted and categorized the visual aspects that stood out in the data. Three participants mentioned that the interface was either calm, discreet, or non-intrusive, and most participants mentioned the size or amount of pictures as a positive influence on their experience. The neutral, photo-centric interface was believed to present the images more clearly, as one participant stated, *"The picture was the one that caught my eye. It's probably because of the layout"* (IP1). While the participants appreciated the amount of data included in the application, it also exhausted them.

As for innovations and suggestions for improvements, the participants expressed a need for more languages, such as Sámi languages. At the time of testing, there was only Swedish and English present. Participants deemed English necessary, but adding more languages could add to the accessibility and inclusivity. Some participants had knowledge of the local culture and identity, e.g. one participant recognized a familiar name on the list of manufacturers and was visibly delighted. One of the participants pointed out that the height of the screens should always be set to the standard and be adjustable for better visibility, e.g. stating " ..I would like to be able to adjust the height where the screen is placed. The screen's viewing angles are such that when the screen is not at eye level, the colours start fading at the edge" (IP1).

# 6  Discussion

The design process and the results of user experience evaluation in situ using multiple methods have been presented. Next, we reflect on our findings and design considerations and discuss the limitations. Both UEQ and SUS data showed "excellent" results, suggesting that the program's user experience and perceived usability worked well in the wild. Some features were not easily found by the participants in the interview and user evaluation. The positive aspects reported by the participants were the visual aspects and the amount and size of photos, and the familiar icons and interaction method were seen as helpful. The results also indicate that people could connect to the culture (e.g. feeling proud) when looking at it on display. When designing interactive screens in a museum environment, one should take accessibility, understandability, and learnability into consideration, in addition to the cultural aspects. In the co-design process, listening to the substance experts was found critical when choosing the direction to proceed with development.

## 6.1  Indigenous Museum as a Design Context

Indigenous museums are a particular design context, requiring special care and methods. The research presented in this paper was part of a larger work effort focusing on developing a shared *Sámi Museum Language*, to be used in the future for all the Sámi museums working on the topic, featuring museum partners from Finland, Sweden, and Norway. The process involved creating shared icons for the museums and imagining and prototyping different ways of presenting cultural heritage content in museums with digital technologies. Perhaps through co-design methods, interactive technologies can provide a contemporary interpretation of the Sámi culture, which Silvén [44] calls for in order to create new meanings for traditions. To enable safe and fruitful collaboration, much thought had to be put into the design work from ethical and cultural viewpoints [11]. This case example operates as a starting point for the work, but further work needs to be done, as there are multiple museums with varying needs, resources and cultural areas. As noted in the literature [23], both usability and content experts are needed to evaluate an interface; therefore, multidisciplinary development should be encouraged.

Some of our results indicated the feeling of cultural identity and the participants being proud of seeing their culture shown positively. Thus, museums can have a remarkable role when building a picture of peoples, cultures, and areas, both for the community and outsiders. As emphasized by Harlin [12], for the Sámi people, material culture, including objects such as clothes, is important and a way to express things like ethnicity and where one is from. So they can be an important way of expressing identity, which can also be showcased through digital storytelling and enhancing traditional physical exhibits with technology. The literature suggested that sometimes digital technologies can be left out entirely [22] if a suitable way of including them is not found.

## 6.2    Familiarity Supporting the User

We found that the overall user experience in terms of pragmatic and hedonic aspects is positive for the program. Two items in the pragmatic quality, "confusing/clear" and "complicated/easy," received the highest positive values (i.e., 2.58 for "clear" and 2.28 for "easy"), and we identified potential factors that affect the user experience from additional questions. The icon was selected by 88% of participants (23 out of 26 participants), which could imply that the icon significantly influenced the positive results. A few participants chose the colour differences for UI components and familiar UI layout designs. Since familiar design elements (e.g., UI layout and icon design) are helpful in building an intuitive interface [4,39], the icon design and UI layout are designed to present a friendly image that the participants might have experienced before. The questionnaire results implied that the UI designed with familiar images might help participants get used to the program through an easy experience. The participants preferred to interact with their fingers due to the intuitiveness and familiarity of touch interaction. Although some participants sought an alternative interaction modality instead of touching a screen due to the concern of hygiene after the COVID-19 pandemic, more than half of the participants (17 out of 26) preferred to use touch interaction. Hand or body gesture-based interactions require knowing specific motions to give a command properly.

## 6.3    Typography for Multi-line Text

We identified that font size and text alignment are impactful elements for reading in a dim exhibition space. As bigger font size and larger line spacing could improve the readability [40], tests were performed on readability starting with size 20 font, 1 line spacing, and various design elements in typography, including font size, colours, and line and letter spacing. A virtual prototype was used to test different sizes and types to find a font size that is readable even if the user wears glasses or their eyesight is not good.

The screens are installed at a height of about 100 cm to enable interaction for people of different heights, therefore, the taller participants have to look downward. We concluded that the font size 30 with 1 line spacing and sans serif typeface is suitable for texts with multiple lines. White colour for the text and dark green for the background was used to give a higher contrast. Positive feedback was received regarding the font size for reading from most participants. However, some noted low readability for various reasons, including lengthy text and typography-related issues. People are diverse in terms of height, sight, concentration, and preferences. Accordingly, a possible solution to improve the readability could be to support customizable font sizes with different line spacing [8].

### 6.4   Updates and Design Considerations for the Future

After the user tests were conducted at the exhibition, the UI and the system received small changes, taking into consideration the results (Fig. 7). The biggest changes included having the top buttons look more like buttons to increase the UI's intuitiveness and slowing down the rotation speed for easier interaction and a better view of the Gapta's details and adding a 360-icon under the doll to indicate that it can be rotated freely with a swipe gesture. Small adjustments were also made, such as an updated icon and changing the term for manufacturer to artisan for clarity. The participants wished for the inclusion of Sámi language(s), which was the initial plan but was cut out for resource reasons. We hope that in the future, they can be added. Other desired features included adding audio and narration, which the museum could consider.

Although the program aimed to offer inclusive design [37] for visitors of all skill levels, a participant not being able to finish the usability testing tasks without assistance could indicate that touch-based interaction method (i.e., press and swipe) might be too much for some. Perhaps they can benefit from a shared experience and join others who navigate the technology in a shared experience. Several participants wished for audio output while viewing the content in the program. We decided to omit any sounds from our program due to the environment in the exhibition room. However, if a directional speaker could be used, the program could enrich the overall experience Furthermore, adding another channel to deliver the content to the museum visitor could support people with disabilities, or if a supported interaction modality is not applicable to the museum visitor.

### 6.5   Limitations

We acknowledge that our work is limited by the number of participants. In our study, the demographic was not balanced in genders and ages, but the regular visitors of the museum have to be considered. As this was a study only on one exhibition, more extensive work could be conducted on different exhibits and museums to get a broader view of the topic. Also, as mentioned earlier, users' expectations of the experience will affect their perception of the experience [23], and as our participants had already chosen to go to the museum, they might have some positive expectations on the visit.

None of the authors in this paper was Indigenous; thus, we approached the topic as outsiders looking in. We communicated actively regarding the program design between the UI designers, program developers, and Sámi museum experts. An even better understanding of each other's domain could have been included if we had more chances to share knowledge.

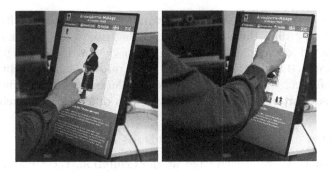

**Fig. 7.** The program being tested after making the changes.

## 7    Conclusion

Our case study has shown an example of an HCI development process in the Indigenous design context. Our results implied that the program was received well by the participants in general as part of the renewed exhibition. We found some perceived usability issues related to features and finding them, which were then used to update the program. We also presented suggestions on what to develop in the future, if possible. We discussed the meaning of applying technologies to promote cultural identities and heritage, allowing people to learn, appreciate and recall cultural aspects at a museum. There needs to be more work between different disciplines in order to showcase Indigenous cultures in museums in the best way possible.

The process was based on the needs of the museum and the Sámi community, focusing on clear information and simple interactions. We feel this topic is essential in making the HCI community think about specific design considerations related to Indigenous HCI topics, e.g. when working with Indigenous museums. We hope we can give them insight, on what things to focus on in such a context. More work is needed around the world in regard to Indigenous HCI.

## References

1. Aikio, Á.: A window into vanishing sámi culture?: visual representations of sáminess in the shared siida exhibition by sámi museum siida and northern lapland's nature centre 1. In: The Sámi World, pp. 21–38. Routledge (2022)
2. Antoniou, A., De Carolis, B., Kuflik, T., Origlia, A., Raptis, G., Gena, C.: AVI-CH 2022: workshop on advanced visual interfaces and interactions in cultural heritage. In: Proceedings of the 2022 International Conference on Advanced Visual Interfaces, pp. 1–3 (2022)
3. Barbieri, L., Bruno, F., Muzzupappa, M.: Virtual museum system evaluation through user studies. J. Cult. Herit. **26**, 101–108 (2017)
4. Blackler, A., Popovic, V., Mahar, D.: Intuitive interaction applied to interface design. In: New Design Paradigms: Proceedings of International Design Congress (IDC) 2005, pp. 1–10. International Design Congress (2005)

5. Brooke, J., et al.: SUS-a quick and dirty usability scale. Usability Eval. Indus. **189**(194), 4–7 (1996)
6. Ciolfi, L., Damala, A., Hornecker, E., Lechner, M., Maye, L., Petrelli, D.: Cultural heritage communities: technologies and challenges. In: Proceedings of the 7th International Conference on Communities and Technologies, pp. 149–152 (2015)
7. Cocq, C., et al.: Traditionalisation for revitalisation: tradition as a concept and practice in contemporary sámi contexts. Folklore: Electr. J. Folklore **57**, 79–100 (2014)
8. Darroch, I., Goodman, J., Brewster, S., Gray, P.: The effect of age and font size on reading text on handheld computers. In: Costabile, M.F., Paternò, F. (eds.) INTERACT 2005. LNCS, vol. 3585, pp. 253–266. Springer, Heidelberg (2005). https://doi.org/10.1007/11555261_23
9. Gestwicki, P., McNely, B.: A case study of a five-step design thinking process in educational museum game design. In: Proceedings of Meaningful Play (2012)
10. Häkkilä, J., Paananen, S., Suoheimo, M., Mäkikalli, M.: Pluriverse perspectives in designing for a cultural heritage context in the digital age. In: Artistic Cartography and Design Explorations Towards the Pluriverse, pp. 134–143. Routledge (2022)
11. Häkkilä, J., et al.: Design sensibilities-designing for cultural sensitivity. In: Proceedings of the 11th Nordic Conference On Human-computer Interaction: Shaping Experiences, Shaping Society, pp. 1–3 (2020)
12. Harlin, E.K.: Repatriation as knowledge sharing-returning the sámi cultural heritage. Utimut: Past Heritage-future Partnerships: Discussions On Repatriation in the 21st Century, pp. 192–200 (2008)
13. Heimgärtner, R.: Reflections on a model of culturally influenced human-computer interaction to cover cultural contexts in HCI design. Int. J. Hum.-Comput. Inter. **29**(4), 205–219 (2013)
14. Heukelman, D., Obono, S.E.: Exploring the African village metaphor for computer user interface icons. In: Proceedings of the 2009 Annual Research Conference of the South African Institute of Computer Scientists and Information Technologists, pp. 132–140 (2009)
15. Hinderks, A., Schrepp, M., Thomaschewski, J.: User Experience Questionnaire (UEQ) (2018). https://www.ueq-online.org/
16. Hornecker, E., Nicol, E.: What do lab-based user studies tell us about in-the-wild behavior? insights from a study of museum interactives. In: Proceedings of the Designing Interactive Systems Conference, pp. 358–367 (2012)
17. Hornecker, E., Stifter, M.: Learning from interactive museum installations about interaction design for public settings. In: Proceedings of the 18th Australia Conference on Computer-human Interaction: Design: Activities, Artefacts and Environments, pp. 135–142 (2006)
18. Hugo, J., Day, B.: Business: government, business, HCI, and technological development in South Africa. Interactions **8**(4), 25–32 (2001)
19. Hutchinson, R., Eardley, A.:'I felt i was right there with them': the impact of sound-enriched audio description on experiencing and remembering artworks, for blind and sighted museum audiences. Museum Management and Curatorship, pp. 1–18 (2023)
20. Karoulis, A., Sylaiou, S., White, M.: Usability evaluation of a virtual museum interface. Informatica **17**(3), 363–380 (2006)
21. Kelly, L.: Measuring the impact of museums on their communities: the role of the 21st century museum. Intercom **2**(4), 11 (2006)
22. Kelly, M., Taffe, S.: When digital doesn't work: experiences of co-designing an indigenous community museum. Multimod. Technol. Inter. **6**(5), 34 (2022)

23. Konstantakis, M., Caridakis, G.: Adding culture to UX: UX research methodologies and applications in cultural heritage. J. Comput. Cult. Herit. (JOCCH) **13**(1), 1–17 (2020)
24. Laiti, O., Harrer, S., Uusiautti, S., Kultima, A.: Sustaining intangible heritage through video game storytelling-the case of the Sami game jam. Int. J. Herit. Stud. **27**(3), 296–311 (2021)
25. Lawrence, C., Leong, T.W., Brereton, M., Taylor, J.L., Bidwell, N., Wadley, G.: Indigenous HCL: Workshop at Ozchi 2019, Perth. In: Proceedings of the 31st Australian Conference on Human-Computer-Interaction, pp. 17–19 (2019)
26. Lazem, S., Giglitto, D., Nkwo, M.S., Mthoko, H., Upani, J., Peters, A.: Challenges and paradoxes in decolonising HCI: a critical discussion. Comput. Support. Cooperat. Work (CSCW) **31**, 1–38 (2021). https://doi.org/10.1007/s10606-021-09398-0
27. Loureiro, S.M.C., Roschk, H., Lima, F.: The role of background music in visitors' experience of art exhibitions: music, memory and art appraisal. Int. J. Arts Manag. **22**(1), 4–24 (2019)
28. Lucero, A.: Using affinity diagrams to evaluate interactive prototypes. In: Abascal, J., Barbosa, S., Fetter, M., Gross, T., Palanque, P., Winckler, M. (eds.) INTERACT 2015. LNCS, vol. 9297, pp. 231–248. Springer, Cham (2015). https://doi.org/10.1007/978-3-319-22668-2_19
29. Magga, S.M.: Gákti on the pulse of time: the double perspective of the traditional sámi dress 1. In: The Sámi World, pp. 39–52. Routledge (2022)
30. Magnani, M., Guttorm, A., Magnani, N.: Three-dimensional, community-based heritage management of indigenous museum collections: archaeological ethnography, revitalization and repatriation at the sámi museum Siida. J. Cult. Herit. **31**, 162–169 (2018)
31. Micoli, L.L., Caruso, G., Guidi, G.: Design of digital interaction for complex museum collections. Multimod. Technol. Interact. **4**(2), 31 (2020)
32. Otto, K., Wood, K.: Product design: techniques in reverse engineering and new product development (2001)
33. Paananen, S., Suoheimo, M., Häkkilä, J.: Charting experience categories for museum exhibitions. In: Ardito, C., et al. (eds.) INTERACT 2021. LNCS, vol. 12936, pp. 372–376. Springer, Cham (2021). https://doi.org/10.1007/978-3-030-85607-6_40
34. Paananen, S., Suoheimo, M., Häkkilä, J.: Decolonizing design with technology in cultural heritage contexts-systematic literature review. In: Bruyns, G., Wei, H. (eds.) With Design: Reinventing Design Modes. IASDR 2021. Springer, Singapore (2022). https://doi.org/10.1007/978-981-19-4472-7_119
35. Pallud, J.: Impact of interactive technologies on stimulating learning experiences in a museum. Inf. Manag. **54**(4), 465–478 (2017)
36. Parsons, M., Fisher, K., Nalau, J.: Alternative approaches to co-design: insights from indigenous/academic research collaborations. Curr. Opin. Environ. Sustain. **20**, 99–105 (2016)
37. Persad, U., Langdon, P., Clarkson, J.: Characterising user capabilities to support inclusive design evaluation. Univ. Access Inf. Soc. **6**(2), 119–135 (2007)
38. Peters, D., Hansen, S., McMullan, J., Ardler, T., Mooney, J., Calvo, R.A.: "participation is not enough" towards indigenous-led co-design. In: Proceedings of the 30th Australian Conference on Computer-Human Interaction, pp. 97–101 (2018)
39. Raskin, J.: Intuitive equals familiar. Commun. ACM **37**(9), 17–19 (1994)

40. Rello, L., Pielot, M., Marcos, M.C.: Make it big! the effect of font size and line spacing on online readability. In: Proceedings of the 2016 CHI conference on Human Factors in Computing Systems, pp. 3637–3648 (2016)
41. Saldaña, J.: The coding manual for qualitative researchers. SAGE, Los Angeles; London, 3rd edn. (2016). oCLC: ocn930445694
42. Schrepp, M., Hinderks, A., Thomaschewski, J.: Design and evaluation of a short version of the user experience questionnaire (ueq-s). Int. J. Interact. Multimed. Artif. Intell. 4(6), 103–108 (2017)
43. Silvén, E.: Nomadising sami collections. In: Current Issues in European Cultural Studies; 15–17 June; Norrköping; Sweden 2011, pp. 271–275. no. 062, Linköping University Electronic Press (2011)
44. Silvén, E.: Constructing a sami cultural heritage. Ethnologia Scandinavica 44 (2014)
45. Tlostanova, M.: On decolonizing design. Design Philos. Papers 15(1), 51–61 (2017)
46. Valkonen, S., Alakorva, S., Aikio, Á., Magga, S.M.: Introduction: introduction to the sámi world. In: The Sámi World, pp. 1–18. Routledge (2022)
47. Wang, G.G.: Definition and review of virtual prototyping. J. Comput. Inf. Sci. Eng. 2(3), 232–236 (2002)
48. Webb, S.: Making museums, making people: the representation of the sámi through material culture. Public Archaeol. 5(3), 167–183 (2006)
49. Winschiers-Theophilus, H.: Bridging worlds: indigenous knowledge in the digital world. In: Proceedings of the 22nd ACM/IEEE Joint Conference on Digital Libraries, pp. 1–2 (2022)
50. Wolf, K., Reinhardt, J., Funk, M.: Virtual exhibitions: what do we win and what do we lose? Electronic Visualisation and the Arts, pp. 79–86 (2018)
51. Xu, X., Kang, J., Yasin, I., et al.: Effect of music tempo on duration of stay in exhibition spaces. Appl. Acoust. 207, 109353 (2023)
52. Yalamu, P., Chua, C., Doube, W.: Does indigenous culture affect one's view of an LMS interface: a PNG and pacific islands students' perspective. In: Proceedings of the 31st Australian Conference on Human-Computer-Interaction, pp. 302–306 (2019)
53. Zaman, T., Falak, H.: Framing indigenous knowledge in digital context: technologies, methods and tools. Int. J. End-User Comput. Develop. (IJEUCD) 7(2), 36–51 (2018)

# Design Paradigms of 3D User Interfaces for VR Exhibitions

Yunzhan Zhou[1](✉)(iD), Lei Shi[2](iD), Zexi He[1](iD), Zhaoxing Li[1](iD),
and Jindi Wang[1](iD)

[1] Durham University, Durham, UK
{yunzhan.zhou,zexi.he,zhaoxing.li2,jindi.wang}@durham.ac.uk
[2] Newcastle University, Newcastle upon Tyne, UK
lei.shi@newcastle.ac.uk

**Abstract.** Virtual reality (VR) technology capably complements exhibitions. Despite the considerable attention to the development of VR exhibitions, corresponding 3D user interface (UIs) design is in strong need. In this paper, we focus on the design of 3D UIs for VR exhibitions based on head-mounted displays (HMDs). The paper presents two workshops: one explores UI design paradigms that improve the user's perceived usability and sense of immersion in the VR space, while the other examines ergonomic arrangements of the UI to address spatial layout issues. We aim to assist designers and developers by suggesting design choices, thus saving them time and avoiding the need to start from scratch.

**Keywords:** VR exhibitions · Design paradigms · 3D user interfaces

## 1 Introduction

Virtual reality (VR) technology facilitates access to exhibitions in an innovative way [1]. With VR exhibitions, visitors can remotely experience digital artefacts and exhibits without having to physically visit the exhibition site [15]. In physical exhibitions, visitors are accustomed to specific interaction patterns, such as navigating around exhibits and reading text or multimedia information on labels or posters. However, in VR exhibitions, visitors engage in 3D interaction within the VR space, where visitors perform 3D selection and manipulation tasks, or navigate by walking or controllers. Although some initial issues in 3D UIs (i.e., UIs that involve 3D interaction [14]) have been addressed within the context of VR environments recently [13,28], there is still a need for research on design paradigms for 3D UIs that are tailored specifically for VR exhibitions.

The sense of immersion [10] is a crucial factor in exhibitions, as it has been shown to lead to a greater potential for learning and pleasure [3]. This sense of immersion is even more important in VR exhibitions, where VR itself functions as an immersion technology for simulating real-world experiences. Therefore, designing 3D UIs that enhance the sense of immersion in VR exhibitions should

J. Abdelnour Nocera et al. (Eds.): INTERACT 2023, LNCS 14143, pp. 618–627, 2023.
https://doi.org/10.1007/978-3-031-42283-6_33

be a top priority. Poorly designed 3D UIs can reduce the sense of immersion and even cause VR sickness or disrupt the virtual environment. Moreover, designers must consider usability and ergonomic requirements during the design process to ensure a positive user experience.

In this paper, we target head-mounted displays-based (HMD-based) VR environments, where VR exhibitions are 3D modelled for visitors to freely navigate and interact with 3D virtual objects [7,18,19]. Our goal is to offer a collection of design paradigms for 3D user interfaces in HMD-based exhibitions. These paradigms will help designers and developers save time by suggesting design choices, eliminating the need to start from scratch.

We first conduct an interview to investigate the challenges people face when designing 3D UIs. We then organise two workshops: a paradigm workshop to explore the ideal templates for 3D UIs in VR exhibitions, and a layout workshop to explore their optimal ergonomic arrangements. Based on the outcomes of the workshops, we contribute to the design paradigms for 3D user interfaces specifically tailored for HMD-based exhibitions.

## 2   Related Work

The current state of research on VR exhibitions can be viewed from three primary perspectives. Firstly, some researchers have concentrated on analysing the general structures and experiences associated with VR exhibitions [21,24]. Secondly, attention has been given to the development platforms [12,30]. Lastly, there have been comprehensive reviews conducted on VR exhibitions [26,29]. In this work, we particularly focus on the design of 3D UIs in VR exhibitions.

The topic of UI design for VR exhibits has not been extensively explored in research. Previous works have mainly focused on UI design in physical exhibition environments, which may not necessarily be directly applicable to VR ones. Many researchers have studied UIs on PDAs or other mobile devices, [11,17]. For instance, Li et al. [17] presented a prototype for an interactive user interface based on a mobile platform to enhance on-site museum experiences. Additionally, some researchers have designed and implemented UIs for web platforms, as exemplified by [27] or for AR platforms [9,23]. However, overall, there is still a gap in research when it comes to UI design specifically for VR exhibitions.

Furthermore, existing works on UI design in VR environments are not typically customized for exhibition environments. Some of these works focused on examining various interaction methods that support VR manipulations, including tablet interaction [6], object selection [16], 3D gestures [5], and gaze input [4]. Some of these works conducted case studies and presented UI designs for evaluation. Bhowmick et al. [2] proposed an HMD-VR interface to help students understand atomic structures, while Weiss et al. [28] designed 2D, 3D, and speech interfaces for completing predefined furnishing tasks in VR environments. Some studies [8,20] focused on the comprehensive UI evaluation of VR environments. Lastly, some works, such as [22], aimed to obtain guidelines for VR UI design. Our paper focuses on studying the 3D UI design specifically for VR exhibits, with the goal of achieving high usability and immersive user experiences.

# 3  Methods

We aim to identify the general design issues in developing 3D UIs for VR exhibits and proposed solutions by exploring the UI paradigms. The study lasted five weeks and contained one interview and two workshops. We first conducted the interview to investigate the difficulties people may have when designing UIs. The following two workshops were held to explore UIs' optimum templates and ergonomic arrangements, respectively.

## 3.1  Exhibition Scenarios and Participants

We built exhibits in two different example exhibitions: an *Egyptian Exhibition* presenting the historic Egyptian culture, and a *Computer Exhibition* presenting the technology development of computers. In both exhibitions, we set up several exhibits related to the exhibition themes, which were well arranged. We designed the locations and sizes of the exhibits and the stands and kept the space in a good balance as if in a real-world exhibition. Both exhibitions were developed on *Unity* platform and were deployed on the *HTC Vive Pro Eye* device [25]. All the exhibit models originated from open-source databases.

There were two groups of participants recruited in this study. The first group had four experts with rich experience in VR or museum design: three HCI practitioners in VR and one museum researcher. They were all fully experienced with VR platforms and familiar with the VR device. In this study, they participated in the interview and the two following workshops. The second group consisted of five experienced VR users recruited from the computer science department of a university. All participants had rich prior experience with VR spanning over three years and were regular users of the VR device. In this study, they took part in the evaluation of the design choices in the first workshop.

## 3.2  Interview

The interview was conducted to learn the issues people may have when designing VR UIs. We first asked the four experts in the first group to design UIs freely for the exhibits from scratch. We provided them with background information (including videos, images, and text) introducing each exhibit. During and after that, we recorded their design process and asked them questions on two aspects: the workflow of developing UIs and the difficulties they had when designing and developing UIs. We summarize our findings as follows:

**Workflow of Developing UIs.** Based on the feedback from the interviewees, the process for UI development typically involved two main stages. The first stage involved creating or selecting UI elements. For instance, they designed UI elements such as image and video components, as well as operational panels. Additionally, they chose *raycasting* as the hand-controlling method for the UIs. The second stage of the process involved arranging the selected UIs around an exhibit, which involved determining their spatial layout in relation to the exhibit.

**Design Difficulties.** When discussing the issues in creating and selecting UI elements in VR, one interviewee commented that there were too many options when deciding how UIs looked, which cost a lot of time for him to hesitate and make a choice. They argued that there were few previous cases concerning UI design for VR exhibits, except for realistic exhibits. One interviewee mentioned that it would be better if there had been some UI templates already validated as the ideal form of VR exhibit UIs. When discussing the issues in arranging UIs around an exhibit, all interviewees commented that it was very time-consuming and exhausting to arrange every UI element near an exhibit properly.

### 3.3   UI Paradigm Workshop

The goal of this workshop was to explore the UI paradigms for VR exhibits, based on design difficulties articulated above in Sect. 3.2. We invited those four expert participants to brainstorm possible UI types in VR. After brainstorming, they designed and implemented these UIs for exhibits in both exhibitions scenarios. We conducted the evaluation of UI choices to explore the UI paradigms.

**Preparation.** To provide consistent VR experiences for participants, we standardised participant avatars' parameters when they start navigating. In the VR scene, we set the initial height of the camera (i.e., the avatar's eyes) to $1.75m$, as the expected average height of a person. This height standardisation was kept along all the VR scenarios in this paper afterwards.

**Brainstorm and Implementation.** In the brainstorming session, participants were asked to find the UI paradigm solutions. They first came up with four common UI element types for VR exhibits, including video UIs, image UIs, text UIs, and operation UIs. They also discussed the 3D manipulation (3D touching, selecting, and clicking) and spatial navigation methods that could highly impact the interaction experience in VR. Later, when asked about the specific design choices for each of the UI types, they concluded with different design paradigms for image UIs and operation UIs. They also agreed on several common 3D manipulations and spatial navigation methods. In the end, they implemented these design choices in the two example scenarios, as shown in Fig. 1. They also agreed on one typical type of text UIs and one typical type of video UIs as the UI design choices, as illustrated in Fig. 2.

**Evaluation.** We invited five experienced VR participants as stated in Sect. 3.1, to evaluate the proposed design choices. They went through three rounds of evaluation given a set of UIs for one random exhibit. To control the variables, at each round, except the UIs or interaction methods to be evaluated, other UIs or methods in the set were randomly given. At round I, participants were given two operation UIs associated with two 3D manipulation methods, forming four combinations (**O1-S1, O2-S1, O1-S2, O2-S2**). At round II, participants were

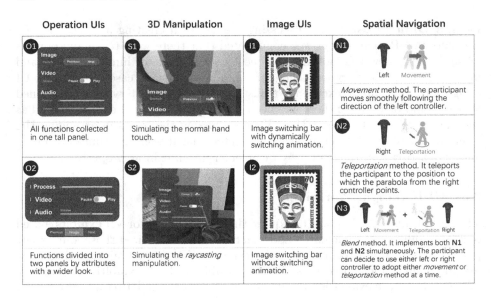

**Fig. 1.** Design options for UI paradigms in VR exhibitions. **O1** and **O2** are representative operation UIs. **S1** and **S2** are representative 3D manipulation methods. **I1** and **I2** are representative image UIs. **N1**, **N2**, and **N3** are representative spatial navigation methods.

given two image UIs (**I1** and **I2**). At round III, participants were given three navigation methods (**N1**, **N2** and **N3**). Participants ranked UI choices by the extent to which they would like to use this UI based on their perceived level of usability and sense of immersion, and provided feedback in a brief interview after each round. We will present the evaluation results in Sect. 4.1.

### 3.4    UI Layout Workshop

The goal of this workshop was to explore the optimum ergonomic arrangements for UIs in VR exhibition scenarios as part of the UI layout problem discussed in the previous interview. As there is usually an optimum area for participants to stand and observe the exhibits in the real world, we aim to find this optimum area for the VR ones. Furthermore, we target UI design for an individual exhibit, we concentrate on looking for the ergonomic arrangements for it when participants stand in its optimum observed area.

**Procedure.** We invited the four experts to brainstorm the UI ergonomic arrangements. During the process, they proposed three key points that are commonly concerned nowadays when designing UIs in VR: viewer-UI distance, the field of view, and text size. Despite some similar guidelines summarised by designers previously (published on blogs or video websites by designers from VR companies), we aimed to discover the specific ergonomic arrangements for VR exhibits. As the complexity of ergonomic issues, we asked the participants to try as many options as possible and give their feedback on the optimum ergonomic arrangements through experimenting on several exhibit UIs. We will present the workshop results in Sect. 4.2.

# 4   Results

We present the results from the above two workshop studies. The summary of our findings is illustrated in Table 1.

**Table 1.** Summary of the design paradigms and optimal ergonomic arrangements for 3D UIs in VR exhibitions.

| | Operation UI & Manipulation Methods (O-S) | Image UIs (I) | Navigation Methods (N) | Viewer-UI Distance | Depression Angle for Operation UIs | Font Size for Text UIs |
|---|---|---|---|---|---|---|
| **Participant Feedback** | O1-S1 (0%); O2-S1 (0%); **O1-S2 (100%)**; O2-S2 (0%) | **I1 (100%)** I2 (0%) | N1 (0%) N2 (0%) **N3 (100%)** | Demonstration UIs 3.5m; Operation UIs 2.6m | 9.8 degrees | 0.1 under Scale 1 |

## 4.1   UI Paradigms

We present results from the paradigm workshop. 100% of the participants ranked **O1-S2** the most favourable UI design out of four choices. They reached an agreement that **O1** was easier to use than **O2**. Some commented *"having all functions in one panel makes O1 clean and compact"*. Concerning the 3D manipulation methods, they thought that the hand touch method (**S1**) required a closer distance between UIs and participants preventing the content on UIs from being clearly seen. One added that the hand-touch method demanded higher selection accuracy. On the contrary, they concurred that the *raycasting* manipulation method (**S2**) was more convenient and easier to use, since it allowed participants to control manipulation wherever they stood. When ranking image UIs, 100% of the participants preferred the animated image-switching bar (**I1**). They liked its smooth image-switching effect and commented that it was more interesting and interactive, compared to a typical image-switching bar (**I2**). When ranking the spatial navigation methods, 100% of the participants voted to choose **N3**. They mentioned that the movement method (**N1**) was closer to real-world walking circumstances and more precise, but it could cause dizziness problems. The teleportation method (**N2**) had higher efficiency in movement but lacked precision. **N3** took advantage of both methods and facilitate a more immersive experience, while one participant mentioned that it might require more learning costs. Based on the results from the paradigm workshop, we proposed the UI paradigm solution for individual VR exhibits. We implemented the UI paradigms in the example scenarios, as shown in Fig. 2. We adopted intuitive text UIs and

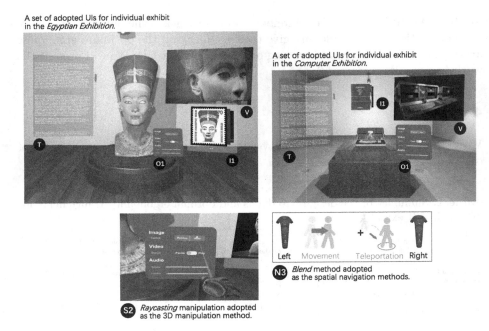

**Fig. 2.** Illustration of the UI paradigms from the workshop conclusion. **T** are adopted text UIs, **O1** are adopted operation UIs with all elements in one panel, **I1** are adopted image UIs with dynamic switch, and **V** are adopted video UIs. **S2** are adopted *raycasting* manipulation method. **N3** are adopted *blend* navigation method.

video UIs proposed by the participants' designs in this workshop. We also implemented the chosen operation UIs with all elements in one panel and the chosen image UIs with dynamic switch. Lastly, we applied the 3D *raycasting* manipulation method and the *blend* spatial navigation method combining both movement and teleportation approaches.

## 4.2    Ergonomic Arrangements

We present results from the layout workshop. For each exhibit, participants reached a mutual result on the optimum viewer-UI distance. When standing in front of an exhibit, the participants' best distance to demonstration UIs (such as video UIs, image UIs, and text UIs) is around $3.5m$, while the best distance to operation UIs is around $2.6m$, as operation UIs had a stronger interactive need. According to the participants' comments, long distances decreased a sense of participation in the exhibit, while short distances discomforted them with squeezed interaction space. The current viewer-UI distance reached a good balance between the sense of participation and free space. For each exhibit, the participants also found the optimum depression angle for operation UIs is around 9.8 degrees, fitting the participants' comfortable field of view and hand-controlling posture. Higher operation UIs are unfriendly to hand-controlling postures, while

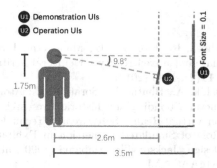

**Fig. 3.** Illustration of the ergonomic arrangements for UIs of VR exhibits.

lower operation UIs are unfriendly to the angle of the participants' heads or eyes. Lastly, the participants found that the suitable font size for text UIs is around 0.1 under Scale 1 defined by the *Unity* platform. This text size was proven to satisfy participants' recognition and aesthetic requirements of text description in VR, given the optimum viewer-UI distance. The overall ergonomic arrangements are shown in Fig. 3.

## 5 Discussion

We have presented a set of design paradigms for 3D user interfaces in VR exhibitions, encompassing operation UIs, demonstration UIs, 3D manipulation methods, and spatial navigation methods. These paradigms aim to provide designers and developers with suggestions for design choices, reducing the need to start from scratch and saving time. We have also provided recommendations for ergonomic arrangements of 3D UIs, taking into account viewer-UI distance, the field of view, and text size.

As the initial study in the field of 3D UI design for VR exhibitions, it is important to acknowledge that there exist additional types of 3D UIs that were not covered due to the time and scope limitations of the study. Furthermore, the evaluation study conducted was of a small scale and had a brief setting. Conducting more in-depth qualitative studies could offer more valuable insights into the design of 3D UIs. In addition to ergonomic arrangements, it is also important to address design issues on the spatial arrangement of 3D UIs around the exhibition object in VR. One significant challenge is the absence of spatial constraints within these UIs. Moving forward, our future work involves two aspects. First, we aim to explore and study other diverse and multi-modal 3D UI types, such as speech interfaces, haptic interfaces, and hand-tracking interfaces. Second, we plan to conduct more in-depth user studies to examine how different UI choices impact users' perceived usability and sense of immersion in VR exhibitions.

# References

1. Bekele, M.K., Pierdicca, R., Frontoni, E., Malinverni, E.S., Gain, J.: A survey of augmented, virtual, and mixed reality for cultural heritage. J. Comput. Cult. Heritage (JOCCH) **11**(2), 1–36 (2018)
2. Bhowmick, S., Kaushik, A., Bhatia, R., Sorathia, K.: Atom: HMD-VR interface to learn atomic structure, bonding and historical research experiments. In: 26th ACM Symposium on Virtual Reality Software and Technology, pp. 1–2 (2020)
3. Bitgood, S.: The Role of Simulated Immersion in Exhibition. Technical report Center for Social Design, Jacksonville, Alabama (1990), https://books.google.co.uk/books?id=VR3KtgAACAAJ
4. Choe, M., Choi, Y., Park, J., Kim, H.K.: Comparison of gaze cursor input methods for virtual reality devices. Int. J. Hum. Comput. Interact. **35**(7), 620–629 (2019)
5. Davis, M.M., Gabbard, J.L., Bowman, D.A., Gracanin, D.: Depth-based 3D gesture multi-level radial menu for virtual object manipulation. In: 2016 IEEE Virtual Reality (VR), pp. 169–170 (2016). https://doi.org/10.1109/VR.2016.7504707
6. Drey, T., Gugenheimer, J., Karlbauer, J., Milo, M., Rukzio, E.: VRSketchin: exploring the design space of pen and tablet interaction for 3D sketching in virtual reality. In: Proceedings of the 2020 CHI Conference on Human Factors in Computing Systems, pp. 1–14 (2020)
7. Enros, M.: Development of an interactive VR experience for an art museum (2020)
8. Granić, A., Nakić, J., Marangunić, N.: Scenario-based group usability testing as a mixed methods approach to the evaluation of three-dimensional virtual learning environments. J. Educ. Comput. Res. **58**(3), 616–639 (2020)
9. Hammady, Ramy, Ma, Minhua: Designing spatial UI as a solution of the narrow FOV of microsoft HoloLens: prototype of virtual museum guide. In: tom Dieck, M. Claudia., Jung, Timothy (eds.) Augmented Reality and Virtual Reality. PI, pp. 217–231. Springer, Cham (2019). https://doi.org/10.1007/978-3-030-06246-0_16
10. Harvey, M.L., Loomis, R.J., Bell, P.A., Marino, M.: The influence of museum exhibit design on immersion and psychological flow. Environ. Behav. **30**(5), 601–627 (1998)
11. Jimenez Pazmino, P., Lyons, L.: An exploratory study of input modalities for mobile devices used with museum exhibits. In: Proceedings of the SIGCHI Conference on Human Factors in Computing Systems, pp. 895–904 (2011)
12. Kiourt, C., Koutsoudis, A., Pavlidis, G.: Dynamus: a fully dynamic 3D virtual museum framework. J. Cult. Herit. **22**, 984–991 (2016)
13. Kyritsis, M., Gulliver, S.R., Morar, S., Stevens, R.: Issues and benefits of using 3D interfaces: visual and verbal tasks. In: Proceedings of the Fifth International Conference on Management of Emergent Digital EcoSystems, pp. 241–245 (2013)
14. LaViola Jr., J.J., Kruijff, E., McMahan, R.P., Bowman, D., Poupyrev, I.P.: 3D user interfaces: theory and practice. Addison-Wesley Professional (2017)
15. Leong, C.K., Chennupati, K.R.: An overview of online exhibitions. DESIDOC J. Libr. Inf. Technol. **28**(4), 7–21 (2008)
16. Li, J., Cho, I., Wartell, Z.: Evaluation of cursor offset on 3D selection in VR. In: Proceedings of the Symposium on Spatial User Interaction, pp. 120–129 (2018)
17. Li, R.Y.C., Liew, A.W.C.: An interactive user interface prototype design for enhancing on-site museum and art gallery experience through digital technology. Museum Manag. Curatorship **30**(3), 208–229 (2015)
18. Lugrin, J.L., et al.: A location-based VR museum. In: 2018 10th International Conference on Virtual Worlds and Games for Serious Applications (VS-Games), pp. 1–2. IEEE (2018)

19. Ma, L., Lu, X.: The VR museum for Dunhuang cultural heritage digitization research. In: Conference Proceedings of Conference on Cultural Heritage and New Technologies, pp. 1–4. ICOMOS, Austria (2021)
20. Naranjo, J.E., Urrutia, F.U., Garcia, M.V., Gallardo-Cárdenas, F., Franklin, T.O., Lozada-Martínez, E.: User experience evaluation of an interactive virtual reality-based system for upper limb rehabilitation. In: 2019 Sixth International Conference on eDemocracy & eGovernment (ICEDEG), pp. 328–333. IEEE (2019)
21. Popoli, Z., Derda, I.: Developing experiences: creative process behind the design and production of immersive exhibitions. Museum Manag. Curatorship **36**(4), 384–402 (2021)
22. Regazzoni, D., Rizzi, C., Vitali, A.: Virtual reality applications: guidelines to design natural user interface. In: International Design Engineering Technical Conferences and Computers and Information in Engineering Conference, vol. 51739, p. V01BT02A029. American Society of Mechanical Engineers (2018)
23. Rodrigues, J.M.F., et al.: Adaptive card design UI implementation for an augmented reality museum application. In: Antona, Margherita, Stephanidis, Constantine (eds.) UAHCI 2017. LNCS, vol. 10277, pp. 433–443. Springer, Cham (2017). https://doi.org/10.1007/978-3-319-58706-6_35
24. Schofield, G., et al.: Viking VR: designing a virtual reality experience for a museum. In: Proceedings of the 2018 Designing Interactive Systems Conference, pp. 805–815 (2018)
25. Sipatchin, A., Wahl, S., Rifai, K.: Eye-tracking for low vision with virtual reality (VR): testing status quo usability of the HTC vive pro eye. bioRxiv (2020)
26. Styliani, S., Fotis, L., Kostas, K., Petros, P.: Virtual museums, a survey and some issues for consideration. J. Cult. Herit. **10**(4), 520–528 (2009)
27. Tong, Y., Cui, B., Chen, Y.: Research on UI visual design of intangible cultural heritage digital museum based on user experience. In: 2018 13th International Conference on Computer Science & Education (ICCSE), pp. 1–4. IEEE (2018)
28. Weiß, Y., Hepperle, D., Sieß, A., Wölfel, M.: What user interface to use for virtual reality? 2D, 3D or speech-a user study. In: 2018 International Conference on Cyberworlds (CW), pp. 50–57. IEEE (2018)
29. Wolf, K., Reinhardt, J., Funk, M.: Virtual exhibitions: what do we win and what do we lose? Electronic Visualisation and the Arts 79–86 (2018)
30. Zidianakis, E., et al.: The invisible museum: a user-centric platform for creating virtual 3D exhibitions with VR support. Electronics **10**(3), 363 (2021)

# Multisensory Diorama: Enhancing Accessibility and Engagement in Museums

Leandro S. Guedes[1]([✉]), Irene Zanardi[1], Stefania Span[2], and Monica Landoni[1]

[1] Università della Svizzera Italiana (USI), Lugano, Switzerland
{leandro.soares.guedes,irene.zanardi,monica.landoni}@usi.ch
[2] Cooperativa Sociale Trieste Integrazione a m. Anffas Onlus, Trieste, Italy
https://www.luxia.inf.usi.ch

**Abstract.** This paper describes the design and evaluation of a Multisensory Diorama (MSD) intended as a tool to provide an alternative learning environment for people with intellectual disabilities (ID) in museums. The MSD is designed to be interactive, engaging, and accessible to accommodate the specificities of participants with ID, and to help contextualize and consolidate previous knowledge. The MSD is a portable box with RFID readers, LEDs, a fan, a photoresistor, a button, an Arduino Uno, an MP3 shield, a speaker, and an external battery. The MSD offers two different ways of engagement and interaction via exploration and gamification: visitors can explore the augmented landscape and play a matching game that reinforces their knowledge of the food chain in the forest. In a formative evaluation approach focusing on the accessibility and engagement with the MSD, a study was conducted with 12 adults with ID, who provided valuable feedback to improve the design and make necessary adjustments for future implementations. The MSD proved to be a successful tool for engaging visitors and reinforcing their understanding of the food chain in an interactive and accessible way.

**Keywords:** Multisensory Experiences · Diorama · Accessibility · People with Intellectual Disabilities · Museum · Inclusion

## 1 Introduction

Museums are spaces of knowledge and cultural heritage, offering a range of experiences that aim to inform, educate, and entertain visitors. Unfortunately, many people face barriers when accessing and enjoying museums, including people with intellectual disabilities (ID). The barriers include the complexity of information and lack of inclusive interpretation. To address them, there has been growing interest in developing inclusive practices and accessible environments in museums. In particular, there has been a focus on enhancing the multisensory experience of museums by engaging multiple senses and modes of communication [11].

J. Abdelnour Nocera et al. (Eds.): INTERACT 2023, LNCS 14143, pp. 628–637, 2023.
https://doi.org/10.1007/978-3-031-42283-6_34

Multisensory experiences can facilitate learning and engagement and can enhance the accessibility of museums for people with ID. One approach to creating multisensory museum experiences is through dioramas, which are three-dimensional models or displays showing a scene or an event. Dioramas, which can provide a rich and immersive experience, allow visitors to explore different perspectives, time periods, and cultural contexts while promoting and enhancing learning and critical thinking.

This paper explores the potential of multisensory experience dioramas to enhance accessibility and engagement in museums for individuals with intellectual disabilities. Specifically, in Sect. 2, we will review the literature on intellectual disabilities, museum accessibility, and multisensory experiences. Further, Sect. 3 will present our objectives, implementation, and interaction and gamification plan. Section 4 will present the evaluation of a multisensory experience diorama designed for a museum exhibition. We will also discuss our findings in Sect. 5. Finally, we conclude this paper and highlight limitations and future considerations in Sect. 6.

## 2   Background and Related Work

Intellectual Disabilities (ID) are neurodevelopmental disorders characterized by deficits in cognition and adaptive functioning [1]. The severity can vary widely, with some people facing minor issues and being able to live relatively independently with the right support, while others may need significant and permanent assistance [26]. Assistance is especially needed in the context of formal and informal education [20], as learning can be difficult for individuals with ID without accommodations or modifications [15]. This is due, in part, to intellectual function limits, which may include issues with abstract concepts, memory, problem-solving, planning, reasoning, and generalization [1,9,32].

In recent efforts to provide inclusive interactive technologies, the multisensory approach has received special attention [16]. Multisensoriality for people with disabilities has been employed with different applications, ranging from multisensory smart objects [2,13,24] to multisensory environments [5,18,25], and with different goals, such as relaxation [10], communication [24], and learning [2]. Indeed, multiple sensory modalities can benefit learning [29] as they present information that can be more accessible according to the preferences of the learner [21], enhancing learning opportunities for everyone [4]. Multisensory experiences can also be found in museums, where multisensory technology creates immersive experiences and empowers imagination [11]. Regarding accessibility, multisensory solutions typically focus on visual impairments [19], as visual information constitutes the majority of museums' content [11], and visitors with ID received less attention in HCI technologies.

When it comes to enhancing learning experiences, natural history museums frequently employ dioramas [12,31], which are "three-dimensional depictions of animal-landscape sceneries that include real or artificial models of animals in combination with background paintings and natural or artificial requisites" [14]. Because of their educational value [30], their potential in relation to HCI has been investigated to understand how technology could enhance dioramas.

Although museums are the most common setting for digital dioramas, there are also applications set in schools to provide hands-on experience with science concepts [3,6,27]. Aside from traditional physical ones [3,27,28], there are virtual reality dioramas [6,22,23], augmented reality dioramas [7,17,23], and mixed reality dioramas [8]. Interaction is typically achieved through external controllers [6,8,22,23,27,28], with only a few opting for physical interaction [3,7,17], highlighting a lack of multimodality. Similarly, there is a lack of multisensoriality. The sensory output of digital dioramas is primarily visual, with occasional incorporation of auditory feedback [3,7,28] and even less frequent incorporation of haptic output [28]. The latter is the only one designed specifically for people with disabilities, explicitly those with visual impairment. The target users of digital dioramas are not always specified because they are appealing to a wide range of people [8,22,23], but when the design is specific to a defined population, targets are usually children [3,6,7,17].

## 3    Design

### 3.1    Rationale and Objectives

Thanks to informal learning, museums can provide an effective informal alternative learning environment for people with ID. In particular, dioramas can provide explicit and immersive representations of information that can be more easily understood. After visiting a Natural History museum with people with ID and observing their reactions to playful interactions, we conducted a focus group session with a psychologist, educators, and the museum's researcher. Together we explored the feasibility, requirements, and features of a tangible interactive object to place inside the museum. Inspired by the literature and the museum's content, we envisioned a Multisensory Diorama (MSD) focused on the food chain. As the group of participants was going to learn content about wolves and reindeer, the educator suggested focusing on that topic and proposing an activity that could be placed inside their learning process. Following the focus group, the content of the museum, and accounting for the learning objectives of the participants, we extracted the key considerations that should have been taken into account during the design phase:

1. **Engagement:** The diorama should be designed to be interactive and engaging for the participants, to involve them in a memorable and meaningful learning experience;
2. **Accessibility:** The diorama should propose multisensory feedback to accommodate the specificities of the participant with ID. It should leave the participant the possibility to choose how to engage with it and should be easy to use;
3. **Learning:** The diorama should help contextualize and consolidate previous knowledge.

## 3.2 Implementation

The MSD presented in this paper is a portable box with the scenery on top and the electronics inside. To recreate the landscape, a green textured cloth miming grass covers the surface. On the front are three cards with pictures and names of mouse, moss, and reindeer. Each card has its own RFID reader housed inside the box. Red and green LEDs are on the left side of the box and next to the cards. Statuettes of wolves and reindeer occupy the middle portion of the surface, and two of them stand on a white card-shaped RFID tag. Paper trees with thin branches and leaves that can easily shake with wind serve as a backdrop for the game. The wind is generated by a small fan located directly behind the trees. It can be activated by a photoresistor placed among the trees and a button on the diorama's left side. RFID readers, LEDs, the fan, the photoresistor, and the button are all connected to an Arduino Uno, which is equipped with an MP3 shield, a speaker, and an external battery. Figure 1a shows the components.

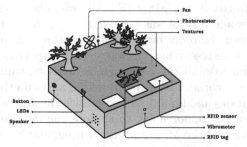

(a) Components available on the MSD.

(b) MSD in the Museum.

**Fig. 1.** MSD: Components' description and the box inside the museum.

## 3.3 Interaction and Gamification

The MSD offers visitors an interactive experience in a forest setting, where they can observe wolves and reindeer. The diorama is designed to provide two different ways of engagement and interaction, allowing visitors to choose their own experience and make their visit more memorable. Visitors can explore the augmented landscape, where they can touch the MSD's elements to discover their textures, activate the wind, and move the animals. This allows visitors to experience the forest environment hands-on and understand the different elements that make up the ecosystem. They can also play imaginative games set in the forest, which will make the experience more fun and creative.

In addition, visitors can play a matching game that reinforces their knowledge of the food chain in the forest. The game is based on the prompt "Who eats what?" and visitors can pick up the animals from the scenery and place them on top of the image of their food. The answers provided are mouse, moss, and reindeer. If the participant selects the wolf, the correct answers would be mouse and reindeer. However, if the participant selects the reindeer, moss is the correct answer. When the answer was wrong, a red LED lit up, and a feedback sound was played, encouraging participants to try again. On the other hand, if the answer was correct, a green LED lit up, and the speakers played a sound associated with the animal. Every time a match was made, the diorama vibrated. The game is designed to reinforce knowledge about the different animals and their role in the ecosystem in an interactive way. The simple mechanic and interaction are meant to enhance accessibility and improve understandability.

## 4    Evaluation

### 4.1    Method

To evaluate the accessibility and engagement of the MSD, we conducted a study at a Natural History museum. Participants were first given a tour of the museum room with the wolf and the reindeer and were given a brief refresher on the animals featured in the diorama. Afterward, the MSD (Fig. 1b) was placed on a table between the animal statuettes and a stool was provided for participants to sit on. The participants then entered the room individually for a one-on-one session with two researchers present. One researcher was leading the experience and was standing beside the participant to guide them through the activity, while the other researcher was standing in the corner of the room, taking notes on the participant's interactions and observations and filming the experiment for further analysis. Participants were first given the opportunity to explore the diorama freely. We then provided a brief overview of the MSD and its purpose, and later, the leading researcher presented the matching game promptly. The researcher handed the animal with the tag and asked the participant to place it on its food. At the end of the session with the MSD, the researcher showed participants any interaction that they hadn't tried at the beginning of the session. Finally, we requested that participants exercise their free will in selecting between the MSD and other familiar options, including a Museum app, an Augmented Reality app, printed easy-to-read text, and augmentative and alternative communication (AAC) pictograms. They were asked to choose their preferred option in sequence until the final alternative. After the session, participants were interviewed by an educator in a separate room, where they were asked to describe the diorama, the activity, and express their opinions about it. This approach allowed us to gather valuable feedback on the accessibility and engagement of the MSD and make any necessary adjustments for future implementations.

### 4.2    Participants

The study involved a sample of 12 adults with ID, 8 women and 4 men, who were chosen to participate in a museum visit by their educator from the same association. It was made possible by an ongoing agreement between the participants' association and the research organization involved and formal approval from the ethical committee of the researchers' institution. The association ensured that both legal guardians and participants knew the research purpose and that participation was voluntary. This was an important aspect of the study as it ensured that all participants were willing and able to participate in the experience. Three participants had a mild disability (P3, P5, P10), eight had a moderate disability (P1, P2, P4, P6, P8, P9, P11, P12), and one had a severe disability (P7), providing a representative sample of the population. Regarding age, 2 participants were under 40, 4 were between 40 and 50, and 6 were over 50. To ensure that all participants were comfortable during the study, frequent reminders were given that they could opt out of the activity at any time. This was an important step as it ensured that participants were not feeling pressured to continue the activity if they were uncomfortable with it. For non-verbal or minimally verbal participants, their educators were present to ensure that their needs were understood and that they felt comfortable throughout the experience.

## 5   Findings and Discussion

### 5.1   Initial Observations

Participants were initially free to explore the diorama. We analyzed and clustered data based on similarities in behavior. Some participants (P1, P3, P7) focused more on physical interaction with the elements, such as touching and feeling, while (P2, P4, P5, P6, P8, P9, P10, P12) focused more on verbal expression and describing what they see or experience. P11 is initially more cautious and skeptical of the diorama and needs help to relax and understand what we are proposing.

   We now look at accessibility, engagement, and learning during exploration and playing with the diorama via participant observations and feedback.

### 5.2   Exploration

Several similarities were observed in participants' exploration behaviors. A few participants described the elements they saw, such as in P1, P4, and P5, while others pointed at them and named them, as seen in P6 and P12. Many participants interacted with the wind, expressing enjoyment, surprise, or fascination with it, as evidenced in P2, P3, P4, P6, P8, and P12. Some participants explored the exhibit independently, as observed in P8 and P9, while others needed some prompting, such as in P6 and P10. P10 mentioned, "I am confused with the mouse" and later on highlighted when the fan was activated "as if it was the wind of nature." Ultimately, P11 expressed curiosity about the exhibit's purpose or mechanisms.

### 5.3   Independence and Accessibility

Most participants were able to access the diorama and complete their assigned tasks independently. Nonetheless, some participants required different levels of assistance to complete the game. Three participants (P7, P8, P12) were found to be primarily independent but required some form of guidance or assistance, such as specifying where to place a statuette or correcting the placement of a tag on the reader. One participant required scaffolding to complete the game (P9), and another needed help to start (P11).

### 5.4  Understanding and Learning

Participants showed a good understanding of the feedback provided in the game, either through sound or light. Some participants found the light feedback more immediate and noticeable than the sound feedback. When prompted P12 said, "It's not right because red means mistake." Several participants used the feedback to correct their following answer, while others understood that the green light meant a correct answer and moved to the next spot. P1 says when playing, "One reindeer doesn't eat another reindeer. That doesn't make sense." One participant (P11) required scaffolding to understand the game. The vibration was the least noticeable. Participants could feel it when touching the statuettes during the game's feedback.

### 5.5  Gaming Experience

Most participants demonstrated an understanding of right and wrong answers by saying out loud what was going to happen, before waiting for the matching game feedback. P12 is sure about her answers and proud to get them right, saying: "You see?!?" Two participants (P9 and P11) needed help playing the game. P3 explained the gaming experience "I didn't know if it was correct, but I wanted to try. The light told me it was right."

### 5.6  Emotions and Engagement

Participants exhibited a range of emotions during gameplay. P1, P7, and P12 were surprised and enthusiastic, with P1 expressing excitement at discovering new features "I really liked the box, did you know?" P2, P4, P6, P10, and P11 smiled during gameplay, with P6 smiling specifically at the feedback, P10 while playing with the reindeer statuette, and P11 while discovering what the box did. P5 was generally serious, while P9 was curious and spent time looking closely at the objects.

### 5.7  Preferences

We asked participants to freely choose which solution they would like to use to learn more about the museum content. They had five alternatives, three high-tech (Museum app, Augmented Reality app, and the MSD) and two low-tech (printed easy-to-read text and AAC pictograms). MSD was the second preference of 5 participants (P3, P6, P7, P11, P12), the third preference of 3 participants (P1, P2, P10), and the fourth (P5 and P8) and last (P4 and P9) of two. When placed as second or third place, the MSD was always chosen after a high-tech solution, proving the engagement and interest in technology by people with ID.

## 5.8  Interview

After each one-on-one session, the participants were asked about what they saw without any extra prompt, they were free to express what they remembered. They all described the box and various animals, the reindeer and the wolves. P3 mentioned "stickers" indicating the game alternatives glued on top of the box, while P4 and P5 provided detailed descriptions of the LEDs, fan, and wind, as well as their interactions with the box. P9 noted the presence of "fake moss," and P10 mentioned the "reindeer and wolf family."

We asked participants to describe their experience with the MSD in detail and prompted, if necessary, with the following questions: were there any noises or sounds? Did you have something to read? Were there any pictures? Were there any lights? Could you do something with the box? Many participants mentioned lights that turned green when they gave a correct answer and red when they gave an incorrect answer. Some participants also reported hearing animal sounds, such as the wolf howling or the reindeer making noise. Several participants described feeling the wind on their hands or seeing leaves move when they touched a specific box area. Participants appeared engaged and enjoyed interacting with the various elements, such as guessing which animals the wolf and reindeer should eat. However, there were also some differences in their experiences, such as one participant who reported not hearing any noises (P3) and another who did not see any lights in the box (P11).

Lastly, during the interview, the educators asked about the participants' favorite technology. A few participants said they enjoyed the tablet (with the museum or AR app) and the easy-to-read texts. P2, P6, P7, P8, P9, and P10 highlighted the box and its features. P4 answered, "I liked the pictures," which could be related to any of the alternatives they had in the hall. Additionally, one participant (P3) noted that he liked everything.

## 6  Conclusions

This study aimed to propose and evaluate the effectiveness of a MSD designed to enhance accessibility and interaction in the museum environment. The MSD was an innovative and inclusive way for people with ID to learn about the museum content, providing participants with multisensory experiences that allow for interactive and fun informal learning. Nevertheless, the study had limitations, such as noise inside the museum that disturbed the audio feedback experience and the museum hall with stimuli everywhere. As a result, future work should focus on evaluating new multisensory feedback and increasing speakers' volume. Overall, the results of this study suggest that the MSD successfully engaged participants and elicited a range of responses and behaviors, making it a promising approach for enhancing museum learning experiences.

**Acknowledgments.** We would like to thank our amazing participants from ANFFAS and SNSF for funding this research.

# References

1. American Psychiatric Association, A., Association, A.P., et al.: Diagnostic and statistical manual of mental disorders: DSM-5, vol. 10. American Psychiatric Association, Washington (2013)
2. Brule, E., Bailly, G., Brock, A., Valentin, F., Denis, G., Jouffrais, C.: Mapsense: multi-sensory interactive maps for children living with visual impairments. In: Proceedings of the 2016 CHI Conference on Human Factors in Computing Systems, pp. 445–457 (2016)
3. Cools, S., Conradie, P., Ciocci, M.-C., Saldien, J.: The diorama project: development of a tangible medium to foster STEAM education using storytelling and electronics. In: Mealha, Ó., Divitini, M., Rehm, M. (eds.) SLERD 2017. SIST, vol. 80, pp. 169–178. Springer, Cham (2018). https://doi.org/10.1007/978-3-319-61322-2_17
4. Eardley, A.F., Mineiro, C., Neves, J., Ride, P.: Redefining access: embracing multimodality, memorability and shared experience in museums. Curator: Museum J. **59**(3), 263–286 (2016)
5. Frid, E., Lindetorp, H., Hansen, K.F., Elblaus, L., Bresin, R.: Sound forest: evaluation of an accessible multisensory music installation. In: Proceedings of the 2019 CHI Conference on Human Factors in Computing Systems, pp. 1–12 (2019)
6. Gambini, A., Pezzotti, A., Broglia, A., Poli, A.: The digital diorama project: the design. Procedia-Soc. Beh. Sci. **182**, 470–476 (2015)
7. Harrington, M.C.: Connecting user experience to learning in an evaluation of an immersive, interactive, multimodal augmented reality virtual diorama in a natural history museum & the importance of story. In: 2020 6th International Conference of the Immersive Learning Research Network (iLRN), pp. 70–78. IEEE (2020)
8. Hayashi, O., Kasada, K., Narumi, T., Tanikawa, T., Hirose, M.: Digital diorama system for museum exhibition. In: 2010 IEEE International Symposium on Mixed and Augmented Reality, pp. 231–232. IEEE (2010)
9. Henry, L.A., MacLean, M.: Working memory performance in children with and without intellectual disabilities. Am. J. Ment. Retard. **107**(6), 421–432 (2002)
10. Hogg, J., Cavet, J., Lambe, L., Smeddle, M.: The use of 'snoezelen' as multisensory stimulation with people with intellectual disabilities: a review of the research. Res. Dev. Disabil. **22**(5), 353–372 (2001)
11. Hornecker, E., Ciolfi, L.: Human-computer interactions in museums. Synthesis lectures on human-centered informatics **12**(2), i–171 (2019)
12. Insley, J.: Little landscapes: dioramas in museum displays. Endeavour **32**(1), 27–31 (2008)
13. Jost, C., Le Pévédic, B., El Barraj, O., Uzan, G.: Mulsebox: portable multisensory interactive device. In: 2019 IEEE International Conference on Systems, Man and Cybernetics (SMC), pp. 3956–3961. IEEE (2019)
14. Kamcke, C., Hutterer, R.: History of Dioramas. In: Tunnicliffe, S.D., Scheersoi, A. (eds.) Natural History Dioramas, pp. 7–21. Springer, Dordrecht (2015). https://doi.org/10.1007/978-94-017-9496-1_2
15. Kauffman, J.M., Hallahan, D.P., Pullen, P.C., Badar, J.: Special Education: What It Is and Why We Need It. Routledge (2018)
16. Kientz, J.A., Hayes, G.R., Goodwin, M.S., Gelsomini, M., Abowd, G.D.: Interactive technologies and autism. Synthesis lectures on assistive, rehabilitative, and health-preserving technologies **9**(1), i–229 (2019)

17. Kyriakou, P., Hermon, S.: Can i touch this? Using natural interaction in a museum augmented reality system. Digit. Appl. Archaeol. Cult. Herit. **12**, e00088 (2019)
18. Lancioni, G., Cuvo, A., O'reilly, M.: Snoezelen: an overview of research with people with developmental disabilities and dementia. Disabil. Rehabil. **24**(4), 175–184 (2002)
19. Lloyd-Esenkaya, T., Lloyd-Esenkaya, V., O'Neill, E., Proulx, M.J.: Multisensory inclusive design with sensory substitution. Cogn. Res. Principl. Impl. **5**, 1–15 (2020)
20. Mastrogiuseppe, M., Guedes, L.S., Landoni, M., Span, S., Bortolotti, E.: Technology use and familiarity as an indicator of its adoption in museum by people with intellectual disabilities. Stud. Health Technol. Inf. **297**, 400–407 (2022)
21. Mount, H., Cavet, J.: Multi-sensory environments: an exploration of their potential for young people with profound and multiple learning difficulties. Br. J. Spec. Educ. **22**(2), 52–55 (1995)
22. Nakaya, T., et al.: Virtual Kyoto project: digital diorama of the past, present, and future of the historical city of Kyoto. In: Ishida, T. (ed.) Culture and Computing. LNCS, vol. 6259, pp. 173–187. Springer, Heidelberg (2010). https://doi.org/10.1007/978-3-642-17184-0_14
23. Narumi, T., Kasai, T., Honda, T., Aoki, K., Tanikawa, T., Hirose, M.: Digital railway museum: an approach to introduction of digital exhibition systems at the railway museum. In: Yamamoto, S. (ed.) HIMI 2013. LNCS, vol. 8018, pp. 238–247. Springer, Heidelberg (2013). https://doi.org/10.1007/978-3-642-39226-9_27
24. Neidlinger, K., Koenderink, S., Truong, K.P.: Give the body a voice: co-design with profound intellectual and multiple disabilities to create multisensory wearables. In: Extended Abstracts of the 2021 CHI Conference on Human Factors in Computing Systems, pp. 1–6 (2021)
25. Parés, N., et al.: Mediate: an interactive multisensory environment for children with severe autism and no verbal communication. In: Proceedings of the Third International Workshop on Virtual Rehabilitation, vol. 81, pp. 98–99 (2004)
26. Patel, D.R., Apple, R., Kanungo, S., Akkal, A.: Intellectual disability: definitions, evaluation and principles of treatment. Pediat. Med. **1**(11), 10–21037 (2018)
27. Ritzel, C., Sentic, A.: Investigating energy prosumer behaviour in crowd energy using an interactive model/diorama. J. Electron. Sci. Technol. **16**(4), 341–350 (2018)
28. Samaroudi, M., Rodriguez-Echavarria, K., Song, R., Evans, R.: The fabricated diorama: tactile relief and context-aware technology for visually impaired audiences. In: GCH, pp. 201–206 (2017)
29. Shams, L., Seitz, A.R.: Benefits of multisensory learning. Trends Cogn. Sci. **12**(11), 411–417 (2008)
30. Tunnicliffe, S.D., Scheersoi, A.: Dioramas as important tools in biological education. In: Tunnicliffe, S.D., Scheersoi, A. (eds.) Natural History Dioramas, pp. 133–143. Springer, Dordrecht (2015). https://doi.org/10.1007/978-94-017-9496-1_11
31. Tunnicliffe, S.D., Scheersoi, A.: Natural History Dioramas. History Construction and Educational Role, Dordrecht (2015). https://doi.org/10.1007/978-94-017-9496-1
32. Wehmeyer, M.L., et al.: The intellectual disability construct and its relation to human functioning. Intellect. Dev. Disabil. **46**(4), 311–318 (2008)

# Museum Visitor Experiences Based on Hyperspectral Image Data

Markus Löchtefeld[1]([✉]), Eleftherios Papachristos[2], and Hilda Deborah[2]

[1] Aalborg University, Aalborg, Denmark
mloc@create.aau.dk
[2] Norwegian University of Science and Technology, Gjøvik, Norway
{eleftherios.papachristos,hilda.deborah}@ntnu.no

**Abstract.** Hyper- and multispectral imaging allows to collect data from specific wavelength ranges or across the electromagnetic spectrum, including frequencies that are imperceivable for humans. As non-invasive imaging techniques, it has been used in the field of art conservation and art history extensively in the past. In these areas application of hyperspectral imaging include for example conservation monitoring or pigment identification. In the context of museum exhibits, hyperspectral data of artworks offers a unique opportunity to enhance visitor experiences by providing new ways of engaging with artefacts, artworks, and cultural heritage. This paper presents design concepts for creating immersive and meaningful experiences using hyperspectral data. We used an expert led design workshop to explore the possibilities of museum experiences with such data, including considerations such as suited technologies, visitor types and visitor experience.

**Keywords:** Hyperspectral Imaging · Museum Experiences · Augmented Reality · Virtual Reality · Multispectral Imaging

## 1 Introduction

The human visual system is limited in its ability to perceive the electromagnetic spectrum as it is only sensitive to a narrow range of wavelengths [18]. However, with the recent developments in hyperspectral imaging (HSI) technology, that allows to capture and analyze the spectral information of objects or scenes across a wide range of wavelengths, it is possible to gain more detailed insights into the properties and characteristics of materials. With this technology it is possible to take advantage of the fact that differing materials have unique spectral signature, allowing for identification and characterization [17]. By analyzing the different spectra in a hyperspectral image, valuable information about the constituents and surface properties of the material can be obtained. The technology has gained traction across a variety of fields where precise material analysis is critical for understanding the composition and condition of objects or surfaces, such as remote sensing, archaeology, forensics and especially art [17].

J. Abdelnour Nocera et al. (Eds.): INTERACT 2023, LNCS 14143, pp. 638–647, 2023.
https://doi.org/10.1007/978-3-031-42283-6_35

In art conservation and art history HSI has gained increasing popularity for nearly three decades, as it is a non-invasive technology, that allows to gain insights about specific material properties without damaging the artworks [19]. For example, if the specific pigments of an artwork need to be identified, to restore the artwork as closely to the original as possible, chemical methods such as gas chromatography or microscopy, require to take a small physical sample from the work, thereby damaging it. HSI on the other hand allows to determine the specific pigments by comparing the spectral properties to known pigments completely non-invasive [2,7]. These possibilities led to the proliferation of the technology in art conservation [21] which means that an increasing number of museum are in possession of HSI data of their artworks.

Only little work has so far focused on using multi- or hyper spectral imaging in the field Human-Computer Interaction (HCI) to create interactive experiences or applications [11,23]. The primary reason for the limited adoption of HSI in HCI could be attributed to the high cost (which can exceed $20,000) as well as the intricate nature of these systems. We propose that HSI data can be utilised to create immersive interactive experiences that could allow museum visitors to engage with artwork in new ways that foster exploration. However, developing meaningful experience requires not only a deep understanding of the art but also the technological capabilities of HSI. This work represents a first step in the exploration of HSI in which we develop a first mapping of application possibilities through an expert led design workshop.

## 2 Background

HSI has seen an increase in interest across a variety of different fields, however in this paper we only focus on the use in art and museum cases, for a more comprehensive overview of HSI application domains consider [17]. One of the most common application is to reveal information that is hidden under other parts of the painting, so called pentimenti. This can include, artworks that are painted on top of another painting on a canvas, original pencil sketches outlining the artwork, or major changes in the composition that were made during the painting [19]. It should also be mentioned that such investigations have been made since the 60's by using an infrared camera [4]. With its ability to capture both spatial and spectral information which relates to physical characteristics of materials, HSI also allows for the far more complex identification of pigments and their spatial distribution across the painting [6,7]. As discussed above already, this is crucial in conservation and restoration of art works similar to the detection of damages and past interventions through inter-band comparisons [19]. This analysis can also be used to detect potential forgery [14]. Furthermore, old paintings also often exhibit cracks, also known as craquelure, which occur when the paint or pigment layer, as well as the substrate or varnish layer, break. These damages are primarily caused by aging, drying, and mechanical factors such as vibrations and impacts. Crack detection is crucial as these cracks diminish the perceived image quality of a painting and HSI has been used to detect these this as well [8].

Another application with a focus on art is to enable rendering of colour accurate images of paintings under any lighting conditions. Unlike a normal RGB image which can only capture an accurate colour image under the specific illumination used at the time, HSI data can be render in a variety of lighting condition. However, a major problems that arise from having hundreds of spectral bands available in HSI, is the visualization of them. They can only be made digitally visible for the human eye using three spectral channels for red, green, and blue (RGB) colors. Magnusson et al. presented an algorithm which creates realistic color images out of HSI data, using the CIE 1931 XYZ color space and D65 as the reference illuminant [20]. When replacing the illuminant it is also possible to create renderings of artworks that simulate other lighting conditions. Chen et al. even explored the possibilities to generate hyperspectral data from standard RGB imagery of artwork using deep neural networks with some success [5]. While we in this work focuses on museum that often have proper HSI data, such inference could enable similar experience for hobbyists and private art collectors.

Only a limited amount of prior work focused on using multi- or hyperspectral imaging in HCI. In comparison, the use of a limited amount of bands of the electromagnetic spectrum - for example using near-infrared for spectroscopy of sucrose contents drinks [15] - is much more common in HCI and UbiComp as such devices are cheaper, smaller and easier to integrate into end-user devices [13, 15, 16, 22]. An example of using multi-spectral imaging is SpeCam presented by Yeo at al. [23]. SpeCam uses the front-facing camera of a smartphone and the display as a multi-spectral light source to infer the material underneath the face-down lying smartphone. HyperCam by Goel et al., provides a low-cost implementation of a multispectral camera including software to automatically analyzes a scene and provide the user with a set of images that try to capture the salient information of the scene [11]. They demonstrate in two application cases how this can be used. In the first application case they identify individual users through the venous structure on the back of the users hand, that becomes visible in the near infrared area of the HSI data. For the second case they again used multiple bands of the near infrared spectrum to determine th ripeness of different fruits. To the best of our knowledge no previous work explored the use of HSI data as a basis for interactive experiences in a museum.

## 3    Design Concepts

The goal of this paper is to develop design concepts for interactive museum experiences that are based on the HSI data and knowledge available in museums.

### 3.1    Method

To investigate the possibilities of HSI data as the basis for novel museum experiences, we organized a full-day expert-led design workshop. Given the complexity and multiple approaches required to analyze HSI data, we decided to have an expert in this field guide the design workshop. Besides the expert we involved five participants that were never exposed to HSI technology before. The participants consisted of two female (aged 26 and 40) and three male (aged 36, 37 and 46) all coming from interaction- and graphic design background. The expert in hyperspectral image processing had a particular focus on its use in cultural heritage and art conservation (female, aged 34).

After the expert's introduction to HSI and its capabilities, we began with an initial brainstorming session to identify potential areas of interest for museum visitors based on HSI data. A number of application ideas were generated, which were subsequently organized into five themes, namely: *invisible information, human visual perception, alternative perceptions, art modification,* and *revealing the artistic process.* The participants were then challenged to create design concepts that included technical implementations for the different ideas. Additionally, they were asked to identify which of the five museum visitor types (Explorer, Facilitator, Experience seeker, Professional/Hobbyist, and Recharger), as presented by Falk [9], would be most interested in each concept and explain why. In the following section, we will discuss each theme and its associated designs and their relevance to specific types of museum visitors.

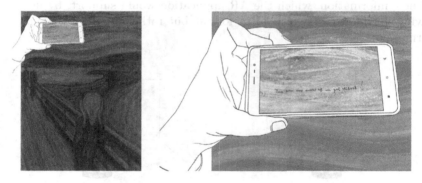

**Fig. 1.** Augmented Reality Example: Edvard Munch's Scream (1983) contains a pentimenti in Norwegian "Kan kun vre malet af en gal Mand!" (English: "Can only be painted by a mad man!") written with a pencil, which can be made visible in the near-infrared spectrum. Here it is conceptualized how this could be utilized in a mobile AR application.

## 3.2   Invisible Information

The first experience that was conceptualized was providing access to concealed layers of an artwork that are not discernible by the naked eye but that can be revealed in HSI data. Thereby fostering a more immersive and enriched exploration of the artwork. Especially elements such as pentimenti (underdrawings) and underlying revisions or changes made by the artist in the original image, were deemed to be of high interest for museum visitors. Also, the results of more complex HSI analysis methods such as Principal Component Analysis (PCA) of short wave infrared data [12], which can for example reveal patterns in the substrate that a picture is painted on where deemed as interesting content in this application area. Another element, that were discussed, where anomalies that can be identified in HSI data should be highlighted, even if they are human visible. One example that peaked interest here specially bird droppings and wax stains that are on Edvard Munch's Scream (1893) [12]. While they are visible to the human eye they are unlikely to be identified as such, but rather mistake for accidental paint droppings.

While different technologies, such as project mapping or larger touch displays were discussed, there was reached consensus that the most suited technologies that was identified for this is the utilization of mobile Augmented Reality (AR) to spatially correct overlay HSI data onto the camera view, thereby effectively unveiling the underdrawings in the paintings (compare Fig. 1). By leveraging AR to reveal these subtle modifications in the artwork, visitors can gain a deeper insight into the artist's creative process, potentially elevating their appreciation and enjoyment of the artwork. This concept was particularly seen as suitable for the visitor type of Explorer. These are driven by curiosity and the ability to find new information, which the AR application would support, by not simply showing all information in a plain format but rather let the user explore the information.

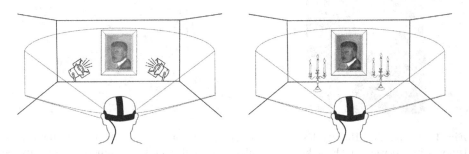

**Fig. 2.** VR Rendering Example based on Edvard Munch's Selfportrait (1905). Left: The user experiences the painting with artificial illumination that is common in museums. Right: The user experiences the painting in candle light, as Munch would have.

## 3.3  Human Visual Perception

The second larger theme that was discussed is the reflection on the human visual system, as through HSI data, the term colors became quickly quite abstract. Above, we discussed the issue of how to render visible images out of the HSI data [20], however, this issue can be used as an advantage. It can be used to render images with a variety of different illuminants, thereby imitating how the artwork would look in these different lighting conditions. Most museums use artificial light to protect the artworks from taking damage from too strong radiation of natural light [10]. However, this is stark contrast to how many artists experienced and created the artwork. For example, Munch was known for preferring natural light, and even leaving paintings out to fade as part of the artistic process [1], which resulted in the above discussed bird droppings.

The technology that was deemed most suited for this was Virtual Reality (VR). VR recently gained some traction in museum experiences [3], as it enable user-centred presentation and make cultural heritage accessible, especially in cases where physical access is limited or impossible. This would even enable remote experiences, independent from the original artwork, however, it was conceptualized by our participants as an experience that is supposed to be contrasted with their own real world experience. In order to give the audience the best impression to what the artist originally intended and present renderings of the artwork using different luminants, multiple other technologies, such as a public large display would be also suited. However it was agreed that through the use of VR the visitors would not only get a more immersive experience but also it would allow to present it in proper contextual environments showing the lighting sources (compare Fig. 2). By doing so, visitors would be given the opportunity to perceive the impact of different light sources on the artwork and compare it against their real-world encounters. Such an immersive experience could facilitate contemplation on the intricate interplay between pigments and the human ocular visual system, fostering a deeper understanding of the artwork's visual dynamics. Here besides visitor type of Explorer, it was also highlighted as important for Facilitators as means to use it as an educational tool to reflect on the human visual system for example. Furthermore, Professional/Hobbyist could also benefit from this, reflecting on their own practice and light use.

### 3.4 Alternative Perceptions

The preceding discussion concerning the impact of the human visual system and its role in art perception generated a closely related theme: the possibility of rendering HSI image data to mimic the visual systems of other animals. This application could expand on the previous concept by generating renditions of the artwork as it would be perceived through the visual systems of various animals, providing visitors with a distinctive perspective, such as observing the artwork through their dog's eyes. For example, Fig. 3 illustrates the variations in false-color images of "The Scream" (1893) as it would be perceived by different animals. This approach would permit visitors to explore how the artwork might appear from diverse visual standpoints, thereby deepening their appreciation for the subjective nature of perception and expanding their understanding of the artwork's visual impact across various species. While VR technology would be a fitting choice, participants suggested that a large interactive display would be even more appropriate. In contrast to the previous concept of different illuminants, context is less relevant here, and it would be simpler to compare the various visual systems. Moreover, this idea was seen as highly promising for Facilitators and the visitors they cater to, as it would enable a more in depth discussion involving multiple visitors simultaneously. For example, in the case of a teacher visiting the museum with their students, everyone simultaneously perceiving the same different renditions, could allow for deeper reflections on visual systems. Additionally, this would be suitable for Experience Seekers who are typically drawn to the most prestigious exhibits, and this could potentially attract their attention if it was a highly visible feature positioned near these artworks.

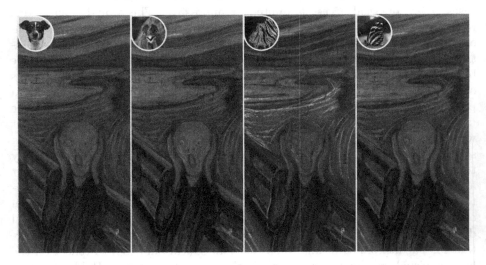

**Fig. 3.** Four examples of how animals would perceive Edvard Munch's Scream (1893). From left to right: Dog, Chicken, Zebrafish and Butterfly.

### 3.5   Art Modification

Another application that was considered involves the identification of specific pigments using HSI data. As pigments tend to fade over time, the visual appearance of the artwork also undergoes significant changes. A prime example of this is cadmium yellow, a pigment that is particularly susceptible to fading and becoming transparent, resulting in a dramatic alteration of the artwork's overall appearance [1]. By identifying the various pigments in the artwork through spectral analysis [6,7,12], the corresponding spectral values of the pixels can be substituted with the original pigment values. When rendered as an RGB image [20], the resulting visualization would more accurately resemble the original appearance of the artwork. This idea also sparked discussions about giving visitors the ability to swap various pigments and create their own rendition of the artwork. In addition, the aforementioned application could be further extended to include the ability to generate the new image using different luminants or based on different visual systems. By incorporating these three concepts, visitors would have access to a vast array of possibilities and ample room for experimentation. A large multi-touch display was deemed the most suitable technology for this purpose, as it would enable multiple users to assess various versions simultaneously. This application would mostly appeal to the Facilitator visitor type, as well as Explorers. Finally, the large multi-touch display approach was also seen as a quick and easily accessible method that may also entice the Recharger visitor type, provided it is implemented in a manner that supports "peace and psychological uplift" [9, p. 176].

### 3.6 Revealing the Artistic Process

Finally, the idea to disclose the creative process, encompassing the transient order of the painting, as well as elements such as brushstrokes inferred from the HSI data, was discussed. Although this idea did not receive significant attention during the preliminary phase, it emerged as a highly favored concept for visitors categorized as Hobbyists/Professionals during the subsequent phase. These visitor types typically seek information that is content-oriented, a criterion that this idea precisely fulfills. However, the expert pointed out that while this is feasible to a certain extent, it may be challenging or even impossible to reconstruct underlying pigments in cases where dark and highly opaque pigments are applied over lighter ones, as these absorb a significant portion of the electromagnetic spectrum. Moreover, it soon became apparent that obtaining additional insights from experts such as art historians and conservationists (e.g., see [1]) would be necessary to appropriately explicate the process and create a potential explanatory application.

## 4    Conclusion

In this paper we presented design concepts that utilize HSI data as there basis, namely: *invisible information, human visual perception, alternative perceptions, art modification,* and *revealing the artistic process,* that are the result of an expert led design workshop. We outline the rich possibilities that these hold to create unique experiences for museum visitors, and discuss which museum visitors types would be most receptive to them. Although our participants were unable to reach a consensus regarding the most appealing concept, it was observed that the first three options garnered the greatest degree of interest among the participants. For future we aim to implement these applications and gather real museum visitor feedback, furthermore these concepts will enable other researchers and museum curators to develop new experiences and refine these concepts. Another important aspect that emerged during the design workshop was the recognition that the development of such experiences necessitates the involvement of experts in cultural heritage and art conservation, which luckily was present in our case. Nonetheless, as previously noted, the knowledge and HSI data required for these purposes are frequently accessible within museums; their full potential, however, remains largely untapped as our design concepts clearly outline.

# References

1. Aslaksby, T.: Edvard munch's painting the scream (1893): notes on technique, materials and condition. In: Public Paintings by Edvard Munch and His Contemporaries: Change and Conservation Challenges, pp. 52–71 (2015)
2. Balas, C., Papadakis, V., Papadakis, N., Papadakis, A., Vazgiouraki, E., Themelis, G.: A novel hyper-spectral imaging apparatus for the non-destructive analysis of objects of artistic and historic value. J. Cult. Heritage **4**, 330–337 (2003)
3. Bekele, M.K., Pierdicca, R., Frontoni, E., Malinverni, E.S., Gain, J.: A survey of augmented, virtual, and mixed reality for cultural heritage. J. Comput. Cult. Herit. (JOCCH) **11**(2), 1–36 (2018)
4. Asperen de Boer, J.V.: Reflectography of paintings using an infrared vidicon television system. Stud. Conserv. **14**(3), 96–118 (1969)
5. Chen, A., Jesus, R., Vilarigues, M.: Hyperspectral image reconstruction of heritage artwork using RGB images and deep neural networks. In: CBMI 2022, New York, NY, USA, pp. 97–102. Association for Computing Machinery (2022). https://doi.org/10.1145/3549555.3549583
6. Deborah, H., George, S., Hardeberg, J.Y.: Pigment mapping of the scream (1893) based on hyperspectral imaging. In: Image and Signal Processing: 6th International Conference, ICISP 2014, Cherbourg, France, June 30-July 2, 2014. Proceedings 6. pp. 247–256. Springer (2014)
7. Deborah, H., George, S., Hardeberg, J.Y.: Spectral-divergence based pigment discrimination and mapping: A case study on the scream (1893) by Edvard munch. J. Am. Inst. Conserv. **58**(1–2), 90–107 (2019)
8. Deborah, H., Richard, N., Hardeberg, J.Y.: Hyperspectral crack detection in paintings. In: 2015 Colour and Visual Computing Symposium (CVCS), pp. 1–6. IEEE (2015)
9. Falk, J.H.: Identity and the Museum Visitor Experience. Routledge, London (2016)
10. Garside, D., Curran, K., Korenberg, C., MacDonald, L., Teunissen, K., Robson, S.: How is museum lighting selected? An insight into current practice in UK museums. J. Inst. Conserv. **40**(1), 3–14 (2017)
11. Goel, M., et al.: Hypercam: hyperspectral imaging for ubiquitous computing applications. In: Proceedings of the 2015 ACM International Joint Conference on Pervasive and Ubiquitous Computing. UbiComp 2015, New York, NY, USA, pp. 145–156. Association for Computing Machinery (2015). https://doi.org/10.1145/2750858.2804282
12. Hardeberg, J., George, S., Deger, F., Baarstad, I., Palacios, J.: Spectral scream: hyperspectral image acquisition and analysis of a masterpiece. In: Frøysaker, T., Streeton, N., Kutzke, H., Hanssen-Bauer, F., Topalova-Casadiego, B. (eds.) Public Paintings by Edvard Munch and His Contemporaries: Change and Conservation Challenges (2015)
13. Hu, H., Huang, Q., Zhang, Q.: Babynutri: a cost-effective baby food macronutrients analyzer based on spectral reconstruction. Proc. ACM Interact. Mob. Wearable Ubiquitous Technol. **7**(1) (2023). https://doi.org/10.1145/3580858
14. Huang, S.Y., Mukundan, A., Tsao, Y.M., Kim, Y., Lin, F.C., Wang, H.C.: Recent advances in counterfeit art, document, photo, hologram, and currency detection using hyperspectral imaging. Sensors **22**(19), 7308 (2022)
15. Jiang, W., et al.: Probing sucrose contents in everyday drinks using miniaturized near-infrared spectroscopy scanners. Proc. ACM Interact. Mob. Wearable Ubiquitous Technol. **3**(4) (2020). https://doi.org/10.1145/3369834

16. Jiang, W., , Kostakos, V.: User trust in assisted decision-making using miniaturized near-infrared spectroscopy. In: Proceedings of the 2021 CHI Conference on Human Factors in Computing Systems. CHI 2021, Association for Computing Machinery (2021). https://doi.org/10.1145/3411764.3445710
17. Khan, M.J., Khan, H.S., Yousaf, A., Khurshid, K., Abbas, A.: Modern trends in hyperspectral image analysis: a review. IEEE Access **6**, 14118–14129 (2018)
18. Land, E.H., McCann, J.J.: Lightness and retinex theory. JOSA **61**(1), 1–11 (1971)
19. Liang, H.: Advances in multispectral and hyperspectral imaging for archaeology and art conservation. Appl. Phys. A **106**, 309–323 (2012)
20. Magnusson, M., Sigurdsson, J., Armansson, S.E., Ulfarsson, M.O., Deborah, H., Sveinsson, J.R.: Creating RGB images from hyperspectral images using a color matching function. In: IGARSS 2020–2020 IEEE International Geoscience and Remote Sensing Symposium, pp. 2045–2048. IEEE (2020)
21. Picollo, M., Cucci, C., Casini, A., Stefani, L.: Hyper-spectral imaging technique in the cultural heritage field: new possible scenarios. Sensors **20**(10), 2843 (2020)
22. Sharma, A., Misra, A., Subramaniam, V., Lee, Y.: SmrtFridge: IoT-based, user interaction-driven food item & quantity sensing. In: Proceedings of the 17th Conference on Embedded Networked Sensor Systems, pp. 245–257 (2019)
23. Yeo, H.S., Lee, J., Bianchi, A., Harris-Birtill, D., Quigley, A.: Specam: sensing surface color and material with the front-facing camera of a mobile device. In: Proceedings of the 19th International Conference on Human-Computer Interaction with Mobile Devices and Services. MobileHCI 2017, New York, NY, USA. Association for Computing Machinery (2017). https://doi.org/10.1145/3098279.3098541

# Author Index

J. Abdelnour Nocera et al. (Eds.): INTERACT 2023, LNCS 14143, pp. 649–651, 2023.
https://doi.org/10.1007/978-3-031-42283-6

Printed in the United States
by Baker & Taylor Publisher Services